AMERICAN
POLITICS

KENNETH M. DOLBEARE
University of Washington

MURRAY J. EDELMAN
University of Wisconsin

D. C. HEATH AND COMPANY
Lexington, Massachusetts   Toronto   London

AMERICAN POLITICS

Policies, Power, and Change

SECOND EDITION

Introduction

Why are we here? Where are we going? These questions may occur to students confronting a new textbook, as well as to Americans facing multiplying social problems. This introduction tells where the book is going and why. *American Politics,* properly used, will help to explain why our political system works as it does, what difference its workings make to people and problems, and where *it* is going. If we are successful, it should also help readers to ask the right ques-

Why are we here? Where are we going?

tions, and either to get what they want or to reconstruct the system so that they can. These are not modest goals. But neither are they mere boasting on our part. We express them this way less in pride in this book than in the confidence that readers will share our sense that politics in the United States today is a deadly serious business, and will apply themselves equally seriously.

This is not a book for counter-culture dropouts, nor for those who think they can avoid or transcend the effects of politics. It is sheer self-delusion to think or act as if the sometimes-nasty facts of power and politics can somehow be rendered unimportant. No one in the world (let alone in the United States) can escape the impact of the uses of power in this country. Politics need not be, and often is not, either dirty or degrading. The moral dilemmas of mankind, and the failures and successes of human efforts to build a decent world, deserve our best understanding and active responses. We think this book can help. We shall describe our goals, themes, and strategy, and then let readers decide for themselves—about the book and about American politics.

Goals

If this were a traditional American government textbook, it would be very different in approach and substance. Our primary purposes are to help people see their political system more clearly, to develop their skills of analysis and evaluation, and to enable them to act more effectively to gain their ends in politics—whether through, around, or in spite of the established political system. To do these things honestly has forced us to look critically upon many of the revered institutions and values of the United States, to challenge some familiar myths, and to depart from some of the standard approaches of academic political science.

Naturally, this book is biased. Every textbook is. There is no such thing as a "neutral" or "objective" textbook. Some books may *appear* "neutral" or "objective" because they say things we have heard many times before. That is, they repeat dominant beliefs and familiar interpretations, and the familiarity causes us to respond favorably. But that says only that we have not *recognized* the biases that lie hidden in those dominant beliefs and orthodox points of view, or that reside unconsciously in our minds and shape our responses. The most scrupulously "neutral" authors must select certain "facts," present them within a particular conceptual framework, suggest ways of interpreting them so that they become meaningful, and so on. At every stage, the authors' assumptions and preferences—in short, their biases—determine what will be presented as truth to their readers. The best that authors can do is to declare frankly where they stand and warn their readers to be skeptical—another of the purposes of this introduction.

But if all books are thus biased, why read any except those we agree with? What can a serious reader expect to gain from a biased book? This brings us to a vital point. We believe that it is possible, even necessary, to be both honestly critical and frankly biased without sacrificing intellectual quality, rigor, or utility. The key lies in our conviction that readers must become independent thinkers, and in our determination to provide them the tools to do so. The first step toward independence is to escape from the thick fog of unexamined assumptions, myths, and ideology with which our society has enveloped our minds. A critical stance that points up the culture-bound, parochial, self-congratulatory, or otherwise limiting elements of standard American beliefs is absolutely essential for this purpose. Only then can people begin to analyze where power is located, how it is used, and for whose benefit. A number of concepts and other tools are available for these purposes. One of our goals is to present, apply, and evaluate these tools. Only by seeing them at work can the reader determine whether the tools have merits that make them worth acquiring.

Finally, becoming a truly independent person requires that one make repeated value judgments—about particular policies and practices, about the political system itself, and about alternatives to both. Change is constant, and more drastic changes appear to lie ahead. Choices must be made, and conscious action taken, to shape the future. To do these things, people must learn to identify their present values and preferences, and to ask the right questions about both present and future so that they can effectively further those values that they conclude are desirable. A substantial portion of this book is devoted to presenting these questions systematically and to exploring their implications and possible answers. Thus, although we readily acknowledge the biases of this book, we argue that such biases are functional—in fact, necessary—for the purpose of forcing questions to the surface and equipping the reader to become a truly independent thinker.

Thus, this is not the usual civics book. But neither is it a mere polemic, another in the long series of attacks on things American. It is a set of tools and questions, applied to the real world of American politics, to enable readers to gain a better understanding of the political system and of themselves—in short, to help them decide what they want and how to get it. It is heavily burdened with evidence, for we must begin with what is concrete. But to understand the meaning of "facts," we need to use ideas as frameworks. These ideas are presented carefully, so that readers may decide for themselves whether and how to employ them. "Central questions" are asked, and their uses and implications examined, so that readers may see where we are taking them. The prospects of change are considered in relation to the conditions that lead to particular forms of change. As an aid in the process of developing critical judgment skills, we describe from time to time the judgments *we* make from a particular set of facts, or between alternative values. If we have done our job, and if readers do theirs, the result should be the development of more independent persons, better able to cope with the deepening crises of the American future.

Themes

The book has three major themes or arguments. The first, which has already been suggested, is the United States is facing a severe social crisis, one that may be unique in our history because of the many different forces and factors that have converged upon us. The term "crisis" is much overworked these days, to the point that it may seem meaningless. A kind of popular self-hypnosis also exists, which causes people to agree complacently that things are very, very bad, and then to go about their daily routines as always. But we invoke the term "crisis" precisely, deliberately, and in all seriousness. Moreover, we see this crisis as such an overwhelming convergence of economic, racial, international, ecological, intellectual, technological, and moral problems that only substantial change can ensue.

In other words, we believe that the one thing that cannot be predicted is a future that automatically incorporates the basic outlines of the present. Throughout our history, it has always been safest to predict that tomorrow will look very much like today, only slightly more so. We do not believe this is true any longer. We may well come to a crossroads, for example, at which the only choices will be socialism or fascism. But this does not mean that there is nothing people can do, or that results are predetermined, or that such powerful forces are at work that individuals cannot affect the outcome of events. Men and women make history, and this is a time when history is malleable, open, and subject to the determined efforts of knowledgeable individuals.

Our second theme is that a relatively few persons possess the bulk of the wealth, status, and power that exist in the United States. They hold such stature in part through their class and family origins and in part through their positions in the major economic and social institutions of the society, from which they can affect nearly all of the major political decisions that are made at the national level. Their interests are principally those of maintaining and furthering the American economic system. To fulfill the basic needs of that system, they act in a united way and tolerate no significant opposition. With respect to less important matters, there may well be conflict within the ruling group, and political decisions may be made favoring first one group or interest and then another.

The domination of the ruling group is not grossly or blatantly carried out, however, and sometimes is not even publicly visible. Social control is accomplished in many subtle ways—through the educational system, the media, legal rules and procedures, the symbolic rituals of leaders, and the like—and only infrequently is it necessary to resort to outright coercion. Drastic repression may create a sense of hopelessness among people. Management of the society is, therefore, usually a peaceful process.

Our final theme is that the process of political change can only be understood through the identification of a wide variety of relevant conditions, particular combinations of which will produce specific consequences upon the political system. It is the way that these conditions converge that determines the scope, character, and direction of change. Some conditions that would appear to make for change do not, in their usual combinations, have that effect. Fundamental change in the United States is not easy to envision, but it is far from impossible. Nothing is predetermined, and there are many areas where the actions of people can have profound consequences. The important task is to develop the theoretical perspective that permits us to recognize that the odds on change are relatively high, and what sorts of change are possible under which circumstances.

Strategy

What is distinctive about this book? The intent to help others become independent thinkers is often voiced, though rarely implemented. Indeed, we anticipate that only full study of this book will convince those who have heard this litany regularly that we are indeed serious about this goal. Though our critical posture toward the American political system, and our view that it is dominated by the needs of the economic system, is not unique to this book, it is distinctive in its systematic and evidential demonstration of how and why this happens.

The method of presentation that we have chosen is unprecedented. We feel that it is a major breakthrough toward clear understanding of American politics. Part One of the book briefly presents some basic tools for analysis and evaluation. In each of the four chapters in Part Two, we examine what the United States government has actually done in regard to a particular problem in the last few years. By looking at the actual consequences of public policies on real problems experienced by people, and by asking who was affected and in what ways by a government action, we shall understand for whom government works. We believe that the performance of government can best be measured by results, and that is why we focus on the consequences of government actions. Our questions in Part Two will be: Who wins and who loses as a result of this policy? What effect did this policy have on the problem or goal involved?

Once we can recognize who gets what from government policies, and how people and problems are affected, we shall be in a position to ask why this is so. Our inquiry proceeds in two ways. First, in Part Three we look at contrasting ideological justifications or explanations of these outcomes. What values, assumptions, and goals are apparent in these policies and their effects? The orthodox American ideology, dominant for decades, is plainly visible in the practices of government and in the words and actions of leaders. A radical-populist challenge to the validity or propriety of this established ideology is also apparent, however, though usually in the complaints of deprived groups and the writings of a minority of intellectuals. The contrasts between these two sets of beliefs are sharp, and they raise some vital questions of fact and interpretation for us as analysts. They also, quite obviously, indicate some of the reasons for continued conflict in American politics today.

Then, in Parts Four and Five, we turn to an analysis of power and decisionmaking. There we look not just at the institutions of the national government, but at the structure of power in the society generally. This is because much of what is done by government institutions reflects needs and preferences flowing from the economic or social structures of the society. In these sections, we shall try to understand how elites shape popular opinion, and to what extent non-elites are able to influence decisions. In seeking to understand the relative balance of power and influence between elites and masses, we shall not have to guess about who benefited ·from various policies that have been enacted—we shall know what the patterns of benefit were from our previous analysis. In the context of that knowledge, and of our broad analysis of power distribution in the society as a whole, the actions of the institutions of the national government will become more understandable and more meaningful.

In effect, we will be using our knowledge of the consequences of public policies as a kind of prism through which to look at power and decisionmaking. We are convinced that we can see far more clearly how power is distributed and used in this way than by focusing on elections or politicians' rhetoric. Certainly it is better than merely describing how government institutions work in isolation. Many benevolent assumptions and democratic myths may be exposed as false, but that is both necessary and proper in an accurate political analysis. Moreover, this approach will avoid many of the fruitless arguments between social scientists about who actually made or influenced particular decisions. Such arguments normally cannot be resolved, because the necessary evidence about a specific decision cannot be obtained by analysts, and because that decision can only really be understood in a context of many other similar decisions. Where we know what the long-term patterns of benefit and burden from government policies have been—who consistently wins and loses—and we find that the beneficiaries have the apparent power to shape decisions as they wish, we have a solid basis for inferring that they in fact do so for their own benefit. This is the primary focus of analysis in this book.

A final and important feature of our approach is its concern with the process of political change, a concern that culminates in the three chapters of Part Six. Why do we try to discover who rules and for whose benefit, except to ask whether and, if so, how this situation should be changed? And yet, very few analyses of American politics systematically explore the conditions and actions that permit, promote, or impede change in this society. Our analysis, from the first chapter on, is undertaken from the perspective of these findings' implications for change. In Part Six, we first reach some conclusions about the structure of power in the United States. Then we look at the many ways in which the symbols and appearance of change often substitute for the reality. Finally, we propose a general theory of change, and apply it to our present circumstances to develop some forecasts of possible change in the United States in the next decade. This is a potentially controversial endeavor, but we think it is a necessary and desirable sequel to the analysis undertaken earlier. Moreover, it should be both rigorous and provocative enough to enable readers to test their skills of independent political judgment.

This book may be difficult in spots. If the writing is at fault, we are to blame. But more often, we think, the difficulty is due to the complexity of the subject matter, and to misconceptions and incapacities produced by the dominant American ideology, which not only teaches that all is well and need not be examined closely, but also erects verbal and conceptual barriers against doing so. We must establish factual points thoroughly, on the basis of data and other evidence where possible; thus there are many tables and charts in this book. To meet a high standard of proof, some precise definitions and carefully detailed considerations are essential. We must comprehensively synthesize and interpret a vast body of material—the totality of the American econopolitical system and process—and so repeated conceptual clarification is necessary. For all these reasons, we ask that readers respond to difficult sections by trying a little harder. The end product—understanding of how and why the system works as it does, and for whom, and what can be done about it—is surely worth the trouble.

One aid in developing independent skills and gaining greater depth of insight into many of the problems, issues, and processes discussed in this book may be the reader designed to accompany it. Entitled *Institutions, Policies, and Goals: A Reader in American Politics*, it contains several case studies of decisionmaking in national institutions, conflicting interpretations of the nature of problems and what government has done about them, and several contrasting prescriptions, conflicting interpretations of the nature of problems and what those we present in this text, in both conservative and radical directions, and thus may serve as a check on our arguments.

We hope that this introduction serves as a map of what lies ahead in this book, and of the perspective from which we shall examine policies, power, and change in the United States. We have had many interesting and useful reactions from students and teachers to the first edition of this text, and this revision takes most of them into account. We welcome further comments, suggestions, complaints, and denunciations at any time. Although the road to political insight and understanding may be a hard one, it is an exciting and mutually rewarding process, and the goal is one for which all of us strive. We do so together. Thus armed, let us begin.

CONTENTS

TABLES

FIGURES

AMERICAN
POLITICS

PART ONE

THE STUDY
OF POLITICS

Chapter 1

Let us begin with a brief illustration of why a careful approach is essential, using a problem that will remain with us throughout the book. Then we can move on to develop the necessary tools of analysis.

The United States States is a capitalist society. This is one of the most meaningful statements that can be made about American politics. It is not a very startling or original observation, but Americans react to it in sharply contrasting ways. Most people never

Politics: Some Tools of Analysis

do understand its implications. Others are so shocked by the discovery and its implications that they believe there is nothing more to be said. Much recent talk about American politics falls into the latter category, interpreting all political attitudes, behavior, institutions, processes, and prospects exclusively in terms of the (bad) characteristics of capitalism.

Neither of these two responses satisfies the demands of sophisticated political analysis. Both result from a lack of understanding of the interrelationship of economic, social, cultural, and ideological factors in shaping politics. These two types of intellectual failure define our task in this book. We must develop the concepts, methods, and other tools of analysis that enable us to go beyond these responses to the point of understanding, for example, how much of our politics is traceable to the capitalist nature of the American social order, and how much is due to other factors.

What does it mean that the United States is a capitalist society? First, it means that the productive resources of the society—farms, factories, mines, and so on—are all owned by private individuals or corporations and operated so as to produce profits for those owners. Services such as transportation, advertising, communications, and the like, are also privately owned and operated for profit. Most people are not owners, and must earn their livelihoods by working for those who are.

Next, it means that the social structure is shaped in important ways by the patterns of wealth and income distribution created by that economic system. A relatively few people—mostly owners, but also some salaried managers and other persons—receive a large share of all the wealth and income produced. A bigger group of people with specially useful skills—engineers, lawyers, accountants, salesmen—also receives a substantial proportion. A still larger number of people, mostly blue-collar workers and minorities, receives a smaller proportion of income. They are not highly skilled, and hold only those jobs that are both low-paying and most likely to be eliminated during economic recessions. Status and power in the society are distributed in the same stratified manner, giving rise to a class system.

A capitalist society also has certain cultural and ideological characteristics. The values of the society support the kinds of behavior that are consistent with the economic system and social structure. Individual self-seeking, materialism, the work ethic or profit motive, and respect for private property are both basic American values and necessary principles of behavior in a capitalist society. The way of thinking within that culture is also (but less obviously) consistent with that form of social order. It assumes the continuity of existing patterns of ownership, social structure, and values, and unconsciously tries to fit all it sees or imagines into that mold. It asks only questions that are answerable in these terms, and employs only words that express attitudes appropriate to such a society. For example, it looks at higher education chiefly as a means to prepare young people for jobs and income in a technological society. It either cannot imagine other purposes or considers them uneconomical "frills"—or possibly even subversive.

Finally, although all societies generate self-congratulatory and justifying ideologies, that associated with a capitalist society has certain special features. It holds that economic activity is separate from (and morally superior to) politics. And it teaches that human nature itself is the basis of capitalism: people are naturally competitive and self-seeking, and thus capitalism is the "natural" economic system. American ideology includes many other beliefs as well, as we shall see in a later chapter; but the principles just identified are specially linked to the capitalist nature of the American system.

All of these economic, social, cultural, and ideological characteristics play significant parts in our politics. They are not the only major factors in politics, of course. But they are often so familiar as to pass unrecognized, or so much a part of our way of thinking as to control our perceptions and judgments. How do we identify precisely the part played by different factors in our politics? Clearly, we must cast

our analytical net wide enough to include all major causal factors—
and we must be alert enough to see them after we have caught them.
Part of the answer lies in some careful definitions, and another part
in clarification of what is involved in analysis and evaluation. After
setting forth some key points, we shall return at the end of this chapter to the issue of understanding the shaping role of capitalism in
our politics.

Some Preliminary Reflections on Politics

In order to live together on a continuing basis and to achieve their
various goals in life, people seek and employ power in ways that
affect the lives of their fellows. In other words, they engage in
politics. They erect governments to maintain order, further mutual
goals, and promote general well-being. Around and within the framework of that government, they continue to seek their individual and
group goals. People can no more live without politics in this sense
than they can dispense with food, love, or other basic human needs
and desires. Politics is the activity by which they seek their goals,
maintain the kind of context that allows them to pursue those goals,
or defend what they have already gained through their previous
efforts. For many people, of course, politics serves all three purposes.

Those persons who possess the resources of power—such as
wealth, prestige, strength, or oratorical talent—are often easily able to
persuade or compel others to alter their intended patterns of behavior. Others, by combining their lesser resources, may influence or even
reverse the decisions of the more powerful. In the broadest definition
of the term, political activity occurs whenever an individual or group
of people brings resources of power to bear, not only on government,
but on any other individual or group whose behavior they desire to
change. If tenants withhold rent payment in order to induce a land-
lord to make needed improvements on a building, they are, in a general sense, engaging in political activity.

But regardless of how seldom individuals employ their own political resources to influence the actions of others, they cannot escape
the consequences of political decisions in the modern society. If only
as a consumer of the political products generated by the actions of
others, every one of us is involved. Thus, we are all in politics,
whether we like it or not, inevitably and permanently.

Because war has been a continuing fact of history, politics has
always held life-or-death importance for at least some people. With
the advent of nuclear weapons, politics has come to have such meaning for practically everybody. But it is not only in relation to other
countries that politics holds life-or-death significance. The more powerful elements within a society prescribe the behavior that is in their

eyes consistent with the established order of things and fix punishments for those who break their rules. Further, thousands of men are hired and equipped with weapons to enforce such codes of behavior. For those whose situations or preferences make them able and willing to accept the rules, the political preferences they reflect and the power exercised to enforce them create no great problems. For those not satisfied with the *status quo,* however, the same rules may serve as apparently unjust obstacles to desired change. But violation of the rules, or even talk of the justice of doing so, often brings swift retribution in the form of imprisonment, physical injury, or death.

But politics is also routine. At every hour of the day, in practically any activity in which an individual engages, he or she is affected by the consequences of politics. Consider so prosaic an act as driving to a drugstore to buy a pack of cigarettes. The driver (licensed by the state) gets into his car (licensed and registered with the state; fitted with safety devices according to federal specifications; sold at prices reflecting the manufacturer's response to federal antitrust laws, labor-management relations practices, and interstate commerce rate controls; and taxed by federal, state, and local governments). He drives (according to local and state ordinances, and subject to local traffic officers) to the drugstore (where the state-licensed pharmacist is closely regulated as to the hours he may do business and the prescriptions he may sell to customers). He buys (with federal currency) the cigarettes (which have been the subject of extensive federal testing for danger to health, carry a required warning to users, and are taxed by both federal and state governments). And so forth.

The point is that the relationship of the individual to politics never ends. And every instance of contact with politics implies a prior history of conflict and governmental choice made according to the preferences of those with the greatest amount of power at a particular time or over a particular issue. Thus, the individual exists in a world shaped by the decisions of others, and not even the most determined effort to extricate oneself from such effects can be successful.

Politics: A Definition and Its Implications

Politics is a process (1) in which power is employed to gain rewards, and (2) through which the interests of broad segments of the population are affected. We like the shorthand phrasing of a leading political scientist, who characterized politics as "who gets what, when, and how."[1] This is a wide-ranging definition (which we shall have to refine shortly), for it takes us well outside "government" or

[1]Harold Lasswell, *Politics: Who Gets What, When, How* (New York: McGraw-Hill, 1936).

"the state" to focus on other holders of power in the society and the way they achieve their goals and create effects on people.

Nothing is more tedious, or more important, than the precise definition of what we are talking about. This is particularly true of the emotion-encrusted subject of politics. We have deliberately adopted a distinctive definition of politics in order to employ the widest possible, and least ideologically shaped, frame of reference for our inquiry. But even at the risk of tedium, we must spell out in detail what is implied by our definition, and how it differs from the more familiar and more limited (and more self-congratulatory) definitions usually employed.

We believe that we must include extragovernmental activity that bears on who rules, who benefits, and how change comes about, because government is only one of several channels through which vital goals are obtained. Its use therefore implies change or confirmation of pre-existing patterns of benefits—either of which is of vital concern to political participants. More fundamentally revealing uses of power are often prompted by the question of *whether* government should act in a given area than by *the way in which* government is to act. For example, the "natural" residential pattern in most areas is one of racial segregation. Neighborhood schools thus tend to be enclaves of whites or minorities. Some like this situation, but others do not. Should there be national governmental involvement in this area? Some will gain and some will lose in either event. The consequences for ordinary people, who inevitably feel the impact of this struggle in one form or another, may be very great—and eminently a product of politics.

Further, a concern for the nature of problems and the character of extragovernmental activity will alert us to the processes by which an issue becomes recognized as a possible subject for political debate or governmental action. Some subjects are routinely understood as appropriate for governmental action, some (such as poverty or racial discrimination) are seen as problems for government only at very late stages, and some (nationalization of major industries, compensation for victims of crime) not at all. Sometimes a subject at first appears quite outside the range of "practical" political consideration, but after a period of years moves into the field of political debate and finally takes a place among the policies of government. This was the case, for example, with medical care for the aged and, more recently, with the guaranteed annual wage or "negative income tax."

Throughout the period when some political actors are trying to move a subject from the unthinkable stage to the stage of debate and even action, many forces are at work to shape opinion about whether the issue should be a subject for government and, if so, what should be done about it. These shaping forces reach deep into the underpinnings of our politics. Our understanding of what is proper for government action, for example, is strongly affected by the cultural values and assumptions we have acquired during the process of growing up.

But these values and assumptions are not coincidental: somebody or something has taught them to us. The result is that some participants in politics are better able than others to gain their ends—usually those who do not need governmental protection or might be hindered by it in some way. Nevertheless, some issues and problems do rise to public attention and are acted upon by government. Which issues do this, and why, and under what conditions? And when they do, who acts in what way to shape our understanding of the nature of these issues? What is at stake in such areas?

The temptation is strong to try to understand too much, to treat almost every event and pattern of social and economic activity as if it had political implications. The fact is, of course, that almost everything does. But we must exclude much of this activity in order to be able to cope concretely with some of it. We shall limit ourselves to matters that have a direct and proximate relation to the present character or future prospect of government action. Our definition of politics then becomes: *the process by which power is employed to affect whether and how government will be used in any given area.* Power is the possession of those resources, ranging from money and prestige to official authority, that cause other political actors to modify their behavior and conform to what they perceive the possessor of the resources prefers. The resources need not be tangible; what counts is others' perceptions of one's resources. They need not actually be mobilized and employed in any particular situation, because others may act in anticipation or expectation. Indeed, much politically significant behavior occurs because of "voluntary" conformity with what one takes to be the expectations of others.

One of the major resources of power, of course, is *legitimacy.* Legitimacy is a status conferred by people generally upon the institutions, acts, and officials of their government. When people believe that their government is the right one—that it works properly and for desirable ends—they place their trust in it and grant it their obedience. Elected officials, bureaucrats, and law enforcement personnel all acquire some of this special status by virtue of their institutional positions in that government. This enables higher officials, at least, to exert considerable influence over what people believe, to draw support for their actions, and (under normal circumstances) to shape the agenda of politics so as to gain their ends more easily.

But legitimacy is a fluid and intangible attribute. It can be diluted by frequent requests for uncritical support, by actions inconsistent with expectations or traditions, and by extreme misconduct. It may be withdrawn by some segment, or even by most, of the people.

Under such circumstances, voluntary compliance with the acts of government and normal cooperative routines may cease. If this occurs among large proportions of the population, people in government may have to fall back on outright coercion to achieve their ends. The shift to this form of power, of course, means that the political system is close to breakdown.

Thus, politics is a vast interactive process of power applications which, although sometimes unintended, nearly always have consequences for others. From our early acquisition of ideology to the present process of defining a "problem" for government, we are subject to the effects of past and present power. Fortunately, our limited definition of politics as those uses of power that bear directly on whether or how government will be employed makes it unnecessary for us to trace the entire web of power transactions in society. The line marking the boundaries of what bears "directly" on the use of government will not always be clear-cut. But we shall try to hold on to what is tangible and demonstrable, and thereby keep our definition manageable.

Political Analysis: The Central Questions

How should analysts approach the problem of understanding this process? We believe that three central questions lead most directly and efficiently to understanding. Because these have already been alluded to in the Introduction, our discussion here will be brief.

1. What does government do with respect to various subjects, and what difference do its actions make for people and problems? In order to answer this question, we shall carefully assess the consequences of recent governmental activity in four subject areas. Our principal tool will be bodies of data about changes in peoples' lives— for example in their wealth, status, or power—as a result of specific government actions. We shall treat each subject area separately, and then ask whether the patterns of benefits and burdens from governmental action that are visible in one area are similar to those in others.

2. What interests, forces, or people cause government to act in such ways? Or, more briefly, **who rules?** In order to answer this question, we shall do three different but related things. First, we shall look at the explanations offered by the dominant American values and ideology, and contrast them with the charges made by radicalism-populism. This will tell us what some people consider the right answers to this question, and alert us to some things we must be sure to look at. Second, we shall start with the knowledge of who wins and who loses as a result of government action, and ask whether those people who win regularly may not be, in practical terms, the real rulers of the society. Third, we shall undertake to identify the people, groups, corporations, or other political participants that have large supplies of the resources of power, and try to see how their resources affect the actions of government.

These three approaches complement each other usefully. The contrasting ideologies suggest who and what to look at, as do the patterns of winners and losers from governmental actions; and our fresh analysis of where the resources of power lie serves as another independent focus. The final answer to the question, of course, can only emerge from the evidence and from the reader's interpretation of that evidence.

3. **How does, and how might, change come about?** Note that this question is partly factual (how has change happened in the past?) and partly speculative (what can be concluded from an analysis of power distribution and usage today to shed light on what might happen in the future?). There is a further component, one readers must resolve for themselves, that necessarily intrudes upon any speculation about change. This is the question of whether change is desirable, and, if so, what sort of change—a value-preference issue properly considered in our section on evaluation.

In order to answer this third central question, we shall draw on theory and experience to construct categories for investigation. We first note that most political change is *marginal* change, i.e., change that takes place without altering the basic outlines of established social and economic systems, or the distribution of wealth, status, and power within the society. *Fundamental* change, i.e., change in structures, basic distribution patterns, or the underlying values of the society, is much less frequent. Presumably, the latter is what we seek to understand, for marginal change may occur at any time, as a result of a wide variety of frequently unpatterned causes.

Let us suggest, quite crudely at this early stage, that fundamental change is dependent upon (1) certain preconditions like an unsatisfactory level of economic well-being, social tensions such as race conflict, or international tensions; and (2) the political impact of those preconditions on the attitudes of people toward their government, the behavior of elites, and the power potential of change-seeking groups. We shall look closely throughout our analysis at developments relating to each of these preconditions, and at the political impact of such developments. By the close of our analysis of power and decision-making, we should be ready to expand greatly our understanding of how and when fundamental change occurs.

Evaluation in Politics: Standards of Judgment

Explaining how and why governmental policies take the form they do, and what difference that makes to people and problems in the society, is an interesting and important task. But it is only a preliminary for the person who wants to be more than a helpless consumer of the products generated by the power and activity of others. One must decide whether a particular policy is good or bad, whether the political system is working well or not, and whether and how to seek improvements. To do this on a sound basis may seem to require more knowledge and greater wisdom than any person can really expect to develop. But this problem can be rendered manageable.

Several simplifying approaches can make it possible for a person to judge and act in politics in a responsible and still timely manner. One does not need to be intimidated by the fact that some scholars spend a lifetime studying particular governmental procedures or narrow subject areas. It is often enough that there be some solid evidence, especially if it pertains to the performance of government with respect to problems with which the person is familiar. People can specialize in certain areas of the greatest interest to them. And they can avoid being diverted by rhetoric, ideology, or elaborate explanations about how the procedures of government operated to prevent accomplishment of their goals.

But perhaps the most important act in preparing oneself for sound evaluation in politics is clarification of the standards to be used in making judgments. Often, the standard applied contains the judgment within itself. For example, a standard that emphasizes maintaining established procedures or traditions is likely to lead to a status-quo-supporting judgment. So is a standard that emphasizes what is "practical" or "pragmatic" under the circumstances of today's power distribution. Today's procedures, of course, promote the interests and preferences of those who hold the balance of power now. What is "realistic" is what they can permit to take place without serious danger to their own predominance. In both cases, therefore, the use of such standards inevitably directs judgments toward minimal changes, which have the effect of supporting the basic outlines of today's power distribution.

On the other hand, standards that emphasize efficiency or economy in the solution of problems are likely to lead to severe judgments of the need for drastic change, often at the cost of important human values. Useful standards require explicit specification of the relative priorities to be assigned to each of several desired results. In the case of "equality," for example, it must be clear whether one means equality in the formal, legalistic sense or in the actual social and economic conditions of individuals. In the case of "democracy," it must be clear whether one means merely full participation in civil rights, or also consistency between popular needs and desires and the products of governmental action.

The key to all evaluation, however, is one's personal political philosophy, which each of us must construct and apply. This is easier said than done, of course. Developing one's own view of what should be is even more difficult and frustrating than understanding what is in politics. Most people can acquire facts about their political system, although they sometimes do so in the fashion of spectators at a game or passive memorizers in the classroom rather than as analytical, purposeful, and independent persons. Relatively few people make the effort to survey, self-consciously and comprehensively, alternative ends and means in politics and to arrive at their own set of standards and goals for political action. But not to do so is to commit onself in advance to a passive role in the processes that determine the shape of the future. In effect, it means acquiescence in the decisions of those now in power about what is best for themselves, and perhaps for others. The person without an independent basis for analysis and evaluation in politics must be somebody's pawn, and the only remaining question is *whose*.

Centuries of reflection and writing by the great political theorists have not produced agreement among them, or among their respective followers, for reasons that are by now obvious to readers. But analysis of their work reveals remarkable consistency in the kinds of problems they found it essential to face. Because these problems also accord with our view of the intellectual issues involved, we shall use some classic categories to indicate the central questions that must be faced by a student of politics seeking to establish his own independent judgmental framework. Each individual must answer three basic questions, however temporary those answers may be, in order to evolve an independent political stance.

1. What is the nature of people and of their relationship to their society and environment?

To some extent these are factual questions, but for the most part we must simply assume or speculate, which means that our answers are more or less frank expressions of our value preferences. Some assume that human nature is fundamentally good—that a human being is essentially a cooperative, rational creature. If so, governing processes should be designed to maximize openness and participation, in confidence that the right decisions will be made. Others assume that people in general are selfish, emotional, likely to follow short-range interests, and subject to demagogues, but that some people possess superior talents. According to these assumptions, a strong government run by the talented few is necessary to civilize people and maintain order and justice in the society. In other words, a whole series of conclusions and preferences is built upon one's assumptions about human nature.

Assumptions must also be made about the character of society and the extent to which both people and their society are incapable of, or resistant to, change. For some, "society" is a term with real meaning—an independent entity with a life of its own, distinct from the people who happen to make it up at any given time. Such people are likely to value the "needs of the society" above any particular member's preferences. But some device for ascertaining those needs must be found. The net result is likely to be a form of government dominated by a relative few of the better-qualified persons in the society. A less mystical use of the term "society" is as a synonym for all, or a majority, of the individuals who happen to be present at any moment within the nation's geographical confines. According to such usage, the needs of the society and majority preference are one and the same, and an entirely different decision-making process is suggested.

Another set of assumptions concerns the extent to which people are irretrievably the product of something innate within their nature, or, alternatively, the product of their environment. If the latter is true, they can be improved (at least to some extent, but with accompanying risks) through manipulation of the environment. If the former is true, of course, such efforts are both hopeless and potentially very dangerous.

Which of these sets of alternative assumptions is better or more soundly based? At the moment, there seems to be no way in which a case for one or the other can be conclusively established or "proved." There are scraps of evidence regarding aspects of these issues, but they often can be used to support equally plausible and contrasting interpretations. People are therefore forced to adopt what seems to them the most reasonable set of assumptions. Because this is just another way of expressing one's preferences, such position-taking tells the listener or reader little about human nature but a great deal about the speaker's or author's political values.

2. What are the proper goals of social and political life, and with what order of priorities and at what cost should they be sought?

This is the area in which evidence is of least assistance. People must answer these questions in response to their own preferences and with only their personal values for guidance. Such questions are rarely put so bluntly, of course: they arise in the context of familiar concepts or establishing priorities among familiar and generally shared goals. For example, the concept of "freedom" carries several alternative meanings. To some, it may mean freedom from government interference, and lead them to seek severe limitations on the activities of government. To others, it may mean freedom to do what one could if only the handicaps of poverty and ignorance were removed. This would lead them to seek broad expansion of the social welfare activities of government.

The concept of "equality" is equally pliable according to one's preferences. It may mean the right to use one's talents, whatever they may be, in the pursuit of one's goals. Or it can be expanded slightly to include the right to at least a minimal education and standard of living. Or it can be broadened still further to signify that all persons are entitled to full social and economic parity with one another.

Economic equality is a much more ambitious goal than mere political equality, but even within the latter concept there is room for considerable difference of viewpoint. In the eighteenth century, some defined political equality in terms of *suffrage*—the right to vote— which was limited to males who owned a certain amount of property. More recently, sharp controversy has developed about whether this generally agreed-upon goal requires the observance of "one man, one vote" at all levels of government. The fact that people who strongly subscribe to the goal of political equality can sincerely argue that some people should have more votes than others indicates that there is wide room for disagreement even when the basic goal is shared "in principle." Thus, it is determining the specific content of familiar terms that is critical in setting up one's own independent framework. No definition is necessarily preferable or "correct," for no person is the ultimate arbiter of the meanings of words. They mean for each citizen what he or she says they mean, and that is why there is bound to be disagreement in politics.

These differences in meaning may become apparent only when an issue arises that requires the concept to be put into practice (or "operationalized"). At other times, generalized agreement on the undefined concept of "freedom" or "equality" or "justice" may create the illusion of consensus. A similar illusion may be fostered by the widespread acknowledgment of these goals, despite sharply differing views as to which should be given first priority. Once again, the illusion is dispelled only when it is sought to actually *do* one or the other.

Consider the dilemma of the person who subscribes strongly to both "liberty" and "equality": at some point, he or she will have to decide which is paramount, because they frequently conflict. In order to provide equality for some, it may be necessary to limit the liberty of others to do as they wish with their property or their talents. If equality is defined as rough parity of opportunity to compete for the goals of life, and if it is a paramount goal, one must reluctantly conclude that in this instance liberty must be limited. But if one holds to a more restrictive view of equality, or considers liberty to be the goal deserving of first priority, this would be an utterly wrong way for government to act. The same type of problem is involved in recent controversies over the proper priority rankings of "justice" and "order," two goals readily acknowledged as vital by all. To some, nothing is more important than order and tranquility, while to others the rights and privileges that are components of justice deserve precedence.

When neither specific meanings nor priority rankings have been established for these concepts, they are not much more than glittering generalities in citizens' minds. As such, they are aspects of ideology; we tend to believe that since all right-thinking people share the same views, all that needs to be done to resolve conflicts is to sit down and "reason together." Or we may believe that our leaders hold the same views as we do because they use these words in their explanations or exhortations. Clearly, these concepts offer us nothing but symbolic satisfactions and complacency until we undertake to define their specific content and relative valuations.

3. **What means—institutions and processes—offer the best prospects of reaching the goals we establish, given our assumptions about human nature?**

In other words, how can we get from specific assumptions about the nature of man to the characteristics of the good life? What logically consistent and empirically practicable means are there for reaching the goals desired? This is the area where we should be able to get the most assistance from factual knowledge about the workings of political institutions and processes. In seeking to establish some coherent connection between the nature of man and the realization of his goals in life, we have for guidance considerable evidence about how particular institutions work and why. We know, for example, that all congressmen in the House of Representatives are not equally influential in determining the provisions of new statutes, and we would not rest our hopes for goal attainment on the illusion that they are. Thus, one of the first necessities in this area is to become familiar with some of the basic facts and processes that determine how the political system presently works, and to use this understanding to establish certain landmarks around which value preferences are to be exercised.

A second requirement in this area, as suggested above, is logical consistency. If man is irrational and selfish, for example, one can hardly expect to achieve equality for all through political mechanisms that are highly responsive to individual preferences. The nature of each set of institutions and processes depends upon the characteristics of the people who design and operate them, and in turn shapes the kinds of goals that can be attained through them. This is a crucial point: the nature of people, the character of institutions and processes, and the goals that can be realized, are interdependent in politics. When we study institutions and processes, we do so with the realization that they have been structured by the values and natures of the people who created and animate them, and also with the knowledge that their character determines in major ways the nature of the goals that can be achieved through them. Because this is so, we must organize our personal political positions to take this interdependence into account.

This is not to say that we must proceed consecutively from a definition of human nature to a vision of an ideal world, and finally to institutional tinkering necessary to link the two together. Most political thinkers probably start with certain highly valued goals and some convictions about what does and does not work in the real world, and then seek to fill in the gaps more or less consistently and adequately. Nor do all the possible questions and problems in these three areas have to be resolved before a personal framework becomes functional. It is enough to be aware of the interdependencies between them and, therefore, to perceive what is at stake when considering one area in apparent isolation, and to see the implications that findings or assumptions in one carry for the others. What *is* important is to begin to build a map in one's mind of what is, can be, and ought to be in politics. This, in turn, will make it possible to respond rationally and selectively to the urgings and pleadings of others and to shape one's own independent course in politics.

Problems in Analysis and Evaluation

It is time to become more rigorous about how one seeks to achieve understanding of a subject like politics, so embedded in emotions, patriotic loyalties, threats, and symbolic diversions. How can we assure ourselves that the understanding we acquire consists of valid interpretations, and not merely uncritical projections of our assumptions, hopes, or fears about American politics? We shall consider some of the technical problems of data collection and interpretation as they arise in later chapters. The more serious problems of nonobjectivity and misinterpretation, however, are conceptual in character. Let us try to identify some of them now, in the hope that we may reduce or avoid their effects throughout our analysis.

Culture-Bound or Ideological Premises and Assumptions

We are all more or less captives of our culture and products of years of indoctrination in its values and assumptions about what is right and good: what is, is right. And what exists in the United States is necessary, desirable, or at least the best that is practical under all the circumstances. These initial (and often subconscious) premises, to say nothing of social or official pressures to adhere to them, or the economic self-interest we may have in endorsing the *status quo*, cause even sophisticated observers to introduce approving evaluations into their supposedly objective "descriptions."

Every person who would be an objective analyst must go through a process of wrenching himself loose from such premises, assumptions, and conceptual blinders. The process is a lengthy and difficult one, for ideology reaches deep into the culture—into stereotypes (or "pictures in the mind"), symbols, even the language we use. Positive images are conjured up in most of us by such phrases as "Constitution," "free enterprise," "the rule of law," "free speech," and the use of such terms to describe what exists may lead us to believe that reality fits into such "good" patterns. Sometimes reality may indeed be what the words implicitly suggest, but reality is not determined by the words or assumptions used to describe it. Reality has its own independent set of characteristics and causes, and it may bear little resemblance to what the familiar words urge us to believe. If we are diverted from objective perception by symbols, stereotypes, and loaded words, we may never come to know reality as it is.

The Nature of Evidence

What do we need to know in order to say that a political institution or process works in a particular way? We cannot accept assumptions or speculations, exhortations about how they *should* work, or the self-serving assurances of their sponsors. No matter how hallowed and revered the authority that prescribes or declares how things work, we cannot accept such characterizations as truth. Instead, we must demand precise specification of who actually did what, when, and with what effects. We must be able to say with confidence that thus-and-so is the way the Congress works, or that voters respond to factors X, Y, and Z in deciding which candidates to support. To be able to do so, we must have enough data on hand for a comprehensive characterization—one that leaves no gaps to be filled by ideology-affected assumptions.

When we have achieved exhaustive and accurate description, we are ready to attempt explanation: *why* do people do what they do in politics? Again, we rest primarily on factual evidence—on cause-and-effect relationships that are demonstrable to us or at least inferable from the evidence—rather than on other people's explanations or wishful thinking. It is tempting, once one adapts to exclusively data-based analysis, to assume that the collection of empirical data is all-important and that we can accurately come to know and understand politics and the political process simply by building up larger amounts of more concrete and rigorous data. In seeking explanation for empirically identified patterns of behavior, however, analysis must be aided by theory. In this sense, theory means hypotheses (informed guesses about causes, which can be tested against available evidence) reflecting experience and sophistication about politics. In order to arrive at hypotheses, we must employ our knowledge of the wide range of possible causes, the many forces at work within a context, and the structure of relevant power relationships.

The Focus of Analysis

We must look comprehensively at the acts of all (or at least most) of the powerholders who are active in any given area, and not direct our analyses exclusively at the acts or words of leaders or the official decisions, laws, or regulations of organs of government. The easiest way to observe and analyze politics is to look at the public acts and words of political leaders, on the assumption that they make the key decisions and set the goals their followers accept. The political leader acts in public. One of his chief functions is to make a strong and widespread impression. Because he has a stake in being dramatic, he makes good copy for journalists. Journalistic accounts of politics consist very largely of descriptions of the statements, actions, and interactions of political leaders.

But the political analyst who confines his attention to leaders is likely to be led astray at every turn. If there is a riot, he assumes that ringleaders or outside agitators must have "caused" it. The social scientist looks deeper: at the social, economic, and political conditions that explain the willingness of rioters to engage in violence, to follow leaders who advocate it, and to ignore potential leaders who counsel patience or peaceful courses of action.

Another pitfall is the assumption that everything important in politics and policy formation takes place in the formal institutions and organs of government. A high proportion of decisions is made outside the corridors of government buildings, though their outcomes are closely tied to people's assumptions about how great the political power of the participants is. Even the actions that can be observed taking place within governmental institutions often convey a very superficial or misleading notion of what is going on. One reason formal government acts can be misleading is that they are frequently not put into practice. Almost twenty years after the United States Supreme Court had declared racial segregation in public schools unconstitutional, it still existed in a very high proportion of American classrooms. What goes on in courts, legislatures, bureaus, and United Nations meetings certainly has to be observed. But merely observing it usually reveals little about its meaning. To understand the significance of formal governmental actions, the political analyst has to observe many other activities as well. And he must have in mind a theoretical framework that tells him how the activities he observes are related to each other.

The Analytical Frame of Reference

A final barrier in the way of accurate analysis is a narrow frame of reference within which, or the level at which, the analysis is conducted. Every effort at research and analysis must begin with some premises, or givens, about the world. But the act of making such beginning assumptions (an act that is frequently unconscious) may sharply confine the kinds of conclusions that can be reached. For example, if we assume the validity (or perpetuity) of existing American values, and if we assume that the present structure of power in government is fixed, then the only object upon which to focus analysis or evaluation would be the details of policies and the way in which they relate to the problems involved. This could be a relatively superficial analysis, because it might not penetrate to the real causes of a policy, or to the roots of the problem. Applied to the Vietnam War, for example, such an approach might conclude that its failure was due merely to tactical mistakes or errors of judgment on the part of particular policymakers, and that the whole matter could be rectified by replacing those men with better-informed individuals.

But perhaps a more probing analysis would suggest that more fundamental causes were involved. Analysis might go one step beyond policies to look at the political system itself: perhaps the relative freedom of the President to commit the country, or over reliance on military assurances of capability, or the impotence of Congress in the area of foreign policy, or the influence of economic interests with investments in the Third World nations are more significant causes of the Vietnam situation. None of these potential explanations, of course, would have been suggested by an analysis limited in scope to policy alone. Or analysis could go further still and look at the underlying values that give rise to both the political system and the policy.

Using the same example, the causal origins of the Vietnam War may lie in fears of communism, cultural or racial arrogance, or the needs of the American economic system. The point is that exploration of such possibilities would have been unlikely unless the analyst's frame of reference extended beneath the policies to the political system itself and finally to the underlying values that sustain both. Only then, with such a deliberately broadened and deepened approach, could he or she be sure of including all possible sources of explanation and avoid building in an ideological endorsement for the existing state of affairs. In some cases, clearly, the causes of problems lie at very fundamental levels, and failure to realize this may result in omitting from analysis the very characteristics or values that gave

The Last Laugh

rise to the problem in the first place. A wide frame of reference that probes all three levels of analysis must be part of our approach.

Politics in Capitalist America

We return now to the problem with which we began this chapter—that of understanding the significance of capitalism for the character of American politics. The analysis we are about to undertake has been designed to be broad enough to include the ways in which capitalism—and other social, cultural, and ideological factors—affect politics in the United States.

In Part Two, we will analyze four problem areas and the effects of government policies in each. All four problem areas are ones in which the nature of the economic system is relevant; it would, in fact, be difficult to find important areas in which it is not. But the potential role of the economic system and associated values and ideology in each area could be quite different. Chapter 2 takes up the broad problem of maintaining economic stability—perhaps the most important continuing problem of government. Chapter 3 explores a special policy area that may at first appear unrelated. But national security policy—military spending—is clearly a part of the larger problem of maintaining economic stability. Closely related is the problem of unequal income distribution and poverty, addressed in Chapter 4. The status of racial minorities is the final problem area, in which noneconomic factors might prove more significant.

Taken together, these four problem areas encompass much of the content of American politics. One of our tasks is to see (1) these problems, (2) the characteristics of the capitalist economic and social system, and (3) the actions of government, as one large and connected whole, an interrelated entity. One way to do this is to focus on the patterns of policy consequences (burdens for some, benefits for others) that may be linked to characteristics of the larger social system. But first we concentrate simply on the effects of government policies in each area. Some basic questions that readers should try to answer clearly are:

What does the United States government *do* in these areas?

Who gets what as a result of government policies?

What, if any, patterns of (1) government actions, and (2) effects of such actions, are evident in the four areas taken together?

It is not too soon to speculate about *why* things happen as they do, of course, but it is essential to keep in mind that the evidence has yet to be assembled. One further set of questions, similarly speculative, may be more directly applicable at this point:

Are there identifiable purposes or goals (consistent or conflicting) that may fairly be inferred from the answers to the first questions? If so, what are the priorities among such purposes or goals: which are foremost, and which are secondary?

After we have explored each of these areas, we shall turn to the task of understanding why things happen as they do. Our first inquiry will be directed at two standard explanations. One is a version of capitalist ideology, strongly held by most Americans, and the other is a counter to it perhaps best known as radicalism. Each of these ideologies offers a complete explanation for the pattern of American public policies, one justifying and the other condemning. We shall explore each in detail. Among other purposes, this will help us to generate appropriate questions for the subsequent analyses of power and decisionmaking. But we are getting ahead of our story.

PART TWO

PROBLEMS
AND POLICIES

Chapter 2

To understand politics, we must confront the most important problems that governments face. That is how we will proceed in the next four chapters, starting with the greatest problem of all.

Economic well-being is a major goal of most societies. Physical survival, social harmony, and political stability are all closely linked to the levels of productivity and employment, and the patterns of wealth and income distribution, achieved by the economic system. In

The Basic Problem: Economic Stability

the United States, paramount importance is attached to profit-generating opportunities for businesses and investors and to jobs for a growing labor force. There must be profitability, for that is the central goal of capitalism. There must also be jobs, to maintain consumer demand, provide mass satisfactions, and prevent unrest.

What does this mean for governmental priorities? First, threats to the smooth functioning of the economic system, such as inflation or trade barriers, must be controlled or overcome as quickly as possible. Second, several long-range needs must be promoted. Steady growth in output of goods and services must be maintained so that new profit-making opportunities and new jobs are constantly developing. Consumer demand must be maintained, so that such goods and services find buyers. The whole system must be kept functioning in a predictable way, so that businessmen and investors can plan five- or ten-year projects in confidence that conditions will assure their ultimate profitability.

No other continuing issue or problem—only the most dramatic national emergencies—rises to a similar level of importance. Most other policy problems, such as poverty or racial tensions, promptly recede to secondary status when compared with this overriding necessity. They are dealt with only in ways that are consistent with this basic need. Failure to serve this need adequately, of course, would have profound—perhaps ultimately destructive—consequences for the society.

But maintaining the smooth functioning of the economy is never a simple task. Contradictory theories, conflicting interests, lack of full information, and the impact of international developments all contribute to making the job difficult in the best of times. In the 1970s, however, several factors have converged to make the task more difficult than it has ever been. Indeed, although almost forgotten after two decades of relative stability, the possiblity of a worldwide depression has once more entered the range of policymakers' vision.

We shall first examine the basic elements of the current problem, and note the stakes that various people have in its solution. Then we shall review the tools that government has available to promote growth and stability. Finally, we shall explore the policies applied in the 1970s, and their consequences for both the economy and for people. We shall see that the policy choices that government officials make necessarily result in benefits to some people and burdens to others. For example, all people do not gain or lose equally when the government acts in certain ways to control inflation. In most cases, and particularly in the early 1970s, working people pay the price— in the form of lost jobs, lower real wages, and reduced government social programs. Corporate profits, however, rose to record levels in late 1971 and 1972.

The Elements of Economic Stability

What threatens the stability, predictability, and confidence that are necessary to general and long-term profitability? War and domestic turmoil are highly destabilizing factors, but government seeks to avoid them for other reasons as well as to maintain profitability. The more specifically economic problems that threaten stability—which government addresses with the principal goal of maintaining profitability —are inflation, unemployment, growth, and the balance of payments between the United States and the rest of the world. We shall examine each in turn.

Inflation

Inflation is a general rise in the prices of goods and services, such that the *real value* (or buying power) of money is reduced. Three dollars are necessary today to buy what only two dollars bought yesterday. Inflation may be caused by one or a combination of three sets of forces. One is "demand-pull" inflation, in which an excess of money in the hands of consumers bids up the prices of goods. This may happen during periods when consumer goods are scarce, such as wartime, or as a result of governmental spending in excess of its revenues —in which case it is injecting new money (or increased demand) into the economy. A second source or type of inflation is "cost-push" inflation, in which the rising costs of production (raw materials, interest on loans, wages, and the like) force producers to charge more for their products.

The third form is "profit-push" inflation, in which those producers or investors who have sufficient control over the market for their products or capital to flourish seek to make more profit by raising prices, or by maintaining them at an artificially high level when other prices are declining. In this type of inflation, of course, a noncompetitive market situation is assumed. As we shall see later, this is the case for many American industries, dominated by a few large corporations. Thus, the prospect of this form of inflation, while new, is real.

Combinations of these three types of inflation are also possible. For example, producers may use slight rises in the costs of production as grounds for large price increases. Or a period of inflation may be initiated by one form of inflation, such as governmental spending in excess of revenues for a sustained period (such as the Vietnam War), and continued through one or both of the other forms.

What difference does it make whether inflation is of one or another kind? Don't all people suffer equally from all types of inflation? The simple—and perhaps already obvious—answer is that people do not all or equally suffer from inflation. Rather, one's situation depends on the type of inflation, as well as on one's source of income. (The type of inflation is also relevant to whether and how government can control inflation; we shall take up this aspect of inflation in a later section.) In the case of demand-pull inflation, for example, the need for more workers to produce more goods may result in the sudden availability of jobs or higher income for people who are usually unemployed or earn only minimum wages. For these people, a period of this type of inflation may be the only time that they experience full employment or decent wages. Clearly, such people benefit from inflation. If one's income is derived not from wages but from ownership of corporate stock, the question is whether corporate profits and/or stock value are rising at a rate in excess of the general price rise. If they are, or if the combination of a person's salary, dividend income, and gain from the increase in stock value rises faster than prices (which they normally do), such people also benefit from inflation. Their real income is increasing: they can buy more, relatively speaking, with their income than they could before inflation, despite price increases.

Most wage earners, and all those (such as retired people) on fixed incomes, stand to lose from inflation. Unless they are able to secure wage increases proportionally greater than price rises, their standard of living will be reduced by inflation. It is very difficult for such people to keep pace. Employers do not willingly increase wages at any time, and do so even less willingly during periods of inflation. Only those workers who are members of the most powerful unions are usually able to keep pace with inflation, and even they have difficulty. Those who are not unionized (about *three-quarters* of all workers) are likely to fall further and further behind. Thus, it is highly probable that most wage earners, and certain that all people on fixed incomes, will lose from inflation—at least in relative terms. The exceptions are few: those who can only find employment when demand-pull inflation creates extra jobs, and those who make increased wages—wages, that is, proportionally greater than the rate of inflation.

But inflation also creates problems of predictability for businessmen and investors. In order to be certain of making profits, they must be confident that the returns on their investments will be enough to keep ahead of the rate of inflation. Loans or other investments made this year, if repaid ten years from now in money of substantially lower value, will return insufficient real profits to investors—and soon there will be no willing investors. Similarly, businessmen must be confident that their investments in plant and equipment today will lead to sales at prices that will mean real profits tomorrow. Thus, it is not so much the prospect of inflation itself (which can be planned for), but the prospect of uncertainty—uneven or unpredictable rates of inflation—that is most troublesome to business and financial interests.

Inflation also has several combined economic and psychological effects. If the expectation of inflation is widely shared, people may act to protect themselves against its effects and thereby generate a self-fulfilling prophecy—a prediction that comes true because people act as if it were true. Such attitudes and behavior fuel the upward movement of prices, but at uneven and unpredictable rates. Moreover, inflation in one nation reduces the value of that nation's currency in relation to that of countries not experiencing inflation. Speculators may anticipate the devaluation of the nation's currency, and thus sell their holdings of that currency for a stronger currency—thereby creating further devaluative pressure. The result of such speculation may be instability throughout the international monetary system, interfering with normal world trade—and causing unemployment in various countries. (We will discuss this in more detail later.) Finally, inflation, if prolonged, is likely to have an unsettling effect upon broad segments of the population. Those who have fallen behind economically, and even those who by dint of special efforts have managed to stay even, begin to feel the pressure and to express resentment of the economic and political system that has permitted such conditions. After a long enough period, their resentment may turn into rejection of that system and action to fundamentally change it.

Unemployment

Unemployment has a similarly destabilizing effect, though it is more clearly focused on workers. Prolonged unemployment may generate unrest and resentments among workers, and build up pressure for some kind of action to correct the situation. Not only are poverty and hunger destructive of individual and family life; they also imply reduced consumer demand in the economic system as a whole—hence reduced need for production, and further reductions in employment. In short, employment levels are an important clue to stability *and* profitability within the economic system.

Unemployment may occur because of rapid technological changes in the economy, as when a new productive process renders the skills of a special group of workers no longer relevant. Or it may occur— as is so often alleged—simply because certain potential workers lack all of the basic skills necessary to hold even simple jobs, or because certain people are not really willing to work regularly. Perhaps most commonly, unemployment results from the fundamental fact that there are not enough jobs in the economy for all the people who wish to work. This is another way of saying that the level of demand— purchasing power in search of goods and services—is not high enough. If wages and employment levels were higher, the argument goes, demand would rise and jobs would be more plentiful. Of course, profits might be proportionally lower. Profits are not necessarily highest when employment and wages are at their peak, as we shall see later.

Who are the unemployed? Who suffers when unemployment rises? In the case of technological unemployment, even highly skilled middle-class people may be unemployed. Normally, however, they can find reemployment within a reasonable time, if necessary by moving to another part of the country. This is what happens when government cutbacks in defense spending leave thousands of highly skilled engineers and craftsmen unemployed. But for the most part, the unemployed are the lower echelons of workers—those without skills, women, and minorities. They are the last hired and the first fired as businesses expand and contract their work forces.

To maintain consumer demand, and to keep such people at a basic minimum level of existence, government has initiated a number of social welfare programs. The maintenance of consumer demand is not the only reason for such programs; there are also humanitarian motives involved. But the effect is to keep demand within a predictable range, and above a certain minimum floor. Of course, there are often considerable expenses involved in such programs, and it becomes both economically and politically difficult for government to maintain them at high levels of cost for long periods of time.

Growth

In economic terms, *growth* means continued expansion of the production of goods and services, and hence continued increase in the number of jobs available for people. Growth is necessary to have continued opportunities for profitable investment, and continued expansion of businesses. Without such increased opportunities, a capitalist system ceases to be profitable, which is another way of saying that it ceases to exist. And without such opportunities, there will not be the increasing number of jobs needed to employ the increasing number of people who each year seek work in the American economy.

When an economy fails to produce the growth needed to absorb the capital available for investment or to provide the jobs needed to keep people employed, it is said to be stagnant. *Growth rates* express the pace at which such opportunities are generated. In general, a rate of from 5 to 7 percent per year is considered good, while a rate of 3 percent or less is considered too low to provide the needed opportunities.

It might appear that everybody stands to gain from growth, much as everybody initially appears to lose from inflation. But once again, it depends on the sectors of the economy that are growing, and who bears the burden of assisting whose growth. If growth is government-subsidized, for example, it may ultimately benefit those who own or are employed by certain industries, but at the cost of additional tax burdens on those whose taxes are the source of such subsidies. Those who buy goods whose prices are kept high by means of protective tariffs are burdened, while those who own the companies producing or marketing such goods are benefited. Or, if corporations are allowed special tax benefits designed to spur growth, ordinary taxpayers— who must therefore pay a higher share of the overall tax burden —may well feel that they are being forced to contribute to the profitability of such corporations.

For many years, growth seemed to be a relatively uncontroversial way to expand the economic product and to give "have-nots" something more without depriving the "haves." Recently, the means of promoting growth have come to be seen as favoring some at the cost of others, and thus have become controversial. But an even greater source of controversy has been the uncritical assumption that growth is completely and unqualifiedly *good*. Some opposition to growth was expressed by those concerned with the developing ecological crisis.

They argued that further or unselective growth under present conditions could only hasten the rapidly approaching depletion of natural resources and destruction of the environment. Others saw growth as taking place at the cost of further exploitation of Third World nations, and as provoking tensions or conflict with them. Thus, growth too has come to be seen as involving choices in which some will be winners and some will be losers.

The Balance of Payments Between the United States and Other Nations

A country's *balance of payments* is the net total of all its transactions—trade, aid, loans and investments, profits returned, and so on—with all the other countries of the world. A continuing deficit means that the nation is paying out more than it is taking in, and the difference will at some point have to be made up either from its reserves of gold or through the devaluation of its currency. If trading partners in other countries, and/or the international bankers who control the rates at which the currencies for such transactions are set, lose confidence in the predictable future value of that currency, they may simply decline to deal with the nation in question. They cannot be sure of making a profit because they cannot know the value of the currency involved at the future date when payment is to be made. International trade may thus be greatly reduced, with consequent reductions in profits, levels of production, and jobs. Uncertain or shifting currency valuations also reverberate through the international monetary system, setting off waves of readjustments that similarly threaten trade between other nations. As trade declines, stagnating conditions become worldwide.

In such circumstances, it again may appear that all lose equally. But some people are more dependent on export industries than others. And some people can survive periods of unemployment or inflation better than others, for reasons we have examined. Thus, some stand to gain or lose more than others from fluctuations in the level of international trade. And clearly, only those with large sums of money to invest are immediately affected by changes in currency values. It is not until the general level of economic activity is affected that most people begin to feel the consequences of such changes.

We have now described the major threats to economic stability and profitability that exist in the 1970s. In every case, what government does—the choices among policy options that officials make—causes some people to gain and others to lose. What they gain or lose may be money, jobs, or the means of survival itself. We shall now look briefly at the kinds of policy options governments have available to maintain stability, and at some of the prospective winners and losers from each.

The Basic Theories for Coping With the Problem

Since the Great Depression of the 1930s, governmental action to support and expand the economy has become familiar and accepted. Less recognized is the degree to which the national government and the corporate economy have become interdependent. We shall explore the nature and implications of this integration in Chapter 8. But it is important to note now that the management of the economy by the government described in this chapter is not an antagonistic relationship between two distinct parties. It is more like the purposeful activity of two experienced partners, who so fully share goals, strategies, and risks—and the knowledge that they can only succeed or fail together —that their actions are almost indistinguishable. To say that "the government" takes a step is only to identify the member of the partnership which acts, usually after consultation and with attention to joint needs.

Faced with repeated cycles of inflation and depression, American policymakers and economists have gradually developed a body of conventional wisdom about the government policies that should be applied to stabilize the economy under various conditions. Three types of remedies for destabilizing threats to profitability make up this conventional wisdom: monetary policies, fiscal policies, and "incomes" policies. Each rests on distinctive assumptions about economic conditions, and each normally has strong supporters in and out of government. The three types of policies also represent increasing degrees of government "intervention" in the economy.

Monetary Policies

Monetary approaches to stabilizing the economy rest on the premise that the actual supply of money in circulation powerfully affects income, output, and prices. To prevent or control inflation by this approach, government should simply reduce the amount of money in the country, by not printing new bills to replace worn-out currency, by promoting higher interest rates, and by tightening up on credit. The result will be reduced employment, lower output, and lower prices. In periods of stagnation, government can induce higher levels of each by increasing the amount of money in circulation, by printing additional new bills, reducing interest rates, and so on.

One advantage of this type of remedy is its impersonality. It appears to avoid the situation in which government must choose the segments of the population that will gain and lose from the impact of inflation-controlling policies. By using only contraction or expansion of the monetary supply as a tool, government in effect lets the workings of the private economy determine who shall bear the inevitable burdens resulting from slackening of demand and reduced investment. Normally, of course, this translates simply into unemployment for millions of people at the lowest levels. Another apparent advantage is the limitation on government intrusion in the workings of the economy: monetary policies are relatively slight and indirect thrusts, and are felt by various sectors of the economy only after being transmitted by the standard sources of guidance—the supply of and demand for money. But, perhaps for these reasons, monetarists concede that the effects of such policies are not immediate. Under ideal conditions, they take from six to nine months to develop measurable consequences, and sometimes longer before their effects are significant. Thus economic or political conditions may make other measures necessary.

Fiscal Policies

Fiscal policies involve somewhat more direct and immediate effects on the economy. The various forms of fiscal policy all have to do with the way the government manages its own finances, i.e., how much money it raises in taxes, how much it spends, and for what. The fiscal-policy approach to stabilization and growth was originated by the English economist John Maynard Keynes. Writing in the 1930s, Keynes argued that it is possible for a capitalist economy to become stabilized at low or depression levels of productivity and employment, and that the key to both levels *and* fluctuations lies in the amount of total consumer demand being generated in the economy. Because the budgets of modern governments are primary sources of impact on the private economy, he urged the conscious use of government expenditure-revenue policies to promote or decrease demand and thereby spur or retard the economy.

Such policies could take the form of a large budgetary deficit or surplus, tax reductions or increases, expenditures for new projects such as public works, or cancellation of similar projects already under way. The first item in each of these pairs would stimulate demand, and the second would contract it. To spur the economy, for example, government should under this approach cut consumers' taxes, run a budget deficit, and invest heavily in public-works projects. When these ideas were first introduced, resistance both to the unorthodoxy of a deliberately unbalanced government budget and to purposeful government intervention in the private economy ran high. But avoidance of a depression since 1946, despite Keynesian rhetoric and practices, has gradually made such policies a standard part of the accepted role of government. Who gains and who loses from fiscal policy actions depends on the specific actions taken (e.g., whose taxes are cut or raised, by what relative amounts, and so on).

Incomes Policies

The third more or less conventional approach, reserved as yet for what are perceived as "emergency" conditions, is an *incomes* policy. It assumes that circumstances (inflation, profit levels, and the like) require direct government controls over wages and prices to produce the desired economic conditions quickly and effectively. This means that the government must make not only an annual estimate of the direction in which the economy should be guided, as under the Keynesian system, but also a conscious choice of the segments of the economy that should gain or lose proportionally in profits or income during the year. The controls are then applied in such a way as to accomplish the wage and/or price increases or decreases that will bring this about. Clearly, this type of policy involves direct and extensive government management of the economy, and (though practiced in wartime) was unprecedented in the peacetime United States before 1971.

What is distinctive about each of these types of economy-managing policies? We have seen that they reflect increasing degrees of government "intervention" in the economy. They are also distinguishable by the assumptions on which they are based, and on the degree of choice on the part of government as to who will gain and who will lose from their effects. The first two—monetary and fiscal policies—both assume the same "package" of economic problems. For example, both see inflation, low unemployment, and active growth as comprising one set of consistent symptoms: an active, booming economy in which the problem is to dampen expansion so that inflation does not get out of hand. Both see depression or recession, high unemployment, and low growth as typical of the opposite or stagnating end of the business cycle. The problem there is to get the economy growing again. Each type of policy has a remedy for each package of characteristics or problems. They differ chiefly in the aggressiveness with which they use the instrument of government for that purpose. Fiscal policies are the more aggressive, but both make major use of the workings of the private economy (properly stimulated by government) for the purpose of bringing about the desired result.

The problem of the early 1970s, however, did not fit the assumptions of monetary and fiscal theory. Inflation was associated with high unemployment and low growth, an unprecedented combination. It was not a demand-pull inflation. This was particularly serious because the remedies prescribed by each theory (intended to reduce or stimulate demand) were rendered counterproductive or contradictory. A remedy designed to combat inflation would do so by promoting unemployment and further impeding growth. And a remedy designed to counter unemployment and spur growth would do so only by promoting inflation. Any action by policymakers in accordance with either theory would only make some part of the existing problem worse.

An incomes policy, of course, is not necessarily bound to any particular assumptions about the economy. It simply asserts government control over the economy. It is a much more direct and complete control system, in which the degree of choice about who wins and who loses is much greater. Those who believe, for whatever reason, that a minimum of government control over the economy is desirable tend to be opposed to an incomes policy. But so do those who suspect that, if it is applied at all, it will probably be applied in the interests of the dominant economic sectors of the society and not of working people.

In the circumstances of the 1970s, therefore, the stage is set for vigorous debate over the proper policies to be applied to the management of the economy. The challenge to the first two types of policies argues that they are based on faulty or outdated economic concepts, such as competition or a free market, and hence will not work. The "parable of pigs" on pages 36 and 37 is a none-too-subtle allegory that presses that argument. The challenge to the incomes policy argues simply that policymakers either do not know or care how the burden of fighting inflation is distributed—or that, if they do know, they are deliberately placing it on working people. Let us see how policies and their consequences reveal both the nature of the problem and the distribution of gain and loss from government actions.

Problems and Policies of the 1970s

Stage One: Through July 1971

The Nixon Administration came into office in 1969 to find inflation rising rapidly, apparently as a result of massive spending on the Vietnam War and resulting budget deficits. Table 2-1 shows the patterns of growth, inflation, unemployment, and budgetary deficits or surplus for the 1960s and 1970s. It is important to note not just the fluctuations within each column, but also the relationship between columns (i.e., how changes in one area precede or follow changes in another). For example, inflation was at a very low and steady level (column 4, the Consumer Price Index growth rate) through 1965, and did not begin to rise until 1966. During the same period, unemployment stayed rela-

A PARABLE OF PIGS
(THE INFLATION/UNEMPLOYMENT DILEMMA)

Douglas Stutsman

There once was a pig farm that was operated by an old farmer, his son, and a hired man. The farmyard was filled with hundreds of pigs of all sizes, and they all ate their swill from a huge trough. The big hogs ate faster than the little ones, but they had bigger bellies to fill, and when the swill was finally gone, all the pigs were content. One day some of the biggest hogs jumped into the trough, and the swill spilled over the sides. Some of the little pigs did not get enough to eat, because they could not lap up all the spilled swill before it soaked into the ground. The farmers saw the swill overflowing and they were greatly upset.

The old farmer had learned his agricultural theory in the old Classical School, and he knew that when swill overflowed a trough there was too much swill in the trough. He did not see the big hogs in the trough and he did not notice that some of the little pigs were hungry, because he had been taught that hogs do not jump into troughs and that little pigs do not go hungry (unless they are just too lazy to eat).

The farmer's son had been educated in the new Keynesian School of agricultural theory, but he saw the problem much as his father did, for he too had learned that spilling the swill means too much swill, and, like his father, he did not see the big hogs in the trough, for he too had been taught that hogs do not jump into troughs. But unlike his father, he knew that little ·pigs sometimes were forced to go hungry. (He was fond of joshing his father by reminding him of the notorious pig famines of the past and thus revealing the absurdity of the Classical "hungry pig = lazy pig" theory). But at first the son did not notice the hungry pigs either, because he knew that pigs do not go hungry unless there is too little swill, when quite obviously the present problem was too much swill, i.e., spilling swill.

The son had recently reached manhood and had taken over management of the farm, and so the problem was his to solve. The next day he put less swill in the trough, and sure enough the overflowing stopped. Both father and son were delighted, and each was sure that the happy results supported his school of agriculture theory; however, they soon noticed that some of the little pigs were starving. The father argued rather weakly that these must be lazy little pigs, but the son wore a broad smile of anticipation, for he knew how to solve this problem too. Here, at last, was an opportunity to demonstrate to his father the superiority of the "new" agricultural theory. He patiently explained to his father that the starving little pigs were not lazy; they simply could not get enough swill. He poured more swill into the trough, and sure enough the little pigs stopped starving. The father was amazed and he became a convert to the "new" agriculture. (The father was somewhat senile by this time.)

But soon they noticed that the trough was overflowing again, and they were greatly distressed. When they put in enough swill to feed all the pigs the trough overflowed, and when they took out enough to stop the over-flowing some little pigs starved. They knew nothing in either the Classical or the Keynesian theory to explain and solve the problem. They worried about it constantly and came to call it the "spilled swill/hungry pig dilemma." They became desperate and tried all sorts of ingenious proce-dures in an attempt to find a solution. They tried pouring in the swill from either side of the trough and from both sides simultaneously, they poured swill in one end while the hired man scooped it out the other, and they even tried running up to one side of the trough and acting as if they were going to empty their buckets and then hurrying around and pouring them in the other side, but still the dilemma remained; and it appeared to be getting more severe, because more hogs were jumping into the trough. (Of course neither father nor son noticed the big hogs in the trough, because they both had learned that hogs do not jump into troughs.)

Finally desperation turned to resignation and they lost all hope of finding a solution. Instead they tried to find some balance, some acceptable com-promise. They sought that combination of spilled swill and hungry pigs that would be preferable to all other combinations, but they could not agree. When the son was at the farm he instructed the hired man to pour in enough swill to keep all the pigs from starving, for if the "new" agricultural theory had taught him anything, it was that pig famines were unnecessary. But when the son had to be away and the father was in charge, he instructed the hired man to pour in less swill so that the trough would not overflow, for the father still suspected that hungry little pigs were lazy little pigs.

The simple hired man had never been to school and was completely innocent of agricultural theory. He had great respect for both father and son and was awed by their obvious learning, but sometimes he wondered quietly why they did not pull the big hogs out of the trough.

From Douglas Stutsman, "A Parable of Pigs (The Inflation/Unemployment Dilemma)," *Review of Radical Political Economics*, August 1972.

tively high. As the former rose in 1966–1969, however, the latter dropped; both were probably responding to the large Vietnam War spending, which resulted in the massive deficits of 1967 and 1968.

The Nixon Administration's first acts were standard anti-inflation policies. Cuts were made in federal spending, particularly in the pur-

TABLE 2-1
The Big Picture: Basic Trends in the Economy, 1960–1972

Year	Growth		Inflation		Unemployment	U.S. Government Budget
	GNP* (billions of 1967 dollars) 1	GNP Growth Rate (percentages) 2	CPI† (1967=100) 3	CPI Growth Rate (percentages) 4	Rate, all Workers (percentages) 5	Surplus/deficit for year ending July 1 (billions of current dollars) 6
1960	573.5	2.5	88.7	1.6	5.5	+ .3
1961	584.7	1.9	89.6	1.1	6.7	− 3.4
1962	623.0	6.6	90.6	1.1	5.5	− 7.1
1963	647.9	4.0	91.7	1.2	5.7	− 4.8
1964	683.3	5.4	92.9	1.3	5.2	− 5.9
1965	726.5	6.3	94.5	1.7	4.5	− 1.6
1966	773.9	6.5	97.2	2.9	3.8	− 3.8
1967	794.0	2.6	100.0	2.8	3.8	− 8.7
1968	830.4	4.6	104.2	4.2	3.6	−25.1
1969	852.2	2.6	109.8	5.4	3.5	+ 3.2
1970	846.6	−0.6	116.3	5.9	4.9	− 2.8
1971	869.6	2.7	121.3	4.3	5.9	−23.8
1972						−38.8 (est.)

Source: *Economic Report of the President, 1972.* Column 1: Tables B–1, B–2, B–3, pp. 195–199; Column 2: calculated from annual change; Column 3: Table B–45, p. 247, Column 4; calculated from annual change; Column 5: Table B–24, p. 233; Column 6: Table B–63, p. 269.
*Gross National Product
†Consumer Price Index

chase of war supplies (by this time, American forces in Vietnam were being reduced), and interest rates were raised as part of a contraction of the money supply. The federal budget deficit was reduced by the cuts in war spending, and revenues were increased by the tax increase of 1968, so that a small surplus was possible in 1969. The figures for 1970 show the results of these policies very clearly: economic growth was sharply curtailed, dropping to a minus figure for the first time since the Great Depression of the 1930s, and unemployment took the sharpest jump in more than a decade. But inflation did not respond: it continued to rise. Thus the problem of the 1970s took shape—low growth, rising unemployment, and high and still-rising inflation, an unprecedented combination of stability-threatening factors.

Another way of grasping the nature and meaning of the problem of the 1970s is illustrated in Table 2-2. Here we examine the profit levels of business and the wage levels of workers during the same years. Notice that corporate profits (column 3) were at their highest during the boom period of the early years of the Vietnam War, and then began to drop steadily, falling to their lowest levels in more than a decade at the time of the initial budgetary cutbacks. The utilization of plant (the extent to which factories and machinery were working, in relation to their capacity) was highest in 1965 and 1966 also, no doubt linked to the high profit levels. The sharp drop in utilization to the 1970 and 1971 levels is another way of saying that the rate of economic growth was very low in those years. A contrast may also be drawn between wages and corporate profits as proportions of national income. As unemployment dropped in 1966–1969, workers' share of the national income (although trailing slightly) rose steadily, and corporate profits fell commensurately. Thus, the problem of the 1970s as seen by the Nixon Administration could also be defined as low utilization of plant and low corporate profit rates (whether measured as a percentage of stockholders' equity or as a share of national income).

Stage Two: August 1971 through December 1972

In preparing the federal budget for fiscal year 1971 (the year ending June 30, 1971), the Nixon Administration saw typical recession characteristics in all respects except for persistent and still-rising inflation. When growth is low or nonexistent, and the general level of business activity is depressed, federal revenues are also lower. But Vietnam War spending was not eliminated, the defense budget absorbed nearly $78 billion, a wide variety of subsidies and other obligations required funds, inflation pushed federal government costs up, and so on, keeping spending pressures high. The result of this combination of factors was the largest peacetime budgetary deficit in

TABLE 2-2
Who Gets What: Business Activity and Profits, Workers' Jobs and Income, 1960–1972

Year	Utilization of Plant (percentages) 1	Productivity — Output per Man-hour (1967=100) 2	Corporate Profits — Percentage of stockholders' equity, manufacturing corporations 3	Corporate Profits — Percentages of national income 4	Jobs and Income — Wages & Salaries as percentages of national income 5	Jobs and Income — Unemployment Rate (percentages) 6
1960	80.1	78.2	9.2	8.4	73.8	5.5
1961	77.6	80.9	8.9	8.3	73.5	6.7
1962	81.4	84.7	9.8	8.9	73.1	5.5
1963	83.0	87.7	10.3	9.1	73.2	5.7
1964	85.5	91.1	11.6	9.6	73.0	5.2
1965	89.0	94.2	13.0	10.6	72.2	4.5
1966	91.9	98.0	13.4	10.6	72.2	3.8
1967	87.9	100.0	11.7	9.5	73.3	3.8
1968	87.7	102.9	12.1	9.2	74.8	3.6
1969	86.5	103.4	11.5	8.2	76.3	3.5
1970	78.2	104.3	9.3	7.2	77.5	4.9
1971	74.5	108.1	9.6	7.7	77.2	5.9
1972						

Source: *Economic Report of the President, 1972.* Column 1: Table B–38, p. 238; Column 2: Table B–34, p. 234; Column 3: Table B–75, p. 282, Column 4: computed from Table B–12, p. 209; Column 5: computed from Table B–12, p. 209; Column 6: Table B–24, p. 223.

American history (to that point) in 1971. The effect of this, of course, was another massive push toward future inflation, or, to put the matter more charitably, a "major investment to spur future economic growth."

The Nixon Administration had not sought such a massive deficit, of course. It had been applying standard anti-inflation policies prescribed by monetary theory, but they were not working. Together with spending cutbacks, they had slowed growth, reduced profits, and forced unemployment upon more than two million persons—but they had not stopped the rising rate of inflation. At this point, another major factor entered the picture, raising the problem to the crisis level. The value of the American dollar began to drop rapidly on the international monetary exchanges, threatening the stability of all other currencies and raising the possibility of the collapse of international trade. Where stable currency values cannot be assumed, trade may not be profitable. It will then either be curtailed, or governments will raise tariffs to protect their own key industries. In either case, the prospect is reduced levels of business activity and thus reduced employment— and eventually worldwide depression.

The reasons why the dollar dropped in value in 1971 may at first appear difficult to grasp. But they must be understood, because the dollar crisis of 1971 will be repeated at intervals throughout the 1970s unless causal conditions change substantially—and such dollar crises are a crucial factor in the American economic problems of the decade. Behind the dollar crisis lies the stagnating character of the American economy (low growth, unemployment) and inflation—the combination of which leads both foreign and American investors and speculators to feel that the American dollar does not represent a stable, continuing unit of value. In West Germany, for example, growth in 1971 was steady and inflation slight. The German *deutschmark*, therefore, appeared to be stable in value but rising in strength relative to the American dollar. These contrasting national economic factors make it unlikely that *exchange* rates (the ratio at which dollars are convertible into marks) can remain constant. And yet international transactions, on which the stability and growth of all national economies in the capitalist countries depend, require nearly constant exchange rates.

Although its roots lie in the long-term trends just noted, the immediate precipitating cause of dollar crises is the nation's balance-of-payments situation. Several types of payments are involved. The *balance of trade* (the difference between value of exports and value of imports) is perhaps the best-known component of a nation's balance-of-payments situation. For many years, the United States had exported more than it imported, and thus had a favorable balance of trade, receiving more payments than it paid out. But by the late 1960s, foreign-made goods were selling briskly in American markets, and

American exports were decreasingly competitive overseas. As Table 2-3 shows, the balance finally tipped against the United States in 1971.

Table 2-3 also shows the fluctuations in other payment flows that led to the crisis of 1971. Military grants and foreign aid, principally designed to bolster friendly governments against foreign or domestic threat and to maintain a climate of opportunity for American business and investors, run at a steady level of $6 to $7 billion per year. Long-term private investment continues to rise, as American corporations become increasingly international in scope. There are substantial and increasing returns on this private investment, of course, which reduce the net outflow substantially (and might, in time, neutralize at least those types of outflow just discussed).

TABLE 2-3

The Balance of Payments Crisis of 1971: What Happened

	1968	1969	1970	1971
Balance of Trade	+ .62	+ .66	+2.11	−1.74
Military grants, foreign aid	−7.18	−7.17	−6.70	−6.70
Long-term private investment	−2.89	−2.42	−3.47	−5.88
Income on long-term private investment	+6.05	+6.82	+7.36	+8.01
Short-term private investment and income	+7.69	+9.55	−5.84	−10.17
Miscellaneous (mostly unrecorded transactions)	−2.65	−4.74	−3.28	−14.69
Balance of payments	+1.64	+2.70	−9.82	−31.17

Source: Adapted from Frank Ackerman and Arthur MacEwan, "Inflation, Recession and Crisis, Or, Would You Buy a New Car from this Man?" *Review of Radical Political Economics*, IV (August 1972), Appendix A, Table 2, p. 31; and *Economic Report of the President, 1972*, Table B–87, p. 296.

The most decisive changes in the balance-of-payments situation in 1971, however, appear in the short-term investment and miscellaneous categories. (The difference between the two categories lies mainly in the recorded or clandestine nature of the investments made.) Those with large sums of money to invest for short periods of time (certain wealthy speculators, banks, and the treasurers of American multinational corporations) naturally seek to make the highest possible profits on their money. When inflation is high, they can earn more money and incur less risk that it will be reduced in value by investing it overseas. In particular, if one anticipates that such inflation will eventually force the U.S. government to officially devalue the dollar, quick profits may be obtained by buying another nation's currency and holding it until the devaluation occurs.

Devaluation means that the U.S. government officially fixes the value of the American dollar at a lower level than before in relation to the price of gold and to other nations' currencies. For example, a 10 percent devaluation would have its effect of changing the dollar's ratio to the West German mark from, say, one dollar = three marks to one dollar = 2.7 marks. The speculator, banker, or corporate treasurer who had invested in marks at the rate of three for each of his (perhaps millions of) dollars would, after devaluation, have made a profit of 10 percent in as little as a few days. The attractiveness of such rapid profits draws much speculative investment, and naturally has a self-fulfilling effect in building pressure for the anticipated devaluation.

"And so, extrapolating from the best figures available, we see that current trends, unless dramatically reversed, will inevitably lead to a situation in which the sky will fall."

In August 1971, American and foreign speculators, bankers, and corporate treasurers began to see inflation and worsening balance-of-trade conditions in the United States as foreshadowing inevitable devaluation of the dollar. Waves of speculation, in which dollars were sold for gold, for the West German mark, for the Japanese yen, and for other sound currencies, hit the markets of Europe and Japan. Because the American dollar was the basic unit of the entire international monetary system, such rapid shifts in the dollar's trading value threatened to disrupt trade between all nations. Unless trading partners can confidently predict the value of the currency in which payments are to be made at some future time, they cannot be assured of mutual profit in the transaction and thus will not engage in trade. And if they stop trading for any period of time, national levels of growth and employment immediately drop. If monetary uncertainty continues and trade is reduced or halted for very long, the entire capitalist world is threatened with depression.

In the face of these dangers, the Nixon Administration abandoned the modest monetary and fiscal policies that had been employed, but apparently proven inadequate, for the past two and one-half years. The problems of low growth, unemployment, and continued inflation now were accompanied by serious international complications, the solution to which demanded much more drastic action. But the theoretical confusion still persisted. Neither economists nor policymakers had a consistent explanation or remedy for the conditions that existed. That national policy had to be undertaken amidst great uncertainty is shown by the words of the President's Council of Economic Advisers, who noted with respect to this occasion:

> While these facts (low growth, high unemployment) were clear, their reasons and their implications were unclear. . . .
> Why the slowdown in the inflation was so halting and uncertain is another question which has not been clearly answered. . . .
> The third part of the picture, the great enlargement in 1971 of the balance of payments deficit, also had its share of unanswered questions. . . .
> Policy in the summer of 1971 had to address the uncertainties as well as the obvious facts of these three interlocking problems. The relations among the problems greatly complicated the choice that had to be made.[1]

Nevertheless, the government had to act. By guesswork, sheer ideology, or shrewd insight, a compelling crisis had to be averted if possible.

The Nixon Administration undertook three major policy departures. The first was a set of international actions. The United States severed

---

[1]*Report of the Council of Economic Advisers, 1972* (Washington: Government Printing Office, 1972), pp. 65–66.

the relationship between the U.S. dollar and gold, in effect telling the world that it would no longer back the value of the dollar with gold from its rapidly diminishing reserves. It then called for an international monetary conference, at which new exchange rates and other agreements would be set. It also imposed a 10 percent surcharge on all imports into the United States, thus pushing up the price of foreign goods in American markets. This combination of measures had the effect of putting pressure on other countries to help solve the United States' balance-of-payments problem, by giving up some competitive trading advantages and/or absorbing some of the American inflation through acquiring more soon-to-be-devalued American dollars.

The second and third components of the package of new policies were directed at controlling inflation and spurring growth and employment. Here is how the Council of Economic Advisers described administration reasoning and actions:

> The steps decided upon for dealing with the international situation introduced a potent new argument into the Administration's consideration of the merits of a comprehensive system of controls. Improvement of our international position would require effective and convincing action on domestic inflation, in addition to the action the United States was seeking in the international sphere. Such action on the domestic front would assure our trading partners of our intentions and provide the framework for a cooperative approach to the solution of international problems.
>
> These considerations, combined with others already present, led to the decision to institute a powerful, but temporary, price-wage control system. Once this decision had been made it altered the balance of considerations with respect to a more expansive fiscal policy. Action to make fiscal policy more expansive had been limited by the need to avoid intensifying any inflationary expectations and stepping-up the inflation. The establishment of the direct wage-price controls created room for some more expansive measures, because it provided a certain degree of protection against both the fact and the expectation of inflation. This situation had to be approached with caution, because excessive expansion could make the price-wage control system unworkable. Still there could be no doubt that the tolerable rate of expansion had been increased.
>
> Thus, the decisions of August 15 consisted of a three-part, integrated package: (a) international measures aimed at the balance of payments; (b) controls aimed at checking inflation; and (c) fiscal measures aimed, in combination with the international measures and controls, at speeding up economic expansion and reducing unemployment.[2]

[2]*Report of the Council of Economic Advisers, 1972* (Washington: Government Printing Office, 1972), pp. 68–69.

The intent of the wage and price controls was to clamp a lid once and for all on the persistent problem of inflation. This classic "incomes policy" was authorized by the Democratically controlled Congress in the Emergency Stabilization Act of 1970, but probably without the real expectation that it would be used by the Republican administration. The complete freeze on wages, rents, and prices lasted 90 days, after which it was supplanted by a control system administered by new Presidential agencies. The growth-spurring (and inflation-generating) federal budget deficit, then projected at $34 billion, was increased still further by means of tax credits to businesses and the acceleration of certain deductions for individual taxpayers.

By means of this package of policies, several potentially contradictory forces were set in motion—and all three types of economy-managing policies were put to work at the same time. The 10 percent surcharge on imports represented a clear threat of a mutually destructive trade war in which the relatively stronger American economy would probably be a relative victor. Thus European countries were under pressure to grant trade or monetary concessions to prevent the United States from having to absorb all the damaging effects of its inflation-stagnation crisis. If the United States could get its inflation under control by the time of the monetary conference, it might be able to emerge with less damage to its relative trading and monetary status than at first seemed possible. But because it sought not only to control inflation but also to spur growth, the Nixon Administration was simultaneously applying monetary and fiscal policy in a manner that could not help but create major inflationary pressures for the future. Additional money was put into circulation, and greater deficits were incurred—necessarily resulting in greatly increased inflationary pressure, almost certain to become effective when and if the direct price and wage controls of the incomes policy were removed.

By December 1971, inflation did appear to be slowing. The monetary conference held that month resulted in new international monetary agreements hailed by President Nixon as "the most significant monetary agreement in the history of the world." The United States devalued the dollar by 7.89 percent, and certain other countries agreed to revalue their currencies upward by various lesser amounts (thereby accepting trading disadvantages to aid the American balance-of-trade problem). A new system of international monetary relationships, more flexible but still related to the dollar, was established, and the United States rescinded its surcharge on imports. A temporary stabilization was thus achieved, dependent on the longer-term developments in the U.S. balance-of-payments and inflation situations. Bankers, traders, and national governments alike expressed satisfaction that stabilization was at hand.

The domestic consequences of the combined package of policies initiated in August 1971 began to come clear in 1972, and by the end of that year were fairly well established. The rate of inflation at first appeared to slow, finally dropping below 3 percent during parts of 1972. But it remained stubborn, with several areas showing continued rises despite price controls. Wages were easier to control because employers resisted increases generally, and only the most powerful unions succeeded in challenging the guidelines laid down by the presidential enforcement agencies. On those occasions when wage increases exceeded federal guidelines, they were reduced by action of the government. Price increases, however, faced no such systematic hurdles. The

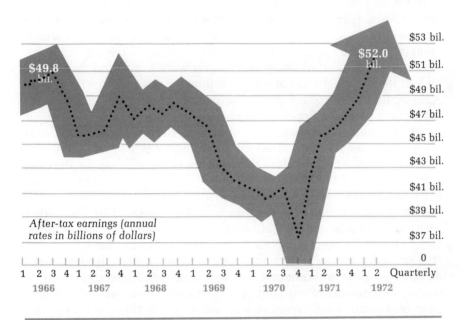

Source: Through first quarter 1972, U.S. Dept. of Commerce, Second Quarter, 1972 estimate by USN & WR Economic Unit. Copyright © 1972, U.S. News & World Report, Inc. *U.S. News & World Report,* 7 August 1972.

FIGURE 2-1
THE PROFIT SURGE OF '72

price control system had a number of loopholes, for which unorganized consumers were no match. The growth rate was clearly picking up in the latter part of 1972, such that predictions of a coming economic boom were made repeatedly during the presidential campaign of 1972. Unemployment, however, remained at nearly the same levels it had maintained for the past two years, dropping only slightly.

But the greatest impact of the new economic policies was on corporate profits. Spectacular rises were reported by nearly all of the major corporations as early as the end of 1971, and the second quarter of fiscal 1972 (marking the end of the new policies' first year) saw corporate profits reach a record annual rate. Not all of these profits were due to loopholes in the price control system. Some were due to the large tax write-offs offered to corporations in 1971. And profits can increase even if prices remain constant, provided that productivity increases and makes more goods available to be sold at the fixed cost.

Stage Three: January 1973 and After

In January 1973, President Nixon surprised businessmen and economists by scrapping the new presidential agencies and the entire control system. In effect, he reverted to exclusive use of the fiscal and monetary policies in effect before August 1971. In keeping with the principles of those theories, interest rates were raised and the federal budget sharply slashed in order to continue efforts to control inflation. Apparently believing that enough momentum lay behind the increasing growth rate, the President presented the Congress with a budget in which many social programs were completely eliminated and others cut back substantially. Defense spending, however, was increased to a new high. The President declared that he would apply the persuasive power of the White House to keep prices and wages below inflationary levels.

The American balance of trade for 1972, revealed at about this time, stood at a record $6.5 billion deficit, the worst in history. Why were American goods suddenly less successful in overseas markets? One possible answer is that American workers earn such high wages by contrast with workers in other countries that American products cannot be priced competitively. Many business and government officials, and some labor leaders as well, subscribe to this view. The remedy they propose is some form of trade limitation to protect domestic markets, and increases in the productivity of American workers and/or government subsidies to render exports more competitive.

The problem with this analysis is that American workers have always earned more than foreign workers, and the difference is probably less now than it has been in the past. At least two other factors also appear to be involved: the loss of technological superiority on the part of domestic American manufacturers and the internationalization of American corporations. The technological superiority of American manufacturing used to allow such high productivity per man-hour that American goods could be priced competitively at home and abroad despite relatively higher labor costs. This technological edge has now been greatly reduced, in major part because of the massive investment of American capital in building new plants abroad. The modernization of American productive techniques is apparently less profitable as an investment than establishing new facilities abroad. Meanwhile, European manufacturers have invested in new technologies and accepted lower profit levels than American companies in order to break into new markets.

Thus, American companies can now produce abroad for sales abroad—thereby helping, together with European producers, to reduce the market for exports of goods made in the United States. In some instances "foreign" goods and, more often, major components of apparently "American-made" goods sold on the American domestic market have actually been made by overseas units of American multinational corporations. Employing the newest technology and foreign workers, such American corporations can detach themselves from dependence on American workers, but still maintain their sales position in American markets—and simultaneously increase their profit margins. The effect on the balance of trade for the United States conceived as a national economy, however, is pressure toward increasing deficits. In short, there are more imports, and fewer successful exports, every year; the internationalization of the world capitalist economy, not the greed of the American worker, is the major cause.

Also in January 1973, new manifestations of the continuing surge of inflation appeared. Food prices in particular were rising rapidly, but so was practically every other measure of inflation. Whether this was due to the suspension of the price control system or to the accumulated pressure of the massive federal budget deficits of previous years was unclear. It was clear, however, that wages were not the source of the renewed visibility of inflation: wages were actually dropping in some cases, and in all cases real wages were decreasing.

Perhaps predictably, the worsening American balance of trade and the rise in inflation triggered speculative activity on world money exchanges, and by early February 1973 the dollar was trading at record lows. The central banks of other countries were forced to acquire billions of weakening American dollars to support its price and maintain it as the core of the international monetary system. Every dollar acquisition under such conditions transfers some of the American inflation to other countries by forcing them to put more of their own money into circulation. It also threatens to make them the sources of major profits by speculators if and when the dollar is devalued. Thus, there is a limit to how long other countries can continue to buy dollars. In mid-February 1973, the pressure on the dollar rose to a point that forced the Nixon Administration again to act. This time it unilaterally devalued the dollar by a full 10 percent, and called for the Congress to authorize the President to employ substantial trade barriers as a means of forcing other countries to grant new trading concessions to the United States. The monetary agreement of December 1971 ("the most important . . . in the history of the world") lay in shambles, and the American dollar had lost 17.89 percent in official value in the space of about a year and a half.

Summary and Implications

The Continuing Problem

The United States government faces, as its most important continuing problem, the task of insuring steady growth, minimal unemployment, low inflation, and a sound balance of payments. In the 1970s, this task has become both crucial and difficult. It is crucial because of the growing interdependence of the government and the economy, and because the combination of national and international conditions makes worldwide depression a real possibility. It is difficult because of the changing character of the newly internationalized capitalist economy, and because of the differences of interest between sectors of the American economy and population.

More specifically, the basic economic problem of the 1970s is controlling inflation and restoring a sound balance of payments. Inflation, running at an average rate of about 5 percent for the first four years of the decade, is steadily eroding the value of the dollar and reducing the real standard of living of all but a fortunate few Americans. Massive deficits and continuing price rises in basic commodities suggest that more is yet to come. The devaluation of the dollar will improve the American balance of trade, because export goods will now be cheaper in foreign markets. But mutually damaging trade wars may well result.

Another aspect of the economic problem of the 1970s is continuing high unemployment. Americans have long been accustomed to accepting relatively high unemployment rates (from 3 to 4 percent) as "normal" or "full employment." West Germany, for example, has an unemployment rate of less than 1 percent, and most European countries define "full employment" as unemployment rates of less than 2 percent. But the American rate has been above 5 percent throughout the first four years of the decade, and has reached 6 percent on occasion. That there are apparently just not enough jobs is in part the result of stagnant growth. As the rate of expansion in the economy picks up, however, it does not seem to result in significant reductions in unemployment. This may be due to the increasing numbers of people seeking jobs, or to the increasingly technological character of the new jobs that become available. In any event, unemployment and underemployment remain serious.

But this summary only brings us to the special problem of the 1970s —the fact that inflation is accompanied by high unemployment. This unprecedented combination means that either new remedies or new combinations of remedies must be found, and/or that unusually high costs will have to be paid by some sector of the economy before real stability is achieved. All known remedies for inflation tend to increase unemployment and impede growth, while known remedies for unemployment and insufficient growth tend to spur inflation.

Choices Amidst Uncertainty

Government policymakers understand that something must be done to restore stability, predictability, and profitability. The balance-of-trade deficit and dollar weakness place continuing strain on an already unsatisfactory—and potentially dangerous—situation. But neither economic theory nor past experience appears to offer a coherent explanation or a consistent remedy. Policymakers' choices must be made amidst factual uncertainty and a lack of understanding of the dynamics of the new economy. In such a situation, old assumptions, ideology, basic preferences, and sheer guesswork are the likely bases of decisions.

What are some of the assumptions and preferences that will shape policy, and what difference do they make? One set of assumptions has to do with the causes of inflation. If inflation is seen as due to excess demand, or to increasing costs of production, the remedy is to reduce the amount of money in the hands of the consumers through tax increases or tight money policies that also promote unemployment. If wages are seen as a major source of cost-push inflation (as they usually *are*, despite the fact that wage increases normally trail price rises), the remedy is wage controls. In either case, lower-class and working people will bear the brunt of the cost of controlling inflation. But if inflation is seen as caused by the profit-push actions of market-dominating corporations, the remedies would be price and profit controls. In such a case, the costs would be borne by the owners and managers of the major corporations and banks.

Another set of assumptions and preferences has to do with the manner in which growth should be promoted. One school of thought holds that prosperity is dependent on the profitability of business, and that if government insures increased profits there will soon be jobs and opportunities for all. President Nixon stated this position well in 1971:

> ... let us recognize an unassailable fact of economic life. All Americans will benefit from more profits. More profits fuel the expansion that generates more jobs. More profits means more investment, which

will make our goods more competitive in America and in the world. And more profits means that there will be more tax revenues to pay for the programs that help people in need. That's why higher profits in the American economy would be good for every person in America.[3]

Some economists label this the "trickle-down" theory of economic distribution or recovery. It has almost uniformly been the strategy for government stimulation of the economy. Tax cuts to induce invest-ment and other business-spurring provisions are traditionally more acceptable to the Congress than any other remedies.

The opposite approach assumes that increased demand is the key to growth, and is preferable for the well-being of working people. Transfers of spendable income to the lower echelons of workers, the poor, and the unemployed—by means of drastic revision of the tax laws or significant new government investment in employment-generating public works programs, or perhaps both—are advocated. This school of thought sees wage controls as a governmental effort to depress the real wages of workers while corporations enjoy increased trading competitiveness and rising profits.

Two major points should be clear in this illustrative contrast of two sets of assumptions and preferences involved in economic policy-making. 1. Assumptions and preferences can play a large part in shaping policy; it is not a field in which facts are undisputed and theory universally shared. 2. The choices made, methods employed, and priorities established (between controlling inflation and curing unemployment, for example) carry massive financial meaning for millions of people. In other words, what policymakers assume about the causes and appropriate remedies, and what they prefer about who should pay the costs and reap the benefits, shape their economic poli-cies and determine whether working people will have jobs and at what income.

Some Key Questions

We have argued that the matters addressed in this chapter lie at the heart of all government policymaking, except in the direst national emergencies. In subsequent chapters, we will take up the government's record in some of the other high-priority policy areas. Each raises issues that bear upon long-term profitability, and policy-makers must make repeated choices based on their assumptions and preferences. We shall focus as much as possible upon the long-continuing patterns and consequences of their policies. A key ques-tion thus is: who bears the burdens, and who reaps the benefits, from

[3]Richard M. Nixon, Address to the Nation, 7 October 1971.

government policies—over time, and in various policy areas? Or, stated differently, what assumptions and preferences about profitability may be imputed to policymakers from the results of their decision-making over a long period of time? More simply, why do they do what they do? In the latter forms, this question will be the basis for intensive exploration of both justifying ideologies and actual decisionmaking later in the book.

Another set of possibly even more important questions underlies the analysis in this and the next three chapters, and also bears on the major issue raised in Chapter One. How much of what policymakers do is necessitated by, strongly induced by, or merely consistent with, the nature of the evolving American capitalist economic system? In other words, are the actions of policymakers primarily directed toward serving the profitability or income needs of a single sector of the economy? How often do their actions run counter to the interests of long-term profitability? How completely are their actions explained by the nature of capitalism as such?

In this chapter, we have seen that the consequences of policy have tended to work to the advantage of corporate stockholders and managers by maximizing profits. Workers experienced reductions in real wages, and, in the case of several million people, unemployment. Is this result (1) unique to this economy-managing situation, (2) unique to this policy area, or (3) dependent on the particular choices of today's policymakers? In any of these cases, it would not appear to be directly related to the nature of capitalism. But if this outcome is consistent with other situations in this and other policy areas, and thus is not attributable to the choices of particular policymakers, we may be led to conclude otherwise. Continued maximization of profits at the cost of workers' income and well-being does not establish conclusively that capitalism is responsible (it might result from some convergence of power not wholly synonymous with the capitalist economic system), but it makes such a conclusion a strong contender.

These questions are at issue in the next stage of our inquiry.

Chapter 3

Since the end of World War II, the policy of the United States government has been to seek national security by maintaining military power superior to that of the major communist nations. In recent years, however, at least some aspects of this basic policy have been challenged. Concern over mounting military expenditures, reports of the wasting of billions of dollars in military procurement practices, and allegations about a "military-industrial complex" have become familiar features of American politics. Some have argued that the military is no longer under effective civilian control, either overseas or at home. Others insist that only the awesome might of American weaponry, alertly managed and constantly poised, has prevented nuclear war and protected the "free world" against communist expansion.

National Security Through Military Superiority

In this chapter, we shall first examine the basic assumptions that have led to the broad policy of national security through military superiority. As we shall see, the concept of "security" itself is open to contrasting definitions. Next, we shall review the major trends in American strategic and military policies, including the arms-limitation agreements of 1972, and offer a general forecast of the problems to be encountered during the latter years of this decade. Then we shall explore the various consequences of this continuing package of policies, particularly for the domestic economy. In a final section, we shall weigh some of the competing explanations for this heavy commitment to military supremacy.

Military Superiority: The Basic Assumptions

Conventional wisdom has it that German aggression prior to World War II occurred because of the military weakness of potential opponents. Military preparedness, it is therefore assumed, is the key to peace and stability in an uncertain and amoral world. This assumption led to the conclusion that the security of the United States required maintenance at all times of military strength superior to that of the major communist nations, which were perceived as expansionist and implacably hostile to the United States. In order to guarantee security, this military superiority would have to be sufficient to cause unacceptable (if not total) destruction of the Soviet Union, and recently China as well, even if such nations should first launch a surprise attack on the United States. Instituted in 1946 in the aftermath of World War II, the policy of security through military superiority still rests on these basic assumptions.

Security is an elusive and frustrating goal. For several reasons, it can never be finally assured. And, paradoxically, the more it is sought, the more it may recede. At any moment, a potential enemy may reach a scientific breakthrough enabling him to achieve military supremacy through technology. Or he may drastically alter the strategic situation through a sudden diplomatic success, subversion, or other means. The more a nation seeks assurance of security by military means, the more it must commit its resources to weapons, research and development, procurement of multiple attack and defense systems, alliances with the governments of other nations, economic and military support for such governments if necessary, and anticipatory intelligence and subversion activities throughout the world. Every such act, of course, provokes the potential enemy to undertake or expand similar activities, and these in turn reduce the first nation's security and require countering moves. Nearly three decades of "Cold War" marked by the continuing threat of nuclear annihilation, combined with the fear of communism, have made such commitments almost unquestionable among American policymakers.

The achievement of security through such means thus presents inevitable and apparently unending difficulties. On the one hand, it may be costly to the point of financial, if not moral, exhaustion. On the other, it may be so provocative that it causes the enemy to do as expected, and attack first in the fear that his survival depends on such a move. One alternative, of course, is to seek nonmilitary means of achieving security. The basic assumptions just reviewed, together with American perceptions of our own and Soviet behavior and intentions, have foreclosed real efforts in such a drastic new direction. A second alternative, however, is regularly argued and sometimes pursued, particularly in times of budgetary stringency. This is the principle of military *sufficiency*, rather than supremacy. In other words, all that is necessary is the sure capability to destroy all possible enemies, even if they strike first and no matter how well they might defend themselves. In addition, of course, policymakers would have to reach agreement on such matters as the number of conventional weapons and manpower needed to fight lesser wars and maintain domestic security.

The range of discussion among strategic planners thus tends to be between military sufficiency and military superiority. But the difference may be more apparent than real. What is enough? Who will take responsibility for assuring the American people that our military capability is sufficient to deter a Soviet or Chinese attack, when we cannot know for sure what new scientific breakthrough is about to occur or what the Soviet or Chinese planners are up to?

The Strategic Problem

If there is a factual base for resolving this dilemma, it lies in a nation's "second-strike" capability. The principle of deterrence holds that no nation will launch a "first strike," or "preemptive strike," against another if it knows that the attacked nation will still have the capability to retaliate with unacceptable levels of destruction. If all major antagonists believe that about each other, mutual deterrence will take effect and relative peace (or a "balance of terror") will reign. Second-strike capability requires that the necessary missiles be located so that they cannot be destroyed by the prospective enemy in any kind of first-strike attack. In practical terms, this has meant intercontinental ballistic missiles (ICBM) in heavy concrete ("hardened") silos and submarine-launched ballistic missiles (SLBM) stationed in undetectable submerged submarines around the enemy's coast. All missiles at above-ground locations, and all heavy bombers not actually in the air, are potentially applicable only to first-strike use, and thus serve to provoke rather than to deter. Even ICBM at hardened sites now may be vulnerable to accurate first-strikes with heavy new warheads, and deterrence is coming to depend more exclusively on submarine capabilities. In computing second-strike capability, of course, planners must provide for the defensive capabilities of an alert enemy, particularly through its antiballistic missile (ABM) system. Although these have yet to be proved effective, there is always the possibility that some incoming missiles might thus be rendered ineffective.

Thus we come to the business of calculating the destructiveness of the second-strike capabilities of the United States and the Soviet Union. (China as yet has no such capability; France and Britain will soon each have about 64 missiles in submarines.) Table 3-1 presents Defense Department estimates as of mid-1972. The American missile total has been stable since 1967, partly because of the need for funds for the Vietnam War and partly because it is perceived as sufficient. The Soviets, drastically outdistanced by the Amercan buildup of the 1960s, have recently closed the gap in number of missiles.

But in number of warheads—the nuclear-armed "payloads" of such missiles—the United States is far ahead. This is because the United States initiated a major new program in 1969 to produce multiple independently targeted reentry vehicles (MIRV), which permit each missile to carry several warheads, each of which can be aimed at a separate target. Most ICBM and submarine missiles are now being equipped with these MIRV, while some will have three warheads that spread in flight toward the same target. When this program is complete in the next few years, the number of American warheads will have been more than doubled with the addition of no additional missiles. The Russians have no such program, although they may in several years. Instead, they have a lead in the so-far ineffective ABM system, with 64 launchers in place around Moscow.

What does this stock of missiles and warheads mean in terms of second-strike capability? According to Defense Department estimates, 200 nuclear warheads landing on major Soviet targets would kill 52 million people (21 percent of the population) and destroy 72 percent of Soviet industrial capacity. In addition, millions would be injured or homeless, the physical environment contaminated, and social organization thoroughly disrupted. We may take this as representing "unacceptable" levels of destruction, sufficient to deter Soviet policymakers from launching a surprise attack on the United States. Assuming that five times the required number of missiles must be launched from protected land sites and from under the sea to assure that 200 missiles penetrate Soviet air defenses and reach their targets, it still appears that the United States possesses enough nuclear armament to destroy the Soviet Union several times over. The reverse is also true, of course. No matter how large the U.S. strategic forces grow, not even an American surprise attack could prevent the

TABLE 3-1

The Basic Comparison: Strategic Capability, 1972

	United States		USSR	
	Hardened Sites	Submarines	Hardened Sites	Submarines
Available missiles	1054	656	1550	580
Total number of warheads	5700		2500	

Source: "Strategy of Realistic Deterrence," Department of Defense Annual Report, Fiscal Year 1973 (Washington: Government Printing Office, 1973), p. 40.

Soviet Union from launching a prohibitively destructive second strike from its protected sites and submarines.

In terms of numbers alone, it would appear that the United States has more than achieved military sufficiency, and perhaps superiority as well, in its efforts to assure security. But, of course, these figures are only a small—though highly visible and important—part of the total picture. The relative destructive capabilities of each side can be greatly enhanced by research and development of new defensive and offensive systems. And the national interests of both sides can be advanced by developing and maintaining other weapons that make the cataclysmic use of nuclear arms unnecessary in conflicts of lesser importance. Accordingly, there is active competition between the United States and the Soviet Union in many other categories of military capability as well. Thus, the question "What is enough?" is not answerable exclusively by means of comparison of the superpowers' existing second-strike capabilities.

The Financial Problem

Another way in which "enough" is often measured is by its cost. In order to maintain military capabilities at the level deemed necessary, the United States invested more than $700 billion in direct military expenditures during the decade ending in 1973. At its recent peak during the Vietnam War, military spending exceeded $80 billion, amounting to 43 percent of the entire federal budget and 29 percent of all spending by all governments in the United States (federal, state, and local). A brief comparison of types of expenditures over most of the post-World War II period is presented in Table 3-2. Much of the increases shown are due to inflation, of course, but the comparison shows that military and space expenditures have consistently outstripped government investment in the other major functions combined. Not included are the payments on veterans' benefits or interest on that portion of the national debt incurred to finance past military spending.

One critic of military spending summarizes this situation as follows:

> Each year the federal government spends more than 70 cents of every budget dollar on past, present, and future wars. The American people are devoting more resources to the war machine than is spent by all federal, state, and local governments on health and hospitals, education, old-age and retirement benefits, public assistance and relief, unemployment and social security, housing and community development, and the support of agriculture.[1]

What is all this money spent for? Why is the total so high? For one thing, the military establishment amounts to a very large capital investment, both in the United States and overseas, and it requires commensurate operating costs each year. Department of Defense holdings in the United States, valued at their acquisition cost, total over $40 billion; personal property, such as plant and equipment, valued at their current cost, add another $162 billion. Overseas, the Defense Department has built or leased more than 2,000 bases in thirty countries. Their total operating cost is more than $4,000,000,000 per year, and they house more than a million service personnel and half as many dependents. In 1973, active-duty personnel totalled roughly two and a half million, with another million civilians directly employed by the Defense Department and about three million more working for the nearly 100,000 companies supplying goods and services to the military.

Aside from the sheer size of the military establishment, costs are high because of inflation, the rapid rise in costs of weaponry and manpower, and certain military procurement practices. In constant dollars, the $76 billion expenditure proposed in 1973 was actually *less* than the $51 billion spent as recently as 1964! The cost of increasingly sophisticated weapon systems has leapt well ahead of inflation and comparable commercial products. While the prices of industrial commodities rose about 23 percent between 1961 and 1971, the cost of many weapons rose 300 percent or more in the same period.

TABLE 3-2

Selected Public Purchases, by Function, in Billions of Current Dollars

	National Defense*	Space	Federal, State, and Local Governments Combined			
			Educa- tion	Health and Hospi- tals†	High- ways‡	Police and Correc- tions‡
1955	$38.6	—	$11.9	$ 2.8	$ 6.3	$ 1.8
1960	44.9	0.57	18.7	4.4	8.9	2.7
1965	50.1	5.6	29.1	6.5	11.9	3.8
1970	76.6	3.5	52.5	12.4	15.9	6.8

*National defense purchases category includes military assistance and atomic energy programs, but not space program.
†Includes federal veterans program, 1970.
‡State and local only, 1970.
Source: Calculated from U.S. Department of Commerce, *National Income and Product Accounts of the United States, 1929–1965*, Table 3–10; and U.S. Department of Labor, *Manpower Report of the President*, 1971, Table G–12.

Major items, such as fighter aircraft, cost five or six times more in the 1970s than in the 1960s. Military payrolls, the largest single item in the defense budget, are rising despite the fact that the number of persons in service in the 1970s is substantially less than during the height of the Vietnam War. The reason, of course, in addition to general pay increases for federal employees, is the effort to establish the military as an all-volunteer force. Despite reductions of nearly a million persons, therefore, the total amount spent on manpower has remained about the same, climbing from 43 percent of the budget in 1964 to 56 percent in 1973. Weapons procurement practices that have been severely criticized even by the military's friends in Congress include pushing new weapons systems into production before development is complete, adopting excessively sophisticated technology, and allowing lack of competitiveness and waste in the defense contracting industry. Because of all these factors, the once-expected drop in military expenditures after the end of the Vietnam War (the "Vietnam dividend" counted on by some social planners) simply did not materialize.

Time for a Change?

For nearly three decades, the same basic assumptions about the utility of military superiority and the danger of communism have dominated American thinking about national security and have justified granting military needs highest priority among federal expenditures. The 1970s have witnessed the first stirring of public challenge to the desirability of these priorities. Congressional disclosures of vast waste totalling billions of dollars in military procurement activities were one source of this concern, but more fundamental developments in the world-wide context also contributed to the new mood of questioning. The concept of security itself, at least as it had been understood in the past, appeared to be undermined by these changes.

The emergence of many newly independent nations, the rise of some secondary powers to nuclear or near-nuclear status, and the development of serious tensions among the communist nations all contributed to a much more volatile and uncertain world situation. With power widely diffused and multiple conflicts likely, some quite unrelated to competition between the superpowers, "security" would require preparation for many more contingencies, and would be far more difficult to assure. Also, the advance of technology creates two contrasting forms of pressure on established definitions and policy. On the one hand, highly sophisticated but vastly expensive new attack and defense systems appeared possible. Their efficacy was not proven, but if they worked, both sides would be tempted to develop them, and thereby greatly increase their armaments expenditures.

On the other hand, highly destructive nuclear weapons were becoming cheaper and easier to manufacture. In fact, they were so readily available that private groups or individuals might be able to acquire them. The only distinction remaining to the established superpowers, therefore, was the capacity to deliver thousands of tons of nuclear destructiveness by intercontinental rockets.

THE SOARING COST OF WEAPONRY

	Unit cost (millions of dollars)
Strategic Bombers	
B-29 [World War II]	$ 0.7
B-52 [1952–1961]	7.9
B-1 [in development]	30.0
Air Force Fighters	
P-47 [World War II]	0.1
F-105 [1954–1963]	2.5
F-15 [in development]	10.0
Aircraft Carriers	
Essex class [World War II]	4.7
Enterprise [1961]	451.3
CVAN-70 [planning stage]	900.0
Attack Submarines	
Conventional power [World War II]	4.7
Nuclear power [1968]	77.0
Nuclear power [1971]	175.0

Source: Data from Senate Armed Services Committee and the Defense Department, *Business Week*, 19 February 1972.

Finally, and perhaps most important, serious domestic needs became highly visible. Rebuilding the cities, restoring the environment, repairing worsening race relations, and generally reconstructing the American social order appeared to demand high priority. But none of these goals would be attainable within reasonable time limits, unless they received priority rivalling that of military expenditures. Moreover, "security" need not be merely an externally oriented concept. It seemed in many peoples' eyes to be applicable to domestic problems as well, and to justify placing such needs alongside military demands.

But, despite considerable rhetoric, very little was actually done to reduce military expenditures. Even under heavy criticism, the military budget endured, an achievement that demands investigation. For years, a variety of explanations for heavy military spending have been offered, only to be challenged by defenders of the military's needs or refuted by advocates of another explanation. The *strategic* explanation insists that all of the various weapons systems, in the amounts assembled, are necessary to the security of the United States. The *bureaucratic* or decisional-process explanation sees the military budget as the product of competition between the services and their allies in Congress, and of the momentum built up by the needs and power of the defense contracting industry, working through the military and the Congress. (Allegations about a "military-industrial complex" draw on the latter explanation.) Finally, the *systemic* explanation places responsibility on a combination of the capitalist nature of the American economic system and the values and ideology of Americans as a people. In the sections that follow, we shall examine recent policy trends and then the consequences of this long-established policy pattern. In conclusion, however, we shall return to the issue of the military's success in maintaining its high priority and heavy funding. The subject is too important and potentially revealing to defer, and we shall consider each of the possible explanations outlined above. Readers may wish to assess the next two sections with such alternatives in mind.

Policy Trends in the 1970s

The buildup of military manpower and purchasing for the Vietnam War began in 1965 and escalated steadily until its peak in 1968. In that year, there were 3,548,000 persons in the armed forces, and a total of 8,037,000 civilian and military jobs were generated by defense spending. In other words, 1 in every 10 jobs in the country stemmed from defense spending, which exceeded $79 billion. The purchase of arms alone topped $31 billion, compared to just over $18 billion in 1965.

The Nixon Administration began to reduce military spending in late 1969 and 1970, partly because of reductions in the number of men actually in Vietnam and partly as a means of combatting inflation. Much of the insistence in Congress and the nation upon cutting the military budget stemmed from opposition to the Vietnam War, and the administration was also responding to these pressures. Substantial cuts in the purchase of arms and other supplies were made

—about $3 billion in each of the first two Nixon budget years. By the end of 1970, the armed forces had been reduced by about 500,000 persons, and roughly another 500,000 workers had lost their jobs at defense plants. By mid-1971, only 1 in every 13 jobs in the country was defense-related, a reduction of nearly 1 out of every 4 defense jobs. Employment in the space industry also dropped sharply as expenditures were cut almost in half.

By the end of 1971, however, military spending was on the way up again. Inflation, payrolls, and new research and development used up the savings realized from reduced purchases and lower manpower. Even though military personnel had been reduced by a total of more than a million, and another 500,000 defense-related civilian jobs had been eliminated, the budget was up. One reason, clearly, was reduced congressional opposition and a lessening of the public pressure for cuts in military spending. In turn, this may have been due to the heavy impact of previous cuts on several states, and the generally high level of unemployment in the country—much of it traceable to previous defense cutbacks. The military budget rose in both 1972 and 1973, principally for research and development of new weapons and procurement of new missiles, aircraft, and ships—long-term strategic weapons, as opposed to the expendable supplies given priority in the Vietnam War period.

The most significant development of the early 1970s was the successful negotiation in 1972 of strategic arms limitation agreements between the United States and the Soviet Union. The basic purpose of these negotiations was to limit construction of more offensive weapons. Each side having more than enough to destroy the other, both could save money by not building more; but apparently neither could unilaterally take such action amidst domestic political pressures. To preserve the existing supremacy and capability of offensive systems, defensive systems too had to be limited. The two major agreements froze the deployed strength of both sides at then-current levels (see insert for details). This gave the Soviets a probable lead in number of missiles, but left the United States well ahead in number of warheads (see Table 3.1). The agreements did not apply to armaments other than long-range strategic missiles, leaving the United States with hundreds of medium-range missiles ringing the Soviet Union and more than 500 heavy bombers with nuclear armament, compared to less than 100 Russian equivalents. Nor did the agreements restrain the United States from its program of increasing the number of warheads per missile, or from expanded research and development of new systems.

Reaction to the agreements in the United States provide an interesting insight into the present state of military policymaking. Substantial congressional criticism was directed at the numerical lead

FACT SHEET ON AGREEMENTS

Following is the text of a fact sheet, released by the White House May 26, 1972, on the strategic arms limitation agreement.

The Current Agreements

The ABM Treaty

Limits each side to one ABM site for defense of their national capital (Moscow and Washington) and one site for each side for the defense of an ICBM field.

There will be a total of 200 ABM interceptors permitted each side, 100 at each site.

Radars will be limited to Modern ABM Radar Complexes (called MARCs), six for each side within a circle of 150 km radius around the national capitals; (MARCs are a circle of 3 km diameter, in which radars can be deployed; in practice they can accommodate about one large radar or a few smaller ones).

For the ICBM defense fields there will be a total of twenty radars permitted; two of them can be about the size of the two larger radars deployed at Grand Forks; the other eighteen radars will be much smaller.

The Soviet ICBM protection site will be at least 1300 km from Moscow. Our comparable site will be at Grand Forks, North Dakota.

in offensive missiles granted to the Soviet Union, particularly since the Soviet missiles are capable of carrying much heavier warheads than the American ones. Defense Secretary Melvin Laird informed the Congress that he could not support the agreements unless it approved increased funds for the development of new undersea missile systems and another manned bomber to replace the aging B-52s so heavily used in the Vietnam War. These new systems alone would cost over $25 billion during the five-year term of the agreements. In backing up his argument, Laird revealed for the first time that the Soviet Union was testing missiles that could lead to a MIRV system of multiple warheads much like the existing American system. The Joint Chiefs of Staff of the military services made clear their insistence that research and development, particularly of vast new weapons systems, not only be allowed to be maintained at levels superior to the Russians' but be funded as necessary to do so. Calls for reduced military spending as a result of the new agreements were limited to a few scattered congressmen and newspaper columnists.

The long-range effects of the arms limitation agreements thus appeared in doubt. On the one hand, present deployments and expan-

Other large non-ABM radars that may be built in the future will be restricted to space tracking or early warning and limited in size so as not to create a clandestine ABM potential.

The treaty will be of unlimited duration with withdrawal rights if supreme interests are jeopardized, and on six months notice.

The Interim Offensive Agreement

Limits ICBMs to those under construction or deployed at the time of signing the treaty or July 1. (This will mean about 1618 ICBMs for the USSR and 1054 for us.) The USSR will field about 300 large SS-9s, but they will be prohibited from converting other ICBM silos to accommodate the large SS-9 types. Other silos can be modified, but not to a significant degree. Modernization is permitted.

Construction of submarine launched ballistic missiles on all nuclear submarines will be frozen at current levels. The further construction of SLBMs on either side, can only be accomplished by dismantling of an equal number of older land based ICBMs or older submarine launchers.

The Interim Agreement will run for five years (compared to the original Soviet proposal of 18 months), and both sides are committed to negotiating a permanent and more comprehensive agreement.

Both sides will abide by the obligations of the agreement once it is signed, though formal implementation will await ratification of the ABM treaty.

---

sion of existing missile systems were frozen. On the other, the race for technological supremacy continues, and duplicative and supplementary weapons systems not limited by the agreements are being developed at a faster rate than they otherwise would have been. Costs continue to escalate rapidly, as each of the new and proposed systems on the military drawing boards turns out to be significantly more expensive than the last. Very little change in the basic military-supremacy assumptions appears to have occurred. Whether any real prospect for a change in these policy patterns exists is at least an open question. Nothing in the response to the arms limitation agreements or the continuing pattern of funding suggests that it does. The explanation for this may lie in the strategic situation, but seems more likely to lie at one of the levels cited earlier.

Three Decades of Military Priorities: The Consequences

We must observe immediately that there has been no nuclear war. Whether this is because of or in spite of the American policy of strategic superiority is not so clear. We have approached the brink of mutual annihilation with some frequency, in Berlin, in Vietnam, in Cuba, and in the Middle East. Whether, under different strategic conditions, American policies would have been less intransigently anticommunist, and Soviet policies more or less provocative in response, is a question that—if answerable at all—requires much deeper analysis than is possible here. But we can say with assurance that the *domestic* consequences of assigning the highest budgetary priority to military expenditures have become readily indentifiable. And increasingly, they appear to many to outrank international consequences in importance. Let us explore some of these domestic consequences before returning to the strategic scene.

Since World War II, a large new industry has been created.[2] During the war years, the bulk of federal expenditures went to long-established companies, which simply sold their usual products to the government for the duration of the emergency. Some companies developed products to meet defense needs or adapted existing models for military purposes. Automobile manufacturers diverted production to tanks, and aircraft manufacturers shifted to military aircraft. Many firms expanded production facilities, but few new industries were created. Even for those that modified their productive processes, postwar conversion to civilian production was practical, anticipated, and consistent with prior experience and expertise.

Developments in electronics, nuclear power, and rocket propulsion, however, have changed the character of military needs. Since the mid-1950s, the technological complexity of military requirements has spurred the rise of new companies (or substantially independent subsidiaries of established corporations) which specialize in such work—sometimes to the exclusion of all other products. Thus, over time there has developed a segment of the economy with an exclusively military focus, with no background experience of production for civilian needs or competitive consumer sales.

Characteristics of the New Defense Industry

Table 3-3 presents some summary data on the new defense industry of the 1960s and 1970s. The predominance of a relatively few companies is clear: in 1971, fewer than thirty companies received more than half of all defense dollars awarded. These companies are primarily engaged in only a few manufacturing industries. In 1964, for example, more than half of all defense dollars went to aircraft

[2]The most comprehensive analysis of the economic impact of defense expenditures is found in the work of Murray Weidenbaum, recently an Assistant Secretary of the Treasury. The next paragraphs draw particularly from his "Defense Expenditures and the Domestic Economy" in *Defense, Science, and Public Policy*, ed. Edwin Mansfield (New York: W. W. Norton, 1968).

and missile makers; about 25 percent to electronics firms; between 2 and 5 percent each to automobile, oil, rubber, construction, chemical, and educational institutions; and the remainder, less than 6 percent, was shared among all other industries.[3] These ratios have remained essentially unchanged since, although the Vietnam buildup shifted expenditures somewhat toward expendable supplies (food, clothing, and other consumables.) There has also been continuity among the leading contractors, chiefly aircraft manufacturers; the top five contractors of the mid-1960s remain among the leaders in 1971. Only a few drastic shifts have occurred, and these might be caused by specific features of the single year 1971.

Although the major contractors differ greatly in the proportion of their business that is dependent on defense contract awards, the data for the 1960s show that some of them do almost all of their business with the military arms of the U.S. government. These are, again, principally the aircraft and missile manufacturers. The leader, for example, is Lockheed Aircraft, which received more than ten and a half billion dollars in government contracts in the mid-1960s, a figure amounting to 88 percent of the company's total sales for that period.

The major defense contractors are located in two sections of the country. The aircraft and missile manufacturers and their related subcontractors tend to be centered in the southwest and Florida, while the electronics industry is chiefly located in the northeastern states. In 1972, for example, the three states of California, Texas, and Florida received almost 34 percent of all defense expenditures. The five northeastern states of New York, Connecticut, Massachusetts, New Jersey, and Pennsylvania received almost 20 percent. The other 42 states shared the remaining 37 percent of the defense budget, with none of them receiving as much as —any one of the five leading companies doing business with the Defense Department. This concentration of expenditures in a few regions means that the impact of defense spending is greatly multiplied in those areas. One estimate holds, for example, that 43 percent of the economy of the Los Angeles area depends on direct defense expenditures and the jobs and other services they generate indirectly.[4] Cutbacks in Boeing's prime contracts in the 1969–1970 period led ultimately to unemployment levels approaching 20 percent in the Seattle area.

The profitability of the defense industry is a matter of disagreement. Instances have been documented of particular contractors compounding profits among subsidiaries and subcontractors to attain real profit levels of 100 percent[5]. In other cases, contractors have been

[3]*Ibid.*, p. 20.
[4]*Ibid.*, p. 25.
[5]Julius Duscha, *Arms, Money and Politics* (New York: Ives Washburn, 1964), p. 78.

TABLE 3-3

30 Leading Defense Contractors, 1961–1967 and 1971, Showing Shares of Total Business and of Defense Spending (in millions of dollars)

		Cumulative Contract Awards, 1961–1967		Fiscal Year 1971		
Rank	Company	7-year Total	Percent of Total Sales	Rank	Contract Amount	Percent of U.S. Total
1.	Lockheed Aircraft	$10,619	88%	1	$1,510	5.08
2.	General Dynamics	8,824	67	2	1,489	5.00
3.	McDonnell Douglas	7,681	75	7	897	3.01
4.	Boeing	7,183	54	9	733	2.46
5.	General Electric	7,066	19	5	1,041	3.50
6.	North American-Rockwell	6,265	57	13	478	1.61
7.	United Aircraft	5,311	57	8	733	2.46
8.	American Telephone & Telegraph	4,167	9	3	1,200	4.03
9.	Martin-Marietta	3,682	62	26	187	0.63
10.	Sperry-Rand	2,923	35	16	359	1.21
11.	General Motors	2,818	2	17	344	1.15
12.	Grumman Aircraft	2,492	67	4	1,098	3.69
13.	General Tire	2,347	37	32	159	0.54
14.	Raytheon	2,324	55	14	454	1.53
15.	AVCO	2,295	75	29	171	0.57
16.	Hughes	2,200	u	12	516	1.73
17.	Westinghouse Electric	2,177	13	15	437	1.47
18.	Ford (Philco)	2,064	3	24	218	0.73
19.	RCA	2,019	16	21	251	0.84
20.	Bendix	1,915	42	31	162	0.55
21.	Textron	1,798	36	18	325	1.09
22.	Ling-Temco-Vought	1,744	70	10	725	2.44
23.	Internat. Telephone & Telegraph	1,650	19	23	233	0.78
24.	I.B.M.	1,583	7	19	316	1.06
25.	Raymond International	1,568	u	45	98	0.33
26.	Newport News Shipbuilding	1,520	90	6	913	3.08
27.	Northrop	1,434	61	34	151	0.51
28.	Thiokol	1,301	96	43	102	0.34
29.	Standard Oil of N.J.	1,277	2	27	187	0.63
30.	Kaiser Industries	1,255	45	71	57	0.19

TABLE 3-3—Continued

Contractors in Top 30 in 1971, but Not Among Top 30
Contractors 1961–1967

Cumulative Contract Awards, 1961–1967				Fiscal Year 1971	
Rank	Company	7-year Total	Percent of Total Sales	Rank	Contract Amount	Percent of U.S. Total
35	Litton Industries	1,085	25	11	516	1.73
31	Honeywell	1,129	24	22	237	0.80
*	American Motors	*	*	20	251	0.84
*	Teledyne	*	*	25	216	0.73
*	TRW	*	*	28	177	0.59
*	Olin	*	*	30	163	0.55

u = unavailable
* = not included by original data source
Source: Data for period 1961–1967 from Ralph E. Lapp, *The Weapons Culture* (New York: W. W. Norton, 1968), pp. 186–187; for 1971 from Department of Defense, as reported in *Aviation Week and Space Technology*, 6 December 1971, pp. 50–66.

able to persuade the government that profit levels were so low that contracts should be renegotiated. Precise general conclusions are impossible, because separate records on defense contracting, subcontracting arrangements, the actual costs of capital employed, and related matters are not kept or made available for analysis. But it is clear from studies made by the General Accounting Office of the Congress that the aerospace industry, at least, earns high profits (28 percent on equity capital, a figure considerably higher than commercial profits).[6] And it has been demonstrated that the profitability of these contractors, at least as measured by the prices of their stocks, is substantially higher than the averages of other stocks traded on the New York Stock Exchange.[7]

The Effects of Defense Priorities on the Domestic Work Force

Nearly 7 percent of all American workers hold jobs directly dependent on defense expenditures. Probably an equal or larger num-

[6]Richard F. Kaufman, "MIRVing the Boondoggle: Contracts, Subsidy, and Welfare in the Aerospace Industry," *American Economic Review* LXII (May 1927), p. 290.
[7]George J. Stigler and Claire Friedland, "Profits of Defense Contractors," *American Economic Review* LXI (September 1971), 693.

ber owe their jobs to the indirect or "multiplier" effects of this direct spending. We may guess that many of the latter are in sales, retail, or service occupations, but it is impossible to analyze this group precisely. The work force directly engaged in defense-generated work, however, is readily identifiable. Table 3-4 analyzes the non-military defense work force, and compares it with the general characteristics of the U.S. labor force. Predictably, defense employment engages a disproportionate number of professional persons, primarily engineers; there are relatively few sales, service, or laborer-farmer jobs among defense employees. Perhaps less obvious, however, is the fact that a highly disproportionate number of defense jobs are blue-collar jobs.

TABLE 3-4

Characteristics of the Defense-related Labor Force, 1968

| | Defense Employment | | U.S. Employment | |
Occupation Group	Total in Defense Work (in thousands)	Proportions of Defense Workers in Each Group (percentages)	Proportions of All Workers in Each Group (percentages)	Defense Workers as Proportions of Total Employment (percentages)
Professional	680	14.4	12.8	6.9
Managers, officials, proprietors	414	8.8	10.0	5.4
Sales	112	2.4	16.8	2.4
Clerical	830	17.6	6.4	6.0
Craftsmen, foremen	949	20.1	13.2	9.3
Operatives (semi-skilled)	1,233	26.4	18.4	8.8
Service workers	219	4.6	12.3	2.3
Laborers and farm workers	260	5.5	10.5	3.2
Totals	4,700	100	100	6.1

Source: *Monthly Labor Review*, February 1970, p. 12.

Skilled workers and production workers together make up nearly half the defense-related labor force, a much larger proportion than they bear to the American working population as a whole. In these two categories, defense employment represents nearly 10 percent of all jobs.

But the real significance of defense-generated employment is not evident until specific occupations are examined. Here we find that key skill areas have become much more fully dependent upon defense expenditures. In 1970, for example, one out of every five engineers employed in the United States was engaged in defense-related activities.[8] Among aeronautical engineers, the proportion was nearly one out of two. Figure 3-1 lists several occupations in which high proportions of jobs were tied to defense spending. Many scientists—chemists, physicists, and other natural scientists particularly—are concentrated in defense work. In 1970, nearly one-fourth of the country's physicists were in defense work.

The defense-related work force is thus a very special slice of the American working population, both occupationally and geographically. Certain occupations are highly dependent upon military spending, as are certain parts of the country. As a result of the cutbacks of 1969 and 1970, for example, severe unemployment developed among physicists, a group one might consider to represent an important national resource. In six states (Utah, Alaska, Hawaii, Washington, Virginia, and California), defense expenditures account for more than 10 percent of all personal income.

Consequences for the Larger Economy

What do these and other characteristics and effects of defense spending mean for the economy as a whole? First, it should be obvious that a considerable volatility is built into the economy by such substantial dependence upon government spending. When this spending rises, the economy is sharply stimulated; when it is cut back, employment and growth are sharply curtailed. The Vietnam buildup and cutback is a good illustration. From 1965 to 1968, about 1,400,000 new jobs were created by increased defense spending. Each billion dollars of defense purchases from the private sector is estimated by the Bureau of Labor Statistics to have created about 80,000 jobs in 1965 and 74,000 jobs in 1968.[9] These figures mean that nearly all of the roughly 2 percent drop in national unemployment during this period was attributable to increased defense spending, and that the cutbacks of 1969–1970 were a major cause of the unemployment of the early 1970s. In other words, the difference between full employment and recession may now be quite simply the extent of military spending.

[8]Richard Dempsey and Douglas Schmude, "Occupational Impact of Defense Expenditures," *Monthly Labor Review* 94 (December 1971), p. 13.

[9]Richard P. Oliver, "Increase in Defense-Related Employment During Vietnam Buildup," *Monthly Labor Review* 93 (February 1970), p. 3.

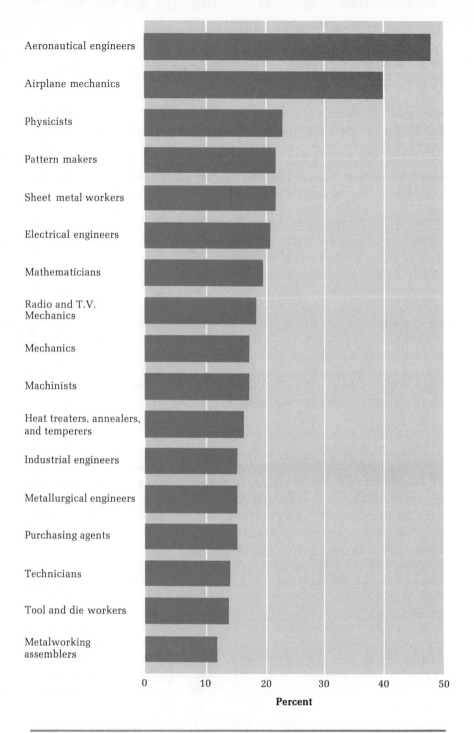

Aeronautical engineers

Airplane mechanics

Physicists

Pattern makers

Sheet metal workers

Electrical engineers

Mathematicians

Radio and T.V. Mechanics

Mechanics

Machinists

Heat treaters, annealers, and temperers

Industrial engineers

Metallurgical engineers

Purchasing agents

Technicians

Tool and die workers

Metalworking assemblers

0   10   20   30   40   50

Percent

Source: *Monthly Labor Review* **94,** (December 1971).

FIGURE 3-1
Proportion of Employment Resulting from Defense Spending, Selected Occupations, 1970

Second, it seems equally clear that the federal budget has been thrust sharply upward by the combination of defense priorities, the costs of the new weaponry, and the nature of the industry created to develop and produce these systems. It is the latter point that concerns us here. A noncompetitive industry whose activities are extremely costly and subject to politicomilitary management and decisionmaking develops certain special features. One of these is the tendency to underestimate the costs of major units, and another is to overestimate speed of delivery. According to a staff economist for the Joint Economic Committee of the Congress:

> An analysis of 45 selected major weapons systems now being built shows that they will cost $35.2 billion more than the original estimates, after adjustments are made for increases and decreases in quantities. From June 30, 1970, to June 30, 1971, the costs of these programs increased by $7 billion. . . . An examination of 57 selected weapons systems revealed program schedule slippages of from six months to three years in 34 of the systems.[10]

In other words, costs rise—and the federal budget is pressed constantly upward—not just because of inflation and sophisticated weapons, but due to the nature of the industry itself. We might also add that, because of the character of this industry, the Defense Department buys much of its equipment on a "cost-plus" basis. In other words, suppliers are permitted simply to add up all their costs, add on their margin of profit, and bill the government for the total. Competitive bidding may be impractical because only one company has the research and scientific skills to produce a certain product. (In 1968, for example, 58 percent of all contracts awarded by the Defense Department were by negotiation with a single supplier.) Or it may be ignored because the Defense Department wishes to allot its expenditures to several different companies or regions for technical or political reasons.

A third and broader consequence of the vast sums regularly appropriated for defense purposes is their impact on the national sense of priorities. That such expenditures tend to be self-validating, to the point that they develop an almost unchallengeable momentum and position among the activities of government, is evident in the failure of efforts in 1969–1971 to reduce military spending. Domestic social welfare expenditures receive far more challenge and investigation in the Congress, perhaps because they are more visible and intrude more upon vested interests in domestic politics. It seems clear that three decades of military priorities have set in motion a spending

[10]Kaufman, *op. cit.*, p. 289.

pattern that may now be irreversible. Whether this is true and—if so—why, are the subjects of speculation in the next section.

But sudden recognition of the significant domestic consequences of military priorities should not preclude awareness of some of the international effects of the American strategic superiority policy. As noted earlier, we cannot prove that this posture was responsible for the avoidance of massive nuclear war. But neither should we dismiss the possibility that the balance of terror of the past decades was a major contributor to the relative peace of those years. "Small" wars have been kept relatively small, even though tensions among the superpowers have occasionally been very high. The mutual deterrence of the superpowers has permitted many smaller nations to gain independence and attract assistance for their own goals, which they might otherwise have been unable to do.

The core of America's strategic problem today is still the definition of "security." But the contextual conditions—international, technological, and domestic—are so different from those of the early Cold War as to change totally some of the factors to be weighed and to introduce quite new alternatives. We may have reached a point at which *less* security, rather than more, is produced by the development of new weaponry, because several nations will possess the power to destroy each other without the certainty of suffering retaliatory destruction in return. The same outcome may occur if the domestic society, its problems unattended to, erupts in civil conflict or degenerates into a police state. What is "security"? Must it include the kind of domestic order and tranquility attainable only through general acquiescence in some version of justice? If so, then national security itself may demand a reordering of national priorities away from military "strategic superiority" and an accelerated arms race toward provision for domestic needs. But would the accumulated momentum of the Cold War and the influence of the "military-industrial complex" permit such a change in priorities? Or is it really unwise and dangerous to do *anything* to alter the policy of "erring on the side of American superiority" that characterized the previous decades—even though the sums involved might require a slighting of domestic needs and problems?

These issues were raised during the first Nixon Administration, as vastly expensive new weapons were proposed amidst demands for federal action to cope with problems in race relations, the cities, and the environment. As the debate wore on, the Congress continued steadily to appropriate military funds with the same paramount priority as before (though with somewhat more headline-attracting inquiry). Analysts and participants alike sought explanations and urged solutions for this apparent disinclination to consider the consequences of escalating military expenditures. Did the international situation require it? Or was the nation in the grip of a military-industrial complex so powerful that it could not be thwarted? The continuation of the policy of military superiority, and the consequences of that policy, raise questions about the possession and use of power within the American system that this book seeks to answer. Let us explore some explanations by way of illustration.

Military Priorities: Contrasting Explanations

Earlier, we introduced three contrasting "models" that are often used to explain the continued high level of American military spending: the strategic explanation, the decision-process or "military-industrial complex" explanation, and the systemic explanation. In this section, we shall explore certain features of each of these explanations.

We cannot really hope to understand military expenditures and policies fully until we know much more about the character and workings of the American political process, a subject analyzed in detail in Chapters 8 through 16. But because we want to make some important suggestions to readers at this early stage of policy analysis we will offer a brief preview of some matters elaborated on later. First, we want to suggest some ways of searching for possible explanations for the patterns and consequences of policies. Second, we want to illustrate the difference in *levels of analysis,* which we referred to in Chapter 1, in a concrete situation. Finally, we want to show the interpretive and evaluative implications of the scope of questions asked and frame of reference employed.

The Strategic Explanation: Analysis at the Level of Officials and Their Decisions

Much political analysis assumes that the causes of governmental actions are to be found exclusively in the merits of issues as they are perceived by the government officials responsible for the subject areas in question. This leads to the view that faulty or mistaken policy can be corrected by providing better information or voting better and wiser people into public office. The strategic explanation for military supremacy policy fits in this category. Its character, and its utility as an explanation, are well described by a political scientist as follows: "Strategic explanations are familiar enough: they argue that weapons procurement results from rational calculations about foreign threats or from the reciprocal dynamics of arms races. Not surprisingly, policy makers and officials offer strategic explanations. They are less favored, however, outside of official circles."[11] In other

[11]James R. Kurth, "The Political Economy of Weapons Procurement: The Follow-on Imperative," *American Economic Review* LXII (May 1972), p. 304.

words, outside of government, relatively few analysts believe that American security requires the production of so many duplicative and costly weapons systems. Some other explanation for continued high budgets and the construction of apparently unnecessary, obsolete, and wasteful weaponry seems to be necessary. Thus, we will move on to the two other explanations offered.

The Decision-Process or "Military-Industrial Complex" Explanation: Analysis at the Level of Institutions and Processes

Reaching somewhat deeper, this analysis focuses on the relationships between individuals and the social and organizational settings in which they operate, rather than on their private judgments. It is a more comprehensive approach; not satisfied with the observation that decisions are made by individuals, it goes on to ask what factors, in addition to the supposed merits of the issue, led them to make such decisions. There are many illustrations of this level of analysis in the current debates about the "military-industrial complex" and its power. Some see a community of interest among military officers, their friends in Congress, and the managers of the major military contractors and suppliers. Others include militarized civilian leaders drawn from business and the legal profession in this interlocking relationship. Analysts differ as to whether the initiative rests chiefly with the military or the industrial managers, but the principal thrust of their arguments is that the relationship between these holders of power in interdependent institutions is the real cause of military ascendancy.

Some basic characteristics of the decisional process lend support to this explanation. The military services are in a position to exercise powerful influence within the government, for at least three related reasons analyzed in detail in Chapter 12. In brief, the military is able to apply various forms of pressure to which congressmen in particular are vulnerable.

One illustration of this type of analysis is drawn from John Kenneth Galbraith's How to Control the Military.[12] As suggested by the title, the well-known Harvard economist sees the self-maintenance needs of the military as providing the impetus for this nonconspiratorial but shared-interest aggregation of power. He is convinced that military leaders are sometimes carried away by their anticommunism, that they seek excessive levels of security, and that they are often wrong in their assessments of both American capability and foreign nations' intentions and capacities. Their ascendancy in Washington is such that, with their allies in industry, they exert a nearly independent control over major aspects of American foreign and domes-

[12]John Kenneth Galbraith, How to Control the Military (New York: New American Library, 1965).

tic policy. Galbraith goes on to argue that this unhealthy influence gives the military a kind of sovereignty over the American people, which should be broken by restoring their power to Congress.

After reviewing the sources of the military's strength, he argues that conditions now make the military-industrial complex vulnerable. Essentially, this is because the communist world has fragmented, and the American people are no longer as tense about the communist threat as they once were; the American population is alerted to military indiscretion because of the Vietnam War; domestic problems are visible; and divisions of interest make some businessmen opposed to military expenditures. Galbraith's solutions follow from his analysis and his political experience: electoral action at the presidential and congressional levels; pressure tactics (particularly with regard to placing new members on the Congressional Armed Services Committees); a target goal of eliminating $5 billion per year in the production of weapons that encourage an arms race but leaving the space program intact; and an independent body of scientists to audit military needs.

Galbraith's argument has the merit of grounding itself in an analysis of the sources of military-industrial ascendancy, and of seeking to take such factors into account in developing countermeasures to bring about change. As he admits, however, his view of the extent of circumstantial change that is likely, and of the probable efficacy of his proposals, is highly optimistic. All of his proposals require substantial popular mobilization and involve electoral action—which would demand that millions of people learn to see this issue as more crucial than any other. They also assume that other forces (such as military persuasiveness or the economic well-being of particular areas) will not intervene and lead decisionmakers back to the established priorities. Modest and traditional as his proposals are, they appear to depend on forces and events not now powerful or probable. And there is an element of self-contradiction in them: if the military-industrial complex is as powerful as he says it is, it must have deep roots in the values of the society and in the economy. But if so, can it then be controlled through an electorally based attack focusing chiefly on the military?

Another type of institutional analysis sees the causes of military policy in the ideology of major civilian decisionmakers in various institutions of government, or in the developing "military socialism" inherent in the close and continuing relationship between the Defense Department, its holdings of land and equipment, and its major suppliers. In *The Economy of Death*,[13] for example, Richard Barnet—formerly an official of the U.S. Arms Control and Disarmament Agency—makes both of these points. Much like Galbraith, he argues

[13]Richard J. Barnet, *The Economy of Death* (New York: Atheneum, 1969).

that, regardless of the individuals who hold office and make decisions, the existence of the "national security ideology" and the dependence of institutions upon help from one another make military policy safe from attack. The remedies that he adds to those urged by Galbraith involve reallocation of powers and responsibilities among the institutions of government, placing more initiative in the hands of Congress.

Similar arguments are made by Senator William Proxmire in his *Report From Wasteland.*[14] He argues that the United States has developed much more than a military-industrial complex—that universities rank among the top 100 defense contractors and are heavily involved in military work, for example, as are other nonprofit institutions. Thus, the system of interlocking institutions extends well beyond the manufacturers of defense supplies into many other areas of social life. What has been achieved is an integrated power system, involving both "public" and "private" institutions. One telling illustration offered in Proxmire's book is the blue-ribbon panel of "private" citizens appointed by President Nixon to review Pentagon policies and practices.[15] Composed of 16 members, the Commission included nine members who held official positions with 13 different companies doing business with the Pentagon; many of these men had held high positions in the Department of Defense or the military before attaining their present positions. The chairman of the panel was also chairman of the board of directors of an insurance company with more than a billion dollars' worth of loans outstanding to 24 defense contractors and more than $30 million worth of stock in defense contracting companies. The other members of the commission included a labor leader, a close friend of President Nixon who was president of *The Reader's Digest,* a former professional football halfback become a beer company public relations man, and four other persons with no background in military affairs. The chief of staff for the commission, and several other staff members, were Pentagon assistants loaned to the commission for its study. The prescriptions that Proxmire offers, however, are aimed chiefly at greater economy in procurement practices.

The Systemic Explanation: Analysis at the Level of Economic Imperatives and Underlying Values

This type of analysis locates causes at a still deeper level. It says in effect that regardless of the individuals in positions of official responsibility, and regardless of institutional changes, the policy of military superiority will prevail until there are changes in the kinds of values that Americans hold and/or in the nature of the capitalist

---

[14]William Proxmire, *Report from Wasteland* (New York: Praeger, 1970).
[15]*Ibid,* pp. 141–150.

economic system.[16] One example of this type of analysis is an essay by Marc Pilisuk and Tom Hayden, the former an academic and the latter an activist, entitled "Is There a Military-Industrial Complex Which Prevents Peace?"[17] The authors first deny that available evidence can support the idea of a conspiracy, or even of a closely coordinated elite, at the apex of military and industrial leadership ranks. They then argue that the convergence of opinion and behavior evident at these levels permeates government, and is widely diffused throughout the society as a whole. They see certain "core beliefs" as unquestioned ("by any potent locus of institutionalized power"), widely shared by the entire population, and therefore animating decisionmakers and supporters alike. These shared premises, according to the authors, are convictions that (a) efficacy is preferable to principle in foreign affairs (causing military means to be chosen over nonviolent means); (b) private property is preferable to public property; and (c) government patterned roughly according to the American model is preferable to any other system of government. The problem of world order and security, they argue, is that the United States seeks to protect these premises or assumptions at any cost. It does not devote resources to finding routes toward change, nor to establishing the conditions of world peace, but to the preservation and effectuation of these values. The authors conclude their analysis by noting that they do not visualize American society as containing a military-industrial complex, but as *being* a military-industrial complex.

This analysis can hardly be faulted for failure to probe deeply enough into the origins of present power distribution, nor for lack of comprehensiveness. But Pilisuk and Hayden do not carry it to the point of prescription. They quite properly note that proposed solutions must rest on a basis of sound analysis and careful planning, but, like many other academics, they then declare that the necessary research has not yet been done; instead of prescriptions for change, they offer suggestions for accomplishing this research. This is not to denigrate the potential insight of their analysis, but merely to note that the absence of prescription leaves the argument open to a wide range of possible interpretations. Most damaging of all, perhaps, is the possibility that the argument proves too much—either that the

---

[16]See, for example, Victor Perlo, *Militarism and Industry: Arms Profiteering in the Missile Age* (New York: International Publishers, 1963), which argues that a full analysis must discuss the profits American corporations make from foreign investments protected by the American military shield; and Carl Oglesby, *Containment and Change* (New York: Macmillan, 1967). Perhaps the best concise argument concerning business-dominated military and foreign policy, and the manner in which this leads to apparent society-wide "consensus" (thus obviating conspiracies) is Gabriel Kolko's *The Roots of American Foreign Policy* (Boston: Beacon Press, 1969).

[17]Marc Pilisuk and Thomas Hayden, "Is There a Military Industrial Complex Which Prevents Peace?" *The Journal of Social Issues* 21 (July 1969), pp. 67–117.

roots of militarism lie so deep that nothing short of miraculous or cataclysmic change will suffice to redirect American priorities, or that the American military posture is a product of the will of the American people.

An example of a more exclusively economic analysis is an article by economist Michael Reich entitled "Does the U.S. Economy Require Military Spending?" He presents his own argument more incisively than we could summarize it:

> The growth and persistence of a high level of military spending is a natural outcome in an advanced capitalist society that both suffers from the problem of inadequate private aggregate demand and plays a leading role in the preservation and expansion of the international capitalist system. In my view, barring a revolutionary change, militarism and military spending priorities are likely to persist for the foreseeable future.
>
> In what follows, I shall present three principal propositions on the role of military spending in the U.S. economy. (1) In the period beginning in 1950, if not earlier, the U.S. economy was not sufficiently sustained by private aggregate demand; some form of government expenditure was needed to maintain expansion. Without such stimulus, the growth rate of the United States as well as the international capitalist economy would have been substantially lower. (2) The U.S. government turned to military spending as the outlet for needed government expenditures precisely because it provides the most convenient such outlet; in a capitalist context, spending on the military is easily expandable and highly attractive to corporations. Military spending supplements rather than competes with private demand, more is always "needed" for adequate "defense," it is highly profitable to the firms that receive weapons contracts, and no interest group is explicitly against it. (3) Federal expenditures on socially useful needs on a scale comparable to the military budget are not a feasible substitute. Massive social expenditures would tend to undermind profitability in many sectors of the private economy, remove potential areas of profitmaking, interfere with work incentives in the labor market, and weaken the basic ideological premise of capitalism that social welfare is maximized by giving primary responsibility for the production of goods and services to profit-motivated private enterprises. In short, military spending is much more consistent than is social services spending with the maintenance and reproduction of the basic social relations of capitalism. . . .
>
> Military spending is acceptable to all corporate interests. It does not interfere with existing areas for profit making, it does not undermine the labor market, it does not challenge the class structure, and it does not produce income redistribution. Social spending does all these things, and thus faces obstacles for its own expansion. . . .
>
> This brings me to a final point regarding the meaning of the ques-

tion, is military spending really necessary to capitalism? I have tried to frame the answer to this question in the following way. A capitalist economy with inadequate aggregate demand is much more *likely* to turn to military than to social spending because the former is more consistent with private profit and the social relations of production under capitalism. If this military outlet were cut off, say by massive public opposition, it is possible that a capitalist economy might accommodate and transform itself rather than commit suicide. But such reasoning misses the point. Military spending is favored by capitalists and is likely to be defended with considerable vigor, as recent years have shown. Perhaps a parallel with imperialism will clarify this point. It is not essential to a capitalist economy that it be imperialist, for growth can be domestically based. But so long as there are lands to be conquered and markets to be penetrated, it is natural to expect that capitalism will have an imperialist character. Similarly, so long as there is profit to be made in military spending, capitalists will turn to it.[18]

Summary

The strategic explanation, which addresses itself to the merits of officials' perceptions and decisions, does not appear to be a sufficient explanation for military policies in the postwar world. The only prescription that could result from it would be for more information or better and wiser office holders. The other two types of explanations dig progressively deeper. Authors who subscribe to them draw on premises about the American political process to prescribe actions to correct the problems they identify. Because they have different premises, operate at different levels, and in effect ask different questions, they arrive at different prescriptions. Those who blame a military-industrial complex urge popular awareness and reform of a basically sound system. Those who see the system itself as the cause fail to offer explicit prescriptions, but implicitly are either calling for change in the system or arguing that change is hopeless.

Does it make any difference at what level analysis is conducted? What assumptions should be made about policies, processes, or the nature of the system itself before undertaking analysis? These are unavoidable questions. Readers must begin to decide on what level to operate, and what assumptions to make in their effort to understand American politics.

[18]Michael Reich, "Does the U.S. Economy Require Military Spending?" *American Economic Review* LXII (May 1972), pp. 296–297, 302, 303.

Chapter 4

Income and wealth are paramount goals of individual economic and political activity in the United States. It is hardly news that some people are more successful than others. This is due to a variety of factors, including individual talents and opportunities, the systematic effects of government policies, and the nature of economic forces in a highly industrialized capitalist society. The combination of factors may be different for each individual. *Patterns* of distribution of income and wealth, however, offer a means of analyzing the social consequences of all of these factors taken together. Patterns of distribution of income and wealth are a kind of snapshot of the results of many public policies and the way they have combined with "private" forces to shape individual attainments.

Income Distribution: Inequality, Poverty, and Welfare

As we have seen in the last two chapters, many government policies serve to allocate economic benefits and burdens among segments of the population. But some bear more directly than others on who has how much spendable income at any given moment. By focusing on such policies as taxation, subsidies, and welfare—areas in which the actions of government bear directly on the vital income and wealth goals of all individuals—we should be able to see clearly for whom governement works.

This chapter therefore operates on two levels of analysis. First, and rather briefly, we will sum up the combined effects of public policies and private forces in this crucial area by analyzing the basic patterns of distribution of income and wealth in the United States. Second, we will explore in some detail those government policies that bear most directly on such distribution. In separate sections, we will look at taxation, subsidies to different sectors of the population, and welfare. The larger problem addressed by the chapter is that of income inequality and its sources, but a major subsidiary problem is poverty and its alleviation by various means—chiefly welfare. We conclude with an analysis of the alternatives to, and probable future of, the nation's welfare programs.

Patterns of Income and Wealth Distribution

We begin this analysis with three basic facts: (1) The United States is a sharply stratified society, in which a very few people receive very large proportions of income and wealth, the majority share a relatively modest proportion, and a substantial number receive very little indeed. (2) This pattern has persisted for at least the last 60 years, and has changed only negligibly in the last decades; indeed, recent change has tended to widen these gaps rather than close them. (3) Income inequalities are closely related to *sources* of income (those who gain their income from stocks and dividends and from capital gains are at the top, and wage-earners at the bottom, of the scale), sex (men earn more than women in the same jobs; women are disproportionately concentrated in the lower-paying jobs), and *race* (nonwhites earn less than whites with comparable education in comparable jobs; nonwhites are highly concentrated in the lower-paying jobs). Poverty and racism are so closely linked in the United States that it is very difficult—almost arbitrary—to talk about them separately; we do so only for the sake of analytical clarity, and do not mean to suggest that they are extricable.

The Basic Patterns

Table 4-1 presents the income pattern that has prevailed since at least the early years of this century, on the basis of the most recent national census. It shows the proportion of national income received by each fifth of the population. Stratification—that is, inequality—is evident, and may be summarized in a variety of ways. The top 5 percent of the population, for example, earns more than twice as much as the bottom 20 percent. Or, the top 20 percent earns more total dollars than the bottom 60 percent, though the latter group includes more than three times as many people! The data for unrelated individuals show even greater disparities. The meaning of these figures in human terms, of course, is that a substantial number and proportion of Americans live in poverty or near-poverty. The precise number depends on a series of definitions and calculations, which we shall explore in a later section; but by any reasonable assessment, at least 40 million persons are at or below the poverty level.

Wealth—financial resources not derived from income—is even more concentrated at the top of the social and economic pyramid. The top 1 percent of adult wealth-holders own more than 25 percent of all personal property and financial assets in the country.[1] The top 5 percent of family units holds more than 40 percent of all wealth. Most of this wealth is in the form of financial assets (stocks, bonds, mortgages, and the like), real estate, and business capital equipment. Using data from a survey of American households, one major study found that the top 1 percent held 31 percent of the nation's wealth and 61 percent of all corporate stock; the top 20 percent was found to hold 76 percent of all wealth and 96 percent of all corporate stock.[2]

TABLE 4-1
Shares of National Income, 1969 (percentages)

	Bottom 20%	Next 20%	Middle 20%	Second 20%	Top 20%	Top 5%
Family income*	5.6	12.3	17.6	23.4	41.0	14.7
Unrelated individuals' income*	3.4	7.7	13.7	24.3	50.9	21.0

*"Family income" is the combined income of all wage-earners in a related family unit, while "unrelated individuals' income" is the earnings of individuals not members of such units; the former exhibits less inequality because more family members work at lower levels. All figures are before taxes (but see Table 8).
Source: U.S. Bureau of the Census, *Current Population Reports*, Series P–60, No. 75 (Washington: Government Printing Office, 1970), p. 22.

These distribution patterns are well summarized in Figure 4-1 from *Business Week*. Not known for exaggeration, the editors of *Business Week* nevertheless declare flatly: "Personal holdings of wealth, to a much greater extent than shares of income, are dramatically concentrated at the top of the population heap."[3] In the same article, the editors note that this pattern of wealth-holding persists by virtue of inheritance, and that the rich get richer faster than others can rise by virtue of their headstart. Citing a study of the top 1 percent of wealth-holders—"the rich"—the editors estimated that $326 billion in corporate stock and a total of $753 billion in all was held at this level.[4]

[1]James D. Smith, Pennsylvania State University, cited in *Business Week*, 5 August 1972, p. 54.
[2]Dorothy Projector and Gertrude S. Weiss, *Survey of Financial Characteristics of Consumers*, Federal Reserve Board, 1962, pp. 110–114.
[3]*Business Week*, 5 August 1972, p. 54.
[4]*Ibid.*, p. 55.

The Permanence of These Patterns

Again in the words of *Business Week,* "... income distribution seems to be one of the few real constants in the U.S. system."[5] A study of the proportion of national income received by the various

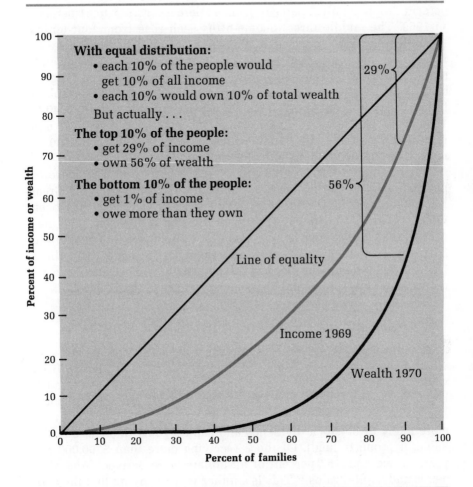

Source: *Business Week,* 5 August 1972.

FIGURE 4-1
U.S. Income is Shared Unevenly, but Wealth Distribution is More Unequal.
By plotting percentages of income and wealth recipients on the horizontal axis and percentages of income and wealth on the vertical axis, both expressed in cumulative form, it is possible to see at a glance that the bottom 50% of income recipients, for example, drew 23% of personal income in 1969, while the bottom half wealthholders in 1970 survey accounted for only 3% of net worth.

[5]*Business Week,* 1 April 1972, p. 56.

levels of income-earners, according to the U.S. Census Bureau, reveals that the poorest 20 percent of Americans has gained only six-tenths of one percent since 1947.[6] That is, the share of national income received by the *lowest* fifth of income-earners rose only from 5.0 percent to 5.6 percent in the recent period of more than twenty years. At the same time, the share of national income received by the *top* 20 percent dropped only 2 percent, from 43 percent in 1947 to 41 percent in 1969. The middle three income-fifths each rose from four-tenths to six-tenths of one percent in the same period. The continuity of these basic patterns could hardly be clearer. Moreover, because all real incomes have been rising, but since the rich start from a higher base, the gap between rich and poor has actually widened in absolute terms. Citing a recent study, *Business Week* reports that, from 1949 to 1969, "the gap between average real incomes of the poorest and richest fifths of the population widened from less than $11,000 to more than $19,000 in constant 1969 dollars."[7]

Nor has there been any closing of the wealth gap. The share of national wealth held by the top 1 percent did drop during the Great Depression and in World War II, but since that time it has been widening again. Starting at 32 percent in 1922, it dropped to 28 percent in 1933 and as low as 21 percent by 1949; but it was back up to 26 percent by 1956 and is now estimated to be higher than that.[8] On the other hand, the poorest 25 percent of Americans have no net worth at all—their total debts equal or exceed their "assets."[9]

The Sources of Income and Wealth Disparities

The most obvious source of income differentials is the way in which people gain their income. Those who earn their income from wages and salaries, while they are many in number and earn a much larger dollar total than others, are concentrated at the lower income levels. At the higher income levels, the source of income is much more likely to be stock dividends and capital gains (increases in the value of property held). Of those receiving more than $100,000 per year, for example, 67 percent of all dollars were derived from dividends and capital gains.[10] This is another way of saying that the con-

---

[6]U.S., Bureau of the Census, *Current Population Reports*, Series P–60, No. 75, p. 22.

[7]*Business Week*, 1 April 1972, p. 56.

[8]Robert J. Lampman, *The Share of Top Wealth-holders in National Wealth* (Princeton, N.J.: Princeton University Press, 1962), p. 24.

[9]*Business Week*, 1 April 1972, p. 56.

[10]U.S., Internal Revenue Service, *Statistics of Income, 1966: Individual Income Tax Returns*, tables 7, 11, and 19. Cited in Frank Ackerman, *et al.*, "Income Distribution in the United States," *Review of Radical Political Economics* III (Summer 1971), p. 28.

centration of wealth (financial assets that give rise to dividends and capital gains) in a few rich people results in sharp income differences.

Income and wealth are related in many and obvious ways, some of which are mutually reinforcing. Theoretically, it is possible that the patterns we have identified could be permanent but that the particular persons or families composing each level could vary over time. In other words, people who were in the top fifth in one period could be in the second or middle fifth twenty years later. Or people whose families were once at the bottom could rise until they reached the top fifth. But the evidence we have examined so far makes this very unlikely. Those who were rich in one time period appear more likely to be even richer in the next time period, because the sources of great fortunes lie in types of wealth-holdings that are handed down within families or transferred only to others with great wealth. Only a few very unusual or fortunate individuals appear likely to rise to the levels of the great incomes within one or two generations, and the amount of mobility between the lower fifths may not be much greater. As we are about to see, other factors are also at work to hold people at their existing levels of income-earning capacity.

A second major cause of income differentials is the occupations of income-earners. Professionals, managers, and other white-collar workers earn substantially more than blue-collar, service, or farm workers. Both categories tend to be self-perpetuating. The former requires greater education; hence a white-collar family is likely to have greater financial resources and the social status or upward identification to make college education appear appropriate for its children. In other words, white-collar families are likely to produce white-collar children. Conversely, other people enter blue-collar occupations in part because their parents held such jobs, were relatively poor, and could offer neither the money nor the social support necessary for further education and occupational mobility. The extent of government investment in education and other economic opportunity-providing policies affects the extent of real mobility across class lines that exists in the society. Despite much mythology occupational mobility remains limited.

Another major cause of income differences is sex. Culturally imposed limitations on educational opportunities and career expectations, and systematic discrimination in both employment and wage or salary levels, have combined to severely limit the income-producing capabilities of women. The result is that women find many jobs closed to them, and are paid less than men for comparable work when it is available.

But the single greatest and most enduring cause of income differentials—one that persists across time and regardless of all individual efforts to fulfill the requirements of mobility within the society—is racism. Nonwhite Americans have always been among the last hired and the first fired; they are systematically excluded from educational and other opportunities; and they are paid less for every job than equally or less well educated whites in the same jobs. The effects of occupation, sex, and race on income are summarized in Table 4-2. Here we come a little closer to understanding the human dimensions of the discrepancies in income between groups of people. The weekly wages of each group decline as the occupational level declines. The wages of white men are greater than those of nonwhite men in the same job levels. The wages of women trail those of men in the same job levels and within races, so that nonwhite women are the lowest paid of all. Thus, race combines with sex and occupation to create a self-perpetuating cycle of income limitation for the majority, while special sources of income provide a vastly greater level of income for the favored minority.

TABLE 4-2
Usual Weekly Earnings by Occupation, Sex, and Race for
Full-Time Workers, 1971*

	White		Nonwhite	
Occupation	Men	Women	Men	Women
White-collar	$199	$114	$156	$115
Blue-collar	152	88	120	81
Service workers	132	72	105	70
Farm workers	80	68	61	58
Incomes for year 1969, all occupations	$9,000	$5,200	$5,900	$4,100

*Figures reflect *medians* (half of the applicable population earns more, and half earns less, than the figure shown) rather than means or averages (total earnings divided by number of earners.) Figures do not include part-time workers.
Source: Weekly income: Bureau of Labor Statistics, as quoted by Paul O. Flaim and Nicholas I. Peters, "Usual Weekly Earnings of American Workers", *Monthly Labor Review* 95 (March 1972), Table 5, p. 34. Annual income: U.S. Bureau of the Census, *Current Population Reports*, Series P–60, No. 70, p. 5.

In this context, the question with which we began becomes even more crucial. How do governmental policies affect income distribution? Do they contribute to greater equality, or to increased inequality? Left alone, the private economy appears likely to work toward considerable (perhaps increasing) inequality. But it is not yet clear whether governmental policies accelerate that process, control it, or retard it, and (in either case) how this comes about. It is to these issues that we now turn.

Taxing and Spending

The U.S. government raises and spends roughly $250 billion per year. Nearly all of this amount is raised through taxation, mostly in the form of individual and corporate income taxes. It is spent on a wide variety of functions, the major items now being national defense, social security, and interest on the national debt. The U.S. government is, in effect, a massive transfer agent, drawing money from certain people and activities and transferring it to other people and other activities to fulfill public purposes.

The act of raising and spending sums of this size has profound consequences for the economy as a whole and for the individuals involved at both ends of the process. *It is no exaggeration to say that government taxing and spending policies quite literally determine the income level at which most Americans will live.* We do not mean merely that these policies make differences of from $500 to $1,000 in a person's net income, though that is the case for some; in many cases, these policies are the difference between spendable income and no income, or between comfort and marginality or poverty. This is because tax provisions may determine whether a business will be profitable or not, whether it will be expanded or contracted, whether it will enter a new line of production or marketing or not, and so on. Spending decisions may create new jobs, terminate others, provide or foreclose educational or economic opportunities of various kinds, and so on.

When such stakes are at issue, there are likely to be sharp value conflicts and much controversy. At every stage of the taxing and spending process, it must be decided who is to pay and on what basis, and who is to receive and for what specific purposes. There emerges a vast array of inducements and rewards, penalties and punishments, which have—and are *designed* to have—the effect of shaping the economic behavior, attitudes, and opportunities of nearly everybody in the society. If some people fail to see this, it is because they do not look at the totality of the process, the pattern of benefits and burdens, and the values, purposes, and applications of power they represent. We shall survey only a few representative illustrations of the major tendencies of taxing and spending policies.

Taxation

How should a tax system be designed? Almost inevitably, principles of equity become enmeshed with long- and short-range social and economic goals and plain political expediency. The basic principle of equity upon which the national tax system is grounded is that of progressive income taxation. This means that people are to be taxed in accordance with their ability to pay, and assumes that those with the most income can afford to pay at higher rates than those with limited incomes. Rates thus vary from zero on the lowest incomes to more than 50 percent on the highest. If the system actually worked this way, the higher income brackets would have their share of national income reduced, and those at the bottom would gain ground in relative terms.

But this does not happen. Table 4-3 shows that changes in the share of national income received by the various income-fifths as a result of the "progressive" income tax are very slight. The poorest fifth of the population, for example, gains only three-tenths of one percent, while the highest fifth loses less than 2 percent. Another study conducted in the 1970s and aimed specifically at poverty-level people found that those with incomes under $4,000 gained only 1.4 percent of the national income (from 5.0 percent to 6.4 percent when after-tax income was compared with before-tax income).Those earning over $15,000 dropped 2.4 percent, from 37.7 percent to 35.3 percent.[11] This taxing arrangement clearly has very little redistributive effect, no matter how it is calculated. Other studies show that nonprogressiveness has been characteristic of the tax system since its inception more than a half century ago.[12]

Why does this happen, and what does it mean for the distribution of income and wealth in the country? Essentially, it means that the "progressive" income tax is progressive in name or image only; people

TABLE 4-3

Shares of National Income, Before and After Federal Income Tax, 1962* (percentages)

	Bottom 20%	Next 20%	Middle 20%	Second 20%	Top 20%	Top 5%
Before Tax	4.6	10.9	16.3	22.7	45.5	19.6
After Tax	4.9	11.5	16.8	23.1	43.7	17.7

Source: Edward C. Budd, *Inequality and Poverty* (New York: W. W. Norton, 1967), pp. xiii, xvi.

*Family units and unrelated individuals combined.

[11]S. M. Miller, "Income Redistribution and Economic Growth," *Social Policy* 2 (September-October 1971), p. 36.
[12]Gabriel Kolko, *Wealth and Power in America* (New York: Praeger, 1962), p. 34.

think it is something that in most respects it is not.[13] What then does this system do, and how? One answer is that, by means of a varied package of tax exclusions, deductions, exemptions, credits, write-offs, and reductions—most of which are applicable only to large corporations or the very rich—privileged potential taxpayers are allowed to pay sharply reduced shares of the tax load. The burden thus avoided must then be shifted elsewhere, and the only alternative is the individual wage- and salary-earning taxpayer. Examples of tax-avoiding exemptions include the opportunity to deduct a proportion of the value of resources drawn from the earth (the oil industry's famous "depletion allowance"), the opportunity to deduct sums invested in new equipment ("investment credits"), and reduced rates on certain kinds of income (such as that gained from the rise in value of stocks and real estate, or "capital gains"). The list could be multipled at great length; such selective advantages led in recent years to an outcry against "tax loopholes" and calls for tax reform.

The attack on the existing pattern of loopholes has produced a number of spectacular illustrations of apparent inequities. Some of these have to do with disparities between individuals of different income levels. In one study, the *real* tax rate on families earning $50,000 per year was found to be the same as for families earning $5,000 a year, because of the variety of deductions open to the higher-income people.[14] An Undersecretary of the Treasury admitted to the Congress that those making between $7,000 and $20,000 per year pay a higher proportion of their incomes to the federal government than do the richest 1 percent of Americans. Each year, many taxpayers with large incomes pay no taxes at all; in 1970, this was true of 112 persons with incomes over $200,000, including three with incomes over $1 million.[15] Because of the tax advantages granted for home ownership and for certain kinds of business expenses, persons making identical net incomes can face totally different tax obligations. A wage-earner who lives in a rented house, for example, pays much more than a person who lives in his or her own mortgaged house and earns the same amount from an increase in the value of stocks.

[13]Note that only the federal income tax makes any pretense of being progressive. State and local governments raise more revenue than does the federal government, and do so primarily from the property tax and/or sales tax. Both of these are regressive, in the sense that they take about the same absolute amounts from each taxpayer—or, in effect, a much larger proportion from the relatively poor than from the affluent. When state and local taxes are combined with the federal income tax, the effect is to remove any vestige of progressiveness from the total American tax system.

[14]Jack Newfield and Jeff Greenfield, "Them That Has, Keep: Taxes" *Ramparts* 10 (April 1972), p. 34.

[15]William Proxmire, *Uncle Sam: The Last of the Bigtime Spenders* (New York: Simon and Schuster, 1972), p. 168.

Another category of inequities involves special opportunities for businesses to reduce their taxes. Some companies making large profits have very low rates. For example, the large oil companies earned profits of $8.8 billion in 1970, and paid an average tax rate of only 8.7 percent. Some of them paid much lower rates: Standard Oil of California paid only 5 percent, Gulf 1.2 percent.[16] (By contrast, a wage-earner near the poverty level pays about 16 percent of his earnings in taxes.) In the case of the oil industry, this situation is made possible by depletion allowances and generous credit for a variety of business expenses. Other industries benefit from opportunities to deduct new investment from their tax obligations, or to increase their allowable deductions for depreciation of equipment by large sums; in both cases, profits can be large but taxes minimal. In 1971, for example, the Nixon Administration changed certain tax rules for businesses, making it possible for them to "write off" millions of dollars in equipment and greatly reduce their tax liabilities. At the same time, congressional enactment of the administration's tax proposals provided $7.5 billion in varied forms of tax relief to large corporations.

Both types of tax-avoidance advantages are justified by appeal to long- and/or short-range social goals. In the case of individuals, such goals include the encouragement of property ownership and investment, or rewards for hard work, thrift, willingness to take business risks, and the like. In the case of large corporations, the theory is that increased investment and higher profits will lead ultimately to more jobs and faster economic growth. Each type of tax advantage has powerful defenders in and out of government; each network of support normally succeeds in retaining or expanding its particular advantage.

For many years, each type of tax advantage has been justified or attacked on its own merits, and in terms of the equities and goals involved. Very little study has been done of the entire pattern of tax advantages as a whole. In a major study released in 1972, however, the Joint Economic Committee of the Congress introduced the concept of "tax expenditures" or "tax welfare payments."[17] This concept views tax-avoidance opportunities as costs to the government— money that the government would otherwise have raised if the blanket provisions of the tax laws had been followed. The Committee's purpose was to make the analysis of tax advantages clearer by making it possible to compute the losses incurred by the government and relate them to the goals and purposes involved on a comparative basis. One of the Committee's consultants estimated that some $73 billion a year was "distributed" by such avoidance opportunities. In

---

[16]Cited in Newfield and Greenfield, "Them That Has," p. 34.
[17]U.S., Congress, Joint Economic Committee, *Economics of Federal Subsidy Programs* (Washington: Government Printing Office, 1972.)

other words, loopholes and other tax forgivenesses provided some
people with untaxed income. The 6 million families whose annual income is $3,000 or less got only $92 million of this, and families with
incomes of less than $15,000 per year (more than 70 percent of all
families) received only 25 percent of these benefits. By contrast, the
three-tenths of one percent of families with incomes over $100,000
per year received 15 percent of such untaxed money.[18] In effect, the
Committee argued, the Congress was voting the nation's richest citizens annual "welfare" payments amounting to tens of billions
of dollars.

Spending

Let us focus on the other side of government's activities as a "transfer agent," and ask who gets what the government spends. Once
again, principles of equity compete with long- and short-range social
goals and sheer political expediency. The broad patterns of expenditure are shown in Figure 4-2, which compares totals in various categories in 1972. Military expenditures are the largest single item, for
example, and the combined total for health, education, and welfare
expenditures is only about half that amount.

Within these classifications by function, of course, government is
actually engaging in many different activities. In the case of national
defense, it is paying salaries to military and civilian employees, buying supplies, conducting research, and countless other things. In the
case of foreign aid, it is transferring money to other countries in the
form of grants or loans or export goods. Under commerce and transportation, it is making grants to the states for road building. Under
education, it is transferring funds to local school districts for a variety
of purposes. Under social security, it is paying elderly citizens directly
from a trust fund created by the payments of all working people and
their employers over several decades. Under veterans' benefits, it is
supplying services and making payments to veterans out of the general tax revenues. It is also paying interest on the national debt, incurred for the most part in World War II but greatly increased since
then, to banks and investors who hold such investments. Under general government expenses, it is paying its own officials and employees
and conducting day-to-day business. And, finally, it is simply transferring a portion of its revenues to the states to do with as they wish.

The broad totals thus do not reveal the specific uses or, in many
cases, recipients of government money. It is very difficult, as the
Congress has learned over and over again, to tell exactly who gets
how much from government spending. Frequently, the various oper-

[18]Proxmire, *Uncle Sam*, p. 181.

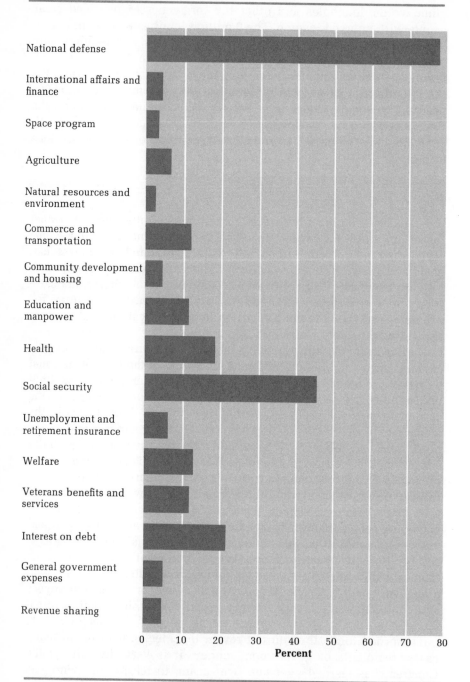

Source: Office of Management and Budget, *The Budget in Brief,*
Washington D.C.: U.S. Government Printing Office 1972.

FIGURE 4-2
WHERE IT GOES
U.S. Government Expenditures by Function, 1972 (in billions of dollars)

ating arms of a single agency do not even know what the others are doing, and the Secretaries of cabinet-level departments can only guess at the real beneficiaries. The inability or unwillingness to identify systematically the actual recipients of federal funds, of course, may permit more benevolent interpretations than are really justified. If there is no clear evidence to the contrary, for example, we may assume that the intentions of a funding program have been fulfilled.

But this is often not the case. One area in which some investigation has been conducted is housing and urban renewal.[19] The Housing Act of 1949 pledged decent housing for all, and more than $10 billion has been spent on urban renewal. Urban renewal has destroyed some 400,000 housing units that once housed the poor, but only 20,000 units of public housing have been built in their place. More often, urban renewal has meant systematic exclusion of nonwhites and the construction of business or civic center facilities for use by entirely different classes of people. The real beneficiaries must be identified as the construction industry, real estate brokers, downtown businesses, and suburban dwellers—not those in need of housing or the original residents of the area.

It seems likely that similarly tracing the consequences of government expenditures in ostensible public-benefit areas would show the real beneficiaries to be investors, builders, and other major units of the private economy. Where data are available on the usage of public services provided by government, such as education, health care, research information, and the like, the beneficiaries tend to be middle- and upper-class persons rather than the lower-class or poor people for whom such services are often said to be provided.

Another way to characterize the purposes and beneficiaries of federal spending is offered by the Joint Economic Committee of the Congress.[20] Applying their concept of "tax expenditures" to the spending side of governmental fiscal activity, the Committee identified three other kinds of "subsidies" being provided by the government. *Subsidies* are payments or other assistance, *not* for services the recipients do for the government, but for the support of the ordinary and necessary business activities of private (mostly profit-making) companies or individuals. Thus, governmental purchase of military goods would not be considered a "subsidy" under this definition; only payments and other assistance for which the government got nothing in return would qualify. Even with this limited definition, however, the Committee found about $25 billion per year being distributed in cash or in kind to private businesses and individuals.

[19]*Ibid.*, p. 191 ff.
[20]Joint Economic Committee, *Federal Subsidy Programs.*

Each of the three types of subsidies is briefly described and illustrated below.

1. *Cash subsidies.* These are direct payments from the U.S. Treasury, running upwards of $13 billion per year, designed to increase the profits or reduce the losses of various businesses. Cash subsidies also make up for airlines' losses, support construction of merchant shipping, send students to college, and support a wide variety of other activities. The government's program of farm price supports alone now approaches costs of $10 billion per year. In order to protect farmers against price drops due to increasing production, the government instituted a program of supporting prices by purchasing some foods and paying farmers *not* to produce others. Once again, however, it is the largest farms that receive the overwhelming proportion of such subsidies; small family farms get very little assistance of this kind. One percent of all farms got 18 percent of all cash receipts in the 1960s, for example, while half of the farms in the country got only 12 percent. In 1969, 396 farms received government checks for more than $100,000; twenty-five giant farms received checks ranging from $360,823 to $4,370,657. For the most part, the big winners from the price and crop-control programs are the cotton, wheat, and feed-grain growers of California, Arizona, and Mississippi.

2. *Credit subsidies.* These are low-interest loans for housing, farming, rural electrification, education, veterans' needs, hospital construction, and purchase of military supplies; and guarantees of privately issued loans for an even wider variety of business activities. If the government makes a low-interest loan itself, it loses a proportion of the usual interest rate and thus, in effect, subsidizes the recipient by that amount. If the government guarantees or insures payment of a loan that is privately issued, it is using its credit to obtain something for the borrower that he or she could not otherwise obtain.

Loans and guarantees made by the Federal Housing Administration and the Veterans Administration account for about 62 percent of all U.S. credit guarantees, now totalling about $150 billion; they were responsible for developing and sustaining the housing industry and private mortgage market for many years. At present, the government is doing considerable loan-guaranteeing to fulfill the needs of major businesses that are experiencing economic difficulties. When Lockheed Aircraft neared bankruptcy, for example, the government stepped in to guarantee the $250 million in loans needed to keep the company afloat. The reasoning was that nearly $1.4 billion had been invested by various banks and airlines in the development and production of the Lockheed L-1011 "air bus," that Lockheed was needed as a leading defense contractor, and that the solvency of thousands of subcontractors and the jobs of thousands of employees depended upon such action.

3. *Benefit-in-kind subsidies.*   These are services provided by government to private companies or persons that they would otherwise have to pay for in some way. Grants of public lands, postal subsidies (absorption of much of the cost of running the Post Office or moving certain kinds of mail), airport construction, grants of the use of government-owned machinery, research and development services, information-gathering and other analytical services, and the like are of benefit to some but not to all. In fact, the Committee found, most of the recipients of these services are profit-making firms, if not provided by government, the services would have to be paid for by such firms at the cost of lower levels of profit.

Much of the expenditure that we have identified, and all of the tax advantages, appear to benefit the wealthier segments of the population. In effect, we have described the relationship between government and the top of the income-and-wealth pyramid. In the next section, which focuses on the problem of poverty, we shall examine the relationship between government and the bottom of the income-and-wealth pyramid.

Poverty and Welfare

This chapter began with a series of findings about the concentration of income and wealth among the relative few. Since then, we have seen that governmental taxing and spending policies do little to modify this advantage, and in many respects appear to bolster it. In this section, we shall turn a spotlight on that portion of the population at the lowest levels of the income-and-wealth pyramid. First, we shall try to identify the people who are located at the bottom, and why they are there. Then we shall explore the various government policies that specifically affect these people. Many such policies, it should be noted, have already been described in this and preceding chapters. The effects of these policies have already been examined; there remains only analysis of the consequences of deliberate anti-poverty policies.

Who Are the Poor?

The extent of poverty in the United States depends on the definition used. The first official definition, used by the President's Council of Economic Advisers in the Economic Report of 1964, held simply that all families with a cash income of less than $3,000 and all individuals with a cash income below $1,500 were "poor." By this definition, one fifth of the people of the United States were "poor" in 1963. One-third of all poor families were headed by a person over age 65; one-fourth were headed by a woman; and over eleven million children were included among the poor. Twenty-two percent of the poor were non-white, and nearly half of all nonwhites were below the poverty line. Such numbers may be less meaningful than comparisons. One observer points out that "the Other America," with its roughly 35 million poor people, can be viewed as an underdeveloped nation within the United States. As such, it would be exceeded in population, among the underdeveloped nations of the world, by only six nations. He continues:

> Of 19 Latin-American republics, only Brazil and Mexico were larger than our own "nation" of the poor. In Africa, only Nigeria had more people. All the rest of some 35 underdeveloped African countries had far fewer. There was no country in the Middle East as large; Egypt with 28 million came closest of the thirteen countries in that area. Our own internal "nation of the poor" has twice as many people as Canada. As a matter of fact, a separate nation of American poor would constitute the fifteenth largest nation of the world.[21]

Since 1964, a series of new definitions exhibiting greater sensitivity to family size and composition has come into use. In 1971, the government's official "poverty line" was set at $4,137 for a nonfarm family of four. This meant that 25.5 million people, or 12.5 percent of the nation's population, were living in poverty. Another basis for defining the poor, preferred by some analysts, is a comparison of earnings with the cost of living in various cities. The Bureau of Labor Statistics publishes three levels of budgets for families living in urban areas, imaginatively termed "lower," "intermediate," and "higher" budgets. These budgets are intended to represent the cost of living at these levels. The lower-level budget for a family of four in 1971 was $7,124,[22] considerably higher than the Office of Economic Opportunity's "poverty line." By the former standard, about 20 percent of all families, or between 40 and 50 million people, were below the lower level and living in poverty.

The only available data concerning the poor use the official government definitions, however, and it is these on which our analysis must rest. The characteristics of the nation's poor in 1971 are outlined in Table 4-4. More than half of the poor are either children or the eld-

[21]John C. Donovan, *The Politics of Poverty* (New York: Western Publishing Company, 1967), p. 96.

[22]Elizabeth Ruiz, "Urban Family Budgets Updated to Autumn 1971,"*Monthly Labor Review* 95 (June 1972), p. 46.

erly; of the working-age population, most are women; thus, children, the elderly, and women comprise about 80 percent of all poor persons. Nonwhites make up only about 15 percent of the nation's population, but 30 percent of the poor; nevertheless, seven out of every ten poor persons are white. This group, with more than 25 million members, may be considered the "hard-core" poor, inasmuch as these are the people who remained poor during the temporary drop in numbers of the poor in the late 1960s. After a period of years in which relatively full employment and narrower definitions combined to reduce the official poverty population, the recession of 1969–1971 caused this number to begin to rise again in 1971 and 1972.

TABLE 4-4
Characteristics of the Poverty-level Population

Age			Race		
	Number	%		Number	%
Under 16	9,917,000	38.8	White	17,780,000	69.6
Age 16–24	10,990,000	43.0	Nonwhite	7,780,000	30.4
Over 64	4,652,000	18.2			

Residence
(in numbers of families)

Region			Urban-Rural		
	Number	%		Number	%
Northeast	916,000	17.3	Central Cities	1,781,000	33.6
North Central	1,191,000	22.4	Suburbs	1,189,000	22.4
South	2,356,000	44.4	Outside		
West	840,000	15.8	Metropolitan		
			Areas	2,333,000	44.0

Source: U.S. Census Bureau.

Some other facts about the poor are worth noting.[23] Many poor people work, but do not earn enough to escape poverty. More than half the heads of poor families held jobs in 1971, for example, although only one-fifth of them were able to find full-time employment. Only 12 percent of all poor people who did not work were physically

[23]The data in this paragraph are drawn from *U.S. News and World Report*, 14 August 1972, pp. 23–25.

able to hold jobs, and most of these were mothers with small children. Only 1.5 percent of all nonworking poor people were able-bodied men. Thus, the poor population—even those who are physically able to work—either cannot find jobs for which they are qualified, or are paid such low wages that they are unable to avoid poverty. In one study, conducted by the Senate Subcommittee on Employment, Manpower and Poverty in 1971, it was found that more than 30 percent of all inner-city residents were paid less than the $80 per week required for a family of four to stay above the poverty line. Many of the families above the poverty line managed by having two or more working members. The Subcommittee identified 22 large cities where at least a third of the inner-city labor force was paid less than $80 per week.

Why are these people poor? Many factors contribute to poverty, but the two major ones are unemployment (or subemployment, which is defined as work at a part-time job or a job that pays less than one is qualified for) and racial discrimination. Unemployment among the poor usually runs well above the national averages. Lacking education and skills, they are among the last hired and first fired as the economy expands and contracts. For nonwhites, unemployment rates run upwards of 20 percent; for younger nonwhites, figures over 30 percent are common in most large cities. As the Senate Subcommittee survey documents, low pay and a shortage of jobs reduces the prospects that the poor can help themselves. In 1966, for example, a year of relatively low unemployment, nearly 10 percent of the working population was subemployed. The rate for white men, however, was only 8 percent, while it was 22 percent for nonwhites. *In ten major urban slums, the rate for nonwhites rose to 34 percent.* Clearly, much of the explanation for low income and poverty is structural in character. That is, it has to do with the characteristics of the economic system and the racial biases of the society, rather than the personal failures of poverty-level people.

The Nature of Governmental Policies

In one sense, low income and poverty are consequences of the combined workings of the private economy and government policies for the last hundred years. For many years, slavery was enforced and defended by governments at all levels. After the Civil War, many public policies defended the rights of employers and promoted the opportunities of various businesses, while only a few aided workers or minorities. The dominant ethos of *laissez faire* ("hands off") in the private economy limited the capacity of government policy to benefit low-income people, though it did not inhibit self-interested actions on behalf of wealthy individuals or large corporations. It was not until the Great Depression that federal social welfare programs sought to deal comprehensively with the problems of low-income persons.

BILLS SWAMP NON-WELFARE COUPLE

Laurie Johnston

Beulah and Ralph Watkins did not know that a pothole lay ahead of their 1965 Oldsmobile as they were driving home through Queens Village after church and Sunday dinner at the home of friends.

"A river of rain was hiding that hole," Mrs. Watkins recalled in her bright, wry manner as she described an incident at Springfield Boulevard and Murdock Avenue. "My head hit the roof of the car twice, and I'm still going to the doctor for neck treatments."

The jolt was enough to break the couple's grasp, once again, on their personal will-o-the-wisp—financial solvency. As with countless blue-collar families who struggle to keep within their meager budgets, such things as a hidden pothole, a leaky roof or a steep medical bill can plunge them into red ink and desperation.

At the age of 59, Mrs. Watkins is not old enough for Medicare or quite poor enough for Medicaid, despite her chronic kidney disease and diabetes. "I have to go and fight with the clinic for some kind of reduced rate," she said.

In addition, the day she missed from work cost her half of the $60 a week she still earns doing part-time housework on Manhattan's Upper East Side—commuting nearly three hours a day.

Mr. Watkins, who is 68, gets a $58.94 monthly union pension as a retired plasterer and $212 in monthly Social Security payments. He needs a hernia operation, but he still owes $60 from three months in the hospital after stomach surgery last year.

"Every month, I think I can pay that bill," he said, "but some emergency always comes up."

In search of "some green and a little space," the couple left Harlem 10 years ago for an $18,500, three-bedroom house near the Queens Village-Hollis boundary. They were the fourth black family on their street.

Mrs. Watkins was making $80 a week as a full-time housekeeper, plus extra for serving at parties. Her husband earned at least $150 a week. Their daughter, Linda, was at Emma Willard Academy, a fairly exclusive girls' school in Troy, N.Y., on a scholarship. They themselves were able to pay for "about $1,000 worth of singing lessons" for her over the years, and she now sings with the Harlem Chorale.

The decade has left the family shaken, still proud and confirmed in a basic blue-collar belief: that society places more potholes in the precarious upward path of the struggling than it does for either the affluent or the indigent.

"We were always trying to better our lot," Mrs. Watkins said. "No gimmicks, just hard work. Welfare is degrading, but the working people who are not on welfare are caught in a tight economic squeeze. We're really being used. They keep us poor to keep others rich.

"Even the clinic says we must be doing all right—don't we have our own house?"

"I helped build the city," said Mr. Watkins, who now has Parkinson's disease, "East Side, West Side, the Bowery to the Bronx. I paid income tax, too." With a short laugh, he added, "I considered myself middle income. Now I'm not even working poor.

"But when the property tax goes up for Mr. Rockefeller, it goes up for me too. Ten years ago we paid $104 a month on this house. Now we pay $150, but I think only about a third of it goes to pay off the mortgage. The rest is for taxes and sewers and all that."

Mr. Watkins, self-supporting since he dropped out of the seventh grade, came to New York in 1926 from Virginia. Mrs. Watkins, who is from Louisiana, finished the ninth grade and "always wished for more."

Linda, 24 years old, attended Barnard College on a scholarship, dropped out and now need only complete summer school to get a bachelor's degree in anthropology from Columbia.

"But what can you do with it without a Ph.D.?" she said. "And I'm tired."

In the carpeted living room, on the baby grand piano, a gift from a wealthy employer, an Emma Willard graduation picture shows a very "finishing school" Linda with straightened hair.

Recalling those days, she remarked: "That was a nice interlude—very plush, and I wasn't used to that—even though I had to repeat English and history because I was so badly educated in Harlem."

Now Linda wears her hair Afro-style and talks longingly of a future in Senegal. But she has a 4-year-old son, Charles, from a broken marriage to a Columbia student who is now disabled. Charles lives with his grandparents during the week, and the family's most immediate worry is how to keep the boy in a city-sponsored day-care center so his grandmother can go on working.

The day-care center families are convinced that H.R.1, the Federal welfare reform bill passed by the House and now before the Senate, takes aim —as usual—at them, despite proposed Social Security increases.

"The new bill is designed to do away with the kind of center Charles is in," Mrs. Watkins said. "It won't be for community children, only for people on welfare, so the welfare families can work."

As a taxpayer, Mr. Watkins does not grudge pensions for policemen and firemen—"those fellows gamble their lives for us"—but he sometimes wishes he had worked for the city instead of for private contractors. And he wishes the city would come up with some tax relief "to help us maintain and hang on to our property."

He once thought he could sell his house "for a few thousand more than we paid," since he built a patio and added other improvements. Now it needs paint, gutters and leaders, and he can no longer do the work himself. The collapse of the old heating system last year put him $1,000 in debt for a new one.

Source: *The New York Times*, 2 July 1972.

The assumptions on which the New Deal programs were structured are of crucial importance. Not only do they still shape the pattern of government action in regard to poverty, but they also help to explain the present character of poverty and the nature of American attitudes toward ameliorative action. The basic purpose of the New Deal social legislation was to protect individuals against hazards beyond their control—both natural and biological hazards (aging, blindness) and economic hazards (unemployment, disability through accident on the job). The assumption was that if individuals were given certain minimal assurances of economic security, a revived and prosperous economy would do the rest.

Thus, the basic approach was a series of *social insurance* programs (a federal system of old-age, survivors', disability, and health insurance; and a federal-state system of unemployment insurance) which working people and their employers would pay for throughout their working lives. Men and women in eligible occupations were entitled to benefits, the amounts of which were based chiefly on their earnings while employed.

Supplementing these systems, on what was assumed to be a temporary basis, were *public assistance* or "welfare" programs, assisting the blind, disabled, elderly, families with dependent children, and others; these programs were administered by the states but utilized federal funds to a great extent. They were expected to "wither away" as an expanding economy drew more and more people back to work and social insurance programs were expanded.

A strictly temporary program of government employment was instituted, in which many new public works—bridges, highways, public buildings, and the like—were built. The rights to form unions and to engage in collective bargaining were also protected by new laws. The final major component of this package of policies was minimum wage legislation, which required that employers in certain fields must pay at least the specified minimum hourly wage to all employees.

Throughout, the assumption was that the minimum needs of the population could be met adequately by the workings of a reasonably prosperous economy, provided only that certain minimum assurances were legally established. There was no provision for assistance to those who did not work, except under stringent conditions. Fearing that the incentive to work might otherwise be weakened, or that moral damage might be inflicted, public assistance programs required that disability or destitution be proven as conditions for receiving aid.

The social insurance programs, chief among which is social security, have for the most part fulfilled expectations. About 90 million people now contribute to social security, and 90 percent of the population aged 65 and over is eligible for monthly social security benefits. In 1973, a monthly avarage of 28 million people received benefits of $45 billion. A very large proportion of employed people now have protection against loss of income from several important causes. In 1971, 8 million people received $5.2 billion in unemployment compensation. The benefits are not ample enough to enable most people to support themselves without further income, and are paid only to those who have previously paid into these funds, but minimal sums are available to such people under specified conditions.

The public assistance programs, however, have not lived up to expectations. Not only has there been no "withering away," but the numbers of people in need of such assistance has steadily increased. And the costs of these welfare programs have multiplied rapidly. The most dramatic rise has occurred in the large cities, and in the category of Aid to Families with Dependent Children (AFDC). In New York City in 1971, one out of every six persons was on welfare. In Newark, unemployment was running at 11 percent, and 30 percent of the population was on welfare. The total number of persons on welfare in the nation in 1972 was over 15 million and the total costs exceeded $10 billion. Ten percent of all American children under 16 were receiving welfare aid under AFDC, more than double the proportion only five years earlier.

The makeup of the welfare population is much like that of the poverty-level population, for obvious reasons. Nearly 60 percent are children, and another 19 percent are their mothers; these stark proportions suggest the contribution of the AFDC category to the rising costs of the program. Another 16 percent are aged, and 9 percent are blind or disabled. Less than 1 percent of welfare recipients are able-bodied men.

The costs of welfare shot up in the 1960s for several reasons. One was that the number of eligible families and children increased. Another was that the level of payments increased. Between 1965 and 1970, payments rose 19 percent. According to one set of experts, the most important reason was that welfare was used as a means of reducing discontent and as a direct response to urban rioting.[24] In any event, the great increase occurred between 1965 and 1970. During the 1960s, the population increased 13 percent, but the welfare rolls went up 94 percent and the number of families receiving AFDC more than doubled. Still, many poor people do not qualify for welfare payments. And the kinds and amounts of benefits vary greatly among the states. AFDC benefits for a family of four now range from $332 per month in New Jersey to $55 in Mississippi.

The Current Policy Dilemma

From one end of the political spectrum to the other, there is intense dissatisfaction with AFDC. Some resent its cost and believe that it discourages recipients from working. Others point to its failure to provide aid for many who need it, the inadequate benefits it provides, and the repressive administrative practices that control the number and behavior of claimants and stigmatize them in the process. Its unpopularity and ineffectiveness have given rise to some supplemental "welfare reform." Each of these deserves consideration, for they imply far-reaching change in the whole system of public policy toward low-income people.

One political consequence of the unrest of the 1960s was enactment in 1964 of the Economic Opportunity Act, the so-called "War on Poverty." Chiefly through community action agencies established in approximately 1000 communities, programs providing educational, vocational, medical, legal, and other social welfare services were begun. But by 1972 it was apparent that this "war" had generated a great deal of talk and political controversy, several programs that had had an impact upon small numbers of the poor, but only a relatively small investment of money and other resources—an investment that represented experimentation in attacking poverty rather than an effort to eliminate it or reduce it substantially. Most program funds were cut back sharply or eliminated in the late 1960s. The more important continuing programs involve "in-kind" services to the poor to supplement cash assistance.

Benefits to the poor in forms other than money are justified politically on several grounds: that some recipients cannot be trusted to spend money as they should; that some goods and services can be offered more efficiently in the form of in-kind programs; that these programs benefit the suppliers of the commodities and services offered; and that they are less likely than cash grants to discourage the poor from working. Though there is good reason to doubt the validity

[24]For an elaboration of this point see Frances Fox Piven and Richard A. Cloward, *Regulating the Poor: The Functions of Public Welfare* (New York: Vintage Books, 1971).

of most of these arguments, in-kind benefits have increased sharply in recent years. In fiscal 1971 they cost $9.6 billion, almost as much as the cash assistance programs.

The least effective in-kind programs have been such "social services" as counselling, family planning, and manpower training. Resented by many poor people as demeaning or pointless, counselling is now stressed less than efforts to prepare the poor for work. Attempts at "rehabilitation rather than relief" have done more to frustrate the poor than to help them.

Other in-kind programs provide necessities. People certified as eligible by a local welfare agency can buy food stamps at a price below their face value, but because the recipient must have enough cash to buy the stamps, the poorest often cannot afford them. The surplus commodity distribution program requires no cash, but recipients cannot choose what they get; such items as lard and peanut butter are most easily procured, and balanced diets are hard to achieve. A national school lunch program provides lunches free or at reduced prices to children certified by local officials as unable to pay the full price.

While they unquestionably help, these programs also present problems. Because of the "means test," they stigmatize recipients. Some localities choose not to participate, and this is especially likely to hurt the rural poor. A study published late in 1972 found that half of the country's 25 million poor people were still going hungry; 43 percent were getting no federal help for food.[25]

Everyone over 65 is covered by the "Medicare" program, which pays some, but far from all, the costs of medical services. The program has provided a substantial benefit to the elderly poor, as well as to the middle-class elderly population. Far more controversial has been "Medicaid," which offers a federal subsidy to the states for medical aid to the poor of all ages. Because of rising costs, Congress has cut back sharply both the quality of Medicaid benefits and the number of people eligible for them.

There are other in-kind programs. Federal housing assistance rose sharply in the 1960s, but helped the working poor more than welfare recipients and did not go far toward meeting the overall housing need. Legal aid has also been useful, but politically controversial and trivial in comparison to the demand. In some cases it provided the interesting spectacle of lawyers paid by one government agency (the Office of Economic Opportunity) to challenge in court the denial by other government agencies of benefits to the poor. Under such programs as Headstart and Upward Bound, poor children have been given special educational opportunities to try to compensate for the disadvantages with which they start their educational careers.

[25]*The New York Times*, 27 October 1972, p. 22.

Though every significant sector of the American public is dissatisfied with the motley set of welfare programs in effect, and especially with the rise in the welfare rolls, there are sharp differences over what to do about it. The objective that has received most attention has been an effort to provide work incentives for AFDC recipients. In 1967, the law was amended to provide small payments for participation in job training programs and to enable welfare recipients who find jobs to retain some of their welfare benefits if their total income remains low. Experience with the "WIN" (Work Incentive) program was disappointing; it did little either to encourage job training or to provide jobs for people on welfare. In 1971 the WIN program was made compulsory for every able-bodied person on AFDC aged 16 or over, except some specifically exempted groups such as mothers of children under the age of 6. The 1971 amendments also encouraged the states to force recipients to work by providing more federal funding and by making funds available for a relatively small number of public-service jobs.

Opponents of this emphasis on "workfare" are convinced it will continue to be ineffective because only a very small percentage of recipients are physically able to hold jobs. Also, research has demonstrated that welfare recipients are already eager to work if they can only find jobs.[26] The basic problems, according to opponents, are high unemployment levels and the number of jobs paying so little that those who hold them are still poor. It is the failure of the economy to provide enough jobs and to pay subsistence wages that creates the need for welfare, they argue, not individual laziness or the character of the welfare programs. The chief function served by work requirements in this view is a psychological one: to create and reinforce the belief that welfare recipients do not want to work.

Those who see the problem as primarily economic, rather than psychological, and who do not like to vest arbitrary power over recipients in bureaucrats, favor automatic "income maintenance" programs under which some minimum income is guaranteed to all American families. An approach winning support from some conservatives, as well as many liberals, would establish a "negative income tax"—an arrangement whereby families with incomes under the poverty line would receive money from the government in amounts sufficient to maintain a subsistence standard of living. As an incentive to work, the grants would be decreased by *less* than a recipient earns so long as his total income is under a fixed amount. Some favor allowances to families for the support of children. Another income maintenance proposal would assure government jobs to those unable to find work in the private sector. Behind all of these

---

[26]Cf. Leonard Goodwin, *Do the Poor Want to Work? A Social-Psychological Study of Work Orientations* (Washington: Brookings Institution, 1972).

elaborate proposals, of course, is the stark fact that the transfer of only 1 percent of the national income—$10 billion—would raise *all* of the nation's poor above the poverty line.[27]

Poverty Policy: A Summary Analysis

There seems little doubt that the various policies enacted to cope with widespread poverty embody very different assumptions, and attempt to do quite different things. There is no coherent plan, nor any clear understanding of the nature of the problem, underlying either current policies or proposed remedies for the present problem. Many of the complaints voiced against the welfare system are based on ideological assumptions, rather than fact. The welfare rolls are not made up of lazy chiselers or minority-group members luxuriating at the expense of white working people, nor is life on welfare a comfortable existence. Yet many people think and act as if these charges were true. Apparently, the fact that some people require welfare assistance is a matter of psychological importance for certain other people. One analysis extends this argument to the point of saying that the maintenance of many people at the poverty level is not just a psychological necessity for certain others, but an economic necessity for the society as well—in that somebody must be available to do the "dirty work" of the society, and to provide a reserve supply of labor to undercut the demands for higher wages and better working conditions of employed workers.[28]

What we have seen, therefore, is a very mixed package of policies directed at low-income persons. For the most part, these policies embody the assumptions and preferences of the more affluent sectors of the population—i.e., that work is available if people will only look for it and, in effect, that people are poor because of their own personal faults. Some policies provide assistance to poor people only after rigorous investigation, and then so grudgingly that the recipients are stigmatized and resentful. Some are more concerned with disposing of surpluses, or otherwise serving the goals of nonpoor people or interests, so that they do not really address the problems of the poor. The money that is transferred to the poor through this package of policies is substantial, but it is hard to be confident that it is well employed—in terms either of coherent national intentions, or of the best interests of the poor themselves.

[27]Sar A. Levitan, Martin Rein, and David Marwick, *Work and Welfare Go Together* (Baltimore and London: Johns Hopkins Press, 1972), p. ix. For recently published accounts and evaluations of American welfare policy, see this book and also Bruno Stein, *On Relief: The Economics of Poverty and Public Welfare* (New York: Basic Books, 1972).

[28]Herbert J. Gans, "The Uses of Poverty: The Poor Pay All," *Social Policy* 2 (July–August 1971), pp. 20–31.

Chapter 5

This chapter, like Chapter 4, is a kind of composite summary of many public and private policies over a long period of time. Racial minorities—blacks, native Americans (American Indians), Chicanos and Puerto Ricans, Asians, and others—are at the bottom of the American social and economic pyramid. They are there because of centuries of often deliberate and systematic discrimination and exploitation both by government and private forces. This can be stated bluntly to-

The Status of Racial Minorities

day as little more than a truism, although it would have seemed extreme or provocative only a decade ago. In the last ten years, primarily as a result of the exasperated insistence of minorities themselves, there has been growing recognition of the status of minorities in the United States. Some of the many resulting governmental and private efforts to promote their opportunities have been effective, and in several ways the decade has been one of significant progress for minorities.

But this has only served to bring the depth and complexity of the problem of racial minorities in the United States into focus. Racism is deeply embedded in the American culture, and erects barriers far more difficult to surmount than those faced by immigrant groups in the past. Moreover, the governmental policies undertaken to assist minorities have run up against two serious obstacles with roots in the character of American society itself. Even with the best intentions, there is only so much public policies can do in an individualist, capitalist, and property-conscious society to advance the economic and social status of an entire group in any prompt and substantial way. Certainly we have not even approached those boundaries in any comprehensive way. But even the modest acts undertaken so far have generated substantial—and sometimes violent—resistance from the great majority of people. Finally, some members of each of the racial minorities do not seek mere admission into full participation in the existing American system, but rather legitimacy and autonomy for the perspectives, values, and way of life of their independent cultures. In effect, they seek to live in their own ways, even though that may be inconsistent with the values and practices of the dominant society.

This chapter, therefore, will focus equally on the conditions of minorities today and on the real problem exposed by efforts to improve those conditions—the gap between the needs and goals of minorities and what American society can and does offer them. The policies that brought both the dominant society and the racial minorities to the present situation will be briefly reviewed first. Current policies and their consequences will be examined after we have characterized the conditions and the needs and goals of minorities.

Four Centuries of Public Policies Toward Minorities

What have governments done with respect to nonwhite races on the American continent—and why? And what has this practice meant, not only for the affected minorities, but also for the dominant society? We will touch only upon certain basic policies, to illustrate practices that are general and long-established.

Indians

When Columbus "discovered" America, there were probably about 1 million persons living on the North American continent. Believing himself to have reached India, Columbus mislabelled those he met "Indians"; this was to be the first of many instances of the white man's failure to understand native Americans except in his own terms. The "Indians" of the time were a highly diverse people. But they shared the beliefs that land was a resource for all to share, and that man should live in harmony with nature, appropriating only those animals needed for food and clothing. As waves of land-hungry white settlers arrived, the Indian was promptly introduced to the concepts of private ownership of land and the use of nature for commercial purposes (e.g., fur trapping). Indian lands were either "bought," acquired by governmental decrees or soon-violated treaties, or despoiled by the hunting and trapping of commercially oriented whites.

By 1840, Indians had been displaced from practically all of their lands east of the Mississippi. In some cases, broken treaties were followed by forced marches (or "removals") in which thousands of Indians were resettled further west because their remaining lands were wanted by whites. In a series of "Indian Wars," thousands of Indians were killed, injured, or rendered homeless to make first the South and then the West available for commercial and homesteading

opportunities. On the Great Plains, millions of buffalo were slaugh-
tered by white hunters for commercial purposes, depriving the Indians
of their major source of food and hides. Indians were confined to reservations of then-unwanted lands, and caught between the Army's
urge to exterminate them completely and the Bureau of Indian Affairs'
preference for simply managing their affairs and making good Americans out of them.

By 1900, displacement, removals, wars, and disease had reduced
the Indian population to one sixteenth its original size. Reservation
schools enforced the dominant society's customs and religions, preventing Indians from coming to know their own heritage. Not until
1924 was the right to vote extended to Indians, and other forms of
political redress were virtually unavailable. Many treaties made over
the years were broken to serve the needs or desires of governments
and private economic interests.

Blacks

The first blacks arrived on the American continent in 1619 and
were sold as slaves in Virginia. Slavery was incorporated into the
legal structure of the Southern colonies somewhat later in the century. Jefferson's proposal to abolish slavery found no place in the
glowing language about the rights of men in the Declaration of Independence, and the Constitution specifically provided for representation based on slave-holding and for protection of the slave
traffic for a period of years. Slavery was too important to the economic and social structure of the Southern states, and too fully in
accord with general beliefs in the North as well, to be seen as inconsistent with the assumptions and goals of either document.

The abolition of slavery, accomplished during the Civil War, did
little to change the practical effects of previous policies. The war was
justified as a means of preventing the spread of slavery to the new
western states, i.e., keeping the territories free for the wage-earning
white working man. The Emancipation Proclamation was thus more
a tactical act of warfare than a principled policy. The Fourteenth and
Fifteenth Amendments to the Constitution were intended as much
to build the political strength of the struggling Republican Party as
they were to assure freedom for blacks. The swift passage of Jim
Crow segregation laws, whose constitutionality was confirmed by
the Supreme Court in the famous case *Plessy* v. *Ferguson* (1896),
officially and legitimately subjected black people to a condition only
abstractly better than slavery.

Official segregation continued to be the law of the land until 1954,
when a well-orchestrated legal campaign by blacks finally caused the
Supreme Court to rule segregated education unconstitutional. The
federal government practiced segregation in the armed forces until

after World War II. Aside from these official policies, governments at all levels condoned and/or practiced systematic discrimination against blacks. Educational systems were not only segregated and unequal, but actually taught that blacks were inferior; other agencies and activities of governments were almost equally "whites-only."

Chicanos

The population now known as Chicanos, or Mexican-Americans, owes its status as Americans chiefly to the conquest of the Southwest in the Mexican War, and particularly to the Treaty of Guadalupe Hidalgo in 1848. Spanish explorers, settlers, and missionaries were the first whites to enter New Mexico, Texas, and California, in the late 16th, 17th, and 18th centuries respectively. Contacts with the surrounding Indians of the Southwest and with Mexico, where the Spanish had intermarried with Aztecs and other Indians, led eventually to a mixed Spanish-Indian-Mexican population in these areas. In some cases, vast landholdings existed in relative isolation.

And then came the Anglos. The influx into Texas was followed by the acquisition of the entire Southwest in the Mexican War. The Treaty of Guadalupe Hidalgo, however, confirmed all existing land titles as it granted the ostensible subjects of Mexico living in those areas American citizenship. But in the words of one historian, "Mexicans quickly became the Negroes of the Southwest."[1] Although they were not officially slaves, the conditions of peonage and officially condoned discrimination were not far from slavery. Land was divested, stock stolen, voting rights denied, and physical violence employed to intimidate and prevent efforts at redress.

The discovery of gold in California led to the rapid Anglicization of that territory, and once again the Mexican-origin population was displaced and reduced to near-peonage. In both law and practice, the Republic and then the State of California aided the rapid private exploitation of a captive population while denying them effective redress. It was not until the advent of mass farming techniques and the resulting need for cheap labor that Mexican-origin people were in demand, and then only as the lowest form of laborers. Whenever they were not needed, Mexicans and Mexican-origin people were uprooted from their homes and deported.

The Mexican-origin population of New Mexico and Arizona was brought into the American system somewhat later. The lack of resources and opportunities for development permitted rural areas to remain essentially unchanged until the end of the 19th century, and in some cases later. At that time, a somewhat modernized version of the

---

[1]Paul Jacobs, Saul Landau, and Eve Pell, *To Serve the Devil: Volume 1, Natives and Slaves* (New York: Vintage Books, 1971), p. 237.

familiar process began; eventually family land titles were completely replaced by Anglo ownership and Anglo forms of organization had been imposed on whole communities.

Puerto Ricans

The Puerto Rican population, located principally in major East Coast cities, is the other, smaller body of Spanish-speaking Americans. The island of Puerto Rico too was acquired by conquest, in the Spanish-American War of 1898. Although legally American citizens, Puerto Ricans have suffered from the same officially condoned and systematic practice of peonage and discrimination as have the Chicanos. The lack of economic opportunities on their native island has led many to seek jobs in New York and Philadelphia, where until quite recently they were ignored by governments at all levels.

Asians

Asians have experienced changing government policies toward them, on top of a consistent pattern of governmentally condoned private discrimination and exploitation. Thousands of Chinese were imported as cheap labor to build railroads, for example, but when no longer needed (and when white workers' demands that they be prevented from undercutting wage levels erupted in riots and lynchings), they were excluded by law. The same exclusion applied to the Japanese after 1907. California's land laws prevented Asians from acquiring title to property for many years. And the federal government, as late as 1942, uprooted American citizens of Japanese descent from their homes and businesses to relocate them in camps in Utah and Nevada on grounds of their probable disloyalty in World War II.

Why has there been a consistent pattern of public policy of this kind toward racial minorities? Neither economic necessity nor racism is a sufficient answer in itself, though both are major causes. That is, they are *mutually reinforcing* but independent factors. It is not necessary to speculate on which is more important, or whether economic interests lead to an increase of racism. It is enough to see that neither could function without the other. A recent history sums up four centuries of American policy as follows:

> ... The colonizers came to the New World believing that colored people were inferior, and used that ideology to justify the enslavement of blacks, the killing of Indians and Mexicans and the importation of Oriental labor for work considered unfit for whites. The identification of colored skin with evil, with the devil, with inferiority, infused the entire culture of the Anglo-Saxons during the first centuries of colonization.

In each case, the racism coincided with economic need for slave labor and for land. At the same time, racist attitudes were institutionalized as laws, religion, and everyday practice. Each school child learned, along with the principles of republicanism and democracy, about the inferiority of colored people. Ministers explained to their flocks that slavery was God's will.

Racist law and racist behavior became an integral part of American culture. . . . Racist attitudes not only made whites feel superior by virtue of their skin color, it also made all colored, colonized people feel inferior because of their skin color. . . .[2]

This passage implies that it is not only minorities who experience the consequences of racially discriminatory public policies. Members of the dominant society are also powerfully affected, both in the circumstances of their individual and social lives, and in the ideology and mythology they subscribe to. Belief in the superiority of whites and the "natural" inferiority of other races can come to serve as an underlying principle of social order. Without a myth of this kind, no discriminatory public policy can long persist; and the institutionalization of the myth in such policies serves in turn to sustain and validate it. If today most whites concede that they are not biologically superior to other races, they still tend to believe that they are socially, economically, or culturally superior. Some members of racial minority groups have also come to believe in the supremacy of whites and their culture. Once established, the myth penetrates all levels of society and serves to justify subordination as well as supremacy. Many in the dominant society, and those among minorities who share such myths, do not even realize that the bases of their actions lie in such assumptions. They may believe that they are merely "following the rules" or being "realistic" or "practical." Yet they act out essentially racist assumptions because they cannot escape them.

But the effects of racial myths are the least visible consequences of American policies toward racial minorities. Another primary consequence is the actual social and economic condition of such minorities today.

The Contemporary Circumstances of Minorities

The physical circumstances of minorities—their shared low levels of education, income, and employment, for example—are increasingly the subject of documentation. We will undertake no exhaustive catalogue here, in part because the conditions, attitudes, and behavior of minorities are discussed at every appropriate opportunity elsewhere in this book. We shall touch only upon certain basic characteristics of the black, Spanish-speaking, and Indian populations, emphasizing in each case those features that are distinctive to each minority. Not

[2]*Ibid.*, p. xxi.

all of the deprivation experienced by minorities is accounted for by the social and economic gaps visible in these data, however. To concentrate exclusively on these tangible aspects of minority status would be to miss the important point that much of the difficulty of minority/dominant-society relations flows from less tangible factors, particularly the distinctive ways in which each minority looks at the world. Thus, in a sense, the characterizations that follow are only a preliminary to the effort to understand the differences in the cultures and values that separate minorities from the dominant society—which we shall discuss in the succeeding section.

Blacks

As the nation's largest minority, blacks have for many years set the pace in minorities' struggles for recognition and status. In the 1970 census, blacks numbered 22.6 million, or 11.2 percent of the American population. Blacks as a whole were both younger and growing more rapidly than the white population: they made up 13.8 percent of the under-15 population, and were increasing at the rate of 19.6 percent between 1960 and 1970, compared to 11.9 percent for whites. Increasingly, blacks are concentrated in the cities: in 1970, they made up 21 percent of all center-city residents, up more than 4 percent since 1960. Blacks accounted for 27 percent of all center-city residents under 15 years of age. Twenty-five major American cities, only seven of which are in the South, have more than 100,000 blacks.

The migration patterns of black people constitute one of the major social phenomena of the 20th century. This is in part due to the general movement from agricultural to industrial jobs, but it also represents a movement away from the South toward the big cities of the North and Midwest. Between 1960 and 1970, as the trend continued, three cities (New York, Chicago, and Los Angeles) all had a net gain of more than 100,000 blacks. New York drew a net increase of 435,000 black residents. The rate of these increases is shown in Table 5-1. The dramatic increases in the proportions of blacks are not due just to black in-migration, of course; they also reflect the exodus of whites from the central cities. This does not undermine the basic point, however: the proportion of blacks in the South is dropping steadily and the actual number of blacks outside the South has increased sharply. Between 1960 and 1970, the number of blacks in the Northeast increased by 43 percent; in the North Central states, by 33 percent. There is no escaping the implication that these migration patterns are combining with other factors to concentrate the black minority in the nation's major cities. This fact has profound import for future urban, transportation, and welfare policies.

But perhaps the most distinguishing feature of black peoples' lives in the United States is the extent to which they trail whites in income,

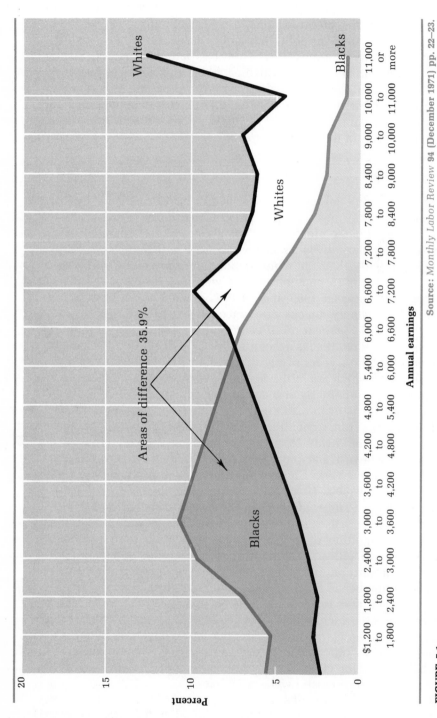

FIGURE 5-1

Percent Distribution of White* and Black Men with Four Quarters of Earnings, by Total Private Nonagricultural Sector Earnings, 1966

Source: *Monthly Labor Review* 94 (December 1971) pp. 22–23.

*Includes workers of all races other than Negro

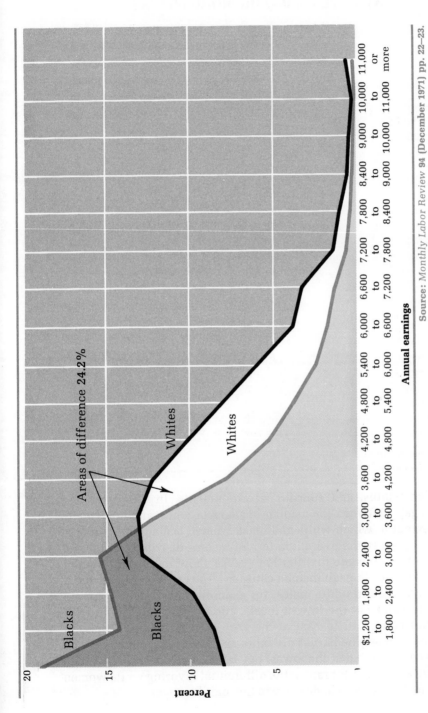

Source: *Monthly Labor Review* 94 (December 1971) pp. 22–23.

FIGURE 5-2
Percent Distribution of White* and Black Women with Four Quarters of Earnings, by Total Private Nonagricultural Sector
Earnings, 1966
*Includes workers of all races other than Negro

25 CITIES THAT HAVE 100,000 OR MORE BLACKS

	Black Population	Black Percentage of Total
New York, N.Y.	1,666,636	21.2
Chicago, Ill.	1,102,610	32.7
Detroit, Mich.	660,428	43.7
Philadelphia, Pa.	653,791	33.6
Washington, D.C.	537,712	71.1
Los Angeles, Calif.	503,606	17.9
Baltimore, Md.	420,210	46.4
Houston, Tex.	316,551	25.7
Cleveland, Ohio	287,841	38.3
New Orleans, La.	267,308	45.0
Atlanta, Ga.	255,051	51.3
St. Louis, Mo.	254,191	40.9
Memphis, Tenn.	242,513	38.9
Dallas, Tex.	210,238	24.9
Newark, N.J.	207,458	54.2
Indianapolis, Ind.	134,320	18.0
Birmingham, Ala.	126,388	42.0
Cincinnati, Ohio	125,070	27.6
Oakland, Calif.	124,710	34.5
Jacksonville, Fla.	118,158	22.3
Kansas City, Mo.	112,005	22.1
Milwaukee, Wis.	105,088	14.7
Pittsburgh, Pa.	104,904	20.2
Richmond, Va.	104,766	42.0
Boston, Mass.	104,707	16.3

Source: Census Bureau figures of April 1970.

employment status, and educational attainments. In Chapter 4, we noted the gaps between the median incomes of white and black men, and the extent to which white and black women trailed both. Figures 5-1 and 5-2 portray the overall pattern of income distribution for men and for women. Income distribution curves show the proportions of blacks and whites in each income category. The contrast between the curves for black and white males, for example, shows that there are many more blacks at the lowest levels, and a substantial number of whites (but almost no blacks) at the very highest income levels. In the case of women, the curves are more similar: most women of both races are concentrated at the lowest pay levels. Only a very few white women are at the highest ranks; the differential favoring white women is due almost entirely to higher pay in the middle ranges.

TABLE 5-1
Black Proportion of Total Increase in Population,
Major Cities (percentages)

	1950	1960	1970
New York	9.5	14.0	21.2
Chicago	13.6	22.9	32.7
Detroit	16.2	28.9	43.7
Philadelphia	18.2	26.4	33.6
Washington	35.0	53.9	71.1
Los Angeles	8.7	13.5	17.9
Baltimore	23.7	34.7	46.4
Cleveland	16.2	28.6	38.3
St. Louis	18.0	28.6	40.9
Newark	17.1	34.1	54.2

Source: U.S. Bureau of the Census, *The Social and Economic Status of Negroes*, 1972.

Spanish-Speaking Americans (primarily Chicanos and Puerto Ricans)

The second-largest American minority group is that loosely classified as Spanish-speaking. We include it among racial minorities for the powerful reason that it consists primarily of persons who identify themselves as Mexican-Americans or Chicanos, referring to their mixed Spanish, Mexican, and Indian origins. Some Puerto Ricans, too, trace their origins to the mixture of Spanish, West Indian, and black strains. But analysis is rendered difficult by the fact that nearly all Spanish-speaking persons are officially classified by the Census Bureau as white. The only readily identifiable shared characteristic is their propensity to speak Spanish as their native, home, or family language. They also share a certain level of poverty and deprivation, as we shall soon see.

Table 5-2 is an official Census Bureau table. It shows the breakdown of Spanish-speaking people into major categories, of which the Mexican or Chicano is by far the largest. Including those "other Spanish" who are probably Mexican in origin (see footnote to Table 5-2), the number of Chicanos approaches six and a half million. Puerto Ricans number approximately another million and a half, perhaps more. The majority of Chicanos is understandably located in the five southwestern states (Texas, California, New Mexico, Arizona, and Colorado), and to some extent in the Midwest south of and including Chicago. The majority of Puerto Ricans is, equally naturally, located in the northeastern coastal cities.

Black and Spanish-speaking Americans: some comparisons with whites. By means of some special analyses, the Census Bureau has finally begun to sort out the characteristics of minority groups. Predictably, they fall well below the attainments of members of the dominant society, but certain comparisons among all groups are worth noting. For example, 44 percent of white men held white-collar jobs in 1970, while only 23 percent of Spanish-origin men and 22 percent of blacks held such jobs. The unemployment rates for Spanish-origin persons and blacks were about the same, roughly twice those for whites. Spanish-origin families achieved a median income, however, somewhat above that of blacks but still well below whites. Tables 5-3 presents some basic income comparisons. It shows, for example, that the median income of Spanish-origin families ran about $1,000 ahead of that of blacks, but was still barely 70 percent of that of whites. Families with a younger head-of-household, however, appeared to trail whites to a lesser degree than did the older generations. At the same time, substantially larger proportions of white families were headed by full-time, year-round workers—suggesting that income differentials are built into many aspects of family and work life.

Blacks were found to have somewhat more education than Spanish-origin persons. Among persons 25 to 29 years old, probably the best educated stratum of the American population, 80 percent of all whites

TABLE 5-2

"Spanish Origin" Population for the United States and for the Five Southwestern States, November 1969 (in Thousands)

	United States Number	Percent	Southwest Number	Percent	Southwest as a Percentage of United States
Mexican	5,073	55.0	4,360	79.2	85.9
Puerto Rican	1,454	15.8	61	1.1	4.2
Cuban	565	6.1	82	1.5	14.5
Central or South American	556	6.0	170	3.1	30.6
Other Spanish*	1,582	17.1	835	15.2	52.8
Total	9,230	100.00	5,507	100.0	59.7

*This category includes persons identifying themselves as "Spanish-American" or "Spanish" and also persons reporting themselves as a mixture of any of the Spanish-origin categories. It seems clear from their predominantly southwestern location that they are chiefly of Mexican origin.
Source: U.S. Bureau of the Census, *Persons of Spanish Origin in the United States,* November 1969. Population Characteristics, Series P-20, No. 213, February 1971, Table 1.

are high-school graduates. But only 58 percent of blacks, and 48 percent of Spanish-origin persons, had reached that level. About 1 in 5 persons of Spanish origin over 25 had completed less than five years of school, compared with 1 in 25 whites. Blacks tended to stay in school somewhat longer than did Spanish-origin students. In a series of tests of specific accomplishments, such as reading levels, blacks and Spanish-origin children regularly scored below Oriental Americans and those American Indians who were tested.[3] They averaged three full grades below white children, which may indicate that the tests are oriented toward whites, that minority children are badly educated in the school system, or both.

TABLE 5-3
Median Family Income in 1970, by Age of Head and
Ethnic Origin: March 1971

Age of Head-of-Household	Total Population			Spanish Origin	
	All Races*	White†	Black	Total‡	Mexican
14 to 24 years old	7,037	7,294	5,013	5,697	5,534
25 to 34 years old	9,853	10,187	6,605	7,324	7,567
35 to 44 years old	11,410	11,790	7,569	8,345	8,058
45 to 54 years old	12,121	12,626	7,357	8,146	7,491
55 to 64 years old	10,381	10,737	6,438	7,482	7,997
65 years old and over	5,053	5,263	3,282	3,756	(B)
Total	$ 9,867	$10,236	$6,279	$7,334	$7,117
Head year-round, full-time worker: Median family income	$11,804	$12,016	$8,880	$9,309	$8,946
Percent of all families	64.1	65.5	51.4	57.4	57.0

B Base less than 75,000.
*Includes persons of "other races," not shown separately.
†Includes almost all persons reporting Spanish origin. About 97 percent of persons of Spanish origin, about 99 percent of persons of Mexican origin, and 96 percent of persons of Puerto Rican origin were classified white in this survey.
‡Includes persons of Central or South American, Cuban, and other Spanish origin, not shown separately.
Source: U.S. Bureau of the Census, *Persons of Spanish Origin in the United States, November 1969.* Population Characteristics. Series P-20, No. 213, February 1971, Table 1.

[3]Tetsuo Okada, et al., *Dynamics of Achievement: A Study of Differential Growth of Achievement Over Time.* Tech. Note No. 53 (National Center for Educational Statistics, U.S. Office of Education, 1968).

Indians

Because of the lack of agreement about who is an Indian, and absence of concern for the question until very recently, it is not possible to say precisely how many Indians now live in the United States. Estimates range from 600,000 to 1 million. The best estimate is probably that of the Bureau of Indian Affairs (BIA), which puts the number of Indians on reservations at about 450,000, with at least another 200,000 or so living in cities. In recent years, there has been substantial migration from reservations to the cities, partly as a result of federal programs aimed at reducing the reservation population (and its landholdings). More than 112,000 Indians, or from one-tenth to one-sixth of the total Indian population, migrated to the cities in the period 1952–1970 when the programs were in effect. Los Angeles is thought to have the largest number of urban Indians (about 60,000), followed by San Francisco-Oakland, Dallas-Fort Worth, Oklahoma City, Minneapolis-St. Paul, Phoenix, Cleveland, Chicago, and New York.

The economic and social conditions of Indians are probably the worst of all American minorities. The average annual income per Indian *family* is about $1,500 per year; unemployment is very high, reaching ten times the national average in some areas. The life expectancy of Indians is one-third less than the national average, and incidence of tuberculosis among Indians is eight times the national average, infant mortality rates are twice the national average, and the suicide rate is double that of the general population. According to Senator Edward Kennedy, 50,000 Indian families (that is, nearly half of all Indian families) live in unsanitary, dilapidated dwellings; many live in huts, shanties, or abandoned automobiles. Those who migrate to the cities often find that they are untrained for employment and unable to adapt to urban life. The average educational level for all federally educated Indians is under five years, and dropout rates are twice the national average in both federal and local public schools.

A recent Senate subcommittee study examined the history of, and current policies toward, Indian education and issued a scathing indictment of both policies and their underlying purposes.[4] It not only found failures of education to lie at the root of current Indian conditions, but also—far more important—declared the whole approach to education to exemplify what is wrong with American policy toward Indians. In a sense, this report is applicable to the dilemma facing all racial minorities; thus a brief review of it may serve to highlight the problem to be dealt with in the next section.

[4]U.S. Senate, Subcommittee on Indian Education, *Indian Education: A National Tragedy—A National Challenge,* 91st Cong., 1st sess.

In its opening sentences, the subcommittee report declares: "A careful review of the historical literature reveals that the dominant policy of the Federal Government toward the American Indian has been one of forced assimilation which has vacillated between the two extremes of coercion and persuasion. At the root of the assimilation policy has been a desire to divest the Indian of his land and resources."[5] Referring to the federal statute dividing reservations into 160-acre parcels so that Indian families would learn about property ownership and become successful farmers—which resulted in the sale or abandonment of much of the acreage because such principles were totally inconsistent with Indian culture—the subcommittee next declared:

> ...During the 46-year period it was in effect it succeeded in reducing the Indian landbase from 140 million acres to approximately 50 million acres of the least desirable land. Greed for Indian land and intolerance for Indian cultures combined in one act to drive the American Indian into the depths of poverty from which he has never fully recovered.
> From the first contact with the Indian, the school and the classroom have been a primary tool of assimilation. Education was the means whereby we emancipated the Indian child from his home, his parents, his extended family, and his cultural heritage. It was in effect an attempt to wash the "savage habits" and "tribal ethic" out of a child's mind and substitute a white middle-class value system in its place....[6]

The subcommittee's basic points are that racism and economic interests have combined to place the Indian at the very bottom of the socioeconomic pyramid, and that the only route by which the Indian is allowed to rise out of poverty and degradation—education—has required that he abandon everything unique to his culture. In other words, the purpose of education has been to make the Indian over into a person whose attitudes and goals are consistent with white capitalist American society. Naturally, the Indian resisted such "education," and instead fought a continuing battle to maintain his cultural heritage and integrity.

The situation is not very different for most other minorities, although the process is somewhat less visible. "Progress," in the sense of the increasing capacity to earn income and gain status in the dominant society, has been available only for certain individuals among minorities, and only at the cost of abandoning the distinctive features of their cultures. Unless they give up, at the very least, those values

---

[5]*Ibid.*, p. 9.
[6]*Ibid.*

and habits of thought that are inconsistent with competitive individualism and materialistic self-seeking, they will not succeed in American economic life. How much of a cost does this represent? Clearly, some minority-group members would gladly pay the price in order to gain the material and other benefits of full participation in American society. But for others the cost is too high. The gap between the values and habits of mind of their cultures and those of the dominant society is too great, or they prize their own values and cultures too highly, to give them up in favor of those of the dominant society. We shall explore the nature of this gap and the distinctiveness of certain minority views in the next section.

The World-Views, Values, and Goals of American Minorities

We use the term *world-view* here to denote (1) the understanding of the world that is characteristic of a given minority—that is, how it sees the workings of American society—and (2) the *way in which that minority culture thinks*—that is, the concepts, language, and habits of mind that characterize the thinking process in that particular culture. The latter is of primary importance. Every culture takes certain things for granted, attaches particular meanings to words, employs specific concepts, and thus tends to think in particular ways. Understandably, these ways of thinking are consistent with the kind of society that has given rise to that culture; they embody the values that underlie the social order, and provide its members with an understanding of what life is about.

But cultures differ. They do not all employ the same ways of thinking. We shall explore the basic values of the dominant American orthodoxy in some detail in Chapter 6. For the moment, we need only note certain familiar characteristics of the world-view widely shared within American society. It is founded on individualism, and the sense that it is natural for individuals to compete and to seek to satisfy themselves through material gain. It assumes that all people will or should want to amass a certain amount of property, with which to render their economic situation more secure. It takes for granted that man has to struggle against nature and other obstacles until he masters or is mastered by them. It analyzes situations or problems by means of tangible evidence, or "hard facts," which must be related to each other step-by-step to "prove" that something is or is not true. And it assumes that white skin, Western culture, and the Judaeo-Christian religious tradition are superior to all other brands.

This world-view is characteristic of nearly all nonminority Americans. It is characteristic also of many members of racial minorities, because they too are subject to the pervasive influences of American culture—its educational system, mass media, public rhetoric, and official practices. But it is not shared by at least some members of each of these minorities. Within each minority, there are some who hold to the distinct way of thinking characteristic of their own culture. In a variety of ways, they have resisted assimilation into the world-view and habits of thought of the dominant society. On occasion, this may take the form of an exaggerated attachment to peripheral aspects of the minority's heritage, or even of efforts to rediscover an indigenous culture that has been long forgotten. It may be quite deliberately calculated as a response to the pervasiveness of the dominant culture, and as a means to draw other members of that minority away from the values and ways of thinking that spell assimilation into the dominant society. For the most part, such adherence to elements of an independent minority culture appears odd or incomprehensible only to those who fully subscribe to the dominant world-view and are impatient with all else. In any event, there are significant numbers of Indians, Chicanos, and blacks who hold world-views and ways of thinking that stand in sharp contrast to those of the dominant culture.

What is distinctive about minority world-views? To begin with, they consciously reject many things—basic values, assumptions, preferences, and the like—that the dominant society simply takes for granted. Individualism, competition, materialism, the concept of struggling against nature, the concept of private property, and many other basic principles of the American social order are completely rejected by some or all of the three minority cultures we have been discussing.

The Indian World-View

The distinctiveness of the Indian world-view may be seen in two excerpts from *We Talk, You Listen*,[7] a major work by Indian spokesman Vine Deloria, Jr. He first points to some basic differences in the ways that Indians and white Americans conceive of the nature of man and of individualism:

> The vital difference between Indians in their individualism and the traditional individualism of Anglo-Saxon America is that the two understandings of man are built on entirely different premises. White America speaks of individualism on an economic basis. Indians speak of individualism on a social basis. While the rest of America is devoted to private property, Indians prefer to hold their lands in tribal estate, sharing the resources in common with each other....[8]

[7]Vine Deloria, Jr., *We Talk, You Listen* (New York: Macmillan, 1970).
[8]*Ibid.*, p. 170.

The Indian concept of land, and of human life as inextricably bound up with nature, are major distinguishing features of the Indian world-view. Man is to live in harmony with nature, to preserve and restore it, to be part of its ecological balance—and not to struggle against it or exploit it for commercial purposes. Deloria contrasts the Indian view with the white man's developmental mania as follows:

> The Indian lived with his land. He feared to destroy it by changing its natural shape because he realized that it was more than a useful tool for exploitation. . . . All of this understanding was ruthlessly wiped out to make room for the white man so that civilization could progress according to God's divine plan.
>
> In recent years we have come to understand what progress is. It is the total replacement of nature by an artificial technology. Progress is the absolute destruction of the real world in favor of a technology that creates a comfortable way of life for a few fortunately situated people. Within our lifetime the difference between the Indian use of land and the white use of land will become crystal clear. The Indian lived with his land. *The white destroyed his land. He destroyed the planet earth.* (Italics in original.)[9]

The distinctiveness of the Indian world-view extends also to ways of knowing. Indian understanding does not depend on logic or evidence, but rather on a sense of wholeness with nature, a perhaps intuitive or mystical insight. Relative isolation has apparently made it possible for Indians to preserve substantial portions of their indigenous culture, and it stands in sharp contrast to the dominant society in a variety of ways.

The Chicano World-View

In many respects, the Chicano world-view is grounded in similar concepts. This is understandable in light of the close bond between Chicanos and their Indian forbears; the Indian heritage is stronger than the Spanish heritage among Chicanos. But there is also a deliberate effort among some Chicanos to recapture the unique combined heritage and employ it as a means of uniting "la Raza" into a more effective force. Special emphasis is placed on the sense of brotherhood and community that should and did exist among Chicanos, and the need to reject Anglo values in order to realize these ideals, again. In his *Chicano Manifesto,* for example, Armando Rendon declares:

[9]*Ibid.,* p. 186.

Our ideals, our way of looking at life, our traditions, our sense of brotherhood and human dignity, and the deep love and trust among our own are truths and principles which have prevailed in spite of the gringo, who would rather have us remade in his image and likeness: materialistic, cultureless, colorless, monolingual, and racist. Some Mexican-Americans have sold out and become agringandos, . . . like the Anglo in almost every respect. Perhaps that has been their way of survival, but it has been at the expense of their self-respect and of their people's dignity.[10]

There is no ambiguity in Rendon's insistence that Chicanos should reject the thought of assimilation into white society:

The North American culture is not worth copying: it is destructive of personal dignity; it is callous, vindictive, arrogant, militaristic, self-deceiving, and greedy; . . . it is a cultural cesspool and a social and spiritual vacuum for the Chicano. The victims of this culture are not merely the minority peoples but the dominant Anglo group as well; everything that passes for culture in the United States is symptomatic of a people so swept up in the profit motive and staying ahead of the Joneses that true natural and humanistic values may be destroyed without their knowing it.[11]

In part, this strong antipathy to Anglo society and its values is intended to provide a sense of identity and personal worth to enable Chicanos to better withstand the assimilative pressures of the larger society. But it is also intended as a rallying point around which several minorities combine. The Chicano emphasis on community leads to the idea of a multi-minority cultural pluralism, in which all minorities would have status and legitimacy equal to that of the dominant society. Few steps have been taken to put such an idea into effect, though there have been some tentative overtures, particularly between Chicanos and Puerto Ricans.

The Black World-View

Blacks are obliged to look harder for their independent cultural heritage because they have undergone a longer and heavier exposure to the dominant culture and its social system. But for those blacks who have either rejected or become frustrated by integration, the task is relatively easily accomplished. In many respects, that heritage has

[10]Armando Rendon, *Chicano Manifesto* (New York: Macmillan, 1971), p. 46.
[11]*Ibid.*, p. 178.

been maintained intact but simply not understood as such by whites or by those blacks who accepted white world-views and values; in others, it has been rebuilt out of the life of the ghettoes and the needs of millions of blacks for a sense of personal worth and self-respect. In any event, many blacks share a unique understanding of the white world, and of what is necessary to change it into a world where blacks can live in dignity and comfort.

The "Black Power" era of the mid-1960s marked an important stage for the black movement. It was partly a result of recognition by many black leaders that the mobilization and ultimate liberation of black people required change at the cultural level. In their eyes, it was necessary for blacks to reject and/or purge themselves of the dominant society's values, and to learn to see themselves as worthy because of, and not in spite of, being black. Blacks were the first to see that integration meant integration *on the white society's terms.* To maintain one's own identity, it is necessary to avoid being caught in another's definitions; in turn, this requires clear understanding and commitment to distinctive values. Stokely Carmichael made these points in 1967:

> ...How much easier it is to keep a man in chains by making him believe in his own inferiority! As long as he does, he will keep himself in chains. As long as a slave allows himself to be defined as a slave by the master, he will be a slave, even if the master dies....
>
> Black Power attacks this brain-washing by saying, WE WILL DEFINE OURSELVES. We will no longer accept the white man's definition of ourselves as ugly, ignorant, and uncultured. We will recognize our own beauty and our own culture and will no longer be ashamed of ourselves, for a people ashamed of themselves cannot be free....[12]

Speaking before Third World audiences, particularly Latin Americans, Carmichael regularly emphasized the role played by independent cultures in the process of change. In this regard, both language and symbols become vitally important; a people who would be free must not subscribe to those of their oppressors:

> ...When African slaves were brought to this country, the Anglo saw that if he took away the language of the African, he broke one of the bonds which kept them united and struggling. Africans were forbidden to speak to each other in their own language. If they were found doing so, they were savagely beaten into silence.

[12]Stokely Carmichael, "Black Power and the Third World," *Readings in U.S. Imperialism,* ed. K. T. Fenn and Donald C. Hodges (New York: Herder and Herder, 1971), p. 351.

Western society has always understood the importance of language to a people's cultural consciousness and integrity. When it moves into the Third World, it has moved to impose its own language...

The white man hardly needs to police his colonies within this country, for he has plundered the cultures and enslaved the minds of the people of color until their resistance is paralyzed by self-hate. An important fight in the Third World, therefore, is the fight for cultural integrity....

One of our major battles is to root out corrupt Western values, and our resistance cannot prevail unless our cultural integrity is restored and maintained....[13]

Certain continuing themes are evident in these varying calls for cultural independence from the dominant American world-view and values. Resistance to the overwhelming pressure of the dominant society's values is urged by all, and all insist that assimilation is offered only at the price of abandoning what is distinctive and worthwhile in minority cultures. Each insists that its own culture and world-view has important contributions to make to a reconstructed version of the larger society. Indians would probably seek merely to be left alone to pursue their own ways, but the other minorities appear to recognize that their status and legitimacy depend on changes in the dominant culture and social system. Chicanos tend to envision a genuine cultural pluralism. Those blacks who emphasize the uniqueness of black culture tend to do so as a prelude to more far-reaching change, including revolution itself—which many see as necessary to eliminate racism.

Thus the dilemma for minorities becomes somewhat clearer. Not only are the dominant world-view and values promulgated forcefully and variously; they also pervade the policies that seek to aid minorities. The cost of acquiescence in them is loss of cultural integrity and of the uniqueness of one's heritage. And yet this is the only (though still uncertain) route to "progress" for minorities. The gap that we have been seeking to understand is not just social and economic. It is also a gap in self-definition, between one identity and another. Minority persons who are conscious of this must in effect choose between the world-views and values of the culture and communities in which they grew up and those of an alien and often cold society that forces them into a competitive enterprise in which the cards are stacked against them. Thus, deprivation is not measured by mere facts and figures concerning income and employment. Indeed, those are the kinds of measures that are valued chiefly by the dominant society. Important as they are in terms of sheer physical survival, they do not measure the pain and desperation that are felt as one's very identity

---

[13]*Ibid.*, pp. 353–354.

and way of thinking is cast aside. Nor can public policies conceived within the dominant culture and system go very far toward alleviating that kind of deprivation. As we shall see, such policies can create a better life for certain individuals; but whether they can do so for minorities as a whole, and without exacting the cost of cultural submission, remains doubtful.

Minority-Related Policies of the 1960s

We come now to the larger problem posed by the current status of racial minorities in the United States. It involves the sharp contrast between the *limits* set by the dominant culture and econopolitical system and the *needs and goals* of minorities. The limits are defined by the dominant society's perceptions of the "problem" of minorities; its options within the established framework of laws and property rights and the basic premise of individualistic self-help; and the odds against its doing *anything*, given the many powerful defenders of the *status quo* who oppose significant advances for minorities. The needs and goals of minorities involve both vast advances in tangible social and economic conditions of life and, for many, the desire for true cultural pluralism and legitimacy for their values and way of life.

Bases for the Policies

The policies of the 1960s were based on some characteristic assumptions of the dominant society. Central among these was the belief that the poverty and low status of minorities was the product of a lack of opportunity, and that they could be alleviated by providing better educational and vocational opportunities. Related was the belief that discrimination in such areas as housing, employment, and voting operated to reduce individual opportunities. Faith in legal remedies for such discrimination was widespread. Thus one primary response to minority demands and pressure in the 1960s was a series of Civil Rights Acts providing legal remedies for various forms of discrimination against individuals. The other was a set of new educational and training programs (the "War on Poverty") designed to enable minorities to compete more successfully for employment and, hence, income.

The premise underlying such beliefs and programs is that the economic system can and does provide ample jobs and income opportunities, and that if minority-group individuals were only qualified they would be able to raise themselves through their own efforts. But at best this would require a long slow process of upgrading skills, finding jobs, and eliminating discrimination on a case-by-case basis. Quite possibly, the jobs might not exist, or only a very few individuals might qualify for them, or broad-scale discrimination might

"We are pleased, Running Bear, that you will attend Harvard Business School.
For over 2,600 moons, what our people needed most was a damned good real
estate specialist."

prove impervious to individual attacks. Even more likely, substantial proportions of minority persons might be unaffected by such programs, or might become discouraged by the time and effort required for self-help against such entrenched odds.

Not all the burden of bringing about change fell on public policies, of course. The enactment of highly visible Civil Rights Acts and the institution of the much-publicized War on Poverty also had the effect of symbolizing a change in national sentiment. One result was a greater willingness on the part of private businesses to hire at least some minority group members. Educational institutions developed minority recruitment programs, and various governmental and private agencies initiated hiring and other aid programs specifically directed at minorities. In place of unconcern and disinterest, there appeared in many instances at least a superficial sensitivity to advancing the status of minorities. At the same time, the new statutes and programs led to greatly increased expectations on the part of minorities in general, and to deep resentment on the part of lower- and middle-class whites of the "special favors" being granted to minority groups, apparently in response to minority pressure.

Thus the dilemma repeats itself over and over again. Limited public policies do create opportunities for a relatively few individuals. But the process is slow at best, and dependent on the speed with which the private economy is able to absorb new workers. And the fanfare with which the new programs are instituted both leads minorities to expect real assistance (and to become frustrated when it is not forthcoming) and creates the impression among whites that massive efforts are being made by their government to raise minorities above them on the socioeconomic ladder.

Consequences of the Policies

It is in this context that the consequences of the programs of the 1960s·must be analyzed. That there has been progress cannot be doubted. But the scope, permanence, and intangible dimensions of its impact cannot yet be seen. Nor is it clear whether the visible advances are due to public policies or to broad private response to the militant pressures generated by minorities during that period.

Progress can best be measured in terms of the advancement of blacks, because of their numbers and relatively higher visibility as a deprived minority. Apparently dramatic progress is visible in the ratio of income earned by black families to that earned by white families:[14] in 1959, the median family income of blacks was only 51

[14]Data on income in this section are drawn from U.S. Census Bureau, *Differences Between Incomes of Whites and Negro Families by Work Experience and Region: 1970, 1969 and 1959*, Series P-23, no. 39 (Washington: Government Printing Office, 1971).

percent that of whites, but in 1970 it had jumped to 61 percent. Better yet, outside the South the ratio was 74 percent. And in the North and West, the median income of black families with both husband and wife present was 88 percent that of whites. If the head of the family was under 35, the median income was 96 percent that of whites; if both husband and wife were working, median family income for blacks in this category was 4 percent *above* that of whites.

This sharp overall rise, and the extent of equality among the youngest population, suggests that minority pressures and/or programs had a substantial impact in the 1960s. It is clear that blacks' share of the higher-paying, higher-status occupations increased substantially, and at a rate well above that of whites.[15] At the highest level—professional and technical positions—blacks showed a 109 percent gain between 1960 and 1970; 8 percent of such occupations are now filled by blacks. During the same period, the number of whites in such jobs increased only 31 percent. The gain in middle-level (clerical, sales, skilled blue-collar) jobs was 64 percent for blacks, compared to 21 percent for whites. At the same time, the number of blacks in the lowest-paid jobs dropped, while that of whites gained slightly. Blacks also narrowed the educational gap, reaching the point in 1970 that young black adults as a group trailed whites of similar age by only a half year of schooling, as compared with a year and a half in 1960. Unemployment among blacks was 8.2 percent in 1970, but the shift toward the higher-paying (and more stable) jobs means that this figure was lower than it would have been in previous years.

Some qualifications must be registered, however. For one thing, the income advances appear to be due in large measure to the fact that more black women are now working. In the North and West, for example, where the greatest advances were made, the number of young black families in which husband and wife both worked almost doubled between 1960 and 1970. Black women were working at considerably higher rates than were white women in 1970: 63 percent of black wives held jobs, while 52 percent had year-round jobs; only 54 percent of white wives worked at any time, and only 36 percent had year-round jobs. Moreover, the earlier figures are drawn from a period of particularly high black unemployment, higher proportions of Southern residence, and lower educational levels generally. Thus, the real advance between 1960 and 1970 was probably less than the data seem to indicate.

How much of this advance should be attributed to government

[15]Data on occupational and educational status in this section are drawn from U.S. Department of Labor, Bureau of Labor Statistics, *Black Americans: A Decade of Occupational Change, Bulletin 1731* (Washington: Government Printing Office, 1972).

policies? In the best years of the War on Poverty, less than $3 billion per year was invested by the federal government, little over 1 percent of the federal budget. The Civil Rights Acts of the 1960s were enforced by a mere handful of attorneys in the Justice Department although a series of cases were tried and won so that the Acts themselves were legitimated constitutionally. With the advent of the Nixon Administration, funding for the War on Poverty dropped substantially, and much of the thrust toward school integration was undermined by the President's opposition to busing for racial equality. As minority measures slackened, so did the momentum of national policies.

The extent of real progress, even in socioeconomic terms, appears to remain an open question in the mid-1970s. Achievements to date appear fragile and perhaps temporary, and so far limited to the advancement of a relatively few individuals. They appear to depend on the mobilization and militancy of minorities themselves, but the massive efforts of minorities in the 1960s may have been a unique and unrepeatable episode. If the various business, governmental, and educational initiatives of the 1960s were merely short-term responses to ghetto riots and other violent confrontations, the costs of "progress" will ultimately be seen as very high. Nor will the situation then appear promising for other minorities, or for those among all minorities who seek legitimacy and equal status for their own cultures and life styles.

PART THREE

CONTRASTING IDEOLOGIES

Chapter 6

At the start of our analysis of public policies, we posed certain key questions. We asked who gets what from government action, and whether there are patterns of burdens and benefits—predictable winners and losers—in the four problem areas taken together. And we urged speculation about why such patterns exist.

There seems little doubt that patterns have been identified. The same people, mostly blue-collar workers and minorities, are at the bottom in every category. They bear the brunt of inflation control, experience repeated unemployment, make the least income, and (in the case of minorities) suffer the effects of racism as well. Government policies do little to change these conditions; indeed, their net effect seems more likely to maintain them. On the other hand, the larger corporations and wealthier individuals occupy systematically favored positions. Their investment opportunities are fostered, expansion and profits are encouraged and subsidized, and tax avoidance opportunities are made available. Whatever the policy area—economic stabilization, military preparedness, income distribution, or even race relations—it is not an exaggeration to say that the rich get richer and the poor get poorer. And government policies, on balance, appear to play a causal role.

But what explains this pattern of consequences? An immediately accessible explanation is offered by *ideology*—those beliefs about how government does and should work that are held by the members of a society. Ideology links basic political values to the day-to-day operations of government. It maintains that institutions and policies embody and apply those values (or, in the case of ideologies other

Ideology and Public Policies: American Orthodoxy

137

than the dominant one, that they should do so). Ideology may be an accurate, or totally incorrect, description of reality. Ideology only incidentally rests on analysis: for the most part, it merely asserts that things function in a particular way or for specified reasons. This is because it is a set of beliefs that an individual acquires quite independently of analysis of the true state of affairs. Ideology is acquired early, from one's family and schools. It is reaffirmed in a variety of ways as the individual grows older—by the media, the rhetoric of politicians, and the beliefs and actions of others. That it conforms to reality in one or another instance may be only coincidental, for it has a life and a continuity of its own.

In most societies, one particular belief system is predominant. The United States is no exception. Indeed, the depth and strength of the orthodox American ideology are so great that some people do not even recognize it as ideology. Their beliefs about politics and government seem so natural and self-evident that they can imagine no other possibilities; they are convinced that they see only the truth and nothing else. This total short-circuiting of independent analysis is the supreme achievement of an ideology.

American orthodoxy, for example, insists that wealth and income are distributed roughly in accordance with individual talents and effort, and that nearly everybody is or could be reasonably affluent in this highly productive system. Such disparities as may exist do not affect the distribution or usage of political power. Thus the American political system is democratic, works well, and regularly produces policies that are appropriate to the problems in question or at least the best accommodation possible under the circumstances. Armed with such convictions, most Americans see only good or necessity in the acts of government. Economic and political systems both therefore merit the full support of all good Americans.

This strongly held orthodoxy is clearly consistent with all the major principles of capitalism. Although it is not synonymous with capitalism, American orthodoxy is so fully fused with capitalist values and beliefs that many Americans do not even realize how completely the latter has been incorporated into their thinking. Thus, *capitalism and Americanism may seem to be one and the same.*

But some Americans reject the dominant orthodoxy. When confronted with the pattern of policy consequences just identified, their immediately available explanation is a form of radicalism. Radical ideology holds that powerful economic interests are using government for selfish purposes, to exploit the masses of people while controlling them with a combination of marginal economic benefits, ideology, and coercion. Radicalism too is shaped by the values and beliefs of capitalism, if only because it rejects them and searches for appropriate substitutes. It also draws on some traditional American values and beliefs that are less fully integrated with capitalism. To some extent, but far from completely, radicalism has succeeded in introducing alternative explanations, values and beliefs into the American political dialogue.

To see how capitalism affects both orthodoxy and radicalism, we must again cast our analytical net widely enough to understand the general nature of ideology. In this chapter, we shall first look at the functions performed by ideologies—how they operate to shape understanding of the workings of government. Then we shall examine the two major components of the pervasive American orthodoxy: the basic political values of the society, and the dominant ideology that emerges from them. Finally, we shall summarize the relevance of capitalism to orthodoxy, and the meaning of orthodoxy for the character of our politics. In Chapter 7, we shall explore the radical challenge to this orthodoxy, and compare the two in some depth.

The Functions of Ideology

Three primary functions of ideology are worth noting here. First, ideology affects our perception of problems. Because we are used to thinking in certain ways, and because we habitually make certain assumptions, we tend to "understand" new problems only in a particular (limited and narrow) context. Second, ideology not only explains why policies take the form they do, but also justifies (or condemns) these patterns. It may do so on the grounds of the rightness (or wrongness) of the political system that produced them, the structure of power that animates that system, or the basic values underlying it. Third, ideology serves broadly to organize people and to provide them with a coherent sense of the relationship between themselves, their values, and the workings of their government.

1. *Ideology and the Perception of Problems*

What is a "problem?" Clearly, how we understand the character and causes of problems relates directly to what we regard as acceptable public policies to solve problems. Social problems have both an *objective* and a *subjective* character. Their objective character has to do with the tangible realities of conditions, such as the fact that air and water are polluted. Their subjective character involves the way our minds perceive and interpret those conditions. Is the pollution of air and water, for example, such a drastic threat to the enjoyment of life, or to the long-term ecological balance of nature, that severe measures should be taken to control the industrial sources of pollution? Or is it a necessary price to be paid for the continued expansion of the economy and the provision of jobs for a growing labor force? One's answer depends only partly on objective facts. Part of the "answer," probably some of the "facts," and certainly much of the "solution," depend upon one's ideology.

Thus, the subjective understanding of a problem may be more important than its objective characteristics. This subjective understanding is a direct product of one's values and ideology. Much of the difference between various ideologies' analyses of problems may be summed up in their respective conceptions of the nature of social life and problems generally. Particularly important is the extent to which they see various aspects of social life as interrelated and forming a whole. Let us imagine a continuum, at one end of which social problems are seen as integrated, and soluble only by taking into account their multiple causes and intimate relationship with the structure and operating characteristics of the economy, society, and political system. At the other end of the continuum, problems are seen as separate and discrete, each having specialized and independent causes and solutions. Some of these problems are in the economic realm, others in the political sphere. At this end of the continuum, problems are more likely to be seen as the results of officials' mistakes or specific institutional failures (i.e., Congress did not declare war in the Indochina situation). At this end of the continuum, no relationship between a given problem and the underlying values or characteristics of the economy and social structure is recognized.

In the first case, one understands problems as surface manifestations of deeper conflicts between the basic organizational principles of the economy and society, and/or basic political values. One is led deeper and deeper, past the problems themselves and their apparent surface "causes," in search of an underlying unity—a single cause or explanation of many visible problems viewed as a whole. In the second case, one might be satisfied with the first level of explanation, and seek to "solve" the surface manifestations of a problem as if they themselves were the causes, and it had no roots deeper in the economic and social systems. Or, taking all underlying values and structures as fixed and unchangeable, one might declare the problem either insoluble or inevitable.

This interpretation suggests why adherents of a challenging ideology often completely fail to communicate with those who hold to the dominant ideology. They are simply not talking about the same "problems" at all. It also raises some potentially revealing questions to be addressed to each of the two major ideologies under examination here. The effort to see how these ideologies shape understanding leads in turn to some profound questions for all of us who would be analysts of politics. We shall try to deal with each set of questions at the close of Chapter 7.

a. Where is each of the two contrasting ideologies on this continuum? How deep does it go in explaining causes of problems and offering solutions? *Which values and assumptions have what effects on understanding?*

b. How far should an objective analyst search for unifying explanations of problems—isn't there always some prior cause, probably one that cannot practically be dealt with by government? Is there a truly objective way to understand the real causes and character of a problem? Or are all versions of "reality" merely projections of ideological premises?

2. *Ideology and Explanation-justification*

Ideology does not just affect what we see and understand in the world around us; it also—and simultaneously—implies that what we see conforms to either our hopes or our fears. Things not only *are,* they are also *good* or *bad,* because ideology teaches us to understand them in both dimensions at the same time. By connecting newly perceived events with long-established and deeply held convictions, and by insisting that the former are consistent with the latter, ideology filters all events through a particular perceptual screen. In the view of the dominant ideology, for example, the rightness of the American political system and the propriety of our basic political values make it inevitable that public policies will benefit the society as a whole. If in some specific regard they do not, the matter can be promptly corrected. Of course, because there are some limits to what government *should* do for people, certain conditions simply cannot be corrected. The liberty of some should not be unduly restrained so that the equality of others can be advanced, for example; the latter must do for themselves, as others have done.

3. *Ideology and Organization of People*

What does it mean to shape what people see, and whether they see it as good or bad? Clearly, it implies at least organization of, and potentially control over, those people. By providing a coherent and comprehensive understanding of their world, ideology organizes people; it molds them into particular relationships with other people, with government, and with events. They need not be aware of what is happening to them, nor is it the same as if they were marching in a column of thousands with explicit orders from their leaders. But they *are* organized in the sense that they see and think the same things at the same time as do many other people. In the case of the dominant ideology, the life situation and experience of most individuals implicitly reinforce (and reward) acceptance of American orthodoxy, and political leaders explicitly call for behavior in accordance with it. Thus, the ideology becomes a powerful instrument of social control on behalf of those people or interests served by its teachings. It is easier, and more effective, if people voluntarily behave in ways that are congenial to the existing social order; coercion can then be held to a minimum. A challenging ideology may similarly organize people's lives and serve many of the same functions on behalf of group leaders. In both cases, people perceive and behave in certain ways, and believe in their acts and perceptions, because they consciously or unconsciously hold a particular ideology. And everybody holds *some* ideology, in greater or lesser degree. The only question is *which* ideology, and how it affects understanding and action.

Basic American Political Values

Political values are the most fundamental commitments that people hold about what is right or wrong in politics. They are the building blocks for thinking about how political systems should be organized, and why. We shall touch upon five political values that have had major impact on American political thought and practice.

Individualism

The focal point of political thought in the United States is the individual. From this beginning, all other relationships and values follow. The individual is the basic unit of politics, for whose benefit the political system is erected. Individuals are viewed as naturally competitive, and their competiton makes for personal fulfillment and social progress. The principal goals of political life have to do with providing a suitable context for the individual's satisfaction and happiness. Self-fulfillment is sought, and principles of government are deduced, from assumptions about what is needed to serve the individual's needs. In the mid-eighteenth century, for example, the chief impediment to individual self-attainment seemed (with good reason) to be governmental power wielded by royal or aristocratic authorities. The principal means of assuring individual opportunity, therefore, was a firm set of limitations on the power of government and an equally determined *laissez faire* approach to the role of government in the society and economy.

The "Natural Rights" of the Individual

As part of his entitlement on earth, due him solely by virtue of his existence, the individual has certain rights. These are (1) the right to property—to be secure in the possession of goods and land, to be able to rely upon the value of money, and to be able to collect debts owed; (2) the right to life and liberty, in the sense that one cannot be deprived of either without being granted the due processes of law (hearing, trial, fair procedures, etc.); (3) the right to participate, to some degree at least, in the decisions of government; and (4) the right to equality, whether it is defined as equal treatment before the law or equality of opportunity.

Although property rights are only one of several natural rights, political thinkers and practical politicians have frequently tended to elevate them to first place on the priority scale and sometimes to exclusive entitlement. Alexander Hamilton, an eminently practical thinker, was very blunt about his priorities: "Money is the vital principle of the body politic." Vital as his efforts toward nation-building must be acknowledged to be, his writings concede little comparative importance to equality or other "human rights" among the natural rights. The problem is, of course, that property rights often conflict with other natural rights, particularly equality; thus the issue of priority is crucial. The deep and bitter conflict over slavery may serve to illustrate this point and demonstrate the power and ascendancy of property as an American political value. None of the Framers of the Constitution seriously doubted that slaves were property, to be provided for as such. The early debates over limited slavery versus emancipation foundered on the appropriate amounts of compensation (the propriety of which was never questioned) for the loss of property. The Abolitionists were bitterly resisted by most Northerners, at least partly because of the antiproperty implications of their position. And when emancipation came, it was as a limited expediency in the course of a difficult war. In this sequence of events, relatively few voices were raised on behalf of granting equality priority over property, and it was only the commitment to preserve the Union that finally mobilized the use of force.

This conflict between property and other natural rights is real and repeated—in debate over the progressive income tax, social security, the poverty program, and the regulation of the economy generally. But such conflict is anticipated and feared by those who hold property far more than actual inroads upon their possessions would seem to justify. The Framers and the early Federalists feared attacks upon property and radical redistribution of wealth if majorities were allowed to work their will through the political system. Consequently, they built in a series of restraints upon the power of government.[1] In justifying this principle, they developed and promulgated the idea of "majority rule *and* minority rights." By minority rights, of course, they meant property rights. But the two are logically

---

[1]For a full presentation of the Framers' ideas, one should examine the *Federalist Papers*, available in many inexpensive editions.

inconsistent: no political system can provide *both* majority rule *and* minority rights in the absolute sense. An effective limit upon majority rule on behalf of minority rights means that there is no real majority rule. Conversely, if majority rule succeeds in working its will in all cases, the system *cannot* always be protecting minority rights. Nevertheless, most Americans subscribe to both principles and acknowledge such limitations on the power of majorities— testimony, perhaps, to the success of the Federalists in establishing their view as an integral component of American political ideology. Or possibly *all* Americans—not just the propertied but nervous Federalists and their successors—have accepted property as a primary value and have therefore imposed limitations upon themselves and not sought the anticipated redistribution. This is certainly the view preferred by the orthodox ideology.

Limited Government

At least as far as eighteenth-century thinkers were concerned, a necessary corollary to individualism and natural rights (in which property rights hold primacy) is the principle of limited government. If the individual possesses rights flowing from the laws of nature, then government is his creation. Its powers must be consistent with his natural rights and must have been conferred upon it by the collectivity of individuals who together possess all powers. Its sphere of action is defined both by the limited scope of the powers granted to it and by the inviolability of the rights of individuals.

In this view, government is a marginal and semi-illegitimate enterprise. Regardless of the fact that the society (or collectivity of individuals) has no other agent capable of acting on behalf of the whole, each effort to employ government for particular purposes is viewed with suspicion and its necessity and propriety are challenged. To justify their proposed use of government as an instrument to accomplish (presumably) majoritarian purposes, supporters of the contemplated action must prove a special need not being (or capable of being) served in other ways. They must show cause, in other words, why circumstances are so unusual as to legitimate the use of government on this specific occasion and in this particular manner.

Materialism and the Business Ethic

From the earliest days of this nation, observers have repeatedly commented on the special disposition of Americans to seek private economic gain. Acquisitiveness and profit-seeking are sometimes related to a so-called "Protestant ethic," according to which ultimate salvation depends upon striving and attainment in this world.

National celebration of such motivations reached its height at the end of the nineteenth century, in the days of Horatio Alger and the robber barons. Although it would be little more than caricature to attribute such motivations to most Americans today, it is clear that the United States is a business-oriented society. The underlying value system strongly supports such capitalist principles as the value of consumption by individuals, the measurement of the propriety and desirability of new ventures by their profitability, and the measurement of individual achievement by the accumulation of wealth.

These values and motivations, broadly shared, affect the criteria used to determine the priorities and programs of government. Because private profit and consumption are valued so highly, public expenditure is suspect. Government outlays for such public purposes as schools, hospitals, and welfare may be seen as "spending" and therefore undesirable, while corporate expenditures for new and perhaps unnecessary consumer products are "investments" and therefore good. Government action may be judged with a kind of tradesman's approach, in which short-range questions of profitability dominate: Can the Post Office be run as a business and bring in enough income to balance its costs? Will the proposed bridge earn enough income to pay off the cost of building it in a fixed period of years?

Racism

Almost equally long-lived and pervasive in American society is the assumption of white supremacy. Perhaps originating in Western culture centuries ago, the sense of superiority of the white race has been an animating feature of Americans and their governmental policies throughout our history. Neither the American Indian nor the Afro-American was thought fit for full citizenship until very recently. Recent scholarship indicates that nearly all of the major leaders at the time the Constitution was framed, as well as in subsequent periods, held white-supremacist assumptions.[2] However unconscious such notions may have been, they were instrumental in shaping policies that massacred Indians, oppressed slaves, and built a sometimes unrecognized racist strain into the American value system.

After centuries of official action in accordance with these premises, it is not surprising that those who seek evidence of the degradation of the nonwhite races are readily able to find it. Efforts to remedy the work of centuries, however, run up against denials of personal responsibility and failure to perceive the racist bases of existing

[2]Thomas F. Gossett, Race: The History of an Idea in America (New York: Schocken Books, 1963).

policies, as well as normal resistance to change. Most Americans do not understand the extent to which subtle and not-so-subtle racial barriers served as artificial constrictions that prevent the nonwhite poor from rising via the routes taken by the immigrant poor of the nineteenth and early twentieth centuries. Given such widespread and deep-seated racism, it is not difficult to see why the limited governmental steps taken have nevertheless been highly controversial, and why the tangible signs of change are so few.

There are many important factual questions to be asked about all of these values, of course. We do not know which groups or strata within the society actually held or hold them, how widely shared or intensely felt they are, or whether people who assert them actually act on them. These are questions we shall attempt to answer later.

AN INTERVIEW WITH PRESIDENT RICHARD M. NIXON

... Now, on the domestic scene: I think that the tragedy of the 60's is that so many Americans, and particularly so many young Americans, lost faith in their country, in the American system, in their country's foreign policy. Many were influenced to believe that they should be ashamed of our country's record in foreign policy and what we were doing in the world; that we should be ashamed of what America did, and all.

Many Americans got the impression that this was an ugly country, racist, not compassionate, and part of the reason for this was the tendency of some to take every mole that we had and to make it look like a cancer.

Now, let us understand: This is not a perfect country. There is much that needs to be corrected. But I don't say this in any jingoistic sense—I have seen the world, and I don't know any young person abroad, if he had the chance, who wouldn't rather be here than someplace else.

Moles Into Cancers

What I think we have to do is not simply to reinstill in Americans a pride in country, a majority of the Americans do have a pride in country. You see how they respond.

But they must not do it on blind faith, "My country, right or wrong but my country." We want them to know why this country is right. Now, taking the foreign field, we want to make the American people feel proud of their country's role in the foreign field. I think the trips to Peking and Moscow helped in that respect. I think the people saw that the United States was leading the world in peace and that we were the only ones who could do it. They were proud of our country.

We are going to continue to exert that kind of leadership.

At home, as we move toward equality of opportunity, and it will not come overnight, but as we move toward equality of opportunity, as we move toward dealing with the problems of the environment, whether it is clean air, or a better health system, or improvement in education, as we make progress in all of these fields, I think that we will reinstill some of the faith that has been lost in the 60's.

I think we have somewhat digressed from your question, but I think what we are talking about here is that we have passed through a very great spiritual crisis in this country—during the late 60's, the war in Vietnam by many was blamed for it totally. It was only part of the problem and in many cases it was only an excuse rather than a reason. But we saw a breakdown in frankly what I could call the leadership class of this country.

I am not saying that critically because many lost faith in many of our institutions. For example, the enormous movement toward permissiveness which led to the escalation in crime, the escalation in drugs in this country, all of this came as a result of those of us who basically have a responsibility of leadership not recognizing that above everything else you must not weaken a people's character.

Conservative Judges

Now, let's try to get at it another way. One issue you haven't touched on is the whole area of the courts. I said several times that I intend to continue to appoint conservative judges to the court. I do. The courts need them and they need men like Rehnquist and Burger and Blackmun and Powell on their court, not reactionary judges but men who are constitutional conservatives, because the trend had gone too far in the other direction. I don't mean that there weren't well-intentioned judges calling them as they see them. But I don't believe that that was the right trend for this country and I think we have got to continue to reverse that trend in the whole field of law enforcement.

Drugs, etc.—We are going to continue a very strong program here because the whole era of permissiveness has left its mark.

Now, having said that, I do not mean that we turn to reaction. I do not mean that we turn to an attitude which does not have compassion for those who cannot be blamed for some of the problems that they have. But I feel very strongly that this country wants and this election will demonstrate that the American people want and the American people will thrive upon a new feeling of responsibility, a new feeling of self-discipline, rather than go back to the thoughts of the 60's that it was government's job every time there was a problem, to make people more and more dependent upon it to give way to their whims.

Welfare Mess Deplored

The welfare mess is an example. This escalation of the numbers on welfare, much of it is a result simply of running down what I call the work ethic. Now, I understand that is considered to be reactionary, to suggest people ought to work rather than go on welfare. And I do know there are some who can't work and must go on welfare. But on the other hand, another thing this election is about is whether we should move toward more massive handouts to people, making the people more and more dependent, looking to Government, or whether we say, no, it is up to you. The people are going to have to carry their share of the load.

The average American is just like the child in the family. You give him some responsibility and he is going to amount to something. He is going to do something. If, on the other hand, you make him completely dependent and pamper him and cater to him too much, you are going to make him soft, spoiled and eventually a very weak individual. . . .

We are going to change the way we are going to do this and rather than Government doing more for people and making people more dependent upon it, what I am standing for is Government finding ways through the Government programs to allow people to do more for themselves, to encourage them to do more for themselves; not only to encourage them, but to give them incentive to do more for themselves on their own without Government assistance.

Source: Garnett D. Horner, White House correspondendent, *Washington Star-News,* 5 November, 1972.

The Orthodox Ideology

The dominant political belief system holds that the values just described are realized on a day-to-day basis in American politics. In part, this is the natural function of a nation's political ideology. In effect, ideology is a kind of mental map that tells people how to harmonize what they see with their strongly held convictions about what is good. Because it is simplifying and reassuring, it is also seductive and frequently unconscious. It tends to be strongest among those who have had the most formal education, possibly because their economic interests and social positions act to reinforce what they have heard so often and in so many different forms in the educational process. Others, particularly those who experience more contrast between the ideology and the realities of daily existence, may be less prone to uncritical adoption of it. But because of such ideology-induced confidence, those few who (however accurately) believe a given policy to have disastrous implications will have great difficulty gaining support from a majority of their fellow citizens. Or ideology may serve to divert or frighten people so completely as to distort consideration of various problems. American anticommunism in the post-World War II decades was apparently strong enough to reduce public concern for due process and to prevent rational consideration of priorities and alternatives in policymaking. We shall illustrate two components of the dominant American political ideology in the paragraphs that follow.

1. **The ideology holds that the basic political values of the United States are reflected in the structure of the American government, and that the resulting political system is democratic in character.** American ideology teaches that the core political values are so well represented by the machinery of American government that one may understand government as the manifestation of those values. To a great extent, the Framers did indeed seek to operationalize those primary values, although it is at least questionable (a) whether they did so in such a way that the benefits were to be realized automatically by the entire population, or chiefly by the Framers and others like them; and (b) whether, regardless of their purposes, their product can fairly be termed democratic in character. Each type of question raises some potentially revealing issues.

The core political values—individualism, limited government, natural rights (with property rights ascendant over equality and other human rights), and procedural regularity—are patently manifest within the Constitution and the government it creates. Ideology holds that the institutional forms of these principles will operate as if controlled by an unseen hand, and will deliver the results considered appropriate by those who subscribe to that set of values. The interplay of presidential and congressional power is seen as yielding a mechanistic (and therefore appropriate) product; the decision of the Supreme Court is seen as representing a higher law's mandate, not the preferences of five judges. In short, ideology suggests that the translation of values into institutions and powers has achieved a nonpartisan, depoliticized apparatus that works to the benefit of all.

Next, the ideology holds that this structure creates a situation that allows full play to the "natural" workings of human capacities and wants, and of the economic market, which will result in the greatest good for the greatest number of people. Thus, the established political values are seen as manifested in a particular set of institutions; these institutions interact in a mechanical manner; and the result is the furtherance of a natural order in which talent and effort are rewarded and the incompetent and slothful are carried along by the successful.

The teachings of ideology with respect to the structure and operations of government are that all will benefit equally, or at least substantially, from such procedures. But it seems clear that the character of the institutional setup, and the principles on which it frequently operates, neither benefits all equally nor leaves results to chance. It works to the advantage of those who are situated so as to be able to seize opportunities for gaining power and influence. Separation of powers, distribution of powers between nation and states, and the protection provided for property rights, for example, make it very difficult to enact laws that change the *status quo*. The principle of *laissez faire* means that people with private economic power are free to use that power as they see fit, and it is difficult (and perhaps wrong in any event) for others to try to use government to control such activities. If government works mechanically, of course, nobody should be aggrieved about its actions, because they are inherent in the (good) design of the American governmental structure itself. Thus, it turns out that nothing is responsible for the advantages secured by those with economic or social power except their own talents in the free and open struggle for individual achievement.

Perhaps even more important than the manner in which basic political values are related to the structure and operations of government, however, is the way in which the ideology equates the values *and* the nature of American government with democracy. Democracy is good; the United States is good; the United States is a democracy; democracy is what we experience in the United States. Circularity and poor logic are no obstacles for a powerful ideology, and it may be fruitless—perhaps unpatriotic—to try to unravel the relationships here. What has apparently happened is that the ideology has adapted to the powerful appeal of democracy in the last two centuries and interpreted American values and institutions in this light. Thus, the commitment to private property and individualism becomes a characteristic of democratic man. Or, the institution of judicial review, originally designed to frustrate popular will expressed through the elected legislature, comes to be seen as a vehicle for expression of the democratic values of civil liberties. A statute outlawing political participation by people of a particular viewpoint becomes democratic because it preserves the "freedom" of the "democratic" electoral process. A natural tendency to believe that what we have is good, if not ideal, leads to favorable (democratic) interpretations of whatever we have.

We are not arguing that the governmental system of the United States is necessarily undemocratic, though we may appear to be taking a harsh view of some much-revered things. We are saying that the acts of *assuming* that American institutions are democratic, and *defining* "democracy" as what exists in the United States, are essentially *ideological* in character. In both cases, "American" and "democratic" become synonymous—testimony to the power of ideology to suggest conclusions rather than leaving them to the judgment of the observer.

It is the social control thrust of American ideology—its capacity to disarm analysis and provide benevolent interpretations—that is so significant to contemporary American politics. Few, if any, Americans are fully captured by all the characteristics of ideology we have touched upon, but practically everyone is influenced by at least some of them. In the next section, we shall discuss aspects of ideology held even by some scholars and students of American politics.

2. The ideology holds that the process of political decisionmaking in the United States consists of negotiation and compromise among many factions and groups, and that the product is a reasonable approximation of both democracy and the public interest. In the next five paragraphs, we shall characterize the generally accepted view of the American political process, sometimes termed "democratic pluralism."

To begin with, the system is considered to be open to all those who wish to take the time and trouble to participate. For the most part, Americans actually do participate through the vehicle of voluntary associations, organized around the interests that are real to them: ethnic, religious, occupational, social, economic, political, or other bases of shared concern. A single citizen may belong to several different groups. These groups articulate the needs and desires of the people at all levels of the society, but particularly with reference to government.

In organizing support among the population and presenting their claims upon the government, groups come into conflict with other groups. Each group's efforts to achieve its goals is likely to call into play another group with different or opposed goals in the same subject area. This is sometimes termed the principle of "countervailing powers." The various groups with interests in this field then engage in an elaborate process of negotiation, bargaining, appeals to principle and popular support, pressures on decisionmakers, and finally compromise. Because each group represents a significant segment of opinion and probably has access to some source of power within the governmental structure, it can usually delay if not completely frustrate an extreme demand made by another group. This means that each group is induced to compromise on a solution that falls short of achieving its full goals because, if it does not, it may end up with nothing.

A further spur to harmonious handling of conflict through compromise is the influence of the informal rules for group goalseeking. Each group is assumed to be sufficiently concerned with the fairness and openness of the process (because the attainment of its goals depends on getting a fair hearing from the others) so that all share a strong commitment to defending the procedures of decisionmaking. Above all, parties to the goal-seeking process should be willing to see the other side's problems, and also to compromise at a point not only short of their own goals but also short of absolute disaster for the other side. This is also sound strategy, since those who happen to win today may be on the losing side tomorrow, in which case they can expect the same consideration from their new opponents. Thus, the informal rules promote compromise and help to build a shared feeling of mutual approval for the decisionmaking system itself. An opponent, after all, is a person who plays the game by the rules and is entitled to respect for his views and for the demands placed on him by his constituency. Those who do not accept the rules are not playing the right game, or are cheating, and are properly censured by all the regular players. When the regular groups do find themselves in disagreement, or at other moments when major decisions must be made, the basic outlines of national policy are determined by popular elections. In this way, the day-to-day activities of group goalseeking are channeled; they devote themselves to working out the details of policies decided upon by the mass electorate.

Groups perform many functions within the social and political order. They serve as a major means of representation, providing people with a sense that their voices are heard in the halls of government in ways other than the familiar geographical or party systems of representation. Thus, if a citizen belongs to the minority political party in his state or congressional district, he can nevertheless feel represented in government by the efforts of interest groups that seek to further his goals. In discharging this representative function, groups also root the citizen more thoroughly in the society—giving him a sense of place, status, and fulfillment. Further, in a reciprocal manner, groups give public officials a means of knowing what the people want and need, and a way of communicating back and forth that makes for more responsive government.

There are other democratic consequences that grow out of the pattern of group activity in politics. People who participate in groups acquire the tolerance for others and respect for fair procedures that help to support a democratic system. They may also belong to two or more groups whose interests are occasionally in conflict. For example, one citizen may belong to both the League of Women Voters and the Catholic Church. If the League seeks to take a position contrary to that of the Church on birth-control issues, the citizen may be "cross-pressured" to take a much less extreme position on the issue than she otherwise would have. At the same time, her influence within each organization helps to lead it to a less extreme position. This "cross-cutting effect, multiplied cleavages" many times over for many issues, helps to keep the political system on an even keel by reducing the extremity of pressures on it. The process is both democratic and in the public interest. It is democratic because everybody has a chance to be heard, the procedures for "playing the game" are known and followed, and a general consensus based on compromise and toler-ance for the other side emerges before the decision is cast into final form. It is in the public interest chiefly because it *does* represent a con-sensus that everybody can accept, and that is therefore very likely to be both in harmony with the experience and capacity of the system and responsive to the problem in question.

These five paragraphs sum up a very large body of analysis, inter-pretation, and self-congratulation by journalists, academics, and the general public. Most of it, however pretentiously set forth, is little more than a restatement of the dominant ideology. Taken together, these two major components of the dominant ideology exhibit a very strong commitment to the established order. In particular, they em-phasize over and over again the necessity and propriety of following the rules. Sometimes insistence on procedural regularity is raised to the level of a basic political value, and given a label such as "legal-ism." The importance to Americans of formal written provisions, and of the law generally, has often been noted by observers; the major role played by lawyers in the governing of this society also rests on this procedural-legal bias. Beneath the stress on established rules and legalistic procedures, of course, lies a basic conviction that actions taken in the private sphere are best and should take precedence over (if not be protected against) public policies. Thus, the orthodox ideol-ogy says in effect that if policies are developed by the established rules of the political system, they must be appropriate. Further, if they maximize the opportunities of people to gain their ends through pri-vate rather than governmental means, they are good. This makes it almost unnecessary to examine the actual consequences of policies. Their merits can be determined from the circumstances of their en-actment, and from the extent to which they leave people free to gain their ends through private means.

The Implications of American Orthodoxy

So far, we have analyzed the American orthodoxy as a set of spe-cific values and ideological beliefs held by Americans. We have seen how political images and beliefs are rooted in basic values, and have examined the nature of each. Now it is time to note again how fully American beliefs are fused with capitalist values, and to ask what this orthodoxy means for our politics.

How much of our orthodoxy is capitalism by another name? Indi-vidualism, materialism, competition, the work ethic and profit motive, property rights, and the primacy of private economic activity are clearly capitalist principles. The concepts of limited government, con-tractualism, and legalism are applications of capitalist principles to the political system. Some American values may have had other origins and independent support, but have become intertwined with capitalism throughout our history. Racism is a prime example. It relegates minority groups to artificially low levels of employment and income, and both divides workers and diverts them from making more effective demands for larger shares of wealth and income. Some values, originally intertwined with capitalism, have increasingly diverged from it. Equality, for example, has begun to take on social and economic dimensions that require more than mere opportunities to compete for material gain. Perhaps the best way to conceive of the American orthodoxy is as a hard core of capitalism with certain modifications, ambiguities, and accompanying cultural idiosyncrasies. A capsule characterization, however, would have to emphasize the continuing overlap and parallel with capitalism.

What does this orthodoxy mean for our politics? The *strength* of its influence clearly has several important results. Most Americans are unaware how specific their values and beliefs are, partly because they are rarely challenged effectively. Thus, they consider their values and beliefs natural, inevitable, and self-evident. This can lead to failure to understand others' feelings and opinions, and to impatience with or intolerance of those with other views. Because the orthodoxy exists at such a deep level that it is not always recognized, those who depart from it may appear mentally or morally defective. They can then be imprisoned, hospitalized, or otherwise ostracized legally and with general approval.

The *shared character* of at least the major elements of the orthodoxy has other implications. We do not argue that all sectors of the population hold the orthodox values and beliefs in the same proportions; as we shall see, there are levels at which only certain basic elements of it are observed, and some where other views predominate. But most Americans share the values and beliefs discussed in this chapter to some degree. This means that prominent public officials can draw support for their actions by manipulating revered symbols. They do not have to justify their acts exclusively, or even primarily, in terms of their merits. Instead, they can claim that their acts conform to the values of individualism or preservation of the economic system. In short, the broadly shared character of the orthodoxy facilitates social control. It causes people to believe in and support their leaders, almost without regard to what they are actually doing.

The *content* of orthodoxy combines with its strength and shared character to create certain additional implications. Capitalism becomes insulated from critical evaluation, because most Americans do not perceive the economic system in those terms and, in any event, believe it to be both good and inevitable. Nationalism is enhanced, because many Americans come to feel that our system is clearly superior to all others. Some may carry this to the point of messianism, a feeling that it is our moral mission to bring the blessings of our (capitalist) system to the rest of the world. Those who willfully stand in the way and reject our system—for example, communists or socialists—are thus seen as evil and inevitable enemies.

This characterization may seem harsh or exaggerated. We do not believe that it is; at least, it is thoroughly grounded in the interpretations of generations of reputable American scholars. More likely, such reactions are the result of a lifetime of uncritical acceptance of orthodox values and beliefs, in greater or lesser degree. The strength and character of this orthodoxy also suggest why radicalism has not been very successful in the United States. As we shall see, even radicalism has often been unable to extricate itself from the scope of this pervasive belief system.

Chapter 7

Why do public policies have the character and consequences that they do? The radical answer is a clear contrast to the democratic pluralist-legalist explanation urged by American orthodoxy. It is quite simply that concentrated economic power is, as always, systematically and selfishly exploiting the great majority of the people. Public policies serve the purposes of the powerful, who use government as a tool for private profit. At times, when pressure mounts, the ruling class offers certain pacifying benefits to leading elements among the lower echelons. The dominant ideology is no more than a facade for manipulation by such corrupting interests.

Ideology and Public Policies: The Radical Challenge

"Radicalism" itself means only the call for drastic change at the roots of the social order. The term is applicable to efforts on both the left and the right that seek such change. We will focus here on the radicalism of the left, because it is the major source of challenge to American orthodoxy today. The essence of this American radicalism is concern for equality in some form, and for advancing the cause of the "little man" in some fashion. Ever since the nation was founded, radicalism, in one or another of its evolving versions, has periodically risen to challenge the dominant orthodoxy. Tom Paine's early egalitarianism, the Jacksonian movement, the Abolitionists, the women's suffrage movement, the labor movement, and the recent civil rights movement are all manifestations of this deep and continuing stream in American political thought.

But there are several contending strands in radical thought. One emphasizes participation and opportunity *within* the evolving American capitalist system. It opposes all concentrations of wealth and privilege, and demands reforms sufficient to allow deprived individuals and groups to enjoy the full benefits available or potentially available in the United States. Another challenges American capitalism directly, insisting that the inherent nature of capitalism prevents realization of people's social and personal potential. This anticapitalist strain of radical thought is grounded in the argument that individualism, materialism, and private profit-seeking inevitably result in exploitation, misery, and war for the great mass of people in the world. Only a social system in which people cooperate for the fulfillment of the material and human needs of all can provide a decent and morally justifiable life under current world conditions. A third dimension of radical thought is strictly individualist, or self-oriented, in contrast to the system-orientation of the first two. It holds that no good can be achieved through social action or efforts to reconstruct society as a whole. Instead, people should seek to reconstruct their own ways of thinking and personal lives in ways more truly human and worthwhile. This can be accomplished only alone or in the company of a few other like-minded people.

All three strands have permeated American history. The demand for participation and opportunity is probably the most conspicuous, for it has taken many forms and led to changes in the character of capitalism itself. The Jacksonian, Populist, Progressive, and New Deal periods were all characterized by such protests and by the ultimate transformation of capitalism from one form to another. In effect, the dominant system was able to blunt, absorb, and convert such demands into forms that could serve its own needs because their basic nature was not antagonistic to the principles of capitalism. Direct challenges to capitalism itself began with late nineteenth-century socialists and have continued to the present. They have been notably unsuccessful to date, because of the strength of American orthodoxy and the attacks mounted upon them by governments and others. Individualist withdrawal began with the transcendental individualists' attacks upon the commercial society in the early nineteenth century. It exists today in the form of a kind of libertarian anarchism and in certain versions of countercultural withdrawal. Because it has never been a serious threat, it has never been repressed as have direct challenges to capitalism.

Thus radicalism is not a single coherent system of thought, nor is it the rallying point of a unified social movement. Instead, it is a collection of different (and sometimes conflicting) beliefs, whose adherents share chiefly the conviction that they are deprived, powerless, and victimized by the dominant system. Radicalism begins as a set of reactions against contemporary conditions, and against the values and ideology that rationalize and justify them. Ultimately, it takes the form of an alternative ideology.

People can and do move from one strand of radical thought to another. In the 1960s and 1970s, radicals have tended to shift from demands for participation and reform to rejection of the existing system. Their rejection takes the form either of calls for the replacement of capitalism, or of withdrawal into highly individualistic anarchism or countercultural life styles. At any given moment, of course, some people are sincerely hoping and working for the reforms that will make the system more just in their eyes, while others have despaired of this and are either attacking capitalism itself or abandoning politics and social life to find solace by themselves.

In this analysis, we shall focus on the distinctions between these three strands of radicalism and orthodoxy, and on the evolving views of some of the major sources of today's rebirth of radical ideology. Throughout, we shall be searching for what is general, or shared, among the different strands of thought that make up radicalism. And we shall emphasize the drift from demands for more equitable distribution of the rewards of the American capitalist system to rejection of the system itself.

Radical Political Values and Ideology

Each strand in radical thought rests on a distinctive response to the political values of American orthodoxy. Individualism plays a particularly central distinguishing role. The thrust of the major strand of radicalism, as we have said, is toward participation, reform, and redistribution of rewards within the American system. This strain of radicalism accepts all the orthodox values, including individualism, but redefines and reorders them somewhat. The currently growing trend toward confrontation with capitalism rests on the outright rejection of at least some of these values, including individualism as we understand it, and the substitution of new values. The individualist strand of radicalism raises individualism even beyond its high status among the orthodox values, granting it nearly exclusive standing. It correspondingly reduces emphasis on values that legitimate social or governmental action. We shall briefly characterize what is distinctive about each of these forms of radicalism.

Participation, Reform, and Redistribution of Rewards

This primary strain of radicalism best illustrates the nature and consequences of the radical commitment to equality. Much of the history of tension between radicalism and the dominant orthodoxy can be summarized in the conflict between the values of equality and property as they are understood by the respective ideologies. The argument has involved both the *definition* and the *priority* to be attached to equality. Radicalism of this kind defines equality in broad and steadily expanding terms, moving beyond equality of opportunity to equality in the actual conditions of people's lives. And it gives full priority to equality, raising it above all other political values when they come into conflict.

But it is easy to exaggerate the "radicalness" of the radical argument. At no time in American history, for example, did any significant number of radicals call for the abolition of private property as such, or for drastic action to equalize the conditions of people's lives. They asked only for somewhat greater emphasis on equality in the context of competitive individualism and respect for property rights. They started from the acknowledged principle of political equality, in the sense of voting rights and majoritarianism, and gradually caused restrictions inconsistent with such principles, such as those involving property, sex, and race, to be removed.

Although these are not very drastic steps, they opened up another range of issues involving equality. To what extent should the principle of equality be carried into the extrapolitical dimension? Should it, for example, be generalized to imply at least a minimum level of "human rights" and support for various forms of social-welfare action by government? Or, in other words, should equality have an economic or social dimension? Can there be true political equality without social and economic equality? In the early years of this nation, it was assumed that the individual could attain his economic and social ends through his own efforts. The chief threat to this goal appeared to be the single major source of power that then existed—government. If government were sufficiently prevented from interfering with the natural process of individual self-realization, the result would be a rough equality of opportunity. Jefferson, for example, strongly defended the principle of *laissez faire* on behalf of this egalitarian purpose.

In later years, however, it appeared that sources of power other than government, and other socially produced limitations, prevented the individual from attaining his ends. Radicals, therefore, sought to expand the implications of equality to include government action to preserve opportunity and the provision of sufficient education and social status to enable individuals to compete more equally. Once again, there was strong resistance on the part of others who held to more restrictive definitions of equality. Thus, though equality is symbolically unchallenged, its political and socioeconomic effectuation has been tentative and controversial.

By contrast, attachment to property as a legitimate and paramount value has been widely shared and rarely challenged. No major Ameri-

can thinker, including Jefferson (supposed by some of his contempo-
raries to have been unsympathetic to the wealthy and propertied),
has failed to support strongly the individual's right to whatever land,
goods, and money he could amass. Hamilton and some other Federalists took these to be the central goals of man's motivations and
sought to construct a government to serve these ends. Men like Adams
and Jefferson believed that property gave people political independence, a stake in the society, and the capacity and right to judge—from
which wise public decisionmaking might be anticipated.

To be sure, there have been disagreements about property rights,
but they are different from debates over equality. Debates about property rights have centered on the competing claims of various types of
property, or at times on whether property should be the *exclusive*
(not just the primary) value to be served by the political system.
Jefferson's long struggle with Hamilton and the Federalists illustrates
the former issue. Jefferson opposed the creation of the national bank
and the Federalist program of fostering manufacturing through import
tariffs because he felt that these measures were creating an artificial
form of property—interest on stocks and investments—that did not
reflect labor and merit in the same way as did the cultivation of land.
In part, Jefferson also saw the governmentally fostered accumulation
of wealth by a few people as a potential threat to political equality,
but his challenge and that of his followers was made in behalf of an
alternative form of property.

It should be clear that this strain of radicalism historically affirmed
other traditional values, as well as property rights. The concepts of
individualism, materialism, natural rights, limited government, and
legalism were all taken for granted throughout the effort to expand
and raise equality. The same is true today: what this form of radicalism seeks is a reality that conforms to orthodox American rhetoric,
providing greater opportunity for individuals to compete more successfully and amass larger amounts of the material rewards of the
American system.

To a limited extent, such radicals do see the flaws and limits of
existing values, and would repair these deficiencies. Limited government, for example, though still considered valid in the abstract because people should be free to attain their individual ends, is seen as
much violated in practice. In this view, the worst violations are the
subsidies, price supports, and other financial benefits for those very
economic interests most likely to use the principle of limited government as a defense against proposed policies that would benefit
ordinary people. Individualism is considered to have humanistic
and esthetic, as well as material, dimensions. Material aspirations,
however, are still taken to be the primary motivation of "human
nature," and the basic dynamic of social life. Racism is acknowl-

edged and condemned, but the chief remedy is seen as laws to prevent discrimination.

The ideology that flows from these values contains a profound ambivalence. On one hand, it brusquely rejects orthodoxy's claim that present policies must be appropriate because they are enacted by a system in which rules and widespread participation assure outcomes that reflect a democratic consensus. Economic and social conditions, readily visible to all who are willing to look, completely rebut the claims of American orthodoxy and must be corrected. Concentrations of economic power must be prevented from continuing their exploitation, and ordinary citizens must recapture power over the circumstances of their lives. On the other hand, this ideology holds that these goals can be accomplished if more people become involved, reopen the political processes, and "throw the rascals out." By reforming certain aspects of politics, installing better men in office, and thus rearranging the priorities of government and society, the conditions of the mass of the people can be dramatically improved. In short, things are very bad, but it won't take much to set them right.

The fight against this concentration of privilege—open and covert, legal and illegal—is, we believe, the most important political question of this decade. Its goal is a more equitable distribution of wealth and power; its enemy is the entire arrangement of privileges, exemptions, and free rides that has narrowed the opportunity of most Americans to control their own destiny. This fight for fairness is political; it can be won only by organizing a new political majority in America.

From Jack Newfield and Jeff Greenfield, *A Populist Manifesto: The Making of a New Majority* (New York: Warner Paperback Library, 1972), p. 17.

This ambivalence has its roots in acceptance of most of the orthodox political values "as is," and in the effects of orthodox political ideology. Accepting the values of competitive individualism and materialism, this form of radicalism can only say that the "problem" is the unfair distribution of rewards—and not the wrongness of the nature or workings of the economy as a whole. Thinking within the framework of American political ideology, and therefore convinced of the rightness and legitimacy of the political system as a whole, it can only say that there must be something temporarily wrong. If corrected through the sincere efforts of the people, the national government could again become the agent of the people and the instrument of economic opportunity for all. For these reasons, this version of radicalism remains principally a protest movement, demanding reform and opportunity *within* the existing system.

Challenges to Capitalism Itself

Though not yet primary, this version of contemporary radicalism has grown in proportion to the failure of reformist radicalism to achieve real success for more than a few sectors of the population. It holds that the traditional American values are not just in need of redefinition and reordering, but are themselves the cause of current problems. In particular, anticapitalist radicalism rejects individualism in the orthodox sense. Human nature is not necessarily competitive and self-aggrandizing, such radicals argue; people can learn to share, and to cooperate for the betterment of their mutual condition. When they do, a true sense of community will emerge. Justice in the form of roughly equal distribution of rewards will be available for all.

The key to achieving such results, is seen as the elimination of the private ownership of productive machinery and resources, and the profit-maximizing use that necessarily results. As long as such private ownership and profit orientation exists, masses of people *must* be exploited. Thus anticapitalist radicalism must reject the value of property rights, not necessarily as to personal property or home ownership, but as to large private holdings of land, capital, securities, or other forms of wealth.

The concept of limited government too must be abandoned, because government must serve as a central planning source on behalf of the society as a whole. In order to provide enough goods and services for the qualitative improvement of the lives of millions of ordinary American citizens, and to discharge obligations to the rest of humanity, it will be necessary to employ the society's productive resources in an efficient manner. This requires central planning to determine at least what is to be done where. Local organizations of workers or others may then assume responsibility for deciding how each goal will be reached and by whom.

Materialism is not entirely rejected, for it will be crucial to raise the material standard of living for most Americans, as well as for other people in the world. This is a prerequisite to the opportunity to enjoy other aspects of life, and to develop the creative, esthetic, or other human potential that exists in all persons. But materialism will not be the principal motivating force in people's lives, because they will not seek to amass things for themselves. They will be assured of enough to serve their needs, and instead will work out of a commitment to bettering the lives of others.

Anticapitalist radicalism clearly operates with fundamentally different values from those held by most Americans. The ideology that flows from such values sees the American system today as fundamentally irrational. Private ownership and the profit motive lead inexorably to exploitation, widespread misery, and a sharply stratified class system with a very few rulers at the top. There is a continued need for manipulation of the masses by the ruling capitalist class and its agents. Because the ruling class controls the nation's wealth, it also controls the government, and, through it, the educational system and the political process generally. The major means of manipulation is the inculcation of the ideology we have been calling American orthodoxy. Once fixed in the minds of the people, it makes social control possible with a minimum of conscious effort. Aspiring and competent people are induced to become agents of the ruling class because the ruling class controls the rewards and opportunities they seek.

In this self-reinforcing and self-perpetuating way, the system operates relatively smoothly. The problems that exist arise out of the characteristics of capitalism, but people recognize only their surface manifestations and not their causes within that economic system. The financial problems of cities, for example, result not from the lack of a tax base or too much spending on education or welfare, but rather from the vast sums being spent to pay the interest and principal on loans from capitalist bankers. Because so many people are seen as hopelessly trapped in the orthodox values and ideology, anticapitalist radicals face a serious dilemma. They must either commit themselves to trying to transform the system through revolutionary action with the conscious support of only a minority of the people, or they must await a change of mind on the part of a decisive majority of the people, either through events or persuasion or both. Understandably, this issue remains a subject of debate within this strain of radicalism.

Individualist Rejection of Social Solutions

Reformist radicalism accepts orthodox values and ideology, and asks that rhetoric be made real. Anticapitalist radicalism requires sweeping value changes and a sharp rupture with orthodox ideology. But both of these strains have an ideal social system in mind, in which aggregations of people do certain things in accordance with specific principles, thereby producing a pattern of rewards for individuals. If the rewards or satisfactions are not just or desirable, the remedy is to change the way the social system operates. But the individualist form of radicalism rejects the idea that a large-scale social system can provide what individuals really need: such nonmaterial things as understanding of life and its meaning, harmony with nature and other people, love, and other forms of personal growth and fulfillment.

It is plain that the goal of revolution today must be the liberation of daily life. . . . Revolutionary liberation must be a self-liberation that reaches social dimensions, not "mass liberation" or "class liberation" behind which lurks the rule of an elite, a hierarchy and a state. . . . Out of the revolution must emerge a self that takes full possession of daily life, not a daily life that takes full possession of the self. . . .

If for this reason alone, the revolutionary movement is profoundly concerned with lifestyle. It must try to *live* the revolution in all its totality, not only participate in it. . . . The revolutionary group must clearly see that its goal is not the seizure of power but the dissolution of power—indeed, it must see that the entire problem of power, of control from below and control from above, can be solved only if there is no above or below.

From Murray Bookchin, *Post-Scarcity Anarchism* (Berkeley: Ramparts Press, 1971), pp. 44–47.

Thus, the individualist rejection of what it sees as a corruptly commercialized and destructive world is a personal, not a social, form of radicalism. Emphasis on individualism is greatly expanded and turned inward, away from material acquisitiveness and away from the great mass of other people. The more limited government is, the better, for each individual must seek his or her own solution; real help can come only from the very small number of other persons with whom one has established special relationships.

This form of radicalism can be reached by a direct route from American orthodoxy or from reformist radicalism because it does not require extensive value change. Its emphasis on individualism and withdrawal makes it intellectually accessible to those who tire of struggling against large and impersonal social forces, and to those who conclude that all large-scale social organizations are equally destructive of human freedom and potential. Unless vast numbers of people suddenly embrace the same personalized form of radicalism, it poses no serious threat to the continued operations of the American system or its orthodoxy. Power and its capabilities in a society are unaffected by the withdrawal of a few persons, particularly when their withdrawal is consciously based on the conviction that social efforts toward change are by definition undesirable or impossible. Nevertheless, this form of radicalism is gaining adherents, perhaps because the other two forms of radicalism are frustrating and (in the case of anticapitalism) require greater value change than people can or want to achieve.

The Rebirth of Radicalism

Radicalism again became a major national force in the mid-1960s. It developed first out of blacks' strugles for civil rights, which soon spread to Chicanos, Puerto Ricans, American Indians, Asians, and other minorities, and also drew support from white college students. The latter soon expanded their activities to protests against the Vietnam War and to demand "student power" which in turn generated broad but often superficial student radicalism and emphasis on new values and life styles (the "counterculture").

While these highly visible minority and young people's movements were claiming much national attention, two other potentially powerful social forces were emerging. One is the union of poor and other disaffected people from all classes in a loose general movement promptly labelled by the media as populism. The other is the recognition by women of systematic sexual discrimination, and the consequent pressing of demands for equal status and opportunity. Populism is more protest than program, adding only depth of support to the existing radical critique of American history. It has no new ideological dimensions as such. The women's movement is still in an early stage, with most of its adherents seeking only those rights to which they are legally entitled, and likewise add little in the way of new substance to the basic radical ideologies. But both are highly significant in terms of potential.

... the first demand for any alternative system must be:

(1) *The freeing of women from the tyranny of their reproductive biology by every means available, and the diffusion of the childbearing and child-rearing role to the society as a whole, men as well as women.* . . . To thus free women from their biology would be to threaten the *social* unit that is organized around biological reproduction and the subjection of women to their biological destiny, the family. . . .

(2) *The full self-determination, including economic independence, of both women and children.* To achieve this goal would require fundamental changes in our social and economic structure. This is why we must talk about a feminist socialism: in the immediate future, under capitalism, there could be at best a token integration of women into the labor force. . . .

We have now attacked the family on a double front, challenging that around which it is organized: reproduction of the species by females and its outgrowth, the physical dependence of women and children. To eliminate these would be enough to destroy the family, which breeds the power psychology. However, we will break it down still further.

---

(3) *The total integration of women and children into all aspects of the larger society.* All institutions that segregate the sexes, or bar children from adult society, e.g., the elementary school, must be destroyed. *Down with school!*

These three demands predicate a feminist revolution based on advanced technology. And if the male/female and the adult/child cultural distinctions are destroyed, we will no longer need the sexual repression that maintains these unequal classes, allowing for the first time a "natural" sexual freedom. Thus we arrive at:

(4) *The freedom of all women and children to do whatever they wish to do sexually.* . . . one could now realize oneself fully, simply in the process of being and acting.

From Shulamith Firestone, *The Dialectic of Sex: The Case for Feminist Revolution* (New York: William Morrow, 1970), pp. 206–209.

We shall touch briefly on the two major sources of contemporary radical-populism—black liberation and the student radical movement. It will be evident that the drift from reformist radicalism to anticapitalist radicalism has occurred in both. After that, we shall describe the characteristics that are shared generally among the various elements of radicalism-populism.

1. *Black Liberation*

The first post-World War II efforts by blacks were an attempt to use the system's own values and procedures to raise their legal and social status. Taking the American endorsement of the natural rights of equality, freedom, and justice at face value, the NAACP used the legal process to secure substantial victories in the Supreme Court. But they soon found that these "victories" had little or no effect on the daily lives of ordinary blacks; neither the legal process nor appeals to treasured values succeeded in integrating schools, lunchrooms, or other public facilities in the South. Nonviolent protest marches, sit-ins, and other tactics dramatized the nation's failure to adhere to its oft-stated principles, and eventually resulted in a succession of civil rights statutes prohibiting discrimination in voting, housing, and employment. Once again, however, the consequences for the average black citizen were minimal: subtler discrimination, economic handicaps, training and educational deficiencies, insistence upon following the time-consuming established processes, and other factors combined to hold blacks in the same position as before. Blacks were useful to white society in Vietnam, but otherwise filled no significant role in America.

The black liberation movement grew out of these frustrations and sank its roots in the fundamental conviction that the United States was a racist society.[1] Martin Luther King had come to the same conclusion in the last year of his life,[2] though (chiefly on tactical grounds) he remained aloof from the early Black Power leaders. The premise of basic societal racism in the United States both explains the failure of earlier efforts at achieving equality through the established system and points directions for the future. It says, for example, that it is no accident that the procedures of the American legal system were slow, cumbersome, and ineffective in achieving integration; and that it is not really remarkable that no substantial economic assistance was forthcoming for blacks' education and training. White society did not sincerely *want* to help blacks and never had. The only solution was to build such self-pride and sense of identity among blacks that they could achieve their goals by themselves—or, in other words, *Black Power*. The task would be a staggeringly difficult one, of course. Centuries of deprivation and exploitation had left Afro-Americans at the lowest levels of the economic order, and many held equally low self-images of their worth. Without resources, constituting only 11 percent of the nation's population, enclosed in urban ghettos, and surrounded by both subtle and blatant proofs of white society's attitudes, the situation of American blacks was indeed desperate.

To the black liberation leaders, however, this meant only that they had nothing to lose. There was no hope of real help from white society, and any effort on the part of whites would be destructive in any event: whites would only invite blacks into their society on whites' own terms—terms that defined the black man as inferior. Thus, any integration or accommodation with whites would inevitably mean surrender and perpetuation of blacks' second-class status. Accordingly, they set about to create a black consciousness that was independent of white influences and capable of standing firmly on a distinct set of (black) values. Among other things, this meant elimination of whites from their organizations and causes, rejection of many of the values and practices of the dominant society, disavowal of nonviolence as a technique, and preparation for self-defense when the inevitable white repression began to occur. Other black leaders, believing white support necessary for an 11 percent minority and seeing their only hope in eventual integration, began to draw away from the black liberation movement as such. Their removal left the new

[1]The first, and perhaps still the most comprehensive, articulation of the black power argument is Stokely Carmichael and Charles V. Hamilton, *Black Power: The Politics of Liberation in America* (New York: Vintage, 1967).

[2]Martin Luther King, "Letter From A Birmingham Jail," in *Why We Can't Wait* (New York: Harper and Row, 1964).

and younger leadership with both the opportunity and the necessity to develop their own analysis and ideology.

Two important movements, each with its own ideology, have emerged from the early ambiguities of the call for black liberation. Both seek to instill black identity and pride among their own people, both use the Third World as a model for Afro-Americans, and both seek eventually to alter white society in the United States fundamentally.

Black Pride. One, perhaps best represented for a time by Stokely Carmichael,[3] called for a kind of cultural nationalism among blacks with the ultimate goal of changing the white racist value system. Racism was the key, and their primary target. By awakening their own people to their independent traditions and heritage, blacks would steadily build self-reliance and personal independence from white values. The route by which blacks were to acquire their sense of identification, mutual loyalty, and independent value system was through emphasizing the achievements of black people in the past and reconstructing a distinct black culture. For these purposes, the success of the Third World independence movements was a paramount example. Black and brown people had rid their lands of white invaders, dramatically established their own validity, reasserted their past heritages, and now regularly stood up to the powerful white states in the United Nations and elsewhere.

[3]See Carmichael and Hamilton, *Black Power.*

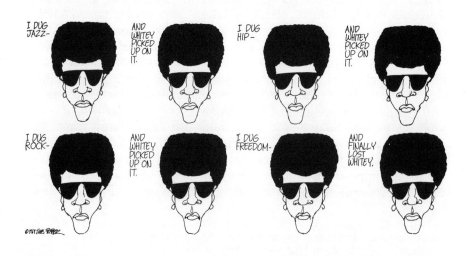

By "thinking black," and helping to build viable economic bases for their own communities, American blacks similarly could *lift* themselves out of their deprived state. Once they had developed real pride and the capacity to accomplish their goals on their own—and not until then—it would be possible to reestabish contact with the white world. Whites, seeing blacks doing as well as or better than they, and becoming aware that blacks neither were nor considered themselves inferior, might be forced to reexamine their own values. This process would probably not occur without some serious clashes as blacks asserted their rights, but Carmichael alleged at one point that it was the only alternative to full-scale guerrilla warfare in the United States. Carmichael himself ultimately despaired of developing the necessary power to achieve these goals in the face of continued white opposition and harassment. He concluded that the active assistance of Africans and Asians would be necessary, and left the country. But others have and no doubt will continue to pursue this essentially nationalist route toward black liberation within the United States.[4]

Black Panthers.   The second position generated by the black liberation movement is associated with the Black Panther Party.[5] Equally determined to achieve black identity and pride, and to create a new set of values that would acknowledge black independence and worth, they mapped out a somewhat different route to follow. Racism was a major target, but not the only one; behind racism, creating and maintaining racist attitudes and systematically exploiting both blacks and whites, was the capitalist economic system. They saw blacks as specially deprived victims at the very bottom of the social and economic order, requiring concentrated self-help efforts to create the capacity to resist and eventually triumph over the established system. But the lowest echelons of whites were also exploited by the capitalist system, and their true class interests, if recognized, would lead to joint efforts to break free. Those few whites who were in one way or another able to extricate themselves from the capitalist-encouraged racist syndrome could become allies—though in practice this was both tenuous and difficult because so many whites were not really free and blacks were naturally suspicious of open-armed whites. The Third World was again a model, but this time both for the triumphs of black and brown over white *and* for its triumphs over capitalist imperialism. Further, the Third World might now provide tangible assistance in a worldwide struggle by undermining the U.S. economy and hastening its breakup.

[4]See, for example, LeRoi Jones, *Home: Social Essays* (New York: William Morrow, 1966).

[5]This version is drawn from Robert Scheer, ed., *Eldridge Cleaver: Post-Prison Writings and Speeches* (New York: Random House, 1969).

These divergencies of emphasis within the militant black liberation movement should not obscure their broadly shared rejection of the basic outlines of the American system. They both see its procedures as facades for white manipulation of blacks. Police are the military power sent to crush legitimate disobedience to exploitative actions by "respected" white businessmen. And the only recourse for blacks is to resist by any means necessary. The consequences of action in accordance with such principles by even a relatively small number of blacks are not limited to those they envision, of course. Far more likely is drastic change in the operating principles of the American political system toward greater repression and more or less constant use of force in isolated ghettos.

2. Student Radicalism

The origins of the white student radical movement, like those of black liberation, lie in efforts to actualize the rhetorically familiar values of equality, freedom, and justice.[6] The last years of the 1950s and the early 1960s saw numbers of northern college students taking part in freedom rides, sit-ins, and voter registration drives in the South. The inability or unwillingness of those who were dominant in the American political system to make equality a reality for blacks led many of them to look more closely at other claims on behalf of the system. Contrasting the affluence of some with the poverty of others, or marginal governmental actions with the depth and breadth of problems, radical students concluded that the familiar values were not only unrealized but that the really operative priorities were all wrong. Private comfort and advantage clearly took precedence over public needs. The escalation of the Vietnam War was one tragic example of outmoded priorities at work.

At first, the roots of the problem seemed to lie in an implacable technology, operating largely on its own momentum and using the media and other teaching vehicles to make people value and want what it found possible to produce.[7] Thus, conformity with materialistic values, and a commitment to seek ever-increasing personal comforts, were gently but completely instilled either through inducement or coercion or both—making the nation into a land of smooth, plastic unfreedom. Much of the originating thrust in the 1960s flowed from efforts to break free of the materialist priorities and self-seeking that seemed to characterize the technological society, to bring meaningful choices back into the lives of ordinary citizens, and to realize the ac-

[6]A comprehensive description of the early stages of this movement may be found in Jack Newfield, A Prophetic Minority (New York: New American Library, 1966), from which this passage is drawn.

[7]This stage of analysis is well represented in Herbert Marcuse, One Dimensional Man (Boston: Beacon Press, 1964).

cepted goals of equality, freedom, and justice first for all members of the American society, and then for others in the world. The principle of decentralization or "participatory democracy" was first conceived as a means of providing citizens with power to control the forces that were affecting their lives. Community organizing, "student power" movements on campuses, and other participatory activities were first based on the same democratic aspiration.

Again like the black movement, the first efforts to achieve these essentially orthodox goals were unsuccessful. Participatory groups were able to secure control only over matters that were insignificant, or in areas where their antagonists were no better off than themselves. When they attempted to obtain new leverage over matters that seemed important, they were met with a barrage of procedural limitations or other restrictions. Racism in both North and South continued undiminished. The capacity of the established order to promise change, and then to delay or frustrate it, seemed unlimited. In the eyes of many, the Vietnam War was the classic example of official hypocrisy. Escalating steadily throughout the mid-1960s and bringing with it the threat of conscription, the Vietnam War seemed to show the American government as callously pursuing an immoral policy under the outmoded banner of anticommunism. Instances of officials' overoptimism, concealment, and insistence upon the citizenry's patriotic obligation to support such policies only made the war a greater violation of supposed American commitments to democracy, freedom, and peace.

The enormity of American deviance from professed goals, and the complacence of both the establishment and much of the population in the face of it, seemed to mandate a more profound analysis than the deterministic technological-society-gone-wrong theory on which the earlier movement had been based. By the late 1960s, supporters and sympathizers had more or less arrived at the conclusion that the answers were to be found in the nature of the American capitalist economic system.[8] They began to see the Vietnam War and other Third World adventures in terms of imperialist efforts to acquire control over raw materials and markets. Black repression was not just the product of idiosyncratic racism, but of a racism partially created and thoroughly encouraged by capitalist values. The upper classes were profiting from the exploitation of the black and other working classes, and thus were quick to defend establishment policies in all essential respects.

For at least some members of this loose coalition, the only solution seemed to lie in eliminating the basic courses of racism and injustice

---

[8]A full statement, based on the Vietnam experience, may be found in Carl Oglesby and Richard Shaull, *Containment and Change* (New York: Vintage, 1967).

at home, and of wars against Third World peoples abroad—in short, in putting an end to capitalism and introducing some form of social-ism. Some saw it as sssential to build alliances with the working classes, despite the difficulties of reaching a group that seemed in large part both satisfied and unsympathetic to middle-class college students, and then to seek to use electoral and other routes to power. Others believed, like some black militants who served as their models, that conditions were so bad that they had nothing to lose from en-gaging in destructive or revolutionary acts immediately. Still others saw the prospective revolution more in terms of a complete change in life style and values, and sought to live out their lives in illustra-tions of those better values. By creating in time a "counterculture," they hoped to recruit others and ultimately to affect the dominant values of the nation. By the mid-1970s, the number of young whites who considered the termination or drastic transformation of the capi-talist economic order to be essential—and by means that included revolutionary violence if necessary—seemed to be still growing. A much larger number, however, dismissed such aspirations as hope-less romanticism. Nevertheless, they shared many of their hopes for equality and democracy and saw these as unattainable without sub-stantial change in the American system.

The Shared Elements of Radical-Populist Ideology

Sparked by these two sources, a substantially broader and deeper movement has evolved. Chicanos, Puerto Ricans, American Indians, and other minorities have each forcefully and steadily pressed their distinctive demands for cultural identity and status. Although the New Left has fragmented into such disparate elements as counter-culture withdrawal, Christian and Eastern religious sects, anarchism, terrorism, community control movements, and others, new layers of serious radicals and revolutionary socialists are joining the general thrust toward change. This movement has gained considerable depth from the growth of populism, which has drawn poor people and many other protest-minded individuals to the point of readiness to act against established practices and interests. The populist surge has little independent theory or ideology, and some elements in it could probably be readily mobilized to attack minorities and the left. But its traditional critique of "economic royalists" and the establishment generally, as well as its demand for a larger share of income and op-portunity, ally its numerous followers with the radical movement.

It is possible to speak of "the radical movement," despite the dis-tinctiveness of its various strands, because some important character-istics are shared among all forms of radicalism, and because all lie sufficiently outside American orthodoxy to constitute together a serious challenge to it.

Many aspects of the radical-populist ideology help to locate it outside the mainstream. For one thing, the new movements took a contextual and comprehensive approach to issues and goals. They did not seek only one or two tangible results from politics, nor did they focus on one problem at a time. Instead, they aimed at several problems simultaneously, looking for their common cause. They began to look behind the apparent sources of problems at the assumptions and power distribution that were even more basic causes; this tended to lead to queries about the nature of political values and the character of the economy as the ultimate source of power.

But perhaps the most distinctive aspect of the approach to politics characteristic of the various new movements of the 1960s was the shift in priority from the procedural side of political decisionmaking to the substantive side—the content of public policies, and their sufficiency in the light of the problems that existed. Previous generations had been caught up in the intricacies of procedures, such as the manner of holding elections, the nature of decisionmaking in the Congress, the proper rules for considering legislation, or the requirements of due process. They saw democracy chiefly as the manner in which people go about making decisions, and assumed that if everything is done according to the rules, the result will be appropriate or at least the best possible under the circumstances. This outlook may have been fostered first by the trauma of the Civil War, in reaction to which some people came to believe that Americans cared too much for the substance of governmental actions, and, that the nation had suffered tragically because of it. Whatever the reason, the nearly exclusive focus on *how* things were done led to greatly reduced regard for *what* was being done.

But the new groups took just the opposite tack. They insisted that the *only* thing that mattered was the results of governmental action. Judged by this standard, the American claim to equality and freedom was a fraud. They disdained complexities as *status quo*-supporting rationlizations, asking in effect: if the system is so good, why is its product so bad? Segregation was unconstitutional, according to the Supreme Court, but the reality of segregation and discrimination was evident to blacks in both North and South in dozens of ways every day. Some of these were lawful, according to courts. Others could not be remedied because due procedures had not been followed. The same pattern existed elsewhere. In Vietnam, the United States talked peace and waged bloody war. Consequences that appeared morally wrong could not be altered because established procedures had not been followed. When the procedures *were* followed, the result was often perpetuation of the *status quo*. When protests were made, the procedures turned out to be effective means of prosecution and punishment. Soon radicals came to see the procedures themselves, as well as the policies they rejected, as synonymous with callousness and immorality. To follow the established procedures was often simply to invite rejection of one's claim, and so the procedures too were condemned. This oversimplified account highlights the essence of the shift from a politics of means to a moralistic politics of ends. No two approaches to politics in the American context could be more fundamentally different.

Nor were the radical demands capable of being readily deflected. Historically, radicalism has been blunted when leading groups achieved material gains and lost their militancy. Although the odds were that material or status gains would be preferred and would have the same effect again, there were noneconomic dimensions to the new demands as well. They could not be deflected by providing more money or more goods and services because the protesters were already affluent, did not care about material rewards, or (in the case of blacks) held fast to status claims that were not limited to economic attainments. Tensions over the war in Vietnam, for example, could not be resolved by increasing the total economic product and distributing more to the protestors. Instead, the prizes under contention were indivisible: if one side won, the other side had to lose. As such, the level of conflict had to be higher than normal. The same held true in the case of blacks' demand for equality in the full sense. Such a demand could not be met entirely by economic solutions but only if whites yielded some of their prerogatives and sense of superiority— which, of course, they were likely to resist bitterly. The noneconomic character of the new demands, and the refusal of their advocates to be caught up in procedural complexities, meant that some of the flexibility of the system was short-circuited and the level of conflict remained abnormally high.

The central part played by race conflicts in the new politics by itself gave them a status unprecedented at least since the Civil War. No issue cuts so deeply into the American consciousness, arousing in both blacks and whites mixed fear, guilt, hatred, sympathy, and helplessness. And yet the issue of race arises again and again today in every arena and in every area of American politics. It can neither be avoided nor (apparently) resolved within the confines of the established values and ideology of the American system, and therefore must be a constant source of threat to that system. As the chief theme of the black movement and a major focus for white radicals, and, from an opposite perspective, for some of their reactionary counterparts, race relations cannot fail to continue to make for a new and potentially much more explosive kind of politics in the United States.

Thus, by taking a deep-probing, contextual approach that focuses on underlying values and sources of power; viewing power as concentrated in a few hands and not broadly diffused among the people; judging American politics not by its procedures but by its products;

asserting demands not readily converted, diverted, or absorbed by the flexibility of the system; and centering on the inflammable subject of race relations, radical-populism has moved outside the range of what the established American system can find digestible. The label "new politics" is not an overstatement. It is an accurate characterization of at least some major new elements that seek significant change.

Black liberation, however, will not come about solely through the activities of black people. Black America cannot be genuinely liberated until white America is transformed into a humanistic society free of exploitation and class division. The black and white worlds, although separate and distinct, are too closely intertwined—geographically, politically, and economically—for the social maladies of one not to affect the other. Both must change if either is to progress to new and liberating social forms.

From Robert L. Allen, *Black Awakening in Capitalist America: An Analytic History* (New York: Doubleday, 1970), p. 281.

Implications of the New Radicalism-Populism

These nontraditional, change-oriented ideologies are important because of what they *stand for* (alliances among the lowest classes to bring about fundamental change in the *status quo*); and for the kind of reaction their beliefs and tactics may *provoke* (rigid policies, repression, a police state). Their reactionary counterparts, increasingly visible and certainly both more numerous and more powerful, seem likely to act in essentially similar ways if and when the radical groups approach success. All of these groups play a different game of politics—an ends-oriented, play-for-keeps kind of game—that neither accepts the traditional standards known and treasured by the "establishment," nor is prepared to abide by them. The extent to which the new groups are indeed engaged in a new and different game may be quickly grasped from some of their tactics. In many cases, these tactics appear—from the perspective of the establishment and old rules of American politics—to be irrational, counterproductive, or simply the senseless self-indulgence of spoiled children. But even if an objective analyst would occasionally agree, these tactics uniformly reflect the ideological premises and goals of the movements and usually are entirely rational and effective in those terms.

Such tactics as deliberate disruption of public speeches, public defiance of laws concerning parades and demonstrations, physical blockades of government or university buildings, and violent resistance to attempts at law enforcement, became familiar occurrences in the late 1960s and early 1970s. At subsequent trials of members of the various movements, the legal system was mocked and defied. The charge of Communist influence or infiltration was met with derision or casual acknowledgment.

Each of these apparently self-defeating challenges to the strongly held American values of procedural regularity, law and order, and anticommunism, however, carries its own rationale. It can surely be argued that resistance is the only moral course for a person who believes the government to be immoral. On more tactical grounds, it is true that such public displays draw attention to the causes at issue and perhaps recruit some new members to the movement. They also have a radicalizing effect on the people who participate: few emerge from violent confrontations or a night in jail with the same benevolent view of the American political system. Moreover, confrontations of this kind are thought to reveal the true nature of the system—that is, its determination to repress any serious effort to accomplish change. In cases in which violent or unlawful tactics have been employed in behalf of black or poor peoples' demands, one of the real purposes has frequently been to mobilize new support among people previously inert and hopeless, and only secondarily to achieve specific results from official decisionmakers.

Broader rationalizations also support such tactics. For one thing, the ultimate success of any change-seeking movement depends in part on withdrawing legitimacy from the established political order, at least in the eyes of a substantial segment of the population. If the government can be shown to act arbitrarily, vindictively, and in violation of its own expressed standards of due process, it will be seen as no better than other contending forces. The acquiescence and cooperation on the part of citizens that makes government possible then begins to break down, and the prospects for drastic change are much greater. Further, a larger perspective would not see violence as initiated by the protesters. Where the state is viewed as exploitative and the police force as the agents of its necessary physical coercion, violence by ordinary citizens may be seen as counter-violence—or, in effect, as legitimate resistance by any means necessary.[9] There is no obligation to submit nonviolently to a police force and a legal system that are deliberately set up to work injustice upon citizens. Nothing is owed to such a system, and nothing is an unfair or improper tactic to be used against it, if it appears likely to contribute to overthrow of that system. The charge of Communist influence, of course, is

[9]For a full statement of the "counterviolence" rationale, see Marcuse, *One Dimensional Man* and *An Essay on Liberation* (Boston: Beacon Press, 1968).

merely archaic. The New Left had little respect for the Soviet brand, which it saw as repressive, bureaucratic, and as technologically dominated as the United States. Communists are conservatives, however, in their tactics and in their timetables. To charge these new groups with Communist leanings or influences is so hopelessly irrelevant to their real goals and purposes as to provoke laughter.

The reactions of the vast majority of still-uninvolved Americans, so far as they can yet be understood, measure the strengths and weaknesses of such tactics. Serious attention has been gained from intellectuals, college youth, and many blacks, but support for generalized goals is much more readily forthcoming than agreement with ultimate purposes or specific tactics. The deepest thrusts into the defenses that standard American values and ideology provide for the established order have occurred when liberals have been mobilized around such comparatively orthodox issues as police brutality or denial of due process. For the most part, however, it appears that the white majority has simply not understood either the demands or the tactics of radical-populism, and when they have, they have been repelled. Some lower middle-class elements, perceiving themselves threatened, have apparently hardened in resistance. The long-heralded "backlash" of lower-class whites appears to be a stronger possibility than the hoped-for alliance of workers, students, and blacks. As the economic dimensions of an enduring crisis become clearer, of course, this could change substantially.

Contrasting Ideologies and the Nature of Social Problems

It should be clear that the orthodox values and ideology lead to a disintegrated view of the nature and causes of problems. Individualism's "every man for himself" approach, for example, or the premise that economics is distinct from politics and should remain so, serve as barriers against seeing problems as interconnected and grounded in both basic values and the fundamental characteristics of the economic and social systems. Not all problems are, of course; but the longer a problem endures, in one form or another, the more we may suspect that its sources lie at these deeper levels. Problems are certainly easier to deal with politically if they are seen as discrete and superficial, but they may not be easier to *solve* permanently. This too is characteristic of the dominant ideology, in that it stresses accommodation and compromise and seeks to avoid basic conflicts at all costs.

Is radical-populism distinctively different in its analysis of the nature and causes of problems? Again, we must be careful not to attribute too much consistency or unity to the disparate beliefs of that loose ideology, but the answer would appear to be a qualified yes. A progression can be traced from relatively superficial analysis toward a view of problems as rooted in basic values and the nature of the economic system. Problems are seen as the combined product of social, economic, and political factors, implying rejection of the compartmentalized approach of the dominant ideology. Problems are also seen as parts of a social totality, not isolatable from each other.

But some features of the radical outlook suggest that certain qualifications are in order, and that it should not be seen as the precise opposite of the dominant ideology. Radical-populism is some distance away from orthodoxy on our continuum, but it by no means marks the opposite pole. For one thing, many of its allegations appear to be facile oversimplifications. Often neither evidence nor logic connects visible issues or problems with the alleged underlying "causes." Also, many of the remedies that radicalism urges presuppose the continuity or efficacy of the very values, systems, and processes that it purports to be attacking as corrupt or fraudulent. To argue that economic exploitation by a callous American ruling class is the central cause of world-wide misery, and then to urge community organizing and electoral campaigns as a remedy, is at best inconsistent and confused, and perhaps hypocritical.

Finally, and perhaps most important for our purposes, radicalism and populism both still operate within the confines of American political consciousness, broadly conceived. American radicals and populists project the future from what they see around them today, and from readings in American history, data about social conditions, and attempts to understand what people actually want. They consider and select alternative courses of action based pragmatically on existing conditions and on what they think others can be induced to accept. Their values are only modestly different, mostly in terms of priorities, from those of most other Americans. In these and other ways, their style of thinking is pragmatic, empirical, and distinctively American—and therefore distinguishable from orthodox values and ideology only in a limited fashion. Nevertheless, this is sufficient to cause great tensions and potentially drastic change in the United States in the next decade.

Though it is not vital to our analysis, we should perhaps note that the beginnings of a fundamentally different political consciousness are becoming visible, and may achieve real significance in the future. These new beginnings lie in some aspects of minority thinking, and in some versions of socialist thought. In no case do they embody elements of mainstream American thought. Nor do they even build their world-view upon the rejection or correction of specific aspects of the dominant values and ideology. In this way, they avoid the problem of so many radicals—unintentionally falling back into an orthodox frame of reference by focusing exclusively on it.

The political consciousness and world-view of American Indians, for example, rest on wholly different premises and values, and on a cultural milieu so distinct as to be unrecognizable to most Americans. The rational, empirical, logical steps of the capitalist-liberal American mind are absent. In their place are intuitive, communal, traditional, holistic thought processes. The same is true of certain segments of the black and Chicano movements. Wholly distinct world-views reflecting sometimes-distant cultural heritages are taking contemporary forms and serving as the basis of self-contained enclaves within the larger society. In all of these cases, the ultimate goal is self-determination, a kind of multicultural pluralism in the United States in which each minority is free to live in accordance with its own standards and principles. Whether this is practical or not, or even attractive to any substantial proportion of each minority, remains to be seen.

But there can be little doubt that, for the present, the focus of political conflict in this country is the tension between the established orthodoxy and its radical-populist offspring. The former may evolve gradually and grudgingly, or the latter may recede in the face of change and coercion. Far more likely, however, in the light of the continuing convergence of problems into a deepening crisis, is an exacerbation of this conflict. In that event, their differences may come to seem very real indeed. We shall note the implications of these differences repeatedly throughout our analysis, and then return to a head-on confrontation with prospects for the future in Part Six.

The Unresolved Questions

A number of questions remain, and some have just barely been touched on. We have not yet determined why American public policies have the forms and consequences they do. The ideological answers are, after all, only that—ideology. They tell us what some people believe to be the answers, but they have no necessary relationship to reality. Only evidence about who does what to bring about which results—and why—can satisfactorily answer this key question. But we *have* raised a series of questions through this analysis of contrasting ideologies. Is power in the United States dispersed and held mostly by the people, as the orthodoxy insists, or is it concentrated in such a manner as to leave the people powerless in most cases, as radicalism argues? What is the relationship between economic power and political power: is it direct, as radicalism claims, or are they separate worlds, as the orthodoxy maintains?

In short, we have before us some clear patterns of policy consequences, and some conflicting "explanations" of them. We shall use both to frame our approach to the study of power and decisionmaking in American politics. From the evidence gathered and analyzed in all the ways suggested by these two types of inquiries, we should be able to reach some conclusions.

PART FOUR

INSTITUTIONS
AND PROCESSES:
THE ROLE
OF ELITES

Chapter 8

We now reach the third, and perhaps decisive, stage of our analysis. We have examined some of the consequences of the policies developed over time by the combined American economic-political system. And we have examined both the orthodoxy's justification of these patterns of policy and the radical-populist attack on the values and system that produced them. Only now do we begin to analyze the ways in which various forces and factors actually converge to shape public policy decisions. We

The Integrated Economic- Political System

shall look at the *structure* of the economic-political system, the *people* who hold power within those institutions, and the *process* by which the two combine to shape decisionmaking in national political institutions. But first we shall describe the key questions to be explored in this and the next part of the book.

Elite Analysis: The Central Questions

The basic question is simple: who rules, and how? But simple questions frequently have no answers or, at best, complex answers. This question is no exception. Elaborate methodologies have been developed by social scientists to try to establish who holds power, how it is used, and for what purposes. But the multiplicity of key definitions, the elusiveness of "power" as an objective quality, and the tenacity of conflicting ideological perspectives have prevented reaching widely shared conclusions. Perhaps the same fate awaits our analysis. But we believe that it is possible to reduce drastically the range of possible interpretations through careful and self-conscious consideration of the evidence.

In our review of the basic disputes between the dominant American political orthodoxy and its contemporary challengers, we said that the former holds a "pluralist" image of power in the United States. This means that power is seen as diffused among many groups, whose competition for support and advantage takes place in a context of fair procedures and is subject to the control of the electorate, acting through public officials who responsively arrange the necessary compromises among the many legitimate interests. Group membership teaches democratic and leadership skills, and prevents extremism. The political system itself is seen as producing policies in the public interest, manifesting widely shared political values, and therefore as democratic. The contemporary challengers, on the other hand, see power as tightly concentrated in a power elite or ruling class, with resultant policies reflecting that group's interests and values and not those of the mass public. The political system not only operates with the wrong values and priorities, but denies realization of the different values and aspirations held by the lower classes. Thus, it is far from a democracy. The gap between the pluralist and the ruling-class or power-elite analyses is substantial and, as we noted earlier, shaped in part by ideological assumptions. Our problem now is to design an inquiry that will enable us to resolve some or most of the disputed issues concerning the structure of power in the United States, while avoiding the effects of ideology.

Images of power range from the relatively democratic pluralist view to the economic ruling-class interpretation[1]. The vital questions, answers to which would add up to a clear characterization of the actual structure of power, may be organized into three major categories: (1) the composition, origins, attitudes, and cohesion of elites; (2) the nature and sources of mass attitudes and unfulfilled aspirations, and the extent and character of mass participation in politics; and (3) the balance of initiative and constraints actually existing in the elite-mass relationship. For example, if elites generate most policy initiatives themselves and are not actually subject to mass constraints, an elite-based structure of power is indicated—and vice versa. We shall consider each set of questions separately.

1. Elites

Elites are those people who hold more of the resources of power than others. Where the line is drawn between elites and non-elites

---

[1]It may be worth noting that no analysts seriously argue the validity of the classic or New England Town Meeting model of democracy, in which informed citizens act on all matters of policy and direct their agents in government to carry out their will. "Democratic" pluralism is the *most* democratic interpretation asserted by empirical political scientists, and its "democratic" nature is disputed even by those who accept most of its empirical findings. See Peter Bachrach, *The Theory of Democratic Elitism* (Boston: Little, Brown, 1967).

(or masses) is not crucial. Everybody has *some* power, of course, but at some point the disparity between a congressman, corporation president, or newspaper editor and a steelworker, welfare mother, or student becomes very clear. Elite status, in our eyes, is defined by the ability to affect the action of others. It is enough that a person *can* affect governmental action, and does not necessarily require that he *do so* in every case. (Whether he does or not is a matter of great interest in regard to any specific policy area, but it does not determine whether or not he belongs in the *general* category of elite. Elite status cannot be limited to those who can actually be shown to have affected a particular decision, for that would make it contingent upon the evidence-collecting skills of the analyst rather than the characteristics of the person himself.)

PEANUTS ®   **By Charles M. Schulz**

© 1958 United Feature Syndicate, Inc.

Elite status may flow from the mere possession of disproportionate wealth, status, knowledge, or any other power-yielding resource, held as *a personal attribute*. Persons in this general category are more capable of exercising influence over public policy than is the ordinary citizen, if they choose to so apply their resources. Or elite status may be conferred on a person who holds an *institutional position* within the society that gives rise to the capacity to directly control or affect the lives of others, such as an officer or director of a major corporation or an official of government. In the latter case, both the voluntary compliance granted to legitimate authority and the availability of means of coercion greatly add to the potential power held.

It is this second category of elite status in which we are most interested, and on which our analysis will focus. First, we need to know who such people are—their age, race, education, income, occupation, and other background characteristics. In particular, we shall be interested to know whether they represent a cross-section of the American population, or, on the other hand, resemble those in the personally-based elite category. If the latter is the case, and those with the greater wealth and status are also the directors of the major economic governmental institutions, we have inferential evidence of general elite domination. Socioeconomic background characteristics, it may be inferred, usually give rise to class-based values and priorities, economic interests, and overall perceptions of the world. A government staffed by wealthy professionals and businessmen would probably not be particulary understanding of the conditions, needs, and desires of workers, housewives, or blacks. But socioeconomic background evidence is only inferential. It is possible that upper-class decision-makers understand lower-class needs and act in accordance with them, or even that their values and interests are substantially similar, so that when they act for themselves they in effect act for all. Common sense and experience must determine the conclusiveness of inferences drawn from socioeconomic evidence of this kind.

The careful analyst, of course, will seek corroboration wherever possible. Thus we should seek to learn how the occupants of the most powerful positions in the key economic and governmental institutions acquired their positions. The underlying issue is whether elite status is accessible to many people, or whether there are specific criteria that tend to determine who can become a major powerholder. If a person was elected, how did he or she acquire the nomination and initial public visibility? In other words, to what set of interests and priorities must people be acceptable before they have a chance to acquire elite status? This will tell us much about the kind of policy orientation a person is likely to have while holding an institutional position. If a person was appointed to office, by whom and subject to what standards? Again, we seek insight into the probable values and interests that will animate him or her while in office. A poor youth, for example, might well attend an Ivy League college and law school on scholarships and rise through a great banking corporation to substantial wealth and membership on the Federal Reserve Board. Such a career, however, would suggest upper-class values and interests rather than those associated with the person's socioeconomic origins.

Third, we could improve on these bases for inference by acquiring direct evidence about the political values and attitudes of such elites. Some studies of the attitudes of elites at various levels have been made, although their comprehensiveness and depth of analysis are not very satisfactory. It is difficult to get comprehensive and accurate responses from individuals in major positions of power, in part because they are rarely available and reluctant to take firm stands on key issues. Where such evidence is obtainable, of course, we have a clear basis for comparing elite values and attitudes with those of the masses. This avoids all the problems of inference and assumption that prevent complete confidence in the apparent implications of socioeconomic background data.

Finally, the most conclusive evidence of all is actual elite behavior.

Socioeconomic background, origins, and general values and attitudes alike may lead in one direction, while the decisionmaker actually acts in the opposite direction. If possible, we should seek to learn to what extent people in power consciously act together, as a single unit with common purposes, and how much they just happen to generate specific policies out of their ongoing conflicts. But it is even more difficult to acquire comprehensive and accurate evidence about actual elite behavior than about their values and attitudes. People in power do not act in public, and their public speeches (or private accounts to interviewers) may be totally at odds with their real be-behavior. Or they (or others) may quite sincerely understand their behavior to have been based on one rationale when they were in fact responding to other motivations. It is because of these evidential difficulties that we have spent so much time defining what people in government have done in the way of public policymaking in our four policy areas. In effect, we *have* a solid characterization of actual elite behavior, ready to be combined with the other elements of this analysis.

The six chapters in this part analyze the character and role of elites. In this chapter, we shall sketch the overall structure of the combined economic-political system, identify some of its major units and power positions, and suggest how all of these are interrelated. Chapter 9 looks at the people who hold such positions of power, and tries to answer the questions posed here about their values and attitudes. Chapters 10 through 13 take up the behavior of elites within the major political institutions. Throughout, we shall be concerned with the capacity of elites to manage the society.

2. Non-elites

Perhaps the most important evidence needed pertains to mass or non-elite values and attitudes. In particular, we want to know how mass values and attitudes compare with those of elites and with the policies that are actually carried out by government. If they are substantially the same, we need to ask next about the sources of such mass values and attitudes. As best we can tell from admittedly sparse evidence, are they genuinely self-generated by masses themselves, or are they the product of elite action or indoctrination? If mass values and attitudes are truly self-generated, *and* similar to elites' and to governmental policies, we have good grounds for inferring at least that the political system does not ignore mass goals.

But if mass desires are *not* similar to those of elites, *or* are not expressed in public policies, or are essentially the product of elite manipulation we must infer that the system is elite-dominated. If elites in effect produce the mass values and attitudes to which they later generously respond, initiative rests with elites. If they fail to enact mass values and attitudes into effective policy, the same conclusion is even clearer. If elites hold dissimilar values and yet act according to masses' preferences, an unlikely combination, we have a system whose official management at least is in the exclusive hands of elites.

A second means of gaining insight into the nature of mass-elite relationships and the real locus of power within the system is to examine the extent and character of mass political participation. By exploring the electoral process, from the presentation of issues and programs by candidates and parties to the bases on which people decide whether and how to vote, we may roughly measure the extent of mass influence over government officials and policies. There are also many other forms of mass political participation, such as protests, riots, and lobbying—and a large number of Americans who avoid all contact with politics. We need to know the reasons for each of these forms of behavior, and particularly the extent to which they are either reactions to elite behavior or responses to masses' life situations. Then we need to know what effect any and all of these forms of political participation have on the subsequent behavior of elites. To the extent that mass actions do lead to effective policy changes, we have evidence that power is widely diffused throughout the system—and vice versa.

In all probability we shall find that mass values and attitudes are segmented according to race, age, religion, income, or other characteristics. Our problem then becomes the slightly more complex one of seeking to ascertain how often the goals of various subgroups are expressed in public policies; which, if any, group most often achieves its goals; and to what extent policies reflect elite goals rather than those of *any* mass subgroup. Regardless of whether or not there are important divisions within masses, a further question is the extent of mass support for the political system itself, as distinguished from particular policies or practices. Strong generalized support may be taken as inferential evidence that, on the whole, other values and attitudes are being served—or that masses are strongly convinced by established ideology.

Mass or non-elite circumstances, values and attitudes, and political behavior are analyzed in separate chapters in the next part. Where relevant, however, certain contrasts between elites and non-elites are noted throughout the next six chapters.

3. *Elite–Non-elite Linkages*

Power involves a kind of transaction between two or more people, in which the greater resources of one cause the other(s) to act in certain ways. Similarly, leadership implies fellowship; one cannot be a leader unless there are those who more or less willingly follow. Institutional elites and masses thus have a reciprocal relationship; initiatives and constraints flow back and forth between them. The actions of elites, taken with a view to probable mass reactions, are perceived by masses, whose responses in turn either suggest new actions to elites or cause them to recognize new limits on their action. Or mass demands, conceived in a context of perceived limits, are acknowledged by elites, who act to contain or promote them as their own interests and expectations of probable mass responses suggest.

The problem for analysis is identification of the relative balance of initiative and constraint between elites and masses. Clearly, if nearly all real capacity to initiate policy changes were coupled with nearly complete capacity to impose constraints, on one or the other side of this continuing power equation, that side would be dominant, and we would have an additional piece of evidence concerning the true structure of power. We must seek to understand when and how elites initiate policy changes, and the extent to which masses are able to impose constraints on them. Conversely, we must also try to find occasions and means of mass initiation of policy changes, and assess the way in which elites are able to impose constraints on *them*.

These questions cannot really be answered until we have combined our analysis of non-elites with the one undertaken in this part. But we shall see several important dimensions of the answer in the next six chapters. Repeatedly, we shall note the breadth of decision-makers' legal and practical discretion, the scope of their capacity to generate popular support for their actions, their relative freedom from effective popular controls—and the forces and factors that *actually* shape their decisions.

Let us reiterate what is at stake in this inquiry. Neither masses nor elites are powerless. We know that each can initiate change, and each can constrain the other, under particular circumstances. Our question presses further: how much power of initiative and constraint characteristically lies on each side, and under what conditions is the normal balance disrupted? When and how can elites impose their preferences on unwilling masses? When and how can masses force elites to change their policies or institute new ones? This phrasing of the question lacks sophistication and subtlety, but it will serve to start us on the path toward greater understanding of the real structure of power in the United States.

The day is long past when clear lines could be drawn between "public" and "private" types of power or spheres of economic and political life. There are many nongovernmental sources of power: corporations, interest groups, foundations, universities, and others.

All of them affect people when they act. And all of them have continuing relationships of various kinds—mutually supportive exchanges—with each other and with government. This society-wide network operates with certain basic values, and in accordance with the needs and goals of its dominant elements.

We have two purposes in this chapter. The first is to set forth this broad image of an integrated economic-political system and to locate political institutions within that conceptual frame. The second is to describe briefly the structure of that system and illustrate some of the continuing relationships or exchanges between "private" centers of power and governments. Both can be served by focusing on the latter.

The American Corporation

The principal source of non-governmental power is the large corporation. The number, character, and needs of American corporations largely determine the context of American politics; corporations are a major element of the structure of the economic-political system. The General Motors Corporation is often used as an example. In economic, political, and social terms, it is comparable only to the more important nations of the world. Its annual sales receipts are larger than the *combined* general revenues of the eleven populous states of the northeastern United States: New York, New Jersey, Pennsylvania, Ohio, Delaware, Massachusetts, and the other five New England states.[2] It has 1,300,000 stockholders and more than 700,000 employees in 46 countries. Although it is the largest of the great American corporations, it is not distinctively different from several others. Here is a government lawyer's characterization of Standard Oil of New Jersey:

> With more than a hundred thousand employees around the world (it has three times as many people overseas as the U.S. State Department), a six-million-ton tanker fleet (half again bigger than Russia's), and $17 billion in assets (nearly equal to the combined assessed valuation of Chicago and Los Angeles), it can more easily be thought of as a nation-state than a commercial enterprise.[3]

These two companies, and a handful of others like them, dominate the American economy in sales, assets, and profitability. In part, this is because two, three, or four giants so dominate key markets that

[2] Richard J. Barber, *The American Corporation* (New York: E. P. Dutton, 1970), pp. 19–20. Unless otherwise indicated, all data in this and the next two paragraphs are from this source.
[3] *Ibid.*, p. 20.

competition is replaced by tacit cooperation. For example, the aluminum market is shared entirely by Alcoa, Reynolds, and Kaiser; more than 95 percent of automobiles are manufactured by General Motors, Ford, and Chrysler; more than 90 percent of telephone equipment by Western Electric; more than 75 percent of steel by U.S. Steel, Bethlehem, and Republic; and 90 percent of copper by Anaconda, Kennecott, Phelps Dodge, and American Smelting. Given this stature and market dominance, many such companies are able simply to set prices at the levels required to produce predetermined percentages of profit. In this and other respects, the decisions of their officers have broad public consequences. The slightest adjustments in the uses to which such aggregates of assets and productivity are put cannot help but reverberate throughout the business, financial, governmental, and consumer worlds.

Nor should the international scope of American corporations be overlooked in this analysis. Table 8-1 lists the *world's* 20 largest corporations, ranked according to their sales in 1968. Eighteen of these are American-based corporations, many of them larger in economic resources than most of the nations of the world. These and other American corporations carry on trade all over the world and have investments abroad which in 1967 totalled over $59 billion. The greatest share of their investments was in Canada (nearly one-third) and Europe (almost the same proportion). But a substantial fraction was in Latin America (over 16 percent), and some in Asia (7 percent) and Africa (3 percent.) In addition to the sheer size and volume of business carried on by these aggregates of economic resources, their international activities impose further imperatives upon governmental policymakers. Any significant interference with the continued profitability of these enterprises, at home or abroad, is likely to send severe shock waves rolling through the American economic and political scene. Unemployment, loss of profits, and general economic decline are only part of the prospect. Political repercussions, including calls for military action, are likely to result as well. Thus, the needs and priorities of major corporations become very much a part of governing elites' perceptions of *their* needs and priorities. And this is true even for individual policymakers who might be relatively less enthusiastic about the profit-seeking activities of American business. The present context is such that a great deal is at stake in even the most marginal troubles that business might experience.

Government Regulation of Business

Not only shared needs bind government and business together, however. Several different kinds of continuing transactions between economic power centers and the national government also contribute

TABLE 8-1
The World's Twenty Biggest Industrial Corporations, 1968 (ranked by sales; $ in millions)

Rank	Corporation	Country of Principal Affiliation	Sales	Assets	Net Income (after tax)	Employees
1	General Motors	U.S.A.	$22,755	$14,010	$1,732	757,231
2	Standard Oil (NJ)	U.S.A.	14,091	16,786	1,277	151,000
3	Ford Motor	U.S.A.	14,075	8,953	627	415,000
4	Royal Dutch/Shell	U.K./Netherlands	9,216	14,303	935	171,000
5	General Electric	U.S.A.	8,382	5,744	357	400,000
6	Chrysler	U.S.A.	7,445	4,398	291	231,089
7	IBM	U.S.A.	6,889	6,743	871	241,974
8	Mobil Oil	U.S.A.	6,221	6,872	428	78,300
9	Unilever	U.K.	5,534	3,432	206	312,000
10	Texaco	U.S.A.	5,460	8,687	836	78,475
11	Gulf Oil	U.S.A.	4,559	7,498	626	60,300
12	U.S. Steel	U.S.A.	4,537	6,391	254	201,017
13	ITT	U.S.A.	4,067	4,022	192	293,000
14	Western Electric	U.S.A.	4,031	2,722	192	176,970
15	Standard Oil (Calif.)	U.S.A.	3,635	5,770	452	47,885
16	McDonnell Douglas	U.S.A.	3,609	1,335	95	124,740
17	Du Pont	U.S.A.	3,481	3,289	372	114,100
18	Shell Oil	U.S.A.	3,317	4,230	312	39,080
19	Westinghouse	U.S.A.	3,296	2,271	135	138,000
20	Boeing	U.S.A.	3,274	2,186	83	142,400

Source: Data from Fortune's 1969 surveys. From p. 258 of the book The American Corporation by Richard J. Barber. Copyright © 1970 by Richard J. Barber. Published by E. P. Dutton & Co., Inc. and reprinted with their permission and the permission of the author.

to their interdependence and mutual support. Government regulation is one of these. Regulation of business usually suggests an image of government as the antagonist of business, or at least implies that the two spheres are distinct. A more accurate image, consistent with the conceptual approach we take here, is that of mutual penetration or partial mutual absorption leading to inextricability. In effect, government and major units of the economy are two sides of the same entity. Let us see how regulation and other continuing supportive transactions have this effect.

Throughout American history, there have been recurring periods of public concern over the potential power of economic concentrations and other "private" power centers. Both national and state governments enacted regulatory laws. With only a few periods of retreat—notably the 1920s—the years between the late 1880s and the entry of the United States into World War II in 1941 were marked by a succession of laws purporting to assure that businesses would be restrained in their power to take advantage of customers, competitors, workers, and stockholders: antitrust laws, statutes curbing unfair advertising, restrictions on public utility rates and services, regulation of labor practices, restraints on securities sales and stock exchange practices, and many others.

Such legislation and the administrative arrangements it established created a link between government and private business that sheds a revealing light on the tie between economic power and political power. It is a relationship both subtle and complex, but two basic points may be made.

First, in the eyes of most people in government and business it is simply impossible to imagine applying the antitrust laws to today's giant corporations. The potential economic and political consequences of such a disturbance are so great that no one takes the prospect seriously. In the late stages of the Johnson Administration, a presidential commission's secret recommendations for new antitrust laws were first suppressed, then denied, and finally ignored. The same fate befell a Nixon Administration task force on antitrust priorities. Its very existence was denied, then its report was treated as confidential, and ultimately its recommendations were ignored. Antitrust legislation is, for practical purposes, no longer relevant to the concentration of economic power, regardless of which political party is in power in the White House.

Second, in one field of governmental regulation of business after another, the "regulation" has served to quiet public doubts and anxieties far more effectively than it has altered the behavior of powerful business groups. The law and the administrative apparatus purporting to carry it out have effectively dampened fears of exploitation by private power centers. They have, that is to say, influenced people's states of mind and served the political purpose of allaying actual and potential dissatisfaction. At the same time policies on pricing, wages, and other economic issues have continued to be determined by essentially economic and organizational considerations stemming from demand-supply relationships and by collusive agreements among sellers; other deliberate restrictions on the supply of goods, services, or labor; and "administered pricing" by firms enjoying a monopolistic or oligopolistic position. Widespread political arousal and conflict based upon fear of business power has thus been replaced by essentially ritualistic administrative procedures to determine "fair" pricing and other practices, while relative economic resources still determine who gets what in profits and in wages. Among the more conspicuous examples of this phenomenon have been regulations of radio and television services; air, railroad, and public utility rates; pure food laws; closed shops; antitrust laws; and income tax laws.

Economists and political scientists who have studied public regulations of business have uniformly concluded that the regulators typically become instruments of the private groups they are ostensibly controlling. This conclusion, however, is not obvious either to businessmen or to consumers. If it were generally evident, the psychological impact of the governmental regulatory procedures would, of course, quickly disappear.

Government Support of Industry

An important facet of our political orthodoxy, and an important basis of governmental legitimacy, is inculcation of the belief that government can be counted on to keep the reins on private power centers and so assure that they operate in the public interest. We have noted that this belief is valid in some respects and that it needs serious qualification in others. Perhaps the major respect in which it is misleading is its complete failure to recognize that government itself is typically a major source of the power held by "private" power centers and a major contributor to their financial resources and political support.

Governmental expenditures and other forms of support that result in the creation of new centers of power have been illustrated at length in our earlier analysis of the military-industrial complex. A less readily visible example of the same general process, but with potentially even broader consequences, is the development of new knowledge and techniques for industrial and social applications. Technological advancement and multiplying social problems have inspired a large ($25 billion per year) new (400 percent growth in the last 15 years) research-and-development sector of the economy. Nearly all of the multiple profit-making opportunities generated by research findings and newly developed products and techniques will accrue to private enterprise, through production and sale of the new equipment (frequently to the government) or through use of new labor-saving techniques or other cost-saving equipment. But, as Table 8-2 shows, the federal government provides more than 60 percent of the funds used for research and development, frequently employing profit-making private enterprises to do the actual work.

In effect, the vast expenses of research and development in the technological age, most of it destined to generate multiple new opportunities for private profitmaking, are socialized. The federal government puts up 62 percent of the money used for these purposes in the United States, and private industry only 33 percent; but private industry does 69 percent of the work, and eventually winds up with the profitmaking opportunities from all of the work. The federal government is thus the provider of future opportunities for business and the chief supporter of the major "think-tank" firms that hold the keys to the character of the future economic and social order. Of the more than half a million professional scientists and engineers engaged in research work in the United States, 82 percent are federally supported.

This is far from the only form of governmental financial support for private industries, of course. But it is an especially useful example of how an entire industry can be quickly generated by governmental investment. And, perhaps more important, it shows how new ties of mutual dependence are rapidly constructed. The government's need for space and defense research and development was a major factor in this phenomenon, but by no means the sole reason. Other burgeoning problems created similar needs, which the universities and a new sector of private industry were glad to serve. But government is now heavily dependent on universities and industry to perform this research, and in turn the university and private researchers depend almost entirely on governmental support for their livelihood and existence. There can scarcely fail to develop a convergence of interest between such interdependent partners, to say nothing of the private producers who stand to profit from the findings of research.

Perhaps the identification of specific convergences of interest and other forms of interdependence between agencies of government and units of private industry is an overly crude way of sketching the government-business relationship. But it is clear and tangible. Other tangible links include, as we have seen, the growing interchange of personnel. Less tangible, but perhaps equally potent, is the fact that elites in government and in private economic power centers perceive and are affected by the same domestic social problems. They both recognize the depth of the problem and the necessity for government to take some drastic steps to solve them, such as instituting vast job-training programs, supporting urban transportation system devel-

Table 8-2
Who Puts Up the Money, Who Does the Work ($ in millions)

Sources	Federal Government	Industry	Universities and Colleges		Other Nonprofit Institutions	Total	Percent Distribution: Sources
			Proper	Federal Contract Research Centers			
Federal government	$3,500	$ 9,100	$1,600	$700	$660	$15,560	62%
Industry	—	8,200	60	—	70	8,330	33%
Universities and Colleges	—	—	840	—	—	840	3%
Other Nonprofit Institutions	—	—	100	—	170	270	1%
Total	$3,500	$17,300	$2,600	$700	$900	$25,000	100%
Percent Distribution: Performers	14%	69%	10%	3%	4%	100%	

From p. 135 of the book The American Corporation by Richard J. Barber. Copyright © 1970 by Richard J. Barber. Published by G. P. Dutton & Co., Inc. and reprinted with their permission and the permission of the author.

opments, or rebuilding the decaying cities. Where government must invest, private industry stands to profit from carrying out the tasks.

Several major corporations have begun to design the construction or reconstruction of entire cities, including their physical settings, the organization of their economic life, and their governing mechanisms. Others have entered the field of education, providing not only books and equipment, but also wholly packaged multidisciplinary curricula and automated means of presentation. Many others have taken on a variety of other governmental functions within the cities, overseeing or performing activities formerly accomplished by politically responsible units of government. Again, mutuality of perspective and interest between public and private power centers seems clear.

But let us not overlook the long-established forms of government assistance to private economic power centers. The large American corporations vary greatly in the degree to which their power is dependent upon government. But it would be impossible to find even one really large corporation to which government does not contribute in a significant degree through tax benefits, subsidies, contracts, and the mobilization of political goodwill by identifying the corporations with widely approved national purposes such as defense and space exploration.

Indirect Accruals to Business

From the very beginning of the nation's history, federal and state governments have subsidized private business enterprises, and this pattern has had far more significant tangible effects than *regulation* of business, which commonly receives greater attention and publicity. Benefits to business have taken the form of outright money payments, but more often occur indirectly as services rendered without charge or for much less than they are worth, exemption from taxes imposed upon others, and the shielding of some business enterprises from competition.[4] In the last instance people pay the subsidy in the role of consumers; in the other instances they pay in the role of taxpayers. Some of the characteristics of subsidies were noted in Chapter 4. But here we stress their effects as links between government and the "private" economy.

In hundreds of ways, governmental agencies serve as laboratories and research agencies for a wide range of business enterprises, the taxpayers providing services the businesses would otherwise have to provide for themselves. Economic statistics giving employers information on wage levels, costs, and other matters in specific markets;

---

[4]The material on governmental subsidies to private business is based in part upon the discussion of that topic in Clair Wilcox, *Public Policies Toward Business* (Homewood, Ill.: Richard D. Irwin, 1968), pp. 429–452.

census data that guide product choice and marketing strategies; maps and other navigational aids published by the Coast and Geodetic Survey; crop estimates by the Crop Reporting Service; and weather information for airlines and shippers are examples. The National Bureau of Standards tests materials for industry. The TVA gives the formulas for new chemical fertilizers to the fertilizer industry. The list of free governmental services could easily be extended.

Subsidies in money are almost as widespread. In the nineteenth century, railroads received extensive grants both of valuable public lands and money, but they are not significantly subsidized today. Other common and private carriers benefit enormously from public grants, however. This is especially true of trucks, which use the public highways—for which passenger cars pay more, and heavy trucks far less, than their proportionate shares. The interstate highway system constructed largely in the 1960s has greatly increased a form of subsidy well established in earlier years.

Both inland and transoceanic shipping have benefitted substantially from public subsidies: by the improvement of harbors, rivers, and canals; by the grant of cargo preferences to American vessels; by a requirement since 1954 that at least half of all tonnage procured by the government or supplied by it to other governments be carried in American ships. The government has sold ships to private operators at a fraction of their initial cost. Construction subsidies for new commercial ships sometimes exceed half the cost. The liner *United States* cost $76,800,000, of which $43,900,000 was paid by the taxpayers. For commercial airlines, the taxpayers provide the capital costs of airports and airways, as well as traffic control and weather reporting facilities. Some airlines also receive operating subsidies.

Through various devices, the federal government similarly heavily subsidizes power companies using atomic energy to generate power, American exports, and newspaper and magazine publishers. Billions of dollars of subsidization to the silver mining industry have taken the form of required purchases of silver by the United States Treasury at a fixed price well above the market price. As a result, the entire domestic output has been diverted to the government, which simply buries at West Point, New York, the silver excavated in the mountain states.

Shifting the Tax Burden

Special tax benefits permit many types of business enterprises to retain large amounts of money and place the burden on other taxpayers, chiefly wage- and salary-earners. When corporations build facilities designated as essential to defense production, they can deduct a large part of the cost from their taxable incomes. Special tax benefits to the mining, oil, and gas industries have cut their taxes about in half, depriving the Treasury of hundreds of millions of dollars and making many large stockholders in these industries wealthy men.

Another form of benefit to the same industries bans or drastically curtails the importation of foreign coal and oil, requiring American consumers of these products to pay higher prices than they would for the foreign fuels. The Export-Import Bank makes loans to American businesses, and to their foreign customers, to stimulate export sales of American goods. These government loans, together with foreign aid grants, furnish the money that has maintained American exports at high levels since World War II.

Public services are often made available to private business at much less than their actual cost: research and education, fire protection, technical assistance to the lumber industry, permission for sheep and cattle to graze on public lands for smaller fees than are charged on private ranges, delivery of newspapers and magazines at a loss. As one writer has put it, "In the postman's bag, as he staggers up the street, are pounds of periodicals that denounce the government for doing many things, but not (it may be safely assumed) for cutting the costs and contributing to the profits of publishers."[5]

Since the middle of the nineteenth century, the federal government has helped farmers; in the last 35 years agricultural aid has increased and predominantly gone to large and commercial farms. Virtually all the methods already mentioned in connection with industry are used to aid large-scale farmers, including loans and purchases, restrictions on competitive imports, subsidizing exports, curbing the supply available for sale, providing free land and services, and making it easy and inexpensive for farmers to secure credit, electrification, and crop insurance.

It is unthinkable that a government would grant a major financial benefit to a business or other affluent group unless it can be justified as contributing to some objective that is widely and strongly supported. Each of the subsidies that gives money, status, and influence to private business groups is bolstered by such a justification—which, in turn, provides the popular support or acquiescence that must underlie the benefits. To encourage exploration for oil (and the construction of defense plants) is to contribute to the national defense; to subsidize newspapers and magazines is to promote education and culture; to subsidize agriculture is to safeguard the vitality of both our food supply and the virtues of rural America; and so on.

Whether a particular subsidy does in fact contribute to these widely supported objectives is often debatable and difficult or im-

[5]*Ibid.*, p. 437.

possible to determine. Some argue that because subsidies are ordinarily granted when losses are incurred, rather than when a business operates efficiently, they reward incompetence. Sometimes they do unquestionably contribute to the establishment or augmentation of an important national resource, though it is usually impossible to say how much, or what the balance of general gains against windfall profits to a business is. Ambiguity about this crucial point is what makes these policies politically viable and feasible. It is probably a safe assumption that those who benefit most from them are also most impressed with their contributions to the national welfare. Those people who do not benefit financially from them, however, are also likely to be only dimly or not at all aware of their existence and to be unlikely to protest against them because of the availability of a justification in terms of national interest.

Regardless of the justification, however, large subsidies help create a concentration of political and economic power in which the distinction between the private organization and the government becomes clouded. In an odd way, there is a "symbiosis"—a relationship of mutual benefit—between government and subsidized industries, just as there is between government and regulated industries. In the one instance, governmental rhetoric and ceremony help legitimate the use of the economic bargaining weapons of private groups. In the other instance, governmental money and power legitimate and augment private money and power. The first process is labelled regulation and thereby publicly justified. The second process is labelled promotion of some honored national goal and thereby also publicly justified.

States and Cities in the System

If the national government and private power centers systematically buttress each other, the state governments are also important components in the same power system. An appreciation of the specfic functions the states serve in the system is necessary to understanding of the combined economic-political system.

Both the legal and the political resources of the state governments have bolstered private power centers most effectively in those states that are most homogeneous with respect to their economic base or ideological complexion. In the states of the deep South, the dominance of the white-supremacist ideology often turned the state governments into effective buttresses of the Ku Klux Klan, the white citizens' councils, and the employers, landlords, and labor unions that benefit economically from exploitation of blacks as workers, as tenants, and as consumers.

Similarly, the state government of Texas has long facilitated the aggrandizement of power in the hands of oil and grazing interests by avoiding significant restrictions upon their operations in the interest of consumers or employees and by minimizing their taxes. In Colorado, the copper mining industry so dominates the state's economy that the state legislature is highly sensitive and responsive to its interests.

Such exchanges of benefits between a state government and an economically or ideologically dominant power complex become less feasible by the degree to which a state is economically and ideologically heterogeneous. Heterogeneity is greatest in the more populous states that include both large urban complexes and rural areas marked by some diversity in crops and in rural industries. In such states there is inevitably a wide range of political opinion and a multitude of overlapping interests and organized interest groups that prevent any one of them from consistently dominating the others. Clothing manufacturers and Consolidated Edison in New York, steel and coal mining in Illinois, and right-wing organizations in southern California are all conspicuous and powerful interests. But none of them can count on the kind of continuing and relatively unchallenged influence in their respective state legislatures exercised by oil and grazing interests in Texas or cotton growers in Mississippi.

Even in the heterogeneous states, dominance in limited policy areas is sometimes created and perpetuated through a complex exchange of symbolic restrictions and tangible benefits between government and private industrial groups. This pattern has already been described and illustrated as it occurs in federal politics, and its dynamics are the same at the state level. Here, too, it is especially likely to occur where there is concern among unorganized consumers about exploitation by industry but no clear way for consumers to tell when rates for services are reasonable. Accordingly, state public service commissions serve in practice to legitimize the charges and quality of service of gas, oil, telephone, and other public utilities; highway departments provide vital benefits for trucking interests; and so on.

Because most states are naturally less heterogeneous than the country as a whole, and because some states are dominated by one or a few interest groups, the net effect that decentralization of policymaking has upon the states is evident. It enhances the influence of particular interest groups to the degree that they have greater power in a particular state than in the national government. Because of business-agriculture coalitions and logrolling—the exchange of political favors—labor policy made at the state level reflects management interests more than national labor policy does, except in a few states with large populations of industrial workers, such as New York and Michigan.

Similarly, the federalizing of all social security and welfare programs and federal control over civil rights legislation, is favored by some and opposed by others because both proponents and opponents recognize that interest group influence over these matters is vitally affected by the level at which policy is formulated. The implications of the slogan "states' rights" for interest group influence are therefore clear. Symbolically, "states' rights" evokes an idyll of local self-rule and democracy. In practice, it rationalizes far greater power for already powerful groups than they otherwise enjoy: greater power for white supremacy in the South, for industrial employers in largely rural states, for the aircraft manufacturing industry in California, and so on.

The Implications of Federalism

During approximately the past fifteen years, the American federal system has changed its character in a far-reaching fashion. Through the nineteenth century and the first decades of the twentieth, the federal government shared some functions with the states. Federal and state law enforcement officers often cooperated with each other, for example, and both federal and state courts granted citizenship to naturalized immigrants. More important is a growing trend in the twentieth century for the federal government to encourage the states to undertake various activities by granting them money to do so. Such grant-in-aid programs were established to promote highway construction, vocational education, employment exchanges, municipal airports, and many other functions. In some cases the federal government provides all the money; more often the states have to match varying amounts of the federal money. Usually, the states have to accept minimal federal standards and surveillance as the price they pay for federal grants. In each of these cases, supporters of a policy who are more powerful in Washington than in some of the states have succeeded in using the grant-in-aid device to accomplish their objectives, even in those states in which they have little influence.

On occasion, even more direct federal pressure than the lure of additional revenue has been employed. The Social Security Act of 1935, for example, imposed a 3 percent payroll tax on all participating employers, but provided that any state that passed an unemployment insurance law would receive this money back, to be used in paying insurance benefits under the law and in its administration. In 1935, only one state, Wisconsin, had an unemployment insurance law; two years later all 48 states did. They were virtually forced to enact them by this "tax offset" device, even in the agricultural states in which enthusiasm for supporting the largely urban unemployed was minimal.

A section of the Taft-Hartley Act of 1947 illustrates still a different form of power deployment based on the federal-state link. Section 14b permits employers and unions to enter into "union shop" agreements, by which employees are required to join a union within a stated period of time. But any state is permitted to outlaw the union shop within its own borders by passing a so-called "right-to-work" law. Not surprisingly, most southern states did pass right-to-work laws, but they are rare elsewhere (and generally ignored in traditionally unionized industries such as printing, even where the laws exist). As this example indicates, any federal-state or federal-local relationship amounts to a determination of which pressure groups will be more influential. What looks at first like a legal question of intergovernmental relations turns out to be a question of politics, influence, and power.

The influence and power of the federal government, it appears, depend heavily upon (1) its far greater ability to raise money through taxes relative to state and local governments; and (2) the extent to which federal policymakers use their money and legal supremacy to promote particular policies at the state and local levels. In the last fifteen years there have been far-reaching changes in the deployment of both these determinants of power.[6] Federal grants to the states and to local governments more than tripled in the 1960s. Some of the money went to activities traditionally regarded as the exclusive preserve of state and local governments: education and local law enforcement. Some of it, as noted in Chapter 4, went to fighting poverty and to creating new political demands and new political conflicts in the cities.

In legal theory, an American city (or county) is a subdivision of the state government and subject to its authority, as defined in the state constitution and laws. The major impact of the vast recent spurt in federal grants, however, has been the establishment of direct federal-city links, often bypassing the state government, giving the cities considerable political independence from the states through their acquisition of federal funds, and creating political cleavages between established political regimes in the cities and the federal policymakers dangling money with strings attached before them.

With the increase in federal money available for spending in the localities, both state and city governments have stepped up their

[6]This discussion of recent changes in the federal structure is based in part upon James L. Sundquist and David W. Davis, *Making Federalism Work* (Washington: Brookings Institution, 1969), and upon *Legislators and Lobbyists* (Washington: Congressional Quarterly Service, 1968), pp. 63–64.

lobbying in Washington and must now be counted among the major pressure groups on the national government. By 1967, at least 11 states and 8 large cities had established Washington offices or representatives, most of them set up since 1961. Officials of other states and of every city of any size must make frequent trips to the national capital to solicit money from many different federal agencies and departments for hundreds of local needs and purposes.

Federal defense, war, and space expenditures have done far more to bring jobs and profits to many communities than the urban development, poverty, and welfare programs explicitly designed to improve economic and social conditions. This is true, obviously, because Congress appropriates many times more money for national security and space. Competitive lobbying for these contracts is brisk, and in some measure the outcomes reflect the influence of key figures on the congressional committees overseeing defense and space programs. They also reflect the administration's political strategy. A revealing, if extreme, example of the ability of an influential congressman to buttress the prosperity of his district is the case of Representative L. Mendel Rivers, Chairman of the House Armed Services Committee. By 1970, the South Carolina district Rivers represented had an estimated federal payroll and federal contracts with more than three billion dollars a year. In the district were an air force base, a Polaris missile facility, a submarine training base, a navy supply center, a naval weapons station, a naval hospital, an army depot, a marine corps air station, and a marine corps recruiting depot. Corporations that established branch plants in the district after Rivers became Committee Chairman in 1965 were Lockheed, McDonnell Douglas, Avco, and General Electric.[7]

Conclusions

Though national institutions carry the misleading labels "private" and "public," no clear-cut divisions exist. Interpenetration and mutuality of interest bind national elites together and unite them with their lesser partners in the states and cities. Occasionally, idiosyncratic constituency pressures or competition over profitable opportunities cause tensions or even brief eruptions. The general pattern, however, is that the transactions of the business of government and of business are enacted within the channels of accommodation and mutual interest. The source of initiative in this situation—whether private elites press government into service to gain their ends, or vice versa—may not even be really crucial. The purposes to be served, it appears, are so similar that it makes very little difference on which side the bal-

[7]*The Nation* 210 (19 January 1970), p. 41.

ance of initiative actually lies. But what of the vast majority of persons, who are not engaged in these day-to-day transactions? They are, in effect, spectators, and what they see may be only a small portion of what takes place. The national government's relationships to private power centers and to state and city governments are usually justified in such terms as the encouragement of private or local enterprise; "partnership" with outside groups or with state governments; the accomplishment of such widely supported objectives as national security or effective law enforcement; and administrative feasibility and simplicity.

We have here touched upon only the most essential units of the integrated economic-political system. In subsequent chapters, we shall examine the parts played by universities, the communications media, foundations, and other institutions. But this brief sketch should be enough to create a frame of reference for the analyses that now follow. *All* major institutions, of which political institutions are only a fraction, give rise to positions of power and influence. Political institutions are units in an extensive web of relationships, animated by forces beyond their control. Because they are staffed by the same kinds of people who are dominant elsewhere in the system, and because they respond principally to its dominant needs and goals, they should be seen as linked *horizontally* to the upper layers of that system. It is a form of tunnel vision to see the Congress, presidency, and Supreme Court as a separate set of institutions linked vertically to "the people." Such democratic mythology, which suggests that popular wants and needs are communicated to political decisionmakers through political parties and elections and are ultimately expressed in policymaking, obscures more than it reveals.

This is not to say that nothing of consequence occurs within political institutions. Much does, but it must not be understood as the whole story of politics, or as the major source of initiative or control over the rest of the system. We shall analyze these institutions both as units of importance in their own right, and as parts of the large context that gives them real meaning. First, however, we shall look at the people who hold power in various sectors of the combined economic-political system.

Chapter 9

This chapter explores certain characteristics of the people who occupy positions of leadership in the major institutions of the American political economy. We shall focus on such elites' (1) social backgrounds, (2) values, interests, and attitudes, and (3) styles of behavior. In particular, we shall seek to specify how and where such background, values, interests, and attitudes *converge,* and how and where they *diverge.* Convergence suggests some form of elitism, of course, while divergence suggests pluralism.

Elites: Composition and Attitudes

In the first section, we analyze evidence bearing on the question of whether elites come from a distinctive social group, and how they reached their positions. Next, we explore some of their attitudes and ask how the latter compare with those of other people in the society. Not surprisingly, we shall see that elites are drawn from a distinctive social group, do not normally rise through popular elections, and hold attitudes that are shared but often at odds with those of the general public. But what does this mean? It suggests merely that the basic preconditions of elitist rule have been met, and not necessarily that elites do in fact act for their own benefit and not that of the larger public. To know whether the latter is the case, we must know how elites act, and the extent to which they can act free of mass influence. We have already seen the results of their actions, of course, in our analysis of the patterns of policy consequences; thus our main concern in subsequent chapters will be the manner in which non-elites can and do influence that action. But let us proceed on a step-by-step basis.

206

Social Backgrounds of Decisionmakers

The social backgrounds of people in major governmental positions have always been highly unrepresentative of the population as a whole.[1] Despite notable exceptions, the historical pattern has been for key governmental positions to be filled by upper-status people. This is confirmed by a variety of empirical studies. They show that political decisionmakers are quite disproportionately white Anglo-Saxon Protestants with high incomes, many of whose families have been active in politics for generations. Their occupations are almost entirely the upper-status ones, principally the law. Although they make up less than 1 percent of the adult population, lawyers usually constitute about 60 percent of the two houses of the Congress and the entire Supreme Court. Lawyers constituted 70 percent of all Presidents, Vice-Presidents, and Cabinet members between 1877 and 1934. Such lawyers are far from representative even of their own profession: in most cases, wealth, family political involvement, or a large corporate law practice (or some combination of these) also prefigure high political position. The education of nearly half of all decisionmakers took place in Ivy League schools—chiefly Harvard, Yale, and Princeton—or in the elite eastern small colleges modeled on them. What emerges from this body of research, despite contrasting definitions, time periods, and offices studied, is a composite picture of government conducted by a narrow slice of the population—and one reflecting the very characteristics of income, status, and education that we have described as "elite."

A particularly good analysis illustrating these general propositions

[1] The major source of the data in this paragraph is Donald Matthews, *The Social Background of Political Decision-Makers* (New York: Random House, 1955).

By Permission of John Hart and Field Enterprises, Inc.

The Wizard of Id

is Donald Matthews' study of members of the U.S. Senate during the period 1947–1957.[2] Matthews found that 84 percent of the 180 senators had attended college (at a time when only 14 percent of the white population over 25 had done so) and that 53 percent had been to law school. Sixty-three percent of the Democrats were lawyers, and 45 percent of the Republicans; 17 percent of the Democrats were businessmen, and 45 percent of the Republicans. The other occupations represented were those of farmer, professor, and other professionals such as minister and physician. There were no representatives of any blue-collar occupation, only one woman, and no blacks. The senators came from families of the upper and middle class, as measured by their fathers' occupations; Matthews notes that "the children of low-salaried workers, wage-earners, servants, and farm laborers, which together comprised 66 percent of the gainfully employed in 1900, contributed only seven percent of the postwar Senators."[3]

The implications of such a pattern of origins and occupations for the operation of the Senate as an institution may be seen in Table 9-1, which shows the occupational makeup of Senate committees. All proposals for constitutional amendments and all nominations for the Supreme Court, for example, must pass the scrutiny of the Judiciary Committee, 81 percent of whom were lawyers. Businessmen made up more than half of the membership of the Banking and Currency Committee, even though they constituted only about a quarter of all senators. There emerges a pattern whereby each occupational grouping asserts control over governmental action in the areas of special concern to it. We shall see further implications in a later chapter.

The Senate, of course, is only one institution of government. Its counterpart, the House of Representatives, is somewhat—but only somewhat—less aristocratic in origins and occupations. Although it normally includes a few low-status occupations, it frequently has a higher proportion of lawyers. In general, it displays essentially the same income, status, and occupational characteristics as the Senate. The Supreme Court reflects a greater preponderance of high-status backgrounds, in part because it has been made up of the upper echelons of the legal profession.

The executive branch, which most analysts see as now possessing the important initiative and decisionmaking capacity within the federal government, displays some variations of the same basic characteristics. A major study covering 1,041 individuals who held 1,567 executive appointments from March 1933 through April 1965 was

[2]Donald Matthews, *U.S. Senators and Their World* (Chapel Hill: University of North Carolina Press, 1960). Page citations are from the Vintage Books edition (New York: Random House). The educational and occupational data are from pages 26–36.

[3]*Ibid.*, p. 19.

TABLE 9-1

Occupational Distribution of Members of Senate Committees

Committees	Lawyers	Businessmen	Farmers	Professors	Other Professionals	
Foreign Relations	59	16	6	16	4	= 100 (38)
Appropriations	55	27	12	0	5	= 100 (31)
Finance	46	36	11	4	4	= 100 (28)
Armed Services	55	32	6	3	3	= 100 (31)
Agriculture & Forestry	50	19	27	4	0	= 100 (26)
Judiciary	81	6	6	6	0	= 100 (31)
Interstate & Foreign Commerce	60	29	6	0	6	= 100 (35)
Banking & Currency	28	55	3	10	3	= 100 (29)
Interior	52	27	14	0	7	= 100 (29)
Public Works	50	35	6	3	6	= 100 (34)
Labor & Public Welfare	50	25	4	14	7	= 100 (28)
Government Operations	53	26	8	3	10	= 100 (38)
Rules & Administration	51	29	8	3	8	= 100 (38)
Post Office & Civil Service	56	20	13	4	7	= 100 (45)
District of Columbia	62	27	4	2	4	= 100 (48)
All Senators	54	27	7	5	7	= 100 (167)

Occupations (in percentages)

Note: Data represent the 80th through 84th Congresses. Committee assignments of less than one year's duration are omitted. Reprinted from Donald Matthews, *U.S. Senators and Their World* (New York: Vintage Books, 1960), Appendix E, p. 290. Copyright © 1980 by the University of North Carolina Press.

published in 1967 by the Brookings Institution.[4] The study reports that 39 percent of these leaders had gone to private school; the total for the Department of State was 60 percent. Upper-status origins are indicated also by the fact that 26 percent of all appointees were lawyers and 24 percent were businessmen at the time of appointment. Sixty-three percent of all Cabinet secretaries (86 percent of the military secretaries), 66 percent of all under-secretaries, and 50 percent of all assistant secretaries were either businessmen or lawyers at the time of appointment.[5]

Pattern of Circulation

Other studies, focusing on smaller numbers of strategically located decisionmakers, have produced findings that shed further light on the social background of executive officials. For one thing, a pattern of circulation appears to be developing in which decisionmakers are neither individuals with lifelong careers in government service nor close associates of the man who is elected to the presidency. Instead, they are people who move back and forth between the upper echelons of business or law and government. Historian Gabriel Kolko studied the backgrounds and career patterns of 234 major decisionmakers in the foreign policy field during 1944–1960.[6] He found that individuals whose career origins were in big business, investment banking, or law held 60 percent of the positions studied. Table 9-2, drawn from this study, shows that individuals with such origins held many more foreign policy positions than did those who rose through the ranks of government service. The implication Kolko draws is that an overlap of attitudes and interests can hardly fail to arise under such circumstances of circulation back and forth between business, law, and government.

Nor is the convergence of upper-echelon personnel between government, business, banking, and law at any point a product of electoral decisions. In another study of top political decisionmakers, it was found that only 28 percent of the more prominent politicians in 1933–1953 rose largely through elective office; 62 percent were *appointed* to all or most of their political jobs before reaching top positions.[7] These findings imply that the executive branch represents an even higher-status echelon than does the Congress, and one that is even further detached and insulated from popular electoral control.

[4]David T. Stanley, Dean E. Mann, and Jameson W. Doig, Men Who Govern (Washington: Brookings Institution, 1966).

[5]These are apparently recalculations by Gabriel Kolko, in The Roots of American Foreign Policy (Boston: Beacon Press, 1969), note 6, p. 141.

[6]Ibid.

[7]C. Wright Mills, The Power Elite (New York: Oxford University Press, 1956), p. 230.

In part, this may be due to the increasing need for expert knowledge in the generation and implementation of governmental programs. But the apparent circulation of decisionmakers between government and high-status specialized occupations in the corporate, legal, and financial worlds occurs under both political parties, and seems to imply at least an opportunity for certain "private" preferences to exert significant influence.

What have we gleaned from this analysis of the social background characteristics of elites? The existence of a relatively small group of people who are especially favored with key resources of power seems undeniable, as does the fact that those in the major positions of government are drawn chiefly from this group. We may infer, though it has by no means been established, that people in the general category of elite share some values and interests that are distinct from those of the majority of the people, and that governmental elites may also hold such commitments or unconscious perceptions. A shared high level of income, wealth, and status—and, most likely, family histories of similar standing—does not necessarily mean that even governmental elites will hold similar views on all matters. Indeed, at times their economic interests or their conceptions of the public interest may be diametrically opposed. The occasions and nature of the conflicts that result constitute one of the crucial issues of political analysis.

The Pluralist View

The pluralist view holds that conflicts among institutional elites are frequent, and that the basic directions of public policy are determined by the people in elections. Supporting this view is evidence of the distinctive social backgrounds among subgroups of elites. For example, Andrew Hacker surveyed the backgrounds of the presidents (as of 1959) of the 100 largest industrial corporations, and compared them with the backgrounds of the 100 senators in 1959.[8] Presidents were somewhat more likely to have gone to private school (28 percent to 15 percent) and an Ivy League college (29 percent to 15 percent) than senators, and to have exchanged their town and state of origin for metropolitan residence and national mobility. Hacker concluded that these and other similar findings helped to explain the existence of significant tensions between the major economic and political institutions. Without denying that conflicts do arise, the opposing view holds that such differences in origins and life experience, and in current institutional responsibilities, do not give rise to fundamentally conflicting perceptions or preferences. Both groups of

---

[8]Andrew Hacker, "The Elected and the Anointed: Two American Elites," *The American Political Science Review*, 55 (1961), pp. 539–549.

TABLE 9-2

Occupational Origin of Individuals, by Number of Government Posts Held, 1944–60

Occupational Origin	Individuals with Four or More Posts			
	# of Individuals	% of all Individuals	# of Posts Held	% of all Posts Studied
Law Firms	12	5.1	55	8.1
Banking and Investment Firms	18	7.7	94	13.9
Industrial Corporations	8	3.4	39	5.8
Public Utilities and Transportation Companies	0	.0	0	.0
Miscellaneous Business and Commercial Firms	7	3.0	32	4.7
Nonprofit Corporations, Public Service, Universities, etc.	7	3.0	37	5.5
Career Government Officials (no Subsequent Non-Government Post)	15	6.4	85	12.5
Career Government Officials (Subsequent Non-Government Post)	8	3.4	38	5.6
Career Government Officials (Subsequent Non-Government Post and Return to Government Post)	8	3.4	45	6.6
Unidentified	1	.4	5	.7
Totals	84	35.8	430	63.4

TABLE 9-2 (Continued)

	Individuals with Less Than Four Posts			
	# of Individuals	% of all Individuals	# of Posts Held	% of all Posts Studied
Law Firms	33	14.1	72	10.6
Banking and Investment Firms	24	10.3	24	3.5
Industrial Corporations	31	13.2	49	7.2
Public Utilities and Transportation Companies	4	1.7	4	.6
Miscellaneous Business and Commercial Firms	17	7.3	35	5.2
Nonprofit Corporations, Public Service, Universities, etc.	7	3.0	12	1.8
Career Government Officials (no Subsequent Non-Government Post)	11	4.7	19	2.8
Career Government Officials (Subsequent Non-Government Post)	12	5.1	13	1.9
Career Government Officials (Subsequent Non-Government Post and Return to Government Post)	6	2.6	15	2.2
Unidentified	5	2.1	5	.7
Totals	150	64.1	248	36.5

people, for example, would be strongly defensive of orthodox political values, the present distribution of wealth, and the basic structure of the economic system. In this context, their differences would be over the particular shares to be distributed among established claimants, or over the means of more effectively serving such agreed-upon ends.

The extent to which values and interests are in fact shared among elites, and how much such values and interests differ from those of the masses of non-elite people, are empirical questions. Inference from the existence of similar and distinctive social background characteristics, while suggestive, is not conclusive. Similarly, the existence of internal conflicts between subgroups of elites can only be inferred from differences in social background. On larger questions, their essential homogeneity and difference from the mass public may be more determinative. In the next section, we shall begin to analyze potentially more conclusive attitudinal and behavioral evidence.

Elite Values and Attitudes

The utility of socioeconomic background analysis lies in the gross comparison of the characteristics of two groups of people (here, elites and non-elites). Extreme differences in background may lead to situations in which values and attitudes may differ consistently between the groups—as aggregates, at least. But within such general confines, many other factors also contribute to shaping values and attitudes. For example, specialized family or personal experience, loyalty to a political party, occupational role orientation, individual personality or ideology, or the characteristics of particular issues, may lead to a wide variety of specific priorities and preferences within each group. There may thus be many different configurations of political values and attitudes among members of even a relatively small group such as our general category of elites. The influence of resources and life style may in some cases be overcome by such factors, so that an individual's political perceptions and orientations may resemble those of subgroups of the general population more than those of objectively "elite" persons. Unfortunately, little is known about the extent to which these apparently reasonable possibilities are actually borne out in practice.

Understanding of elite values and attitudes is inhibited by two types of problems. One is the inherent complexity of human belief systems and cognitive and perceptual processes. The subjective impact of apparently clear objective circumstances is apparently very different for different people; for some, it is direct and consistent, while for others it may seem to be just the opposite. The concept of socioeconomic status—class—illustrates this lack of "fit" between objective and subjective "reality." Subjective class identification is probably more relevant to attitudes and behavior than such objective factors as income, education, or status. But Americans are known to hold subjective class identifications that contrast with the apparent implications of their actual socioeconomic circumstances. Before their values and attitudes can be understood, the presence and relative importance of such factors must be sorted out and characterized, along with the effects of such other factors as political party loyalties, occupation, and ideology in regard to different subject areas and specific issues. The complexity of the problem is obvious.

The second problem has to do with the kinds of analytical tools and efforts that have been directed at the task. Very little survey analysis has been directed at elite values and attitudes. We know much more about mass sociopsychological processes than we do about those of elites, perhaps partly because of access problems. Values—the commitments of people to abstract but fundamental principles such as individualism or equality—are hard to explore in brief questionnaire surveys. For such information, there are only impressionistic accounts by the chroniclers of the upper class.[9] Survey-oriented social scientists tend to concentrate on more easily pinpointed attitudes toward specific issues. But even in this area, information is very scarce. Surveys of cross-sections of the national population do turn up a proportionate number of people with high income, education, and status, and to an extent such data can be used to describe the attitudes of our general category of elites. But our category is relatively limited, and its members would be a very small number of even the highest-income, -education, and -status group of national survey respondents. Better survey evidence is available at the community level, where researchers have more deliberately sought out the relatively wealthy. Here also, however, the number of those who would fit into our general category of elite is very few.

In regard to institutional elites, the lack of reliable quantitative data is no less acute. Again, the best sources are the more or less impressionistic accounts of informed observers of particular institutions, processes, or individuals.[10] There are some careful survey studies of the attitudes (and, to some extent, the values) of specialized subgroups of elites, such as delegates to national presidential nominating conventions, corporation presidents, or community officials and leaders. Except for the corporation presidents, however, these insti-

[9] See, for example, Ferdinand Lundberg, *The Rich and The Super-Rich* (New York: Lyle Stuart, 1968), or E. Digby Baltzell, *Philadelphia Gentlemen: The Making of a National Upper Class* (Glencoe, Ill.: The Free Press, 1958).

[10] The biographical and case-study literature is vast; a particularly good example of perceptive revelation of values is Alpheus T. Mason, *Harlan Fiske Stone, Pillar of the Law* (New York: Viking Press, 1956).

tutional elites are at subordinate, rather than decisive national, levels of decisionmaking. For the values and attitudes of major national governmental elites, the best sources are case studies, memoirs, and biographies. The product of their views and actions—the public policies followed by the government—may also shed some light on their values and attitudes. But, for many reasons that we shall explore in later chapters, it is a very gross and uncertain means of characterization.

In the paragraphs that follow, we shall use the evidence available to sketch briefly the pattern of values and attitudes of both our general category of elites and that of institutional elites. In the final section, we shall fall back on the great body of qualitative research and journalistic observation, and extract some frankly speculative interpretations about elite orientations and styles.

1. The General Category of Elites

According to a large body of national attitude research and studies of voting behavior, people of high socioeconomic status may be broadly characterized as more informed, more ideologically oriented, and more involved in politics than others.[11] They are also distinguished by greater orientation to issues, greater support for the political system, and a higher sense of capability to affect action in politics. In general, they tend to hold conservative views on both domestic and international issues, although an identifiable minority is decisively liberal in regard to governmental services and civil rights.

To what extent do they conceive of themselves as a class distinct from others? In a national study made through the facilities of the American Institute of Public Opinion (Gallup Poll) in 1964, Lloyd Free and Hadley Cantril sought to explore class identifications.[12] They asked a cross-section of the population, "In the field of politics and government, do you feel that your own interests are similar to the interests of the propertied class, the middle class, or the working class?" The responses were:

Propertied class	5%
Middle class	37%
Working class	53%
Don't know	5%
	100%

[11]Unless otherwise noted, characterizations are drawn from Angus Campbell, Philip Converse, Donald Stokes, and Warren E. Miller, *The American Voter* (New York: John Wiley, 1960).

[12]Lloyd A. Free and Hadley Cantril, *The Political Beliefs of Americans: A Study of Public Opinion* (New York: Simon and Schuster, 1968), p. 18.

But this self-identification was not consistent with the respondents' other characteristics. The authors note:

> ... more than one-fourth of those with incomes of $10,000 a year or more identified their interests with the "working class," as they defined the term, while more than one-fifth of those with incomes under $3,000 associated themselves with the "middle class." Similarly, three out of ten of the professional and business group identified with the "working class," while more than one-third of the blue-collar workers saw themselves as members of the "middle class."[13]

The question nevertheless reveals some matters of importance. Very few people associate themselves with a "propertied class," but those who do display some distinctive characteristics. For example, the people who saw themselves in the propertied class were only 40 percent "liberal" on the authors' scale of support for various types of governmental assistance to ordinary people, while middle-class people were 57 percent liberal and working-class people were 74 percent liberal. Of the propertied class, 57 percent characterized themselves as either moderately conservative or very conservative, as compared to 35 percent of the middle class and 31 percent of the working class. Table 9-3 shows attitudes toward the use of govern-

TABLE 9-3
Class Identification, Attitudes Toward Government Power, and Political Party Identification

	Propertied Class	Middle Class	Working Class
Government power:			
Has too much	53%	33%	18%
About right as is	30	39	39
Should use more	16	25	34
Don't know	1	3	9
Political party:			
Republican	54%	33%	16%
Democratic	22	38	62
Independent	23	26	21
Other, don't know	1	3	1

Source: Free and Cantril, *Political Beliefs of Americans*, pp. 218 and 234.

[13]*Ibid.*, pp. 17–18.

mental power and political party identification of the various self-described class levels. Given the thorough blurring of subjective class identification in the United States, and the enduring but frequently cross-cutting pull of long-established political party loyalties, these distinctions are fairly sharp. When we recall that this national survey could include only a small sprinkling of those high enough in income and status to qualify for our general category of elites, the implication is that class-based and distinctive policy orientations do in fact exist.

Greater insight can be generated from focusing on special subgroups of elites, even though there is considerable risk in generalizing from small and possibly unique populations. One of the few studies that deliberately sought to include a large enough number of very wealthy people to be able to analyze their attitudes responsibly was conducted by two sociologists in a medium-sized (100,000) Michigan city.[14] Together with a random sample of the community, they included a special group of people whose income in 1960 (over $25,000) placed them in the top 1 percent of wage earners and, for comparison, a special group of poor people with incomes ranging from less than $2,000 upward, depending on the number of dependents involved. Among other queries, they asked all respondents which interest groups in the country ought to be most powerful in shaping government policy. Many people (44 percent of all respondents) volunteered that all should be equal. But 64 percent of poor blacks said that all should be equal, while 14 percent nominated labor unions and 8 percent suggested some other group. Only 39 percent of rich whites, however, endorsed equal status for all groups, while 30 percent nominated big business for supremacy and 27 percent favored some other group. No poor black suggested priority for big business and no rich white endorsed priority for labor unions. The authors concluded tentatively that rich people are less egalitarian than the lower classes, preferring government by their own kind.

A more specific and tangible comparison is provided by answers to three questions about government assistance to poor and black citizens. Table 9-4 shows these results. The first question had to do with providing temporary incomes for poor people who would take job training, the second was a general inquiry about all forms of assistance to the poor, and the last concerned the open-housing provisions of recently enacted civil rights legislation. In each case, opposition rose with income. Rich whites were decisively more opposed to all three forms of government assistance, in stark contrast to black attitudes and substantially distinct even from middle-income

---

[14]William H. Form and Joan Rytina, "Ideological Beliefs on the Distribution of Power in the United States," *American Sociological Review* 34 (1969), pp. 19–31. The data in this paragraph are from p. 26.

TABLE 9-4
Opposition to Federal Help for Disadvantaged (in percentages)

Income	Race	Government should not pay poor to go to school (a)	Government has done too much for poor (b)	Government should stay out of open occupancy (c)
Poor	Negro	30	8	8
	White	46	23	62
Middle	Negro	17	15	8
	White	64	32	73
Rich	White	78	72	96
Total,	%	52	31	57
analytic sample	Number	350	351	344

Reprinted from William H. Form and Joan Rytina, "Ideological Beliefs on the Distribution of Power in the United States," *American Sociological Review* 34 (1969), p. 28.

whites' attitudes. It is possible to attribute too much significance to one study of a single city, of course, but the implication of distinctiveness again seems clear.

Other studies based on national surveys show distinctive attitudinal characteristics among the best-educated echelons. Because education generally correlates with pre-existing family income, these results are suggestive of at least the general direction of elite orientations (though not of the specific causal origins of particular attitudes). Higher education usually leads people to have greater confidence in and support for governmental action, possibly due to faith in the capabilities of technical experts or of people like themselves — or perhaps because educated people are more likely to read or hear about and absorb the explanations of government officials. At the same time, events or new pronouncements by government officials tend to have greater effect on highly educated people. An example of both parts of this apparent phenomenon is the trend of opinion on whether or not it was a mistake for the United States to become involved in the Vietnam War. Less educated people were more dubious at the start, while college people denied that an error had been made. As time went on, however, college people responded much more drastically, and by 1969 they believed that a mistake had been made in larger proportions than did less educated people.[15] The same sequence of opinion change is visible in many other policy areas and it is usually the most educated people who are both highly supportive of government action and most ready to change with shifts in government policy or new events.

2. Institutional Elites

Understandably, institutional elites are distinctly well-informed, issue-oriented, ideological, and self-confident about their ability to influence political outcomes. Although most of the survey evidence available deals with subgroups of institutional elites, this finding is characteristic of practically all research on such elites. Their basic values are also explored in some subgroup analyses. One major study contrasted the responses of delegates to the 1956 presidential nominating conventions of both the Democratic and Republican parties with those of a national cross-section of Democratic and Republican voters.[16] As part of an effort to probe the extent to which both sets of respondents understood and were committed to the value of equality, they were asked to agree or disagree with statements thought to be indicative of political, social and ethnic, and economic equality.

[15]This evidence is reviewed in detail in Chapter 15.

[16]Herbert McClosky, "Consensus and Ideology in American Politics," *The American Political Science Review* 58 (1964), pp. 361–382.

The political equality statements turned out to measure chiefly political cynicism, and the political "influentials" (delegates) proved to be considerably less disenchanted than the voters. On matters of social and ethnic (racial) equality, the two groups were very similar. But on economic issues, the "influentials" were much less likely to feel that "labor does not get its fair share of what it produces" (21 percent agreement, versus 45 percent for voters); that "the government should give a person work if he can't find another job" (24 percent to 47 percent); and that "the government ought to make sure that everyone has a good standard of living" (34 percent to 56 percent.)[17] These contrasts are the more remarkable because they reflect the combined consensus of both Republican and (presumably more liberal) Democratic delegates. They suggest strong economic conservatism among this subordinate level of elites.

Economic conservatism on the part of convention delegates may be explained in part by their high degree of politicization and absorption of orthodox ideology, which may cut through party loyalties and otherwise relevant liberalism. It is also, we may assume, rooted in their highly atypical income levels. The income distribution of convention delegates in 1964, according to one study, showed that almost 39 percent of the Republicans and 30 percent of the Democrats had incomes over $25,000, and thus were among the top 1 percent of American wage earners.[18] The nominating conventions, moreover, are usually seen as one of the areas of political decisionmaking where lesser elites predominate. If this is true, it suggests that the higher elites may be even further removed as far as any form of representativeness in background or attitudes is concerned.

Another group of institutional elites for which attitudinal data are available is the upper echelon of businessmen, bankers, and other executives. Detailed studies of business ideology have been made by analysis of the speeches of corporate presidents, and by long-term examinations of corporate reports, advertising, and public statements. Even in an era of large-scale organization and technological complexity, these studies find that top businessmen laud individualism, materialism, the work ethic, the free market, profit-orientation, and the other elements of classic capitalism. This is tempered somewhat by the recognition, particularly on the part of the highest levels of the Eastern corporate and financial world, that some governmental assistance to the less advantaged is permanent, desirable, and eminently preferable to what might happen if the economic system operated without such backup support. One excerpt from a speech by the presidents, buildings, and equipment to performance of research and teach-

[17]*Ibid.*, Table 5, p. 369.
[18]Kevin L. McKeough and John Bibby, *The Costs of Political Participation* (Princeton, N.J.: Citizens Research Foundation, 1966), p. 84.

toward government but the tension between the Eastern managers of the larger businesses and the more conservative business elite.

> Much as we may dislike it, I think we've got to realize that in our kind of society there are times when government has to step in and help people with some of their more difficult problems. Programs which assist Americans by reducing the hazards of a free market system without damaging the system itself are necessary, I believe, to its survival. . . .
>
> To be sure, the rights and guarantees that the average man believes in and insists upon may interfere, to some degree, with our ability to manage our enterprises with complete freedom of action. As a result, there are businessmen who either ignore or deny these claims. They then justify their views by contending that if we were to recognize or grant them, the whole system of free enterprise would be endangered
>
> This, it would seem to me, amounts to an open invitation to exactly the kind of government intervention that businessmen are trying to avoid. For if we businessmen insist that free enterprise permits us to be indifferent to those things on which people put high value, then the people will quite naturally assume that free enterprise has too much freedom.[19]

Survey evidence regarding the same institutional elite is also available. *Fortune* magazine's 500 survey is a continuous sampling of more than 300 chief executives of the 500 largest industrial corporations, plus the 50 largest banks, insurance companies, retailers, transportation companies, and utilities.[20] It demonstrates that such top businessmen are alert to, and to some extent concur with, contemporary definitions of problems in the society. Confronted in 1969 with the flat statement that "we are a racist society," for example, 15 percent of these key executives agreed strongly and another 31 percent agreed with reservations; the comparable figures for a sample of college youth were 38 percent and 40 percent, and for all youths 18-24 years of age, 28 percent and 46 percent. When the issues are economic, however, the gap is much greater. Two-thirds of top businessmen saw fears of the military-industrial complex as greatly exaggerated and opposed shifting funds to domestic uses; at exactly the same time, 52 percent of respondents to a national Gallup Poll said that too much was being spent on defense and only 8 percent said that such expenses were too low. The general pattern of similarity and dif-

[19]Thomas B. Watson, cited in Robert Heilbroner, *The Limits of Capitalism* New York: Harper and Row, 1966), p. 34.

[20]*Fortune* 80 (September 1969), contains a description of the sampling procedure and all the data reported here with the exception of those comparing executive attitudes with youth attitudes, which are from the October 1969 issue.

ference between corporation presidents and national cross-sections may be seen in a comparison of their respective definitions of the greatest problems facing the United States in 1969. The presidents were asked for the "most pressing and critical problems" and the national sample was asked for the "most important problems."

Despite some problems of comparability in categories and in respondents' propensity to give multiple responses, the top businessmen take a broader and more proprietary overview, in which economic problems receive special attention. And their orientations toward solutions are distinctive also. When asked what level of unemployment they regarded as unacceptable under today's social and economic conditions, more than half of the responding executives gave answers of 5 percent and up. By contrast, national samples regularly rank economic security and insecurity as crucial factors in their lives. These differences in viewpoint are exactly what we would expect, given the institutional responsibility of the top executives. But this is just the point. Decisionmakers can only act on their perceptions— on the problems they understand to exist and require solution. If governmental actions are shaped by the circulation of elites from top levels of business to government, or by government officials who take their cues from businessmen's definitions, then such actions will be in tune with public concerns on some issues but not on others. Whether they *should* be on any given issue, of course, is another question entirely.

The top businessmen also appear to be distinctively concerned about communism. Asked in 1969 whether the communist threat was greater or less than a decade earlier, 31 percent said it had increased, 41 percent said it was the same, and 26 percent said it had decreased.[21] Those who saw it as having decreased based their views chiefly on the decline of Soviet hostility and relative power on the international scene. Those who saw it as increasing, however, were thinking chiefly in terms of an internal threat; two-thirds of such respondents traced the rising danger to communist involvement in student and black protest movements.

Confirmation that institutional elites tend to be more fearful of the dangers of communism is available in the major study of American attitudes toward communism and tolerance of unorthodox political behavior, Samuel Stouffer's *Communism, Conformity, and Civil Liberties*.[22] Conducted at the height of Senator Joseph McCarthy's anticommunist activity in the 1950s, this study sampled a national cross-section and selected community leaders in small cities across

[21]*Ibid.*
[22]Samuel A. Stouffer, *Communism, Conformity, and Civil Liberties* (New York: Doubleday, 1955). Page citations are from the Science Editions paperback (New York: John Wiley, 1966).

the country. The community leaders, local rather than national institutional elites, nevertheless saw communism as a more pressing problem and a greater threat than did ordinary citizens, very few of whom considered it a threat at all. By a nearly two-to-one majority, they expected communism to be rooted in the lower classes and the less educated. And they were much more likely than average citizens to view communists as "crackpots," "queer people," or "warped personalities."[23]

But the most salient finding of the study, and one that is reinforced wherever the investigation is made, is that institutional elites appear more tolerant of unorthodoxy and more supportive of the democratic liberties of free speech and assembly than do ordinary citizens.[24] It may be attributable merely to a quicker recognition of the relation of hypothetical situations to standards of civil liberty, more elaborate ideology, greater confidence in their capacity to manage events, or a sense of responsibility as public officials. Or it may be that education and socialization in the life of politics have promoted genuine respect for the rules of the game of democratic politics. In any event, elites uniformly endorse the traditional civil liberties more emphatically than do non-elites; what they *do* in particular circumstances, of course, is another question.

These findings about the values and attitudes of institutional elites substantially exhaust the available evidence. The themes they suggest include a generally conservative class-altered attitudinal posture that emphasizes economic problems and priorities but encompasses such civil liberties as racial equality and established procedures as well. We may have what is sometimes called an "activist subculture," in which wealth and status are high, ideology is well-developed and both interest and confidence in managing government are marked. This does not suggest insensitivity to what others in the society want, but rather the rudiments of consensus on how, when, and to what extent such desires should be served.

How Elites Influence Society: The Case of Higher Education

The structure of the American political economy and the characteristics of those who hold positions of power within its institutions combine to provide repeated opportunities for the latter to influence public opinion *and* the policy-making process. This could be illustrated by analyses of the management and actions of various institutions, including the communications media, foundations, political parties, and many others. We have selected higher education as an illustration because it is both very important and close at hand.

---

[23]*Ibid.*, pp. 172–175.
[24]*Ibid.*, Chapter 2. See also McClosky, "*Consensus and Ideology.*"

In this example, we shall see how the combination of public and private institutions, and their control by particular types of people, leads to opportunities for managing the society. There are more than 2,200 institutions of higher education in the United States, ranging from junior colleges to institutions with 30–49,000 students and an equal number of faculty, staff, and administrators, which offer a variety of Ph.D. and other professional degrees. They are not usually seen as involved in the ongoing political processes, except as recipients of large proportions of state budgets or sites of student outbursts. But they are an integral part of the configuration of power in the United States and serve some vital functions for it. Any analysis that seeks to locate sources of elite influence or to trace uses of power must make a point of analyzing the political role of institutions of higher education. We shall sketch the outlines of this political role briefly, using the major universities as our principal source of illustration. In general, our thesis is that elites dominate these institutions more fully than most other institutions within the society, and use them to serve their needs and influence both rising near-elites and the mass public toward support of established structures, policies, and practices.

The parameters of the university's functions are set by four factors: the people who govern it, the sources of its financial support, the purposes which these and other forces encourage it to serve, and the people who execute these tasks—i.e., the faculty. A recent study by the Educational Testing Service, the well-known and authoritative testing arm of American higher education, sheds comprehensive light on who trustees and regents of colleges and universities are, and what they think about higher education.[25] Table 9-5 highlights some major aspects of the socioeconomic backgrounds of these trustees, categorizing the institutions they serve as selective private universities (selective in regard to admissions, such as the Ivy League and similar schools) and public universities. It suggests quite simply that the governance of universities, more than any other institutions we have examined, is in the hands of persons in our general category of elite.

University Trustees as Elites

Nearly two thirds of all college and university trustees in the nation are in the top 1 percent in income level; in the case of the selective private universities, 43 percent earn over $100,000 per year. The occupations of trustees are nearly all the highest-status ones, with business executives making up 35 percent of the total. The prevalence of

[25]Rodney T. Hartnett, *College and University Trustees: Their Backgrounds, Roles, and Educational Attitudes* (Princeton, N. J.: Educational Testing Service, 1969).

TABLE 9-5
Socioeconomic Backgrounds of Members of College and University
Governing Boards, 1967 (in percentages)

	Total, Trustees of All U.S. Colleges and Universities	Trustees of Selective Private Universities	Trustees of Public Universities
Age			
under 40	5	1	3
40–49	21	11	20
50–59	37	42	34
over 60	36	46	40
Annual Income			
below $10,000	8	2	2
$10–$19,999	18	3	13
$20–$29,999	15	6	15
$30–$49,999	19	18	27
$50–$99,999	20	26	24
over $100,000	16	43	16
Occupation			
Lawyer	10	13	20
Merchandising executive	7	3	7
Manufacturing executive	17	27	18
Bank or insurance executive	11	14	12
Professional	32	21	19
All Other	23	22	24
Number of corporations, traded on a stock exchange, for which trustees served on board of directors:			
None	78	53	76
One	10	15	11
Two	5	13	5
Three or more	5	18	6

Source: Rodney T. Hartnett, *College and University Trustees: Their Backgrounds, Roles and Educational Attitudes* (Princeton, N.J.: Educational Testing Service, 1969), pp. 57–59.

businessmen helps to explain the fact that 20 percent of all trustees—
including all the trustees or regents of junior colleges, community
colleges, and small private colleges—are members of the board of
directors of one or more corporations whose stock is traded on a
stock exchange. A total of 46 percent of the trustees of the selective
private universities overlap with boards of directors of these major
corporations, and 18 percent serve on three or more such corporate

boards. In general, the selective private universities tend to have the wealthiest, highest-status trustees, perhaps partly because board positions are filled chiefly by the boards themselves on a kind of self-perpetuating basis. The typical board member of a public university is most often a lawyer, perhaps because open positions are filled chiefly by appointment by the governor, who may tend to pay political debts in this way.

Trustees' political attitudes may be determined from their political party identifications and self-described ideological orientations. Of all trustees, 58 percent were Republicans and 33 percent Democrats; 21 percent described themselves as conservative, 15 percent as liberal, and the remainder as "moderate."[26] The proportion of each remained roughly constant among the various types of institutions. But perhaps of more immediate relevance are their attitudes toward issues likely to arise in the university context. Responses to several such issues, posed in the form of statements, are highlighted in Table 9-6. It is clear that the trustees believe higher education to be a privilege and not a right, and that one of the functions of the university is to train faculties and students in accordance with established standards and procedures. In response to other questions, the trustees made clear their determination to maintain control over all major decisions within their universities. Beyond doubt, the structure of university governance indicates firm guidance and charting of basic directions by elites.

Links to Government in University Funding

The pattern of financing most institutions of higher education provides a major link to the more formal governing structures of both federal and state governments—and, presumably, to those dominant in such circles. Public institutions, of course, receive most of their financal support from state (or, in some cases, local) governments. They characteristically charge relatively low tuitions, with the deficit made up from public tax revenues. (A provocative and carefully detailed analysis of the sources of revenue and actual recipients points out that, overall, this amounts to working-class financing of low-cost educations for middle-class youth.[27]) The dependence of these institutions on the largesse of state legislatures makes them especially anxious to serve the needs and preferences held by individual state legislators and the interests dominant in the state generally. Thus, there is a strong desire to be "useful," as defined by key businesses

---

[26]*Ibid.*, p. 65.

[27]Lee Hansen and Burton A. Weisbrod, *Benefits, Costs, and Finance of Public Higher Education* (Chicago: Markham, 1969).

TABLE 9-6
Trustees' Attitudes on University Issues (percent agreeing or agreeing strongly)

	Total, Trustees of All U.S. Colleges and Universities	Trustees of Selective Private Universities	Trustees of Public Universities
Attendance at this institution is a privilege, not a right	92	98	80
All campus speakers should be subject to some official screening process	69	45	68
Students who actively disrupt the function of a college by demonstrating, sitting-in, or otherwise refusing to obey the rules should be expelled or suspended	81	71	83
Students involved in civil disobedience off the campus should be subject to discipline by the college as well as by the local authorities	49	29	46
The requirement that a professor sign a loyalty oath is reasonable	53	33	52

Source: Hartnett, *College and University Trustees*, p. 60.

and industries, and to avoid the taint of unorthodox political ideas or behavior that might antagonize established powers in the state. Despite these pressures, of course, tensions between the larger state universities and their legislatures are frequently high.

Both public and private universities also rely heavily on financial assistance in various forms from the federal government. Public universities such as the University of Michigan and the University of California receive about 50 percent and 40 percent respectively of their annual budgets from the federal government. at private universities such as the University of Chicago and Harvard, the totals were roughly 65 percent and 40 percent respectively in the late 1960s. Federal assistance takes many forms from loans and grants to students, buildings, and equipment to performance of research and teaching functions (ROTC, for example) on the campus, or provision of contract services. In the latter case, the university in effect acts as a direct arm of the United States government, whether in experimental programs of crime control or poverty amelioration in the United States or in the development of agriculture or training of police and bureaucrats in developing countries. In every case, these funds are valued by universities, and a major university must place and keep itself in a position to compete successfully for such grants if it is to retain its status. Not only does the capacity to hire and provide research opportunities for well-reputed faculty members depend on funds of this type, but a substantial share of the operating budget of the university is also contributed in this way. Some university administrators see this as a welcome chance to be of service to the society, others are less enthusiastic, but none deny the reality of the pressure.

Purposes of the University

The purposes of the university are much less concretely demonstrated than the last two parameters, but we can begin to identify the kinds of pressures that contribute to defining them. Three basic purposes may be identified, though how most universities rank them in terms of priority may be disputed. First is the purpose of providing social mobility for students and well-trained functionaries for the economy and society. These goals are complementary: students and their parents visualize college education principally as a means of getting a good job, and the economy and society require alert, aspiring, adaptable men and women to perform a multitude of tasks. The result is a vocationally oriented program of instruction whose chief criterion of success is the student's acquisition of a job offering prospects of income and status. To prepare students for such jobs, the current structure of the economic and social order must be taken as a given, their needs assessed and extended into the future, and students shown how to adapt to and fulfill those needs.

Second is the purpose of providing knowledge that will help solve problems facing the society. To be of assistance, the definitions of such problems must be similar to those of the relevant policymakers; otherwise the results of the research will not be used and the purpose will not be served. The result is that much research effort is devoted to finding ways for those who are currently dominant better to carry out their policies. In seeking to solve problems of social disharmony, this perspective may lead to defining those who for one reason or another do not accept orthodox behavior standards and life styles as "maladjusted" or "criminal," and to developing techniques for better controlling such "deviants." In the case of problems perceived by private industry, university efforts amount to socializing the sometimes high costs of research and development, while benefits accrue chiefly to the user industries.

Third is the intellectual purpose of the university—to transmit the culture and wisdom of the past, to adapt it to the needs of the present and the future, and to help students develop the capacity to think critically and independently about themselves, their society, and their world. This is the most difficult, least accepted, and least accomplished of the university's purposes. To think critically and evaluatively about oneself and one's surroundings requires severe effort self-discipline, and the destruction of a lifetime's complacent assumptions. It provokes sharp reaction from an insecure but financially vital outside world. And so it does not often occur, and if it does, it is not often sustained for long.

Standards for the Faculty

The faculty must operate within the context defined by these various factors. Men and women who teach, let us assume, seek advancement and security in much the same degree as others in their society. To be well regarded in one's own institution and profession, to do the research that makes for visibility and mobility, and to avoid the controversies that spell an end to advancement, faculty members must accept the basic standards that trustees, financial sources, and accepted university purposes have set for them. The real deviant soon becomes uncomfortably visible, pressures focus on him, and he either returns to his accepted role or loses his university status. Nor is this established role uncongenial to many university faculty members. Their class origins; identification with a prestigious profession; need for access to people of knowledge, money, and power, and current positions of authority lead them to adopt the perspective of the "is." Their task is to explain, rationalize, and project the present into the future.

What is the impact of these various forces upon the students who pass through American institutions of higher education? In general, survey evidence suggests that the long-term effect has been to induce them to trust and support the acts of government more fully than do ordinary citizens. College graduates are better informed, take part in politics more, and are more fully imbued with orthodox ideology than those of comparable age and life experience who do not attend college. To some extent, the effects of college education may be mistakenly attributed to the effects of either youth (the proportion of college educated people is higher in each new generation and age group) or economic status (college students come from wealthier families and earn more income after college).The autonomous influences of these separate factors are seldom made distinct. College education has repeatedly been shown to have an independent effect, aside from the fact that it usually coincides with both youth and wealth. Taken by itself, it correlates with greater confidence in the established political system and its current policies. Nor is the reaction to the Vietnam War really an exception to these general propositions. As we saw in Figure 8-2, college graduates at first supported the war more strongly than others and only shifted to greater conviction that the U.S. had made a mistake *after* President Nixon began to withdraw troops. The campus-based dissent against the war began as a very small movement; its escalation took several years and repeated provocations, and even then in many cases seemed to be limited exclusively to opposition to the single policy of war in Southeast Asia.

It is clear, therefore, that the universities offer elites a major means of developing long-term influence, both by shaping vocational orientations and skills and by instilling the political ideology and broad behavioral cues that will lead to later support. Nevertheless, some universities, some faculty members, and some students do not fit these general descriptions. How and why some do not, and how normally impotent students generated such undeniable political impact in the late 1960s and early 1970s, will be examined in a later chapter.

The Nature and Implications of the American "Establishment"

What follows is a frankly speculative commentary on patterns extracted from the foregoing evidence, many exhaustive case studies and biographies, and our own political experience and intuition. We think that the character of leadership in the American political system may fairly be characterized as an "establishment," if the proper definitions are used, and that this situation carries profound implications for both the structure of power and the process of change in the United States.

The concept of an "establishment," though vague and subject on occasion to overtones of conspiracy, has an expressiveness that justifies its use. For us the term encompasses that large proportion of individuals holding positions of power (in government *and* private affairs) who have come to share roughly the same values, interests, political ideology, and sense of priorities about what government should be doing. Most of all, "establishment" denotes a shared proprietary concern for the continued success of the enterprise— meaning the American system, in its familiar social, economic, and political dimensions. Admission to the "establishment" is not easy, and it is never automatic. It is contingent first upon possession of some distinct power resource, such as institutional position (in politics, business, education, etc.), talent, money, family status, and so forth. Among the many men and women with such resources, some are distinguished by their concern for the success of the enterprise, their willingness to play by the familiar rules, and their talent for finding and articulating the compromise or making the sacrifice that insures conflict reduction. These are the crucial attributes. It is such people whom established leaders will invite into the loose and highly informal "establishment." Members recognize each other not by labels or lapel pins, but by the orthodoxy they share—for example, the readiness with which they can negotiate with each other, even across class lines or occupational boundaries. Establishment types are "regular guys" who try to understand the other fellow's problems, avoid "rocking the boat" publicly, and instead do what they can to reach accommodations in which all end up better off than when they started. Mutual trust, mutual support, and mutual advantage knit the establishment together; but it is never so self-conscious and coherent as when challenges arise to the very system that has made possible this relaxed and congenial arrangement.

The establishment recognizes its antagonists on both left and right, uses their complaints to demonstrate its own middle-road propriety, but acts against them only when they "go too far." In part, this is because the establishment has loose margins at either side, with some useful part-time members moving back and forth, and it prefers to act only at such late stages that practically all its members and supporters will concur that "something must be done." (This was true, for example, when conservatives took the lead in the late stages of undermining Senator Joseph McCarthy in the 1950s, and it was true again when liberals formed the cutting edge of prosecution of radicals and peace movement leaders in the 1960s.) Within the establishment itself, consensus is highly valued. Members may disagree on occasion, particularly over the *best* route by which to preserve the system in times of crisis, without risking their membership unless their convictions lead them to take anti-system instead of system-preserving actions.

Public Conception of the Establishment

Thus, our concept of "establishment" does not suggest that a unified upper social class dominates the nation's political structure, though great wealth and upper-class connections give many a platform from which they can achieve such a status. Nor do we see economic imperatives as the sole or even prime determinants of establishment actions, though in the absence of compelling reasons to the contrary they will often be the "natural" principles of behavior. We do not even envision much explicit consultation among establishment members about positions on issues, partly because none is necessary. Our concept of an establishment is, therefore, not the tight ruling group of some elite theories, but neither is it the benevolent representative statesmen envisioned by some democratic pluralists. Our establishment ranges between the two, depending on the type of issue involved. On most routine issues and decisions, it may function much as the latter view suggests. But on fundamental questions, or when the system itself is threatened, it acts in ways characteristic of the former.

Nor is our model of an "establishment" intended as a final characterization of the American structure of power. It is no more than a working hypothesis, grounded in a substantial but not conclusive body of evidence. But it carries vital implications concerning the process of political change in the United States.

We do not imply that there is necessarily anything sinister about this "establishment." We do not even suggest that this group is doing anything conspiratorially, or even contrary to the public interest. But the clear evidence that governmental decisionmaking is dominated by a small circulating elite—consisting chiefly of the upper echelons of big business, banking and investment, and the law—most of whom share many social and economic background characteristics, lends credibility to the hypothesis. We asserted our belief that individuals in government share certain orthodox values and ideology also held by those at the top in private affairs, and that such values and ideology lead them to mutual support for the established rules of the game of politics and to a shared concern for the preservation of the basic outlines of the economic and political systems. We have not "proved" this assertion, nor can we from the evidence available. But the similarity of background and interest implies strongly that shared ideology and shared concern for defense of the system are likely to exist at this level. On fundamental questions, in other words, we expect nearly all members of the establishment to be of one mind—i.e., that the American system as it now operates should be preserved in all its essential characteristics.

But social background and shared responsiblity for the management of public affairs are not the only factors operating to cause decisionmakers at this level to see issues from a single perspective. Most people in key positions are of roughly the same generation, and they thus became politically "aware" at the same period in American history. All of us tend to be structured permanently by what was happening in politics at the time we happened to tune in to such matters. For one generation, Vietnam has meant opposition to a callous and wasteful foreign policy. For many of their teachers, however, political socialization occurred during the early days of the Cold War or the late years of World War II, when one did not question the need to defend the "free world" and resist the spread of communism. For those who made up the establishment in the 1960s, the structuring experiences dated back to the pre-World War II failures at containing Hitler; and they showed that they remembered those lessons. The analogy to Munich and the inevitable failure of appeasement was offered again and again as a rationale for American policy in Vietnam.

The image of international communism as a unified, monolithic force was shared by most decisionmakers. Thus, wherever trouble broke out in the world, including the United States, the guiding hand of Moscow was discerned. An oft-cited classic example is the allegation by Dean Rusk, made two years after the Chinese Revolution while he was in charge of Far Eastern operations for the State Department, that Mao Tse Tung was a Russian agent. Mao's regime, he asserted, was "a colonial Russian government—a Slavic Manchukuo on a large scale—it is not the government of China. It does not pass the first test. It is not Chinese."[28] The point is not that any man can be wrong on occasion. It is that each generation shares a basic image of what is going on in politics, and what is likely to happen, largely produced by the lessons they have drawn from experiences at the outset of their careers. As such, the establishment of the 1960s and 1970s shares an understanding of the world derived from the 1940s and before.

The Establishment View of the World

The convergence and rigidification of beliefs and principles of action among the top echelon of decisionmakers is further aided by some characteristic features of large-scale organizations. Once a position has been taken and the organization has become committed to it in terms of allocation of resources and the career investments of personnel, it is very difficult to modify its methods, purposes, or actions. Many large agencies of the national government, such as the FBI or the State Department, are now committed to a view of the world, a

---

[28]Dean Rusk, as quoted in Ronald Steel, *Pax Americana* (New York: Viking, 1967), p. 129. In 1961 Rusk became Secretary of State, serving in that capacity until 1969.

set of procedures, and an understanding of how things should work that reflect and support the establishment's principles. They see, and report to their superiors, what is consistent with their expectations and career aspirations. One classic example of the triumph of organizational commitments over evidence is the experience of strategic bombing during World War II.[29] The Air Force and its supporters had insisted for years that bombing could by itself destroy German war production, cripple the armed forces, and eliminate the German people's will to fight. The U.S. Air Force accordingly had been designed and trained for strategic bombing, which was carried out with high optimism and massive loads of explosives. But, according to the careful post-war Strategic Bombing Survey undertaken by the Air Force itself, strategic bombing never seriously affected war production, had little or no effect on the capacity of the armed forces or the will of the population, and incurred heavy losses in the bargain. Intelligence failures, equipment failures, and faulty analysis of the German economy and society were also involved, but the chief explanation was simply the incapacity of bombing to accomplish the goals set for it. The same conclusion was arrived at from a similar official study in Japan after the end of hostilities there. But the Vietnamese experience suggests that lessons about the limited capabilities of air power have still not been learned.

An establishment of relatively small size thus receives many self-confirming and supporting messages from its environment. Its approach to politics and its view of the world are validated by almost every trusted source—in bureaucratic memoranda, in the communications media, and at the country club. Attitudes and practices may, under such circumstances, become hardened. Supported by belief in the rightness of their actions, and even in the sacred nature of their responsibility to defend the system against those who would undermine it, members of the establishment may become highly resistant to basic change.

But this does not mean that they are insensitive or inflexible. Indeed, long-term stability is promoted by short-term flexibility (within limits) and adroit channeling of thrusts toward change—in part through judicious use of available coercive power. Although one major characteristic of the establishment is its shared basic beliefs and principles of political action, it would be a gross misinterpretation to see such agreement extending to rigidity of *membership* or of *specific policies*. Indeed, one of the most stability-producing features of American ideology and practice—of the American system, in other words—is its flexibility. By opening itself to new members,

[29]This account is drawn from Herbert Wilensky, *Organizational Intelligence: Knowledge and Policy in Government and Industry* (New York: Basic Books, 1967), pp. 24–34.

new ideas, and new policies, the American system incorporates thrusts toward change into its upper-level consensus. *Such new members, ideas, and policies must, however, accept the basic framework of political values, ideology, structure, and style on which that system is based.* To the extent that they do, of course, extra-systemic movements for change are effectively blunted. Popular movements lose their leaders and their platforms. New governmental policies include enough of their proposals to give the appearance of progress— and reasons for unusual political activity no longer exist.

Co-optation

The process by which rising leaders with new ideas or programs are drawn into the establisment is known as *co-optation.* Many aspiring young men and women seek leadership positions and try to display their ideas and talents in such a way as to put themselves in a position to become candidates for co-optation. Others find that their efforts on behalf of a particular constituency gain attention and produce opportunities to take on governmental responsibility and carry out some of the programs they have been urging. In both cases, establishment-arranged appointments to offices or aid in electoral advancement lead to rise in stature and responsibility. The sobering consequences of responsibility then combine with the real difficulties of achieving goals through the complex political process to induce the candidate to practice the skills of accommodation and mutual support that are the hallmark of the establishment. If he demonstrates these skills and concern for the maintenance of the esssential outlines of the system, he will rise further, if he does not, he will soon decide to leave government, thereby losing his prospective establishment status.

Co-optation does not mean that the new leader gives up his independence, ideas, or program entirely. He retains substantial proportions of each, but learns to adapt them to the framework of the established system so that they are compatible with it. He frequently does succeed in changing things, if he is a skillful advocate of his causes, but not as much as he might originally have wished (and for reasons that he—and we—might rightly consider fully persuasive). The directions of public policy may shift in response to such initiatives after strenuous efforts by the new leader, his supporters, and the new allies his establishment status has made available to him. When the process has run its course, some new policies have been instituted; the basic complaints against the system have been reduced; the establishment has absorbed new members and the system has acquired new defenders. The basic outlines of the system have again survived. Flexibility in the short run, in other words, means permanence in the long run.

Other types of flexibility also contribute to the stability of the American political system. Many layers of government make for many alternative ways to achieve particular goals, and those who seek ends unacceptable to those in power may be directed from one government to another, from one type of approach to another, or from one branch, committee, or department to another. Demands that at first seem indigestible or extreme may be converted into another form and thereby rendered satisfiable. A minority group's demand for status and recognition may be salved by appointing a prominent leader to a visible position, or by naming a public monument or park in their honor. Or, if not quieted by such costless tactics, they may be diverted by channeling their claims into aggression against another minority religious or racial group. Some claims can be converted into economic demands, or largely settled in such terms.

The materialistic orientation of the people and the abundance of the economy have made this a recurring tactic throughout American history. By merely increasing the size of the total economic product and directing the new surplus toward the demanding group, their claims could be satisfied without depriving those who were already advantaged of any of their possessions or expectations. In the history of labor-management conflicts, for example, an increase in total production and therefore total profits (or an increase in price to the consumer) made it possible to grant higher wages without reducing owners' returns. Workers, for their part, tended to be satisfied by higher wages and to abandon any other goals, such as control over the means of production.

Flexibility is thus a means of absorbing, blunting, and deflecting thrusts toward change. But flexibility does not operate alone to promote stability. It operates in tandem with other factors to induce or compel behavior into the established channels. American political ideology emphasizes procedural regularity, and insists upon working through the means provided for the attainment of political goals. The "law-and-order" ethic legitimates action against those who do not follow such prescribed procedures. And, under the conditions of the late twentieth century, the official agencies of law enforcement have a vast monopoly over the power that is necessary to compel obedience. Thus, there is a considerable array of inducements at work to direct political activity into forms that can be dealt with by the established order without serious threat.

The Stability of the System

In effect, the political system offers many routes by which to seek one's goals, most of which lead to conversion of those goals into forms compatible with the basic outlines of the system. Its flexibility tends to absorb both leaders and goals, and to result in incrementally modified elites and policies. Many pressures channel political action into these approved forms, and when they fail there are both accepted grounds for legal compulsion and the requisite power to prevent disobedience. Against this resourceful complex of containing forces and the broad support they apparently evoke from wide segments of the population, it is very difficult to generate fundamental change.

Over the years, these factors have helped to render the American system stable—not in itself an undesirable characteristic for a political system to enjoy. Most people probably would assess the costs of this stability (in terms of lost opportunities, unfulfilled aspirations, poverty for some, etc.) as entirely tolerable. To many, stability is the highest priority in politics. Whether stability continues to be equally desirable today, measured against possibly greater costs and more challenging conditions, is a more acute and more controversial question. After an extended period of stability, unabsorbed pressures for change may build to explosive potential. Or issues may arise that even the most flexible system will have difficulty containing.

Chapter 10

The Constitution: Structure, Symbol, and Political Style

Very few of the present effects of constitutional provisions are prescribed by the words of the document itself. Some parts of it are strictly followed, but some are outrageously tortured to authorize acts not only unimagined by, but anathema to, the original Framers. In nearly 200 years of spirited goal-seeking by individuals, groups, and other entities with influence in politics, the original values and preferences of the Framers have interacted with shifting balances of power to produce a new Constitution. The current Constitution is more an accumulation of traditions and styles of behavior than a written document.

The present Constitution is a partly enabling, partly legitimating construct in the minds of political elites, with some echoes filtering into the minds of the general public. From time to time, the Constitution takes a tangible form, as when a Supreme Court decision operates to change political relationships, or when a third-party presidential candidate appears likely to gain enough votes to force an election into the House of Representatives. In each case, those who are sufficiently motivated and powerful may exercise their influence to revise things in their favor. Congress may modify the Supreme Court's decision, or the two major parties may agree to cast some of their votes so as to foreclose the third party's chances of gaining leverage. Provisions of the document only set the stage on which the interplay of power among political participants takes place. Some are enabled to get what they wanted by means of those provisions, or through the initial interpretation of them, while the previous actions of others are legitimated by the same process. Thus, the real determinant of events is the relative power of participants,

239

and the Constitution is only one of several tools political participants use in search of their ends.

But this is not to say that the Constitution is meaningless with respect to who gets what and how in American politics. The express provisions of the document and authoritative interpretations by Congress, the Supreme Court, the President, and other institutions are persuasive and sometimes conclusive devices in shaping political action. People in government as well as the general public may be persuaded of the necessity or desirability of an action if it is associated with the Constitution. They frequently seek to conform their behavior to constitutional norms when the latter do not conflict with their goals and preferred methods. Let us look at several illustrations of the effects of constitutional provisions on the practice of politics today, as a means of establishing the range of consequences the Constitution has on both politics and public policies in the contemporary context.

Contemporary Effects of Constitutional Provisions

The Inability to Act

Perhaps most readily demonstrated of all consequences is the Constitution-caused incapacity of the national government to perform various types of actions normally associated with governments in the modern world. In the early years of the United Nations, for example, many of its members believed that a proper goal of a purportedly civilized international community would be to assure that such barbaric acts as Hitler's systematic extermination of more than 6,000,000 Jews did not recur. In this first flush of post-World War II idealism, a multination treaty known as the Genocide Convention was drawn up. It provided in part:

> In the present convention, genocide means any of the following acts committed with intent to destroy, in whole or in part, a national or religious ethnic or religious group, such as:
> (a) Killing members of the group;
> (b) Causing serious bodily or mental harm to members of the group;
> (c) Deliberately inflicting on the group conditions of life calculated to bring about its physical destruction in whole or in part; . . .[1]

If the signatory nation failed to prosecute the officials, individuals, or groups engaging in the act of genocide, an international tribunal would be empowered to do so. There would thus be no problem of

[1]Article II, Convention for the Prevention and Punishment of the Crime of Genocide (Resolution 260 of 9 December, 1948, U.N. doc. A/810, p. 174).

legitimacy as occurred with the Nuremburg Trials in 1946. Forty-odd nations of the world ratified the convention, and some saw it as a step toward acknowledgment of community responsibility for raising the moral standards of nations' behavior.

When the treaty was presented to the United States Senate for approval, however, it was referred to the Judiciary Committee and never heard of again. No hearings were held, nor was it the subject of serious consideration at any time. This was not just the work of recalcitrant Southerners: few others were willing to support the treaty, despite its clear purposes, because it might have been construed as applicable to black people. In such a case, attempts to apply it in the United States would run afoul of several constitutional incapacities. For example, the Sixth Amendment provides for a trial in the district where the alleged crime was committed, and by a jury of one's peers. International tribunals would hardly qualify. Further, the national government has no constitutional power to define acts as crimes unless they come within the scope of some other granted power. In other words, the national government cannot make murder a federal crime, though it can make murder of a federal official pursuing his duty a crime because it has power to carry out the tasks assigned to it and that particular murder would be an interference with its assigned task. Thus, the treaty provided a means whereby the national government and not the states would be defining crimes, and this too ran contrary to established constitutional limitations. For these reasons, the United States declined to entertain the Genocide Convention, despite the urging of other nations.

Nor is this an isolated episode. Throughout the 1960s, civil rights workers attempting to register black voters in the South were harrassed and intimidated by local whites, sometimes to the extent of beatings and murder. Appeals to state law-enforcement authorities were unproductive, on occasion because they were the very persons engaged in the intimidation. Appeals to the federal government, however, were equally unavailing. In the absence of federal power to make such local acts a crime, the only applicable constitutional power of the national government was to prosecute such specific acts as preventing a citizen from voting or having his vote counted; it did not include murder or beatings of those who sought to encourage citizens to vote. In several cases, FBI agents stood powerlessly by while (state) crimes were committed; the extent of the FBI agent's capacity was to investigate whether any federal laws had been broken. In effect, individual citizens were left entirely on their own in a hostile environment.

Countless similar instances could be described, but the point has been made. Perhaps it is also clear that the lack of constitutional power was not the *only* cause of these patterns of national government inaction. The preferences of some political participants strongly supported inaction, and there was apparently not enough motivation or strength in those who favored action to reverse the trend. Constitutional incapacity was a convenient and persuasive means to prevent an act which many opposed. That this need not always be the result, or at least not when there is general agreement about the desirability of an apparently unconstitutional action, may be seen from the next illustration.

Auxiliary Means to Agreed Ends

Where a sufficient number of relevant political participants care enough, it is usually possible to achieve desired goals despite apparent constitutional incapacities. One of the conclusions emerging from the celebrated crime investigations of the early 1950s was that the individual states were unable or sometimes unwilling to cope with organized local betting rings, and that federal support would encourage or embarrass them into action. But as we have seen, there is no federal power to make local acts crimes, and the FBI can only investigate such matters to determine whether there are some related aspects over which the national government has jurisdiction. In this instance, however, there was a will to act, and so a way was found. The constitutional authority to raise revenue was used to levy a $50 tax on all bookmakers in the country. Those who paid the tax and filed an address to which the revenue stamp would be sent were promptly reported to the local police, and a follow-up could be made to see whether the local police had acted or not. If a bookmaker elected not to pay the tax, of course, he was in default of a legal obligation to the federal government. He could then legitimately be made the subject of direct FBI investigation, and ultimately prosecuted—not for bookmaking but for failure to pay the tax and obtain the stamp.[2] National governmental capacity to gain agreed ends was in this case limited only by the priority given to the prosecution of cases and the financial investment (in bookmaker-investigation personnel) the Congress was willing to make.

Although the means are somewhat awkward, the national government makes itself capable of many things through this or similar types of rationalization. In the early years of the twentieth century, for example, one of the major goals of social welfare advocates was the elimination of child labor. Efforts to obtain prohibitory laws from the states, which had clear constitutional power to legislate such statutes, were generally unavailing. This was sometimes because state legislatures were under the influence of the very industries over

---

[2]*United States v. Kahriger,* 345 US 22 (1952), is the Supreme Court decision that upheld this arrangement.

which regulation was sought. Or they were reluctant to put their industries at a competitive disadvantage by forcing them to pay higher wages than companies in other states.

The movement therefore turned to the national government, but found that the only available federal power was that of regulating interstate commerce. Under then-current Supreme Court definitions of "interstate commerce" (the Framers having failed to provide any clues to the meaning of the term), the mere production of goods was not sufficient to define a factory as "in commerce"; the issue was therefore outside the scope of federal power. But a resourceful Congress nevertheless enacted a law forbidding the *shipment across state lines* of any goods made with child labor, thereby achieving nearly the same ends as if it had possessed the power to eradicate child labor in the first place. An equally resourceful Supreme Court, however, held that the statute was too palpable in its intent—that is, a subterfuge intended to achieve prohibited ends—and was therefore void as being in excess of congressional powers.[3]

And so the matter rested[4]—the political system being legally powerless to eliminate the practice of child labor—until a new and bolder Congress enacted an analogous statute that sought to regulate labor relations in factories. A newly chastened Supreme Court then reversed past precedent and upheld such regulations as a legitimate aspect of the power to regulate commerce.[5] Since then, the congressional imagination and the Supreme Court's acquiescence have enlarged the definition of commerce to the point that Congress can now constitutionally require little luncheonettes in the backwoods of Georgia to serve blacks, even if the luncheonette never sees a person who is traveling in interstate commerce and never buys supplies from another state. The supporting argument is that even though the luncheonette itself is not "in commerce," it has "an effect" on commerce because people who eat in the luncheonette do not go to eat in restaurants which *are* in commerce.[6]

If this sounds like an elaborate way to say that the Supreme Court is currently unwilling to limit congressional power to regulate commerce, consider the case that provided the basis for the decision just described. A farmer who was growing his full quota of grain under crop limitations (an exercise of the power to regulate commerce) decided to grow more, solely to feed his chickens and not for sale. He was held to be in violation of the limitations on growing neverthe-

[3]The case was *Hammer v. Dagenhart*, 247 US 251 (1918).

[4]A constitutional amendment to authorize child labor laws was passed by the Congress, but it did not receive ratification by a sufficient number of states to become effective.

[5]*National Labor Relations Board v. Jones & Laughlin Steel Corporation*, 301 US 1 (1937).

[6]*Heart of Atlanta Motel v. Maddox*, 379 US 241 (1964).

less, because the grain he grew himself he would not buy in commerce; he thereby had "an affect" on commerce and was subject to congressional power.[7]

In these instances, constitutional incapacities were overcome, at the cost of some awkwardness and some rational credulity as far as the Supreme Court is concerned. The support of sufficiently influential and strategically located interests committed to the goals of such policies made possible a different result than in the earlier series of illustrations. Both the strength and location of supporters is critical, for the Supreme Court (or other institutions) can block attainment of goals for considerable periods of time (though clearly not permanently).

The States and the Nation

The Constitution divides between the states and the national government the power to tax various types of goods and activities. A brief outline of the consequences of these allocations suggests another way that constitutional provisions can have an impact on contemporary politics. Since the states have the power to tax all objects within their jurisdictions except imports, the national government was effectively kept from tapping the most lucrative source of income —property, including both land and personal property. But as the need for governmental revenue grew, and the states encountered severe resistance from property-taxed citizens, the national government's end of the bargain began to look better. The income tax provided a means for acquiring revenue sufficiently remote from the taxpayer to be relatively immune to resistance. Further, the national government ran none of the risks that a state did when it sought to reach taxable resources within its boundaries. States, on the other hand, were constantly faced with a competitive situation in which other states would offer tax benefits to encourage industries to move from one state to another. Many states, therefore, were naturally reluctant to take full advantage of the available resources lest a company move elsewhere. Thus, a provision originally designed to prevent the federal government from garnering enough revenue to overawe the states ultimately had the reverse effect, due to changed economic conditions.

By the mid-twentieth century, the federal revenue-raising capacity was so much greater and more efficient than that of the states that some form of centralizaion was practically necessitated. Even with grants-in-aid to the states and other more drastic revenue-sharing practices, it was clear that revenue-raising capacity alone would make possible federal involvement in (if not control over)

[7]*Wickard v. Filburn,* 317 US 111 (1942).

the activities of state and local governments for the foreseeable future. What had begun as a deliberate scheme to promote decentralized government had become a powerful inducement to centralization. In this and other ways, economic developments have outdated and reversed precise constitutional provisions. The provisions themselves are faithfully observed, but the consequences are far from what the Framers intended.

The Constitution's Effect on the Character of Party Politics

Observers of American politics are fond of characterizing the two major political parties as decentralized, locally oriented coalitions of divergent elements that coalesce only in the few months before a presidential election. Because of this, the American party system is capable of promoting intraparty compromise and moderation, but is less effective at providing a coherent link between the wishes of majorities and government action. These characteristics of party politics are caused by some very basic structural provisions of the Constitution: federalism, separation of powers, and the electoral college.

Federalism is the division of powers between constituent units (the states) and a single central unit (the national government) such that each has defined powers and is supreme in its own allotted sphere. It implies a balance and a certain amount of tension between the two, with the deliberate purpose of permitting local majorities, or other interests not dominant in the central government, a base of power from which to seek their own ends. Although the Constitution does not expressly provide for federalism as such, it does confirm it as a fact of life (indeed, the Framers had no choice, given the independence and power of the states in 1787) and specifies the powers and obligations of each level of government to the other.

That is all it needs to do, however, for several natural effects immediately follow: the existence of real power to do important things at the state level means that those who seek the benefits of governmental action, as well as those who seek power, must focus on the states. Those who successfully control or influence the actions of a state government for their own ends have a strong vested interest in maintaining and defending that control. Therefore, the political parties in each state may well become more concerned with state affairs than national affairs. State elections and the subsequent uses of state patronage (both jobs and contracts) are frequently more vital to political party activists than are national issues, candidates or policies.

Because each state party has a distinctive set of interests and priorities, the national party is not much more than a very loose coalition of 50 state parties, each with a unique view of what the national party should do and why it should do it. Party activists, used to a local struggle for control of their major source of rewards and benefits, retain their localism and private-interest attitudes even when they enter the national political arena. The fact of federalism almost by itself mandates internal divisions and conflict within the major political parties, and assures a decentralized and locally oriented ethos as well.

Separation of powers is the division of specific national governmental powers among the institutions of the national government. A more accurate description of the American system is "separated institutions sharing powers."[8] This is because the separation is not accomplished precisely according to the nature of powers; instead each type of power (legislative, executive, judicial) is scattered among the major institutions. The President, for example, has the (legislative) power of veto, and the Senate has the (executive) power of confirming appointments of ambassadors and department heads. Most of the legislative powers of the national government, of course, are located in the Congress, most of the judicial in the Supreme Court, and so on.

What the separation of powers does is to assure that the power of government is placed in several hands, each of which has a distinctive constituency. The probability is high that the several constituencies represented will not share the same values or priorities, and conflict will inevitably result over all but the most innocuous questions. Although many people in government belong to the same political party, the fact that they are located in different institutions and respond to distinctive constituencies leads them to disagree with each other.

Thus, the party is divided again, and not even its national officeholders share a clear position on its programs. Instead, each fragment of the party claims that its views are representative of the entire party, and then proceeds to seek allies within the other party who share its views on a given issue. Separation of powers in effect assures internal conflict among both majority and minority officeholders in the national government, and encourages attempts at temporary alliances between like-minded elements across party lines.

The Electoral College

The *electoral college* is one of the Framers' peculiar compromises, a device that allots ballots for President and Vice-President among the states according to the size of the state's total congressional delegation (two for each, representing the two senators, plus an additional

---

[8]This apt phrase was coined by Richard Neustadt in his *Presidential Power: The Politics of Leadership* (New York: John Wiley, 1960).

number equivalent to the number of representatives from that state in the House of Representatives). In order to maximize its weight in national party circles, each state has provided that all of its ballots will go to the winner of the popular vote for President in that state. This means that the heavily populated states (the urban and industrial states such as New York and California) represent very critical prizes in the eyes of any presidential candidate. The gain or loss of a few votes in those states could mean the difference between gaining or losing large blocs of electoral ballots, while the smaller states represent much lower risks and opportunities. Consequently, presidential candidates become specially attuned to the needs and goals (and ethnic minorities) of the urban states, with important effects on both the character of the political parties and the government itself.

For example, both political parties become split between the urban (and liberal) orientation of the presidential candidates and their supporters on the one hand, and the more rural (and conservative) orientation of the congressional officeholders and small-state members on the other. Within the government, the split continues—a President is forced to contend with reluctance and opposition within his own party to his efforts to obtain the kinds of programs sought by his special urban constituencies. For the political parties, the electoral college means an inevitable source of internal divisions.

But there are some compensations from the electoral college, at least for the two major parties. Because the electoral college works on a winner-take-all basis in each state, it makes it difficult for a new third party to compete successfully for the single most important prize in politics, the presidency. To have a chance to win the presidency, a party must seek to gain a majority of votes in the electoral college for its candidate. This means that the new party must try to build a base in *all* the states, not just a particular region in which its candidates might be very popular, because no region has enough electoral votes to make up a majority of the electoral college ballots. In trying to compete in all the states, however, the new party runs into difficulties getting on the ballot, great financial burdens, and the prospect that one or the other of the two established parties will have a majority in most states anyhow. Thus the electoral college, by shifting the actual decision in the presidential election from total popular vote to a winner-take-all state-by-state system, preserves the established two-party structure and discourages the development of third parties.

However sketchy, these illustrations point up some important consequences of the provisions of the Constitution on American politics and public policy. We have seen that the words of the Constitution in and of themselves contain few imperatives and do not normally determine the outcome of specific issues. Instead, constitutional provisions are a kind of a starting-point, which political activists use as their values and interests and relative influence dictate. The lack of constitutional power to perform a particular act may be decisive, if enough strategically located individuals oppose it and those who do support it are not willing to make a special effort to see it succeed. But a similar lack of power in other circumstances may be successfully (though awkwardly and perhaps inconsistently) circumvented, if enough individuals and other interests strongly desire particular goals.

Tradition and Prospect

This is not to say that the provisions of the Constitution are *merely* instruments, to be used by various political activists as they see fit. There are traditions and expectations surrounding many specific provisions; and these traditions and expectations are felt very strongly by political elites, whose careers and prospects are deeply committed to the need for consistent and predictable behavior on the part of other men and women in government. As a result, many provisions take on an independent status and meaning, which *in the absence of compelling reasons to the contrary* will probably control the outcome in any given case. When determined and powerful people or groups seek particular goals, however, constitutional words are not likely to prevent them from attaining their ends. In time (if they are successfull), their preferences will become the new and accepted interpretation of the Constitution's meaning, and new generations will begin their political goal-seeking from this new departure point.

We have also seen that extragovernmental forces may over time (1) totally reverse the intent and original effects of constitutional provisions, and (2) create an almost irreversible necessity for federal governmental involvement in the affairs of other governments in the nation. The taxing powers of state and national governments, originally allocated to preserve the most lucrative and accessible source of revenue for the states, have been totally reversed in effect by the new conditions of a nationalized, mobile economy. At present, practical economic realities make the national government the only efficient vehicle of revenue-raising, and thus the focus of all governmental effort to cope with societal problems that require the expenditure of money. Finally, we have seen that the constitutional structure is echoed in the characteristics of political parties and the relationships between people in government, which shape the nature of the final output. Perhaps the present character of the American party system would have evolved under any circumstances, but it has surely been fostered and is presently supported by the provisions of the Constitution.

The most vital single point to be made when considering the implications of the American Constitution is thus implicit in these illustrations: there is simply no mechanical inevitability about American politics inherent in the Constitution. Nothing *necessarily* follows because of the wording of the document, and *everything* depends to a greater or lesser degree on the preferences and priorities of the more powerful political activists of the period. This realization lends crucial significance to the process by which the Constitution is interpreted and applied to contemporary politics. Whoever manages to affix his preferred interpretation to the Constitution receives the

---

ON KEEPING CONSTITUTIONS CURRENT

Some men look at constitutions with sanctimonious reverence, and deem them like the ark of the covenant, too sacred to be touched. They ascribe to the men of the previous age a wisdom more than human, and suppose what they did to be beyond amendment. I knew that age well; I belong to it, and labored with it. It deserved well of its country. It was very like the present, but without the experience of the present. . . . laws and institutions must go hand in hand with the progress of the human mind. As that becomes more developed, more enlightened, as new discoveries are made, new truths disclosed, and manners and opinions change with the change of circumstances, institutions must advance also, and keep pace with the times. . . . Each generation is as independent as the one preceding, as that was of all that had gone before. It has then, like them, a right to choose for itself the form of government it believes most promotive of its own happiness; consequently, to accommodate to the circumstances in which it finds itself, that received from its predecessors; and it is for the peace and good of mankind that a solemn opportunity of doing this every nineteen or twenty years, should be provided by the constitution; so that it may be handed on, with periodical repairs, from generation to generation, to the end of time, if anything human can so long endure. . . . This corporeal globe, and everything upon it, belong to its present corporeal inhabitants, during their generation. They alone have a right to direct what is the concern of themselves, alone, and to declare the law of that direction; and this declaration can only be made by their majority. That majority, then, has a right to depute representatives to a convention, and to make the constitution what they think will be best for themselves.

Thomas Jefferson, Letter to Samuel Kercheval, July 1816.

aura of legitimacy and traditionalism that the Constitution evokes from others in government and in the general public.

Who interprets the Constitution is therefore a more important issue than what the document says. Nor is it clear in any given instance which institution or other participant will win the battle for establishing the authoritative constitutional interpretation. There are many participants in the grim but sometimes invisible struggle within the national government for the power to determine what the Constitution "requires" on any particular issue, and much is at stake in each of these contests. As we examine this struggle and the stakes involved in it in succeeding chapters, it will become clear that the Supreme Court is an intensely politicized organ of government—and by no means the only interpreter of the Constitution.

But the values, standards, and procedures written into the Constitution by its Framers have given it an important shaping power over American legal and political practices. Indeed, the original document can be read as a catalogue of orthodox American political values, and as a major instrument by which those values are projected into the present.

The Original Constitution: Limited Government, Property Rights, and Antimajoritarianism

Limited Government

The underlying theory of the American Constitution fully embodies commitments to the values of limited government and contract. The national government, even today, is a government of delegated powers, and it can perform no acts unauthorized by the text of the Constitution or "necessary and proper" to its effectuation. In addition, several types of actions are expressly prohibited. The document prescribes all the powers and limitations of government, and as such is the complete contract between the collectivity of individuals making up the society and the governmental agent. Legalism is inherent in the so-called "supremacy clause" in which the Constitution declares itself to be the supreme law of the land, binding upon all governmental officials at all levels.

Against this general background of shared political values, several compromises between divergent interests reflect the nature of the political conflict that existed among the Framers. Men from small states resisted exclusively population-based representation in the legislature, and managed to secure equal status in the Senate. Southerners extracted a prohibition against interference with the importation of slaves for a fixed period of time. And the electoral college was constructed to balance the weights of the small and large states in selecting the President. Because of these and other differences between some of the Framers, the document is not logically consistent or precisely symmetrical, and it has often been called a "bundle of compromises." But it is easy to overestimate the extent of conflict and the scope and difficulty of compromise at the Constitutional Convention. Much was shared in the way of political values, and the Framers had very definite convictions about certain critical principles of government—all of which made compromise on the limited differences of interest among them more attainable.

Generations of historians have battled over the proper interpretation of the Constitutional Convention and the goals and purposes of the men who attended. To some, it was a conservative counterrevolution in reaction to the excesses of liberalism inherent in the Declaration of Independence. To others, it was a far-sighted, bold experiment in expanding the frontiers of democracy. Politicians disagreed from the very moment that the veil of secrecy was lifted from the proceedings of the Convention, Patrick Henry, for example, declaring that he had "smelled a rat." James Madison, the chief notetaker at the Convention, did not publish his records until more than fifty years after the Convention was over, and he has been accused of polishing them to assure that they lent support to his changing views.[9]

Nineteenth-century historians, perhaps sympathetic to Federalist principles, tended to be specially struck by the Framers' accomplishments, occasionally implying that they were divinely inspired. In reaction to this school of Constitution-worship, Charles Beard lent support to Progressive Movement realism in 1913 with the publication of his *An Economic Interpretation of the Constitution.*[10] Beard very nearly turned American history upside down by arguing first that the Framers were men who had acquired vast holdings of bonds and scrip (issued by the Continental Congress during the Revolutionary War) at the low values to which they had fallen because of the inability of the Congress to pay its debts. He implied that they had then constructed a powerful government that could raise revenue and pay off the bonds at full value—to their great personal profit. This debunking was viewed by some as in very bad taste, but it helped others to look at the Constitution as a value-laden document with quite human strengths and weaknesses. Not for four decades did scholars seek to verify Beard's allegations, and when they did it appeared that he had

[9]For a thoroughly revisionist view that is very hard on both Madison and Marshall, see William Crosskey, *Politics and the Constitution in the History of the United States* (Chicago: University of Chicago Press, 1953).

[10]Charles Beard, *An Economic Interpretation of the Constitution* (New York: Macmillan, 1913).

at the very least overstated his argument.[11] But few now deny that
there was at least a shared upper-class ethos among the Framers and
that economic interests played some part in shaping the Constitution.
Thus, although we cannot expect to reach a final interpretation of the
Framers' purposes, it is possible to analyze what they wrote into the
document and to point to two very broadly shared principles of government evident in it. The two themes that apparently united most of
the men present at the Convention of 1787 were the need to protect
property rights and a wish to prevent rampant majoritarianism.

Protection for Property Rights

Much of the motivation for the Annapolis Convention, which preceded the call for revising the Articles of Confederation, and for the
latter as well, came from dissatifaction on the part of businessmen
with the protectionism of the states and the tendency of some state
and lower units of government to promote both inflation and the
avoidance of debts. For financial and creditor interests, the Constitution was a triumph. They gained

1. prohibitions on state import restrictions and taxation,
2. a prohibition on state impairment of the obligations of contracts,
3. a single central agency to coin money and regulate its value,
4. a prohibition against state use of paper money or other legal
   tender,
5. a system of courts operated by the central government, so that
   they did not have to take chances with locally run courts in
   states to which their debtors had fled,
6. a guarantee of full faith and credit in one state to the acts and
   judgments of another, so that they could pursue their debtors
   more effectively, and
7. a guarantee of a republican form of government for the states,
   as well as provisions for putting down domestic insurrections,
   so that they need fear no further incidents such as the celebrated Shays' Rebellion of 1787–1788 in western Massachusetts.

In all of these respects, the Framers acted consistently to promote
the enforcement of contracts, the collection of debts, the maintenance of stable valuation for money, and the promotion of a national
economy. These are surely economy-building goals, at least under
the conditions of the times, but their implementation in the new Constitution was at the expense of many small farmers and artisans. In

[11]The leading counter to Beard is Robert Brown, *Charles Beard and the Constitution* (Princeton, N. J.: Princeton University Press, 1956).

that respect the Constitution favored the interests of one class interest over those of another. Nor was the desire of some of the small farmers to promote inflation or avoid debts or protect their local industries merely an ungrateful rejection of contractual obligation. In their eyes, and perhaps objectively, the Eastern financiers and businessmen were profiting unconscionably from exorbitant interest rates and other forms of economic exploitation of the hapless and frequently penniless farmers and artisans. Shays' Rebellion, and other west-east tensions such as the Whiskey Rebellion of later years, grew out of the perception by Western workingmen that they were being exploited by urban financiers. In their eyes, the Constitution was another means off furthering this exploitation.

Antimajoritarianism

Consistent with the desire to protect property rights, but drawing more specifically on the anticipation of redistribution of property by the masses, the Framers built into the Constitution layer upon layer of obstacles to simple majority rule. It may be instructive to see how fully almost every one of these restrictions has been moderated in subsequent years. If it had not been possible to find ways around these limitations, it seems probable that the Constitution would have enjoyed less widespread and/or more critical reception in recent decades.

The major limitations on majority rule, and the means found to circumvent them, included the following:

1. Amendment to the Constitution is very difficult, requiring a vote of two-thirds of both houses of Congress and ratification by three-quarters of the states. But informal means of amendment have been developed, such as the shifting interpretations of the Supreme Court.

2. The electoral college is a device designed to give discretionary power to the elected delegates and deny the people direct choice of the President. But delegates to the electoral college run on a pledged basis, only rarely violating their pledges; ballots list the names of the presidential candidates and most voters do not realize that an intermediate step is involved at all.

3. Separation of powers prevents the people (supposedly represented in the Congress) from working their will in the government as a whole. But the President and the Court have both become virtually representative of majority will, while the House has fallen into the hands of its senior members from chiefly rural, safe districts. And the party system cuts across the separation of powers to induce some degree of cooperation between the branches.

4. Senators were originally selected by the state legislatures. But direct election of Senators was accomplished by constitutional amendment in 1917, and for decades before that state legislators had run for election on the basis of pledges to vote for one or another senatorial candidate.

5. Judicial review offers a means of applying restraints to the legislature, supposedly the representatives of the people. But Congress and the President together have shown imagination in pressuring the Court or avoiding the implications of its decisions.

6. The division of the legislature into two houses was an attempt to introduce institutional jealousies and constituency rivalries into the popular branch and thereby reduce coherent action. But the party system and presidential leadership have promoted some degree of unity between the two houses.

The catalogue might be expanded, but the point should be clear: this impressive list of conscious efforts to fragment, divide, and neutralize the will of the people cannot be coincidental, nor is it likely that a government thus paralyzed in practice could have long endured. What has sustained the American political system is perhaps not so much the quality of its Constitution as the capacity of political elites to generate a style of political behavior that satisfies the different demands of both the major economic and social interests *and* the masses of average citizens.

What has transpired over the years in the United States is more or less a commentary on *both* the Framers and the flexibility of the American politician. Somehow, amidst this complex process, political activists have apparently found it convenient and practical to perpetuate reverence for the Constitution as the embodiment of wisdom and justice in government. Perhaps we should examine the other side of this vital equation—perceptions about the Constitution in the minds of the American people.

The Constitution: Ideology and Symbol

As an instrument of government, the Constitution appears to have immediate behavior-conditioning effects upon political elite and to serve a more general legitimating function for the general public. Officials in government internalize the precedents and traditions surrounding particular provisions and so enable each other to understand and predict official behavior. People outside of government revere and apparently desire the sense of continuity and propriety the Constitution radiates, and so they seek assurance that new actions are consistent with it. On occasion, this leads officials in government to compete with each other for the power to interpret the Constitution as favoring their position in a political controversy and thereby gain the acquiescence of those less involved. To all political activists, apparently, there is a potential payoff in promoting and sustaining the idea that the Constitution contains all necessary answers to public problems if we will but follow its principles.

In one important respect, the Constitution itself promotes this continuity-symbolizing role. In some provisions, the document is eminently precise, leaving little to chance. But in other respects it is almost unconscionably vague and indeterminate ("the President shall take care that the laws be faithfully executed..."). Careful analysis indicates that the *precise* provisions have to do principally with the manner in which elections are to be conducted, or with the question of who is to hold office. The *vague and ambiguous* provisions, for the most part, have to do with the powers of officeholders, or, in other words, with what the incumbents are to do with their powers once they are in office. Political elites, therefore, may have confidence that officials are duly elected, for there is very little uncertainty about such matters. But the directions in which the officeholders may take the nation are very marginally circumscribed (except for a few specific prohibitions), and they are practically free to do whatever they can justify out of their political mandate and circumstances.

Continuity and symbolic reassurance are furthered also by the fact that contention over the meaning of particular phrases in the Constitution translates political controversies into the less heated arena of legal debate. It also simultaneously reminds both participants and the public of what it is that they share—acceptance of the same Constitution and the accumulated political association it represents. Stifling of political controversy in this fashion has not led to later upheavals, perhaps because differences over division of the economic product were more frequent than differences over such fundamental matters as how the political or economic systems should be organized. Indeed, past reduction of tensions by translating them into legalistic debates has probably added to a tradition of nonfundamental political debates, which is now part of the American political style. Let us look more systematically at the ways in which constitutional provisions merge with established values and ideology to create a distinctive American political style.

Ideology, Constitution, and Political Style

The Constitution, as we have seen, scatters official power across a wide spectrum of positions within the governments of the United States. First, it divides power in important ways between the national government and the various state governments, and further fragments the power of the national government among the three major branches. Subsequent developments have carried this fragmentation well beyond the Framers' intentions, so that significant portions of the capacity to govern are today located (through a combination of tradition, necessity, and aggrandizement) in, for example, the committees of the Congress, the Joint Chiefs of Staff, or the middle ranges of the executive bureaucracy.

This pattern of power distribution, as has often been noted, creates a multitude of pressure points (sometimes less neutrally characterized as veto points) scattered across the map of American government. Not surprisingly, what results is a political system highly sensitive to the *status quo*—one that does not readily produce new policies that would tend to destroy established relationships. Usually, it takes a wide-ranging and determined effort to neutralize all of these veto points, to reach some form of accommodation with their preferences, so that a broadly supported new policy can be instituted.

There is nothing casual about the *status-quo*–enforcing consequences of the Constitution's scattering of power. It is entirely consistent with the Framers' antigovernment biases. It conforms completely to their (and their successors') views about the need for private freedom of action: the only way that individuals can be sure of complete freedom to pursue their own ends as they see fit is through the reduction of governmental action to a "lowest common denominator." Moreover, it follows the more fully articulated political principles of James Madison, often termed the "father of the Constitution," in every basic feature.

The Madisonian Approach

Madison, perhaps the most scholarly of the Framers and at the same time completely attuned to their concern for the threat of majoritarian redistribution of property, provided an intellectual framework for the simpler value preferences of his colleagues. He argued that the dangers anticipated from a rampant popular majority could be checked effectively by enlarging the scope of the republic to create so many different special interests within the potential "majority" that no single coherent majority could form and stay united long enough to do real damage to the *status quo*. By giving each special interest within the potential "majority" a selection of possible power points within the governmental structure at which to aim, their cross-pressuring and mutually containing potential would be realized.

The Constitution thus not only facilitates the realization of the pluralist (many groups, many veto points) image of how government does and should work; it is itself based on a belief in the desirability of such a process. It should be clear that the creation of substantial and necessary units of power at a multitude of places within the political system invites (if it does not impel) various groups to seek to control those that happen to be most available or vulnerable to them. But this inducement to group activity is not coincidental. It is instead the fruition of Madison's hopes for institutionalizing the social process, which he believed would permit the people to take part in government but at the same time assure that the government was still able to do the right thing (i.e., what the better informed and generally wealthier people thought was best).

Madison's thesis is sometimes known as the principle of "natural limits to numerical majorities." This means that when a majority in favor of an action reaches a size sufficient to have a chance of achieving its goals, its internal diversities would be so great as to fragment it. This prospect is made more likely by districting systems that require a very large (and nationwide) majority and result in election of its most moderate representatives. It is aided by multiple power points within the governmental structure that enable each divergent interest to make its opposition felt. And it is supplemented by division of the national government into branches, providing a further level of opportunity for opposition and disabling internal tensions. In this manner, argued Madison, ill-intentioned majorities would be held in check. So would "well-intentioned" majorities, of course, but Madison was arguing to and on behalf of the propertied upper classes of his day. His readers were not democrats, but aristocrats (or plutocrats) who favored more direct and explicit limitations on popular influence over governmental policies. Madison carried the day because he convinced some of them that he had devised a subtler and less provocative means to their goals than they had thought possible.

The pluralist characterization of politics and government in the United States thus has a long and respectable intellectual history. It begins with the intentions and achievements of the Framers of the Constitution, and is carried into effect today by the provisions of the document they produced. It is little wonder that this image should have such ideological power by now, or that it should be effective in shaping the American political style. Madison's thesis, and the Framers' intentions as they constructed the new government, sought to preserve the capacity of the wealthy, propertied aristocracy to shape the nation's policies. These purposes lay behind the origin of the pluralist interpretation, though of course they may not hold true today. But it is not unreasonable to think that some portion of the consequences they sought may still inhere in their combined ideological and constitutional achievement. These underlying assumptions, for example, lead to some distinctive characteristics of politics in the United States.

Politics: The Rules of the Game

For one thing, American politicians tend to engage in a balancing act, in which they measure the weight, determination, and potential governmental access of groups that seek something from government, and act according to this calculus instead of on the basis of the merits of the claim. Officeholders assume the posture of referees, despite the fact that they are products of the system's power equations themselves. As referees, they uphold the "rules of the game," which amount to the specified ways in which groups seeking influence are supposed to go about their efforts. Theoretically at least, fairness, hearings, due process, and tolerance of opposing positions are part of these rules of the game.

Concentration on the rules of the game, however, may obscure two crucial aspects of the process of politics. The nature of the rules is to allow certain kinds of competition among certain established players, and also to foreclose and label illegitimate some other kinds of conflicts. Bargaining, negotiation, compromise—which are the leading characteristics of the American political style—are possible only when the "antagonists" share certain assumptions about what the game is about and how it should be played. Management and labor can agree to submit issues to arbitration only when the issues at stake are sufficiently confined within shared value premises to be soluble by factual analysis or compromises that do not deprive either side of its essential holdings. Wages or specific assembly-line grievances offer this potential, but the nationalization of the factory or the workers' right to hire the company president do not. Similarly, the rules of the game of politics allow only those types of disagreements that acknowledge shared value premises. These are disagreements within the basic framework of the *status quo*—disagreements about who gets how much of a particular economic product, for example, or over the application of an accepted rule. To play by these rules, in other words, is to acknowledge the premises and continuity of the basic economic and political structure of the American social order.

Not only the validity of all that lies behind them, but also the kinds of results that can be obtained, are shaped by the rules. Behind the rules lies a particular *status quo*, not an ideal form of political order. When the rules limit the scope of challenge they eliminate much of the possible range of alternatives and specify that the *status quo* can only be changed by a certain amount. Thus, if only limited changes are possible, the rules become part of the means of maintaining the *status quo;* and to defend the rules as if they were neutral is really to defend the substance of the *status quo*. This gives new significance to the American penchant for concentration on procedure—how things are done—rather than *substance*. It is as if it were more important whether all the established procedures were followed than whether the right thing was done. Countless tragedies have been written centering on this dilemma, from classic drama to contemporary works, but the issue has not yet been widely recognized as relevant to American political principles.

The inducements to engage in politics under the essentially pluralist rules of the game are very strong. The constitutional structure and intentions and present political styles all militate in this direction. Just as there are strong attractions, however, there are strong auxiliary coercions for those who do not comply. The widely shared popular commitment to the established rules—which usually overlooks the fact that such rules shape what can be done—first creates a social support for such behavior. Next, a reputation for breaking the rules may lead to social or economic sanctions—ostracism from established society, exclusion from economic opportunities, loss of a job. If deviant behavior persists, legal reprisals are likely to be followed (or perhaps paralleled) by physical coercions such as jail or other injuries. Those who seek substantial change in the policies of government may thus appear to be nothing but rule-breakers, and may well suffer serious punishments in the bargain.

It should be clear that this discussion of the rules of the game and the American political style only superficially confirms the pluralist characterization of the American political process. That the rules promote, and the style endorses, such an image of the political process does not take it out of the realm of hypothesis and/or ideology. The function of ideology, after all, is to explain, rationalize, and promote behavior in accordance with an established structure. Such group conflict as does occur may be over marginal matters, such as who gets how much of the economic rewards of a plentiful economy, and not over fundamental questions. In the latter case, all groups may concur and hew to a single line; or superior sources of power may channel their actions so fully that the result is the same. Thus, the chief consequence of their interaction for our purposes may be that they serve as an effective barrier to efforts toward change generated by new groups or segments of the general public.

Conflict and the "American Way"

We cannot conclude this discussion without commenting on the label that the rules and the American political style have put on conflict as a social process. We have seen how the rules and the style combine to discourage behavior inconsistent with the premises behind the rules. Action at odds with the rules—in short, provoking serious conflicts of values or challenging behavioral norms—is deplored as violating "the American way." But there is nothing inherently immoral or socially reprehensible about conflict as such. Conflict of a fundamental kind (i.e., conflict over ends and not just over means) may sometimes be essential to release contructive forces in a society and remove restraints that simply will not eliminate themselves.

Nor is the distinction between nonviolent and violent types of conflict sufficient to permit moral or historical judgments. To take a very obvious example, slavery would not have been eliminated in the United States without violent conflict—unless one wishes to argue that blacks should have been willing to wait another two centuries until white plantation owners were persuaded of their own immorality so strongly as to overcome their economic interests. Conflict, in short, must be judged not on the basis of its existence, and not on the basis of its nonviolent or violent nature, but in the light of the entire context in which it takes place. If, on balance, it serves to further social and humanitarian progress, and other means toward these ends are blocked by dominant forces within the society, then disapproval of conflict is essentially a vote on behalf of one's private interest in maintaining the *status quo*. Widespread consensus within a society may be similarly good or bad, depending on what the consensus supports and how general are the interests that profit from it. If consensus maintains conditions or policies that are in the special interest of a few and not in the general interest, it is surely undesirable. A broadly shared consensus on either goals or methods that most of the society conceived to be in its interest would be valuable.

This is not intended as an unequivocal call for conflict instead of consensus. It is simply intended to point up the fact that political systems can find both functional at different stages in their development, and that too much of either is likely to be destructive. In the American case, at least for the past decades, both the rules of the game and the general political style have strongly insisted upon consensus and denigrated or repressed conflict. We may, and perhaps should, be en route to redressing that balance in the 1970s. Soon, perhaps, the validity of *avoidance* of issues may again be open to debate.

The American style of not facing issues, of insistence upon following the rules and letting the results fall where they may, has the merit of reducing conflict. Some conflicts may be potentially disastrous: they may be of such a fundamental nature as to be insoluble without mass violence. Where this is the case, the prospect of seriously self-destructive mass violence may suggest that avoidance of issues and deflection of attention elsewhere is morally and politically preferable. The crucial variable is the nature of the context: neither conflict nor consensus has meaning except in terms of goals and existing conditions, and what is useful and desirable in one setting may be disastrous in another. For the present, of course, we operate with the political style and the rules we have been describing.

Chapter 11

Law takes many forms, from constitutional and statutory provisions through regulations and ordinances to court decisions. Law emanates from a variety of institutions: legislatures, administrative bodies, executives, the people, courts, and accumulated social practices. It serves multiple functions at various levels. These range from resolution of the most fundamental (or *constitutional*) questions to the day-to-day management of thousands of routine economic and political transactions between individuals, corporations, and governments. All are politically significant, for in many respects law is merely politics by another name.

Law and the Courts

We shall examine the law and the courts in terms of their political significance, starting with the major problems of constitutional interpretation and working our way down through the court systems to an assessment of the part played by law in the process of social control. In general, we shall see that the workings of law are closely bound up with the values and goals that are dominant within the society, normally meaning those of its more powerful members. Law and the legal order are the vehicles by which the relatively more powerful effectively establish their values and priorities as controlling factors within the society. Almost by definition, law must be non-neutral—it is a conserving force that works in a wide variety of ways to sustain the established social order. Its principal task, after all, is to maintain order—that is, continuity of the existing structures and procedures, which have the effect of helping some people far more than others. But both the law and its applications are usually strongly supported by the great bulk of the people, for whom they may also serve important though different needs.

Interpreting the Constitution

Law plays a larger role in organizing the basic structures and procedures of government in the United States than it does in most political systems. This is because the Constitution is a written document, and by its own declaration the supreme *law* of the land. Fundamental —constitutional—issues are thus removed at the start from the realm of open value choices made according to their merits and the felt needs of the times. They are translated into the language and procedures of the law as *it* exists at the time. Thus, issues must be fitted into the concepts and forms that the law happens to make available, and trusted to a particular (generally upper-class) skill group, lawyers. In the American system, this means that a powerful role is played by pre-existing contractual obligations, property rights, and precedent— the decisions and practices of a perhaps irrelevant past. It also makes for a contest over the right to say what the law "really means"—a contest which, however vital to all, must be decided only by the backward-looking men and methods of the law. In particular, as we noted earlier, this contest focuses on the capacity to affix an authoritative interpretation to the Constitution. Whoever succeeds in doing so gains real advantage in shaping the future policies and practices of government.

Most Americans, if pressed, would probably say that the Supreme Court is the proper vehicle for interpretation of the Constitution. Moreover, it would be difficult for them to imagine a basis for challenging the right and power of the Court to do so. Such is the triumph of Alexander Hamilton's argument, written into constitutional doctrine by the adroit opportunism of Chief Justice John Marshall. The complete acceptance of Hamilton's argument today, however, should not obscure the bitter clash of values and competing philosophies between Hamilton and Jefferson over the question of who was to interpret the Constitution. Hamilton's total victory brought with it mixed costs and benefits, and has had fundamental consequences for the nature of the American system of government. We shall first review the stakes in the conflict and then examine the effects of Hamilton's victory.

The Hamilton-Jefferson Positions

Hamilton had argued for a limited monarchy at the Constitutional Convention, but supported the final product as acceptable for the economy-developing purposes he had in mind. Together with John Jay and James Madison, he authored several essays designed to promote ratification of the Constitution in New York and known by the collective title The *Federalist Papers*. For the most part, Hamilton stressed the utility of union and the need for a strong central government as reasons for accepting the document, but he saved his special enthusiasm for two innovations included in the Constitution which improved upon the old Articles of Confederation. These were a strong and vigorous executive to carry out the laws with force where necessary, and an independent judiciary with the power of judicial review (the power to declare acts of Congress unconstitutional).

In arguing for judicial power to declare acts of the other branches unconstitutional and therefore void, Hamilton employed the legal analogy of the relationship between principal and agent.[1] The people (the principal) having granted the agent (the national government) only certain powers and not others, Hamilton argued, any act in excess of those granted powers must be void. But this left the problem of how the invalidity was to be determined: how does anybody know when an act of a legislature is in excess of the powers granted to it? Certainly sincere and knowledgeable legislators had decided that the act *was* within their powers, or they would have chosen another means of attaining the end they had in mind. Hamilton argued that these determinations were questions of law (again, the Constitution conveniently *declares* that it is the law of the land) and as such ought to be decided by the Court. Jefferson insisted that the question of whether the principal had delegated a particular power to the agent ought to be decided by the principal himself, and certainly not by the agent. In other words, he wanted the people to determine in every instance whether the act of the legislature was authorized or not. The Constitution itself does not specify by what means its provisions are to be interpreted, and so the issue evolved into a test of logic, persuasiveness, and power between the two positions. Analysis of the debate suggests that two major disagreements divided the parties, and that both of these disagreements were rooted in the same conflict of values.

First, Hamilton and Jefferson had quite different views of the nature of a constitution. To Jefferson, it was a fundamental allocation of the people's powers, superior to the ongoing acts of government. For these reasons, it was not law in the ordinary sense of

---

Some perplexity respecting the rights of the courts to pronounce legislative acts void, because contrary to the constitution, has arisen from an imagination that the doctrine would imply a superiority of the judiciary to the legislative power. It is urged that the authority which can declare the acts of another void, must necessarily be superior to the one whose acts may be declared void. . . .

. . . The interpretation of the laws is the proper and peculiar province of the courts. A constitution is, in fact, and must be regarded by the judges, as

---

[1]See essay number 78 of the *Federalist Papers*.

a fundamental law. It therefore belongs to them to ascertain its meaning, as well as the meaning of any particular act proceeding from the legislative body. If there should happen to be an irreconcilable variance between the two, that which has the superior obligation and validity ought, of course, to be preferred; or, in other words, the Constitution ought to be preferred to the statute, the intention of the people to the intention of their agents.

Nor does this conclusion by any means suppose a superiority of the judicial to the legislative power. It only supposes that the power of the people is superior to both; and that where the will of the legislature, declared in its statutes, stands in opposition to that of the people, declared in the Constitution, the judges ought to be governed by the latter rather than by the former. . . .

Alexander Hamilton, *Federalist Papers* Number 78, 1788.

It is emphatically the province and duty of the judicial department to say what the law is. Those who apply the law to particular cases, must of necessity expound and interpret that rule. If two laws conflict with each other, the courts must decide on the operation of each.

So if a law be in opposition to the constitution; if both the law and the constitution apply to a particular case, so that the court must decide that case conformably to the law, disregarding the constitution; or conformably to the constitution, disregarding the law; the court must determine which of these conflicting rules governs each case. This is of the very essence of judicial duty.

If, then, the courts are to regard the constitution, and the constitution is superior to any ordinary act of the legislature, the constitution, and not such ordinary act, must govern the case to which they both apply. . . .

Chief Justice John Marshall in *Marbury* v. *Madison* (1803).

. . .The Constitution and the right of the legislature to pass the Act, may be in collision. But is that a legitimate subject for judicial determination? If it be, the judiciary must be a peculiar organ, to revise the proceedings of the legislature, and to correct its mistakes; And in what part of the Constitution are we to look for this proud pre-eminence? Viewing the matter in the opposite direction, what would be thought of an Act of Assembly in which it should be declared that the Supreme Court had, in a particular case, put a wrong construction of the Constitution of the United States, and that the judgment should therefore be reversed? It would doubtless be thought a usurpation of judicial power. But it is by no means clear, that to declare a law void which has been enacted according to the forms prescribed in the Constitution, is not a usurpation of legislative power. It is an act of sovereignty. . . It is the business of the judiciary to interpret the laws, not scan the authority of the lawgiver; and without the latter, it cannot take cognizance of a collision beween a law and the Constitution. . . .

Chief Justice Gibson of the Pennsylvania Supreme Court, in *Eakin* v. *Raub* (1825).

. . . I ask for no straining of words against the General Government, nor yet against the States. . . .

But the Chief Justice says, "There must be an ultimate arbiter somewhere." True, there must; but does that prove it is either party? The ultimate arbiter is the people of the Union, assembled by their deputies in convention, at the call of the Congress, or of two-thirds of the States. Let them decide to which they mean to give an authority claimed by two of their organs. And it has been the peculiar wisdom and felicity of our constitution, to have provided this peaceable appeal, where that of other nations is at once to force.

Thomas Jefferson, in a letter to Justice William Johnson, June 1823.

a statute or code, but rather the people's instructions to their government about the goals and purposes it should pursue. These goals and purposes would be changeable over time, of course, as circumstances changed, and Jefferson insisted upon the right of the people to change their Constitution regularly. Hamilton, on the other hand, saw the Constitution as a technical legal document with more or less fixed meaning, requiring legal expertise for interpretation. He argued that the Court was more likely to possess the expertise and wisdom necessary to divine the meaning of the document's words. Although he acknowledged that the Constitution flowed from the people he insisted that their ratification had carried with it authorization of the Court as interpreter.

Second, the two men disagreed over the nature of the act of interpretation. Since Jefferson viewed interpretation as requiring value-based choices, it followed that the choice should be made by the people themselves. But if that was not feasible, it should be made by the institution closest to the people—normally their elected representatives in either state or national legislatures. He was particularly unwilling to be subjected to the value choices of a body of men not elected but appointed (and for life terms) by members of the very national government whose exercise of powers was being questioned. Hamilton blandly declared that there was no act of choice involved in interpretation of the Constitution. He argued that it was simply a matter of comparing the statute with the words of the Constitution and registering the mechanical judgment that would be apparent from the comparison. He expressed confidence that the independence and life terms of judges would enable them to rise above the petty strifes of the day and render decisions true to the basic intent of the document.

What really divides the antagonists in this debate is a wide gulf between their respective value premises and priorities. Jefferson feared the self-serving tendencies of the financiers and businessmen represented by Hamilton and the Federalist Party. Thus he sought to prevent them from staffing and using the Supreme Court to legitimate their aggrandizing schemes. His trust in the people was by no means complete, but he preferred their judgments to those of any self-selected elite. Hamilton feared the property-redistributing tendencies of the masses, and so sought to keep control over the scope of legislative powers in the hands of a trustworthy body sympathetic to property rights. Lawyers, already accustomed to reverence for the traditions and practices of the past, would be—particularly if well selected—another bulwark in defense of the Constitution's protections for the established order.

In principle, Jefferson's position appears the more logical and the more democratic. If, as seems evident, the act of interpretation involves value choices, then choice by the people or their recently elected representatives seems more democratic than choice by an appointed body that is not accountable to the people in any way. But Hamilton's view was made into authoritative doctrine by Chief Justice John Marshall in the case of *Marbury* v. *Madison* in 1803.[2] To add insult to injury, Marshall accomplished his feat while Jefferson was President, with a Republican majority behind him in the House of Representatives. He did it by declaring that an act of Congress was contrary to the Constitution. The institution restrained by the declaration of unconstitutionality was the Court itself, so Marshall faced no problem of failure to comply. Despite some wavering in the face of Jefferson's pressures, Marshall stuck to the principle of the Court's power of judicial review throughout the remaining thirty years of his term on the Court. He had the political sophistication not to exercise the power, however, and it was not until 1857 and the *Dred Scott* case[3] that the second test of judicial review occurred. This too met with strong political reaction, and the principle of judicial review did not become firmly established in practice until after the Civil War. By then, the Court had proven to be an effective defense against the experiments of several states with social legislation, but the acceptance of the Hamiltonian position was widespread.

---

[2] *Marbury* v. *Madison*, 1 branch. 137 (1803).
[3] *Dred Scott* v. *Sanford*, 19 Howard 393 (1857).

The Hamilton Victory

Why did Hamilton win the argument so fully that it is now difficult to convey the significance of the choice that was unconsciously made? Surely the American penchant for legalism and the law is both cause and effect here. Americans were a receptive audience for Hamilton's legalistic approach to political problems. Further, the group to which Hamilton first appealed was made up chiefly of the upper and upper middle classes of propertied people. They may have perceived the same advantages in the prospective role of the Court as he did. Business and wealthier interests consistently supported the Court's power of judicial review right up through the famous Court-packing conflicts of the New Deal period.

The latter event suggests another reason why Hamilton's argument may have succeeded in the long run. There is nothing inevitable about what the Court will do in any given situation, for the real determinant of a decision is less the power of the Court than the particular preferences of the judges who happen to be sitting on the Court at the time. The presence of liberal judges leads to liberal decisions, as the Warren Court era demonstrated; thus the Court may become a Hamiltonian instrument that acts on behalf of Jefferson's ideals. This realization may lead to acceptance of the Court's power of judicial review by *all* political activists, each of whom hopes to control the presidency and thus the channel of appointment to the Court. Careful choice of appointees to the Court—and longevity on their part—may permit greater impact on the directions of public policy than some Presidents generate in four years in the White House.

There seems little doubt, however, that the bestowal of the power of judicial review on the Supreme Court adds an important dimension to the character of American politics. For one thing, it tends to depoliticize some issues and convert them into a form in which only some people—lawyers and their clients—rather than the entire citizenry, are the relevant decisionmakers. Taking some of the great value conflicts of the society to the Supreme Court for resolution probably siphons off some of the tensions and bitterness from our politics and perhaps renders them more stable. But this can be a mixed blessing, for people probably *ought* sometimes to become engaged in vital questions affecting their futures. The Supreme Court is not the final authority on any question about which a large number of people care strongly. There are many ways to combat or circumvent a single decision. It is nevertheless, even as a contingent decisionmaker, able to structure public understanding of some issues and to resolve many others without much public attention. Again, the desirability of this depends on one's attitude toward popular participation and the need for a preliminary decisionmaker in a large society with many public issues of considerable complexity.

Nonjudicial Factors in Interpretation

In any event, the Supreme Court is not left to do the job of constitutional interpretation by itself. Many other institutions and political participants take part in shaping the meaning of the Constitution in any particular situation. The Court is, after all, an essentially passive institution, requiring several prior decisions by a variety of interested parties before a case even reaches it. Why and under what circumstances do some people or interests decide to sue others? Litigation is not the most direct and sure way of gaining one's political ends, and therefore it must be utilized because other routes appear blocked or unpromising. The courts thus become a kind of supplementary political level—a means of moving other institutions to action, or occasionally a route to limited specific ends. Other choices within the legal arena include decisions as to whether or not to appeal, decisions by the Department of Justice as to the position it wishes to take on cases that are appealed to the Supreme Court, and all the decisions of trial and lower appellate court judges on aspects of a case both before and after the Supreme Court decides it.

Nor are the many participants in the legal process allowed to decide important questions through interaction alone. Neither the Congress nor the President has been supine before the Supreme Court in American history. Both have reacted strongly to decisions they considered inappropriate or undesirable. Congress can pass a new statute only marginally different from one ruled unconstitutional. It can initiate constitutional amendments to overrule decisions. Or it can and does express its displeasure by modifying the Court's jurisdiction or severely challenging and perhaps rejecting confirmation of newly appointed justices. The President's cooperation is usually necessary to enforce Court decisions, so he is often in an even stronger immediate position to prevent the Court's interpretation of the Constitution from becoming definitive or final. Presidents have ignored the Court, flatly refused to obey its decisions, or simply nominated judges with totally different views from those that previously prevailed. Thus, even when the Court does receive and decide a case in such a way as to pronounce a particular interpretation of the Constitution, the other institutions may reverse, modify, or ignore its determination.

Much of the time, questions of the Constitution's meaning are resolved without the involvement of the Court at all, as when the President, the Congress, the political parties, and others establish precedents and traditions that are unchallenged or unchallengeable in courts. For example, the President is solely responsible for determining when the Constitution's guarantee to the states against domestic insurrection should be invoked. The political parties decide through their accumulated years of practice how the electoral college shall work, and so forth. Thousands of lower court opinions generate a wide variety of constitutional interpretations. In addition, statutes and regulations specify the jurisdictional boundaries of courts and agencies, particularize the generalities of the Constitution in infinite numbers of ways, and authorize or preclude the bringing of claims to enforce constitutional "rights."

The history of interactions among the many participants in American politics suggests that the interpretation of the Constitution is considered too important an act to be left to the Supreme Court. Even if it were capable in practice of hearing cases on all the disputed aspects of the Constitution, the other political participants are too vitally concerned about gaining their ends to defer to the preferences of the judges. The contest over who shall affix his preferences as the established meaning of the Constitution involves great stakes—perhaps the winning or losing of major prizes of politics—and so it is on occasion bitterly fought. The final, authoritative meaning of the Constitution (assuming one ever finally emerges) is thus more a product of relative political power than of legalistic analysis alone.

Even if the Supreme Court is only a preliminary, or contingent, authority on the meaning of the Constitution, its role remains a powerful one. In analyzing the Court as an institution, we shall interpret it in political terms. For example, we shall be concerned with the internal distribution of power and influence in order to come to grips with the reality of its operation.

The Supreme Court as a Political Institution

After two decades in which the Supreme Court has had major impact on a wide range of public matters—segregation, political freedoms, defendants' rights in criminal cases, state legislative and congressional districting, to mention only a few—it hardly seems necessary to stress that it plays a major policy-making role within the national government. Although it can make decisions only on cases that are brought before it, the Court's powers to interpret the Constitution and judge the acts of other branches render it an integral part of the political process. In order to decide what a statute or an executive regulation means, whether an act by a government official is consistent with authorizing legislation, or whether either is consistent with the Constitution, the justices must make choices. These choices are inevitably based, at least in part, on their personal values, preferences, and goals. Nor is it a coincidence that the same issues that have been before the Congress or the executive branch are also brought before the Supreme Court. Thus, the Court is different from the other institutions in form, but not in political character or impact on the society.

The Supreme Court consists of only nine persons, each of whose votes is of equal weight. It has no committees, and (with rare exceptions) all of the justices personally hear arguments on, discuss, and vote on every case. Nevertheless, there are ways in which influence becomes concentrated within the Court. Not all justices are equally determinative in shaping the Court's policy positions. Official status, the division of labor among the justices, and their reputations, personalities, and styles as individuals are the chief reasons for sometimes sharp differences in their real power.

The Chief Justice

The position of Chief Justice offers the principal opportunity within the Court to affect the nature of its decisionmaking. In nearly two centuries under the present Constitution, there have been only 15 Chief Justices, as compared with 38 Presidents. A politically astute Chief Justice who assumes his position at a relatively early age and enjoys a long life may leave a more lasting imprint on the public policies of the nation than some Presidents. Chief Justice John Marshall (1801–1835), for example, probably had considerably more effect on the development of the United States than several of the Presidents who held office during the nineteenth century. Not all Chief Justices have left the mark of a Marshall, a Hughes, or a Warren. Some have found the tasks of the office, the strongmindedness of other justices, or the issues of the times to be more than they could manage. To be effective, a Chief Justice must employ the political skills of bargaining and accommodation. He must develop and use the formal powers of his office in harmony with the more personal techniques of small-group leadership in order to bring a majority of the justices into agreement with the positions he favors.

The formal powers of the Chief Justice are few. But tradition and practice have combined with an increasing caseload to make them important sources of leverage within the Court. For example, the Chief Justice presides over the conferences at which the justices select the cases on which they will hear arguments and write opinions expressing new or clarified rules of law. Of the many thousands of cases appealed every year, the Court must of necessity decline to hear the great majority and allocate its time to the 150–200 cases involving what the justices see as the most important issues. Although each justice has the right to review all of these potential cases, the Chief Justice has a larger staff and therefore makes it his responsibility to see that all appeals are reviewed. He suggests the cases that should be selected for further hearings and those that should be rejected. Discussion at these conferences thus proceeds according to an agenda and a preliminary selection set by the Chief Justice. If he has done his work carefully, the cases actually chosen for the Court's subsequent calendars will closely resemble his original list.

The Court's practice is to hear oral arguments on cases for two-week periods and then to take the next two weeks for research, decisions, and opinion-writing. Decisions on cases are made at regular conferences of all justices, again presided over by the Chief Justice. At these conferences, the Chief Justice normally structures the issues for resolution in each case, and then opens the floor for discussion among the justices. Voting on the case, however, proceeds from the most junior justice (the most recent appointee) up to the Chief Justice. Because he votes last, the Chief Justice has the decisive vote in closely-divided cases. Although each vote in a 5–4 majority is of equal importance to the outcome, the final vote cast gains a trump-card status by virtue of its conclusive effect.

Perhaps more important than casting the last vote is the Chief Justice's power (when he is in the majority) to decide who will write the majority opinion in the case. If the Chief Justice wants to state the rule of law applicable to the case in terms consistent with his own policy preferences, he may write the opinion himself. Or he may assign it to another justice of like views. In some cases in which the outcome has been decided before the Chief Justice's turn to vote, he may decide to vote with the majority even if he does not wholly agree with them. This gives him control over the writing of the opinion and thus prevents the dissemination of an extreme statement that he would oppose.

Writing the Majority Opinion

The writing of the majority opinion is a crucial stage of the Court's work. Through this opinion, other political activists and the public will learn of the Court's position and its reasoning, and a new bit of substance will be added to the body of law and precedent that supposedly guides or controls behavior in the nation. The scope and nature of the rule laid down by the Court in an opinion is normally more important than who wins or loses the case itself. The opinion exercises the justices' broad discretion as to whether their decision will be grounded in a new, perhaps drastic, interpretation of the Constitution, or in a narrow interpretation of a statute or a minor omission by one of the figures in the case. Further, the author of the opinion can write it in such a way that the reasoning behind the decision appears to apply to many similar or analogous situations. Or he can confine it so sharply that no other cases or behavior need ever be affected.

The justice who is chosen to write the opinion in a crucial case thus acquires substantial influence within the Court, at least in that subject area. (He also achieves public and professional visibility and the satisfaction of the judicial ego, a fact that gives the politically astute Chief Justice a kind of patronage to bestow on associate justices who vote with him.) There are limits to this power, of course. If an opinion writer seriously misrepresents the views of the other justices who voted with the majority, any one or more of them may decline to join in the opinion. In some cases, this may mean the loss of the necessary vote(s) to make up a majority. Drafts of the opinions are circulated within the Court for comments by the other justices, and the process of negotiation and compromise over the wording may take weeks. In some instances, the majority-uniting solution is an opinion in which conflicting or ambiguous positions are taken—in effect, postponing precise formulation of new rules of law to some future time or other institution.

The Chief Justice has some other powers, mostly of a housekeeping nature, which he can use to make the daily routines of the other justices relatively more pleasant. He also serves as head of various bodies having administrative responsibilities over the lower federal courts, thus giving him opportunity to influence the opinions of lower federal court judges in a number of issue areas. Within the Supreme Court, however, he must rely for further influence on the personal support and regard he generates from the other justices.

The only other institutional positions of importance within the Court derive from seniority relationships among the associate justices. When the Chief Justice votes with the minority in a case, the senior associate justice in the majority chooses the writer of the opinion. The justice with the longest tenure on the Court may acquire some added prestige, particularly because he is most likely to select opinion-writers when the Chief Justice votes in the minority, but he rises above his fellows only slightly by virtue of such prerogatives.

Influence of the Justices

This analysis is not intended to suggest that the other Supreme Court justices are without means of developing significant influence as individuals. Instead, we stress that power within the nine-member Supreme Court is very much the product of individual reputation, effort, personality, and style. There are many ways in which justices can maximize their influence. By developing expertise in difficult subject areas, for example, or earning a reputation for hard and effective work on the Court, a justice may end up writing far more than his share of opinions. Or by joining with other justices through pre-conference "caucuses" or simple logrolling, a justice may help form coalitions that establish Court policy positions of great significance. Four votes are required to select a case to be heard on appeal, for example. Justices convinced that particular aspects of existing law should be changed may simply vote to hear any cases raising such issues, regardless of the Chief Justice's suggestions. The history of the Court's decisions shows that justices have frequently coalesced to form blocs for or against certain national policy developments. During some such periods, one or two "independent" justices have shifted back and forth between the blocs, casting the deciding votes first on one side and then the other.

Extra-Court prestige, such as intimacy with a President, may contribute to a justice's capacity to exercise influence on the Court. More often, his real power depends on the persuasiveness with which he argues cases among his fellows and the personal esteem in which they hold him. If he is almost always accurate, incisive, and un-abrasive in intellectual discourse; if he is tolerant of the views and mistakes of others; if he is able to combine policy disagreement with personal friendship; and if he understands what is possible and practical for the Court and does not seek decisions that are inconsistent with the underlying nature of the system, he may become highly influential. In short, the Court places a premium on an accepted political style in much the same way as do the two houses of Congress. Though here it is much influenced by the language and techniques of legal scholarship, it is as well formed and as institutionally defensive as elsewhere in government. The maverick who challenges the long-established operating procedures of the Court, who fails to do his share of the work, or who advocates actions that are "far out" in the eyes of his fellows is not likely to be effective.

Because of the relatively small number of men who have served as Chief Justice, or even as justices of the Supreme Court, it is difficult to generalize about the types of men and political preferences that have been dominant. All of the justices have had legal training, and most have been either prominent in the law or in political life. The President consistently nominates men likely to follow his policy preferences, and senators just as consistently resist confirmation when a nominee holds views contrary to their preferences. Republican Presidents tend to nominate men from the ranks of the federal or state judiciary or from large private law firms, while Democrats are more likely to nominate from political life, such as the Congress or the Cabinet. Presidents have occasionally guessed wrong about a nominee's probable actions on the Court, or have paid political debts instead of seeking policy support. Eisenhower's nomination of former Chief Justice Warren and Kennedy's appointment of Justice Byron White are only the latest in a series of such examples. But by and large, the best cues to the political preferences of the Chief Justice and the other members of the Court are the goals of the Presidents who appointed them. Since Roosevelt appointees gained full control of the Court in 1941, it has been generally liberal, with the exception of a short period of Truman-appointee dominance in the late 1940s and early 1950s. The character of several Nixon Administration appointees and the prospect of more to come, however, suggests that the next decades will see a much more conservative Court.

The Federal and State Court Systems

One of the most conspicuous illustrations of American federalism is the dual court system. The national and state governments each maintain distinct and complete court systems with separate jurisdictions and powers. Both are hierarchically organized, i.e., trial courts are superseded by a series of appeals courts rising to a single authoritative highest court. Each set of courts has both civil and criminal jurisdictions—that is, they hear and decide cases involving disputes between private persons, corporations, and governments *and* prosecutions brought by governments against those who are alleged to have violated criminal statutes.

The Federal System

The federal court system consists of 89 District Courts, at least one in each state. These are the trial courts of the federal system, and they hear both civil and criminal cases. The kind of civil cases that are brought to such courts involve federal laws, such as antitrust issues, or suits between citizens of different states. The criminal cases in their jurisdiction involve violation of federal statutes, in which the federal government is the prosecutor, such as income tax fraud or transporting narcotics across state lines. A single judge presides in such District Court trials, although many judges are normally assigned to each District to keep up with the volume of business. Juries are a regular feature of such trials only in criminal cases. In roughly two-thirds of all civil trials the litigants waive their rights to jury trials, while only one-third of criminal defendants do so.

The federal government also has several specialized trial courts to hear income tax questions, claims against the federal government, and customs or patent cases. For certain constitutional issues involving state or federal statutes, three judges are convened to form another special kind of court. This procedure is designed to speed the hearing of important constitutional questions, and direct routes of appeal to the United States Supreme Court are available after their decisions.

Above the District and specialized courts in the federal system are the federal Courts of Appeal. Eleven such courts exist in the country, each in a separate geographic "circuit," from which trial-court cases may be appealed to them by losing litigants. Not all issues may be re-examined at this level; only matters of law, that have been specifi-cally raised at the trial-court level may be raised on appeal. This means, for example, that a question of fact (whether the defendant performed a particular act or not), once decided by a jury, is forever conclusive except under very special circumstances. The kinds of questions that can be raised involve such issues as whether the judge correctly instructed the jury as to the applicable law in the case, whether certain evidence was or was not lawfully admitted into the case, and so on. No new evidence may be presented on appeal, nor does an appellate court listen to any of the parties to the case. It may not even hear their attorneys, but may limit itself instead to reading the "briefs" they are required to file on the disputed points of law.

The highest federal court is, of course, the United States Supreme Court. It exercises supervisory authority over all federal courts, seek-ing to standardize their actions and procedures across the country. It also hears appeals from losing litigants in the Courts of Appeals. It should be obvious that several screening procedures operate to make it unlikely that any given case will ever reach the Supreme Court. First, only losing litigants can appeal, and then only on points of law that they have explicitly raised at the trial-court level. Second, it is a very costly process to appeal, because skilled attorneys must be re-tained and expensive briefs prepared; only wealthy or broadly supported litigants can normally afford to carry an appeal to the Supreme Court. Finally, as we have already noted, the Supreme Court does not have to hear every case that is appealed to it. It uses its right to choose the cases it will consider to select those involving serious constitutional questions or interpretation of key sections of federal statutes or of the powers or procedures of federal administrative bodies, or those in which two federal Courts of Appeal have ruled differently on the same issue.

The State Systems

Each state's court system has certain distinctive features; very few are alike. In general, however, they parallel the federal system. At the trial-court level, states tend to maintain a great variety of courts with varying names. In some cases, local magistrates or Justice of the Peace Courts handle minor matters such as traffic offenses. Another set of trial courts hears more serious matters, such as felony cases (violations of the criminal laws involving possible jail sentences of more than a year). In some states, civil and criminal courts are combined, as in the federal system; in most states there are separate courts and judges for the two types of cases. Specialized courts for such matters as domestic relations also exist in many states.

Only 22 states have intermediate appellate courts similar to the federal Courts of Appeal. In the majority of cases, appeals from the major trial courts go directly to the state's highest court. Generally, the criteria for the right to appeal are the same as in the federal court system, i.e., only losing litigants can appeal and only on matters of law that they raised at the trial-court level. Each state's highest court fully controls all matters of state law, just as the U.S. Supreme Court does in the federal system. In other words, once the highest court of the state has declared the proper interpretation of a state statute, no other court (including the U.S. Supreme Court) can modify that interpretation. The judgments of such courts are therefore *final,* and all matters of state law are solely determined within the legal system of that state. As a result, the laws and practices of the 50 states vary greatly; matters that are crimes in some are not in others, and the rights of defendants or others may differ greatly also.

If a question of federal law or a constitutional issue is raised in a state case, however, there is a possibility of an ultimate appeal to the U.S. Supreme Court. In these areas only, the U.S. Supreme Court is superior to the highest courts of the states. This is because there must be a single authority to interpret the meaning of federal laws and the Constitution. Once again, however, the Supreme Court decides whether the constitutional or other federal question raised in a case appealed to it is important enough for it to hear. If it does decide to hear the case, it only considers federal questions. Of course, state statutes or practices may be alleged to be contrary to the Constitution; if the Court agrees and declares them void, there is considerable opportunity for conflict between the Court and the state or states involved.

Other Elements of the Judicial Systems

The dual court systems are not the only elements in the United States' judicial systems. The judicial process encompasses not only judges but also lawyers, prosecutorial staffs, police, the organized bar, and segments of the general public. We shall look briefly at who such people are and what they do, with reference to two major functions of the legal system, establishing and maintaining an open and fair political process and maintaining social control through the application of criminal sanctions.

The essence of an open and fair political process, as it is understood in the United States, is the protection of citizens' political rights. The underlying principle is that people should have the right to attempt to convince others of the correctness of their views and thus seek to become a majority—and that their rights to vote and have their votes counted fairly are a part of that process. Of course, the social order also seeks to defend itself against efforts on the part of some to destroy it. At times, the guardians of the established order perceive greater threats than actually exist, or fear that existing threats may become too great to cope with, and thus there are recurring temptations (or actual efforts) to prevent unorthodox political ideas from being heard. This is the point at which the legal system comes into play.

The Bill of Rights

Citizens' basic political rights are set forth in the first ten amendments to the Constitution, known as the Bill of Rights, and particularly in the first six. They provide that the United States government shall not do certain things. In particular, it "shall make no law . . . abridging the freedom of speech, or of the press; or the right of the people peaceably to assemble, and to petition the Government for a redress of grievances." This sounds absolute—it seems to say that there can be no law abridging the freedom of speech, and thus no instance in which government could legally prevent speech of any kind. But, in a series of decisions from the early days to the present, the Supreme Court has interpreted the First Amendment's reference to "the freedom of speech" to guarantee only the particular limited form of freedom of speech protected by law in 1789 when the Amendment was adopted. Thus, the Congress is free to adopt such limitations as it sees fit, provided they meet the Court's standards of reasonableness—which the Court derives from its view of the proper combination of eighteenth-century precedent and current circumstances and necessities. In practice, the Court has only once in its history declared void a Congressional statute on the grounds that it violated the First Amendment.

Notice that these political rights exist only as limitations upon the United States government. In other words, they do not protect citizens against each other's actions. If a gang of hoodlums prevents a person from speaking in a private auditorium, for example, no constitutional rights have been violated; the crimes of assault or trespass may have been committed, but the Constitution provides guarantees only against the acts of government. As originally written, the Constitution did not provide these protections against state governments either. In an early case, the Court held that citizens must look to their state constitutions for such protections. In the 1920s, the Supreme Court decided that at least some of these guarantees *do* apply to the states, and since that time it has in a series of decisions added one after another of the guarantees of the Bill of Rights to the list of individual rights that are protected against state action. The Court did so on its own initiative, holding that the Fourteenth Amendment's provision that the states not deny their citizens "due process of law" made the guarantees of the Bill of Rights applicable to the states. Not all of them are thus applicable, the Court has held, but only those that the Court deems fundamental to the concept of due process.

In practice, the protection of the political rights presents serious problems for many elements of the judicial process. The Supreme Court has declared that speech is to be protected up until the time it presents a "clear and present danger of bringing about an act which government has a right to prevent." This means that if armed insurrection or rioting is about to break out, policemen may legally restrain a speaker and/or the speaker may be prosecuted for such

---

... the character of every act depends upon the circumstances in which it is done.... The most stringent protection of free speech would not protect a man in falsely shouting fire in a theater and causing a panic.... The question in every case is whether the words used are used in such circumstances and are of such a nature as to create a clear and present danger that they will bring about the substantive evils that Congress has a right to prevent. It is a question of proximity and degree....

Justice Oliver Wendell Holmes, in *Schenck* v. *United States* (1919).

---

words and/or action. The principle is that no one should be prevented from speaking or publishing something, no matter how unpopular it might be, but that he or she must bear responsibility for such acts afterwards, such as in suits for libel or slander.

But afterwards may be too late, from the perspectives of both governments and dissenters. Police may unreasonably foresee riots resulting from provocative speeches; licensing authorities may fear that granting a parade permit will make demonstrators vulnerable to attack by a hostile crowd, and either or both may act to prevent speech or assembly. Those who seek to exercise their rights in such circumstances must find an attorney willing to suffer public disapproval for representing their cause, and must try to convince the courts to order the authorities to permit them their rights. Local judges do not willingly expose themselves to popular disapproval either, and so appeals to higher courts may be necessary. By the time all these procedures are concluded, of course, the occasion for exercising one's political rights may be long past. Thus, important discretion remains with the lower elements of the judicial system. The reality of an open political process is a matter not just for the Supreme Court, but also for multiple decisions on the part of local authorities who are often subject to popular pressures—and perhaps only too willing to support or help generate such pressures themselves.

Criminal Sanctions and Social Control

The criminal sanctions system also presents continuing opportunities for social control on the part of various elements in the judicial system. This is particularly important because the criminal laws and the entire criminal justice system are, at least to some extent, extensions or enforcement of the inequalities and injustices of the larger society. Let us grant immediately that any society must have some means of restraining people who wantonly assault or endanger others. But from that point forward, the values and characteristics of the society shape the nature of its approach to restraint. What acts are to be defined as crimes? If it is "legal" to charge 20 percent interest rates for necessities of life, why should it be "criminal" to keep such goods after missing an installment payment? What shall be done to those

who break such rules—should they be helped in any of several possible ways, or should the society exact retribution by killing, confining, or otherwise punishing them? In every case, judgments are made consistent with the values of those who are favored by the existing system, and those who are not favored are limited (or perhaps, in their eyes, exploited) by the provisions of the criminal laws.

Thus, the enforcers of these laws may come to be viewed as the agents of a repressive or exploitative system. Where it also appears that they enjoy broad discretion, serious tensions may result. This is particularly true in the case of minorities, who are likely to feel the restraints of criminal laws far out of proportion to their numbers or to the actual incidence of violation of such laws. As Table 11-1 shows, most large-city police forces are quite disproportionately made up of members of the dominant society. In no major city does the proportion of nonwhite policemen approach the nonwhite proportion of the population. It is not surprising, therefore, that in some cities the police are looked upon as an occupying army by ghetto residents.

The problems inherent in the process of criminal sanctions are exacerbated by conflict within the dominant society itself over the proper approach to enforcement of the criminal laws. One authority puts the issue in this illuminating fashion: there are two contrasting "models" of criminal sanctions. Some people view the process from the perspective of due process. They emphasize the rights of defendants and the social importance of fairness and legality in the arrest and questioning of accused persons, decisions regarding whether to prosecute, conviction rates, sentencing, and types of prison treatment. Others view the problem as one of controlling crime. They emphasize freeing the police to do whatever is necessary to prevent crimes and to punish those reasonably thought to be guilty, and stress protecting society against possible second offenses by criminals. Because there is continuing disagreement over which of these views is to predominate, police, prosecutors, and sentencing authorities vary even more widely in the exercise of their discretionary choices. The result is, understandably, still greater perceptions of arbitrariness on the part of certain sectors of the population.

The social-control function of the criminal process, and the disagreements about the proper way to conceive of the process, combine to make criminal "justice" almost a nightmare of variability and perceived injustice. We should first be clear about the incidence and character of crime in the United States. As Table 11-2 shows, most "crimes against the person" occur among the lower classes and minorities. Crimes against property are also numerous at this level, although the possession of property—that is, wealth—does serve as a spur to such crimes. But there is clearly not a wave of crime by the lower classes and minorities exclusively against the white middle class; instead, it is the lower classes who suffer the greatest incidence of crime, and whom effective crime prevention might benefit the most. And yet, if patterns of conviction and sentencing and the makeup of the prison population are any measure, it is minorities, particularly blacks, who feel the brunt of the criminal system. And it is the mid-

TABLE 11-1
Percent Nonwhite Police and Percent Nonwhite Population
of Some Major Cities

Name of Department	Percent of City's Nonwhite Population	Percent of Nonwhite Police
Atlanta, Ga.	38	10
Baltimore, Md.	41	7
Boston, Mass	11	2
Buffalo, N.Y.	18	3
Chicago, Ill.	27	17
Cincinnati, Ohio	28	6
Cleveland, Ohio	34	7
Dayton, Ohio	26	4
Detroit, Mich.	39	5
Hartford, Conn.	20	11
Kansas City, Mo.	20	6
Louisville, Ky.	21	6
Memphis, Tenn.	38	5
Michigan State Police	9	*
New Haven, Conn.	19	7
New Orleans, La.	41	4
New York, N.Y.	16	5
New Jersey State Police	9	*
Newark, N.J.	40	10
Oakland, Calif.	31	4
Oklahoma City, Okla.	15	4
Philadelphia, Pa.	29	20
Phoenix, Ariz.	8	1
Pittsburgh, Pa.	19	7
St. Louis, Mo.	37	11
San Francisco, Calif.	14	6
Tampa, Fla.	17	3
Washington, D.C.	63	21

*Less than one-half of 1 percent.
Source: Report of the National Advisory Commission on Civil Disorders (1968), p. 321.

dle class that provides most of the political support for tougher administration of the criminal system.

The points of discretion within this system are already obvious. Police must decide whether or not to arrest, and how to conduct questioning. Their status and opportunities for promotion may depend on their records in these respects. Prosecutors must decide whether to bring charges, offer to accept pleas of guilty to lesser offenses in exchange for evidence, carry cases to trial and in what manner, and so on. Often, prosecutors are elected; headlines bring opportunities for reelection or advancement to higher office. Defendants' attorneys must select their cases in part according to whether they think they can win (in order to maintain good records) and whether they can reasonably expect to get paid. The public defender has a large volume of cases, and can be expected to give only minimal time to each one. Judges vary in their understanding of issues, facts, and law, and in their propensity to convict as well as their sentencing behavior. In all of these cases, the biases and assumptions of these elements of the judicial process create patterns in the exercise of discretion. But, of course, the patterns are different for different people, even within the same court district. And so variability multiplies, and with it tension and resentment.

Conclusions: The Elite Orientation of the Law

This chapter implies that elites derive particular advantages from the role of law, perhaps more so in this society than in others. The reasons for this include the makeup and backgrounds of those who apply the law, the unequal availability of access to legal services, and certain structural characteristics of the law itself exaggerated by the American emphasis on legalism as a political value. In the courts as well, a number of factors assure that elite interests will be accorded great weight in decisionmaking. The nation's judges and lawyers are drawn disproportionately from the prosperous and high-status groups in the population. Law school education, like public education generally, consists in part at least of the inculcation of elitist values. Accused persons with money and social status are far more likely than those without these advantages to benefit from competent legal advice and defense. Finally, the elaborate legal code and the established processes for interpreting and enforcing it work in the interests of the advantaged. Each of these points needs to be considered more fully.

The last of these factors is both more subtle and more potent than the others, and it underlies and bolsters them. Americans have always been proud to say that we have "a government of laws, not men." That belief stems from our development of an elaborate code of legal rules that are relied upon to settle conflicts and to determine guilt or innocence, with a theoretical minimum of human arbitrariness and a maximum of impersonal "equality before the law." Justice is portrayed as blind: blind, it is alleged, to differences among litigants in income, color, race, education, social position, and so on.

In a crucial sense, this very blindness to real differences means that the legal code repeatedly offers justifications for dealing harshly with the disadvantaged and leniently with the elite. In the trenchant words of Anatole France: "The law in its splendid impartiality prosecutes

TABLE 11-2

Victimization by Race and Income (rates per 100,000 population)*

	White			
Offenses	$0-$2,999	$3,000-$5,999	$6,000-$9,999	Above $10,000
Total	2,124	2,267	1,685	2,170
Homicide	0	0	0	0
Forcible Rape	58	46	0	17
Robbery	116	91	42	34
Aggravated Assault	146	289	147	220
Burglary	1,310	958	764	763
Larceny ($50+)	378	700	565	916
Auto Theft	116	183	167	220

	Nonwhite		
Offenses	$0-$2,999	$3,000-$5,999	$6,000+
Total	2,894	2,581	3,387
Homicide	56	0	0
Forcible Rape	111	60	121
Robbery	278	240	121
Aggravated Assault	389	420	121
Burglary	1,336	1,261	2,056
Larceny ($50+)	501	300	363
Auto Theft	223	300	605

*Rate per 100,000 population of each specific race and income group.
Source: 1965 Survey by the National Opinion Research Center for the President's Commission on Law Enforcement and Administration of Justice.
Reprinted from U.S. Department of Health, Education, and Welfare, *Toward A Social Report* (Washington: U.S. Government Printing Office, 1969), p. 59.

both the rich and the poor for stealing a loaf of bread or sleeping under bridges." In an essay that has had a wide influence on contemporary social science, the German sociologist Max Weber analyzed the phenomenon more precisely, if less pointedly, than Anatole France's epigram does. He suggested that any system of justice depending upon formal legal definitions and classifications and upon precedent becomes a ready instrument for "rationalizing" the interests of the elite—that is, for finding acceptable reasons to serve the interests of the elite. This is the case because the judges' attention is turned away from the concrete situation and problems of the litigants and their ethical implications and toward unclear, formal categories that can be used to justify any action and are likely to be used in practice to justify the judge's predispositions and prejudices. The man who steals a loaf of bread to feed his hungry family is fitted into a formal, abstract classification—larceny. And the legal code prescribes penalties for larceny, not for a particular person driven to desperate action by his desperate situation. Law makes the concrete abstract and thereby justifies overlooking concrete differences. Weber therefore concludes that "The propertyless masses especially are not served by a formal 'equality before the law' . . . ."[4]

Access to Legal Aid for the Poor

The high cost of legal protection and its unequal availability is another potent factor in fostering the influence of elites in judicial policymaking. The fact that it is largely the fairly affluent and the corporations that employ legal talent reinforces the tendency for lawyers to shape legal codes into rationalizations of elite interests. It is very likely, however, that the sheer inability of a large proportion of the population to buy legal counsel and assistance is an even more telling fact. Many of the individuals charged with crime confess on the spot or in the police station without a lawyer's advice; and this has remained true even since the *Miranda v. Arizona* decision requiring that an accused be advised of his legal rights and his right to counsel.

The unequal availability of legal talent is also a central factor in the formulation of broader public policy. Corporations often provide legislative committees with drafts of proposed bills whose passage would be advantageous to them. An early draft of the Taft-Hartley Act, for example, was prepared by lawyers employed by the National Association of Manufacturers. In the formulation of administrative policies of direct concern to consumers and to businessmen, corpora-

[4]H. H. Gerth and C. Wright Mills, eds., *From Max Weber: Essays in Sociology* (New York: Oxford University Press, 1958), p. 221.

tions also enjoy an advantage. A government agency representing the interests of consumers can typically hire too few attorneys, and those are poorly paid and inexperienced compared to the lawyers representing a large corporation charged with violating a proconsumer law. In three antitrust cases on which one study reports, the lawyers representing the Antitrust Division of the Department of Justice were outnumbered by lawyers for the defendants 5–30, 10–50, and 5–103 respectively. Counsel for the defense receive salaries that may be 10 times as high as those of the government lawyers; and turnover among lawyers for government agencies is typically high.[5] Partly because salaries are low, law school graduates often see jobs in government agencies as ideal training grounds for subsequent lucrative employment by the companies the agencies are supposed to regulate. This expectation in itself may condition the behavior of counsel.

The value systems of all societies support obedience to constituted authorities, but the American emphasis on the character and role of the law seems distinctive. American thinkers have assiduously developed the notion that solutions to problems are to be found within the body of the law, perhaps partly to impose some distance between elites and masses. The unstated assertion behind such a notion is that the quality of being "law" somehow raises a statute or regulation above its original status as the mere expression of the preferences and interests of those who happened to be successful in shaping its ultimate form. When aggrieved, the average American is likely to say, "There ought to be a law . . . ." And when he seeks goals through the political process, his opponents or his leaders are likely to explain that the law requires that he conform to a particular standard, or that he must obey "because it is the law." In both cases moral imperatives have been inserted into the concept of law, suggesting that once value preferences have been written into statute they acquire some exalted status and must now be obeyed without regard to their specific content or the justice of their provisions. Some individuals who are more powerful than others exercise their values and create a statute to their liking; other individuals, also winners in the game of powerseeking, interpret these statutes as their value preferences suggest. In what respect then does it make sense to say that "this is a government of laws *and not of men?*" Clearly, only in the sense that the speaker believes (or wishes his audience to believe) that law is not applied arbitrarily in this system, and that certain standards of fairness and consideration for others may be anticipated. These are empirical (factual) questions, however, on which we might gather data and reach conclusions. But as a preliminary, we must free ourselves of the notion that there is some mystical validity to whatever

[5]Clair Wilcox, *Public Policies Toward Business* (Homewood, Ill.: Richard D. Irwin, 1960), p. 103.

majority or elite preferences find their way into the words of a statute, court decision, or regulation.

Preserving the Status Quo

The effects of the generally accepted assumptions about the sanctity and importance of the law are many. For one thing, they operate to shift consideration of the merits of issues to specialized arenas and persons. If a statute, once enacted, acquires special status and must not be questioned, then the only occasion for real choicemaking in regard to its content occurs in the late stages of its drafting, amendment, and passage in the legislature. In some cases, courts make critical choices in the process of affixing an authoritative interpretation upon the statute. In both cases, lawyers—those with special skills in the drafting and interpretation of legal words and phrases—will exercise considerable influence over the exact provisions and precise applications of the statute. The precedent-oriented training and cautious background lawyers bring to their tasks operate to limit the change (in any direction) from the *status quo* that can be made through a statute or decision. In neither case will the matter be thrown open for broad public consideration of the value choices or questions of priority involved. Thus, expertise is needed by a society that transacts its public business through the provisions of statutes and regulations, and the particular group with the greatest claim to such expertise—lawyers—becomes in effect the brokers of public policy. Issues are issues insofar as they can be phrased as such, and only decisions that can be articulated by the traditional language of the law can be made by the polity. Instead of a public consideration of preferences and goals for present or future, there can be only a technical and professional dialogue on the precise manner in which things are to be done. To an extent, a politics of means gains precedence over a potential politics of ends.

Uncritical adherence to the provisions of the law in regard to the procedures of politics has the further effect of institutionalizing the *status quo*. Every set of rules must be based on certain premises about the right way to do things in politics, and when those rules acquire independent validity as "the law," other kinds of political behavior are foreclosed. But no rules can be neutral: they either support or prevent interference with a present order of things, a present distribution of power and influence within the society. They set limits within which change must take place, and tip the scales on behalf of those who under the existing rules are most successful and most powerful.

Let us take an example, admittedly oversimplified, from outside the American context, where its implications may be more immediately visible. The substance of "international law" was created and developed mostly in Western Europe and the United States. It reached its fullest flower in the late nineteenth and early twentieth centuries when the Western countries were not only dominant internationally but also colonizers of most of the rest of the world. International law recognized the power of nations to expropriate the property or investments of foreign nationals within their boundaries, but provided that such action required compensation at full value to the original owners. This means that a former colony that gained its independence would not be able to take over the mines, plantations, or oil wells that foreign corporations had developed within it unless it was prepared to pay them full value for their holdings. A country with few other resources and a low standard of living would probably be unable to do so, and would be faced with the prospect of watching foreign investors extract its mineral resources and reap great profits from their sale, while its own people bordered on starvation.

Believing that the colonizing countries had exploited their resources in order to build up their own economics, many newly independent former colonies considered themselves justified in acquiring such properties anyway. They either refused to pay any compensation at all or offered token payments over extended periods of time and in their own currency, terms that investors were not likely to find satisfactory. To them, the "international law" that required payment for what was originally and in their eyes rightfully their own property was merely a convenient construct of colonial profiteers, never consented to by them, and therefore not binding upon them. To some Americans, however, it was an illegal and unconscionable interference with property rights, deserving of reprisal in any feasible manner. The point is that the fairness and justice of a procedure established by law depends on the perspective from which it is viewed, and however neutral it may appear to some, it may quite reasonably appear to others to preserve and protect an unjust *status quo.*

Laws limiting dissent, controlling elections, regulating police powers, or prescribing the manner of student participation in universities all may carry the same implications, at least in the eyes of some beholders. Reflecting elite satisfaction with the *status quo,* they provide channels for action and attempted change that are basically consistent with that *status quo,* and outlaw actions seriously at odds with it. In other words, they establish a range of results that are tolerable to the dominant interests and that can be achieved by action in conformance with the rules. Adherence to those rules can mean aquiescence in that limited range of potential results. Those who seek other results, of course, must decide whether to change their goals or to seek them outside of, and probably in violation of, the existing rules. This is the point at which uncritical devotion to "the law" as an abstract entity, divorced from its specific provisions or consideration of whose ends it serves, becomes so important to the nature of American politics. Law and procedural regularity are an effective aid to social control—perhaps a necessary one, depending on one's perspective and whether or not one feels represented by the currently dominant groups. But it is not an aid to clear thinking about the real nature of politics in the United States.

Chapter 12

As any newspaper reader quickly learns, the two houses of Congress do not make up a single-minded, homogeneous policy-making instrument. Each is responsive to a distinctive set of external pressures, each has its own rules and procedures, and each has evolved a unique internal distribution of power. At the same time, the power of the United States government (in the sense of the capacity to act on a matter) is spread broadly among these and the other major institutions. Little coherent governmental action can emerge without some form of affirmative co-operation among most or all of them. Thus, what *does* emerge must succeed in winning the support of, or at least neutralizing the opposition of, the interests that are dominant in each institution.

Congress

But this is only the beginning. The interests and priorities that shape governmental policies are far from representative even of the distinctive constituencies represented in each institution. Instead they reflect, first, the special internal distribution of power created by the nature, rules, and procedures of the institution; and, second, the preferences of the people who hold key positions of power. Further, these men and women use the power of strategic positions in accordance with tradition and political necessity. They identify with the institution through which they wield their power, and seek to represent that institution in transactions with similar power centers in other institutions. They also recognize the investment they share with other governmental powerholders in maintaining the political structures that support them. What results is a style of mutual accommodation and bargaining among the various institutional power centers in which both self- and mutual preservation play an important part.

In this chapter, we shall analyze first the House and then the Senate in terms of their personnel and internal power distribution.

Then we shall summarize the high points of the legislative process and assess the role of the Congress among the policy-making institutions of American government.

The House of Representatives

There are 435 members of the House of Representatives. This fact, straight from sixth-grade civics, has profound significance for the distribution of power and operating procedures within the House. The 435 representatives face a bewildering array of complex problems, a vast national budget, and a sprawling federal bureaucracy. Few of them come to Congress with any special expertise or experience that would enable them to cope effectively with such problems. Their time to acquire such knowledge is limited, both by the demands of service to their constituents and by the imminence of the next election. What little staff they have must devote most of its time to mail, errands, and, again, the forthcoming election.

Even, or perhaps particularly, for representatives with the sincerest intentions of translating constituents' wishes into governmental action, the task is extremely difficult, if not impossible. They must develop two types of capabilities: a subject-area expertise in order to know what should be done, and an administrative sophistication enabling them to recognize whether or not executive-branch employees are acting (and spending authorized funds) to carry out congressional policies in the manner prescribed. In both areas, they can act as independent policymakers only if they are able to acquire knowledge on their own, not if their knowledge depends upon inevitably self-serving voluntary disclosures by the executive branch or private power centers.

For all these reasons, they have little choice but to divide their governmental responsibilities among individuals or committees formed out of the House membership. Through specialization, at least some of the members will have a chance to develop the expertise and managerial capacity to make independent policymaking possible. Presumably, members will exercise such capabilities in accordance with the will of the majority of the House. But when there is a division of labor, a stratification of power results. Special knowledge or responsibility in a subject area gives the possessor the tools and prestige to cause others to go along with his views. Formation of a task group implies leadership within it, and the chairman of a committee may come to exercise disproportionate influence over its work. To a considerable extent, these are the inevitable costs of a necessary division of labor.

It is a mistake, however, to take for granted that the congressmen with the greatest knowledge of an area necessarily have the greatest influence upon policy. Values play at least as great a part as facts;

indeed, the two are not really separable. If a particular set of values or ideology dominates a committee or a house of Congress, it is likely to be a more important shaper of policy than is expertise.

Over the years, the House of Representatives has evolved a unique form of dividing its labor, such that most of its capacity to act lies in the hands of about 25 individuals occupying its key positions. Moreover, such individuals are chosen solely by virtue of their "seniority" (length of service). Although this may appear a mechanical, and therefore politically neutral, means of selection, it in fact places power in the hands of older, usually more conservative men. This is because longevity in the House depends on having a relatively "safe" electoral district. Many such districts are found in the rural South and Midwest, usually the more conservative parts of the nation. Some districts in the more liberal large cities regularly return candidates of the same political party, but the availability of alternative political careers and the volatility of city districts tend to eliminate any given representative before he reaches the higher levels of seniority.

The overall effect of this House system is to create a highly structured game. In this "game," only the oldest members actually hold power; members on the next level have invested many years in moving up the ladder and are more or less patiently awaiting the death or retirement of their elders; and the newest and youngest members are close to impotent. The House has roughly co-equal hierarchies of leadership positions, both reflecting this principle clearly. The first type of position involves leadership of committees, each of which carries responsibility for the actions of the House in a particular policy area; the major position is that of chairman, with secondary status for the ranking member of the minority party. The second type is leadership in the management of the House itself; these positions include the Speaker of the House, the majority and minority leaders (and their "whips," or assistants), and the Rules Committee. Let us briefly examine the powers of these offices and the characteristics of their occupants.

Policy Area Committees

There are 20 standing committees in the House, ranging in importance and prestige from Civil Service and Post Office to Armed Services, Ways and Means, and Appropriations. Most committees have 20-25 members (Appropriations has 50), appointed from each party roughly according to the partisan ratio then prevailing in the House. Each representative usually serves on two committees. Although he naturally seeks assignment to a committee whose work will be of concern to his district, he has no means of appeal from the decision

OUTSIDE BUSINESS AND
PROFESSIONAL INTERESTS, HOUSE MEMBERS, 1971

Nature of Interest	Number of Members	Notes
Stock and/or income, banks and other financial institutions	101	7 of these members are on House Banking & Currency Committee, 6 on Ways & Means Committee.
Income of more than $1,000 from outside law practices	66	
Honoraria of more than $300	145	Highest earners: Rep. Dellums (D-Cal.), $20,675; Rep. Chisholm (D-N.Y.), $14,300; Rep. Abzug (D-N.Y.), $11,975; Rep. McCloskey (R-Cal.), $10,900.
Stock in one or more companies among top 100 defense contractors	59	
Stock in and/or income from oil and gas companies	44	
Capital gains of more than $5,000 from a single transaction (not sale of residence)	54	In most cases, these were single transactions, usually sales of stock or real estate.
Financial interest in radio or TV stations	20	
Financial interest in power and light companies	25	

Source: *Congressional Quarterly,* 17 June, 1972, pp. 1382–1386.

of the party leadership. With seniority, however, he may move to a more prestigious committee when openings arise. It is no coincidence that the two most prestigious policy area committees in the House are those dealing with money matters—Ways and Means with tax bills (including separately financed social welfare legislation such as Social Security and Medicare) and Appropriations with expenditures. Raising and spending money is absolutely crucial to the operation of the government; it is the area in which the Congress wields its greatest influence over policy and the surest route to maximum influence for any individual representative.

The chairman of each committee decides when and if the committee shall meet, sets the agenda, and controls all hearings and executive sessions. From the perhaps hundreds of bills submitted to his committee each year, he chooses which, if any, will be considered by the full committee. He can shape the list of witnesses at public hearings, control the detailed drafting of the legislation in executive sessions, manage the bill when it is debated on the floor of the House, and represent the House in any later negotiations with the Senate over differences in bills passed by the two houses. In all of these activities, of course, his personal preferences regarding the form and desirability of the legislation play a crucial role.

The chairman is not completely autonomous, of course. The President, or the House or party leadership, may bring pressure on him, and the members of his committee may seek to force him to act as they prefer. But the chairman has powerful defenses at his command. Neither the President nor the leadership wants to incur his opposition, for they know that the chairman can cause delay, drastic revision, or even destruction of legislation he dislikes. Nor do the members of his committee wish to lose either the opportunities to obtain special provisions in legislation that the chairman can grant them, or the public visibility that his goodwill makes possible for them. At all times, the chairman also has on his side the traditions of the House, which call for action only in accordance with duly established procedures—in this case, with the recommendations of the standing committee having jurisdiction over the subject area of the bill. The House almost never considers, and even more rarely, enacts legislation that is completely opposed by the chairman of the applicable committee. In part, this is because an alert chairman knows when to join a majority position; but even when he does so, he leaves the clear mark of his preferences on the final product.

The ranking member of the minority party on a committee gains some leverage from representing his party and mobilizing other party members on behalf of specific positions. He becomes the chairman of the committee when his party wins control of the House. Frequently, this prospect gains him a friendly *modus vivendi* with the chairman, for both men have served on the committee for a long time and know that they may be destined to rotate with each other for the rest of their political careers. Having served together for some time, the two men probably also share a strong concern for the "proper" working of the House itself, and for the efficient discharge of the responsibilities of their committee to the House. In many ways, therefore, the two positions complement each other, rather than serving as opposing correctives.

House Leadership Positions

The major leadership positions within the House itself are filled by the majority political party, usually through application of the seniority principle. The key position is that of Speaker of the House. The Speaker presides over House debates on bills, recognizing speakers he considers appropriate by pre-arrangement or preference. He shapes the House agenda, deciding which bills will receive priority. He designates the members of the "conference committees" who will represent the House in negotiations with the Senate. He controls the referral of bills to committees, sending them to friendly or unfriendly receptions in accordance with his preferences. He makes public visibility possible for, or ignores, members as he chooses. Not least, he is privy to the President's preferences and intentions regarding the legislative program for that session of Congress, and can (if he wishes) work in harmony with the President to schedule and obtain passage of desired legislation.

The majority and minority leaders within the House are party leadership positions. In both cases, seniority is a major factor, but policy views representative of the mainstream of the party are also influential in determining election by the party's caucus. The duties of these leaders, assisted by their elected "whips," are to mobilize party members behind legislative positions that the leadership has decided to be in the party's interest. Members of the House are often under pressure to support the position of the President when he is of their party or to join with other members of their party in opposition to a President of the other party. (Many measures before the House are not made matters of party discipline, of course, and in such cases members are free of all pressures to vote with the leadership.)

Another group of positions of crucial importance to the management of the business of the House is membership on the Rules Committee. These are perhaps the most coveted committee positions in the House, and are filled, predictably, with its most senior members. All proposed legislation must go through the Rules Committee en route to the floor of the House. The function of the Rules Committee is to set specific rules for debate and voting on each piece of business, in order to conserve the time and order the transactions of that unwieldy body. In practice, this means that the Rules Committee exercises an important influence over the form in which that bill will be presented and the real prospects for its passage. Particularly at the close of congressional sessions, the Rules Committee (frequently in the person of its chairman) may prevent legislation from reaching the floor. Or it may attach rules for debate and voting calculated to assure its defeat, such as permitting unlimited amendments to a tax bill that represents a number of delicate compromises. At other times, the Rules Committee may content itself with making clear to the chairman of a policy-area committee that certain provisions must not be included in prospective legislation.

Certain other powers inhere in the leadership of the two political parties in the House. Principal among these is the power to fill committee assignments by selecting among new and returning members of the House; the member who receives a coveted, prestigious assignment is likely to be one who has previously demonstrated party regularity, and he or she is expected to be properly appreciative in the future. If he is not, he may be overlooked in future assignments. Development of the expertise necessary to make the House function more effectively is rewarded equally with party loyalty, and the representative who applies himself diligently often finds that he is appointed to more and more visible and rewarding positions of responsibility within the House. The party leadership is also one of the major sources of information for ordinary members, most of whom would otherwise have no better sources than the daily newspapers. Party leaders provide knowledge about the President's plans and make arrangements for joint action by all party members in response to those intentions. No representative can be successful by himself; he must have the support of many other representatives, and the political party machinery is the most promising way to secure it. Thus, the party leadership gains an important kind of leverage within the institution.

Why do the other members acquiesce in the dominance of these two types of leadership positions? The simple answer is that, as a practical matter, there is very little they can do about it. Communication among the balance of the 435 members is very difficult, and it is inhibited by party and ideological differences. Even if they could agree on measures to redirect or unseat the leadership, the total control of the parliamentary machinery by the established leaders would make such action very complicated, requiring a degree of perception, trust, skill, and discipline not likely to exist in any large body. If they did replace the leadership, moreover, the new leaders might be even less desirable than the old ones.

A more sophisticated answer would point out that most members do not even want to extricate themselves from the web of seniority-based leadership management. A representative depends for reelection on achieving certain visibility in his home district, preferably by accomplishing some tangible benefit for his constituents. He can do so in his early terms in the House, when his need is greatest, only through the assistance of established members—such as the chairman of his committee or the party leadership. Almost before he realizes it, he has incurred debts to his senior colleagues. Further, he soon acquires a degree of seniority himself—a kind of investment in perpetuating the established "move-up" system—and he becomes socialized into the House tradition: "to get along, go along." In other words, he begins to find not only that the established procedures contain payoffs for him if he votes with his chairman and his party leadership, but that he too begins to identify with the House and the accommodating, bargaining system to which it is committed. He becomes sympathetic to the constituency problems of other members, giving higher priority to harmonious relationships between members and reduction of conflict within the House than to the solution of the great problems of national public policy.

What types of people hold the key positions in the House? Table 12-1 gives some basic data about the incumbents of major positions in the 1973–1975 House of Representatives. The mere fact that a chairman or House leader came to Congress in the 1920s and is over 70 years old does not necessarily mean that he is either conservative or out of touch with the intervening five decades of rapid changes in American society. But neither is it a reason to be encouraged about the probable responsiveness of the people's legislators.

Many congressmen are much more aware of problems in the management of the House than observers, of course. But acting to install new leadership would not only provoke drastic conflicts; it would constitute an antitraditional act. And so members wait politely for senile leaders to die or retire, seeking in the interim to cover up for their incapacities. This deep commitment to following the hallowed traditions of the House, no matter what the cost in adequate treatment of public problems, we find one of the aspects most completely characteristic of its institutional and social life. Only the most demanding emergencies can wrench members out of traditional behavior, because all of the rewards and penalties of their political lives are based on acting in accordance with that predictable standard. Their capacity to do things for their constituents, and their progress up the political ladder, depend on following tradition. Not to do so, no matter what the issue at stake, normally means severe damage to their effectiveness within the House and perhaps the end of their careers.

The Senate

The Senate has only 100 members, and it prides itself on dispensing with the many formal rules and procedures that characterize the House. In contrast to what it views as "the lower house," the Senate tries to operate with a minimum of organization and a maximum of gentlemanly agreement, in which the objection of one senator

TABLE 12-1

**Biographical Survey of Political Leaders and Committee Chairmen
of the House of Representatives, 93rd Congress (1973–1975)**

Political Leadership

Position	Name	Age (as of 1972)	Business occupation or profession	Religion	Year entered Congress	District (including type of area); percentage of vote in 1972
1. Speaker	Carl Albert	64	Lawyer	Methodist	1946	3rd Oklahoma (8 rural counties) 93.4%
2. Majority Leader	Thomas O'Neill	59	Insurance	Catholic	1953	8th Massachusetts (Cambridge-Boston) 88.7%
3. Majority Whip	John McFall	54	Lawyer	Not Available	1957	15th California (rural) unopposed
4. Minority Leader	Gerald Ford	59	Lawyer	Episcopalian	1949	5th Michigan (urban-suburban) 62.3%
5. Minority Whip	Leslie Arends	76	Banker and farmer	Methodist	1935	15th Illinois (7 rural counties) 57.2%

TABLE 12-1 (Continued)

Committee Chairmen

Position	Name	Age (as of 1972)	Business occupation or profession	Religion	Year entered Congress	District (including type of area); percentage of vote in 1972
6. Agriculture	William Robert Poage	72	Lawyer	Universalist	1937	11th Texas (11 rural counties) unopposed
7. Appropriations	George H. Mahon	71	Lawyer	Methodist	1935	19th Texas (17 rural counties) unopposed
8. Armed Services	F. Edward Hebert	71	Newspaperman	Catholic	1941	1st Louisiana (suburban New Orleans) unopposed
9. Banking and Currency	Wright Patman	68	Lawyer	Baptist	1929	1st Texas (18 rural counties) unopposed
10. District of Columbia	Charles Diggs	50	Mortician	Baptist	1955	13th Michigan (Detroit) 87.8%
11. Education and Labor	Carl D. Perkins	56	Lawyer	Baptist	1949	7th Kentucky (22 rural counties) 61.4%

TABLE 12-1 (Continued)

Position	Name	Age (as of 1972)	Business occupation or profession	Religion	Year entered Congress	District (including type of area); percentage of vote in 1972
Committee Chairmen						
12. Foreign Affairs	Thomas E. Morgan	65	Medical Doctor	Methodist	1945	22nd Pennsylvania (24 rural counties) 59.6%
13. Governmental Operations	Chet Holifield	68	Businessman	Christian Church	1943	19th California (urban Los Angeles) 67.2%
14. House Administration	L. Wayne Hays	60	Teacher of history and public speaking	Presbyterian	1949	18th Ohio (6 rural counties) 70.4%
15. Interior and Insular Affairs	James Haley	73	Businessman	Methodist	1953	8th Florida (7 rural counties) 57.6%
16. Internal Security	Richard H. Ichord	45	Lawyer	Baptist	1961	8th Missouri (15 rural counties) 60.7%
17. Interstate and Foreign Commerce	Harley O. Staggers	64	Teacher and sheriff	Methodist	1949	2nd West Virginia (20 rural counties) 68.3%

TABLE 12-1 (Continued)

Position	Name	Age (as of 1972)	Business occupation or profession	Religion	Year entered Congress	District (including type of area); percentage of vote in 1972
Committee Chairmen						
18. Judiciary	Peter Rodino	63	Lawyer and politician	Catholic	1949	10th New Jersey (urban Essex Co.) 79.4%
19. Merchant Marine and Fisheries	Leonor Sullivan	69	Businessman and banker	Catholic	1955	3rd Missouri (urban St. Louis) 69.8%
20. Post Office and Civil Service	Thaddeus J. Dulski	56	Accountant	Catholic	1959	37th New York (urban Buffalo) 71.6%
21. Public Works	A. John Blatnik	60	Teacher and administrator	Catholic	1947	8th Minnesota (11 rural counties) 76.1%
22. Rules	Ray Madden	80	Lawyer	Catholic	1943	1st Indiana (rural Lake Co.) 50.7%
23. Science and Astronautics	Olin Teague	62	Military politician	Baptist	1945	6th Texas (6 rural counties) 72.6%

TABLE 12-1 *(Continued)*

Position	Name	Age (as of 1972)	Business occupation or profession	Religion	Year entered Congress	District (including type of area); percentage of vote in 1972
Committee Chairmen						
24. Standards of Official Conduct	Charles Melvin Price	67	Journalist	Catholic	1945	23rd Illinois (urban E. St. Louis) 75.0%
25. Veterans' Affairs	William Dorn	56	Agriculture	Baptist	1947	3rd South Carolina (10 rural counties) 75.5%
26. Ways and Means	Wilbur D. Mills	62	Lawyer	Methodist	1939	2nd Arkansas (15 rural counties) unopposed
Major Appropriations Subcommittees						
27. Defense	George H. Mahon	[See No. 7]				
28. Foreign Operations	Otto E. Passman	71	Businessman	Baptist	1947	5th Louisiana (17 rural parishes) unopposed
29. Military Construction	Robert L. F. Sikes	65	Newspaper publisher	Methodist	1945	1st Florida (9 rural counties) unopposed
30. Public Works	L. Joe Evins	61	Lawyer	Church of Christ	1947	4th Tennessee (20 rural counties) 81.1%

Source: *Official Congressional Directory: 92nd Congress, 2nd Session Washington:* Government Printing Office, 1972). Updated.

can prevent or delay the transaction of crucial business. In fact, the Senate has evolved an elaborate set of rules and traditions governing the behavior of members. These standards are maintained by an institutional establishment—an informal group of usually senior senators distinguished principally by their commitment to the Senate as an institution. This group asserts authority not only over internal procedures but also on occasion over the policy positions assumed by the Senate as a body. Membership in the inner circle of the Senate is personal rather than institutionally based. Supplementing this form of leadership is a division of labor that carries many of the same benefits and costs as does that of the House of Representatives. Again, the types of positions may be divided between policy areas and Senate leadership.

Policy Area Committees

The differences between House and Senate committee structure and operation are minor, reflecting chiefly the difference in size of the respective houses. The Senate has fewer, smaller committees, with a somewhat different prestige ranking. Finance and Appropriations, which deal respectively with revenue and expenditures, are (despite the Senate's secondary role in House-initiated money matters) probably the most important committees. Foreign Relations, because of the Senate's special powers in that field, is a more visible committee and one that attracts many senators, but its impact on policy is not great. Judiciary, because of its power to confirm or reject Supreme Court nominees and the Senate's special concern for proposed constitutional amendments, is also a high-status committee. Armed Services and Agriculture follow, and the remainder are reserved for specialists and newcomers.

The formal powers of the chairman of a Senate committee are much the same as those of a House chairman, but in practice they fall short of the autocracy of the House model. Operating with smaller numbers and a more relaxed, gentlemanly ethos—perhaps aided by the relative length of their six-year terms—the Senate chairmen tend to consult more with their members, grant them more visibility and influence within the committee, and proceed on the basis of a general consensus. The chairman is clearly the leader, and no junior senator would be unaware of or dare to ignore that fact; but the operation of the committee is normally more harmonious.

The Senate's traditions of elaborate courtesy among members extend to the manner in which pressure is applied to chairmen to consider legislation, and to the relationship between the ranking minority member of a committee and its chairman. Rising to the chairmanship of a Senate committee implies not only substantial seniority, but also commitment to the Senate as an institution and to its "proper" functioning within the system. No President and no party leader would insult the dignity of the Senate by brash or blatant attempts to coerce a committee chairman. And party differences would ordinarily play a small part in the deliberations of senior members of a committee. In short, in the Senate there is at least the appearance of greater consideration of the merits of issues, and a smaller organizing role for the political party.

Senate Leadership Positions

Although the position of President Pro Tem of the Senate corresponds in form to that of Speaker of the House, it is in practice no more than an honorific title bestowed on a very senior member. The actual managerial functions performed by the Speaker in the House are in the hands of the Senate Majority Leader. This officer is elected by the senators of the majority party at the outset of each session; once chosen, of course, a senator usually retains his position as Majority Leader until he dies, retires, or is defeated for reelection. The choice is influenced, but not controlled, by the relative seniority among senators of the majority party. But more important is the reputation of a senator for commitment to the protection and furtherance of the Senate as an institution, his mainstream position within the party on major issues, his adherence to traditional rules and procedures, his sense of fair play, and his parliamentary skills. Choice of the Minority Leader by the minority party is based on similar criteria.

Both Majority and Minority Leaders serve informing, scheduling, and unifying roles for their respective parties, in effect combining the duties of Speaker, party leaders, and Rules Committee in the House. The Majority Leader coordinates the activities of Senate committees, seeking to bring bills to the floor in accordance with his view of the proper priorities for that session. He selects members of the conference committees that will negotiate differences between House and Senate versions of enacted legislation. He is the chief source of information for other senators, as well as the dispenser of public visibility, additional institutional responsibilities, or improved committee status. He consults regularly with the Minority Leader so that most of the Senate's business can proceed with the support of a broad consensus. Both Leaders are normally consulted and kept informed of major developments by the President, although matters of party strategy or program are reserved for the Leader of the President's party.

Behind the two Leaders of the Senate is the inner "establishment," or "club," of generally senior senators. This group has no precise boundaries, but some senators are clearly inside and some just as clearly outside. Membership is personal, based in part on acceptance of the Senate's traditional ways and in part on the senator's political skills and style. The senator who works hard and effectively on committees and at other tasks assigned him by the leadership, thereby contributing to the work of the Senate, is soon marked as a potential member. If he continues to show tolerance and respect for other senators, demonstrates a strong concern for the harmonious transaction of the Senate's business and the preservation of its reputation, and is not too "far out" on issues, he may be consulted more and more often about important matters of Senate policy. In time, he will be fully socialized and eventually integrated into the social grouping within which most of the major decisions of the Senate are made.

INCOME FROM SPEECHES AND WRITING OF 17 SENATORS EARNING MORE THAN $15,000 IN 1971

Humphrey (D-Minn.)	$83,451.00
Hatfield (R-Ore.)	39,338.40
McGovern (D-S.D.)	37,976.64
Dole (R-Kan.)	35,025.00
Bayh (D-Ind.)	29,575.00
Hughes (D-Iowa)	24,100.00
Packwood (R-Ore.)	23,405.76
Ribicoff (D-Conn.)	21,765.00
McGee (D-Wyo.)	21,750.00
Muskie (D-Maine)	21,600.00
Gravel (D-Alaska)	20,800.00
Tower (R-Texas)	18,000.00
Goldwater (R-Ariz.)	17,390.00
Tunney (D-Calif.)	17,166.00
Proxmire (D-Wis.)	17,085.50
Sparkman (D-Ala.)	16,500.00
Buckley (Cons-R-N.Y.)	15,683.19

Source: *Congressional Quarterly,* 17 June 1972, p. 1379.

The individual senator, whether a member of the inner group or not, is somewhat more capable of making himself felt within the institution than is a member of the House. He is no more likely to be able to redirect or unseat the leadership, nor, again, is he likely to want to try. But he can count on being able to gain the floor and address the Senate, which a representative may not be able to do.

Further, the Senate's tradition of operating on the basis of unanimous consent means that the objection of a single senator can delay or, in some cases, prevent action on matters to which one senator is opposed. The Senate's famous filibuster rule, for example, permits any senator or group of senators to talk for as long as they are physically capable, and some have held the floor in excess of twenty-four hours. Toward the close of a legislative session, a filibuster or even the threat of one by one or more senators can result in a leadership decision to abandon proposed legislation. Thus, the individual recourses of a senator are substantial, though it is questionable whether he can have any greater ultimate impact on policies than his counterpart in the House. In both cases, the leadership's grip on the machinery of the institution is very strong.

The Senate leadership during 1969-1971 is listed in Table 12-2. The key senators are roughly the same age as the key representatives, but they are distributed somewhat more broadly across the nation—and across the ideological spectrum. As a result, the Senate, though clearly the stronghold of Southern defense against civil rights legislation by virtue of the filibuster rule and Southern dominance of the Judiciary Committee, is somewhat more liberal in its basic orientation than is the House.

What do these characteristics of power distribution and incumbency mean for the overall operation of the Congress? Clearly, the individuals of power are far from representative of the national population. They are much older, probably much more conservative, and are motivated by long-established traditions that impose additional boundaries on what they can seriously consider or hope to accomplish in the way of legislation. Because such individuals are rarely challenged effectively in elections, they do not feel pressures for change within the society except as the interests and people with whom they have close contact happen to present such problems to them. Under these conditions, the Congress is normally likely to be responsive to developments in the economy or society chiefly in arbitrary, unpredictable, and conservative ways. Further, what appear to be challenges to the system itself are likely to be met with lack of understanding and severe reaction. On such matters, nearly all men and women of power are likely to be of a single mind.

A second major consequence of the existing pattern of power in the Congress is its great dependence on effective leadership. Unless the President and the party leaders within the two houses establish clear and agreed priorities, and work effectively to coordinate committee actions and floor debates, very little legislation will be produced. At best, the Congress is an institution that operates on a fits-and-starts basis; the number of powerful individuals who must be convinced of the necessity of a particular action, and the difficulty

TABLE 12-2

Biographical Survey of Political Leaders and Committee Chairmen of the Senate, 93rd Congress (1973–1975)

Position	Name	Age (as of 1972)	Business occupation or profession	Religion	Year entered Congress and/or year entered Senate	State (including population in 1970); percentage of vote in most recent election
Political Leadership						
1. Majority Leader	Michael J. Mansfield	69	Professor of history and political science	Catholic	1943 & 1953	Montana 694,000 60.5%
2. Majority Whip	Robert C. Byrd	54	Lawyer	Baptist	1952 & 1959	West Virginia 1,800,400 78%
3. Minority Leader	Hugh Scott	71	Lawyer	Episcopalian	1941 & 1959	Pennsylvania 11,794,000 51.4%
4. Minority Whip	Robert P. Griffin	48	Lawyer	Congregational Christian	1947 & 1966	Michigan 8,875,000 52.2%

TABLE 12-2 (Continued)

Position	Name	Age (as of 1972)	Business occupation or profession	Religion	Year entered Congress and/or year entered Senate	State (including population in 1970); percentage of vote in most recent election
Committee Chairmen						
5. Aeronautical and Space Sciences	Frank Moss	61	Lawyer	Latter-Day Saints	1959	Utah 1,067,810 not available
6. Agriculture and Forestry	Herman Talmadge	58	Lawyer	Baptist	1957	Georgia 4,590,000 77.5%
7. Appropriations	John McClellan	76	Lawyer	Baptist	1935 & 1943	Arkansas 1,923,000 60.9%
8. Armed Services	John Stennis	70	Lawyer & farmer	Presbyterian	1947	Mississippi 2,217,000 88.4%
9. Banking, Housing, & Urban Affairs	John J. Sparkman	72	Lawyer	Methodist	1937 & 1946	Alabama 3,444,000 63.9%

TABLE 12-2 (Continued)

Position	Name	Age (as of 1972)	Business occupation or profession	Religion	Year entered Congress and/or year entered Senate	State (including population in 1970); percentage of vote in most recent election
Committee Chairmen						
10. Commerce	Warren G. Magnuson	66	Lawyer	Lutheran	1937 & 1944	Washington 3,409,000 65%
11. District of Columbia	Thomas Eagleton	42	Lawyer	Catholic	1968	Missouri 4,677,000 51.1%
12. Finance	Russell B. Long	53	Lawyer	Methodist	1948	Louisiana 3,643,000 unopposed
13. Foreign Relations	J. William Fulbright	66	Lawyer	Disciples of Christ	1943 & 1945	Arkansas 1,923,000 59%
14. Government Operations	Sam Ervin	76	Lawyer	Presbyterian	1935 & 1943	North Carolina 5,125,000 not available
15. Interior & Insular Affairs	Henry M. Jackson	59	Lawyer	Presbyterian	1941 & 1953	Washington 3,409,000 82.4%

TABLE 12-2 (Continued)

Committee Chairmen

Position	Name	Age (as of 1972)	Business occupation or profession	Religion	Year entered Congress and/or year entered Senate	State (including population in 1970); percentage of vote in most recent election
16. Judiciary	James O. Eastland	67	Lawyer & farmer	Methodist	1943	Mississippi 2,217,000 57.9%
17. Labor & Public Welfare	A. Harrison Williams	52	Lawyer	Presbyterian	1953 & 1959	New Jersey 7,168,000 54.0%
18. Post Office and Civil Service	Gale McGee	57	Professor of history	Presbyterian	1959	Wyoming 332,000 55.8%
19. Public Works	Jennings Randolph	70	Professor & journalist	Seventh Day Baptist	1933 & 1948	West Virginia 1,744,000 66.3%
20. Rules and Administration	Howard Cannon	60	Lawyer	Latter-Day Saints	1959	Nevada 492,396 not available

Source: *Official Congressional Directory: 92nd Congress, 2nd Session* (Washington: Government Printing Office, 1972). Updated.

of persuading them, together with the multitude of public problems on which action of some kind must be taken, mean that a given subject comes before the Congress for serious consideration only once every few years. Unless the leadership does its job well, the chance for action will pass with the enactment of a half way, or patchwork measure that makes conditions worse instead of better.

Finally, the decentralization of power into the hands of a relatively few congressmen means that many veto points are created from which the positions and prerogatives of well-established groups can be defended even against the wishes of a large majority. Because it is so easy for one or two key congressmen to block legislative action, and so difficult for the leadership to mobilize support at all the necessary points in the legislative process, inaction (and advantage to those favored by the *status quo*) is a frequent result. The other likely result is legislation of the "lowest common denominator" kind—legislation that offends few, usually because it has no serious effect on the *status quo*. One may well ask, of course, whether such legislation is capable of solving problems.

The Legislative Process

Congress does not operate by itself. Its distribution of internal power and special operating characteristics are only meaningful as they are linked with other forces and factors in the larger policy-making context. Interest groups, administrative agencies, and public pressure (or the lack of it) all play major roles in shaping congressional decisions. The most powerful influence, however, is the President. The resources at his disposal, and the focusing effects of his program and pressure, provide much of the impetus toward congressional action. Very little clear indication of popular preferences is available in respect to most issues. Thus, relatively small interest groups are able to work their wills by creating the impression of popular support for their goals. Only when the President undertakes to arouse public pressure is "heat" usually put on the Congress.

The dominance of the President and the executive branch has become so apparent that many observers now ask whether the Congress's function has not changed. Rather than serving as an independent policymaker, according to this analysis, Congress has become nothing more than a critic of the President's programs, limited to occasional modification of the initiatives of the vast bureaucracy and its central leadership. We shall return to this question after a brief review of some of the pressures upon Congress, using the military appropriations process as a principal illustration. We concentrate on the appropriations process because it is the point at which Congress has its greatest relative power. In foreign policy, for example, the President's actions and monopoly on information may give the Congress no real choice but to ratify his actions. But Congress is the sole source of funding for all areas of the federal government, and its will is thus most strongly felt in the appropriations process. If Congress is not independent here, it is not likely to be anywhere.

The General Situation: Low Public Visibility, Legislative Initiative

Basic to legislative policymaking are the allied processes of log-rolling and coalition-building. Only a rare issue, such as a declaration of war or a strong civil rights bill, arouses a farily strong interest, pro or con, in virtually all members of the legislative body. When this happens, it is because there is widespread concern or controversy over the issue in the country at large. On most issues that come before a legislative body, only a relatively small proportion of the members take an active interest. Most have only a mild concern or none at all, largely reflecting the interest or lack of interest among their constituents. A proposal to raise the tariff on foreign coal imports will certainly evoke strong interest in the coal-producing areas of Pennsylvania, West Virginia, and Illinois and thus among legislators representing these areas. But most other congressmen are not likely to be strongly aroused, even though some of their constituents use coal to heat their homes or factories. A proposal to appropriate federal funds to change the flow of the Colorado River will certainly awaken hopes or anxieties in legislators from the states bordering the river, but probably will not deeply stir legislators from Georgia, Alaska, or New Jersey.

Where this combination of strong interest among a few legislators and apathy among most prevails, conditions are ripe for bargaining, logrolling, and coalition-building. The congressman from Pennsylvania who very much wants support for a higher tariff on coal knows he can probably get supporting votes from unconcerned colleagues in return for his goodwill and the resulting expectation that he will support them in the future on some issue on which *they* badly need support. He may have an understanding with congressmen from cotton-growing states that he will vote for higher price supports for cotton: an issue in which he and his Pennsylvania constituents have relatively little interest. It is more likely that there will not be an explicit understanding about vote-trading at all, but rather a gentlemen's recognition that a favor rendered today deserves a return favor in the future.

This process serves to identify the representatives of unaware or apathetic masses with the interests of relatively small economic groups that have a lot to gain from a public policy. It makes it possible for a group that is strongly interested to put together a coalition composed largely of the uninterested or the mildly interested. One of the most common forms of coalition in American legislatures allies urban business groups with legislators from rural areas, which are heavily overrepresented in both houses of Congress and in the legislatures of states with large urban areas. This form of logrolling has frequently given business groups substantial support on labor and welfare issues, where business interests frequently clash with those of urban workers, low-income groups, and the poor. In return, it has helped Southern rural legislators to win support from Northern conservatives for weakening civil rights bills and for legislation to help large farming interests. As this last example suggests, the division of American states into districts for the election of members of state legislatures and national congressmen has often made it easier for the interests of mass publics to be subordinated to those of elites.

A Special Situation: The Military Orchestrates Pressure

Each year, the President submits to the Congress a budget that reflects his judgments and preferences about national priorities for the coming fiscal year. The Congress then reviews the proposed funding for each department and activity of the government, and modifies allocations in accordance with its own priorities before appropriating the money. Underlying this formal description, of course, are some hard realities: each year a bitter contest takes place, first within the executive branch and then in the Congress, among the armed services themselves and also between the military and its supporters and those seeking other priorities for governmental action. Each service naturally believes that its needs are paramount and that with new weaponry it can make an even greater contribution to national security. The cumulative effect of sincere and persuasive arguments for the pressing needs of the Air Force, Army, Navy, and Marine Corps is to force other governmental departments and functions to defend themselves or be content with what is left over. In this competitive process, three factors work to the advantage of the military services.

1. As large and complex organizations, the military services constantly need increased funds merely for self-maintenance. Over the years, they have perfected tactics for effectively influencing the Congress and the public. In this, they have been aided by a general aura of patriotic necessity and selfless sacrifice in the struggle against communism. Not surprisingly, generals and admirals in testimony before Congress, in speeches, and in books consistently endorse the doctrine that only superior military power can keep the peace and assure the security of the United States and the Free World. When budget-cutting pressures build up, they are likely to report new ad-

vances by Soviet military forces and to project dire consequences unless our own appropriations are increased. In all of this, we may be sure that they are sincere in reporting conditions as they perceive them. They believe that it is part of their job, if not their duty, to proceed in this fashion. At some point, however, a natural enthusiasm and confidence in the importance of one's lifework are likely to produce claims that are, from the broader perspective of *all* national needs and resources, out of proportion. But it is not easy for either a citizen or a congressman to resist when confronted by a high-ranking military officer's expert testimony that national security will be endangered unless another $5 billion is provided for a new defense system. Nor do congressmen relish hearing their opponents at the next election attack their records on the ground that they have been "penny-pinching with the nation's security" or "advocating unilateral disarmament."

Below the level of patriotic publicity and exhortation, the military services make effective use of the pressure tactics familiar to American politics. They lobby regularly with supporters and potential supporters in the Congress, explaining in detail the economic benefits to districts and regions resulting from new defense contracts and rewarding their friends with free air transportation or round-the-world trips. Because the Armed Services Committees and the members of the Appropriations Committees of the two houses are so crucial to approval of new spending programs, the military services pay special attention to them. They lobby on behalf of their friends for appointment to these cherished positions, and they build new bases in, and direct defense contracts toward, the districts represented by such members.

The services are also able to call on some powerful allies in their efforts to influence decisionmakers. Private associations closely aligned with each service carry much of the burden of lobbying, particularly in ways that might seem improper for military officers on active duty. These associations are made up of former military officers and reservists, the contractors and suppliers who do business with that service, and some interested citizens. By holding conventions, issuing statements, visiting congressmen, and otherwise engaging in pressure tactics, these associations serve as nongovernmental extensions of the various services. A second and growing body of allies has also recently been found in that segment of the scientific community that is engaged in research-and-development work for the military services and NASA. Some scientists have left universities to set up businesses to provide skills and products for the services, while others retain their university bases. In both cases, their prestige and seeming independence lend useful support to the military argument.

2. The military services can count on powerful and closely coordinated support from major defense suppliers who stand to gain or lose large sums as a result of budgetary decisions. It seems fair to conclude that these companies have a vital interest in the outcome of military appropriations controversies, some because of near-complete dependence and others because of the profitability of this portion of their business. Nor are these companies reluctant to press their efforts to acquire contracts: frank statements of determination to secure shares of this business lie behind extensive lobbying, contributions to the services' associations and institutional advertising in national magazines and scientific and engineering journals. Coordinated lobbying campaigns, as well as close contacts for the purpose of securing contracts and administering them smoothly, are achieved through the contractors' well-established pattern of employing high-ranking retired military officers with procurement experience. Senator William Proxmire of Wisconsin released figures in 1970 showing that, as of February 1969, 2,124 former high-ranking officers were employed by the 100 largest military contractors.[6] The ten largest suppliers employed 1,065 of these retired officers; Lockheed had 210; Boeing, 169; General Dynamics, 113; North American Rockwell, 104; and General Electric, 89. As a group, the top ten suppliers employed about three times as many ex-high-ranking officers in 1969 as they had a decade earlier. The same rate of increase applies to the top 100 defense contractors.

3. The key members of Congress are strong supporters of the military services, and most others are vulnerable to the economic opportunities for their districts represented by military contracts. The members of the Armed Services Committees of the two houses, and their counterparts on the Appropriations Committees, enjoy a virtual monopoly of influence over the substance of military authorizations and appropriations. They have the time and opportunity to become informed about the details of military activities and expenditures. In past decades, they have usually been willing to appropriate more than the services requested. The ordinary congressman is habituated to take the word of his colleagues who are specialists in a subject area, unable to acquire the inside knowledge that permits informed challenge or preparation of sensible alternatives, and vulnerable to the economic needs of his district. This dependence on the evaluations and recommendations of others has several implications.

The geographic concentration of defense business creates both strong defensiveness on the part of congressmen who want to maintain business for their districts, and strong acquisitiveness on the part of others who want to share it more widely. As we saw in Chapter 3,

6Proxmire, op. cit., pp. 153–154.

defense business is monopolized by a few states. Others, chiefly in the Midwest, are especially low in defense business. Although the lack of any real opposition to military budget appropriations makes analysis of congressional voting patterns on this issue meaningless, it is clear that such opposition as exists comes quite disproportionately from the Midwest and some urban areas where the level of defense business is particularly low.

To many congressmen, defense contracts have come to be another (and larger) "pork barrel" like public works. A politician's constant need to be able to show his constituents that he is working effectively on their behalf finds fulfillment in announcing new defense contracts, even if he had little or nothing to do with securing them. The military and the White House have contributed to the gamesmanship and spoils-system aspects of defense contracting by helping to make congressmen "look good" in this respect—by arranging for them to make public announcements of contract awards, for example. The question of who has done or who can do most for the district by obtaining contracts is regularly an issue in many congressional campaigns.

What does this mean? To what extent can it be said that Congress controls the appropriations process, let alone the various other activities of the far-flung federal government? In effect, the division of labor into committees that is necessary to transact business at all has caused the Congress to parcel out vital power to a few members—who then become as much advocates as overseers of the agencies under their jurisdiction. Only rarely can the Congress rise to the level of independent policymaker. For the most part, the sheer volume and complexity of issues force it into secondary, modifying-ratifying roles. And, as we have just seen, it has difficulty performing even these functions rationally and consistently.

But perhaps these are the wrong questions. It may be not that Congress is not in charge, but that nobody is in charge. In other words, the total apparatus of governmental bureaucracy—perhaps even the technological-organizational society as a whole—may be subject to the direction and control of no decision-making institutions at all. Certainly the multitude of factors involved here suggests uncontrollability, not just specific failures of control. We shall explore this issue further in Chapter 13.

Chapter 13

The presidency of the United States is the most visible and apparently the most powerful office in the world. Nevertheless, it is part of an institution, which implies considerable dependence on others and constraints on what one can do without the cooperation of others. The American presidency undoubtedly *is* a uniquely powerful office, but this power is much less focused in one person than often appears; only in rare periods of perceived crisis is truly decisive power concentrated in his hands. For the most part, the President operates in a context of multiple restraints and frustrations, and can only move the decentralized and independently oriented units of government through carefully planned and coordinated campaigns. Most of the time, he must accommodate his program to what can be negotiated with the many power-brokers and veto points throughout the federal establishment. And, all of the time, he must consider the condition and needs of the economic system of which he is necessarily the chief steward.

The Presidency and the Bureaucracy

Major constraints on presidential power flow from such sources as the Congress, the influence of forthcoming elections, and national or international events. But the greatest continuing constraint of all is the bureaucracy—the many federal departments, agencies, and commissions with their more than 2 million employees. They represent many different values, interests, attitudes, and goals. They are institutions that give rise to positions of power from which to seek their goals—which are not necessarily the President's goals. Most of them are strongly tied to the Congress, their clienteles, and/or interest groups in the larger society, and thus can defend themselves ably against the President's efforts to coordinate them for his purposes. At times, the inertia inherent in sheer size and continuity is enough to frustrate presidential or other efforts to introduce new goals or methods into the system.

In this chapter, we shall briefly survey the powers, formal and real, at the President's disposal. Then we shall look at the problem of managing the bureaucracy, and some of the tactics employed to try to gain control. By means of a case study involving foreign policy toward the Third World, we shall explore who is actually in charge of noncrisis policymaking in this area of maximum presidential power and discretion. Finally, we shall summarize the respective parts played by the several institutions we have analyzed in this section of the book.

Formal Powers and Real Powers

Article II of the United States Constitution and various statutes grant to the President a number of important legal powers. He is supposed to "take care that the laws be faithfully executed," recommend legislation to Congress, act as Commander-in-Chief of the armed forces, and appoint a large number of civilian and military officers to their posts. He may remove some government officials for any reason he likes or for no reason, and he may remove others if he can show that they have been guilty of malfeasance or on other grounds for removal specified in the laws creating their offices. He may pardon persons convicted of federal crimes. He may propose treaties to the Senate for ratification, may enter into "executive agreements" with foreign countries without Senate ratification, and may recognize foreign countries or break diplomatic relations with them on his own initiative.

This is an imposing list of formal powers, especially so because some, particularly the first three, are extremely broad in character. To recite such a list, however, is to understand almost nothing about the true powers and influence of the President. If, in taking "care that the laws be faithfully executed," appointing, and so on, he acts only or chiefly in conformity with the information and recommendations provided by top civil servants, a group of congressional leaders, or some combination of these, his formal powers are largely ritualistic and empty. If he arouses wide and intense public concern by creating a sense of crisis and widespread anxiety, the list of formal powers is also largely meaningless because he can then shape the policies of governmental organs that are supposed to check him. To learn what the formal powers of a public official are is only to begin to understand his place in the political system. How he uses those powers depends upon patterns of support and opposition from political participants with resources for influence at their disposal, not upon the legal words or constitutional provisions.

Power Through Issues

Presidential sway over public opinion is greatest on issues that create serious anxiety without pitting clearly defined or organized groups against each other. A threat from a foreign power or a serious and lengthy economic depression makes virtually everyone anxious and at the same time makes people eager for resolute leadership without arousing clear demands for particular lines of action or policy directions. On such matters, it is generally assumed that the President has information and expert advice not available to the mass public and that he should be supported and followed. This is not so when he recommends restrictions on labor-union activity or higher benefits to welfare recipients—policy proposals that predictably pit workers and employers or liberals and conservatives against each other.

When President Kennedy told the country that Russian missile emplacements in Cuba threatened the United States, he created a level of anxiety conducive to arousing general support for his ultimatum to the Russian Premier that they be removed, even though that policy carried considerable risk of nuclear war. In such a crisis situation, the President was able to structure opinion, rather than merely responding to it; and in doing so he carried Congress with him and destroyed any possibility of serious footdragging or resistance on the part of the State or Defense Departments. The same was true of the Tonkin Gulf incident. It was also true of the economic crisis presented by the Great Depression of the 1930s, which produced anxiety in the entire population, including the business community, and gave President Franklin Roosevelt a ready and manipulable audience for the resolute actions which, he confidently told a frightened country, would put us back on the road to recovery.

The conditions for this kind of overriding presidential power are sometimes created by events outside the President's control; but at other times he can create them himself. It was certainly not conscious governmental policy to create the Great Depression, even though ignorance of economic principles may have encouraged public policies that contributed to it. Nor was the Japanese attack on Pearl Harbor in 1941 an effort by the President to give himself crisis powers. The Cuban missile crisis and the Tonkin Gulf incident are not such clearcut cases; many see them as deliberate efforts to create strong public support for presidential policy. President James Polk's deployment of troops into disputed border territory, thus starting the Mexican War, is another example of a presidential action that left little room for an opposition to function.

The conclusion would seem to be that it is simplistic to generalize about presidential power without specifying the kind of issue involved. On most issues of the sort that regularly involve conflicting interests based upon economic position, occupation, and socio-economic status, the President reflects established interest patterns more than he changes them. On the occasional issue that is of deep concern to virtually everyone and evokes strong anxiety and uncertainty (rather than clear but differing ideas) about what should be done, the President's power to shape opinion and policy is very great. In these situations, the formal and legal checks upon him become formalities and not real constraints, for a majority of congressmen and bureaucrats is likely to be swept along with the dominant tide of opinion. That the President is sometimes subjected to overriding constraints and sometimes largely free of them does not necessarily add up to a balanced situation or a "happy medium." For an issue as crucial as variations in presidential power, averages are meaningless. A virtually free hand in a major crisis can come close to destroying the checks that operate in normal times. This is an especially telling consideration when the President can himself create a sense of crisis.

Political Constraints

That the President is chosen by election and has an interest in his own reelection or in keeping his political party in power is the most conspicuous formal constraint upon him, but it is unquestionably minor compared to the others. As Chapter 16 makes clear, the policies a President and his party pursue are not the only reasons people support or oppose him on election day. Party identification, the candidates' personalities, and the advantage an incumbent enjoys over a challenger are all important factors.

Nor is the electoral-college method of selecting him a major constraint on what he does, though it undoubtedly has an occasional influence. Since it is to the President's advantage to carry the most populous states—those with large cities—he has some incentive to appeal to the large-city voters. Remember that rural overrepresentation in both houses of Congress gives those bodies the opposite bias, making them less sensitive to the interests of urban residents. The electoral-college system, however, is at most a minor constraint upon the President. Only three times in our whole history has it produced an outcome different from what would have been the case under direct popular election, though the possibility of a repetition constantly keeps alive an interest in changing the electoral system. Probably more important, the Nixon election in 1968 showed that it is possible, even under the electoral-college system, for a candidate to win an election by appealing chiefly to rural and small-town voters in the South and Midwest. Presidential candidates have to put together some kind of a coalition of supporting groups to win, but they have considerable leeway in deciding to which demands they will be responsive and which they will play down or ignore.

Another and more serious limitation on presidential power is the need to win congressional cooperation for major policies. The President must constantly try to induce the Congress to enact his legislative program and provide the appropriations necessary to carry it out. On domestic policy matters, he frequently does not succeed, even when his own political party controls both houses of Congress and he vigorously pushes his program. Both Harry Truman and John Kennedy found it impossible to induce the Congress to go along with the major domestic policies they strenuously advocated, even though both were Democrats dealing with Congresses dominated by Democrats. When the opposition party dominates even one House, the likelihood of deadlock is of course greater, for both the President and the congressmen then have an incentive to create the impression that their efforts to promote the public interest are being blocked by a recalcitrant, partisan opposition.

When such conflict occurs, either the President or the Congress may espouse the more liberal position. The fairly consistent positions taken by a long series of more or less liberal twentieth-century Presidents left the impression for a time that the Congress could be counted on to take more conservative postures than the President in such areas as labor, welfare, conservation, and civil rights. In the Nixon Administration after 1968, however, the opposite pattern prevailed. Congress still severely limited the President's maneuverability, but now it did so by approving more liberal programs than he wanted on a wide variety of issues: pollution control, welfare benefits, social security benefits, federal aid to education, and desegregation of the public schools, among others.

Managing the Bureaucracy

The most potent constraint on the President is his need to rely upon the information and advice of his subordinates for most of the decisions he makes. The President is one individual, charged by the Constitution with the duty to "take care that the laws be faithfully executed." To do so, of course, he needs help. Figure 13-1 shows the formal structure of the executive branch and lists the administrative agencies. Not surprisingly, the effect of thus parceling out the power and responsibility of the presidency is to create the same kind of division of labor and resulting dispersal and stratification of power that occurs in the other institutions.

Characteristics of Bureaucratic Organization and Procedures

Policymakers are dependent upon others for information on which to act, and subordinates thus acquire a lever, and a potent one, for influencing top-level policy. A President's decision to commit funds

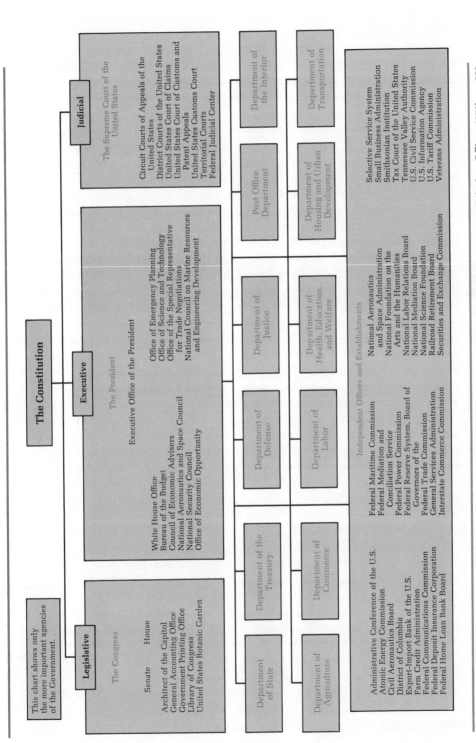

The Constitution

This chart shows only the more important agencies of the Government.

Legislative

The Congress

Senate   House

Architect of the Capitol
General Accounting Office
Government Printing Office
Library of Congress
United States Botanic Garden

Executive

The President

Executive Office of the President

White House Office
Bureau of the Budget
Council of Economic Advisers
National Aeronautics and Space Council
National Security Council
Office of Economic Opportunity

Office of Emergency Planning
Office of Science and Technology
Office of the Special Representative for Trade Negotiations
National Council on Marine Resources and Engineering Development

Department of State
Department of the Treasury
Department of Defense
Department of Justice
Post Office Department
Department of the Interior

Department of Agriculture
Department of Commerce
Department of Labor
Department of Health, Education, and Welfare
Department of Housing and Urban Development
Department of Transportation

Independent Offices and Establishments

Administrative Conference of the U.S.
Atomic Energy Commission
Civil Aeronautics Board
District of Columbia
Export-Import Bank of the U.S.
Farm Credit Administration
Federal Communications Commission
Federal Deposit Insurance Corporation
Federal Home Loan Bank Board

Federal Maritime Commission
Federal Mediation and Conciliation Service
Federal Power Commission
Federal Reserve System, Board of Governors of the
Federal Trade Commission
General Services Administration
Interstate Commerce Commission

National Aeronautics and Space Administration
National Foundation on the Arts and the Humanities
National Labor Relations Board
National Mediation Board
National Science Foundation
Railroad Retirement Board
Securities and Exchange Commission

Selective Service System
Small Business Administration
Smithsonian Institution
Tax Court of the United States
Tennessee Valley Authority
U.S. Civil Service Commission
U.S. Information Agency
U.S. Tariff Commission
Veterans Administration

Judicial

The Supreme Court of the United States

Circuit Courts of Appeals of the United States
District Courts of the United States
United States Court of Claims
United States Court of Customs and Patent Appeals
United States Customs Court
Territorial Courts
Federal Judicial Center

Source: U. S. Government Organizational Manual (Washington: Government Printing Office, 1972), p. 628.

FIGURE 13-1   The Government of the United States

to a new weapon system is based on information from subordinates about the weaknesses of existing defenses, the potential threats posed by enemies, the effects of various policy alternatives on his and his party's chances of reelection, the effects of the decision on jobs and unemployment in various sections of the country, and so on. He cannot possibly know or learn all these things by himself in the hundreds of areas in which he must make decisions. Subordinates are therefore in a position to influence his decisions very powerfully through their own decisions about which data are pertinent and which are not, what is to be stressed and what is to be ignored. They do this every day, often not consciously trying to influence top decisions, but nevertheless doing so.

To a significant degree, a staff member in an administrative agency is limited and guided in his choices and judgment by the role assigned to him and to the unit for which he works. He is not free, if he wants to keep his job and win promotion and the favor of his colleagues and superiors, to put anything he wishes into the reports he writes. If he works for the Extension Service of the Department of Agriculture, he is not expected to develop or emphasize data suggesting that the agricultural price support program chiefly subsidizes wealthy and commercial farmers and fails to benefit small and marginal farmers. People inclined to do so are not likely to accept a position in the service in the first place or to stay long if they do accept one. A staff member in a state conservation department is not normally expected to devote his energies to demonstrating that the economic interests of paper factories that pollute the rivers are more important than conservation interests; but an employee of a state agency to promote industrial development may well be expected to do exactly that. To a considerable extent, then, the very establishment of an administrative unit and the assignment to it of responsibility for a particular job is a way of making sure that certain kinds of information will be gathered and emphasized and that they will come to the attention of decision-making authorities.

This situation offers the resourceful policymaker a way to maximize his own influence over policy directions even though he is dependent upon others for information and guidance. He can exercise control over the range and jurisdictions of administrative units under him. If, in a controversial policy area, information is channeled through a single agency dominated by a particular interest or clientele, the top decisionmaker is in a very real sense the prisoner of that agency and of the interests it reflects. He knows only or largely what it tells him; and what it tells him will predictably further the interests of the groups that dominate it, and ignore or soft-pedal information harmful to them. To some extent this kind of selective attention to information is deliberate, but for the most part it is subconscious,

THE UNDER SECRETARY OF LABOR

Washington

Memorandum to Supervisory Personnel

The 1969 Savings Bond Campaign will commence in the Department of Labor on April 21. In order to demonstrate that Department management enthusiastically endorses the campaign, it is planned to use supervisory employees as canvassers. The basic guidelines under which they will operate are:

1. There will be no pressure put upon employees, but all will be seriously urged to sign up.
2. Please emphasize that in making the Department of Labor a stimulating place to work we are building an *esprit de corps* and unity of purpose. We particularly want to excel in programs where we can be compared with others. Therefore, all employees are urged to respond to this appeal.
3. Payroll deduction is a convenient way of saving, helps support the Government and, of course, is a sound and valuable investment, but the paramount appeal by the Department is *widespread participation* in this joint effort, not investment.
4. The Government has set a goal of 80 per cent participation in the bond payroll savings plan. However, the Department of Labor likes to excel in responding to worthy causes, to do just a little better than other agencies. Therefore, we are setting ourselves a goal of at least 90 per cent employee participation. Many other organizations both in Government and private industry regularly exceed this figure so the target is not unreasonable.
5. Any person who does not sign the card after a discussion with his supervisor will be talked to by the next higher level of supervision to insure he or she is fully aware of the importance the Department places on this program. If discussion at these two levels of supervision does not result in participation, no higher referrals will be made.
6. Employees should be advised that any payroll deduction authorization effective in July will count in this year's drive. Therefore, it is appropriate to point out that there will be a substantial Government-wide pay raise effective in July.
7. It is the fact of participation, not the size of the deduction, that is important in this particular drive, a minimum deduction may be all that some will wish. No encouragement for higher amounts should be extended in such cases.
8. The payroll deduction method is reliable. Employees now receive their bonds regularly and promptly.

Please accept my thanks for your efforts in this program. Only through leadership on the part of its supervision can the Department expect to achieve the leadership position to which it aspires.

/S/ James D. Hodgson
Under Secretary

since people are likely to perceive what they want to see and what serves their interests.

An executive who receives data from two or more agencies with overlapping jurisdictions, dominated by different interests, enjoys far more freedom. He will receive a wider range of information upon which to act; and he will be in the position of umpire for contending groups rather than the captive of one of them. As already suggested, to be able to influence the *organizational pattern* for making policy in a controversial area is to be able to win such freedom and maneuverability and therefore to influence which constituencies will win how much of what. This is a key mechanism through which elites can influence policy.

President Franklin Roosevelt made especially telling use of this kind of strategy and maneuverability. He liked to set up agencies with conflicting and overlapping jurisdictions. This made for confusing organization charts; but it guaranteed that when different groups of people had conflicting interests, a top-level coordinating agency like the Bureau of the Budget or the President himself would be made aware of the problem, preventing it from being settled by a subordinate agency sensitive to only one interest. In umpiring such disputes, the President could consider not only the data and arguments of the contending administrative agencies but also the probable loss or gain of votes for his party in the next election from each possible course of action.

This same principle, relating influence to organizational pattern, has an important application below the level of the chief executive. An economic elite that can win continuing influence over the policy directions of an administrative agency is in a strong strategic position to win mass acquiescence in the favors it receives. A governmental agency at the federal or state level that is established to control the relationship between an organized business group and an unorganized consumer group is bound to come to see itself as responsible for the continuing survival and success of the businesses within its domain. It will become sensitive to the importance of maintaining a profitable operation and will therefore be sympathetic to petitions for increases in charges. It is bound to receive from the organized businesses a stream of messages that have the effect of making the governmental administrators see problems from business' point of view. At the same time, the consumers, being unorganized, can exert no such subtle but powerful psychological influence on the administrative agency. On the contrary, the very existence of the agency is taken as a signal that the consumer is being protected, for that is the reason the agency was established. The net effect, therefore, is that the business groups get much of what they want and at the same time remain relatively protected from public resistance or protest.

Presidential Efforts at Control: The Limits of "Power"

The modern President spends much of his time trying to learn what executive branch employees are doing in his name and trying to persuade or coerce them into doing things the way he wants them done. He is usually aware of how badly he needs capable, independent (and therefore strong-minded) people in positions of responsibility, even at the risk of finding that they have different ideas and priorities from his own.

In trying to set up a staff organization that can make it possible to discharge these responsibilities, a President tends to delegate powers in a highly personal manner. To some extent, allocations of power are implied in the creation of permanent departments and bureaus of the executive branch, but their role may vary according to the President's preference and his confidence in their top management. Three broad classes of people in the executive branch influence presidential decisions and policy. The first consists of incumbents of those positions that are most personal in nature—whose occupants are intended to serve the President's need to know what is going on and to mobilize and apply his power on his personal behalf. Examples of such positions include the major White House assistants, the Director of the Bureau of the Budget, and the office of Attorney General. The second class consists of positions created by statute that have specific and continuing responsibilities, and whose occupants owe their status to their offices rather than to their special relationship to the President. Individuals among the secretaries of Cabinet-level departments may be close friends of the President and enjoy considerable special influence for that reason, but they also have outside or public responsibilities fixed by law that force them to play an independent role at times. Examples of major positions of this sort are the Secretary of Defense, the Secretary of State, the Director of the FBI, the Chairman of the Federal Reserve Board, and members of the independent regulatory commissions such as the Interstate Commerce Commission. The third class consists of staff members at the lower levels of all these types of executive agencies: people who gather and screen the information upon which top officials act and who often themselves make decisions that go far toward shaping the course of future policy.

To a degree that often surprises a newly elected President, all these subordinates limit and influence what he can do. Beset with hundreds of other pressing matters, a President cannot often reexamine in detail a recommendation by his special advisor on welfare policy about an income maintenance program or independently change his attorney general's recommendation that a particular person be nominated for a Supreme Court vacancy. He may, of course, do this sort of thing

NATIONAL LABOR RELATIONS BOARD
Washington, D.C.

Administration Bulletin

TO: All Employees
SUBJECT: Post-Attack Registration of Federal Employees

Civil Service Commission instructions require that government agencies remind all employees annually of their responsibilities under the Commission-operated registration system.

In the event of an attack all National Labor Relations Board employees should follow the procedure outlined below:

If you are prevented from going to your regular place of work because of an enemy attack, or, if you are prevented from reporting to an emergency location—Go to the nearest Post Office, ask the Postmaster for a Federal Employee Emergency Registration Card, fill it out and return it to him.

He will see that it is forwarded to the office of Civil Service Commission which will maintain a registration file for your area. When your card is received the Civil Service Commission will notify us and we can then decide where and when you should report back for work.

Another important reason for mailing in your Registration Card as soon as possible is that it will enable us to keep you on the roster of active employees and enable us to forward your pay.

Even though you complete your Registration Card promptly, it may be a while before you are put back to work. In the meantime, you would be expected to volunteer your services to the Civil Defense authorities.

Approved for issuance:
C.S.W.

---

occasionally on matters about which he feels especially strongly or in response to still other pressures—from powerful elements in his political party, in Congress, or in pressure groups.

Whenever a President tries to put into effect a policy that lacks support among those who have to carry it out, he faces a formidable obstacle. In these circumstances, his formal authority to issue directives may do him little good. Long-term staff members in any large bureaucratic organization learn many devices to delay, reinterpret, or ignore directives they do not like, and they are easy to employ because responsibility for any course of action or lack of action is difficult or impossible to pinpoint. Both Eisenhower in the 1950s and Roosevelt during World War II formally ordered federal officials to be sure that any company awarded government contracts did not discriminate against blacks in hiring or promoting their work forces, and both established commissions to carry out the directive. In both cases, the order was ignored far more than it was observed. In an important sense, the basic power of the President is the power to persuade, the implication being that when he cannot persuade his subordinates to favor what he favors, his power is minimal. This is a crucial point, though there are areas of policymaking, discussed below, in which it has little applicability.

The President and Civil Servants

The constraints civil servants place upon the power of the President are not wholly random or dependent on the whims of subordinates with a variety of values or ideologies. To a significant degree, this form of constraint functions to minimize policy change. Any change disrupts established routines, relationships, and statuses in an agency and so elicits resistance among at least part of the staff. This tendency is enhanced by the psychological and organizational ties a long-established agency develops to particular clienteles. The Visa Division of the Department of State, for example, has attracted and kept staff members who share the view that the nation's security is in their hands and that a significant relaxation of standards for granting visas for entry into the United States is a disservice to the nation. Veterans' groups and other patriotic organizations reinforce this view and help win appropriations and support for staff members who put it into practice. In the face of bureaucratic stubbornness of this sort, even an act of Congress, let alone a presidential directive, has at times brought little change in the actual award of visas.

The difficulties of gaining knowledge and leverage sufficient to manage the bureaucracy effectively have recently led to a rapid increase in the President's personal staff. The Executive Office of the President helps him coordinate recommendations from the vast executive branch and acts upon many of them without his personal intervention. The Bureau of the Budget is particularly concerned with fitting appropriations requests from the agencies into an overall executive budget, screening recommendations for new substantive legislation, and overseeing administrative procedures. The National Security Council serves to accommodate the sometimes disparate interests of the armed forces, the State Department, the intelligence services, and domestic agencies in the field of foreign policy. The makeup of the Executive Office of the President changes from time to time, but these two agencies, together with the White House staff, are its major components. Increasingly, burdened Presidents are adding to the White House staff individuals who advise them on specialized and controversial policy areas such as foreign policy, welfare policy, and pollution of the environment. This amounts to still another form of overlap among agencies concerned with specific policy areas, for the

State Department and the CIA also deal with foreign policy; at least four cabinet departments and the Office of Economic Opportunity deal with welfare policy; and the Interior Department, the Commerce Department, and others deal with pollution.

Who's In Charge? The Case of Foreign Policymaking

The foregoing analysis suggests that Presidents experience great difficulty gaining control over day-to-day actions by elements of the federal bureaucracy. A great number of powerful and independent units appear to be heading in a variety of directions, only occasionally subject to systematic guidance and coordination from their nominal superior. But there *are* patterns to federal governmental activity. All is not haphazard or random. This raises some interesting questions. If the President were really in control, we might have asked whether he was coordinating and managing the bureaucracy to move in directions consistent with apparent popular preferences or needs. He is not usually in direct control, however, and so we must ask other questions. Who (if anybody) *does* control "executive" policy? If no source of control is identifiable, what are the reasons for patterned, regular policies and practices? Are they to be found, for example, in the characteristics of the bureaucracy itself, or in the values of the society, or in the imperatives that flow from the nature of the economic system? In any of these cases, whose interests and preferences are served by the policies and practices in effect?

We have chosen the area of foreign policy toward the Third World as a means of raising these questions, for two reasons. The first is that foreign policy is the area of greatest presidential power and discretion; we should be able to trace the influence of the President most clearly here, where he is relatively free of congressional and popular constraints. The second is that Third World policies do not normally present the kinds of crises that demand and receive the President's personal attention. We know that when superpower relationships are involved, the President or his emissaries frequently assume direct responsibility. But these occasions tell us little about the more routine policies and practices that raise the question "Who's in charge?" The latter are the kinds of policies and practices that establish long-term patterns and create the contexts out of which crises may later arise. We shall first briefly survey the substance of recent policies, and then consider some contrasting explanations for them. The national security dimensions of Third World policies are relevant, of course, even though they involve direct presidential supervision (and, frequently, use of the armed forces as the implementing agency). We shall begin with them, and move on to the longer-range economic and other policies.

The Truman Doctrine

In March 1947, President Truman announced what has come to be known as the "Truman Doctrine": "We cannot allow changes in the status quo by such methods as coercion, or by such subterfuges as political infiltration." This declaration came in the context of the Greek civil war, in which a highly authoritarian government sought to put down a revolution that enjoyed considerable popular support but had strong local communist components. For more than two years, British troops had fought on the side of the Greek government they had set up, finally achieving a measure of stability despite continued official corruption and severe inflation. The British, however, were unable to keep up their efforts; their own financial situation was so desperate that they had no alternative but to withdraw their troops. The United States proceeded to take over the support of the Greek government's campaign by supplying weapons, military advisers, and substantial amounts of money. The decision to intervene was perceived by the President as essential to American security given the context of a global struggle between contrasting ways of life, and it has come to be understood in these terms ever since.

The commitment in Greece was a major turning point in American foreign policy. It effectively marked the beginning of the period when national security concerns led to the use of Third World nations, particularly those on the perimeter of the Soviet bloc, as buffer states, with prevention of the spread of communism seen as more important than the nature of the government or long-term economic development. Ultimately, Greece and Turkey were incorporated into the North American Treaty Organization; but despite massive military and economic assistance, their financial conditions and general economic levels remained low. In the 1960s, continued dissatisfaction led to several changes in the makeup of the government in Greece. Apparently still acting to promote national security, American policymakers tended to support the more conservative factions in each case.

The Korean War of 1950-1953 provides an Asian illustration of this early stage of American policy. South Korea was considered crucial as another testing-ground of what was assumed to be Soviet expansionism. Experts now differ about the extent to which the two crises were instigated or encouraged by the Soviet Union. In the case of Greece, it seems clear that the Soviet Union had declined to help because it considered the revolution a hopeless cause.[1] And it is also apparent that the belligerent threats of the South Korean government to invade the North may have contributed to the North's

---

[1]Based on a quotation from Joseph Stalin reported in Milovan Djilas, *Conversations with Stalin* (New York: Praeger, 1962), p. 164.

decision to send its armies south. In any event, this aggressive act triggered American involvement. When the American army appeared to be pushing toward the Chinese border, the Chinese too became involved. The war then settled into a long-term stalemate. Nearly two decades after the end of the war, South Korea had received such massive economic assistance that it was becoming a showcase of economic growth. The government, however, showed little progress toward more democratic organization or operation.

As the perceived communist threat became global, the Eisenhower Administration set about to tie as many Third World nations as possible to the United States through alliance treaties. Acting on the model of the NATO pact, alliances were formed with Turkey, Iran, Iraq, and Pakistan (CENTO) and, together with Britain and France, with Thailand and Pakistan directly and Laos, Cambodia, and South Vietnam by informal extension (SEATO). Bilateral defense treaties were undertaken with the Philippines and Taiwan. Pursuant to these various treaties, considerable military assistance was extended. Similar help was made available when the key neutralist nation in the world, India, was engaged in border skirmishes with the Chinese. Ironically, the major use of American military assistance occurred not in defense against communist attack but in small wars between nations allied with the United States, such as Pakistan and India.

The Eisenhower Doctrine

When the containment policy was rendered obsolete in the late 1950s by the development of indigenous popular movements all over the world, the United States faced new difficulties in serving its security interests. Any independence movement in an African or Asian colony, or any revolutionary movement in Latin America, might serve as a route to power for communists. Almost without considering the limits of propriety or capability, the global approach to security was extended once again to cover such possibilities (the "Eisenhower Doctrine"). The United States in effect served notice that it might see its security involved, and act accordingly, not only in the internal conflicts of nations with which we had alliances, but also where violence threatened or occurred elsewhere in the world.

One illustration of the meaning of this commitment occurred in Lebanon in 1958 when Marines landed in and occupied the country for four months. The cause of the disorder was an effort by Lebanon's incumbent anticommunist president to change the country's constitution in order to serve another term in office. Arab nationalists, supported by aspiring Lebanese politicians, had formed a powerful coalition in opposition. Calls for the violent overthrow of the government came from Egypt and Syria, but U.N. observation groups could find no major foreign sources of arms or men behind the opposition. There was undeniable fighting, however, and it seemed to be part of a trend toward revolutionary disorder throughout the nations of the Middle East. At the height of the fighting, the president abandoned his efforts to succeed himself, but nevertheless called for American assistance. The Marines had been alerted for months and landed the next day. Soon the U.S. forces, armed with atomic howitzers, numbered seven thousand men. President Eisenhower told Americans in a television address that the situation was like the Greek civil war and various communist conquests of the early 1950's, and that American troops were required to defend Lebanese sovereignty and integrity. They did so by acceding to the election of a new president, whereupon the fighting died away.

But a precedent had been set for the involvement of U.S. troops in the internal affairs of Third World nations, even in cases where the opposition to the local government came not from communists but from indigenous nationalist forces. This precedent was much recalled in 1965, when American Marines again landed in the Dominican Republic. In this instance, there was no solid evidence of communist involvement in the revolution, but the American Embassy thought there was, and President Johnson acted accordingly. The consensus of experts now, however, is that the embassy was either hysterical or acting as the agent of the conservative military forces that were ultimately installed in power through U.S. help. In any event, the United States' commitment to a global view of its security needs, reaching into the internal affairs of Third World nations, began to appear more like a determination to use force to prop up any government that could be induced to request U.S. intervention.

The leading example of American policy under this global definition is, of course, the Vietnam War. Escalating slowly but steadily from the dispatch of the first U.S. advisors in the early days of the Cold War, the American commitment finally became one of maintaining an unpopular government against an indigenous revolutionary movement that enjoyed not only widespread popular support but also the active assistance of a neighboring communist country. To make matters worse for the United States, the site of this insurrection was dense jungle on the Asian mainland, 10,000 miles from the United States. Neither a half million U.S. troops nor bomb tonnages exceeding those dropped by all sides during the entire Second World War succeeded in halting the progress of the revolutionary movement.

These examples of American national security policies toward the Third World are less isolated than they may at first appear. For the sake of brevity, we have not taken up Cuba, the Congo, Guatemala, or other incidents in which the United States made less visible but no less concerted efforts to aid one faction against another, or to help win an election for one side rather than another. All of these interventions stem from a single unifying motivation: concern that unless the United States acted decisively, communist penetration would succeed in gaining control of the government and produce a new ally for the Soviet Union or China. Another factor runs through all of these recent bold assertions of American power, and that is the importance of domestic politics in the formulation of foreign policy. Few policymakers have been willing to give their opponents any ground for charging them with weakness in "standing up to the communists." The dynamics of domestic politics seem to lead decisionmakers to take the strongest possible stances against even remote contingencies that might lead to communist gains. The chagrin at "losing" Cuba is no doubt partly responsible for this bellicosity, but so is an undifferentiated conviction that the security interest of the United States is intimately involved in the domestic difficulties of small nations anywhere in the world.

Economic Development Policies

In the early years of the Cold War, America concentrated its economic aid on the reconstruction of Europe. There was recognition of the development needs of the newly emerging nations, although their proliferation, population expansion, and substantial capital needs were not fully appreciated. Success with the Marshall Plan in Europe and the widening of the Cold War shifted attention to the Third World as early as President Truman's Inaugural Address in January 1949. This was the famous "Point Four" program (so-called because it was the fourth point in the President's program for peace), which pledged American financial aid and technical assistance for economic development. Long-term security and prosperity interests were emphasized, along with the economic benefits the United States could realize from the emergence of prosperous trading partners, and the need for access to crucial raw materials held by the Third World nations.

The policies employed by the United States in the first years after the announcement of the Point Four program were not greatly different from before. Essentially, they involved emphasizing the need for greater effort on the part of the developing nations themselves, and particularly the need to attract private investment. This was a period of selling private enterprise as a doctrine and supporting it with a refusal to make other funds available if private capital could be used for a task. The extension of loans by the United States was governed by standard principles of business risk and prospects of profit. In the words of one of the leading authorities on U.S. economic policies, "American provision of public capital was based on three guiding principles: keep it small; keep it under American control; and mini-mize the competition with private investment."[2]

Proposals were put forward in the United Nations even in this early period for the establishment of "no-strings" multilateral funding of economic development through various U.N. organs. The United States resisted all forms of support by U.N. agencies for the extension of multilateral loans, arguing in effect that the underdeveloped nations had overestimated their need for capital or that they were not doing enough to attract private investment. U.S. cooperation was of course essential, because for practical purposes the United States was always the chief funding source. American policymakers preferred that major funding be through the World Bank, or through more ob-viously bilateral sources (such as our Export-Import Bank or direct loans or grants from the United States government) from which maxi-mum political mileage could be secured. The still-potent resistance of business leaders to any form of foreign aid helped to keep economic assistance on a strictly "businesslike" basis—not tied to military defense needs. Where loans were extended, the terms were ordinarily the same as in any commercial loans transaction, i.e., repayable in dol-lars at competitive interest rates within a relatively short and fixed term of years. Only extraordinary circumstances resulted in outright grants of U.S. funds to developing nations.

The World Bank came in for severe criticism from the under-developed nations in the late stages of the Truman Administration. It was alleged that the World Bank extended loans only on the same conventional basis as did private lenders, and that it withheld funds where it thought that governments should look to private investors for capital. The World Bank had been established to provide funds for international development in the aftermath of World War II, in part on the assumption that the judgment of "hard-headed" bankers and businessmen would create a viable international market without regard for the political pressures of self-interested govern-ments. In practice, however, the directorate of the bank was controlled by the United States—or rather, by the New York financial com-munity. The bank normally functioned in concert with U.S. policy, not necessarily because of prior agreement between it and the U.S. government, but because of assumptions and criteria for judgment shared by the U.S. government and bank officials. At the time the bank was created, however, it was better prepared to take risks on behalf of such political goals as long-term development than either private businesses or the U.S. government. In this way, it ultimately began to set precedents for U.S. government policies, and to inspire

[2]David A. Baldwin, *Economic Development and American Foreign Policy* (Chicago: University of Chicago Press, 1966), pp. 22, 81—an excellent source on the evolution of U.S. economic development policies from 1943 through 1962, on which this account draws freely.

business support for such actions. In part, the creation of the bank was provoked by the U.N. criticism, but it also saw an unfulfilled need and opportunity in the Third World. As a consequence, it began to make "soft" loans, which involved no commitments to export trade in order to secure the funds with which to repay the loans.

The Shift to "Soft" Loans

These circumstances led to a modest change in American policy in the late 1950s. Major emphasis continued to be on lending through the World Bank, and the U.S. government doggedly resisted all multilateral funding arrangements through the United Nations. The Special United Nations Fund for Economic Development (SUNFED), much favored by the underdeveloped nations, was still strongly opposed by the United States, on the grounds that it would be both wasteful and duplicative. But, while continuing to insist upon the need for private investment (and greatly expanding U.S. government guarantees of the security of such investments), American policy began to shift toward acquiescence in "soft" loans. These were extended on an experimental basis only, following the lead of the World Bank. The significance of such loans was that the recipient nation was under less pressure to export in order to repay in American dollars, and the costs of paying the interest would be substantially less in any event. The local currency in which the loan would be repaid could only be spent within that country itself, which guaranteed future spending or investment by the United States government and further spurring of the local economy.

The breakthrough to soft loans was originally due almost as much to the desire on the part of the U.S. government to dispose of agricultural surpluses as to any altruistic goal; but the precedent, once established (like so many others in government), began to expand and legitimate other types of loans as well. In subsequent years, the principle of the soft loan became so well established as to be the primary means of transfer of public capital. But its effects were considerably reduced, though by no means eliminated, by the requirement that loans be spent for (more expensive) U.S.-produced goods and shipped in (more costly) U.S. merchant vessels.

But in the last years of the 1960s, the pressures of the Vietnam War and a growing general disillusionment with foreign aid led to sharp reductions in all American efforts to assist Third World nations. The shift toward greater emphasis on economic rather than military assistance during the early 1960s had been accompanied by a steadily shrinking total expenditure on foreign aid.[3] The United States had

[3]This discussion rests on Max Millikan, "The United States and the Low Income Countries," in *Agenda for the Nation*, ed. Kermit Gordon (Washington: Brookings Institution, 1968).

been investing nearly 2 percent of its gross national product in foreign aid during the early years of the Cold War, and the proportion was 1.5 percent even in the mid-1950s. By the mid-1960s, however, even though the GNP had doubled since postwar days, foreign aid was down to 1 percent. By the late 1960s, it was below 0.5 percent; for countries other than Vietnam, aid resources were very sharply reduced if not eliminated altogether. In 1967, the United States had been tenth among the noncommunist developed nations in proportion of GNP devoted to public and private development assistance, ranking behind France, the Netherlands, Portugal, West Germany, Great Britain, Belgium, Switzerland, Japan, and Australia, in that order. In strictly public capital transfers, it ranked somewhat higher, but still below many European nations. Real per capita income in the United States is about double that of the other developed nations, and it seems obvious that the United States did not carry a proportionate share of development assistance even before the sharp reductions of 1968 and 1969.

Private Investment Policies

In order for private investment to contribute to the flow of capital to the underdeveloped world, several conditions must be met. Private investors must have confidence in the intention and capacity of the recipient nation to repay. This means that the recipient nation must have political stability and a government committed to maintaining an economy in which such contracts are honored. It also means that the debtors, whether governments or private entrepreneurs, must be able to sell in a world market and obtain dollars with which to repay the loan. Stability, determination to repay, and capacity to repay are thus the features of a good "investment climate."

American policies designed to foster such favorable climates have been roughly consistent throughout the postwar decades. The central theme is the efficacy of private enterprise. In the words of one moderate authority on economic policy:

> To representatives of the less developed nations, it must seem that the United States never tires of citing the advantages—real and imagined—of an economic system based on private enterprise. The main advantages of private investment cited by American policymakers were: first, private investment is more "flexible," presumably referring to the relative absence of governmental "red tape." Second, private investment is "non-political," presumably referring to a supposed absence of interference in domestic affairs by private investors. And third, private investment often carried with it technical knowledege and managerial skill.[4]

[4]Baldwin, *Economic Development, op. cit.,* p. 19. Statements of American officials are extensively quoted on pp. 20 and 195 ff.

The specific techniques by which American policymakers reinforced the priority given to private investment in the early years of the Cold War included outright refusal to make government grants or loans if private funds might be available; referral of requests for capital to the World Bank (which itself declined to make development funds available if they might be "competing" with private investors); and determined diplomatic efforts to open various nations to "fair" treatment for American private investors.

Ranged against the American commitment to private enterprise and the means adopted to further private investment were Third World nationalism and a need for central planning and control, as well as the apparent instability of many governments and economies. Relatively little private money was actually invested in developing nations. In the mid-1950s, the U.S. government began to supplement its endorsements of private enterprise with provision of "investment guaranty" contracts to American businessmen. These guarantees insured them against certain "nonbusiness" risks in Third World investments, such as exchange problems or expropriation, and resulted in some increases in the flow of private funds. Investment opportunities in Europe and Canada, however, still attracted much more capital than did those in Third World countries. The efficacy of the guaranty program was indisputable, however, for by the mid-1960s more than a billion dollars' worth of such insurance for Third World investments had been extended. To some degree, of course, U.S. government willingness to employ military force to maintain stability (and hence a favorable investment climate) in Third World nations must also be counted as a factor in private investment patterns.

The one aspect of investment-relevant policy under complete American control—trade and tariff policy—was not brought to bear on this problem in any but marginal ways. Third World nations could only acquire the dollars with which to repay private loans by selling exports, principally in American markets. The executive branch made strong efforts to get the Congress to reduce at least some trade barriers, but no significant reductions were ever achieved. In particular, protections against agricultural products (the most common Third World product) remained fixed at prohibitive levels. In effect, the policies of the U.S. government have centered upon promoting opportunities for private investment, but the terms, problems, and consequences involved in following that route have not been attractive to Third World nations. The private investor, on the other hand, could earn substantial profits from Third World investments if he kept ownership or control of the commodities produced and arranged their sale himself. In addition, of course, he would have his investment insured by the U.S. government.

Some Contrasting Explanations

Many factors, some of them beyond presidential control, are involved in shaping foreign policy. The dominant motivations appear to be, first, national security and then profitability of investment and trade with Third World nations. Major participants include not only the executive agencies nominally responsible for foreign policy—such as the State Department, the National Security Council, and special presidential advisors—but also the Commerce Department, the Treasury Department, and the Department of Labor. Also involved are important elements in the Congress, the American and world financial community, the United Nations, and private companies. Under these circumstances, "Who's in charge?" is a crucial question. Perhaps, as we implied in Chapter 12, *nobody* is in charge, and the engines of government run on essentially unchecked. But—again—there *are* patterns. The same things happen repeatedly, the same people or interests gain and lose over extended periods of time. Why?

We shall consider three explanations. The first is the bureaucratic one, which says essentially that the characteristics of the massive organizations involved (and, frequently, mere accidents within them) shape results. The second explanation rests on analysis of the social and occupational backgrounds of decisionmakers, and their ideology. Finally, analysis at the level of basic systems holds that the needs of the economic system would require *any* American institutions and/or decisionmakers to choose the same policies. These three levels

Rius, Siempre (Mexico City)

Rius-Siempre, Mexico.

of explanation are similar to those explored in Chapter 3; by now, readers should recognize which explanations should be given greater weight.

The bureaucratic explanation.   Policy emerges from the random activities of people in organizations; but those organizations are themselves "programmed" to produce certain kinds of results, and so the system works in a generally acceptable fashion. If it does not, the remedy is to replace the people whose bureaucratic failings have caused mistakes in policy. Here is an example, drawn from the experience of a distinguished foreign-policy scholar in the State Department:

> In 1948 the government had for some years been conducting programs of technical assistance in Latin America, and only there. It seemed reasonable that this novel way of conducting international relations might have its uses elsewhere in the world as well, and I recall one occasion especially, a late evening at the end of the day's work, when the Deputy Director of American Republic Affairs and I talked casually about this possibility.
>
> Then, sometime in November, a routine message from the President's speech-writing assistant in the White House requested the Department to send over, in due course, any proposals it had for the contents of the Inaugural Address that the President was to deliver in January. Following established procedure in these matters, the Director of the Office of Public Affairs called a meeting of the interested divisions, to which my friend the Deputy Director went in representation of American Republic Affairs. A Mr. Ben Hardy, pad on knee, took down the various proposals put forward at the meeting as they were accepted. The first proposal advanced and accepted was a statement of support for the United Nations; second was an assurance that the European Recovery Program would be continued; third, the announcement of an intention to organize a common defense among the free nations of the Atlantic area.
>
> Any more?
>
> There was a pause while everyone searched his mind. The Deputy Director, recalling our evening conversation, ended the pause by asking: how about technical assistance for undeveloped countries (the word "underdeveloped" had not yet been coined), like what we're doing in Latin America?
>
> That's a good idea, said the Director of Public Affairs, put it down, Ben. So "Point Four" was set down without further discussion, and there the meeting adjourned.
>
> When the four points proposed for inclusion in the President's address went up through the Department's clearance-machinery, the fourth was discarded. Here I do not have the details, but I have no difficulty in surmising. Any responsible officer was bound to ask what

thought and analysis had entered into the proposal of a program for giving technical assistance to countries all over the world. What countries specifically? What kinds of technical assistance, specifically? On what scale? How much would it cost? Until at least rough answers to these questions were available, until at least the feasibility of such a program had been determined, it would be irresponsible to have the President announce it. So the first three points, without the fourth, were sent on to the White House.

A few days later, the Director of Public Affairs received a phone-call from the presidential assistant, who complained that, while the three points were OK in themselves, they were mere "boiler-plate" (government slang for the cant statements that are always thrown into speeches). I think, he said, the President would like to have something in this speech that's just a bit original.

At this juncture, without proper time for reflection, the Director of Public Affairs found himself standing on the shore of his own Rubicon. He took a deep breath, and crossed over.

There had been a fourth point, he said, but it had been thrown out.

What was it?

The Director told what it was.

That's great, said the voice from the White House, and "Point Four" went back in again.

If anyone gave the matter a further thought, from that moment until the delivery of the Address on January 20, I find no indication of it. "Point Four" was a public-relations gimmick, thrown in by a professional speechwriter to give the speech more life.

When the newspapers dramatized it in their principal headlines on the morning of January 21, the White House and the State Department were taken completely by surprise. No one—not the President, not the Secretary of State, not the presidential assistant or the Director of Public Affairs—knew any more about "Point Four" than what they could read for themselves in the meager and rather rhetorical language of the speech. No one could answer the pressing questions of the newspaper-reporters, of the Congressmen concerned with appropriations, of the foreign diplomats. It was only now, after the Inaugural Address had been delivered and the "bold new program" acclaimed all over the world, that machinery was set up in the government to look into the possibilities of such a program and make plans. The inauguration of an actual program was not to come until twenty-one months later—twenty-one months of hard-packed confusion in which the careers of good men were broken and ulcers proliferated. . . .

At President Truman's press-conference, six days after the Inaugural Address in which he electrified the world with his announcement of the "Point Four" program, he was asked: "Mr. President, can you give us any background on the origin of Point Four?"

"The origin of Point Four (he replied) has been in my mind, and in the minds of the government, for the past two or three years, ever since the Marshall Plan was inaugurated. It originated with the Greece and Turkey propositions. Been studying it ever since. I spend most of my time going over to that globe over there trying to figure out ways to make peace in the world."

I have emphasized the role of accident in what actually happens. Its role, however, is dominant only in the close-up view. . . .

I cannot believe, however, that this close-up view is right. As someone afterwards said, "Point Four" was "in the air" at the time, as Darwin's theory of evolution had been "in the air" when he published his *Origin of Species*. . . . If the series of accidents that produced "Point Four" had not occurred, another series of accidents would have produced it in another way, under another name.[5]

Decisionmakers and their ideologies. This explanation insists that foreign policy is not a matter of accident nor of things being "in the air," but of systematic and deliberate behavior on the part of relevant decisionmakers. Drawing on the facts (reviewed in Chapter 9) that most key foreign-policy decisionmakers come from the business world and/or have close ties with its major institutions, Richard J. Barnet sees "National Security Managers" operating coherently to produce these policies.

The National Security Manager still tends to look at the "Underdeveloped World" as a vast Gray Area in international politics. No part of it is of intrinsic interest unless, of course, it supplies some vital commodity. Otherwise it can capture the official attention in Washington only if it symbolizes some struggle which transcends the minor turmoil of native politics. To the man of the West, Paris and Berlin are important places in their own right, for they symbolize his own historical heritage. But Danang, Santo Domingo, and Kinshasha penetrate his consciousness, if at all, only as battlefields, and then only if the fight is about something sufficiently important. He has almost no knowledge about such places, their people, or their politics, and little personal commitment to them. They represent either sources of strength, strategic or economic, or points of vulnerability. "Vietnam is not the issue," National Security Managers have frequently confided to critics who question whether systematic bombardment is the best way to secure freedom for the Vietnamese people; "it is the testing ground for the Communist strategy of Wars of National Liberation. If they win here, they will strike elsewhere. If they lose, they will not be so ready to start another."

The National Security Manager is a global thinker. In themselves, local problems of other countries are not worthy of his attention; it is the transcendent importance of local revolutionary struggles that warrants intervention. Interference in purely domestic matters is still unjustified as a matter of law and sound policy. Unfortunately, he hastens to add, the line between domestic and foreign matters has

---

[5]Louis J. Halle, *The Society of Man* (New York: Harper & Row, 1965), pp. 21–23, 29–30.

blurred. When political factions struggle with one another in far-off places, their conflict is an expression of a single worldwide struggle. The real contestants remain the same. Only the battlefield shifts. The battle, which takes the form of a series of guerrilla wars, is not about Vietnam or Greece or the Dominican Republic any more than World War II was about Iwo Jima or Sicily. Wherever men struggle for power, one can always find International Communism, the ubiquitous political scavenger, ready to use genuine local grievances as ammunition in a global holy war. Global strategy, more than local conditions, dictates the site of the next engagement between International Communism and the Free World.

At this point let us try to look more closely at the mental set of the National Security Manager as it bears on the U.S. commitment against revolution. The ultimate bureaucratic dream is the prefect freedom of unlimited power. It is the ability to push a button, make a phone call, dispatch a cable, and know that the world will conform to your vision. The capacity to control, or, as he might put it, to have options, is a much clearer objective for the professional statesman than the purposes to which he would put such power. The guiding stars of the working bureaucrat are not cosmic goals. One can find a few expressions of an official eschatology in flowery speeches on National Purpose, or in the negotiated generalities of the Basic National Security Policy papers representing the collective wisdom of the foreign-policy bureaucracy. Usually, however, the National Security Manager prides himself on avoiding theological and "nonpragmatic" speculation. He has faith in his intuitive grasp of the art of *ad hoc* politics. Yet, in developing official policy on U.S. intervention, he is not quite so free as he thinks. Just as he casts his adversary, the Revolutionary —Castro, Mao, Ho—in the inevitable role of foreign agent, so he has picked out a well-worn part for himself. It is the role of the imperial peacekeeper.[6]

The systemic explanation.   The first two explanations were recognizable as analysis at the level of men and institutions—the kind of analysis, examined in Chapter 3, that resulted in the concept of a "military-industrial complex." A version of the deeper, systemic explanation—which focuses on the character of the economic system— is offered by the work of Harry Magdoff, a socialist. His *The Age of Imperialism*[7] may serve as our example.

Magdoff presents evidence that the United States, as the preponderant capitalist nation, does and must engage in systematic exploita-

[6]Reprinted by permission of the World Publishing Company from *Intervention and Revolution* (pp. 28–29) by Richard Barnet. A New American Library book. Copyright © 1968 by Richard Barnet.

[7]Harry Magdoff, *The Age of Imperialism: The Economics of U.S. Foreign Policy* (New York: Monthly Review Press, 1969). Copyright © 1969 by Harry Magdoff. Copyright © 1966, 1968 by Monthly Review Press. The following excerpts from pages 52–53 and 198 of this work are reprinted by permission of Monthly Review Press. Magdoff is an independent economic scholar and an editor of *Monthly Review*, a socialist journal.

tion of the Third World as a means of maintaining its own prosperity. The motivations for this exploitation are the need for raw materials, the profits to be made from foreign investment (which rose, he alleges, from 10 percent of domestic profits to nearly 25 percent between 1950 and 1965), and the need to sell export goods in the world. Table 13-1 and the accompanying text, both from Magdoff's book, summarize his argument concerning the need for raw materials.

TABLE 13-1
Critical Materials Used for Jet Engine

	Pounds used in jet engine*	Imports as percent of consumption*	Where this material is produced‡
Tungsten	80–100	24%	U.S. (30%) South Korea (19%) Canada (12%) Australia (8%) Bolivia (8%) Portugal (7%)
Columbium	10–12	100%	Brazil (54%) Canada (21%) Mozambique (18%)
Nickel	1,300–1,600	75%	Canada (71%) New Caledonia (20%)
Chromium	2,500–2,800	100%	South Africa (31%) Turkey (19%) Southern Rhodesia (19%) Philippines (18%) Iran (5%)
Molybdenum	90–100	0	U.S. (79%) Canada (10%) Chile (9%)
Cobalt	30–40	100%	Congo (Leopoldville) (60%) Morocco (13%) Canada (12%) Zambia (11%)

*From Percy W. Bidwell, *Raw Materials* (New York: Harper and Bros., 1958), p. 12.
†Calculated from data in U.S. Department of Interior, *Minerals Yearbook, 1966* (Washington: Government Printing Office, 1967).
‡Major producers of the material in the noncommunist world. The percentages in parentheses represent the amount produced in the country in 1966 as a percent of total production in noncommunist countries. The source for this information is the same as that for the previous note.

The facts presented here are of course no mystery to business or to the government planners and coordinators of policy. President Truman established in 1951 the Materials Policy Commission cited above, to study the materials problem of the United States and its relation to other noncommunist countries. The resulting five-volume report was issued with much publicity in the midst of the Korean War. The theme of raw materials sources as an ingredient of foreign policy crops up not only with respect to direct United States requirements but also as it concerns United States responsibility as the leader of the "free world" to see to it that Western Europe's and Japan's supplies of raw materials are assured. Consider, for example, this frank statement by former President Eisenhower:

> One of Japan's greatest opportunities for increased trade lies in a free and developing Southeast Asia. . . . The great need in one country is for raw materials, in the other country for manufactured goods. The two regions complement each other markedly. By strengthening of Vietnam and helping insure the safety of the South Pacific and Southeast Asia, we gradually develop the great trade potential between this region . . . and highly industrialized Japan to the benefit of both. In this way freedom in the Western Pacific will be greatly strengthened.

Magdoff also argues that the techniques by which this neo-colonialist relationship is maintained include (a) control of the international monetary and banking structure, (b) trade restrictions, (c) political and military pressures to maintain friendly governments and permit American private enterprise to dominate local economies, and (d) economic assistance to keep Third World nations in peonage situations. This phase of Magdoff's argument may be illustrated from the following excerpt:

> The chains of dependence may be manipulated by the political, financial, and military arms of the centers of empire, with the help of the Marines, military bases, bribery, CIA operations, financial maneuvers, and the like. But the material basis of this dependence is an industrial and financial structure which through the so-called normal operations of the marketplace reproduces the conditions of economic dependence.
>
> A critical element of the market patterns which helps perpetuate the underdeveloped countries as dependable suppliers of raw materials is the financial tribute to the foreign owners who extract not only natural resources but handsome profits as well. The following comparison for the years 1950–1965 is a clear illustration of the process and refers to only one kind of financial drain, the income from direct investments which is transferred to the United States:

		(billions of dollars)		
	Europe	Canada	Latin America	All other areas
Flow of direct invest-ments from U.S.	$8.1	$6.8	$3.8	$5.2
Income on this capital transferred to U.S.	5.5	5.9	11.3	14.3
Net	+$2.6	+$ .9	−$7.5	−$9.1

In the underdeveloped regions almost three times as much money was taken out as was put in. And note well that besides drawing out almost three times as much as they put in, investors were able to increase the value of the assets owned in these regions manifold: in Latin America, direct investments owned by United States business during this period increased from $4.5 to $10.3 billion; in Asia and Africa, from $1.3 to $4.7 billion.

Magdoff further argues that a mature capitalist economy no longer has choices about such policies. In his words, "Imperialism is not a matter of choice for a capitalist society; it is the way of life of such a society."

Conclusions

The implication seems clear that there is no single source of national policy, and that no one explanation is adequate. A wide variety of interests, entities, and individuals can make their influence felt in the process of shaping policy. But so many of these powerful interests and individuals share the same perspective, and want or need the same things, that coherent patterns of action result. *Each* of the explanations just reviewed thus explains some part of the American policy-making process.

The institutions of government reflect and respond to the power units of the economic system, and each ultimately comes to play a characteristic part in serving the ends of those power units. The larger and continuing goal of the major power units, of course, is to sustain and expand the American political economy. Within this context, we can see each political institution playing a distinct role; let us briefly identify each as a means of concluding our analysis of the ways in which elites manage the society.

We have already seen that the Congress is conservative, operates by fits and starts, and depends heavily on presidential leadership. The Court is usually a passive but not ineffective extension of the views of the President who appointed the Chief Justice and a majority of the other justices. And the President, on whom all action really depends, seeks with an *ad hoc* conglomerate of personal aides to acquire the knowledge and leverage necessary to make the whole eighteenth-century mechanism operable in the modern world. We can express these findings somewhat more elaborately in two complementary interpretations.

Roles of Governmental Institutions

First, the distribution of power and the pattern of incumbency in the institutions of the national government are such as to give each a specific role to play. The President is often the initiator of new policies because only he has the information-gathering capabilities of the executive branch at his disposal. He is the major source of leadership, coordination, and priority-setting for the other institutions, although he may anticipate their demands and values to avoid deadlock. By considering the diverse assessments of the problems and needs of the nation produced within the departments of the executive branch, and comparing these with the analysis of resources needed and available in the Bureau of the Budget, the President formulates a program for action. Because he is the highest official of the government, he can command public attention for his program. Through forceful articulation of such priorities and the drafting of proposed legislation, he can set in motion a process that may result in the desired action.

In this process, the Congress becomes a kind of accommodator and conservator of established features of the *status quo*. Interests that were unrepresented or ineffective in shaping the President's program are likely to have access to one or more veto points in the House or Senate. And because nearly all interests with a major investment in the *status quo* have some form of representation in the Congress, the chances are that nothing truly destructive of their status will be enacted. The Congress therefore performs a kind of adjusting and accommodating function by which proposed legislation is fitted to the preferences and perceived needs of established groups. With provisions for the most far-reaching kind of change thus eliminated from legislation, the Congress makes it acceptable to the great majority of the interests powerful enough to count. That this is not an unpopular legislative function may be seen in public opinion studies, which regularly show higher proportions of public trust in the Congress than in the President or the Court.

The Supreme Court plays the role of legitimator in this involved process of institutional interaction. Interests that are defeated, or not fully victorious, in struggles within the other institutional arenas may seek to challenge acts they oppose in the courts. The Supreme Court may in such instances become their last line of defense, and its upholding of a statute or executive act becomes the official act of legitimation. There is no further appeal but to the people, and that, in the face of the unanimity of the major institutions of government, is a very poor prospect. This is a general interpretation, of course, and not every instance of institutional interaction will fit this mold; but most do, and the reason is that the dominant power centers in each of the various institutions have come to behave in consistent ways to play expected roles.

Levels of Interaction

Two levels of interaction among the branches of government are identifiable. The usual posture is one of wary bargaining among equals, in which each organ is concerned about advancing its own special policy interests and protecting its institutional prerogatives. But constant engagement in this process leads to familiarity, predictability, and a shared commitment to the established style. This bargaining and accommodating serve as a uniting bond among all power centers. When the legitimacy of the system itself is challenged, therefore, nearly all power centers react as one and seek to remove or repress the challenge as quickly and as ruthlessly as possible. Such a challenge is not met with partial measures or promises of future study, as are demands for increased rewards on the part of regular participants in the legislative process. Instead, because the challenge is directed at the existence, shared policy preferences, and practices of the power centers themselves, it appears to the conservative people whose lives have been invested in gaining such positions to be wholly illegitimate, if not revolutionary. And nothing in the established rules of political style and procedure requires that any tolerance be extended to those who voluntarily place themselves outside the boundaries of legitimacy and propriety. Further, effective elimination of such challenges will help induce others to operate within the framework that has given rise to the agreeable distribution of power now in effect among the various organs of government.

PART FIVE

INSTITUTIONS
AND PROCESSES:
NON-ELITE ROLES

Chapter 14

In the next three chapters, we deal with issues and relationships that stand in stark contrast to those examined in the last six chapters. Here we deal with *non-elites*, the overwhelming majority of relatively powerless people who have little or no wealth and no institutional positions. What is their life like? How does it affect their beliefs, attitudes, and actions? How and where do the felt needs of non-elites have impact on public policy? In short, what is the meaning —the political implications—of the *context, attitudes*, and *actions* of non-elites?

The Political Context of Non-Elites

In a sense, we shall now look at the meaning and consequences of capitalism at the mass level, where before we analyzed the workings of the major power units in the system. Immediately, we face the issues of (1) a satisfactory definition of the concept of social *class*, and (2) the political relevance of class and class consciousness in American politics. Our analysis begins in this chapter with an exploration of the objective conditions of non-elites' lives and certain of their subjective reactions, from which we conclude that many of the requisites of "class" and "class consciousness" are fulfilled in this country. In Chapter 15, however, we examine the values, ideology, and other attitudes of non-elites, and tentatively conclude that the dominant orthodoxy has diverted attention from objective circumstances and blunted the thrust toward redress of those injustices that are perceived. Finally, in Chapter 16, we analyze the ways in which non-elites seek fulfillment of their perceived needs. For the most part, the orthodox channels—such as political parties—are managed by elites, and non-elites have only limited choices among their offerings. But alternative channels, such as strikes and demonstrations, also influence policy. Although their use is costly, their effects can often be broad and far-reaching.

The overall thesis of these chapters is that (1) non-elite conditions give rise to real and unfulfilled needs, but orthodox values and ideology inhibit recognition of the depth, scope, and shared nature of such needs ("class consciousness"), and diffuse or deflect the efforts that are made to fulfill them; and (2) that the orthodox channels available to non-elites to seek their ends are managed by elites, and tend to absorb non-elites' thrusts or to convert them into harmless or mutually-cancelling forms. Thus the *status quo* persists, and non-elites appear to generate little explicit or effective action to change it. Some observers are quick to say that they are satisfied, and that the system has fulfilled all their real wants and needs. Let us examine this question step-by-step.

Social Context and Social Class

What is the political significance of the kinds of lives that non-elites lead? In this chapter, we shall try to understand what such lives are like, and how they shape non-elite political ideas and actions. For example, one of our focal points will be the economic status of non-elites. It is sometimes said that non-elites are becoming predominantly affluent and middle-class in income and life style, and that this accounts for the lack of political militance on the part of working and lower classes. The weight of the evidence, however, suggests that non-elite economic status is insecure and marginal, and that we must look elsewhere for explanations of this apparent quiescence. This issue leads to another set of questions: what needs really *do* exist at this level? How fully have non-elite needs actually been satisfied, and what kinds of wants that might be served through public policies still remain unfulfilled?

We shall also be examining the extent to which non-elite life conditions justify conceptualization in class terms, and searching for indications of present or potential class consciousness among such non-elites. In Chapter 8, we saw that the concept of class was meaningful for elites (e.g., those who identified themselves as members of the "propertied class"). But the problem of giving concrete meaning to the concept of class in the case of the much larger and less cohesive body of non-elites is much more difficult. If class and class consciousness were found to be realities at this level, of course, the political implications would be vast: a powerful and cohesive force would exist in the American political arena, potentially capable of significant impact on public policy.

Definitions of Class

What do we mean by "class"? There are many definitions, some with long and emotional histories. Each definition carries a particular set of implications. Some refer only to *objective* characteristics of people, such as their income, education, occupational status, or relationship to the means of production (as owners or non-owners). Others define class in *subjective* terms, arguing that classes exist only to the extent that people think of themselves as members of social classes, or are "class-conscious." The first type of definition often amounts to no more than a set of convenient categories in the mind of the observer: such categories frequently have no meaning for the people involved, and thus do not say anything about their real thoughts or actions. The second type of definition suggests that a class can come into existence only if people see themselves in such terms, but does not connect such perceptions to any objective factors in their lives. According to this view, quite casual shared perceptions might be enough to create a "class," or "classes" might never exist; in either case, the concept becomes practically meaningless. In other words, each of these two types of definition requires supplementation by the other before it acquires real utility.

A useful definition of class for purposes of political analysis adds to these two a third dimension—present or potential political power. The concept of class we shall use posits three conditions. First, a number of people are objectively affected in similar ways by some fundamental dynamic of the socioeconomic system. For example, wealth distribution is a fact of life, and it is caused by that fundamental dynamic, the economic system. But the income of professional athletes is not linked to such a structural pattern, and thus does not locate football or basketball players among the upper class.

Second, groups of people develop similar orientations toward the world, values, and attitudes, which are related to the objective conditions of their lives and distinguish them from those outside the group. For example, they have, and understand that they have, certain patterns of access to education, certain probabilities of future income or job levels, and certain cultural experiences or interests, related to amounts of wealth. If these first two conditions are met, a class exists; its members need not be explicitly conscious of how fully they share their particular situation with other people, or of other factors to be noted.

Third, for a class to have real political significance, its members must become aware that they share their situation *and that the reason for their shared status is that they are similarly affected by the same fundamental dynamic of the economic system.* The realization that their status is systemically caused becomes the primary factor in their political orientation. It leads them to define their political goals and mobilize their political power in order to defend or improve their relative positions. No other goals, interests, or loyalties take precedence over the desire to serve the class' needs in this manner. And people must (correctly) believe that political power can be mobilized and applied, so that they are not, and do not see themselves, engaging in an empty or self-deluding exercise.

Political Class Consciousness

The third condition is what we mean by "class consciousness" in the political sense. It requires four elements: (1) recognition of significant status shared with identifiable others, (2) identification of the systemic cause of this shared status, (3) primary commitment of one's political goals to group action with respect to this status and cause, and (4) perceived access to (real) sources of political power sufficient to make the group an effective force in politics. It is thus possible for a class to exist without class consciousness, though such a class would not have much political significance as an independent force. But it is *not* possible for class consciousness in the real sense to exist without the objective and subjective components of classhood to give it reality and substance. Women will not constitute a class or its equivalent, for example, even if they all become conscious of themselves and of what they share as women, unless they also perceive such characteristics as the most significant defining forces in their lives, define themselves politically exclusively in such terms, and find and apply political power toward systemic reconstruction.

We shall use this concept of class as a means of analyzing the situation of non-elites and its political potential. If a class exists, of course, there is always the possibility of class consciousness. But many forces intervene between the two. If they are strong enough, and sustained enough, class consciousness may never develop. If conditions contribute to the generation of class consciousness, however, dramatic political consequences may follow. One of the continuing arguments in American politics, as we shall see, is over the existence and consciousness of an American "working class." Recently, this debate has centered on the existence of a "new working class" made up of professional, technical, and other higher-level white-collar workers, and students—and on the possibilities that such a class might take over the historical role of the working class as an agent of change. Let us begin by simply describing some of the characteristics of non-elite life, and work our way toward these more complex issues.

Economic and Social Conditions

American affluence is much celebrated, and, in aggregate terms, it is real. Per capita gross national product and real income are the highest in the world. Per capita personal income in 1970 was about four times higher than it was in 1900. But these figures represent averages, not actual patterns of distribution. When the actual incomes of all families are examined, it becomes clear that the majority of Americans are either poor or economically marginal—that is, likely to drop into the ranks of the officially poor in the event of a layoff, illness, or accident.

Monetary and Occupational Circumstances

The measurement and exact characterization of economic marginality presents continuing difficulties of definition and data. One method is to compare income levels with the Bureau of Labor Statistics' regularly published family budgets.[1] These are calculated for families of four living in urban areas, and set at "lower," "intermediate," and "higher" levels according to prices of food and other goods and living standards thought to be common or appropriate to families at these levels. The intermediate budget (formerly termed the "modest but adequate" budget), for example, assumes careful shopping, modest apartment rental, and other frugal habits. And yet, at no time since these budgets were first prepared in the mid-1960s has the income of any category of blue-collar worker except certain skilled craftsmen and foremen reached this level. Characteristically, the incomes of nearly all blue-collar and several categories of white-collar workers fall below the "modest but adequate" standard in their cities, sometimes by as much as $2,000 per year. These facts take on added significance when they are related to occupational patterns. Fifty-four percent of all employed males are in either manual or service work, the typical blue-collar jobs. Nearly 80 percent of all employed women are at these levels or in low-paid clerical or sales positions. Thus, more than half of all employed males and the great majority of employed females earn incomes that do not provide them modest but adequate standards of living. Life is far from affluent at this level, and those whose regular earnings do keep them above this line are faced with the prospect of dropping below it in the event of a recession or other financial reverse.

Some recurring myths about changes in the American occupational structure and about who is poor or economically marginal might well be addressed at this point. Table 14-1 summarizes many of these changes, comparing the proportions of workers in each of the major categories in 1900, 1940, and 1970. It shows clearly, for example, that blue-collar workers are *not* disappearing as a category: the proportion of males in manual work occupations has actually risen since

[1]The basic source of data in this passage is Bureau of Labor Statistics, *Employment and Earnings*, January 1970, p. 67.

TABLE 14-1

Occupations of the U.S. Labor Force (percentages)

	1900			1940			1970			
	Male	Female	All	Male	Female	All	Male	Female	All	Nonwhite % of all
Managers, officials, proprietors, farm owners	30	7	26	22	5	18	17	5	13	4
Professional-technical	3	8	4	6	13	8	14	15	14	7
Clerical & sales	7	8	8	12	29	16	13	42	24	7
Service workers	3	36	9	6	29	12	7	22	12	23
Manual workers	38	28	36	46	22	40	47	16	35	14
Farm workers	19	13	18	8	3	7	3	1	2	12
Total	100	100	100	100	100	100	100	100	100	100

Source: Historical Statistics of the United States; Statistical Abstract, 1970. (Figures may not total 100% due to rounding.)

1900! In 1970 there were only half as many people in the independent, entrepreneurial category of managers, proprietors, and farm owners as in 1900. In other words, more and more people are working for wages and salaries and fewer own their own businesses. Long-term changes have drawn workers away from the farms and toward professional-technical and clerical-sales occupations. Women workers in particular have been concentrated in clerical positions. Black workers, who make up 12 percent of the labor force, are still most numerous in service jobs. They are only slightly disproportionately manual workers.

These data, and other facts about the makeup of the officially poor, demonstrate that both the poor and the economically marginal are predominantly *white*. The myth that poor means black is simply inaccurate, even though it is both long-lived and probably partly responsible for the lack of effective action to raise the standard of living of people at these levels. Fifty-seven percent of *all* employed whites are in blue-collar, service, or clerical occupations, and thus earning low incomes. Of the officially poor in the nation as a whole, only 25 percent are black.[2] The figure rises to one-third in metropolitan areas and one-half in central cities, but this means only that the white poor are disproportionately rural. Nor are the poor unemployed: one-third of the heads of family listed as officially poor work full-time, and others work part-time. In other words, most of the poor and the great bulk of the economically marginal are white and hold jobs.

Financial standing is also measurable in terms of accumulated assets and liabilities. Annual surveys that measure both regularly report very limited funds on hand and extensive debts for the purchase of cars and appliances.[3] For example, an average of about 70 percent of all families have less than $500 in checking or savings accounts—and are thus only two or three paychecks away from public assistance of some kind. Installment debts are steadily climbing, and the great majority of all families with incomes under $10,000 have debts requiring regular payments from current earnings.

Many other factors enter into economic and occupational status. A major one is the prospect of unemployment. Manual workers and other lower-paid workers are most likely to be laid off during recessions or to work only intermittently in the best of times. Less educated and less skilled workers, particularly minorities, are likely to be the last hired and the first fired; economic fluctuations thus have exaggerated effects at these levels. Technological change works par-

[2]George Katona, James N. Morgan, Joy Schmiedeskamp, and John A. Sundquist, *1967 Survey of Consumer Finances* (Ann Arbor: University of Michigan, 1967.) All data in this paragraph are drawn from this source.
[3]Gus Tyler, "White Worker, Blue Mood," in *Dissent*, Winter 1972, p. 190.

ticular hardship on older workers, who may not be able to find alternative employment for which they are qualified. All workers who suffer intermittent unemployment risk losing such fringe benefits as medical and hospitalization insurance. In most cases, of course, the economic ups and downs of business firms occur for reasons unrelated to workers' efforts or competence, but they nevertheless feel the effects.

Working conditions among the working class and the lower middle class are also distinctive. In many cases, employment means hard and exhausting physical labor. Some work on an assembly line, where speed is essential and the number of units produced is the measure of income or the criterion of further employment. Loud noise and danger may be constant. For others, safer and more comfortable settings may mean highly routinized, tedious work requiring intense concentration. Nor are white-collar workers insulated against undesirable working conditions: routine work, highly bureaucratized rules and requirements (and, for women, menial and subservient roles) are characteristic of many low-paid positions. For most working-class people, travel conditions also contribute to insecurity and frustration: public transportation systems are crowded, inconvenient, expensive, and time-consuming; but the cost and upkeep of a car may be a serious drain on family income.

Social Circumstances

Despite national affluence, the United States as a whole does not enjoy a particularly high level of social welfare. In many Western nations, for example, family allowances (payments to help support children) are a common means of sharing this financial burden and marginally redistributing income. Most have broader manpower training and reemployment assistance programs than does the United States, and none either experience or (apparently) would tolerate the levels of unemployment that are standard in this country.

The general health conditions of Americans are not commensurate with national affluence either, and hardships are concentrated in the lower socioeconomic levels. Americans have lower life expectancies at birth than do the citizens of 15 other nations of the world; infant mortality rates are higher than in 14 countries, and rates of death from a variety of diseases are higher than in several other countries.[4] The lower classes, and particularly blacks, experience a higher incidence of infant mortality and higher death rates from infectious disease than do the middle and upper classes. For example, among

[4]U.S. Department of Health, Education, and Welfare, *Toward a Social Report* (Washington: Government Printing Office, 1969), pp. 6–10. The data apply to the mid-1960's.

employed males aged 45–64, those with incomes of less than $2,000 have three-and-a-half times as many disability days as those who earn over $7,000.

People at lower income levels tend not to make use of preventive services or to visit doctors for medical care, no doubt chiefly because of their cost. More than 20 percent of members of families with incomes under $3,000 have *never* visited a dentist, compared to 7 percent of those in families with incomes over $10,000. Fifty-four percent of children under 17 in families with incomes of more than $10,000 had had physical checkups, in contrast to 16 percent of those from families earning less than $2,000. Medical care prices have risen at a rate 50 percent higher than the cost of living in the last decade, and the costs of hospital services have climbed even faster. Medicare covers only about 35 percent of total medical expenses, and then only for those over 65. Nearly half of the remaining population is covered by some form of private health care insurance, but these plans pay, on the average, less than half the costs of medical care. Poor health and its costs, it seems clear, are an acute aspect of lower classes' economic and social circumstances.

The living conditions of the working and lower classes also differ from those enjoyed by the more affluent. The most drastically substandard housing in the country is found in rural settings inhabited chiefly by the poor—and, again, principally by the black poor. Large city neighborhoods are normally crowded, and the cost per square foot of living space is frequently higher than in the suburbs. Blacks in particular have little choice over where they will live, however, as the nation's sharply (and in many cities, increasingly) segregated city ghettos attest.

Moreover, the incidence of crime is far higher in lower-class areas, and particularly in black neighborhoods, than elsewhere. Despite all the concern about crime expressed by middle-class suburbanites, it is the poor—and, again, the black poor—who experience most of the nation's personal crimes. We saw a comparison of the incidence of crime by race and income in Chapter 11. Except for the theft of property, which naturally occurs more often among those who have property, the lower income levels experience more incidents of every kind of crime than do the higher levels. Whether due to the surroundings in which they live or the lack of effective police protection, crime is a condition they must live with to a degree unknown to the middle and upper classes.

Mobility Opportunities

We may well ask to what extent there is real opportunity for individual members of the lower classes to escape from these circumstances. Table 14-2 presents an important overall summary of social mobility opportunities in the United States. It uses responses to a U.S. Census Bureau survey to compare the occupations of working-age men with their *fathers'* occupations, as a means of measuring relative improvement or decline in status. The left-hand column lists fathers' race and occupations, and the horizontal rows represent the respondents' present occupations. In general, white children tend to remain in the same occupations and status levels as their fathers. Today's higher white-collar jobs are filled by people whose fathers had similar jobs. For whites, however, there is some net upward mobility. For example, 36 percent of whites whose fathers were in the "lower manual" occupations are themselves in the same category; but 23 percent have moved up to the "higher manual" level, and 21.3 percent of such children have attained high white-collar status.

But for blacks, there is much heavier initial concentration in the lower occupations, less mobility, and little retention of higher status once gained. Children of lower manual fathers move up at much lower rates than do whites; children of higher white-collar fathers tend to *drop back* into the lower manual category! In analyzing these data, of course, we must keep in mind that the general structure of employment in the country has shifted toward white-collar jobs and away from those classified here as lower manual or farm. Thus, some of this apparent "mobility" is due to broad structural changes and not to the relative striving and achievement of individuals. This realization leads to the sobering conclusion that mobility for lower-status people has been modest at best, and for blacks practically nonexistent.

These aspects of the socioeconomic situation of the great majority of American people establish the context for their political behavior. Economic hardships and insecurity are constant; it takes very substantial effort to maintain existing levels of income and status, and prodigious effort or good fortune to move ahead. There is a substantial lack of health and medical services, educational opportunities, neighborhood and work-place amenities, and protection against crime. What is taken for granted at middle-class levels does not exist for the majority of the population.

The political implications are several. Unfulfilled needs exist, and might be satisfied by elite action or by non-elite mobilization. But non-elites have very little time readily available for political action; the demands of daily living tend to exhaust both time and psychic and physical resources. And a number of external barriers, some already examined and others to be discussed shortly, operate to discourage or deflect mass assertion of group demands. Finally, there is no way of knowing that mass goals would be attainable even if a concerted

TABLE 14-2

Mobility from Father's Occupation by Race for Civilian Men 25 to 64 Years Old, March 1962 (in percentages)

Race and father's occupation	1962 Occupation*						Total
	Higher white-collar	Lower white-collar	Higher manual	Lower manual	Farm	Not in experienced civilian labor force	
Negro							
Higher white-collar	10.4	9.7	19.4	53.0	0.0	7.5	100.
Lower white-collar	14.5	9.1	6.0	69.1	0.0	7.3	100.
Higher manual	8.8	6.8	11.2	64.1	2.8	6.4	100.
Lower manual	8.0	7.0	11.5	63.2	1.8	8.4	100.
Farm	3.1	3.0	6.4	59.8	16.2	11.6	100.
Not reported	2.4	6.5	11.1	65.9	3.1	11.1	100.
Total, percent	5.2	5.4	9.5	62.2	7.7	10.0	100.
Non-Negro							
Higher white-collar	54.3	15.3	11.5	11.9	1.3	5.6	100.
Lower white-collar	45.1	18.3	13.5	14.6	1.5	7.1	100.
Higher manual	28.1	11.8	27.9	24.0	1.0	7.3	100.
Lower manual	21.3	11.5	22.5	36.0	1.7	6.9	100.
Farm	16.5	7.0	19.8	28.8	20.4	7.5	100.
Not reported	26.0	10.3	21.0	32.5	3.9	6.4	100.
Total, percent	28.6	11.3	20.2	26.2	6.8	6.9	100.

*Combinations of major occupation groups. *Higher white-collar:* professional and kindred workers, and managers, officials, and proprietors, except farm. *Lower white-collar:* sales, clerical, and kindred workers. *Higher manual:* craftsmen, foremen, and kindred workers. *Lower manual:* operatives and kindred workers, service workers, and laborers, except farm. *Farm:* farmers and farm managers, farm laborers, and foremen. Classification by "father's occupation" includes some men reporting on the occupation of a family head other than the father.

Source: Unpublished tables, survey of "Occupational Changes in a Generation."

Reprinted from U.S. Department of Health, Education and Welfare, *Toward a Social Report* (Washington: Government Printing Office, 1969), p. 24.

effort were made, and good reason for predicting that they might well be denied.

What Does It Mean? The Subjective Side of Non-elite Life

The preceding brief characterization of the major socioeconomic facts of non-elite life is only part of the story. It says nothing about the feelings that people at this level have about their lives, their jobs, and their prospects. And the latter may be more crucial to the actual life style and potential class consciousness of such people than are the bare facts of income and job status. Let us turn from data analysis for a moment, and listen to a steelworker talking about his job and his world. This excerpt is from a collection of similar interviews with ordinary people conducted by a Chicago journalist. What are the political implications of Mike Fitzgerald's view of the world? In what ways is he class-conscious?

A STEELWORKER SPEAKS:
AN INTERVIEW WITH MIKE FITZGERALD

Studs Terkel

Mike Fitzgerald lives in a two-flat dwelling, somewhere in Cicero, on the outskirts of Chicago. He is 37 years old, works in a steel mill. On occasion his wife, Carol, works as a waitress in a neighborhood restaurant; otherwise she's at home, caring for their two small children, a girl and a boy.

At the time of the first visit, a statuette of Mother and Child was on the floor, head severed from body. Fitzgerald laughed softly as he nodded toward his three-year-old daughter: "She Doctor Spock'd it."

What sort of work do you do?

No trade. Laborer. Strictly muscle work. . . . Pick it up, put it down, pick it up, put it down. We take things off the hook. We handle manually, I'd say, between 40,000 and 50,000 pounds of steel a day. There's nothing automated about it, you just pick it up, put it down. (Laughs) I know this is hard to believe—from 400 pounds down to three- and four-pound pieces. The work I do is part of a dying kind. Manual labor.

You can't take pride anymore. You remember when a guy could point to a house he built, tell how many logs he stacked. He did something physical. He built it and he was proud of it. I don't really think I could be proud if a contractor built a home for me. I would be tempted to get in there and kick the carpenter in the ass (laughs) and take the saw away from him. 'Cause I would have to be part of it, you know.

It's hard to take pride when you work for a large steel company. It's hard to take pride in a bridge you're never gonna cross, in a door you're never gonna open. You're mass-producing things and you never see the end result of it. Whereas, (muses) . . . I worked for a trucker one time. And I got this tiny satisfaction when I loaded a truck. At least, I could see the truck depart loaded. That's small, that's very tiny. In a steel mill, forget it. You don't see where nothing goes.

I know guys that are 50 years old and do my job. I don't think the average college boy could handle it. Your muscles get used to certain kinds of work.

How long have you been doing this work?

Ever since I can remember. Out of the orphan home into the service, out of the service in '54 . . . manual labor until today. The difference is when I was single I could quit, just split. I wandered all over the country. You'd work a week, two weeks. You weren't ambitious. You worked just enough to get a poke, you know, money in your pocket.

Now I'm married and I got two kids. . . . (trails off) I worked on a truck dock one time when I was single. The foreman came over and he grabbed my shoulder like that, you know. just my shoulder and kind of gave me a shove. I punched him and knocked him off the dock. He fell only four or five feet, didn't hurt himself. Just knocked the wind out of him and I think maybe put a knot in his head. I stood on top of the dock and I told him. I said: "I'm prepared to jump on you, too. Any way you want. Leave me alone, I'm doing my work, just stay away from me, just don't give me with-the-hands business."

What made you do it?

Hell, if you whip a damn mule he might kick you. And that's the way I felt about it. Stay out of my way, that's all. Working is bad enough, don't try bugging me. I would rather work my ass off for eight hours a day with nobody watching me than work five minutes with a guy watching me.

There was a feeling you had before he even touched you . . .?

No, not really. Who you gonna sock? You can't sock General Motors, you can't sock anybody in Washington, you can't sock a system. Who'll the kids sock then, their fathers? I'll put it this way: personal violence, yeah, in a minute. But political violence, violence against establishments, institutions, no. That's stupid. For one thing, they don't change. They don't change by violence. I think they change in smoke-filled rooms.

Is the work you're doing dangerous, do you have bruises?

Oh yeah. See. (Shows black and blue marks, burns) I'm 37 years old. I think I can outwork the average 18-year-old kid. I can outpunch him, too. I want my kid to be an effete snob. Yeah. Mm-hmmm (laughs).

I want him to be able to quote Walt Whitman, to be proud of it. To be able to ... just have the kind of job where ... I'll give you an example. I went once to the Playboy Club. During the whole—what do the kids call it, plastic?—setup, I felt uncomfortable. I want my kid to feel comfortable there. You know what I heard from more than one guy at work? "If my kid wants to work in a factory, I am going to kick the hell out of him." If you can't improve yourself, you improve your posterity. It's a continuum. Otherwise life isn't worth a thing. You might as well go back to the cave and stay there. I'm sure the first caveman who went over the hill to see what was on the other side—didn't go there wholly out of curiosity. He went there also because he wanted to get his son out of the cave. Just the same way that I want to send my kid to college.

Do you feel you're in a cave right now ... the work you're doing?
A mule, an old mule. That's pretty well the way I feel.

Do you feel looked down upon by others?
You better believe it. Oh yes, oh yes. I got chewed out by my foreman once. He said, "Mike, you're a good worker, but you have a bad attitude." My attitude is that I don't get excited about my job. I do the work but I don't say whoopee-doo. The day I get excited about my job is the day I go to a head shrinker. How are you gonna get excited about pulling steel? How are you gonna get excited when you're tired and want to sit down? It's like slavery. What was it Malcolm X said one time? They were praying for the master to live. Malcolm X said, "No, they weren't. They were praying for a strong wind to blow his house down."

It always comes back to your work. . . .
Somebody built the pyramids. Somebody's gonna build something. Pyramids, Empire State Building—these things don't just happen. There's hard work behind it. I would like to see a building, say the Empire State, I would like to see one side of it, a foot-long strip from top to bottom with the name of every bricklayer, the name of every electrician, with all the names. So when the guy walked by, he could take his son and say: "See, that's me over there on the 45th floor." Or, "I put the steel beam in." Picasso can point to a painting. I think I've worked harder than Picasso, and what can I point to? A writer can point to a book. Everybody should have something to point to.

It's the nonrecognition by other people. To say a woman is just a housewife is degrading, right? OK. *Just* a housewife. It's also degrading to say *just* a laborer. The difference is that a man goes out and maybe gets smashed. I work so damn hard and want to come home and sit down and lie around. *But I gotta get it out.* I gotta get the inside out. I want to be able to turn around to somebody and say, "Hey, fuck you." You know? (Laughs) The guy sitting next to me on the bus, too. 'Cause all day I wanted to tell my foreman; but I can't. So I find a guy in a tavern. To tell him that. And he tells me, too. Maybe we come to blows. I've been in brawls. He's punching me and I'm punching him, because we actually want to punch somebody else. The most that'll happen there is the bartender will bar us from the tavern. But at work, you lose your job. I lost my job when I punched that foreman off the dock. But I was single then. Now it's different.

This one foreman I've got, he's a kid. He's 25 years old, he's a college graduate. He thinks he's better than everybody else. He had me in the office. I was saying: yeah, yeah, yeah. He was chewing me out. He said: "Whatta ya mean, yeah, yeah, yeah? Yes, *sir.*" I told him, "Who the hell are you Hitler? What is this 'yes, *sir*' bullshit? I came here to work, I didn't come here to crawl. And there's a difference." One word led to another and I lost.

I got broke down to a lower grade and lost 25¢ an hour, which is a hell of a lot. It amounts to about $10 a week. He came over to me—after breaking me down. The guy comes over and smiles at me. I blew up. He didn't know it, but he was about two seconds and two feet away from a hospital. I said, "stay away from me." He just looked at me. He was about to say something and was pointing his finger. I just reached my hand up and grabbed his finger and just put it back in his pocket. He walked away from me. I grabbed his finger because I'm married. If I'd a' been single, I'd a' grabbed his head. That's the difference.

If you were single, you'd have socked him . . .?
For sure. Hell, yes.

So this builds up inside you?
Yeah, oh yeah. For one thing, you're doing this manual labor and you know that technology can do it (laughs). Let's face it. It's a fact that a machine can do the work of a man, otherwise they would not have space probes. Why can we send a rocket ship that's unmanned and yet send a man in the steel mill to do a mule's work? They can go to the moon and do scientific tricks, and yet I still have to go to the steel mill. I'm sure they have things that can lay bricks, too.

The 20-hour week is a possibility today. The liberals, the intellectuals, they always say there are potential Lord Byrons, Walt Whitmans, Roosevelts, Picassos working in construction or steel mills or factories. But I don't think they believe it. I think they're afraid of the potential Hitlers and Stalins that are there, too. What do you think would happen in this country if, for one year, they experimented and gave everybody a 20-hour week? How do they know that the guy who digs Wallace today doesn't try to resurrect Hitler tomorrow? Or the guy who is mildly disturbed about pollution doesn't decide to go to General Motors and shit on the guy's desk? You could become a fanatic if you had the time. The whole thing is time. This is, I think, one reason rich kids tend to be fanatic about politics: they have time. Time, that's the important thing.

It isn't that the average working guy is dumb. He's tired, that's all. Not dumb, tired. That's why it amazed me to find out, years ago—I read Jack London's "Martin Eden"—can you imagine working people at a picnic discussing De Leon and Marx and all that? Today, forget it. I don't know what happened. I think what happened was the people who organized the workingman forgot the spirit and paid more attention to the organization. They became just as corporate as the corporations they were fighting.

I'm saying there should be something to drag a guy down to a union hall. Something *inside* him. To go there to improve his life or somebody else's.

You spoke of tiredness.

I know a guy 57 years old. Know what he tells me? "Mike, I'm old and tired *all* the time." This guy does hard work. He does work a 20-year-old guy should be doing.

The first thing happens: when the arms start moving, the brain stops. I punch in about ten minutes to seven in the morning. I say hello to a couple of guys I like. I kid around with them. One guy says good morning to you and you say good morning. To another guy you say fuck you; that guy's your friend.

I put on my hard hat, change into my safety shoes, put my safety glasses on, go to the bonderizer. It's the thing I work on. They take the metal, they wash it, they dip it in a paint solution and we take it off. It's a whole circle of things. Put it on, take it off, put it on, take it off, put it on, take it off. . . .

You feel, very soon, this work can be done by a machine?

It can be done *right now*. The people in power fear the leisure man. This is the same in every country in the world. Not just the United States. Russia's the same way. About 1 percent of the people make decisions, about 5 percent of the people give us our culture and political stand in general. Maybe another 15 percent give us our drama, our TV, etcetera. I think the top 20 percent are scared shitless that there's 80 percent out there that might disagree with them.

I say hello to everybody but my boss. At 7:00 A.M. it starts. My arms get tired about the first half hour. After that, they don't get tired any more, until maybe about the last half hour, at the end of the day. I work from 7:00 to 3:30. My arms are tired at 7:30 and they're tired at 3:00. I hope to God I never get broke in, because I always want my arms to be tired at 7:30 and 3:00 (laughs). 'Cause that's when I know that there's a beginning and that there's an end. That I'm not brainwashed. It's sort of funny, in between I don't even try to think.

No thoughts at all—between 7:30 a.m. and 3:00 p.m.?

My thoughts are: at 3:30, I get off work.

Can you carry on conversation with the guys while on the job?

Oh, you have to. Not while lifting heavy things. It depends what the guy wants to talk about. Very seldom politics. Maybe the economy a little bit, like things are rough. Maybe about baseball or something like that. Never about work. Unless the guy's a nut. And you do have nuts. I'd say one out of a hundred will actually get excited about work.

Do you daydream, fantasize?

Oh, yeah, I fantasize. I fantasize about a sexy blonde in Miami who's got my union dues (laughs). I think of the head of the union the way I think of the head of my company. Living it up.

Most of your day, though, is a blank?

You try to make it blank. If I were to put you in front of a dock and I pulled up a skid in front of you with 50 hundred-pound sacks of potatoes, and there are 50 more skids just like it, and this is what you're gonna do all day, what would you think about—potatoes?

Does anger get you, bitterness?

No, not really. Somebody has to do it. If my kid ever goes to college, I just want him to realize that when I tell him somebody has to do it, I just want him to have a little bit of respect, to realize that his dad is one of those somebodies. This is why even on (muses)—yeah, I guess, sure—on the black thing.... (Sighs heavily) I can't really hate the colored fella that's working with me all day. The black intellectual I got no respect for. The white intellectual I got no use for. I got no use for the black militant who's gonna scream about 300 years of slavery to me while I'm busting my back. You know what I mean? (Laughs) I have one answer for that guy, Go see Rockefeller. See Harriman. See the people who've got the money. Don't bother me. We're in the same cotton field. So just don't bug me (laughs).

It's very funny. It's always the rich white people who are screaming about racism. They're pretty well safe from the backlash. You ever notice it's always: go get the Klansman, go get the Hunkies, go get that Polack. But don't touch me, baby, 'cause my name is Prince John Lindsay. Park Avenue. Lake Shore Drive. They're never gonna get at 'em, baby, uh-uh.

How the hell am I gonna hate the colored fella when he's sweatin' and I'm sweatin'. We're both working hard. When a strike comes, I carry a picket sign, he carries a picket sign. The difference is he thinks the reason he sweats is because of a white establishment. They actually look at a white guy, sweatin' and bustin' his back just as hard as they are, and yet they still look at that white guy as the white establishment. When I see a black militant with that mental block, I might try for a day or two to break it, but when I can't, I simply say: some fellows at work I can talk to and some I can't.

What happens during your lunch break? Do you talk with some of the guys?

I generally don't bother. Unless I like the guy and he likes me.

What do you think of then?
February in Miami. Warm weather, a place to lie in. When I hear a college kid say, "I'm oppressed," I don't believe him. You know what I'd like to do for one year? Live like a college kid. Just for one year. I'd love to. Wow! (Whispers) Wow! Sports cars! Marijuana! (Laughs) Wild, sexy broads.

Are you jealous?
You better believe it. I sure am (laughs). I'd be a damn nut if I wasn't jealous. Wow!

Back to lunch: you have an hour?
It's a half hour. Sometimes I bring my lunch and sometimes I have a couple of beers. I'd like to sit down and read a book. But you can't pay attention to a book. It's hard to correlate being worn out physically with mental work. That's why most of your weight lifters are office workers (laughs). The athletes are office workers. Do you think I'm going to lift weights in my spare time, loading and unloading 40,000 pounds every day? All that hot steel, that heavy steel, and then go to a gym? Who needs it?

I picked up some books on chess one time. I know how to play the game, the rudiments of it. That thing lay in a drawer for two or three weeks because during the weekdays, you're too tired. During the weekends you have to take care of the family. You want to take your kids out. You don't want to sit there and the kid comes up, Daddy, can I go to the park? And you got your nose in a book? Forget it.

After work, I usually stop off at the tavern. Cold beer. Cold beer right away. There the guys talk about such and such a friend who went out and got drunk the other night. Or he got laid or he didn't get laid. Or close to any layoff, they talk union.

I've heard Vietnam discussed a few times. There are generally two attitudes. The World War II vet tends to be overwhelmed by the thing. He was GI Joe in 1944 and he can't get it through his head that Vietnam isn't GI Joe. Oddly enough, it's the liberals who've brainwashed him. All the flag-waving in World War II is coming back to haunt the liberals now, because they did too good a job. Well, it's true, isn't it?

You're at the tavern. About an hour or so?
Yeah. When I was single, I used to go into hillbilly bars, get in a lot of brawls. I got a thing on the arm here (indicates scar), I got slapped with a bicycle chain. Oh, wow!

Why did you get in those brawls?
Just to explode. I just wanted to explode.

Do you still have that feeling?
Mmm. I'm getting older (laughs). No, not really. You might say I'm

broken in. (Quickly) No, I'll never be broken in. (Sighs) When you get a little older, you exchange words. When you're younger, you exchange the blows. That's the difference.

What happens when you get home?

Oh, I argue with my wife a little bit. That's natural. Turn on TV, get mad at the news (laughs). I don't even watch the news that much, I watch Jackie Gleason. I look for any alternative to the ten o'clock news. I don't want to go to bed angry. I can stand it Sunday afternoon at three o'clock, when I'm rested, sitting back having a cold beer, and I don't have a hard day's work behind me. They can give me all the intellectual jazz they want, and I can think about it. But don't hit a man with anything heavy at five o'clock. He just can't be bothered. This is his time to relax. The heaviest thing he wants is what his wife has to tell him.

You play with the kids . . . ?

Uh huh. Laura is three-and-a-half, Danny is about six months. Laura, wow! She's a hellraiser. God bless her. I don't want an autistic child. It's funny. I look at that colored television, I look at that hi-fi, I look at that clock on the wall. And I tell myself, that's why I'm working. To buy these things. If my kid destroyed any one of 'em, I'd spank her. But I'd buy her things again. So there has to be another reason. Continuum. I'll put it this way. When you're living on green apples, you want to give your kid red ones whenever you can. Whatever you got, you want to make it better. Otherwise, we'd be back in the cave.

When I come home, know what I do for the first 20 minutes? Fake it. I put on a smile. I don't feel like it. I got a kid three-and-a-half years old. Sometimes she says, Daddy, where've you been? And I say, Work. I could've told her I'd been in Disneyland. What's work to a three-year-old kid? If I feel bad, I can't take it out on the kids. Kids are born innocent of everything but birth. You don't take it out on your wife either. This is why you go to the tavern. You want to release it there rather than do it at home. What does an actor do when he's got a bad movie? I've got a bad movie every day.

What time do you hit the pad?

That differs. I don't even need the alarm clock to get up in the morning. I can go out drinking all night, fall asleep at four, and bam! I'm up at six. No matter what I do. (Laughs) It's a sort of death, more or less. Your whole system is paralyzed and you give all the appearance of death. It's an in-grown clock. It's a thing you just get used to. The hours differ. It depends. Sometimes my wife wants to do something crazy like play five-hundred rummy or put a puzzle together.

Till midnight. . . ?

It could be midnight, could be ten o'clock, could be nine-thirty.

Go to movies?
Very seldom.

Go out drinking with the guys at night?
Quite a bit. I went out drinking with one guy, oh, a long time ago, and the bouncer came over. I don't know how the damn thing started. He slapped my friend on the head with a blackjack. I picked up a full quart of Jim Beam, cracked him in the head with it. That's the last thing I remember. It's strange, but it feels good to do a thing like that. Just to cut loose.

There was a college boy working where I work now. Always preaching to me about how you need violence to change the system and all that garbage. Just to show you the difference between rhetoric and what actually happens. This kid was telling me all this bullshit about violence this and violence that. We went into a hillbilly joint. Some guy there, I didn't know him from Adam, he said: "You think you're smart." I said, "What's your pleasure." (Laughs) He said, "My pleasure's to kick your ass." I told him, "I really can't be bothered." He said, "What're you, chicken?" I said, "No, I just don't want to be bothered." He came over and said something to me again. I said, "I don't beat women, drunks, or fools. Now leave me alone."

The guy called his brother over. This college boy that was with me, he came nudging my arm, "Mike, let's get out of here." I said, "What are you worried about?" (Laughs) This isn't unusual. People will bug you. You fend it off as much as you can with your mouth and when you can't you punch the guy out.

It was near closing time and we stayed. We could have left, but when you go into a place to have a beer and a guy challenges you—if you expect to go into that place again, you don't leave. You stay there, put up with what you have to. If you have to fight the guy, you fight. This college boy wanted to leave; but we stayed till closing time. I got just outside the door, and one of these guys jumped on me and grabbed me around the neck. I grabbed his arm and flung him against the wall. I grabbed him here (indicates throat) and jiggled his head against the wall quite a few times. He kind of slid down a little bit. This guy who said he was his brother took a swing at me with a garrison belt. He just missed and hit the wall. I'm looking around for my junior Stalin (laughs), who loves violence and everything. He's gone. Split (laughs). Next day, I seen him at work. I couldn't get mad at him; he's a baby.

He saw a book in my back pocket one time and was amazed. He walked up to me and he said, "You read?" I said, "What do you mean, I read?" He said, "Everybody else reads the sports pages around here. What are you doing with a book?" I looked at him. I said, "I don't know what you're talking about." He said, "All these dummies." I got pissed off at the kid right away. I said, "What do you mean, all these dummies? Don't knock a man who's paying somebody else's way through college." I'll put it this way: he was a 19-year-old effete snob.

Yet you want your kid to be an effete snob. . . .

Yes. I want my kid to look at me and say, "Dad, you're a nice guy, but you're a dummy." Hell, yes. I want my kid to tell me that he's not gonna be like me. I think that's why I didn't even give him my name. I call him Dan. I don't call him Mike. Wholly separate.

Why is it that the Communists always say they're for the workingman, and as soon as they set up a country, you got guys singing to tractors? They're singing about how they love the factory. I wish somebody would explain that to me (laughs). That's where I couldn't buy Communism. It's the intellectuals' utopia, not mine. I cannot picture myself singing to a tractor, I just can't (laughs). Or singing to steel. (Sing-songs) Oh whoop-deedoo, I'm at the bonderizer, oh, how I love this heavy steel. No thanks.

When you were a little kid did you have a dream of what you'd like to be?

A zombie. When I was 12 years old, I asked the social worker at the orphanage who my parents were. She said it was none of my business. I haven't asked since. I have no identity crisis because I couldn't care less. I would not walk across the street to find out who my mother and father is. But I would walk a mile to find out if they left me any money (laughs). To me, from the age of 17 going back, it's B.C.

You blocked it all out?

Everything. I was a zombie. I joined the navy at 17 and ended up in the brig. Soon as possible (laughs). And on the boxing squad. I was going to come out of the service and go into professional boxing. Fighting every day is a natural state of affairs in the orphan home. You put 500 kids together, whattaya got? They are bastards, they are juvenile delinquents, they are half insane. The institutions for children are grab bags. If you're over 21, you go to a state pen. If you're under 18, you go to an orphan home.

I can remember when I was 15 years old, stabbing a prefect. You know what a prefect is? A bum they grab off the street and tell him to tell kids what to do. The guy made a homosexual advance at me and I stabbed him with a knife. They had me talk to a head shrinker and he told me that I was lying. This was an everyday occurrence.

When I went into the service, I automatically assumed when a guy came over to me and said something that I ought to punch him in the mouth. I fought about 70 percent of the guys in my company. I enjoyed boxing, fighting, the whole thing. When I was a young kid, I was strong, hearty, animalistic.

What changed my mind about pro boxing more than anything else was —I seen some kids ring a bell in front of an old man and I seen the old man punching out in the air. I had confidence in my boxing but I didn't think I was that good. You're either gonna be a champion or end up chasing trolley cars.

So from that time on it was labor . . .?

Labor, wandering, yeah. Seen all of the United States. This really pisses me off: why is it when you walk into a place and a guy looks at you and sees you are healthy and can do the work, why should he care whether you're an ex-con, what your politics are, how many other jobs you've had? Why all this application shit?

If I were hiring people to work, I'd try naturally to pay them a decent wage. I'd try to find out their first names, their last names, keep the company as small as possible, so I could personalize the whole thing. All I would ask a man is a handshake, see you in the morning. No applications, nothing. I wouldn't be interested in the guy's past. Nobody ever checks the pedigree on a mule, do they? But they do on a man. Can you picture walking up to a mule and saying, I'd like to know who his granddaddy was?

You've used the word "mule" a couple of times now.

Yeah. Because my kid's gonna be a thoroughbred. Daddy can be a mule (laughs).

What led to your interest in reading. . . . How'd that come about?

If you spend 17 years in orphanages, four years in the service, and out of those four years damn near two of them in stockades—and Korea wasn't a picnic—and then you got out and spent a year in the city jail, you've had 22 years of tight control over your life. Between orphanages, jails, military prisons, etcetera. Then what do you want? You want to explode, baby.

You ever read Ullman's biography of Rimbaud, *The Day on Fire?* That's the closest guy I can identify with. Except he had a different past than I did. He traveled all over the world, I'd like to run a footrace with him, New York to New York, circular. All the way through. Peking, through Cuba, through South America, through Mexico. My fantasy was to get lost, really. If the earth can't swallow you up, all you can do is go around it and look for its mouth.

How did you take to the reading habit?

Pure loneliness. I was a loner. That's one thing you learn when you're raised in institutions. Don't form any friendships, because they are too transitory. Everybody's jockeying for position.

Do you feel these people—the ones you call intellectuals—are looking down at you?

Yes, yes, definitely. Have you noticed the difference between the labor agitator of the '20s as opposed to—let's say, agitator, period. I'm sure guys like Clarence Darrow or Debs or Big Bill Heywood never looked down at working guys. There's an old IWW slogan: Bread and Roses, too.

I been to the IWW headquarters. I'm happy for those old men that the young kids are being radical. They had four or five old men in that little office. I was fascinated, sittin' down, talkin' with this guy, and he was telling me about Spain in the '30s. Now he's got all these young kids that he can talk to and he can get a sounding board. That makes me feel good.

For all your tiredness, there's this curiosity....

Oh yeah. For whatever's over the hill, really. You take a chance with discovery. I'm sure the guy that discovered fire got burned. Maybe the guy who tried to cross the river drowned. The guy that tried to cross over the hill fell down the hill. There's always dangers. You got two choices. If you stay in that damn cave and you bring up your son in it.... (trails off).

You feel there's another way you could be living, another kind of work you could be doing?

Oh sure. I'd like to run a combination book store and tavern (laughs). You could come in dressed however you pleased. No pretensions. I would like to have a place where college kids and steelworkers could come and sit down and talk. Where a workingman would not be ashamed to quote Walt Whitman and where a college professor would not be ashamed that he painted his house over the weekend.

There is a class of people in this country who are ashamed to turn a hand. They might write nice articles in the *Times* or in the *New York Review of Books,* but if you actually told them to get a little grease on their hands, they wouldn't. This might be the type of Marxist who finds himself uncomfortable among the laboring masses (laughs). But he always manages to say something nice about them in some weird magazine. I would like to see that whole dichotomy broken down. This is why I'd like a book store, a tavern, and a boxing ring in the back. I think there are people who are schizophrenic, who are terribly sensitive and terribly violent, too, I would like to give that kind of guy the opportunity.

What's your feeling when you see a young guy in a sports car go by?

If he's an 18-; 19-year-old kid and he's using it as a portable bed, God bless him. But if he's an 18- or 19-year old kid who's using it to go to some radical meeting, then, no.

Why one and not the other?

Why one and not the other? Let's put it this way. There used to be a pope who had what he called worker priests. This was in the 30's, I think. He sent them into the factories in France. He found out they deserted Catholicism for Communism. They were supposed to go in there to turn the working class toward religion, but they got souped up themselves. See, I could respect a bishop or a priest, who takes all the finery off and lives like a workingman, but I cannot respect that priest who drives by in a limousine and says, Oh you poor, enslaved.... The radical kid in the sports car is the bishop in the limousine, the bishop in robes. Same thing.

What do you sense about the guys you work with, their feelings?

They're against Nixon. They like Agnew a little bit. I hate to make the liberals happy, but the average working guy does not like Nixon, and is a Democrat. The point is: they might have voted for Humphrey, but you'd be surprised how many of them, their hearts, belong to George W.

Why do they belong to Wallace?

For the same reason they used to belong to Roosevelt. He used to have these little radio chats and used to pick out enemies like Wall Street. How you gonna pick Wall Street out as the enemy today? Most people on Wall Street, they're the liberals. When Roosevelt attacked them they did have the power, they were—I wish there were another word beside reactionary.

Who do you think has that power today? Who's keeping you doing what you're doing and the guys you work with—not making what they should be making?

People who are actually afraid—oh shit, I sound like Wallace—people who are actually afraid of democracy. Really.

You think Wallace represents democracy?

No, no, no. I would say he's a populist. Huey Long, Gerald L. K. Smith, they were all populists. Now they all had that bad part about them, like either being anti-Semitic or antiblack or what all. But this country today, baby, it's waiting—and not for somebody to crawl out from under a rock. But somebody who is visible out there. Know what I mean? Not a Muskie, because Muskie is too tied in with the whole Administration thing. Let me put it this way: someone who the media hates, who they make fun of. There's an old Arab proverb: the enemy of my enemy is my friend.

The media then—TV, the press—are putting down guys like you . . .?

Oh, definitely. Sure. I know a guy who's a truck driver. He goes to plays with his wife, he reads, a real intellectual-type guy. I mean, you'd never recognize him on the weekend. He's got these sideburns. . . .

This guy told me he's gone to parties where the average person there would be in advertising or in the media. He's met reporters. They'll be discussing, say, automation. He'll point out something, say, the value of work as opposed to the value of money. Oh man, he could get deep in this junk. All of a sudden, they'll say, "What do you do for a living? Are you a professor?" and he'll say, "No, I drive a truck." They would look at him as if he was a freak. I know a lot more people like that.

How do you think I feel if I go into a place where, let's say, if I were to quote Walt Whitman's poem—that thing he has about the labor people, how he sees carpenters and he sees blacksmiths? What do you think would happen if they would listen to me—assuming I'll be dressed—and I said I like Walt Whitman? They would say to me, "What do you do for a living?" "I work in a steel mill." "Are you a supervisor?" "No, I'm a laborer." "What???" You know what I mean.

I don't know if they would say that or not, I really don't.

Well it's happened to me, so I know what I'm talking about.

Way back in the conversation, you mentioned automation. Does it frighten you?

Depends how it's applied. It frightens me if it puts me out in the street. It doesn't frighten me if it shortens my work week. You read that little thing: what are you going to do when this computer replaces you? Blow up computers (laughs). Really. Blow up computers. I'll be goddammed if a computer's gonna eat before I do! I don't know what they'll feed it (laughs). Atomic energy or what all. But I want milk for my kids and beer for me. That's more important to me. It's how they're gonna use the computer. Machines can either liberate man or enslave him, because they're pretty neutral. It's man who has the bias to put a thing one place or another.

What would you do if you had a 20-hour work week?
Mmmm. Get to know my kids better, my wife better. And something else. I was invited by some kid to go on a college campus. 'Cause I gave him my opinion of college kids. He said, "Mike, you're all wrong." I told him, you know, about orgies (laughs). I was putting him on a little, too. He said he was gonna prove me wrong. I was hoping he'd prove me right (laughs). That would've been fun.

He invited me there on a Saturday. It was summertime. Let's face it, if I have a choice of taking my wife and kids to a picnic or going to a college campus, it's gonna be the picnic. But if I worked a 20-hour week, I could do both. Don't you think with that extra 20 hours, people could really expand? Who's to say? There are some people in factories just by force of circumstances. I'm just like the colored people. Potential Einsteins don't have to be white. They could be in cotton fields, they could be in factories.

You feel these possibilities are there?
O yeah, sure. But when people talk about someone's potential, it's kind of like all roads are open. But they're not. A lot of them are closed. I think automation can open some of those roads.

Way back, you spoke of the guys who built the pyramids, not the Pharaohs, but the unknowns. You put yourself in their category?
Yes, I want my signature on 'em too. Sometimes, out of pure meanness, when I make something, I put a little dent in it. I like to do something to make it really unique. Hit it with a hammer; deliberately, to see if it'll get by, just so I can say I did it.

You mean with a piece of steel?
Yeah, anything, anything. Let me put it this way: I think, God invented the dodo bird. So when we get up there, we could tell Him, "Don't you ever make mistakes?" and He'd say, "Sure. Look." (Laughs) I'd like to make my imprint. My dodo bird. A mistake, mine. Let's say a whole building is nothing but red bricks. I would like to have just the black one or the white one or the purple one. Deliberately fuck up.

What do you do on weekends?
Sometimes my wife works on Saturday and I drink beer. Drink beer,

read a book. See that one? *Violence in America.* It's one of the studies from Washington. One of the committees they're always appointing. A thing like that I read on the weekend. But during the week days, gee—I just thought about it. I don't do that much reading from Monday through Friday. Unless it's a horny book. I'll read it at work and go home and do my homework (laughs). That's what the guys at the plant call it—homework (laughs).

You once used a phrase about your job—"mind-dulling."
(Sighs heavily) Yeah. A lot of times you'll find out that unions only inform you about issues when elections come up. You get a synopsis of issues on the news, but you don't have the time to analyze things. Let's say, the workingman who voted for Wallace. Believe me, the only thing that turns me off on Wallace is the black thing. Otherwise, I like the guy. You know what soups me up about Wallace? I saw a picture of him living in a chicken shack. I never seen Lindsay in a chicken shack. When Kennedy— I'm talking about John F. Kennedy and I'm not gonna be a hypocrite, the guy was not my idol—when he went to West Virginia, he said it was the first time he had ever seen a kid without milk. How old was he when he saw that? In his forties. Imagine a man can live over 40 years and all of a sudden get concerned?

This is why I honestly believe if Wallace could get that black thing out of his system, the race thing, he'd be fantasic. This country needs somebody like Wallace. It doesn't need Wallace, but somebody *like* him. Because the workingman today—in the '20s and '30s, the Marxists glorified the workingman to ridiculous proportions, you know? Today, they are ridiculing him to the same proportions. They're kind of making him appear stupid, like in the movie *Joe.*

A liberal made it, I'm positive of that. I can understand the liberals wanting to move the United States Left, Right, whatever you want to call it. They want to open it, broaden it, make it more democratic. But you don't make a country more democratic by hating one class over another.

Do you know the potential? Me and the colored fella are working every day, every day, every day. There is a productive entanglement that can be used. We may live apart, but we have to work together every day. Why isn't somebody making that productive? Why aren't they using that, okay, forced togetherness? No matter how you cut it, it's still togetherness. It's still me and a black guy walking on a picket line, right?

But when I turn on my TV, I see him as a black militant saying, "I'm gonna get all you Hunkies." And he sees me on TV saying, "I'm gonna kill the niggers and the hippies." Neither statement is true. Don't you think the opportunity is open, it's been passed by, of the black and white workingman working together? I don't care if it's a labor leader or I don't care if it's a politician. You get me the guy who can make the black and white workingman stick together, and he's my president.

Let's face it, what McCarthy said about his people is true: "Only the educated will vote for me." Oh, man. I don't own a gun, 'cause if you own a gun, you could shoot somebody (laughs). And I'm impulsive and so's my wife. But if McCarthy were elected president, I woulda' bought a gun. Because that would have been to me a sign that the intellectuals are taking the country over. When the intellectuals start running this fucking world—(a long pause)—right now, I *think* I'm a mule. If McCarthy or anybody like him gets to be president in the United States, then I'd *know* I'm a mule. And that's a big difference, and, baby, I'm gonna buck.

Why would you know you're a mule then?
It'll be, like I say, the intellectuals running the country.

What kind of persons do you call intellectuals?
The type of person who thinks just because he's got a little bit of education and can use bigger words—Agnew, forgive me (laughs)—because he can quote a little poetry, and I'm not knocking poetry—or he can appear urbane or sophisticated—that he's better than a guy who works with his hands.

If a carpenter built a cabin for poets, I think the least the poets owe the carpenter is just three or four one-liners on the wall. A little plaque: "Though we labor with our minds, this place we can relax in was built by someone who can work with his hands. And his work is as noble as ours." No, the intellectual wouldn't say that. The intellectual would assume that God in His benevolence to poets (laughs) sprung up the cabin. I think the poet owes something to the guy who builds the cabin for him.

If I were building a house and Eugene McCarthy walked by, I don't think I'd look over my shoulder. I would expect a spit or a sneer. There's one Kennedy I did like. Robert Kennedy.

Why did you like him?
He wasn't afraid to get his hands dirty. If I left work with my hands full of grease, full of dirty paint, if Bobby Kennedy were along the way, and I reached out and he looked at my hand and saw how fuckin' dirty it was, he'd grab it. I don't think Eugene McCarthy would. I think he would look at that hand and say: redneck! hillbilly! hired hand! jagoff (laughs). Uneducated slob!

Maybe it's mind-dulling that I do think that way, ever thought of that? Maybe if Eugene McCarthy, his type, would stop that kind of shit, who knows?

It's now about ten thirty at night. Suppose tomorrow were Monday. . . .
Would I think of Monday? Hell, no. I don't think of Monday. You know what I'm thinking about on Sunday night? Next Sunday. If you work real hard, you think of a perpetual vacation. Not perpetual sleep. . . . What do I think of on a Sunday night? Lord, I wish I could do something else for a living.

I don't know who the guy is who said there is nothing sweeter than an unfinished symphony. Like an unfinished painting, an unfinished poem. If he creates this thing one day—let's say, Michelangelo's Sistine Chapel; it took him a long time to finish this beautiful work of art. But what if he had to create this Sistine Chapel a thousand times a year? Don't you think that would even dull Michelangelo's mind? Or if Leonardo Da Vinci had to draw his anatomical charts thirty, forty, fifty, sixty, eighty, ninety, a hundred times a day? Don't you think that would even bore Da Vinci?

So it's the sameness of your work, the routine that makes you feel trapped.

I don't know. This is gonna sound square, but my kid is my freedom. There's a line in one of Hemingway's books, I think it's from *For Whom the Bell Tolls*. They're behind the enemy lines, somewhere in Spain, and she's pregnant. She wants to stay with him. He tells her, No. She says, if you die, I die—knowing he's gonna die—But if you go, I go. Know what I mean? The mystics call it the brass bowl. Continuum. You know what I mean? This is why I work. Every time I see a young guy walk by with a shirt and tie and dressed up real sharp, I'm lookin' at my kid you know? That's it.

Mike Fitzgerald has said a great deal, both implicitly and explicitly, about his feelings toward work and life—probably more effectively than any collection of surveys could. Most of his basic reactions and attitudes are widely shared, according to a number of recent studies. Almost all of his feelings have political significance, but we shall defer analysis of his most explicitly political attitudes until we have reviewed reactions to work among today's blue-collar workers.

To begin with, Mike is not alone in finding little meaning in his work. His fruitless search for pride in his work, and his compensatory insistence upon self-respect, are paralleled by the feelings of other manual and assembly-line workers. In a national survey conducted in 1969 by the Michigan Survey Research Center,[5] for example, workers ranked "having interesting work" first among all their job-related desires. Three other dimensions of work-pride (enough help and equipment to do a good job, enough information to get the job done, and enough authority to do the job) were ranked above "good pay." Levels of job satisfaction are also indicated by the data in Table 14-3, which shows the proportions of various kinds of workers who would choose the same work if they could start their careers again.

Such working conditions, and the resulting dissatisfaction with them, can hardly fail to carry over to life outside of work. Mike Fitz-

[5]Neil Q. Herrick, "Who's Unhappy at Work and Why," *Manpower* 4 (January 1972), p. 3.

gerald's sense of being trapped by marriage and children, his frustrations and occasional outbursts of violence, are clearly linked to his work. The same is true of other workers, though their outlets may take a wide variety of forms. Sabotage is frequent in some large

TABLE 14-3
Proportions in Various Occupations Who Would Choose Same Kind of Work if Beginning Career Again

Professional Occupations	Percent	Working-Class Occupations	Percent
Mathematicians	91	Skilled printers	52
Physicists	89	Paper workers	52
Biologists	89	Skilled automobile workers	41
Chemists	86	Skilled steelworkers	41
Lawyers	83	Textile workers	31
Journalists	82	Unskilled steelworkers	21
		Unskilled automobile workers	16

Source: Robert Blauner, "Work Satisfaction and Industrial Trends in Modern Society," in *Labor and Trade Unionism,* eds. Walter Galenson and S. M. Lipset (New York: John Wiley & Sons, 1960).

plants; sometimes it is organized, but often it is simply the result of private resentment against speed-up, monotony, and harsh work. Here is one worker's description of quitting time at an auto plant:

> With a feeling of release after hours of monotonous work, gangs of workers move out from the side aisles into the main aisles, pushing along, shouting, laughing, knocking each other around—heading for the fresh air on the outside. The women sometimes put their arms around the guards at the gates, flirting with them and drawing their attention away from the men who scurry from the plant with distributors, spark plugs, carburetors, even a head here and there under their coats—bursting with laughter as they move out into the cool night. Especially in the summers, the nights come alive at quitting time with the energy of release: the squealing of tires out of the parking lot, racing each other and dragging up and down the streets. Beer in coolers stored in trunks is not uncommon and leads to spontaneous parties, wrestling, brawling, and laughter that spills over into the parks and streets round the factory. There is that simple joy of hearing your voice loudly and clearly for the first time in 10 or 12 hours.[6]

[6]Bill Watson, "Counter-Planning on the Shop Floor," *Radical America* 5 (May-June 1971), p. 7.

Neither Mike nor other workers want their children to spend their lives at similar jobs, or indeed in a factory of any kind. Although Mike himself has little respect for college graduates, he sees education as a route of escape for his children. He wants them to enjoy whatever it is that the higher-ups in society have, such as self-confidence amid the plastic surroundings of the Playboy Club.

Mike Fitzgerald's reactions are shown to be valid on a nationwide basis by the Michigan survey mentioned above.[7] Of a national sample of *all* categories of workers, *one out of every four workers under thirty* expressed dissatisfaction with his or her work situation. The proportions dropped with age, but a total of 17 percent of all blue-collar workers and 13 percent of all white-collar workers expressed such dissatisfaction. Young black workers were the least satisfied, and workers in retail and service jobs were also highly dissatisfied. Among many of the most dissatisfied groups, negative attitudes carried over into their lives generally; nearly 25 percent of those with grade-school educations, in service jobs, or in low income brackets expressed dissatisfaction with their lives as a whole.

Analysis of this pattern of dissatisfaction with work yields some further findings relevant for our purposes. There was no difference between blue-collar and white-collar workers in the under-thirty group: in both cases, 24 percent declared themselves dissatisfied with their work. Nor did college education make a difference at this age level: those with degrees were just as likely to be dissatisfied as those with only limited education. This suggests that job dissatisfaction is not just a blue-collar phenomenon, but a growing characteristic of younger workers in all kinds of jobs. And mere income does not seem likely to make people much happier: the kinds of satisfactions sought tend to be related to the quality of work rather than its wage levels.

Elements of Class and Class Consciousness

Not only socioeconomic characteristics—the objective conditions of life—distinguish Mike Fitzgerald from more advantaged Americans. He clearly has a subjective sense of "we-they," of the "average working guy" (with whom he sees himself having much in common) versus more favored people in the society. He has no difficulty seeing a hierarchy of status superiors above him. But he does not believe that their relative status is a product of innate superiority. Instead, he considers people similar in intelligence and capabilities (and, presumably, in other human qualities as well) and distinguished only by their relative opportunities. He insists, for example, that only lack of time

[7]Herrick, *op. cit.*

distinguishes working people from rich people intellectually and politically. His own conversation supports his outlook; he has literary awareness, historical sense, and political insight. In sum, he believes his status and that of others like him to be due to the workings of *social structure*—the larger system, and the lack of opportunity it provides for such people—and not to their *personal attributes* or shortcomings.

This is an important element in our analysis of the extent of class and class consciousness. If people see themselves at the bottom, in relatively less favored situations, *along with other people and because of characteristics of the socioeconomic system rather than through their own personal faults,* we have the beginnings of potential class consciousness. No national data exist on this matter, but some useful findings are available from a study of a midwestern city in the late 1960s.[8] People of different races and income levels were asked a series of questions about why the rich were rich and the poor poor. Table 14-4 shows the proportions of each group that attributed such differences to personal characteristics (individual strengths or weaknesses) rather than to the social structure. Rich people, it is clear, believe that personal qualities account for their wealth and others' poverty. They are more likely to believe that being on relief is due to personal failings, and that the poor don't work as hard and don't want to get ahead, than are poor or middle-income people. The poor, and particularly the black poor, are much more likely to attribute their status to nonpersonal or structural factors. The accuracy of this judgment is less important for our purposes than is its prevalence —for the latter phenomenon is the root of class and class consciousness as we have defined them.

Nor are such interpretations dependent entirely on the *proportions* in which the respective groups give particular answers. Qualitative statements confirm their significance. The authors of the study, for example, report a rich man explaining why the rich are rich and the poor poor: "...If you have to generalize, it's the self-discipline to accumulate capital and later to use that capital effectively and intelligently to make income and wealth." On the other hand, a poor Black is quoted as saying in answer to the same question, "The rich stole, beat, and took. The poor didn't start stealing in time, and what they stole, it didn't value nothing, and they were caught with that."[9] That difference, we suggest, is the essence of class consciousness.

[8]Joan Huber Rytina, William H. Form, and John Pease, "Income and Stratification Ideology: Beliefs About the American Opportunity Structure," *American Journal of Sociology* 75 (January 1970), p. 713.
[9]*Ibid.*

Views of Power Distribution

Another way of exploring the extent and character of class-grounded thinking is to look at people's images of power distribution within the society. Mike Fitzgerald has a clear sense that a few people on top control things, and that they are afraid of the people like him down below. He acknowledges that there may be grounds for that fear, but makes obvious his own distaste for rule by self-selected intellectuals. Similar attitudes are often expressed by workers at this level. In a study made in the 1960s of skilled and semi-skilled auto plant workers in New Jersey, Lewis Lipsitz found that all categories of workers shared images of vast power disparities in the society, and saw key initiative as in the hands of big business.[10] They believed

TABLE 14-4

Personal Attributes as a Cause of Income by Income and Race (in percentages)

Income and Race	Wealth (a)	Poverty (b)	Being on Relief Last Six Years (c)	Poor Don't Work as Hard (d)	Poor Don't Want to Get ahead (e)
Poor					
Black	17	17	28	3	0
White	34	30	46	13	19
Middle					
Black	29	19	45	4	6
White	35	41	59	30	29
Rich					
White	72	62	78	39	46
Total, analytic sample					
%	37	36	54	21	23
N	(350)	(341)	(347)	(343)	(347)
Total, systematic sample					
%	31	40	57	25	25
N	(183)	(177)	(185)	(186)	(180)

The percentages in the wealth column represent those who saw favorable traits as a "cause" of wealth; in the poverty columns, those who saw unfavorable tracts as a "cause" of poverty. In columns (d) and (e), the percentages are those agreeing with the statements indicated.
Source: Rytina, Form, and Pease, *op. cit.*

[10]Lewis Lipsitz, "Work Life and Political Attitudes: A Study of Manual Workers," in *The White Majority: Between Poverty and Affluence*, ed. Louise Kapp Howe (New York: Vintage Books, 1970), pp. 160–162.

that power was used exploitatively, and exclusively for purposes of maximizing profit, in the context of a society devoted to profitmaking. They also saw government and the mass media manipulating people, partly in the interests of business but also in keeping with the "inherent" selfishness of human nature.

A somewhat more systematic impression of attitudes toward the distribution of power in the United States can be obtained from the survey of a midwestern city noted earlier.[11] In this inquiry, people were given three "models" of power distribution from which to select. One was pluralism, the view that power is widely dispersed and that shifting coalitions of groups and individuals shape the outcome of governmental decisions in each issue area. Another was the elitist model, which holds that a continuing coalition of the same families, corporations, and interests makes most basic decisions and orchestrates popular acceptance of them. The last model was derived from the Marxist image of a ruling class, and termed "economic dominance." According to it, the biggest owners and stockholders control all decisions, either directly or through their agents.

Table 14-5 shows the responses, broken down by educational levels. There is, of course, a close correlation between educational levels and income, and so to an extent both factors are represented here. Given that the pluralist image is a major ingredient in the orthodox American ideology, it is significant that the proportion who subscribe to it drops sharply with educational level. Moreover, the least educated people are the most likely to hold the Marxist ruling-class image; this image becomes less prevalent as the level of education rises, until only 8 percent of college graduates profess it. Does this pattern suggest that the less educated (who are also the lowest in income) hold such images for class-grounded reasons? Or is it just that they have been exposed to less education— or, perhaps, less indoctrination? In any case, their outlook is distinctive from that of the better educated, wealthier people—and that is what counts for our purposes.

It appears that we have identified at least the outlines of class and the beginnings of class consciousness among American non-elites. Their lives share systematically caused characteristics. The life situations, opportunities for mobility, and access to amenities of people at this level are simply not what they are for people at the top of the socioeconomic pyramid. Values and basic subjective reactions appear to be similar: Mike Fitzgerald is not isolated or unique, but is rather typical of a large segment of Americans. He and others like him see themselves as *down here*, below the few people *up there*, because of the social system and not because of personal talent, effort, or qualifications.

[11]William H. Form and Joan Rytina, "Ideological Beliefs on the Distribution of Power in the United States," *American Sociological Review* 34 (January 1969), p. 23.

A New Militancy

How does the "new working class" thesis accord with these tentative findings? The thesis holds that changes in the occupational structure of American life from manual and service jobs toward professional and technical employment, coupled with the growing middle-class attainments of the formerly lowest echelons, have drained the traditional working class of its militancy and created a new grouping of better educated people who must now be recognized as the principal agent of social change. In effect, this argument says that thrusts toward change must now grow out of the rejection by middle-class (and relatively affluent) people of materialism and acquisitiveness. It is perceived as a kind of revolt of the intelligentsia, in which the young and better-educated may show the way to new standards and practices for all.

TABLE 14-5

Selection of Societal Models of Power Distribution, by Years of Education (in percentage)

Years of education	Models of Power Distribution			Total	
	Economic dominance	Elitist	Pluralist	%	(N)
0–7	40	26	33	99	(42)
8–11	28	16	57	101	(141)
12–15	14	19	67	100	(108)
16 or more	8	20	73	101	(40)
Total %	22	19	59	100	
Total (N)	(74)	(62)	(195)		(331)

Source: Form and Rytina, *op. cit.*

Several facts support this thesis. Table 14-1 showed a distinct reduction in the proportions of people who are self-employed, and a commensurate rise in numbers and proportions of people who work for others. These people do not have much control over the conditions of their work, and may thus be resentful of their job situations. Professional and technical employment has risen substantially, from 3 percent of the labor force to 13 percent. The greatest increase in all job categories has occurred in government services—particularly among teachers, office workers, and other semi-professional white-collar workers. It is also true that many white-collar jobs are poorly paid. It is no longer possible to rank all white-collar jobs above all blue-collar jobs in terms of income potential; many skilled blue-collar jobs pay more than routine office work, and are more satisfying as well. The data we examined on job dissatisfaction showed that as large a proportion of young white-collar as young blue-collar workers were unhappy with their work.

But only the last of these findings even begins to address the key subjective dimension. The real question is whether, in the context of American orthodoxy, such middle-class and relatively affluent people can and will develop a sense of shared deprivation—fundamental, systemically caused—equivalent to class consciousness. Individualism is probably stronger at this level than at higher and lower levels, where class feelings have historically been more potent. It will be very difficult for such people to submerge their individualism in favor of shared class sensitivity.

In the meantime, it seems too soon to dismiss the traditional working class as a potential force for change. The manual worker has not disappeared, although the proportions of skilled workers are increasing. Blue-collar workers are still the largest single group in the society, and they are for the most part poor or economically marginal. If the "new working class" has political significance at this point, it appears to be because it is becoming more like the working class—and not the reverse. The pay levels and standards of living of most of this group are dropping, and have been since at least 1966. Inflation is rising, taxes are increasing, and little has been done to ease the burden on either blue- or white-collar lower-middle- or working-class people.

But again, the basic issue is the extent to which people see their fundamental interests as shared and their plight as systemically caused, and commit themselves to seeking remedies as a group. And it is at this point that the dominant orthodoxy enters in. Let us turn now to the meaning of that ideology as it finds expression in the attitudes of non-elites.

Chapter 15

In this chapter, we shall first examine the basic political attitudes and perceived wants and needs of non-elites. In general, they are consistent with the pattern of class-related interests and feelings in Chapter 14. Although many people feel certain satisfactions about their lives and their country, they express many needs and wants that they share with others—and that are not being fulfilled by their government. And yet, there is little concerted thought or action devoted to satisfying such needs. If anything, the political attitudes and behavior of non-elites suggest approval of the *status quo* and opposition to those who take action to change it. Why is this so? What stops non-elites from more actively and effectively seeking their ends in American politics?

The Political Attitudes of Non-Elites

Our next step is to analyze the sources of non-elite attitudes and information. What we find is a series of channels dominated by elites, through which the dominant American orthodoxy is transmitted in a variety of ways. Moreover, the ambiguity of many specific issues and situations leads people to rely on information supplied by, or cues initiated by the actions of, government officials. In a brief case study, we shall trace the evolution of attitudes toward the Vietnam War, and show how even in this apparently exceptional situation, the attitudes of non-elites were strongly supportive, slow to change, and highly dependent upon elite actions or outside events. In other words, we speculate that the transmission and reinforcement of the orthodox belief system, and the opportunities open to elites to affix *their* interpretation to daily events, combine to divert non-elites from cohesive efforts to gain their ends.

Finally, we investigate the result of this process at the present time. We examine certain aspects of ideology professed by non-elites, and their attitudes toward various current trends and issues. We find resentment, distrust, and fear of the future—but little sense of a possible remedy or how to go about seeking it. Needless to say, this situation is not encouraging to political stability in the United States.

Basic Attitudes: Wants and Needs

In analyzing the political attitudes of such a large group of people, we must be sensitive to several principles of interpretation. Although opinion polling is a sound social science tool, its users must exercise care. The form of the question is important, for it may shape answers in several ways. For example, a long checklist of possible answers may result in the impression that people have many strong opinions; a "free-answer" question, in which the respondent must think up his own answer, may come closer to measuring his real knowledge and concerns. Behind this caution lie some even more important facts about the distribution of opinion in a heterogeneous society. People differ greatly in the subjects about which they are concerned, the information they possess, and the intensity with which they hold preferences about particular subjects or issues. In many cases these differentials reflect the relevance of an issue to matters of personal or economic interest to the respondent. This is another way of saying that attitudes are often related to respondents' class status, race, religion, occupation, place of residence, ideology, or political party identification. Some issues appear to touch people primarily in terms of their income, occupation, and education. Others seem to activate loyalties or perceptions along racial or religious lines. Sometimes the same issue strikes different people differently, some seeing it as a simple matter of group economic benefit while others understand it as a question of religious or ideological principle.

On any given subject, therefore, there may be wide variations in interest, information, and preferences—with conflicts of opinion existing not only between groups but also within the same individuals. Further, opinion may shift over time, sometimes steadily as events or campaigns bring new facts or interpretations into focus, sometimes sharply after a single dramatic event or governmental action. Understanding complex and fluid opinion in detail at any given moment may be very difficult or even impossible. But it is not difficult at all to identify and describe the enduring values and attitudes that form the basic structure of non-elite political beliefs. The semipermanent assumptions and preferences are what we examine here. Similarly, we shall point out some consistent features of subgroup attitudes (such as the higher levels of information and support for government among the more educated) as occasions arise.

Support for Social Welfare

It should not be surprising that, when members of the general public are asked to describe in their own words their principal personal aspirations and fears, the answers are cast chiefly in terms of economic security and health. Table 15-1 lists the responses of national cross-sections of the population in 1959, 1964, and 1971. Issues of war and peace enter the picture in important ways, but no other strictly political matters are included among the hopes and fears voiced by 10 percent or more of the respondents. Personal health and economic security account for practically all of the hopes and fears expressed.

TABLE 15-1
Personal Hopes and Fears of Americans, 1959, 1964, and 1971
(in percentages; items specified by 10% or more of sample)

	personal hopes		
	1959	*1964*	*1971*
Good health for self	40	29	29
Better standard of living	38	40	27
Peace in the world	9	17	19
Achievement of aspirations for children	29	35	17
Happy family life	18	18	14
Good health for family	16	25	13
Own house or live in better one	24	12	11

	personal fears		
	1959	*1964*	*1971*
Ill health for self	40	25	28
Lower standard of living	23	19	18
War	21	29	17
Ill health for family	25	27	16
Unemployment	10	14	13
Inflation	1	3	11

Source: Albert H. Cantril and Charles W. Roll, Jr., *Hopes and Fears of the American People* (New York: Universe Books, 1971) p. 19.

These basic concerns seem to lie behind broad support for governmental action in the social welfare field. From the time that responsible public opinion surveying began in the 1930s, large majorities have favored the basic social security and social assistance programs that were ultimately enacted. Often, public support preceded enactment by several years or even decades, as in the case of medical care. The federal social welfare programs of the 1960s enjoyed no less support, with two-thirds of the population favoring most aspects of the poverty program, aid to education, housing, the reduction of unemployment, and so forth. There can be little doubt about the strength of public demand and support for these "welfare state" policies.

But this desire for government to be of service in coping with the problems of daily living in an industrial society does not transcend some basic practical and ideological limits. Nearly equal majorities say that taxes are too high, and the lower income levels are usually most resistant to taxation. The latter fact is sometimes cited as an inconsistency on the part of those who are the probable beneficiaries of much of the social legislation to be funded by such taxes. But it may represent an insistence that those who can better afford the burden of taxation should carry a larger share.

An interesting example of the enduring strength of the work ethic, a continuing element of the American value structure, may be seen in attitudes toward government's role in assuring income for people. When talk of income maintenance plans, negative income taxes, and guaranteed annual wages became prevalent in early 1969, a national sample was asked their views on a governmental guarantee of at least $3,200 per family per year. In the same survey, they were asked their reactions to the idea that government should guarantee enough *work* to assure a family at least $3,200 a year. The questions were posed consecutively, so that respondents did not have to choose between them. Nevertheless, their answers show clearly that people seek only governmental assistance to enable them to do what they feel they should do, that is, work. Table 15-2 presents these totals, which range from nearly two-thirds majority rejection of the guaranteed income plan to nearly four-fifths majority support for guaranteed work. If previous experience holds true, however, support for guaranteed income plans will rise as their desirability is publicly argued and people become more familiar with them. Assuming governmental support for and eventual enactment of such a program, public support would probably reach majority levels by the time it went into effect and would continue climbing thereafter.

The distribution of support for these two types of programs is also significant. The divisions reflect differences of class, rather than race, region, religion, age, or sex. Lower-status persons tended to be more supportive of both, which is understandable (and consistently true for almost every piece of social legislation that is proposed). But not even manual workers, or those earning under $3,000 per year at the time of the survey, gave majority support to the guaranteed income. Even those who stood to gain immediate economic benefits preferred work to an assured income without work. It seems clear that the work-ethic aspect of traditional American ideology is still viable, even at the lowest levels of the economic order.

TABLE 15-2
Attitudes Toward Guaranteed Income and Work, 1969 (in percents)

	Income			Work		
	Favor	*Oppose*	*No opinion*	*Favor*	*Oppose*	*No opinion*
National	32	62	6	79	16	5
Education						
College	26	71	3	75	23	2
High school	31	64	5	77	18	5
Grade school	40	50	10	83	9	8
Occupation						
Professional						
and business	26	68	4	75	20	5
White collar	26	66	8	80	17	3
Farmers	21	74	5	73	23	4
Manual	36	58	6	82	14	4
Income						
Over $10,000	24	72	4	76	16	8
Over $7000	27	69	4	78	15	7
$5–6,999	33	62	5	81	14	5
$3–4,999	40	54	6	77	17	6
Under $3,000	43	44	13	77	11	12

Source: *Gallup Opinion Weekly* (January 1969), pp. 20–21.

The Move Toward Concern for National Unity

When the public's attention is turned to its hopes and fears for the United States as a nation, a more politicized response is elicited. Table 15-3 presents responses given at intervals over the last fifteen years. War and peace and economic issues are dominant throughout. But in 1971, the most dramatic change was a sudden rise in concern for the very existence of the United States as a country. National unity, or the reverse—disunity and instability—was a very prominent concern; law and order is probably a closely related type of response. We shall explore this sudden concern in detail in the last section of this chapter.

Non-elites have very decisive views about the proper uses of government funds. National pride, patriotism, and anticommunism all contribute to support for military and space expenditures. But there is widespread agreement, among all classes, that military spend-

TABLE 15-3

National Hopes and Fears of Americans, 1959, 1964, and 1971
(in percentages; items specified by 10% or more of sample)

	National hopes		
	1959	*1964*	*1971*
Peace	48	51	51
Economic stability; no inflation	12	5	18
Employment	13	15	16
National unity	1	9	15
Law and order	3	4	11
Better standard of living	20	28	11
Solution of pollution problems	—	—	10
Settlement of racial problems	14	15	10
	National fears		
	1959	*1964*	*1971*
War (esp. nuclear war)	64	50	30
National disunity; political instability	3	8	26
Economic Instability; Inflation	18	13	17
Communism	12	29	12
Lack of law and order	3	5	11

Source: Cantril and Roll, *op. cit.* (Table 15-1), p. 23.

ing is too high. In mid-1969, for example, 52 percent of a national sample said that too much money was being spent for military purposes, 31 percent thought that military spending levels were about right, and only 8 percent said that they were too low.[1] Rich and poor, people with college and with grade-school educations, and all ages and races expressed similar views in almost identical proportions.

In the case of space expenditures, the situation is basically the same. Three times as many people wanted to reduce such expenditures as wanted to increase them in 1969, and a majority opposed

[1]*Gallup Opinion Weekly* (July 1969), p. 11.

attempts to land a man on Mars. On this issue, however, there were substantial differences between class levels. College-educated and higher-income people apparently believed that there were uses to the exploration of space, or were simply more interested in scientific adventures than the lower classes. Table 15-4 shows the breakdown by income and education levels of support for increasing or reducing space expenditures. Lower-income people clearly oppose even the present levels of space spending, probably because they see many higher-priority uses for such money.

TABLE 15-4

Attitudes Toward Space Expenditures, February 1969

"The U.S. is now spending many billions of dollars on space research. Do you think we should increase these funds, keep them the same, or reduce these funds?"

	Increase	Keep same	Reduce	No opinion
	%	%	%	%
National	14	41	40	5
Education				
College	19	51	28	2
High School	15	43	37	65
Grade School	9	29	56	6
Income				
$10,000 & over	22	48	27	3
$ 7,000 & over	19	49	30	2
$ 5,000–$6,999	15	37	42	6
$ 3,000–$4,999	7	33	55	5
Under $3,000	8	32	53	7

Source: *Gallup Opinion Weekly* (March 1969), p. 17.

Confirmation that lower-income opposition stems from a strong sense that domestic problems deserve the higher priorities for government spending comes from an important national survey conducted in 1969 under the sponsorship of *Newsweek* magazine. This survey questioned a large number of people in order to obtain a representative sample of Americans earning between $5,000 and $10,000 per year, the so-called "middle Americans." The answers obtained indicate that alternative government spending priorities would be preferred by this large sector of the population. Their responses are shown in Figure 15-1. Domestic economic benefits, followed by "law and order," dominate the list of goals for which they think more government money should be spent. Defense, space, and foreign assistance are areas in which it was believed less money should be spent—and there is little question that these respondents ranked such expenditures very low indeed.

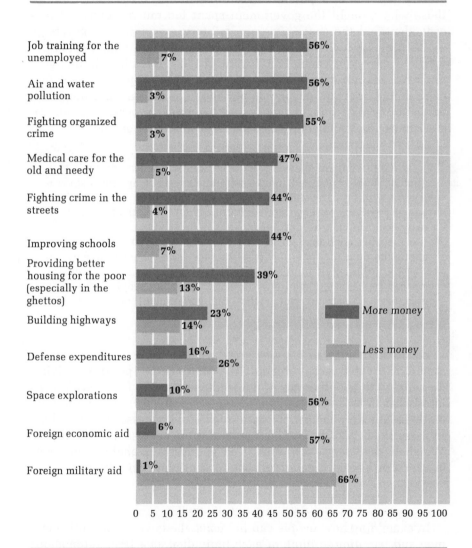

Source: *Newsweek*, 6 October 1969, p. 46.

FIGURE 15-1
Spending Priorities of "Middle Americans," 1969
"On which problems do you think the government should be spending more money—and on which should it be spending less money?"

Thus, there appear to be strong feelings among non-elites that government ought to be doing more to solve domestic problems, and to address some of their economic and personal health concerns. In short, there are significant grievances—unfulfilled wants and needs —at this level. In a subtle and revealing study of 82 poor men in a Southern city, Lewis Lipsitz sought to probe these grievances in greater depth than is possible in national surveys. He found that, of those who thought the government spent too much money, 79 percent identified the space program, military expenditures, or foreign aid as projects for which too much was spent, and *none* named domestic welfare programs. Conversely, of those who thought that government was not spending enough money, only 5 percent said that more should be spent for space exploration, the military, or foreign aid, while 95 percent thought that domestic welfare programs should receive more funds. Summing up his analysis, Lipsitz concludes:

> ... The dominant theme is the sense of being cheated: one's government is not concerned enough with one's well-being; one's government is willing to spend money on what appear to many of these men as frivolous or illegitimate enterprises while it fails to meet their own deeply felt day-to-day needs.
>
> In keeping with this sense of deprivation, we also found a desire among the poor for some sort of assistance from the government, and a series of dissatisfactions with the kind of work the government was engaged in .... we should acknowledge that poor people have many grievances concerning both what the government does and does not do ...[2]

Lipsitz adds that, in his view, one of the reasons such grievances are not expressed more forcefully in politics is that political activists do not always take them up—that is, the elites who frame grievances into issues that can be dealt with have not been concerned with these matters. Nor do poor people with grievances necessarily know how to carry them into the political arena by themselves, Lipsitz argues. We shall keep these possibilities in mind as we analyze the ways in which non-elites receive information and develop attitudes.

Sources of Political Attitudes and Ideology

In examining how people can influence the government, it is common and tempting to think of each individual as a free, autonomous unit expressing his or her desires about what government should do

---

[2]Lewis Lipsitz, "On Political Belief: The Grievances of the Poor," in *Power and Community: Dissenting Essays in Political Science,* eds. Philip Green and Sanford Levinson (New York: Random House, 1970), pp. 165–167.

and should be. Are people really all that free and independent as adults? Or have their ideas been molded early in life to encourage them to have particular political and party loyalties, to see established political regimes and officials as benevolent, or to hold particular values or ideologies about politics and government?

Clearly, these questions deal with a fundamental issue. If people's attitudes and beliefs about governmental officials and political institutions are largely or completely shaped and stabilized by the time they are adults, then governmental responsiveness to the "will of the people" or to mass publics really means responsiveness to what was inculcated into people when they were children. In that case, the only hope for social change lies in changing what children are taught. Such a political system seems largely closed and resistant to forces for change, for the adults from whom children learn are themselves resistant to change. This would be a "system" in a tight and depressingly literal sense of the word.

Shaping Beliefs: The Early Years

There is good reason to doubt that people's political beliefs and values are completely determined by their early experiences. At the same time, the evidence is strong that the family, the school, and other early influences upon children do a great deal to shape their views of the political world and that these initial molding agencies have a lasting impact. The "developmental process through which the citizen matures politically"[3] is called "political socialization."

For some people, induction into the political culture is not a source of pride, but a painful, embarrassing, or demeaning experience that they have good reason to resist. A middle-class white child finds it a source of gratification to be told by his family and his teacher that he is a citizen of the most democratic and powerful nation on earth, that his country's chief magistrate is a benevolent President, and that he or one of his friends may legitimately aspire to that office. A black child is probably taught the same thing in school, but his other experiences, and probably his family, also teach him that blacks can expect to do low-paid and demeaning work and that the likelihood of a black becoming President is virtually nil. Many blacks in the past, given no choice, have had to rationalize this lowly political role and have developed a deep loyalty to the country and its political institutions. Others, especially in recent years, responded readily as they grew older to cues inviting them to refuse to accept this traditional view of the state, its officials, and themselves.

[3]The definition is from Richard E. Dawson and Kenneth Prewitt, *Political Socialization* (Boston: Little, Brown, 1969) p. 17.

If a person clings to particular beliefs, loyalties, and attachments, even in the face of developments that might reasonably give him cause to question them, it may be because those beliefs and loyalties are necessary to his own self-conception. A person who has been socialized as a child to take pride in being a citizen of a democratic country may refuse later to accept evidence that his country's domestic or foreign policies serve the interests of a narrow elite or are not benevolent in the broadest sense of the word. To believe such evidence would hurt his pride and his self-conception. This notion of the "political self" may help explain the inclination to cherish and hold fast to early political loyalties, feelings of attachment or hostility toward political institutions, and even opinions about particular public issues and officials.[4]

Unfortunately, we cannot generalize with much confidence about the extent to which early political beliefs, feelings, and opinions persist into adult life. Clearly, some people do change in some or all these respects while others change very little. Many middle-class Americans who were children in the relatively prosperous and peaceful 1950s developed highly favorable views of the American government and of such officials as the President and the policeman. Some of these people's views changed drastically in the troubled 1960s in response to the Vietnam War, as well as to severe social problems and disturbances in the cities. Others apparently held fast to their earlier views.

People do change with changed conditions, and some more readily than others. The person whose political self does not need the reassurance of old ties is free to learn and to change his or her cognitions and attachments accordingly. Another reason for new patterns of political socialization over time lies in the new sources of information and learning to which a person is exposed as he or she grows older. In place of the family and the school, political observations come largely from the communications media and from associates.

It is from family, school, and friends that a child acquires his or her first ideas about the state and politics. These "agents of political socialization" influence a child both through direct teaching and in indirect and subtle ways that probably have a more powerful and lasting impact upon the child's political beliefs than does direct teaching. The child hears political views and political party attachments stated by parents and friends, and takes them as a model to emulate. Impressions from family, school, and peer group experiences about authoritarian or democratic ways of making decisions are generalized to political objects. Because most families and virtually all schools try to teach the child to believe and to behave in ways that will be widely approved in the culture, their influence is essentially conserv-

[4]*Ibid.,* p. 19.

ative: to inculcate feelings of loyalty to the established regime and to justify prevailing values. The family is most influential when it supports widely held attitudes, not when it inculcates deviant or idiosyncratic ones.[5]

Children are especially likely to adopt the party affiliations of their parents. One study found that 76 percent of a group of high-school students shared their parents' party loyalties when the parents were in agreement.[6] As we might expect, family influence on a voter's preference is greatest when the party outlooks of the members of the family are the same, interest in politics is high, and the same family preference has been maintained for considerable time.[7] Republican voters seem to conform somewhat more strongly to family influence than do Democrats. American parents have strikingly more influence on their children's party affiliations than is true in France. Only 29 percent of French voters can even name their father's political affiliation, while 91 percent of American voters can do so.[8]

Curriculum and Politics

The American public school system does a great deal to reinforce children's attachments to the country and to its beliefs. It trains them for particular roles in politics, according to their class levels. This was the principal finding of a revealing study of the character and effects of the civics curriculum in the Boston area. Courses in civics had little effect upon students' participation in politics, but did make them more chauvinistic and firmer supporters of the "democratic creed."[9] Although the curriculum brought about little change in attitudes, it apparently reinforced existing social-class differences in beliefs about the proper role of the citizen. A study of civics textbooks used in middle-class, lower-middle, and working-class communities of Boston suggests that children are trained to play different political roles depending upon their parents' income level and social status.

Only in the upper middle-class community were the children

[5]Robert D. Hess and Judith V. Torney, *The Political Development of Attitudes in Children* (Garden City, N.Y.: Anchor Books, 1967), p. 113.

[6]Kenneth P. Langton, *Political Socialization* (New York: Oxford University Press, 1969), p. 59.

[7]Herbert McClosky and Harold E. Dahlgren, "Primary Group Influence on Party Loyalty," *American Political Science Review* 53 (September 1959), pp. 757–776.

[8]Phillip E. Converse and Georges Dupreux, "Politicization of the Electorate in France and the United States," *Public Opinion Quarterly* 26 (Spring 1962), pp. 1–24, 13.

[9]Edgar Litt, "Civic Education, Community Norms, and Political Indoctrination," *American Sociological Review* 28 (February 1963), pp. 69–75. The balance of this paragraph draws upon this source.

instructed about the value, utility, and desirability of citizen participation in policymaking or exposed to the idea of conflict and disagreement as inherent in politics. In the working-class community, where political involvement was already low, civic training stressed the view that formal governmental institutions and procedures work in harmony for the benefit of citizens. In the lower middle-class community there was training in the elements of democratic government, supplemented by an emphasis upon the responsibilities of citizenship but not on the dynamics of the political process. A supplementary study of the children in the three neighborhoods found that 70 percent of the upper middle-class children, 55 percent of the lower middle-class children, but only 32 percent of the working-class children had a "most favorable" view of participation. At higher income levels, children are taught to be participants in policymaking; at low levels they are taught to accept the outcomes of the political process as legitimate.

The most persistent finding of socialization research is that children are taught to see the government and public officials as benevolent, have great trust in them, and think they are almost never wrong. The first officials of whom the American child becomes aware are the President and the policeman. Children feel a personal attachment to the President, seeing him as benevolent, dependable, powerful, and possessing leadership skills. They regard the policeman as of slightly lower status but still see him as benevolent and dependable.[10] As the child grows older he or she learns to differentiate the private from the public sector of society, and moves from a highly personalized image of government personified by a few authority figures to a more institutionalized view. Lawmaking and the Congress take on more significance in his or her eyes.[11]

View of Political Parties

The concept of political parties develops rather late. One study found that not until the eighth grade could 50 percent of sampled children think of a single difference between the parties.[12] At all grade levels, the most common view was that both parties do about the same things and contribute equally to national and personal welfare.

The favorable view of government and public officials found by socialization studies may well be overstated, because these studies have dealt almost exclusively with middle-class children. Most of

[10]David Easton and Jack Dennis, *Children in the Political System,* (New York: McGraw-Hill, 1969), pp. 147, 231; Fred I. Greenstein, *Children and Politics* (New Haven, Conn.: Yale University Press, 1965), p. 32.

[11]*Ibid.,* pp. 115–123.

[12]Greenstein, *op. cit.,* p. 67.

them were done in the early 1960s, at a time when there was relatively little popular unrest and civil disturbance. The late 1960s saw the appearance of a "credibility gap," another label for distrust of government, and that in itself raises a serious question about the stability of early political attitudes. This question is especially apt because the most distrustful group in the late 1960s consisted largely of adolescents and young adults from upper middle-class families. We have little data that directly bear on this vital issue, however.

There is other evidence that the early socialization studies may have dealt with a special set of conditions not valid for other times or other groups. The few available studies of poor children and black children found some significantly different socialization patterns. A study of children in the poverty-stricken Appalachian region of eastern Kentucky found them dramatically less favorable to political authority than the middle-class children who were respondents in earlier studies. In their greater cynicism, these children reflected the views of their families, and especially their fathers.[13]

Blacks expect unequal treatment from public officials, especially local officials, far more than do whites in comparable socioeconomic circumstances. Young and northern blacks expect better treatment than older and southern blacks do. These expectations, one can assume, make younger and northern blacks more likely to resent unfair treatment when it occurs and more likely to support protests against it.[14]

It should be no surprise, in view of the research findings already reviewed, that upper-class children exceed those with less status in their capacity and motivation for political participation.[15] The working-class child expresses more emotional attachment to the President and sees government in more personal and less issue-oriented terms. He also sees laws as more rigid than does the child from an upper-income family. Perhaps most important, he has a lower sense of political efficacy, of confidence in being able to affect the workings of government.

The Character of the Communications Process

One image of the communications process is that the media keep citizens informed and enable them to exercise influence over public policy. Another is that the media are a means by which elites

[13]Dean Jaros, Herbert Hirsch, and Frederic J. Fleron, Jr., "The Malevolent Leader: Political Socialization in an American Subculture," *American Political Science Review* 62 (June 1968), pp. 564–575.

[14]Dwaine Marvick, "The Political Socialization of the American Negro," *The Annals of the American Academy of Political and Social Science* 361 (September 1964), pp. 112–127, 119.

[15]Greenstein, *op. cit.*, p. 94.

derive support for their actions. There are ways in which the first image is correct, of course. Without information from newspapers, magazines, radio, and television, most people would have little chance of exercising influence upon government at all, or even of knowing when an issue of concern to them arises.

At the same time, studies of opinion formation and opinion change point unmistakably to a number of mechanisms through which mass publics are placed at a disadvantage and subjected to both deliberate and unconscious influence by elites.[16] First, a substantial proportion of the people have relatively little interest in news of public affairs and do not especially try to expose themselves to it. One study, which questioned people about their knowledge and opinions on eight different public issues, found that from 22 percent to 55 percent of the population, depending on the issue, either had no opinion or had one but did not know what the government was doing.[17] Also relevant is the finding that much political information is "retailed" by opinion leaders to larger audiences. Such a two-step flow of messages in the media gives elites, who are somewhat better educated and have somewhat higher status than the recipients of the messages, a disproportionate influence.[18]

Influence of the Media

Among the opinion leaders who help control the flow of messages are editors and reporters themselves, who are in an especially strategic position to decide which news is emphasized, which soft-pedaled, and which ignored. Further, those who shape the media regularly "create" news, in an important sense, by choosing the questions they ask public figures and by themselves suggesting the answers.

Newspapers and television and radio stations are themselves big businesses, and most are merged into commonly owned chains and business complexes. Television stations are frequently affiliated with newspaper publishers. With few exceptions, such as the noncommercial educational stations, they rely chiefly on advertising by other businesses for their profits. These considerations do not preclude the possibility that reporters and editors will sometimes hold and express competing and liberal views. But the great majority of publishers and editors share the interests of the economic elite. Their vows are typically presented as acceptable and patriotic, while contrary views

[16]Philip E. Converse, "The Nature of Belief Systems in Mass Publics," in *Ideology and Discontent,* ed. David Apter (New York: Free Press, 1964), pp. 206–61; see also Robert E. Lane and David O. Sears, *Public Opinion* (Englewood Cliffs, N.J.: Prentice-Hall, 1964), pp. 57–71.

[7]*Ibid.,* (Lane and Sears), pp. 59–60.

[18]Elihu Katz and Paul Lazarsfeld, *Personal Influence* (New York: Free Press, 1955).

are sometimes treated as suggesting outside, or vaguely un-American, influence.

The influence of political elites over the content of the mass communication media is a powerful adjunct of other devices through which they influence the beliefs, political demands, and affiliations of mass publics. What the President of the United States says and does is automatically news. The same is true in lesser degree of other conspicuous public officeholders and activists: cabinet members, senators, governors, and political party leaders. Because people are curious, anxious, and interested in what such figures say and do, the newspapers, television stations, and popular magazines have strong economic and psychological reasons to keep them in the limelight. It is evident, therefore, that these officials can far more easily convey information, impressions, and arguments to a mass public than can other people. The chief effect of this situation is to intensify and multiply the influence of elites. An administration that thinks it will benefit from a liberal civil rights policy can easily convey to a very large public the impression that the enactment of a new civil rights law represents dramatic progress. Human interest stories about a few striking black advances in employment or housing shape people's thinking even if the cases are not typical.

Public Simplification of Issues

Because controversial public issues are typically highly complex, and it is hard or impossible to sort out causes and effects, people have to simplify them in order to think about them at all. They come to be perceived in terms of a metaphor or a simple model. Urban riots may be viewed as the result of outside agitators stirring up basically satisfied blacks in the ghettos. Or they may be viewed as the actions of aggrieved poor people finally demanding through militance and violence what they deserved long before. Political speeches and public policies help shape the particular simplified view that people adopt, and so do newspaper and television reports. Once a person adopts a metaphor to define a complex situation, he or she tends to fit later developments into the same mold and to see them as offering further support for the view already adopted. People have to make some sense of complicated and threatening situations, and so they perceive selectively in order to bolster the view that serves some emotional function and reassures them.

When people are anxious and have no way to be sure what will help and what will hurt, they are especially willing—even eager—to receive and believe cues from authoritative political leaders that will alleviate their doubts and their fears. This is exactly the situation that usually prevails in many fields of public policymaking. Typically, citizens who see a great deal of unemployment around them and fear it will increase do not know how to restore prosperity. They are therefore eager to believe that the President of the United States and the economists upon whom the President depends for advice do know. It is relatively easy in such a situation for a President to win popular support for spending, credit, or public employment policies that he says will solve the problem.

Similarly, citizens must rely very heavily for their beliefs upon what the government tells them about the friendly or hostile intentions of foreign governments. The creation in 1949 of the North Atlantic Treaty Organization, for the declared purpose of preventing Russia from overrunning Western Europe militarily, was the most direct and persuasive evidence the majority of Americans had for believing that Russia desired to overrun Western Europe and might do so unless prevented by superior military might. The existence of regulatory commissions to protect consumers against unfair prices or other unfair business or labor practices serves to reassure people that they are in fact protected. They have no direct way of learning or knowing what prices or rates are fair and whether the business firms with which they must deal are making excessive profits or exploiting them in other ways. Ambiguity about what is fact and what is fair is characteristic of the complicated issues with which government deals. Thus the susceptibility of mass publics to the influence of leaders is all the greater.

The Process of Attitude Change: The Case of the Vietnam War

The attitudes of the American public changed from a prowar to an antiwar position between 1965 and 1969. But more significant than the fact that attitudes changed may be (a) the way they did so, (b) the length of time it took for them to do so, and (c) the many events, acts of leadership, and other governmental maneuvers necessary before real attitude change occurred. Let us review the process by which attitudes changed during this period.

In some important respects, of course, the political setting of the war in Southeast Asia was distinctive. As a matter of foreign policy in which the armed forces were involved, it fell within an area of presidential discretion and initiative in which the Congress has not sought to assert itself. Given this traditional deference to the President, in part suggested by the Constitution's conferral of substantial power on the President as Commander-in-Chief, there were few ways to enforce limits on his actions. Moreover, neither Congress nor the general public had any reliable information on the situation in Vietnam. In a context of uncertainty, the natural tendency is to accept what the supposed experts decide is necessary; once commitments were made and the necessity for them repeatedly emphasized to the public, the entire development of policy and events was seen in these terms. Not to trust one's elected leaders in an ambiguous situation would have been a drastic departure from traditional patterns of behavior. Finally, the subject of Vietnam raised issues of patriotism, national prestige, and anticommunism. Once national honor was committed and troops deployed, many of these symbols became activated. The presentation of the issues by the Johnson Administration emphasized these concepts strongly, as a means of mobilizing support for policies.

The Beginnings of Dissent

Dissent from these policies began on the campuses as early as 1963, but was still relatively limited in 1964. During that election campaign, the aggressive language of the Republican, Barry Goldwater, made Johnson's policy and assurances about not sending troops to Vietnam sound moderate indeed. The war was not highly salient for the general public, with more than a third of the voters unable to answer survey questions about policy preferences for U.S. action in Vietnam. Of those who had preferences, nearly four times as many preferred "taking a stronger stand, even if it means invading North Vietnam" as wanted to "pull out of Vietnam entirely."[19]

In February 1965, the United States began the bombing of North Vietnam. This was to be the first in a series of acts which campus dissenters perceived as escalations of the war and by which they were provoked into greater activity. The "teach-in" stage of antiwar activity then ensued, with many debates staged on campuses between supporters or members of the administration and prominent dissenters. It is even possible that the Johnson Administration sought to give legitimacy to dissent in this fashion as a means of defending itself against what it expected to be the major pressure in the country —toward greater (and more dangerous) military action in the war.

As the commitment of American forces grew throughout 1965, and the draft began to cut more heavily into American life, the war became much more salient to the general public. In the fall of 1965, it was strongly supported, however, particularly by the better-educated and higher-status people.[20] The first major round of campus outbursts occurred in 1966, with disruptions of speeches by administration members, and demonstrations and sit-ins directed at the draft. The dissenters were still a tiny minority, and the troop commitment in Vietnam was growing.

[19]Philip Converse, Warren Miller, Jerrold Rusk, and Arthur C. Wolfe, "Continuity and Change in American Politics: Parties and Issues in the 1968 Election," *American Political Science Review* 63 (1969), p. 1086.
[20]*Gallup Opinion Weekly* (October 1969), p. 15.

By mid-1967, there were half a million American troops in Southeast Asia, a series of urban riots had swept the country, repeated campus outbreaks were occurring, a balance-of-payments problem was developing, and mounting budget deficits indicated growing inflation ahead. Not all of these were related to the Vietnam War, of course, but they combined to create a context of turmoil and tension. Most of the campus dissent was directed at the war and the draft, and public opposition to the war was rising. Nearly half of the population now said that U.S. involvement in Vietnam had been a mistake, but college gaduates continued to express support for the administration, and self-characterized "hawks" outnumbered "doves" by 5–3 ratios.

A chiefly student-sponsored movement that sought to reach adult voters and affect the course of the war was generated in 1967 as a move to "dump Johnson," and in early 1968 it evolved into a campaign to win the Democratic nomination for Senator Eugene McCarthy, a prominent dissenter. In February 1968, the so-called "Tet offensive" by the Viet Cong shocked Americans into the realization that military matters were proceeding less satisfactorily than most official accounts had indicated. The proportions of voters declaring that the Vietnam War had been a mistake rose to equal the number who still supported the administration's rationale.[21] In the first Democratic primary, in New Hampshire in early March, Senator McCarthy's student campaigners succeeded in winning 42 percent of the Democratic vote for their man, while President Johnson's write-in campaign secured 48 percent. The result was interpreted as indicating great antiwar sentiment among Democrats, and it set in motion a train of events that had immeasurable impact on the election in November. First, President Johnson announced that he would not seek renomination, declaring that this had been his intention all along. Peace talks with the North Vietnamese were started in Paris. Senator Robert Kennedy entered the campaign for the Democratic nomination, after much hesitation.

Subsequent analysis shows that the McCarthy victory in New Hampshire was only partially due to "dove"-style antiwar sentiment. The Michigan Survey Research Center found that New Hampshire McCarthy voters were indeed unhappy with the Johnson Administration, but that a whole range of problems was on their minds. On the issue of Vietnam itself, those who wanted a *stronger* prosecution of the war outnumbered those who wanted to end it by a nearly 3–2 margin.[22] Among all Democrats interviewed in the national phase of

[21]*Ibid.*
[22]Converse, *op. cit.*

the Center's survey before the Democratic Convention, more Mc-Carthy supporters eventually favored Wallace than any other candidate considered in 1968.[23] Thus it seems clear that many observers overestimated the extent of antiwar feeling within the electorate at that time in 1968. Well over half now agreed that involvement in Vietnam had been a mistake, but these totals must have included many who were simply frustrated at not being able to win the war faster.

Chicago, 1968: The Turning Point

The Democratic Convention of August 1968 was the next major event in the expanding student-based movement against the war. Those who went to Chicago probably represented only a relatively small proportion of all students at that time, but the result of the events in Chicago again had powerful effects on the nature of public opinion and on the election itself. Public reaction against the demonstrators and in favor of the police was very strong, as we suggested earlier. Not even those who took "dove" positions on the war expressed significant support for the demonstrators.[24] Only one in six or seven whites felt that the United States had made a mistake in getting involved in Vietnam and that the best course would be to pull out entirely. But even within this group, almost 70 percent denied that "too much force" had been used by the Chicago police, and the main body of opinion was that "not enough force" had been used against the peace demonstrators. Those who were against the war and sympathetic to demonstrations were a tiny minority of the population, about 3 percent. Most other people were adamantly opposed to the demonstrations. It is impossible to tell whether the violence that occurred in Chicago actually gained or lost support for the antiwar cause, but it is clear that it promoted much support for "law-and-order" candidates.

By the time of the 1968 election, much of the indecision of 1964 had of course been eliminated, and the voters had clear preferences on Vietnam. Table 15-5 shows, however, that there had not been a great reduction in the proportion of people who wanted a stronger stand. In three of the four categories, the proportion even went up. Higher proportions favored pulling out entirely, but they were still only about half as large overall as those wanting stronger action. The electorate, in short, did not turn against the war. The signs of revulsion against violent actions, and of trust in the established offi-

---

[23]Ibid., p. 1093.
[24]Data in this paragraph are all drawn from Converse, op. cit. pp. 1087–1088.

cials and practices, suggest that the actions of campus-based dissenters had the opposite effect.

Nevertheless, the proportions of the adult population who said that the Vietnam War had been a mistake continued to rise. As we now realize, this group is composed of both "doves" and "hawks," the latter presumably feeling that it is better not to become involved in wars that we are not prepared to do everything possible to win. Figure 15-2 shows the trend in attitudes toward American involvement. It demonstrates that by late 1968 there was strong consensus that it had been a mistake, and that this sentiment continued into the first year of the Nixon Administration. President Nixon's own ratings remained high for the first year he was in office, showing particular strength after his November 1969 announcement of slow but apparently assured troop withdrawals. His expressed commitment to this goal was actually made earlier in the year, and may have accounted for the rise in proportions believing the war was a mistake.

TABLE 15-5

Attitudes on Vietnam Policy, 1964 and 1968, Whites Only

"Which of the following do you think we should do now in Vietnam?
1. Pull out of Vietnam entirely.
2. Keep our soldiers in Vietnam but try to end the fighting.
3. Take a stronger stand even if it means invading North Vietnam."

	Pull out	Status quo	Stronger stand	Don't know, other	Total
Northern Democrats					
1964	8%	25	29	38	100%
1968	20%	39	35	6	100%
Northern Republicans					
1964	8%	19	38	35	100%
1968	20%	39	36	5	100%
Southern Democrats					
1964	8%	25	28	39	100%
1968	17%	36	38	9	100%
Southern Republicans					
1964	10%	18	42	30	100%
1968	15%	29	48	8	100%

Source: Converse, *op. cit.,* p. 1086.

In mid-1969, 29 percent of the adult population favored immediate withdrawal from Vietnam, but this fell to 21 percent after Nixon's November speech, and rose to 35 percent in February 1970.[25]

Perhaps the most important finding reflected in Figure 15-2, however, is the difference between better-educated (and, presumably, higher-income) people and less-educated, lower-income people. College-educated people were consistently *less* likely to believe the war had been a mistake than were grade-school or high-school people, *until 1969 when it became the official policy of the President and the United States government to pull out of South Vietnam.* In other words, opposition to the war was stronger among the lower classes and less educated; college graduates were apparently readier to trust their government, and to assume that what it was doing must have been right. This is indeed a high level of confidence in one's government, and indicates continued broad discretion for the President in foreign affairs.

In conclusion, it seems clear that most members of the general public continue to trust the established officials of government, and particularly the President, in this type of situation. They are strongly opposed to dissent and particularly strongly disapprove of violent dissent even when it is not initiated by the dissenters themselves; and they are subject to appeals based on patriotism, nationalism, and anticommunism.

Area of Student Influence

But these findings do not mean that the campus-based dissent of the 1960s was without consequence for the character of government policy. Quite the contrary; students had considerable influence, but on elites and opinion-makers, not on the general public. College students are at least near-elites, and people in power seek the approbation of rising generations and their prospective leaders. Highly conspicuous and continuing opposition in the citadels of culture and learning in the nation is embarrassing, if nothing else, for government officials. The issue of the Vietnam War might never have been framed in moral and ethical terms if they had not been emphasized on the campuses, and governmental policymakers would have found it much easier to gain support for escalation of the war if it had not been for the student movement. The McCarthy candidacy, the Johnson withdrawal, and even the relatively moderate public posture assumed by President Nixon, are traceable in important ways to this movement. Its failure to sway most political spectators should not obscure its significant intra-elite effects.

[25]*Gallup Opinion Weekly* (March 1970), p. 9.

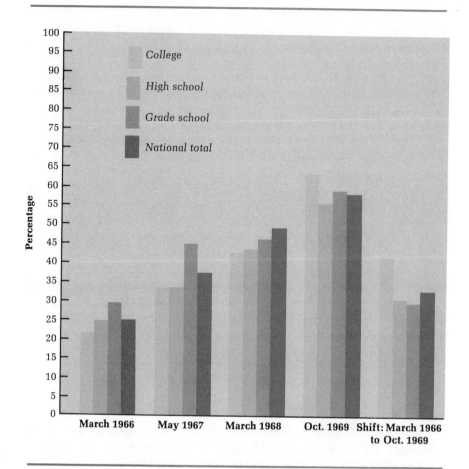

Source: *Gallup Opinion Weekly* **(October 1969), p. 15. By permission
of the American Institute of Public Opinion (The Gallup Poll).**

FIGURE 15-2
Agreement that U.S. Involvement in Vietnam Was a Mistake, by Education Levels

So, too, the mere fact that some segment of the population is engaging in violent actions assumes the stature of a serious threat in
the eyes of national elites, both in and out of government. They see
danger not in the capacity of the dissenters to bring about their goals,
but in the prospect of social chaos and the possibility that other
groups will respond similarly, endangering the structure of order and
civility they consider it crucial to maintain. Even if elites care little
about Vietnam, therefore, it may be preferable to them to end the
war than to have business endangered, inflation rampant, and repeated violence in the streets.

The Results: Ideology and Ambivalence in Non-elite Attitudes

We have seen that non-elites express certain unfulfilled wants and needs, and wish that government would do more about them. At the same time, the sources from which they acquired their basic political attitudes transmitted the orthodox belief system. And the sources from which they receive daily information are dominated by elites and tend to fit new information into the orthodoxy's mold. One result, as we have just seen, is great dependence on, and trust in, the actions of government, a profound reluctance to believe that the actions of revered institutions and high officials could be anything but right and proper. Another is a kind of continuing ambivalence about many things in politics, including those same officials —but not the system itself.

This ambivalence—at times becoming conflict or mutual contradiction—is manifested in many areas of non-elite beliefs and attitudes. The orthodox ideology has been thoroughly absorbed, but reality refutes aspects of it every day. Thus, the system is good, but some of its officials and actions are bad. Change is necessary, but only by legal means. Minorities deserve equality, but have been given too much assistance already.

Ambivalence manifests itself also in simultaneous absorption in race conflicts, intolerance or scapegoating of protesters, antipathies toward leaders, cynicism, and growing fears for the future stability of the country. These apparently unrelated (or, in some cases, "conservative") attitudes are traceable, we believe, to the basic problem of non-elites—a strong sense of unfulfilled needs, but an equally strong generalized support for the system and lack of understanding of specific causes or remedies. We shall briefly survey the current state of non-elite attitudes in these terms.

The Basic Ideology

One interesting illustration of the tension between felt needs and received ideology is provided by Lloyd Free and Hadley Cantril, professional students of American opinion, in a major book entitled *The Political Beliefs of Americans.*[26] Using the responses of a national cross section to a series of questions in 1964, they constructed two "spectrums" of opinion. One was called the "operational" spectrum, and was composed of answers to questions regarding specific governmental actions or proposals in the areas of Medicare, poverty, housing, and aid to education. The other, labeled the "ideological"

[26] Lloyd A. Free and Hadley Cantril, *The Political Beliefs of Americans* (New York: Simon and Schuster, 1968). The analysis in the following paragraphs is drawn from Chapter 3.

spectrum, was made up of answers to more abstract, less tangible questions about how problems ought to be solved and whether the government is interfering too much in private and economic affairs. Those who consistently favored governmental assistance in the specific issue areas were labelled either strong liberals or predominantly liberal, depending on the number of affirmative responses they gave. Opposition to governmental assistance led to classification as predominantly conservative or strongly conservative. The same approach was followed in regard to the ideological spectrum, with endorsement of governmental solutions and denial that the government was interfering too much characterizing the liberal category.

When the two spectrums were compared, some very interesting and revealing findings emerged. In *operational* terms, 65 percent of respondents were completely or predominantly liberal. But in *ideological* terms, only 16 percent were. Fully 50 percent of respondents were *ideologically* conservative, compared to only 14 percent who were *operationally* conservative. This suggests that when it comes to a question of what government should do in a specific situation, people want action to solve problems. But when issues are cast in the form of abstract philosophies or basic values, people endorse the conservative and more traditional assumptions. In other words, the grip of ideology remains strong even in the face of specific needs and desires to the contrary. The questions that gained such support for the conservative side of the ideological spectrum involved standard American nostrums: the federal government is interfering too much, it is regulating business and interfering with the free enterprise system, social problems could be solved if government would keep hands off and let people handle them themselves, anybody who wants work can find it, and we should rely more on individual initiative and not so much on welfare programs. No doubt some people can cheerfully voice such beliefs and then endorse governmental action to solve problems; 46 percent of ideological conservatives were operational liberals. But people of conservative ideology gave only half as much support to liberal measures as did those of liberal ideology. And those who were conservative ideologically made up almost the entire group of those who were conservative operationally. Thus, the conservative nature of the ideology, and its continuing strength, appear to contribute importantly to resistance, even among the general public, to governmental social legislation.

Implications of the Findings

What are the implications of these findings? For one thing, they suggest a gap between rhetoric and performance. For another, they suggest that the ways in which people focus on politics, and what they see as important, may follow such distinctly different dimensions. Those who think and perceive in ideological terms may care most about the abstract principles and rhetoric surrounding government. Those who are operationally oriented may be more concerned with solutions to concrete problems. This implication is confirmed by Free and Cantril's analysis of their respondents' ranking of public concerns. Ideological conservatives ranked such intangibles as preserving economic liberties and states' rights at the top of their list of concerns, while liberals gave first place to specific actions such as aid to education and ending unemployment. Thus, in addition to the familiar divisions among people along class, racial, religious, and other such lines, we must distinguish between them on the basis of perceptual orientations. This phenomenon is related to class status, but is not identical with it.

We should not leave the subject of how people hold an ideology without considering the extent of real concern about communism and socialism. In general, when people are asked to give free answers about their hopes and fears for the nation or their personal worries, communism ranks quite low. One of the most salient findings of a famous study of national opinion in 1954, at the height of the McCarthy era, was that only 1 percent of the population voluntarily listed communism as a concern. But 12 percent of those reported in Table 15-3 listed it as a national fear and the proportion of persons ranking it high as a concern in response to checklist or yes-no type questions is usually fairly high. In 1964, in response to Free and Cantril's twenty-three-question checklist, for example, "combatting world communism" emerged second only to "keeping the country out of war" as a national concern. And, asked how much danger they thought communists represented here in the United States, 62 percent of the same respondents answered "a very great deal" or "a good deal."[27] The uncertainty and conflicting interpretations to which these findings give rise are due in part to the difference between free-answer and checklist type questions, and in part to the difference between the threat of war from international conflict with communist countries and the threat of subversion from internal deviants.

These findings about communism and attitudes toward it may be summarized tentatively and speculatively as follows. First, antipathies toward communism as both international threat and internal menace are strongest among the upper class levels, particularly as we saw in Chapter 9, among top businessmen. The general public fears war, and identifies international communism with that prospect. All retain at least some vestiges of the American ideological commitment to private property and the superiority of American institutions, but

27Ibid., p. 119.

ideological conservatives are particularly moved by these factors and especially strident against communism. There are, therefore, continuing forces within the country, localized chiefly in the upper class levels and the ideological conservatives, which feel threatened by and agitate against communism. From time to time, the general public responds to such elite appeals, or segments of non-elites attribute problems to communism. Thus, when student disruptions or civil rights demonstrations occur, and they are annoying or hard to understand, it may be because of this menace, communism, one hears so much about. No doubt this summary overstates the matter somewhat, but it is intended to make the point that the basic seat of anticommunism in the United States is not the general mass of the people. It finds support among them, but the evidence indicates that there is much stronger support and concern among those in the higher classes who are ideologically conservative.

The American View and Others

We can gain some perspective on the nature of American orientations toward politics and government by comparing them with the views other populations have toward their governments. Such a comparison was made in the mid-1960s in a five-nation study by Gabriel Almond and Sidney Verba, entitled *The Civic Culture*.[28] This analysis explores the orientations of samples of the general population in the United States, the United Kingdom, West Germany, Italy, and Mexico. The extent to which Americans are distinctive in their conviction that their political institutions are right and good is evident in Table 15-6. Whether as a consequence of political ideology or not, Americans professed pride in the Constitution, political freedom, democracy, and similar items much more often than did respondents in other nations. Although Americans were proud of their economic system, Germans outdid them in this respect. On the other hand, Americans were distinctively unlikely to volunteer answers having to do with the arts, sciences, or attributes of the country's environment.

Americans also felt more engaged in the continuing political processes of their country, and drew more satisfaction from voting. Given the criteria employed for measuring the "democraticness" of the political values and expectations of the population, the United States emerged ahead of the other four nations. Great Britain did frequently equal or exceed the United States in some categories. Some

[28]Gabriel Almond and Sidney Verba, *The Civic Culture*, (Princeton, N.J.: Princeton University Press, 1963).

of these responses may be only reflections of dominant ideology. In some cases not encompassed by such ideology, both Germans and Britons saw more democratic conditions in their countries than Americans did in theirs. Table 15-7 compares the fire nations' population samples' expectations of "serious consideration for your point of view" when dealing with either administrative officials or police. Americans, it is clear, are less confident of such treatment than either Englishmen or Germans; the differences with respect to Great Britain are particularly sharp. Of interest also is the fact that for Americans, there is a class-based variation in expectations of consideration for one's point of view. Those with some university education have more confidence in receiving consideration than do those with less education. In Britain, by contrast, higher proportions of the least educated respondents expected consideration from the police than did people with university educations.[29]

TABLE 15-6
Aspects of Nation in Which People Take Pride

Percentage who say they are proud of:	U.S.	U.K.	Germany	Italy	Mexico
Governmental, political institutions	85	46	7	3	30
Social legislation	13	18	6	1	2
Position in international affairs	5	11	5	2	3
Economic system	23	10	33	3	24
Characteristics of people	7	18	36	11	15
Spiritual virtues and religion	3	1	3	6	8
Contributions to the arts	1	6	11	16	9
Contributions to science	3	7	12	3	1
Physical attributes of country	5	10	17	25	22
Nothing or don't know	4	10	15	27	16
Other	9	11	3	21	14
Total % of responses*	158	148	148	118	144
Total % of respondents	100	100	100	100	100
Total number of cases	970	963	955	995	1,007

*Percentages exceed one hundred because of multiple responses.
Source: Almond and Verba, *op. cit.,* p. 64.

[29]*Ibid.,* p. 73.

TABLE 15-7

Consideration Expected from Bureaucrats and Police, by Nation

"If you explained your point of view to the officials (police), what effect do you think it would have? Would they give your point of view serious consideration, would they pay only a little attention, or would they ignore what you had to say?

Percentage who expect:	U.S.		U.K.		Germany		Italy		Mexico	
	bureauc.	pol.	bureauc.	pol.	bureauc.	pol.	bureauc.	pol.	bureauc.	pol.
Serious consideration for point of view	48	56	59	74	53	59	35	35	14	12
A little attention	31	22	22	13	18	11	15	13	48	46
To be ignored	6	11	5	5	5	4	11	12	27	29
Depends	11	9	10	6	15	13	21	20	6	7
Other	0	—	—	—	1	2	6	6	—	1
Don't know	4	2	2	1	8	11	12	14	3	4
Total percentage	100	100	98	99	100	100	100	100	98	99
Total number	970	970	963	963	955	955	995	995	1,007	1,007

Source: Almond and Verba, op. cit., p. 72.

Diversions by Means of Racial Conflict and Scapegoating

Several kinds of diversions operate to deflect non-elites from making efforts to fulfill their wants and needs through coherent political action. War, which causes people to forget their differences and unite in patriotic support for their government, is the classic example. Even if the war is unpopular, it serves as a focus for conflict that aligns people in different ways than do the class-based contests that could bring fulfillment of non-elite wants and needs. Space programs, races to the moon, and other forms of international competition—particularly against communism—serve many of the same functions.

Other forms of diversions divide one group of non-elites from another. Ethnic and religious conflicts and sex discrimination are examples. But the single most important diversion for all Americans is racism. Outbursts of racist violence have provided means of venting non-elite resentments throughout American history. Continuous systematic denigration of minority groups has provided satisfactions for those just above such minorities on the social ladder. In part, such continuing tensions are kept alive by the natural tendency of employers to seek the lowest possible labor costs. Historically, this has meant the use of minorities as cheap labor and as strikebreakers, to the detriment of white working-class wage levels. Aid to the poor has also been interpreted as aid to minorities, particularly blacks; as a result, whites have been less supportive than they might have been if they had understood the potential recipients to be people like themselves.

Racism and racial tensions remain prominent focuses of non-elite attention today. Whites blame blacks for wanting too much too fast, and for not working hard enough to get it. Blacks see whites as unresponsive and racist. The more blacks seek equality, the more whites resent it, and the less either group sees its problems as caused by anything but the other. How rapidly white resistance stiffened in the 1960s can be seen from the shift in whites' opinions about whether blacks "have tried to move too fast":[30]

	Yes: Have tried to move too fast	No: Not fast enough
1964	34%	32%
1965	49	19
1966	85	3

[30]*Public Opinion Quarterly* 32 (Fall 1968), p. 522, citing a Louis Harris survey.

The differences of opinion that separate whites and blacks in the 1970s remain at the high levels to which they were raised by the riots of the late 1960s. A Louis Harris national survey in 1972 showed, for example, that much of the gap still (or again) focused on integration of schools and the use of busing for the purpose.[31] Blacks wanted schools integrated by a 78 percent to 12 percent margin, compared to a 46 percent to 43 percent margin among whites. But whites opposed busing for that purpose by an overwhelming 81 percent to 14 percent margin, while blacks favored it by 50 percent to 36 percent. Similar, but less dramatic, differences were found in a series of other social welfare areas. Blacks also demonstrated lack of confidence in the Nixon administration's record on racial matters, while whites approved it solidly. The overall impression was one of dogged white resistance, and black conviction that whites simply had no real interest in equality between the races.

Other forms of scapegoating also frequently occur in American politics. Youth, protestors, and unorthodox or dissenting people have served from time to time as the objects of such scapegoating. We have already seen the strong disapproval of demonstrations and support for the police that developed after the Chicago Democratic Convention clashes of 1968. Hostility to protestors, and to black demands, tends to be highest among the lower echelons of non-elites. In 1971, one study found that twice as many blue-collar people expressed high hostility toward student demonstrators and black demands as did professional white-collar persons.[32]

Intolerance of dissent or unorthodoxy is a familiar feature of non-elite attitudes. Sometimes it is argued that this shows that non-elites are "undemocratic" or that elites' support for free speech and due process is the main pillar of democracy in the United States. We think it is better understood as evidence of a tendency to scapegoating, brought about by the unfulfilled wants and needs and other ambivalences that we have explored.[33] In any event, the differences between class levels are clear. Table 15-8, reflecting the results of a national poll by CBS News in 1970, is only the latest in a long series of studies showing non-elite intolerance.

[31]Louis Harris survey (November 1972).

[32]H. Edward Ransford, "Blue Collar Anger: Reactions to Student and Black Protest," *American Sociological Review* 37 (June 1972), p. 339.

[33]It is also possible, of course, that the greater education of the higher-echelon people enables them to recognize the rhetoric of free speech more readily. Thus, if the principles of free speech were recognized by the lower levels of non-elites, they might respond differently. Further, the actual behavior of elites might be as inconsistent with free speech principles as that of the lowest level of blue-collar workers. The data alone do not answer these questions. They merely suggest intolerance on the part of lower-level non-elites, which we consider congruent with our scapegoating thesis.

TABLE 15-8
Support for Free Speech and Freedom of Assembly, National Sample, 1970 (in percentages)

Do you think everyone should have the right to criticize the government, even if the criticism is damaging to the national interest?	For complete freedom of speech	Oppose or want limited speech	No opinion
By income:			
$15,000 and over	40	59	1
$10,000–14,999	29	70	1
$5,000–9,999	17	80	3
Under $5,000	13	84	3
By education:			
College graduation	47	50	9
Some college	32	65	3
High school graduation	20	78	2
Some high school	11	87	2
Grade school	8	87	5

TABLE 15-8 (Continued)

As long as there appears to be no clear danger of violence, do you think any group, no matter how extreme, should be allowed to organize protests against the government?

	Favor dissent	Oppose dissent	No opinion
By income:			
$15,000 and over	57	39	4
$10,000–14,999	48	49	3
$5,000–9,999	40	57	3
Under $5,000	33	63	4
By education:			
College graduation	61	34	5
Some college	56	42	2
High School graduation	44	54	2
Some high school	31	64	5
Grade school	28	68	4

Source: Hazel Erskine, "The Polls: Freedom of Speech," *Public Opinion Quarterly* 34 (Fall 1970), pp. 491, 494.

Rising Fear of Instability and Disorder

Perhaps the most dramatic finding of Cantril and Roll's national survey of 1971 was the proportion of Americans who expressed fear of national disunity and political instability.[34] Twenty-six percent of all respondents mentioned it, and it ranked a close second to war as a national fear. All population groups expressed this concern in about equal proportions. Moreover, in a special scale in which the quality of life in past, present, and future is ranked by respondents, the average ranking placed the United States *behind* where it had been five years before. This was a highly unusual result, for such scaling inquiries normally find people feeling that progress has been made from past to present, i.e., that life is getting better. In repeated use of this type of scale in various countries, there had been only one previous instance in which a population had ranked its present lower than its past.

The importance of this finding led the researchers to undertake a special supplementary inquiry into the implications and reasons for this fear. They asked another national sample whether they thought that the unrest and tensions between groups was likely to "lead to a real breakdown in this country" or "blow over soon." Almost half of the respondents—47 percent—said that it would lead to a real breakdown; 38 percent thought it would blow over. Again, all population groups shared this fear in about equal proportions.

Appropriately, the survey also sought to learn whether the reasons for possible breakdown were seen as *systemic* (defined as failures of institutions or deep problems involving values and the character of the economic system) or *personal,* due to the character of those who take part in demonstrations and protests. Table 15-9 analyzes the answers in terms of the occupations and educational levels of the respondents. It shows that there is most support for the conclusion that the *system* is at fault (Statement A), but that it is disproportionately the better-educated and higher-status people who believe this. The blue-collar groups (farmers and manual workers) are least likely to choose this explanation. Further detailed analysis shows that these same blue-collar categories are the most likely to believe that the unrest is communist-inspired. People who have only a grade-school education, probably very similar to the people in the blue-collar category, are *least* likely to blame the system (Statement A) and most likely to choose such protester-related explanations as that protests are communist-inspired or that youth have "gotten out of hand" (Statements D and F). Again, the tendency toward scapegoating seems

[34]Albert H. Cantril and Charles W. Roll, Jr., *Hopes and Fears of the American People* (New York: Universe Books, 1971). The data in this and the succeeding paragraph are drawn from pp. 25, 31, and 70.

TABLE 15-9
Reasons Given for National Unrest, by Occupation and Education, 1971 (in percentages)

	Total All	Occupations				Education		
		Professional & Business	White-collar	Farmers	Manual workers	College	High School	Grade School
A. Our traditional way of doing things is not working and some basic changes are needed if we are to work together.	34	48	40	23	31	53	31	23
B. Some Negroes and other minorities are making unreasonable demands.	31	26	28	33	31	21	34	34
C. Many of the problems our country faces are so big that we can't agree on how to solve them.	19	23	17	17	18	27	17	16
D. The protests are largely communist-inspired.	31	27	37	41	33	20	35	34
E. Our leaders in government and business are not trying hard enough to solve the problems we face and people are losing confidence in them.	31	32	27	30	31	35	30	28
F. Some young people have gotten out of hand and have no respect for authority.	32	27	32	37	32	21	34	40

Source: Cantril and Roll, Jr., op. cit., Appendix, Table A-8, p. 70.

evident: these lower levels of non-elites sense instability and fear breakdown as much as does anybody else, but they blame the protesters and not the (good) system.

Loss of Confidence in the Business System and Leaders

Accompanying the rising fear of national breakdown, and perhaps evidencing a general cynicism, Americans in the early 1970s were losing confidence in business and in leadership in all areas of life. In a lengthy article addressed to its business audience in 1972, *Business Week* magazine compiled a number of findings to paint a picture of the "worst attitude climate in a decade."[35] Approval of companies' performance was low and dropping among all sectors of the population; people favored price and profit controls by increasing margins; pollution was a prominent issue in people's minds; and there was unprecedented support for consumer legislation.

But business was probably not being singled out by the general public for special disapproval. The Louis Harris polling organization found sharp declines in public confidence in the leadership of many areas of national life.[36] A national sample was asked, "As far as peo-

TABLE 15-10
Trend of Confidence in Institutional Leaders (in percentages)

Great deal of confidence in:	1972	1971	1966
Medicine	48	61	72
Finance	39	36	67
Science	37	32	56
Military	35	27	62
Education	33	37	61
Psychiatry	31	35	51
Religion	30	27	41
Retail business	28	24	48
U.S. Supreme Court	28	23	51
Federal executive branch	27	23	41
Major U.S. companies	27	27	55
Congress	21	10	42
The Press	18	18	29
Television	17	22	25
Labor	15	14	22
Advertising	12	13	21

Source: Louis Harris Associates (November 1972).

[35]*Business Week,* June 17, 1972, pp. 100–103.
[36]Louis Harris survey (November 1972).

ple running_____are concerned, would you say you have a great deal of confidence, only some confidence, or hardly any confidence at all in them?" Table 15-10 shows the results—a striking decline from 1966 to 1971, and mixed changes from 1971 to 1972. The levels of confidence are very low, and must be seen as part of the general non-elite malaise, frustration, cynicism, and alienation that is characteristic of the 1970s. Once again, however, we must note that because many of these attitudes are mutually contradictory the overall result is perpetuation of the *status quo*, rather than purposeful action toward change.

Chapter 16

There are many forms of political participation. A substantial proportion of them—such as personal contact with decisionmakers, large contributions to political parties, lobbying, test cases before the Supreme Court, or extensive campaigns for or against contemplated legislation—are monopolized by elites. Non-elite participation may take these forms, but it is for practical purposes limited to those kinds of activities in which a citizen may engage near his home and with limited resources and time. Even with these realistic standards, non-elite participation is distinctly low, whether measured by the resources brought to bear by individuals or groups, the proportion of the people who actually use the officially authorized channels, or the proportion who engage in other types of participation. In the established channels, such as political parties and elections or interest groups, the incidence of participation rises sharply with class status; it varies directly with all three factors of income, occupation, and education.

Participation: Voting and Alternatives

Both political parties and interest groups tend to be hierarchically organized, bureaucratic, and long-enduring forms of organization. Not surprisingly, stable and self-perpetuating leadership elements develop tacit arrangements for conducting business with each other. Often, they pay more attention to their own needs, or to those of their leading supporters, than they do to the interests of the mass of non-elites. Alternative forms of participation, such as demonstrations, petitions, or *ad hoc* campaigns for particular goals, do arise from time to time, sporadically venting demands for change and revealing needs that have gone unheeded within the established channels. But even in these informal processes, participation is low and often reflects the same class biases as do the official channels.

The Electoral Process

The reasons why non-elite political participation is both low and class-related have aroused much speculation since survey evidence first made them analytically clear. It may be that the lower classes are simply satisfied with the higher classes' management of the political system, that they have more economically productive uses for their time, or that they are simply uninformed or too apathetic to care about public affairs. Or it may be that they have been inculcated with the belief that their role is to accept what their betters achieve for them and that all works automatically for the best in this ingenious system. Perhaps they are too busy trying to make ends meet amidst economic hardships, or they may know from past experience or intuition that it will do no good to press their goals through the established system because it is designed to permit elites to deflect, delay, and ultimately deny them. It is worth trying to resolve some of these issues. In this chapter, we shall first explore the orthodox channels, looking particularly at the incidence and nature of participation and its meaning for the system as a whole. Then we shall examine some of the ways in which elites are able to manage these orthodox channels so that non-elite interests do not predominate. Finally, we shall look at some of the unorthodox channels that have been used over the years to express non-elite desires and demands more directly—and at some of the mixed reactions they have aroused.

In general, about 60 to 65 percent of adult Americans vote in a presidential election, despite (a cynic would surely add "or, perhaps, because of") all the publicity and campaigning that urges participation. This proportion is lower than in any other major industrialized nation, and many small, rural, and otherwise "developing" nations. In the normal off-year congressional election, the proportion drops to about 50 percent, and in many state, city, and local elections it falls still further. Only about 10 percent of the adult population ever performs any more strenuous electorally-related act than voting, such as going to rallies, campaigning, contributing, or taking part in primaries.

Voting Patterns

"Turnout," as the act of voting is known to political analysts, is closely related to intensity of preference for one or another candidate or party, and in turn to class level and membership in active political groups. Nearly 90 percent of college-educated persons and nearly 80 percent of high-school graduates vote in a presidential election, but only a little over half of those with only a grade school education do so. The gradation is constant all the way down the status ladder. Skilled workers, for example, vote with greater regularity than do unskilled workers. Union members vote with distinctly greater consistency than similarly situated workers who do not belong to unions. The same is true of other organized groups.

Other demographic characteristics also are associated with the disposition to vote. Men are more likely to vote than women, which almost certainly reflects widely held beliefs about the "proper" role of women in society. This is true in almost all countries. The young are less likely to vote than are older people, due partly to residency requirements that discriminate against the mobile and partly to the greater integration of older people into the political system. Blacks are much less likely to vote than whites even when they are not legally barred from doing so or informally intimidated. People who live in urban areas vote more frequently than rural residents, probably because political life in the cities is more stimulating and there is more social pressure to vote. Voting participation rates are far lower in the South than in other regions, chiefly because of the high proportion of the Southern population that is poor, black, and relatively less educated.

The turnout of voters depends not only upon these socioeconomic factors but also upon people's interest and involvement in party politics. That high-status voters go to the polls more often chiefly reflects their greater belief that it matters how they vote and who wins. Anyone who feels strongly that it makes a difference is obviously more likely to vote than those who do not.

For some, nonvoting is an expression of their rejection of that belife—of their assumption that the major parties present no real choice and that the voters have little influence upon what government does. The proportion of nonvoters who consciously reject the electoral system in this way has probably always been small, but it may be particularly significant because it occurs in the face of such an intense barrage of pressure and propaganda to take part. This pressure is, of course, intended to integrate people into the political system and give them a greater stake in it. The extension of the right to vote —first to propertyless males, then to women, blacks, and finally to the 18 to 21-year-old age group—has never had any significant effect on government policy. But it does seem to have lessened the protests of such groups, and to cause them to believe that remedies for their problems can be found within the orthodox political processes. The right to vote thus helps to commit people to the system and to legitimize governmental actions. Not to exercise that right requires strong resistance to American orthodoxy.

Turnout and participation patterns are clearly fundamental to the outcome of the political process. The sharp disparities in levels of participation that we have seen contribute to the extension of upper-class influence. One leading scholar suggests conceiving of political participation in terms of three types of people: "apathetics" (persons who are uninvolved in any way), "spectators" (people who seek information, vote, talk about politics, etc., but are not themselves active), and "gladiators" (people who go to meetings, become active in a party, etc.).[1] If we then imagine the gladiators (perhaps 3 to 4 percent of the population) battling before a stadium half full of spectators (about 60 percent of the people), while a third or more of the population (the apathetics) simply stay home and ignore the battle, we have a rough characterization of the American electoral process in operation. It might be desirable to add to this characterization that in some cases the spectators are prevented from becoming gladiators, and that the "apathetics" may include some who tried to take part and lost. Thus modified, the characterization is not inappropriate.

The Decision to Vote for a Particular Political Party

How a voter casts his ballot when he does vote depends upon his orientation toward the political parties, the issues, and the candidates. Most Americans identify with either the Republican or the Democratic Party and feel attached to that party, even though they may occasionally vote for a candidate of another party. Such "party identification" typically develops early in life, is fairly stable over time, and is the best single predictor of how a person will vote.

In terms of democratic theory, people's views on policy issues should be the crucial influence upon voting, but studies of voting behavior for the most part show the opposite: that the American public is remarkably uninformed about public issues and about the parties' positions on such issues. Those who are informed, on the other hand, apparently do base their choice of which party to support largely upon the issues.[2] The voters vary greatly in sophistication about issues, ranging from a relatively small proportion (about 12 percent) who have a clear political ideology to about 22 percent for whom politics has no issue content at all. Between these groups are

[1]Lester Milbrath, *Political Participation* (Chicago: Rand McNally, 1963), p. 20.
[2]V. O. Key, *Public Opinion and American Democracy* (New York: Alfred A. Knopf, 1967), p. 461, Table 18.1.

many who see politics as helpful or harmful to labor, farmers, or other groups important to them, and some who simply relate Republicans or Democrats to good times or bad times.[3]

Because relatively few people are attuned to issues, and perhaps also because political parties do not try very hard to take clear and distinct positions on issues, long-standing loyalties to the parties acquire even greater importance in shaping voting behavior. Once identification with a particular party has been established, it tends to continue throughout a voter's lifetime. In effect, the voter makes use of his political party as a "reference group"—that is, he takes his cues as to where he stands on issues from the party and its leaders, rather than the other way around. It is just too time-consuming for the average person to try to form independent opinions about every issue. Besides, each political party might be on his side on five issues and against him on five, with no distinction between them on another ten. How can he know which are going to be more important in the next four years, or which a given party or candidate is going to deliver on? Thus, it is both more efficient and quite rational for him simply to commit himself to the party whose general approach, style, composition, or rhetoric is more to his liking. For most people, this means that the party of their parents and friends is their party.

Two groups of people, however, are relatively free of these generationally transmitted political party loyalties. One group is made up of well-informed people who make choices between parties and candidates on the basis of their positions on one or two basic issues, or who are dissatisfied with both parties for one reason or another. This group is relatively small, perhaps not more than 5 percent of eligible voters, but it includes many people who are in positions to influence others through writing, speaking, and campaigning. The other group is at the opposite pole of knowledge about issues, and is particularly responsive to the characteristics of the candidates. Voters who have strong party loyalties tend to see the major candidates accordingly; their party's man is strong, sincere, competent, and humane, while his opponent is the opposite. But people in this latter group, having no strong party ties, are more likely to react—and vote—according to their personal feelings about the candidates. These feelings are generated by how the candidate looks on television, what he or she seemed to be like in a photograph published in a magazine or newspaper, or by scraps of rumor and conversation.

The importance of the personal image communicated to potential voters leads candidates to take elaborate steps to project themselves favorably. Through careful planning, even to the level of gestures, dress, mode of speech, and the vagueness or specificity with which

[3]Angus Campbell, Philip Converse, Warren Miller, and Donald Stokes, *The American Voter* (New York: John Wiley, 1960), p. 249.

issues are discussed, a particular impression of the candidate is created. Professional public relations consultants have played an increasingly important role in shaping campaign plans and campaign advertising. In the view of many critics, this new emphasis in electoral campaigning tries less to help the voters learn what the candidate is like and what he believes than to construct a synthetic, and possibly quite misleading figure who fits current popular hopes.

National elections in the United States, therefore, represent a contest between essentially permanent social groupings, in which a substantial minority of people shift back and forth between the parties on the basis of particular issues or beliefs about the candidates. The decades since the 1930s have seen the South, urban residents, blue-collar workers, and minority groups disproportionately identified with the Democratic Party, and the wealthier, rural, Protestant, and better-educated people with the Republican Party. The events and conflicts of the 1960s have apparently begun to fragment these coalitions, but we shall first characterize the established patterns and then consider recent changes.

The Meaning of Elections

What significance do elections have in the American political system? The answer depends on whether we are talking about the system itself (in the sense of stability, or national integration, as they are affected in part by political parties and elections), about the impact elections have on mass beliefs about politics, or about their actual influence on governmental policies. A brief exploration of the role of political parties and the meanings of elections will establish some perspective for our analysis of contemporary changes in voting and party identification.

The Two-Party System

For nearly 150 years, the United States has maintained the same basic two-party system. This means that, with rare and temporary exceptions, only two parties have had any serious chance of winning the presidency or even a substantial minority in the Congress. A great many "third parties" have existed over the course of American history, and one of these, the Republican Party, even managed to become a major party. Most American third parties (Know Nothing, Prohibition, Populist, Greenback, Socialist, Communist, Progressive, Liberal, American Labor, Peace and Freedom, and others) have had relatively short lives. They have chiefly espoused policy positions regarded in their times as more or less deviant or "extreme," though many of these positions gained broad popular support and eventually began to look quite conventional. The chief function of these parties for the political system has been to introduce policy innovations: to make it clear that a course of action earlier thought deviant was in fact widely supported and so to induce one or both the major parties to espouse that position itself. Universal compulsory education for children, the progressive income tax, prohibition of the sale or use of intoxicating beverages, the Tennessee Valley Authority, governmental guarantees of the right of workers to organize labor unions, and many other policies first became live issues because a third party made them campaign issues.

Though third parties have occasionally elected candidates to public offices at every level of government except the presidency, the two-party system has remained intact throughout American history. That it has done so tells us something fundamental about mass political belief patterns. It indicates that the American people have never been divided for a long period of time into two well-defined groups that basically and intensely differed on the whole range of public issues regarded as most critical. In Italy and in France since World War II, there has been such a division of the mass public into those with a rightist-center ideology and those with a leftist orientation. People in these two ideological camps have quite consistently differed on foreign policy, economic policy, church-state relations, and educational policy. Within each camp, there are additional differences, and seven or eight distinct political parties have sprung up to compete for the various shadings of the rightist, center, and leftist vote. One can readily understand from these examples that a multiparty system is likely wherever such a "bimodal" pattern of mass political beliefs exist—that is, wherever the voters form two distinct ideological coalitions that take contrasting positions on the range of basic political issues.

Unimodal Political Beliefs

In the United States, and in other countries with two-party systems, mass political beliefs, by contrast, are "unimodal." While people differ on particular issues, they have not formed clearly defined ideological blocs that maintain differing stances on all central policy issues consistently over time. Because people who differ on one issue are likely to agree with each other on others, politics is made less intense emotionally. Given this pattern of mass political beliefs, a political party that wants to win elections is well advised to take a stand near the center of the belief spectrum on the major issues and to remain vague about those matters on which public opinion is seriously divided.

This is precisely the strategy major parties do pursue in countries with unimodal patterns of mass beliefs. In such a system, parties that take a clear ideological position different from the centrist one obviously limit their appeal to a minority, and often a rather small minority, of the voters. On ethical grounds such a stand may be the only tenable one for supporters of these parties; but it has the effect of limiting third parties to an experimental and educational role. Because parties chiefly interested in winning elections must adopt a centrist position, the major parties do not often differ significantly on issues. They each want to elect their own leaders to public office. Sometimes, when it is unclear what most of the public wants, the major parties do differ on specific issues. But often they differ more in rhetorical tone and style than in the policies they actually put into effect.

Both major parties in the United States embrace within their ranks a gamut of policy positions ranging from far right to moderate left—which further underlines the relative unimportance of issues as a determinant of party membership or support. With two parties competing for the center track, where the votes are, still another party trying the same strategy would have little chance of success; it is bound to be absorbed by the major parties in their efforts to broaden their support. Hence, a unimodal pattern of mass beliefs encourages a two-party system.

The strong impact of party identification, the attachment of particular social groups to particular political parties, and the relatively minor effect of issues all suggest that many people take it for granted that either the Republican or the Democratic Party can be counted on to stand for whatever they value most of the time, and that they vote on that assumption, paying little attention to the specifics of particular campaigns. In view of the difficulty any voter might have in sorting out all the pertinent issues and candidates' stands on them, this posture is understandable, and it minimizes the effort and time the voter has to expend in making up his mind. The wide range of policy positions and ideologies in both major parties, and their lack of party discipline, leave some question, however, about the accuracy of judgments reached in this fashion.

The American political party and election system thus contributes to stability and moderation, and apparently to national integration. Whether it is equally effective in promoting public satisfaction (in more than superficial ideological terms) or influencing policy, however, is a more difficult question.

Power of the Vote

For most people, voting is the most potent of all symbols of popular rule and therefore a powerful ingredient in the legitimacy of a regime that holds public office. Whether a group of political participants wins or loses in an election, the fact that it has supposedly been consulted evokes its support for the government. It may not like some policies the government pursues, but it is far less likely to challenge its right to pursue them than would be the case if the government had not been elected. In this critical sense, elections lessen social tensions and inhibit potential civil strife. This is frequently, perhaps usually, the chief function they serve the political system, though that hypothesis is a debatable one and not easily susceptible to rigorous testing. Provisions for compulsory voting in some countries, as well as social pressures to vote in order to prove one is a "good citizen," doubtless reflect an awareness that people who vote are psychologically inoculated against fundamental resistance to the state.

Even more clearly, the use of elections in nondemocratic states reflects the same awareness. Some forms of election do not even offer the *possibility* of defeating unpopular candidates or policies, amounting only to ratification of actions already taken, as in the plebescites of totalitarian countries. It is precisely in such rigged elections, nonetheless, that legal and social pressure to vote has been strongest. The citizen who fails to vote is suspect as a potentially disloyal person and can expect the kind of ostracism that would await a member of a primitive tribe who refused to participate in a communal fertility rite or war dance. Sometimes elections are rigged to eliminate candidates who stand for a genuine alternative on controversial issues, as in many elections in the deep South, some in the North, and virtually all elections in one-party states. The results are nevertheless publicized as mandates for the government and fervently accepted by many as exactly that.

Apart from their uses in promoting and symbolizing social solidarity, to what degree do elections provide policy guidelines for public officials to follow? On the occasional major issue on which the two major parties disagree, they apparently do furnish a clear mandate, though historical examples warn against making this logical assumption without empirical evidence. In 1928, the Democratic platform favored repeal of the Eighteenth (Prohibition) Amendment, while the Republicans were "dry." A Republican victory did indeed delay repeal for four years, even though public sentiment increasingly favored repeal, and in 1932 both parties' platforms reflected that sentiment. In 1964 escalation of the Vietnam War, certainly a major issue, was favored by Barry Goldwater, the Republican candidate, and opposed by Lyndon Johnson, his Democratic opponent. Though Johnson won by a wide margin, he moved quickly after the election to escalate the war. Though this is by no means the only instance in which a major party disregarded what appeared to be a clear popular mandate, elections do in such instances provide a means for evaluating the performance of a regime. This can be an important factor in the following election, as it evidently was in 1968; but there is no guarantee that it will be.

Permanence of the Election Mandate

Even when elections do offer a real choice, however, they are not a sufficient condition of democracy. Election mandates are almost always unclear, and it is always possible to justify departures from them on the grounds that conditions have changed since election day. Even when there is every intention on the part of elected officials to heed the voice of the people as they understand it, election mandates typically furnish only the vaguest kind of guide to administrative officials and judges who have to make decisions in particular cases. Does the fact that the winning political party promised to hold down prices mean that it should institute wage and price ceilings when some economists forecast rising prices and others disagree? Should officials elected on such a plank institute price controls after prices have risen 2 percent? 4 percent? 10 percent? What difference should it make if the winning political party also promised to avoid unnecessary governmental intervention in the economy?

Dilemmas like these face modern governments all the time. The decisions taken to resolve them are bound to reflect a complex set of group interests and guesses about the future political and economic effects of one or another course of action. They cannot be predetermined, or even guided very far, by the votes people cast in election campaigns.

Because of the American parties' avoidance of clear stands on issues, the tendency of candidates (once elected) to act as they consider necessary under the circumstances, and the non-issue-based characteristics of American voting behavior, it is very difficult to say precisely what elections mean in the United States. We have no doubt that it makes a difference which party or candidate wins an election, at least in the general approach to problems of governing, if not in specific policies. But the permanence of the basic social coalitions underlying the parties, and the arbitrariness of both parties' internal processes preceding nominations, preclude exact definition of the role of elections. Events can split the basic social coalitions; indeed, such a process may now be under way. But in the past, only the Civil War and the Great Depression of the 1930s were of sufficient magnitude to realign the major social blocs and redirect the party system. After the Civil War, the Republicans were dominant for nearly 70 years, with only two Democratic intrusions (Cleveland and Wilson). After the Depression the Democrats took over and remained in office, with the exception of the Eisenhower years, until 1968.

Exhaustive electoral analysis has led the experts at the University of Michigan Survey Research Center to distinguish three broad types of American elections.[4] The first and most frequent type of election is the "maintaining" election, in which the party with the numerically larger social coalition is returned to office. The second and least frequent type of election is the "realigning" election or "realigning era" of elections, in which events of cataclysmic proportions succeed in rending the majority coalition and installing a new coalition in power through the vehicle of the other party. Third is the dual category of "deviating" and "reinstating" elections, in which for some reason the minority party wins a particular election without altering the basic underlying social coalitions and is subsequently replaced by the permanent majority party. The Wilson and Eisenhower elections are cited as the kinds of aberrations that constitute deviating elections, and the elections of Harding and Kennedy represent the return of the dominant social coalition.

This is a low-level estimate of the quality of popular impact on government policy directions, of course. It implies that policymakers can count on support for practically anything they wish to do, at least in elections. Mass impact, however, may simply be more subtle than the very gross policy preferences that can be expressed through the instrument of elections. Or more recent elections and contemporary changes may suggest that these characterizations are obsolete. We shall keep these possibilities in mind as we examine recent events.

Electoral Changes in the Late 1960s

The election of 1964 is a good point from which to begin, because it shows the enduring "New Deal coalition" of voters in exaggerated form, as well as the beginnings of race-grounded cracks in that governing social grouping.[5] The Goldwater candidacy provided an unusual event in American party politics, a presidential election based chiefly on sharp ideological differences between the parties. With Goldwater deliberately appealing to conservatives and the South, Johnson was allowed to preempt the middle ground. The result was massive defection from the ranks of traditional Republican voters, particularly college graduates and professionals, and an unprecedented 16-million-vote margin of victory for Johnson. Although ideological conservatives and hardcore Republicans supported him, Goldwater won only the segregationist states of the deep South. Perhaps the long-range significance of this election, however, lies in the

[4]Angus Campbell, Philip Converse, Donald Stokes, and Warren Miller, *The American Voter* (New York: John Wiley, 1960).
[5]This analysis is drawn from Philip Converse, Aage Clausen, and Warren Miller, "Electoral Myth and Reality: The 1964 Election," *The American Political Science Review* 59 (1965), pp. 321–336.

latter fact: several Southern states had been drifting away from the national Democratic Party over racial issues for years, but this was the first time they had been brought into the Republican column on election day. For many Southerners, the Republican Party thus became the new vehicle of segregationist sentiment, and the South acquired greater influence in the Republican Party's internal decisionmaking.

The shifts that occurred from 1964 to 1968 offer lessons in several areas of American politics. They demonstrate unequivocally that neither of the major parties is ever permanently down and out. Events can always restore it, at least as far as winning the next election is concerned, because the party out of power is the only means the electorate has of replacing the people who have been in power and are presumably responsible for the events that have occurred. They also show that the apparent popular will on policy issues may not be effectuated by any given presidential election: elected on the basis of a less aggressive policy in Vietnam, Johnson thereafter escalated the war. Of course, he also accomplished many social welfare programs to which his supporters gave equal priority.

Disruptive Social Events

Many events intervened between the elections of 1964 and 1968, but their relative importance for the election of 1968 can be sorted out.[6] The Vietnam War was a major factor, of course. A long-established image in the minds of the electorate in the 1950s and early 1960s was that the Republicans were the party of peace, but also of economic hardship; the Democrats were the war party, but also the party of economic prosperity. The Goldwater candidacy apparently temporarily reversed the war-peace aspects of this image, but it was restored as 1968 approached. A second and nearly commensurate sequence of events was the series of urban riots occurring between 1965 and 1968. Racial matters have always had the potential of splitting the Democratic coalition, and this seems to have started to occur as a result of the riots and of stiffening white resistance to black efforts to attain full citizenship. A third factor was the increasing public attention to crime and "law and order," perhaps as a means of expressing resentments of blacks that commitment to the abstract principle of racial equality made it difficult to voice directly. Resentment of peace demonstrations also contributed to the momentum of this defection from the Democratic Party. Even those most opposed

[6]This analysis draws on Philip Converse, Warren Miller, Jerrold G. Rusk and Arthur C. Wolfe, "Continuity and Change in American Politics: Parties and Issues in the 1968 Election," *The American Political Science Review* 63 (1969), pp. 1083–1105.

to the Vietnam War strongly disapproved of violent outbreaks and peace demonstrators in general. Those opposed to the war and sympathetic to war protesters made up only 3 percent of the electorate. There was such a wide sense of breakdown in authority and discipline, feeding on militant political dissent as well as on racial outbreaks, that "law and order" ranked with Vietnam and race problems as major factors in influencing the election's outcome. The candidacy of George Wallace, of course, gave concrete focus to these latter complaints.

The results on election day were in all probability the most dramatic shifts that have ever occurred in the United States. The Democratic total dropped from more than 61 percent of the two-party vote in 1964 to less than 43 percent in 1968. Nearly 40 percent of Nixon's votes came from people who had voted for Johnson in 1964, and other Johnson votes (as well as many Goldwater votes) went to Wallace. The detailed analysis conducted by the University of Michigan Survey Research Center led to the conclusion that the Wallace candidacy probably did not change the outcome. Wallace drew as much or more support from sources that would otherwise have gone to the Democratic candidate as from the Republican potential; this may be due, in part, to the deliberate efforts to cultivate Southern support that were made by the Nixon ticket. Disgruntled Democrats, who had previously used the McCarthy candidacy to express their dissatisfaction with the Johnson Administration, abandoned their party, refused to vote for the office of President, or simply stayed home. Only black voters, among all normal Democratic supporters, voted and supported their party more than in previous elections. Ninety-seven percent of all black voters in the country voted for Humphrey, while less than 35 percent of white voters did.

The 1972 Elections

The trends in voter support for the two major parties set in motion in 1968 were confirmed and deepened in the election of 1972. Two major factors can probably be credited with generating President Nixon's massive victory. One is his success in winding down the Vietnam War in an "honorable" manner while developing new and promising relations with both the Soviet Union and China—thereby reducing the threat of larger wars as well. The other is the damage to the Democratic Party and demoralization among Democratic voters wrought by the nomination of George McGovern. We shall look more closely at each of these factors and then analyze the results in detail.

In 1968, most voters did not decide which candidate to vote for until the last two weeks of the campaign. In 1972, however, nearly all voters had made up their minds almost as soon as the candidates were nominated; it was one of the earliest decision-years on record, with the results of the August polls remaining roughly unchanged right up to election day. The effects of Nixon's foreign policy successes are stressed by one major pollster, Daniel Yankelovich,[7] who points out that Nixon's handling of the Vietnam War was disapproved by a majority of the voters through March 1972. In fact, Yankelovich argues, Nixon was in trouble on this issue; voters declared by a 5 to 4 margin that Nixon did not inspire confidence on this question, and it appeared to be McGovern's strongest issue. Then came another of the periodic deteriorations of the military situation in Vietnam, to which Nixon responded with the mining of Haiphong harbor. Opinion surveys at that time showed great concern about a widening of the war, and even fears of a crisis resembling the Cuban missile crisis of 1962. But the Russians did not react. Instead, they went ahead with existing plans for a summit meeting in Moscow, and the American people were treated to television scenes of the Nixons in a variety of friendly exchanges with the Soviets. Clearly, the danger of a big-power confrontation had passed, and in all probability the way was now cleared for a real settlement in Vietnam. Yankelovich summarizes the situation this way:

> . . . . Soviet-Chinese acquiescence in the Haiphong mining had handed Mr. Nixon an overwhelming diplomatic victory, containing the seeds of his subsequent political victory at home. . . .
>
> The results of the Soviet trip were dramatically reflected in the opinion polls. By early July, Mr. Nixon had rebuilt public confidence in his handling of the Vietnam War by an almost two to one margin. Simultaneously, he had undermined Mr. McGovern's major source of public support by converting what had been McGovern's issue into his own principal source of strength among the voters. During the campaign, an unwavering 62% of the voters said "Mr. Nixon is doing everything he can to end the war." They voted for him largely, if not exclusively, for this reason.[8]

George McGovern's candidacy began with his opposition to the Vietnam War in the campaign of 1968. It gained strength from the disillusionment of McCarthy's and Kennedy's supporters and the frustrations aroused by the Chicago nominating convention of that year, and was enhanced in 1969 and 1970 when McGovern and others, seeking reform in the nominating procedures of the Democratic Party, accomplished several changes in the rules for nominating and electing delegates to the party's conventions. State delegations were now re-

---

[7] Daniel Yankelovich, "Why Nixon Won," *New York Review of Books*, 30 November 1973, p. 7. Yankelovich conducts the Yankelovich Election Survey, used by the *New York Times* and other major news media for election studies.
[8] *Ibid.*

quired to include certain proportions of young, minority, and women delegates—exactly the groups most likely to be responsive to the McGovern candidacy. As he began to enter primary campaigns in early 1972, McGovern seemed to be expressing a more generalized opposition to the *status quo*, a kind of modern populism, and apparently gained additional liberal and some blue-collar support on those grounds. To the surprise of the media and the Democratic regulars, the primary elections were a series of victories and near-victories sufficient to give McGovern a commanding lead in delegate strength. Despite last-ditch efforts, there was no way for the outnumbered regulars to deny him the nomination at the convention.

The McGovern Tumble

But the media and his opponents had done their work well. McGovern was perceived as the candidate of the left—radicals, the young, minorities, and activist women. Actually, McGovern was somewhat left-of-center in the Democratic Party, but was hardly the radical he was portrayed to be. His campaign simply never got off the ground. Underfinanced and bedevilled by lack of effective staff work and organization, he was plagued first by the embarrassment of having to replace his Vice-Presidential candidate and then by the image of a radical "can't win" candidate. Seeking to placate such Democratic regulars as Mayor Daley of Chicago—whose support is normally necessary to carry the traditional Democratic strongholds in the nation's cities—McGovern endangered his support among the very activists who had been crucial to his nomination. Labor officially deserted the Democratic Party, and many of its other long-established sources of strength were noticeably absent from the campaign.

The result was a smashing victory for President Nixon. Carrying the entire country except for the District of Columbia and the state of Massachusetts, Nixon rolled up the largest victory since Franklin Roosevelt's landslide of 1936. He received 517 electoral votes and over 61 percent of the popular vote. His foreign policy accomplishments and the McGovern candidacy were enough to overcome some serious economic troubles and continuing inflation, and to further fragment the coalition of minorities, urban residents, rural Southerners, labor, and liberals forged by FDR in the New Deal days. But these factors were not enough to cut deeply into Democratic strength in the Congress, or in the state and local elections held at the same time. In effect, it was a personal triumph for President Nixon, rather than a party victory for Republicans generally.

What happened? To begin with, voter turnout was very low.[9] Less

---

[9] The data in this section are drawn from *Gallup Opinion Weekly* (December) 1972, pp. 11–13.

than 55 percent of all eligible voters actually voted, the lowest proportion since 1948 and one of the lowest since women first received the right to vote in 1920. Part of this can be attributed to the fact that it was the first year in which 18-to-21-year-olds were eligible to vote. Many of them simply did not register, or were unable to do so for various reasons such as residence requirements. Only about 60 percent of all persons in this age group were registered, compared to about 80 percent of all persons. The Gallup Poll made a special effort to learn why so few people voted, in sharp contrast to most other democratic countries. They found that a total of 38 percent of nonvoters were not registered, either because they were unable to or because they did not choose to register. 28 percent said simply that they were not interested in politics, and another 10 percent did not like either candidate. The remainder were either sick, away from home or traveling, or unable to leave their jobs to vote. Clearly, a substantial proportion of Americans has opted out of politics, but we do not really know whether this is because of satisfaction, unconcern, or frustration at not being able to achieve their goals.

The Voter Turnabout

The fragmentation of the New Deal coalition is evident in several ways. Members of labor-union families, for example, normally vote Democratic by roughly 3 to 2 margins; in 1964, the ratio was 73 percent to 27 percent, and in 1968 it was 56 percent to 29 percent, with 15 percent going to Wallace. But in 1972 the ratio was reversed: only 46 percent supported McGovern, while 54 percent went for Nixon. Catholic voters gave a majority to the Republican candidate for the first time since voting studies were initiated. Younger voters (under 30), strongly Democratic in recent years, also returned a majority for Nixon, by a margin of 52 percent to 48 percent. Only black voters among all major population groups remained consistent with prior patterns. 87 percent of all black voters went for McGovern, while only 13 percent voted for Nixon.

Figure 16-1 shows the patterns of change among educational and occupational groups in the 1972 election, and contrasts these with the elections of the 1960s. It is clear that the Republicans' greatest strength is among the upper classes, and the Democrats' among the lower classes. These relationships remain constant. The scope of President Nixon's victory in 1972 is also clear: note the extent of change from the 1964 election. But we cannot say that any new permanent alignment has been forged. Continuing Democratic strength in congressional elections, and the existence of sharp swings (1964 to 1968, for example) in the past, make it premature to declare the end of the New Deal coalition. We can say with some confidence, how-

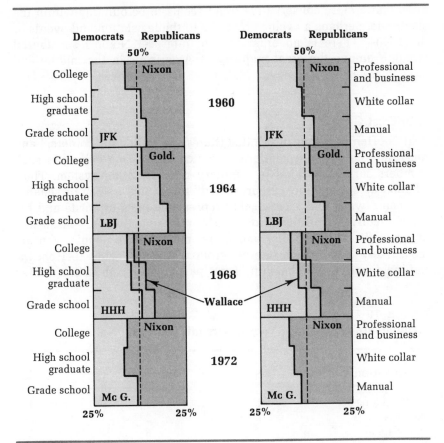

FIGURE 16-1
The Elections of 1960–1972 by Education and Occupation

ever, that a more conservative trend seems to be building within the electorate, perhaps a cyclical reaction to the legislation and events of the 1960s. There is no other way to interpret Nixon's substantial strength among the great majority of Americans in the middle and lower classes.

Interest Groups

It is often said that the United States is a nation of "joiners," and that the voluntary associations to which Americans belong in such numbers serve as a kind of auxiliary representation system. Thus, whether or not one feels "represented" by a congressman or senator, one can always find a group that represents one's interests and become effective in politics through its organized activities. Once again, however, it is the middle- and upper middle-class people who are most likely to join such interest groups. And, as Table 16-1 shows, the incidence of membership is not particularly high in the United

TABLE 16-1

Membership in Various Types of Organizations, by Nation

Organization	U.S.	U.K.	Germany	Italy	Mexico
Trade Unions	14	22	15	6	11
Business	4	4	2	5	2
Professional	4	3	6	3	5
Farm	3	0	4	2	0
Social	13	14	10	3	4
Charitable	3	3	2	9	6
Religious*	19	4	3	6	5
Civic-political	11	3	3	8	3
Cooperative	6	3	2	2	0
Veterans'	6	5	1	4	0
Fraternal†	13				
Other	6	3	9	6	0
Total percentage of members	57	47	44	30	24
Total number of respondents	970	963	955	995	1,007

*This refers to church-related organizations, not to church affiliation itself.
†U.S. only.
Source: Reprinted from Gabriel Almond and Sidney Verba, The Civic Culture (Princeton, N.J.: Princeton University Press, 1963), pp. 246–247.

States. Only 57 percent of Americans belong to *any* voluntary association, as compared with 47 percent in Great Britain and 44 percent in West Germany. If it were not for the distinctive American tendency to belong to church organizations and fraternal bodies (e.g., the Elks, Moose, Masons, Rotary, Kiwanis, and the like), the United States might not rank ahead of the other countries at all.

The groups with the greatest political potential to which non-elites belong are the trade unions. In 1970, more than 19,000,000 people, the largest number in American history, belonged to unions. But the *proportion* of nonfarm workers who belong to unions is dropping. At the high point in 1955, more than 33 percent of all nonfarm workers were union members, but the proportion has fallen steadily to barely over 27 percent in 1970. So many new workers were entering the labor force in the 1960s and 1970s that the unions' proportions fell even as their total numbers rose. As Table 16-2 indicates, the white-collar

TABLE 16-2

The 15 Largest Labor Unions, 1971

	1960 membership	1971 membership	Change
Teamsters	1,484,400	2,020,000	Up 36%
Auto Workers	1,136,100	1,350,000	Up 19%
Steelworkers	1,152,000	1,200,000	Up 4%
Brotherhood of Electrical Workers	771,000	977,295	Up 27%
Machinists	898,100	900,000	Up 0.2%
Carpenters	800,000	808,000	Up 1%
Laborers	442,500	650,000	Up 47%
Retail Clerks	342,000	650,000	Up 90%
Meat Cutters*	436,000	550,000	Up 26%
State, County, Municipal Employees	210,000	525,000	Up 150%
Communications Workers	259,900	500,000	Up 92%
Service Employees	272,000	480,000	Up 76%
Hotel, Restaurant Employees	443,000	450,000	Up 2%
Ladies' Garment Workers	446,600	442,300	Down 1%
Operating Engineers	291,000	400,000	Up 37%

*Meat Cutters figures include those for former Packinghouse Workers Union, now merged.
Source: 1960 figures, U.S. Department of Labor; 1971 figures, union sources: as reported to *U.S. News and World Report*, 21 February 1972.

unions, such as government employees and retail clerks unions, were growing; as the makeup of the work force changes, some traditionally strong unions, such as the United Mine Workers, have shrunk drastically in size. Thus, the trend is toward greater union representation for the white-collar and professional members of non-elites (e.g., teachers, office workers) and reduced representation for the blue-collar worker. This is particularly true for those in isolated or hard-to-organize industries, precisely those that most need organization and broad support to gain their ends. Nor do the established unions, based for the most part in older, labor-intensive industries, appear to want to represent more workers. In a 1972 interview with *U.S. News and World Report,*[10] George Meany (president of the AFL-CIO) made it clear that he preferred to represent only the relatively skilled workers already organized in major industries. The following exchange makes this clear:

Q. Mr. Meany, what is the state of the union movement today? Why is total membership not growing as fast as the country's labor force?

A. I don't know, I don't care.

Q. You don't care? Why not?

A. We have never had a large proportion of the work force in this country—nothing like Britain, nothing like the Scandinavian countries, nothing like the Germans.

Q. Would you prefer to have a larger proportion?

A. Not necessarily. We've done quite well without it. And we are not tied to any political party, and we feel that we've got along without that, too. We've delivered more to the American worker than any labor movement that ever existed—today, yesterday or in the past—and we inherited a good deal of our labor movement: its principles from the Germans and, to a lesser extent, from the British.

With all of our complaints, we have the highest standard of living in the world.

Why should we worry about organizing groups of people who do not appear to want to be organized? If they prefer to have others speak for them and make the decisions which affect their lives, without effective participation on their part, that is their right.

Q. If unions do not keep pace with the growth of the work force, will organized labor's influence be reduced?

A. We made tremendous strides in this country under [Samuel] Gompers, and his percentage of the labor force was very tiny compared with what we've got now.

Frankly, I used to worry about the membership, about the size of

[10] *U.S. News and World Report,* 21 February 1972, pp. 27–28.

the membership. But quite a few years ago I just stopped worrying about it, because to me it doesn't make any difference. It's the organized voice that counts—and it's not just in legislation, it's anyplace. The organized fellow is the fellow that counts. This is just human nature.

Moreover, the leadership of any group (not just a union) requires long-term investments of time and resources, and thus is more likely to be reserved to those with higher status or more skills within each group. Continuing involvement in group leadership also leads to an enduring commitment to the existing structure of relationships among groups and their leaders—that is, commitment to a familiar *status quo*, in preference to a possibly unpredictable future. Day-to-day interaction among groups has the effect of rigidifying their relationships and limiting the extent to which they can serve as instruments of mass participation.

Political Game-Playing

Involvement in political maneuvers for immediate tangible benefits is a kind of game-playing. To win larger tax exemptions or avoid a traffic fine or participate in a local political fight over zoning regulations for business arouses the interest of those affected, often quite intensely; and the most active and adept at this kind of politics express a zest for winning despite obstacles. It is a test of personal and group resourcefulness, as well as of flexibility in meeting challenges and finding a workable solution. This kind of politics necessarily involves willingness to recognize the rights of opponents to exist and to play the political game, willingness to compromise, and a sharing of some underlying values with opponents. Its keynotes are flexibility, opportunism, compromise, and a search for the potentialities in the political situation—for the combination of tactics and resources that will maximize tangible political gains.

This kind of maneuvering is necessarily carried on by relatively small cadres of activists, though one of the major resources at their disposal is the support in votes, money, moral approval, or fighting ability of a mass following. Another resource is the understanding of other concerned activists. The adept political tactician is able to put himself in his opponent's place sufficiently well to understand his needs and wants and the limits of his ability to make concessions. Effective political bargaining within the established rules for political action presupposes as great a bond of empathy with one's opponents as with one's allies. To the degree that a person is flexible enough and free enough of constraining anxiety to be able to see the world from his adversary's perspective, he will be able to devise effective political tactics. Indeed, the very act of responding to another group in this way reassures both sides that their respective interests are being protected. What emotion is involved in such politics springs from the zest of analyzing strategic potentialities as well as from the gratification or disappointment of a tangible payoff or loss.

Group membership is thus the preserve of relatively higher-status persons to start with, and the characteristics of group interaction convert the process from one of representation to one of mass-management. Again, this is well illustrated by the labor movement, whose leadership often serves as the vehicle by which employers manage their workers. By ritualizing conflict, absorbing much of the rank-and-file's resentments, and legitimating the management's wage offers, union leadership may virtually function as an arm of management. This explains in part the rise in wildcat strikes and rejections of contract agreements by rank-and-file workers, particularly younger workers, in the years immediately preceding the imposition of wage controls in 1971. This point may be generalized; it is applicable to both interest groups and political parties, the two major orthodox channels whereby non-elites are said to influence decision-making elites.

Elite Dominance of the Orthodox Channels of Non-Elite Influence

The management of interest groups, as we have already noted, is often the private preserve of those with higher status and other skills and resources of leadership. There are also patterns of association between groups that tend to create a structural advantage for elites and their interests. One is the tendency of people engaged in *making* or *selling* the same product or service to form an organization to promote and protect their interests. Steel manufacturers, broadcast station licensees, trucking companies, physicians, stockbrokers, real estate brokers, cotton farmers, and hundreds of other groupings of people with the same production or sales interests have organized into associations to win favorable governmental policies and sometimes to influence private economic policies as well.

Such interest groups typically represent economic or social elites. Usually, though not invariably, the people who ultimately *buy* their goods or services do not find it natural or easy or even possible to organize themselves into interest groups. The consumers of manufactured or grown products, the patients who pay physicians' bills, the viewers of television programs and commercials rarely organize to promote their interests politically or economically. They find it hard or impossible to do so, for some obvious reasons—their large numbers, their lack of face-to-face contacts or facilities for communicating with each other, and above all, people's tendency not to think of themselves in the role of consumers. They find themselves politically divided by their other interests: economic, ethnic, regional, religious, ideological, and so on. All of this can be summed up in the generalization that people's interests as producers, for which they are paid, are typically seen as primary and are intensely pursued. People's interests as consumers are typically perceived as secondary and are hard to pursue in an organized and effective way.

The Consumer's Problem

Some exceptional groups of consumers do organize effectively. But these groups are themselves elites rather than part of the mass public. Companies that ship their products by truck or rail are organized into interest groups, and the consequence is that their interests, like those of the truck and railroad carriers, are politically protected. But the ultimate buyers of these products, who do not form interest groups, pay for the protection accorded to these elites both in higher prices and in taxes, which often go for governmental subsidies to various businesses. Similarly, management groups, which are consumers of labor, are organized into effective interest groups. Here again the outcome often is that organized labor and management groups are able, through political and economic agreements, to pass the costs of their price and wage gains onto a mass public of consumers that is not organized—at least not as consumers.

The difficulty of organizing interest groups made up of consumers is especially burdensome to the poor—that large part of the mass public least likely to be represented and helped by any kind of interest group of producers or sellers, including labor unions. Fewer poor people vote than do the more affluent, and they do not vote as a bloc in any case. Their main economic resource is their labor, and because they are largely unskilled, intermittently employed or unemployed, and not attached to the mass production industries, they are, for the most part, not organized into labor unions. What political power they do have derives chiefly from the support they get from sympathetic liberals and others who do have political resources. For reasons already considered, however, such support frequently produces largely symbolic benefits for the poor and the disadvantaged: laws declaring their right to vote in a social setting that makes it unlikely they will use that right massively and effectively; laws purporting to protect them from economic exploitation when the agencies administering the laws are influenced chiefly by the economically powerful; civil rights laws that reassure liberals their values are being advanced but that have only token effect in actually making housing, credit, jobs, and social status available to those who suffer from widespread social discrimination.

Interest groups, therefore, serve chiefly to institutionalize and formalize the exercise of political resources deriving from wealth, social status, and the ability to organize effectively—that is, they operate for the benefit of the elite. They are not generally and widely efficacious as a resource for the mass public.

Elite Influence Through Political Parties

To some extent, though not as clearly or consistently, the same must be said of political parties. Two central characteristics of the major American political parties make it easier than it would otherwise be for the elite groups to use them to mobilize support for their interests. Party discipline is minimal or nonexistent; and the locus of power in both major parties is local and decentralized. The implications of each of these characteristics for elite maneuverability are worth attention.

The lack of party discipline in the major American parties means that an elected representative is usually entirely free to support or oppose particular policies regardless of his party's stand on the issues. In disciplined parties, such as those in England, a party member who fails to support the party position on a major issue can expect to be disciplined; sometimes he is even expelled from the party. In the United States discipline is extremely rare, and Republican and Democratic legislators at all levels of government constantly cast votes inconsistent with their parties' platforms or caucus decisions.

One effect of this state of affairs is that the values of those who command political resources are reflected in legislators' votes even when they conflict with the party's formal positions or rhetorical appeals. Southern Democrats consistently vote against civil rights bills even when their party's platform has endorsed them. A congressman from Pittsburgh is likely to vote for a high protective tariff to keep out foreign steel even if his party favors fewer restrictions on foreign trade.

The net effect of such lack of discipline is that an American voter has no assurance that the party he supports will in fact work for the policies or principles it has promised to support in order to attract his vote. On the contrary, he can be quite certain that, as a party, it will do nothing of the kind. More than that, the lack of party discipline makes every candidate and officeholder more vulnerable to pressure from powerful interests in his constituency. In a disciplined party system, pressure groups have to concentrate on influencing the party's platform, for that is what determines the subsequent behavior of party members. In an undisciplined system, the platform becomes largely symbolic, as already noted; the individual candidate or officeholder himself becomes the focus of pressures. It is not surprising, therefore, that there may exist a "senator from Boeing Aircraft Corporation" or that many candidates and legislators from diverse areas should be offered large campaign contributions by conservative Texas oil interests. Elites can take advantage of undisciplined parties to maximize their impact upon individual policymakers.

The second characteristic of the major parties, that is, decentralization of power to the state and local level, makes the kind of pressure and bargaining just described even easier and more effective. There has never been in the United States a national party organization or boss capable of laying down policies that state and local party leaders had to follow. On the contrary, the effectiveness of the major parties' national committees and the success of aspirants for presidential nominations (the only elective office with a national constituency) hinge upon how many local party leaders and organizations they can induce to support them—financially, with votes at the national nominating conventions, and by mobilizing the local constituencies on election day. From the point of view of a county or state chairman, moreover, the chief function of a presidential nominee is to help carry local and state candidates into office with him.

The local party organization cannot afford to be unresponsive to local interest groups that can help finance campaigns or influence voters. The more diverse and conflicting local interests are, the more leeway the party organization has, for it can play them off against each other and gain some maneuverability for itself. A national party organization with real power would, of course, have ultimate maneuverability and freedom from pressure by particular elite groups. The extreme cases of susceptibility to domination by a local interest occur in those constituencies in which one industry significantly surpasses all others in wealth and control over economic conditions. Party organizations in large cities typically fall somewhere between these two extremes.

Alternative Forms of Political Participation

The alternative forms of participation span a wide range of activities. Some of them are as authorized and accepted, though less formalized, as elections or interest-group actions. Others are discouraged or forcefully repressed, but nevertheless amount to major means by which segments of non-elites participate in politics and may influence policy. In the latter case, of course, many consequences may ensue, some quite different from those sought by the participants. In general, however, although the alternative forms are frequently efforts to bypass the established channels, they exhibit many of the same class biases as do parties, elections, and interest-group activity.

One of the most obvious and accepted modes of communication and "pressure" from non-elites to decision-making elites is the simple act of writing a letter, or signing a petition, to be sent to an official or a newspaper. Congressmen are sometimes said to "wait for the mail" before making up their minds how to vote on an issue. There are several problems with this assumption, however. One is that people tend to write or petition those whom they have reason to believe are on their side or at least on the fence. This means that letterwriters favoring a proposal write to decisionmakers who favor it, and those against write to those who oppose it. The net result, even if the decisionmakers take their mail seriously, is no change in positions. Another problem is that decisionmakers become impervious to pressure campaigns organized by perhaps very small interest groups.

But even more important is the fact that the act of writing letters, and to a lesser extent carrying and signing petitions, is more likely to be undertaken by people who are relatively well-educated and upper-class. Moreover, even within class and education levels, it is an act more likely to be undertaken by conservatives than by liberals. In an effort to find out why the 1964 Republican strategists thought there was a "hidden" conservative vote, the Michigan Survey Research Center compared the political preferences of those who wrote letters to officials or newspapers with those who did not.[11] The researchers found, first, that only about 15 percent of the population had *ever* written a letter to a public official, and that two-thirds of *all* letters were written by a total of 3 percent of the population. The 3 percent was distinctly conservative in every ideological dimension; by "vote" of letterwriters, Goldwater would have been elected by a comfortable majority. Thus, if decisionmakers took guidance, or if officials sought to measure the mood of the country, from the views expressed in the mail to officials and newspapers, they would acquire a very skewed image.

"Citizen Participation"

Some alternative forms of participation are built into the process of administering and implementing laws. Juries, for instance, place a significant function in the hands of citizens, and might well serve as means of communicating to higher levels citizens' dissatisfaction with law and/or their circumstances. But juries are drawn from lists of voters or property owners (or, in the case of grand juries, from "blue-ribbon" panels), and thus reflect class orientations. Despite this, juries in many cases involving political figures and issues (Black Panthers,

---

[11] These data are drawn from Converse *et al., op. cit.,* p. 333.

draft resisters, the Chicago 8 trial, and others) have refused to convict or been relatively lenient, suggesting that some potential prosecutions may have been discouraged by these results.

In many areas of governmental activity, there are requirements for advisory boards of citizens. Urban renewal, Selective Service, and other agencies deliberately engage citizens in the implementation of their programs. But they accomplish relatively little on behalf of the preferences of ordinary citizens, because the participants in these programs are drawn from the higher echelons of non-elites. Businessmen, local leaders, and higher-status people generally dominate these positions. Only in the Community Action Agencies of the poverty program has there been a real contest over who is to shape a governmental program. Lower-class citizens did begin to take part, and the result was first an amendment to the law that gave local governments control over the local aspects of the programs, and then such controversy that the funding for many local units was sharply cut back or eliminated.

A much less institutionalized form of participation that has arisen from time to time in American history, and particularly during the 1960s, is the protest demonstration, sit-in, disruption, or deliberate refusal to obey rules. Those who have been unable to make themselves heard through the established channels have resorted to these tactics, often with great success, when their claims were consistent with generally shared values and not at extreme odds with the basic features of the political system. But when they have been unable to find allies, or been perceived as dangerously at variance with established values or familiar political practices, rejection and repression have been very harsh. Successful protest-type activity requires allies, or at the very least the inaction of those who might oppose the protesters. It involves risks of a personal kind for the participants, and is difficult to sustain for a long period of time without a supportive environment. It depends on achieving some tangible goal, usually from an existing political structure.

Another, even less institutionalized, alternative form of participation is the spontaneous riot. Although clearly grounded in the circumstances of ghetto existence, the riots of the 1960s were spontaneous, by contrast to deliberate obstructive sit-ins or other protest tactics. Touched off by one or another form of provocation, they often engaged thousands of participants for days at a time. The immediate consequences were destruction of millions of dollars' worth of property and the deaths of many ghetto residents at the hands of police and National Guard forces. Subsequently, governmental assistance to ghetto and other poor people increased, but so did strong popular support for future repressive measures and political candidates who stood for such action.

Riot and Demonstration Patterns

Patterns of participation in both riots and student demonstrations offer some insight into these alternative forms of participation. In the case of the ghetto riots of 1967, for example, it is clear that substantial proportions of each community were involved. Supplemental studies undertaken for the National Commission on Civil Disorders estimate that participants represented from 11 to 35 percent of the residents of the riot areas in the major cities (Detroit, Newark, New Haven) where riots occurred.[12] The composition of the rioters was roughly representative of the occupational makeup of the ghetto population, with a slight emphasis on the less skilled and the unemployed. Nearly all of those arrested during the riots were residents of the neighborhood involved.[13] The riots thus were fairly broad-based actions by cross-sections of the area populations. They were not caused by the "criminal element," by "outside agitators," or by a tiny minority of militants. They were, it seems fair to say, genuine expressions of community protest of an essentially political kind. Certainly they were perceived as such by most blacks; and several surveys have shown that, while most blacks do not approve of rioting, they see it in many cases as necessary and helpful toward achieving black goals.[14] Younger blacks in particular tend to believe that violence will be necessary before such objectives are attained.

But the same riots were perceived quite differently by whites. We have already seen the electoral consequences of these riots and other race problems. National elites, with some limited exceptions, tended to emphasize theories that outside agitators, a few militants, or habitual troublemakers had caused the riots. The Kerner Report alone blamed "white racism"; it went largely unheard. Table 16-3 lists the causes identified by six key groups within fifteen major cities of the country in 1968. Merchants, employers, and the police saw the riots as primarily the work of criminal elements and nationalists or militants; educators, social workers, and political workers came closer to the explanation offered by blacks themselves. Only small minorities in any category saw the riots as political acts. Consistent with these impressions on the part of local elites, white residents of the same cities perceived the riots in opposite ways from their black neighbors.

---

[12] Robert M. Fogelson and Robert B. Hill, 'Who Riots? A Study of Participation in the 1967 Riots," *Supplemental Studies for the National Advisory Commission on Civil Disorders* (Washington: Government Printing Office, 1968), p. 231.

[13] *Ibid.*, pp. 236, 237.

[14] Opinion data in this section are drawn from Angus Campbell and Howard Schuman, "Racial Attitudes in Fifteen American Cities," in *Supplemental Studies*, pp. 48–52.

TABLE 16-3
"Theories" of Riot Causation Among Six Occupations
(in percentages)

Proportions rating "theory" as "main reason" or "largely true"

"Theory"	Police	Educa- tors	Social workers	Political workers	Mer- chants	Em- ployers
A. Unheard Negro complaints	31	70	72	72	48	47
B. Criminal elements	69	33	27	27	65	42
C. Nationalists and militants	77	46	38	39	65	62
D. Riots as political acts	27	26	25	20	23	24
E. Police brutality	9	33	37	53	21	7
F. Negroes basically violent	28	8	4	8	23	11

Source: Campbell and Schuman, op. cit., p. 96.

Table 16-4 presents these contrasts very clearly. It is as if the two groups of people had seen totally different events—which of course they did. Most whites surveyed saw the riots as opportunities for looting, and a substantial minority said that even orderly marches to protest racial discrimination were unjustified; two-thirds believed that sit-ins were unjustified. In the aftermath of the riots, there can be little doubt that white opinion hardened firmly against further advance by blacks. By comparison, the actions of (essentially white) national elites may well seem generous.

The pattern of participation in student demonstrations shows that very few members of even this relatively activist group had actually taken part in the demonstrations of the 1960s. A CBS-sponsored survey was completed in late 1968, after three years of campus demonstrations, by which time one might expect a pattern of participation to have become fairly well established.[15] Only 12 percent had ever participated in a sit-in, 6 percent in a riot, and only 24 percent in a march, despite the peaceful and legitimate character of the latter. Moreover, the 13 percent of students who were by their attitudes classified as "revolutionaries" or "radical reformers" made up the

[15] Columbia Broadcasting System, "Generations Apart: A Study of the Generation Gap conducted for CBS News" (New York: CBS, 1969). Participation data may be found on p. 29; breakdowns by ideology on p. 39.

TABLE 16-4

Have Riots Helped or Hurt the Negro Cause? (in percentages)

"On the whole, do you think the disturbances have helped or hurt the cause of Negro rights, or would you say they haven't made much difference?"

	Negro		White	
	Men	Women	Men	Women
Helped	37	30	13	14
Hurt	22	24	69	59
Helped and hurt equally	12	11	7	7
Made no difference	21	28	9	17
Don't know	8	7	2	3
	100	100	100	100

"Why do you feel that way?

First reason given	Negro		White	
	Men	Women	Men	Women
Helped:				
Tangible gains (e.g., more jobs)	19	20	8	8
Whites understand Negroes' problems better	14	10	8	8
Show of Negro power	9	5	2	1
Hurt:				
Destruction, injury	8	8	2	3
Increased anti-Negro sentiments	16	19	64	54
Made no difference:				
No tangible gain	19	23	5	12
Negroes are still not satisfied	0	1	7	10
Don't know	15	14	4	4
	100	100	100	100

Source: Campbell and Schuman, p. 49.

overwhelming share of those who had undertaken the more militant actions. Most students were only moderate reformers, confident that the system could be made to work and opposed to militant tactics. There were nearly as many conservatives as there were revolutionaries and radicals combined. The principal implication that can be drawn from these data, therefore, is that campus demonstrations, like many other forms of participation, are indeed the province of a relative few. Many others may share their views, of course, at least on the issue of war in Southeast Asia, but they make little use of any means to make their views known.

The Impact of Non-elites on Policy

Elections are an uncertain vehicle of political participation. Interest groups are highly specialized. The alternative forms of participation are erratic and even counterproductive. And yet needs, claims, and demands *are* introduced into the political arena by the actions of segments of non-elites. At least to some extent, elites feel obliged, or are forced, to respond. Their response may be merely symbolic, negative, or marginal; but there is nevertheless often *some* response, and sometimes one consistent with non-elite demands.

Frequently, a fully satisfactory "solution" is impossible because of perceived conditions, opposition from other segments of non-elites, or because of elites' other priorities and preferences. These determinations are made by elites, of course. Their power, status, and legitimacy enable them to decide how to fit demands that are strongly pressed and supported by established values into the ongoing mix of policy and practice that characterizes the political system. Other demands can normally be deflected or dismissed. In this process, elites are aided by the screening effect of the greater participation and efficacy of the better-educated and higher-status members of non-elites. They cushion or even absorb much of the thrust of deviant, minority, or lower-class demands before they emerge into the national political arena and begin to induce elite response.

In many instances, at least some members of elites *want* to respond; they may even have been waiting for a chance to do so. Elites may support mass demands because they expect to benefit from doing so. Free universal public education is a case in point. Before the Industrial Revolution came to the United States, free public education was an issue that divided Americans along economic class lines. It was a major plank in the platform of one of our earliest third parties, the Workingmen's Party, which gained considerable support among wage-earners in Philadelphia between 1828 and 1832. The issue grew less and less controversial as industrial technologies required that a larger proportion of the work force be literate and possess elementary skills in arithmetic and in what were called the "agricultural, industrial, and mechanic arts." Indeed, many states began establishing normal schools, state colleges, and universities around the middle of the nineteenth century, and in the Morrill Act of 1862 the federal government helped them to do so. As industry and agriculture have required work forces with increasingly complex skills, elite support for education at all levels also increased. To some degree, this trend has been further bolstered by the fact that methods of financing state universities provide a direct subsidy to the largely middle-class students who attend them.

Sometimes elites have even more pressing and immediate economic reasons to support mass demands. In the early years of the twentieth century, a growing number of states enacted minimum wage laws. It was widely acknowledged that if workers were unable to live on their earnings, they should be entitled to a wage that would at least support their families at a subsistence level. This policy was supported both on a moral basis and because it was recognized that people could not even work efficiently when undernourished. A chief reason for the enactment of the first federal minimum wage law in 1938 was its support by some powerful industrial groups, especially New England textile manufacturers. Forced by unions of their workers to pay higher wages than their unorganized Southern competitors, the New England mill owners saw in the minimum wage a device to increase their competitors' labor cost to the level of their own thereby improving their competitive position.

Social security legislation, certainly a significant benefit to a large part of the public, has also enjoyed substantial elite support, for economic and other reasons. Growing worker demands for industrial pension plans, backed by the right to strike, put employers under strong pressure to make some concessions. Governmental old-age benefits, financed by regressive payroll taxes paid chiefly by the workers and by consumers, represented an economical solution. In consequence, frequent improvements in the benefits and coverage of American social security legislation have been relatively uncontroversial since the basic federal law was enacted in 1935.

Elite Fear of Public Restiveness

But there is an even more compelling reason for the success of mass demands for elementary social security protections: anxiety about widespread public restiveness and militancy if large groups of people are denied what they have come to believe every human being deserves. All industrialized countries, including those that have not pretended to be democratic or responsive to mass demands, have therefore instituted social security systems, virtually all of them established earlier and extending wider protections than the American system does. In Germany, for example, Bismarck's highly elitist and authoritarian government provided extensive social security protections as early as the 1880s. Fear of mass restiveness or violence has unquestionably been a major impetus to the enactment of other governmental programs benefitting non-elites. In Chapter 5, we noted that widespread civil disobedience and urban riots mobilized support for voting rights laws and for some concessions, real or symbolic, to black demands for an end to economic discrimination and other affronts. Conspicuous restiveness and civil disobedience must therefore be recognized as another, often potent, tactic through which masses can exert an influence upon public policy.

This discussion has deliberately moved from a consideration of such routine channels of influence as voting and legislative bargaining to those some regard as illegitimate, such as civil disobedience. The analysis and illustrations should make it obvious that there is no clear dividing line between legitimate and illegitimate tactics. Similarly, there is no clear empirical distinction, but only an analytically useful one, between people who feel relatively gratified and those who feel relatively deprived. It is the relatively deprived who are most likely to support political strikes, boycotts, riots, civil disobedience, or civil war as channels of influence.

It is tempting, but misleading, to classify people neatly as content or dissatisfied, as exhibiting a sense of gratification or a sense of deprivation, as perceiving the political system as legitimate or illegitimate, as believing they are efficacious or politically powerless. Test results do, of course, categorize people in these ways; but there is also clear evidence, some of which we have already cited, that people's feelings may vary over time, by issue, and according to the social context in which the question is presented to them. How stable and how consistent any individual or social group is in these respects is an empirical question, to be answered by observation and research. To take stability and consistency for granted is to underestimate the complexity of the human being and to guarantee that some of the most significant political phenomena will not be investigated or fully understood.

People who feel undeservedly deprived in some way that is important to them are likely to resort to civil disobedience or violence as a way of influencing the political system. Occasionally an individual resorts to violence alone, as in the case of the lone political assassin or terrorist or the person who tries by self-immolation to galvanize others into opposition to public policies he regards as immoral. Far more frequent and far more significant politically are the cases in which a substantial group of people feels a strong sense of deprivation with respect to the same issue, such as social, economic, and political equality, the military draft, or the Vietnam War. In such instances violent or nonviolent demonstration is likely; and if it is widely enough publicized and supported, it does win some degree of influence for the demonstrators. Economic boycotts, defiance of official restrictions on mass demonstrations, and riots are all fairly common forms of this tactic. Whether or not they are defined as legal at a particular time or place, they must be regarded by the realistic analyst of political processes as forms of mass action that will predictably occur under the conditions described here. Chapter 5 traces the story of how these tactics have won some gains for the poor and for those deprived of voting rights. We have already noted how the possibility of their occurrence has made elites willing to make concessions in such policy areas as social security and protective labor legislation. In its extreme form this tactic for achieving mass influence becomes sustained violent resistance or revolution, as in the American Revolution and the Civil War.

Militance and Popular Support

The efficacy of civil disobedience and militance in winning benefits for the masses depends ultimately upon how much popular support these tactics stimulate for their cause. When they serve dramatically to call attention to deprivations widely regarded as shocking and unfair, they are effective in rallying such support. Until the civil disobedience campaigns of the early 1960s and the riots of the middle 1960s, a large part of the American people were blissfully unaware of the "other America" living in poverty or denied basic civil rights. The increasingly militant demonstrations against the Vietnam War awakened many Americans to the dubious grounds upon which the Johnson Administration had justified escalation of the war, its high toll in civilian and military casualties, and the corruption and unpopularity of the Saigon regime.

Civil disobedience and violence do, as we have seen, create a "backlash" and so damage the political position of those who engage in them. Militance unquestionably antagonizes some people and evokes repression. The historical record leaves no doubt, however, that it also wins support for righting genuine wrongs. If such real deprivations can be dramatically brought to public attention, these militant tactics are the most potent political device in the scanty arsenal of tactics available to non-elites.

PART SIX

POLITICAL CHANGE

Chapter 17

Before we can assess the prospects for various forms of political change in the future, we must reach some conclusions about today's structure of power. The task of this chapter is to synthesize the separate analyses of problems, policies, ideology, structure, and decisional processes that have been developed in earlier chapters. Do they "add up," so that one or two consistent themes of power and its usage may be formulated? If so, what are these themes? Or are policies, values, and processes so disconnected that the American political system responds unpredictably and unsystematically to shifting, *ad hoc* coalitions of officials, interests, and forces? Each of the many potential answers to these questions implies a particular spectrum of possibilities for the future. Each

Power Structure: Contrasting Interpretations

suggests a distinctive set of prospects and tactics for political change. To omit (or to err in) such basic judgments is to risk irrelevance, the eternal danger of idealism in politics.

In broad historical perspective, events and actions may sustain a variety of very general overall characterizations. But we require a more concrete interpretive base. We shall begin by retreating for a moment to reconsider the concept of power and the ways we may recognize it in action. Then we shall examine some alternative judgments about the distribution of power in American politics that seem supportable from the evidence we have examined. Of course, some important questions remain open, because they have not been asked, or because evidence is not available, or because they involve evaluative premises about which observers are bound to disagree. We shall try to identify and illustrate some of these open questions, so that readers may begin to fit their own experience and observation into one or another of the alternative interpretations. Finally, we shall state our reasons for the opinions we now hold about our political system.

Power as Applied in the United States

The concepts of power and politics used in this book are broad and inclusive. We first defined power as the use of resources in such a way that others are induced to conform to that which the holder of the resources wants. This meant that we saw power as a *relation* between two or more people. There are always some people who are able to shape the behavior of others, sometimes even without deliberate intent; social life is a web of power relationships. For purposes of manageability, however, we did limit our definition of politics to those uses of power having to do with whether and how government is employed.

The intent of casting our analytical net so broadly was to guard against excessively narrow or formalistic images of politics. The institutional framework of government, the authorized processes for filling positions within it, and the formal acts of public officials, though vital objects of study, are only a very small part of political activity. Accompanying them are deep and conflicting currents of value commitments, economic interests, and social aspirations. These and other continuing struggles mean that power is in constant use throughout the society. Occasionally, powerholders achieve and maintain their goals exclusively in private transactions, but frequently their power flows through government, shaping its policies.

Power is a complex concept, open to almost infinite qualification and refinement. Many such efforts result in distinctions that, if effective at all, serve only to channel attention away from the central question: which people hold the resources that enable them to achieve their goals and shape the behavior of others within the society? We did not draw any such distinctions (such as between "power" and "influence," or between "power" and "authority") because they were unnecessary to our broad purposes and use of the concept. Focusing on public policies and their consequences—on power in its applied form—we defined "power" as *all* the uses of resources, outside and inside of government, that culminated in governmental action or inaction. Because we are now about to take up various interpretations of the actual distribution of power in the United States, however, we should make two clarifying observations about the concept.

Forms of Power

First, forms of power differ in character. In its most fundamental form, power involves physical coercion—immediate capacity to cause death or injury, imprisonment, or destruction of property. The much-quoted slogan "power grows out of the barrel of a gun" is no more than a succinctly stated truism. But coercion comes in many forms—economic pressures, social ostracism, legal harassment—that fall short of that ultimate stage. We may imagine a continuum of increasingly subtle forms of coercion, starting with physical force and culminating in the gentle types of social control practiced in some modern societies by means of ideological indoctrination and media management. The form, however, is less important than the fact of power. Whether the carrot or the stick is in use at any particular moment, it is still power that is being exercised.

Second, the power resources of government are distinctive. In most modern societies, private persons and entities have or can develop power resources that enable them to accomplish many of their goals. But some resources are almost exclusively available to government officials. One of these is the entitlement, according to the established constitutional system, to take certain actions—to raise taxes, prohibit strikes, or do any number of other things commonly associated with governments. This type of power is sometimes called "authority," and the acceptance by the people of an existing government's right to do such things is termed "legitimacy." The terms employed are not important, but the idea that certain resources and types of power are reserved for one established government is crucial. It means that the institutions and officials of government hold certain essential components of the total capacity for social control within the society. These components may be bestowed or withdrawn by the people, according to their judgments of how well the system is working, so that they do not exert a constant weight on the power scale.

These distinctions should emphasize the importance and the nature of the part played by government in people's struggles for their goals. A moment's reflection on each distinction reveals that those who would achieve their ends have no choice but to merge themselves with government and use it as an agency for extending and increasing their privately developed powers. In the larger contest for wealth and status, power is a tool, and government's power is a necessary tool.

In the first distinction, we saw that the really vital type of power is physical coercion: the power to kill, injure, jail, or destroy the property of another person. *Legitimate* power to do this, as well as the physical means, rests with government officials. All other such uses of power, and all competing armed forces, are defined, prohibited, and punished as crimes. Government is thus the sole possessor of the most fundamental form of power—not to mention its unique capacity to exercise the lesser forms of coercion.

Our second distinction, between private and governmental power, pointed up the fact that some powers are held only by governments. This means that private concentrations of power must often make use of government's independent power resources in order to secure goals unattainable exclusively through private action. But it also means that they must control government, if only to prevent it from being used by others to take away their gains. Where the means of applying power in its most fundamental form (i.e., the police and other military forces) are monopolized by government, it is imperative for those who aspire to wealth and status to control the uses of that power. Others too may seek to share in determining how government's power shall be used, and the struggle broadens. Thus, again, government becomes the focal point of power usage in the society.

The Holders of Power

This discussion implies, again, that government cannot be neutral. It acts in response to the interests of those with the greatest power resources in the society. Who are these wielders of power? There is ample evidence about who holds the largest private power resources in any society, and this evidence could be used to show that they run the government. From readily available proof of sharp disparities in economic possessions and social status between classes, one might infer government by an upper-class elite. Many studies do just this.[1]

But there are some important intervening questions to be asked, and those who are most determined to view the United States as an operating democracy do not think they have been satisfactorily answered: (a) What proof is there that upper-class elites, despite their comparatively vast power resources, actually *can* and *do* apply that power to control the government? and (b) *Even if they do* (assuming, for example, that their members or agents hold most of the key positions in government and dominate its policymaking), how do we know that their actions are not consistent with the preferences of the people? In other words, these analysts would argue, there need be no inconsistency between elite governance and democracy.[2] The people may freely choose these leaders in elections, or the leaders (however chosen) may in fact accomplish what the people want, or should want, or both. These are demanding questions,

---

[1] G. William Domhoff, *Who Rules America?* (Englewood Cliffs, N.J.: Prentice-Hall, 1967).

[2] For a full discussion of these problems, see Peter Bachrach, *The Theory of Democratic Elitism* (Boston: Little, Brown, 1966). See also Jack L. Walker, "A Critique of the Elitist Theory of Democracy," *American Political Science Review* 60 (1966), pp. 285–295, and Robert A. Dahl, "Further Reflections on the Elitist Theory of Democracy," *ibid.*, pp. 296–305.

perhaps born of ideological resistance to the idea that the United States might be controlled by an upper-class oligarchy. It is extremely difficult to find the evidence necessary to prove elite motivation one way or another. But these questions do point to the fact that those who reach the latter conclusion are making an inference, i.e., that social background and economic interests control behavior. The inference seems plausible to many scholars, but totally unjustifiable to others. The conflict has raged for decades, sometimes politely but sometimes with real emotion, as befits a fundamental question of power and its implications.

We have tried to circumvent this scholarly controversy, and the real evidential problem it highlights, by the approach we have taken in this book. We did not try to identify power in the private sphere and then trace its possible merger with control of, or pressure on, the institutions of government. Instead, we reversed the process entirely. We started with actual governmental policies and their consequences, and then looked into the characteristics of the political system in search of explanations for these consequences. With sufficiently precise description of the beneficiaries and losers from governmental action over time, the priorities actually operative in shaping these patterns, and the manner in which values, ideology, structure, and decision-making processes cause or reinforce them, we emerge with a viable characterization of how power is used and for whose benefit. If this characterization shows that power is used for the principal benefit, and consistently in the exclusive interest of the upper class whose members occupy most governmental offices, *then we are close to resolving the crucial question of whether or not they use their power in accordance with their own needs and preferences.* In other words, we have characterized their *actions,* from which we can much more safely infer their motivations. Comparison with popular needs and preferences is the only remaining step, and one that presents relatively little difficulty.

Our purpose is thus to identify the power structure of the United States by linking a description of the consequences of governmental policies to the goals, interests, and power of a definable segment of the society. In our eyes, these phenomena *do* form an integrated whole.

Policies, Goals, and Decisionmaking: A Coherent Picture

In previous sections, we have identified visible patterns in the consequences of public policies, examined the principles urged in support of such policies, and reviewed characteristics of power distribution and decisionmaking. Now we must try to bring all these issues together. The basic theme running through them, it seems to us, is this: *Governmental policies assume that the existing organiza-*

tion, operations, motivations, and perceived needs of the American economic system must be preserved and furthered in every practical way. No other premises or motivations evident in U.S. public policies effectively displace this basic assumption. Nor can any goal, however desirable in the abstract, be implemented effectively if it conflicts with this presupposition. Given this basic premise, governmental actions and their consequences may be *understood* as a coherent, integrated, and purposeful package. Without such recognition, they can only be *described* with puzzlement at apparent contradictions and chagrin at the mixture of successes and failures, hopes and frustrations.

The needs of the economic order are expressly addressed in the area of economic stability and growth. They are evident in development policies, and again in military expenditures. The military establishment and the space program are also vital to such foreign-policy goals as limiting communist expansion and inducing developing nations to adapt their economies to ours and reach more harmonious long-term relationships. Anticommunism itself rests heavily on the desire to protect the existing economic order and the values surrounding it. Policies to combat poverty encounter resistance because they conflict with values that bolster the economic system (such as self-reliance and rewards according to effort and talent, etc.) and because they threaten the distribution of wealth and power that system creates. Racism lingers in part because stronger measures to enforce desegregation and equal opportunity would run counter to economic values (such as freedom to sell property or hire workers) and perhaps disrupt the current operations of the economic system. In short, although the policy areas we have examined were chosen only because of their diversity and continuing social importance, actual governmental policies in each area seem to flow from the same economic premises. What appeared to be isolated, independent problem areas, each with a distinctive set of characteristics and relevant political forces, now appear to be overlapping, integrated extensions of a single set of priorities and limitations.

Value Priorities in Policy

Can we formulate a rough priority ranking of the values and goals that dominate policymaking in these areas, and perhaps in other apparently "independent" areas as well? Clearly, economic values and property rights are central. The rights to a return on invested capital, protection of that return by armed force if necessary, and the unrestricted use and secure enjoyment of one's property converge to impose imperatives for governmental action overseas and to create imperatives for, and erect barriers against, governmental action in domestic affairs. The United States must stand firm against communism and in favor of an open door in developing nations. It must maximize economic growth but at the same time tread lightly in combatting poverty and racism because of these strong commitments. Associated with property rights are the allied economic values of materialism, profit maximization, and the exaltation of productivity as a sufficient measure of societal achievement. Below this upper echelon of values are some with lower priority but more general applicability, such as anticommunism and the tendency to resort to military force if the dominant economic values are not being adequately served by other means. Still lower on the scale, and subject to a strong general commitment to the existing distribution of wealth and racial status, is the value of equality. Centuries of much rhetoric and some action have given equality real stature as a principle, though it remains subject to the higher priority of other values.

This rough ordering is an operational (as distinguished from historically received, rhetorical, or symbolic) ranking of American political values and goals. The central economic values we have identified and ranked as paramount need not have been explicit in the minds of policymakers. Nor have we yet asked whether they are characteristic of any other group or segments of the population. But they are evident in several apparently independent policy areas and over lengthy time periods. Whether implicit or explicit in the minds of policymakers, they seem to have been prime factors in the shaping of policies.

These chiefly economic values and goals may serve as a beginning framework for understanding the relative weights given to other political values. The latter must be assigned lesser status in the hierachy, and, most appropriately, according to the extent to which they are in harmony with and serve to further the paramount values and goals. Ultimately, we emerge with a serviceable and historically-grounded image of the priority ranking of political values that currently animates the American political system. In brief, it amounts to the protection and promotion of the American economic system and the distribution patterns it has established by various means, culminating in military force. Within this context, equality, humanistic justice, and majoritarianism contend with racism, materialism, and fixed procedures.

Values and the Political Structure

Just as patterns of policy consequence reveal an identifiable hierarchy of political values, so do both of these phenomena show consistent links with characteristics of the political structure and processes. The constitutional structure and institutional arrangement of American government, for example, limit the legal capacity of national, state, and local governments and disperse the total governing power across a wide landscape of levels and branches. The effect of this is to assure primacy for the private sphere on most questions. Those who are able to generate the greatest power out of private sources can shape basic patterns of thought and behavior, because government is unable to act coherently in majoritarian interests. Instead, government is open to penetration by major private interests, which uses its many veto points to establish defenses against the threat of change in economic and social life. Majorities of people are delayed if not prevented from achieving their common goals by their internal divisions and by the complex procedures and limitations that must be transcended. For decisive governmental action to occur, it must either be entirely consistent with the limits and goals of external powerholders, or there must be some highly unusual organizing force (such as an extreme emergency or a charismatic leader, or both) operating to unify its dispersed powers.

Similarly, decision-making persons and processes operate with a set of imperatives and constraints that combine to reinforce the economic priorities. To begin with, many offices are filled by persons who had previously risen to high positions within the legal, banking, or business communities. Their orthodoxy seems assured. Even persons who achieve high official status from extra-establishment positions experience powerful inducements to adhere to accepted priorities. They are normally appointed to governmental offices only because they have acted out their commitments to established values in some way. After doing so for some time, they may find that it is a natural and congenial set of standards with which to operate, and that it is also a way to avoid a rash of complaints from others in high places. More important, nearly every officeholder shrinks from the prospect of national unemployment or depression, and thus finds himself committed almost by default to maintaining the growth and prosperity of the existing economy as a (if not *the*) major priority of government.

Many officeholders are thoroughly familiar with the need for good relations with major sources of wealth. Both political parties, and nearly all candidates for nominations within them, are able to compete effectively only with the support of large contributors. Major senatorial nomination and election campaigns now involve sums approaching $5,000,000 per candidate, and the presidential nomination-and-election process requires hundreds of millions of dollars. Access to the mass media, if not the official support of those who own them, is essential to winning office. Officeholders thus learn the importance of economics early, and in a multitude of ways. Under these circumstances, their decisionmaking cannot help but reflect the priorities of the established economic system. In short, neither structures nor processes are neutral, in the sense of giving rise equally to any number of different patterns of policy. Instead, they contribute to reinforcement of the standards that yield this particular set of results.

At every major stage of analysis, this review suggests that the policy consequences we have examined are not the product of accident or coincidence. They reflect a consistent relationship between policies, values, institutional structures, and the officials and processes by which decisions are made. Each of these political factors independently contributes to, and in effect reinforces, the primacy of property rights and the protection and promotion of the economic system as the basis of policymaking. But there is still a causal question remaining. Our evidence does not establish whether it is the politico-economic institutions themselves, the individuals who happen to hold power within them, or some external force such as extragovernmental elites (or, conceivably, the general public) that dictate these results. In other words, we have defined the consequences and apparent standards of power usage, but we have not yet identified the holders of power who make these policies. That is the task of the next section.

Alternative Interpretations of Power Distribution

This pattern of consequences and of operative values may flow from quite different structures of power. We shall pose, and critically examine, three alternative interpretations: (1) power is located chiefly in governmental offices, whose incumbents respond to a mix of public and interest-group pressures; (2) power is extracted from both public and private resources by an establishment that seeks to shape popular preferences into forms that can be used to support its own basic goals and the system itself; and (3) power is derived from private economic resources by a relatively few persons who influence government in their interest, using it to promote popular acquiescence, discourage resistance, or both. Shorthand terms for the first and last models would be "pluralism" and "ruling-class." The second is a somewhat modified version of a "power elite" model.

Each of these interpretations seems to us capable of explaining the pattern of consequences described, if certain other conditions are taken to be true and other specific assumptions are made. None of them, of course, is likely to be entirely accurate. They are merely abstractions (not caricatures, we trust). But they serve to suggest the directions interpretations may take and the nature of the questions that must be resolved before final conclusions can be reached.

1. *Power as the Prize: Competitive Pressures in the Governmental Arena*

This interpretation denies that there is either a deliberate purpose or a unified power structure behind the making of national policy—except for those instances when practically the entire population is of a single mind on an issue. It holds that each area of public policy involves distinctive problems and separate sets of political agents and forces, such that each action undertaken by government is the result of a unique process of interaction. Accordingly, each action can only be understood by focusing on the particular circumstances and idiosyncratic features of the policy-making processes and individuals involved. In other words, policies vary unpredictably in substance, depending on what the people in office perceived, sought, and did, and on the complex of forces and circumstances that happened to exist at that time. By implication, if the public had strong preferences otherwise, or if the officeholders were different, or if the institutional mechanisms of government were different, the end results would also be different. This interpretation is essentially the one identified earlier as "pluralism." It contains at least six major elements, each of which makes some necessary assumptions about the economic and social setting in which American politics take place.

a. The political system is sufficiently separable from the economic and social systems of the United States that it may be understood chiefly through analysis of the behavior of individuals in governmental offices and in the electoral processes by which they acquire such offices. This premise rests on an especially narrow definition of politics, which considers it nothing more than activity in and bearing on governmental institutions. Further, politics is seen as self-contained, in the sense that practically all important factors influencing it exist in its immediate surroundings. Analysts need never look beyond decision-making processes and elections, for nearly everything else is irrelevant, not amenable to scientific study, or the province of some other social science.

But this restrictive definition itself flows from an image of *boundaries* around distinct systems of relationships—"economy," "society," "polity"—each largely independent of the others. It is this notion of detachment and separation that leads to images of "politics" as no more than the internal machinations of government and the official channels immediately surrounding it. Moreover, it leads to analysis of politics exclusively in its own terms. For example, it becomes difficult to distinguish major issues from minor ones except in "political" dimensions. Either all decisions appear equally significant, or the "important" ones are those on which the voters most often express themselves or on which the Congress debated longest.

b. Government's independent resources give it the decisive balance of power within the society and make it the mechanism through which all other spheres of activity may be managed. Government responds principally to popular preferences expressed in elections, and secondarily to the pressures of organized interests. Thus, it can become an arbiter between conflicting interests or an agent of the general will, essentially in accordance with the people's wishes. This is partly because of the prominence and efficacy of the electoral process, in which all people have equal power—in the sense of one vote. But it is also because the equal power principle spreads further: the American economic and social systems either do not produce serious inequalities of power between individuals or groups, or those inequalities are not translated into effects upon governmental decisionmaking. In short, relevant private power is distributed roughly equally throughout the society. All groups have about the same capacity and opportunity to shape governmental action, and politics becomes a contest (nearly always decided by votes) for the right to shape the direction of governmental policies.

c. The power of government is parceled out into so many component branches, agencies, committees, and offices that every significant interest within the society is able to gain access and affect the course of government action. Each locus of power within the framework of government is capable of delaying or preventing action. Government becomes in effect a much-elaborated system of checks and balances in which opportunities to veto action are broadly distributed, and affirmative action can be taken only when practically everybody concurs in the form it should take and its necessity. The society, instead of being a vast aggregation of individuals, is actually organized into a large number of distinct interests, most of which are represented by groups or associations. All of these have or can gain access to one or more of the many "veto points" among the institutions of government. Thus, there develops a harmonious linkage between governmental and societal structures, with the divisions in one paralleling divisions in the other.

d. Government provides an arena within which the various interests in the society contend with each other for often conflicting goals. Public officials, because they control the use of decisive (governmental) power, must be at the center of these conflicts. They serve as brokers, mediating the differences between competing interests and helping them to find the necessary compromises. This is a broadly representative process because practically every citizen is or can be represented by one or more groups and can thereby have his interests weighed in the process of policymaking. Conflicting pressures are applied to officials in roughly the same proportions that they are felt within the society. Divisions within the society are in effect translated into negotiable claims and adjusted; officials certify the accommodations through their authoritative support for one or another public policy.

e. These accommodations are reached through a set of well-established procedures that assure fairness and opportunity to all; all groups share a commitment to making such a process a continuing reality. Compromises that are just and acceptable to all do not occur by accident: they develop because of strict adherence to principles of procedural due process. These procedures call for full and fair hearings, consideration for others' points of view, and self-limitations if the larger system might otherwise be endangered. Each interest has an investment in preserving a setting in which it can be confident of receiving fair treatment; therefore all act to protect the fairness and openness of the procedures by which decisions are made.

f. The brokerage role played by public officials in reaching accommodations, and the residual choice-making role the situation permits them, means that the public exercises meaningful control over the general direction of public policy through elections. Further, the system as a whole amounts to a stable, satisfied equilibrium of groups and individuals. The officials who serve as mediators of conflicting claims are either elected or directly responsible to those who are. The wide availability and equal weighting of the vote therefore allows the people to choose at least the broad priorities of the government. The entire political system, though with some acknowledged imperfections and time lags, is thus tuned to popular preferences. And it is certainly controllable by the people if they care enough to exert themselves. If they do not, it must be because they are satisfied with its operations. Support for the latter conclusion comes also from the fact that the many conflicting pressures within the society (both between opposed interest groups and within an individual who belongs to two or more perhaps opposed groups) apparently operate to hold the entire society to the middle of the road. Extremes are avoided in this way, as the great majority of people insist successfully upon continued compromise and accommodation. In such a setting, faith in the workings of the established political system is likely to be and remain high.

These six components of the competitive-pressures model make up a familiar and in many ways persuasive image of power in the United States. We all can point to many areas in which there is conflict between interest groups and others, and governmental power is wielded by public officials to mediate and thereby further the public interest. Policy outcomes frequently do favor first one group and then another, and elections indeed often set policy directions for the future.

But there are several barriers to acceptance of this interpretation. One has already been suggested explicitly: it employs a very narrow, tunnel-vision definition of politics, which excludes much of the usage of power in the world (particularly that which determines what can become a political issue, and in what form) and fails to discriminate between more important and less important issues. Others are implicit in our presentation: it rests on the extra-empirical conviction that the United States is an open, democratic political system in which all citizens play roughly equal parts in shaping governmental policy, and it strains to interpret events to conform to this optimistic assumption. It never asks, for example, to what extent the American political parties actually present the electorate with the full range of possible policy choices at elections, nor to what extent both parties are controlled by factors other than popular preferences.

We shall consider two major criticisms of this interpretation. First is the charge that nearly every major assumption it makes about the economic and social structures of the United States is wrong. And second, it is argued that this view fails to explain why a consistent pattern of policy consequences and operative values exists—unless one makes some very agile intellectual leaps or some very unlikely assumptions about the society we live in. The latter criticism interests us most, for the former has been made often and with little effect on those who choose to adhere to this interpretation. But let us consider each in turn.

First, there seem to be solid grounds for challenging almost every assumption about the American social and economic structure that underlies this interpretation of the structure of power. The social and economic systems are not separate from, but intimately integrated with, the political system. We saw earlier in this chapter, for example, that one cannot rise to the top in the former without both acquiring the capacity to, and experiencing the necessity of, exerting power in the latter.[3] Inequalities of social status and economic possessions (and hence of the major resources of power) in the United States are too obvious and too widely documented to require much elaboration. Wealth, whether measured by income or by property holdings, is heavily concentrated in the upper twentieth of the population, with

---

[3]In part, this is a matter of defining what constitutes "power" and what activities are "political." The reader should recognize by now that we are committed to broad definitions of both, and should choose the definitions that strike him as most reasonable under the circumstances. But we do not stand solely on our definition: the empirical verification is also extensive, and we think persuasive.

severe deprivation in the lowest third. Vast accumulations of economic power in the great corporations are under the control of a relative handful of owners and managers.

The social structure clearly represents these facts of economic life: a small upper class dominates the major institutions and controls the corporate economy, while a large middle class takes its cues from them. More than half of the population, however, consists of blue-collar workers, low-salaried office personnel (particularly women), and the unemployed and unemployable. This large proportion of the society is divided against itself, with whites resisting the progress of blacks and men defending their "prerogatives" against women, so that the upper echelon's preponderance of effective power is even greater than its share of wealth and official positions would suggest. Although each system—economic, social, and political—is "open," in the sense that some members of each rising generation are able to penetrate or be co-opted into the upper reaches, the general patterns are *continuity* (those on top stay there) and *concentration and overlap* (those on top in one system merge with those on top in the others). "One man, one vote" thus evokes a democratic illusion: power flows from many sources other than votes, and concentrations of power of various kinds regularly move into government and work their will through it.

Readily documentable social and economic realities suggest much less benign and self-congratulatory *value judgments* about its operation than those implied by the pluralistic interpretation. At the very least, there are substantial grounds to doubt the propriety of terming this system "democratic." More important for our analysis, the crucial assumptions of the competitive-pressures model about social and economic structure seem seriously to lack *empirical accuracy*. And if it is *factually* invalid in these important respects, as well as dubious in its accompanying value judgments, the model itself appears to be undermined.

The second criticism of a pluralistic interpretation is that the consistent pattern of policy consequences and operative values we have identified is left completely unexplained. This is a crucial point, with profound implications for the validity of the competitive-pressures model. The first criticism, examined above, has been made regularly, exhaustively, and with considerable evidential support. But it has not been accepted by most political scientists, because the link between social and economic inequalities of power and the actions of government have not been demonstrated to their satisfaction. It is not enough, in the eyes of those who subscribe to the competitive-pressures model, to show that inequalities result in concentrations of power in the upper echelons of the population, and that these same people hold a very high proportion of the key positions in government. It must also be shown that such people (a) *actually use their* power to cause government to act in ways that are (b) *not only in accordance with their own interests, but also opposed to the public interest.* This is a high standard of proof, perhaps insisted on out of the deep desire to believe in a relatively democratic interpretation of power. It is not an illogical standard, but is a very difficult one to meet given the understandable limitations on acquiring accurate evidence about the motivations of decisionmakers.

The evidence we have developed, however, circumvents this difficulty and addresses the issue of whether governmental action is shaped according to the preferences of private powerholders. Admittedly, our evidence is neither exhaustive nor even comprehensive, but the tentative inferences it permits stand in direct contrast to the interpretation the competitive-pressures model offers. We have seen the consequences of government policies, and we have extrapolated the value priorities that actually dominate governmental action. The central theme was one of action on behalf of the preservation and promotion of the economic order, frequently at the cost of personal deprivations for many millions of people and denial of values that are rhetorically exalted. Such actions are, however, entirely consistent with the interests and power of the upper echelons of the overlapping social and economic structures of the United States.

In the light of such evidence, it seems fair to infer that the patterns we discerned were brought about by *some* consistent and purposeful force operating through the government. We may then demand that alternative interpretations attempt to explain *how* this consistent pattern may have been produced. The competitive-pressures model offers only happenstance, coincidence, or determinism by way of explanation. We think there must be more plausible explanations. Accordingly, we shall reject the competitive-pressures model *except with regard to minor decisions,* and concentrate on the search for more plausible interpretations of the structure of power as it applies to the fundamental issues of politics.

If we assume that *some* consistent and purposeful force is shaping governmental policies, and that there is unequal power inherent in the existing economic and class structure that overlaps into politics, what interpretations of the structure of power then follow? We think there are two major ones, which we shall evaluate after presenting each briefly.

2. *Power as a Social Process: Establishment Orchestration of Econopolitical Life*

This interpretation accepts the competitive-pressures model for minor decisions, though with less optimism about government mediating group conflict in the public interest and more emphasis on special interests' success in achieving their goals. On major issues, however, involving the basic structure of the economic and political order and the permanence of the established patterns of distribution of wealth and social status, a more unified power structure comes into being. Various holders of power coalesce to form a coherent and nearly singleminded force capable of managing major sources of private power, the government, and the general public alike.

The "glue" that holds this coalition together and enables it to work so effectively in defense of the *status quo* comes from two primary sources. One is the class-originated shared values and interests of the establishment, itself consisting of a circulating group of persons moving freely among the upper echelons of the economic, social, and political systems. These people are accustomed to holding and exercising power from their "command post" positions. Their life experiences and current interests have bred in them a strong commitment to orthodoxy and defense of the integrated economic and political structure. They see these values as synonymous with the public interest, not as self-serving.

The other source is the willingness of the general public—or at least the majority of its visible, audible, and active members—to endorse and support the actions of the major officials of their government. This acquiescence has many sources: faith in the institutions established by the Constitution, lack of alternatives, apathy, political party loyalties, hopelessness, fear of coercion. One of its major sources, however, is the wide dissemination and effective inculcation of the familiar American political values and ideology—itself one of the major achievements of the establishment. From twelve or more years of schooling to patriotic rituals and media messages, the individual lives in a context of symbolic assurances, materialism, racism, and benevolent rationalizations about how his government does and should operate. Embedded in this body of myth are the clear grounds of establishment dominance. At least some fragments of this belief system become implanted in the public's mind, available to be drawn upon in times of stress by the status- and legitimacy-exuding establishment.

Under ordinary circumstances, few major issues arise. Most public policies and private practices fit snugly within the approved contours of the established economic, social, and political systems, and special interests are free to seek their narrow ends within this context. When conditions change, and more basic questions are forced to the fore, the establishment begins to rally to the defense of the systems that have served it so well. Despite some disagreements about the best way to preserve the basic framework of the *status quo* (by yielding in the direction of greater equality or by "standing firm"), a consensus usually emerges with little direct consultation. Action then occurs simultaneously on many fronts to mobilize public support for particular forms of governmental action to meet and "solve" the crisis. Taking their cues from the actions of the uppermost echelons, many lesser officials and associated elites (mayors, policemen, Chambers of Commerce, and the like) institute similar (or more drastic) policies and manifest their support for the system-preserving program.

What looks like a consciously synchronized and coordinated movement may be no more than an elaborate follow-the-leader game. And what appears to be slavishly ideological mass support may be no more than silence. But the establishment seems to have managed the situation, and by so doing it improves its chances of succeeding again the next time—unless the social situation has reached a point at which open opposition destroys the harmonious image. Then the issue becomes the capacity to apply coercion to some without losing the public acquiescence and cooperation necessary to make the system operable.

3. Power as a Tool: Economic Dominants Manage the System

This interpretation represents the end of the continuum at which power is most tightly concentrated in private hands and public impact on policy is least. It holds that economic resources are the paramount sources of power, and that those relatively few persons who own or control the uses of them are in a virtually unchallengeable position of power. They set the operative values and priorities in their own private interest. They can direct the actions of people in government or, through control of the foundations, universities, and mass media, shape the attitudes of the general public. Normally, they provide only general direction, but when necessary they can and do assert specific control over governmental action. A principal tool for thus managing the society (and in some respects, the world) for their own benefit is physical coercion. Although efforts are made to present this use of power publicly as necessary and desirable, the lower classes in particular are kept aware of the ready availability of police and other military forces frequently used against them.

There is in this view a distinct structure of power—a more or less definable and self-conscious group of individuals, sometimes labeled "the ruling class." This group uses its extragovernmental resources to control nominations, elections, and governmental decisionmaking, not necessarily by dictating specific decisions but by maintaining boundaries within which action may proceed unrestricted, but beyond which rejection is swift and drastic. The motivations of this group are almost exclusively economic: maximization of the profits of the corporate economy. All areas of governmental activity are subject to that overwhelming goal. Nor is the need for governmental support limited to a desire to defend established domestic prerogatives.

Because of the pressing need of the economy for new opportunities to invest surplus capital, this economic class exerts control of government to assure profitable opportunities in the developing nations.

Selecting Among Alternatives: Questions and Implications

In at least one important respect, these two interpretations are in complete agreement: on all fundamental questions, a unified power structure is ready and determined to defend the *status quo* in drastic and effective ways. But in most other respects, they are quite distinctive. The economic dominants model in effect extracts one dimension —the economic—out of the establishment orchestration model and makes of it a simpler, harsher characterization of the structure of power. The economic dimension is surely central to the establishment orchestration model, and the proper one to build upon if only one theme is to dominate. But doing so posits not only a different basis of power but also a distinctive set of implications for the prospects and tactics of change.

Extensions of the Economic Dominants Model

The economic dominants model sees power arising from economic holdings, tightly concentrated in private hands, and using government as tool. The establishment orchestration model sees power flowing from several resources (of which economic strength is a major one), and thus spread more broadly within the upper echelons of the society. Decisive power in any situation may rest with an *ad hoc* coalition of establishment members, depending on the subject area, the dynamics of specific events and social conditions, the skills of strategically-located individuals, and the particular configuration of popular attitudes toward the government and the issue. Private power merges subtly with government's independent powers after an exchange in which people at the top act and elicit symbol- and ideology-induced support for that action from key segments of the general public. Again, the result may be the same, but the process is different. The establishment orchestration model envisions a somewhat more open process, with interchangeable roles for a larger number of top figures, greater mutual dependence between individuals in and out of government, and greater reliance upon more or less "voluntary" popular support.

The economic dominants model emphasizes economic sources of power and economic motivations on the part of the ruling elite, with capitalism as the source of the values and ideology that facilitate their management of the system. The establishment orchestration model is not only multicausal, but sees an independently generated set of values as more important than economic interests on at least some decision-making occasions. This belief system, perhaps originally influenced quite strongly by the nature of the economic system, is seen as now self-perpetuating. Although it has a strong economic component, it is made up also of the heritage of Anglo-American legal thought, Judaeo-Christian religious postulates, and such values as nationalism, patriotism, and equality. When the establishment acts, it does so on the basis of one or a combination of these received values and beliefs. There is thus more room for uncertainty on its part, and greater need for confidence that key segments of the population concur and support it. To state the point from the perspective of nonelites, the establishment is more vulnerable to popular demands.

The economic dominants model assumes a greater divergence of interests between upper and lower classes and a more distinctive set of values and ideology among those lower classes. Accordingly, although it too sees ideology-based manipulation as a convenient means of managing the masses, physical coercion plays a greater part in maintaining elite governance. In part, because coercion is employed so regularly, the lower classes are kept aware of their different interests. Of course, the middle and upper classes are not normally cognizant of such violence and would probably assume it to be necessary and justified if they were. The establishment orchestration model tends to see lower classes as more fully captured by the values and ideology promulgated by the establishment, so that they do not clearly recognize the divergence of their interests from the middle and upper levels. Thus, management of popular preferences is easier. The underlying value system contributes massively to the stability of the economic and political order because it teaches the population to "genuinely" want, accept—and defend—what is in the establishment's interest. Physical coercion, though necessary at times, is a last resort. Further, indiscriminate use of physical coercion involves the risk of reducing support (and bestowed "legitimacy") from a people who have been taught to revere due process.

The economic dominants model has the virtue of zeroing in on the central theme of power and presenting a clear and coherent interpretation of the American power structure. It permits clearer assignment of motivation and much greater apparent predictability of future elite behavior. The establishment orchestration model, although it posits the same results in crisis situations, envisions those results as flowing from a distinctly more complex structure and process. The differences are not insignificant, in the light of our concern for the prospects of change. Stated briefly, the most crucial issues are: (1) the relative solidarity and singlemindedness of decisive elites and the extent to which they are able to command, as opposed to being obliged to seek to acquire and develop, the power resources of government; and (2) the extent to which their management of the polity is accomplished through consent or quiescence manipulated or coerced from the lower classes, as opposed to drawing more upon apparently "voluntary" support. These are open questions, for which conclusive evidence is still lacking. And much is at stake in the answers tentatively chosen.

Implications for Change

The implications for change may already be obvious. If the economic dominants model is correct, elites are largely impenetrable by non-elites; nor is government a significant means of non-elite access to a share of power. But, at the same time, there is greater consciousness of divergence of interest and deprivation among the lowest classes. Under these conditions, there may be a continuing tension between the desire for change below and the rigid structure of power above. For change to occur, however, drastic reconstruction of the social order from below—by forceful means—may be the only route. However unlikely, and perhaps unattractive to contemplate, no other method of change seems possible in this interpretation.

If the establishment orchestration model is correct, elites' incomplete domination of government, and their need for its legitimating power, opens an aperture for non-elite penetration. If representatives of such non-elites are successful in acquiring key offices and resisting co-optation as establishment agents, they may succeed in short-circuiting accepted practices or even in introducing new priorities. Because the underlying values generate broad and "voluntary" support for the existing economic and political order, and the establishment is genuinely dependent on this support for effective management of the system, two paradoxical results follow. The establishment recognizes that it must at least appear to satisfy changing demands among the major segments of the population, and may even be led to new policies by such changes. But changes in values and ideology require long periods of education, among the principal devices for which is the behavior of leading establishment figures themselves. One implication of this mutually reinforcing situation is that power relationships may remain apparently stable for some time, while shifts in underlying values are actually steadily eroding the bases of that power. When a dramatic event or condition sparks bold action by some establishment figure, he or she may encounter widespread approval and acceptance, much to the surprise of all who remain steeped in the conventional wisdom.

Thus, under the establishment orchestration model, relatively peaceful change seems somewhat more possible. It does require a special convergence of people, events, and conditions, and even then it is likely to proceed only to modest lengths before enough popular demands are satisfied to reduce the situation to a manageable level again. Further, it requires a period of value change to bring broad segments of the people to the point where their desires induce some establishment members to act boldly in unprecedented directions. The few truly change-oriented representatives of non-elites who penetrate the establishment and remain unco-opted are not able to do more than raise issues. Although this is a major means through which segments of the public can adopt new priorities, only determined mass insistence upon doing so will cause the establishment to agree to the wholesale modification of governmental policies.

Which of these two interpretations of the structure of power is the more accurate? Although we felt able to dismiss the competitive-pressures model (except for minor decisions) as conceptually confined and evidentially unsupported, we note earlier that available evidence left two major open questions involving the latter two models. Readers may draw upon their own observations and experience, and perhaps succeed in filling these gaps to their own satisfaction. As may be clear from our analysis, we tentatively accept the more complex establishment orchestration interpretation. We acknowledge the revealing thrust of the economic dominants version, and view it as an often accurate portrait; and we are aware of the utility of clear and direct answers to "Who rules?" But there seem to us to be more currents of power at work, greater uncertainty in the ways power is mobilized and applied, and more (though by no means direct) influence by popular attitudes. For these reasons, our image of the American power structure—pending further evidence—is essentially that of the establishment orchestration model. Perhaps we are also affected by the contrasting implications for the nature and prospects of change; discouraging as it is, the establishment orchestration model nevertheless holds out some hope for a process of change that falls short of full-scale revolution. The latter, as we shall see, remains a possibility. In Chapter 18, we shall look more systematically at different forms of change and the conditions necessary to each, accepting as our premise that the basic structure of power in the United States is that described here as the establishment orchestration model.

Chapter 18

Politics is not simply, or perhaps even primarily, a series of rational decisions and purposeful actions to produce intended results. Neither the powerful nor the powerless can fully calculate or control the actions of others. Many actions are unforeseen or unintended, and so are many results. What seems logical or likely often simply does not occur. One of the most powerful reasons why this is true is discoverable in the part played by symbols in politics. In particular, symbolic processes and effects go a long way toward explaining the sporadic, erratic, and generally unsuccessful nature of thrusts toward change in the United States.

Symbolic Politics and Political Change

In this chapter, we shall explore the nature of symbols and the part they play in our politics. Once again, we shall approach our subject comprehensively, examining many aspects of symbolic politics. But our primary purpose is to understand how symbolism diverts people, reassures them, and thereby deflects or undermines thrusts toward change. There is no direct relationship between the *fact* or even the *perception* of deprivation and rationally calculated action to change that situation. Even if people accurately understand the causes of problems, they may not even consider acting to solve them. Politics is simply not that logical or rational. But it *is* potentially understandable, nevertheless, and a clear sense of the role symbols play will help greatly. We shall first consider the scope and importance of symbolism in our politics, and then some of the ways symbols are created and used. Then we shall move to our major task: an assessment of the effects and implications of symbolism for politics and political change.

The Scope and Importance of Symbolism

The Nature of Symbolism

Government does not just reflect the will of some of the people. It also *creates* public wants, beliefs, and demands, with powerful impact upon who gets what in politics. If some of the major demands and beliefs of mass publics are evoked by what the government does and by what public officials say, then talk of responsiveness to the will of the people means less (or more) than meets the eye.

Governmental actions and rhetoric can reassure people and make them apathetic, or arouse them to militant action. And the messages that reassure or arouse can be either accurate or misleading. Because controversial policies always hurt some people, the temptation is strong for public officials to be reassuring; officials are naturally eager to be reassured themselves and to believe that what they do is in the public interest. Even if political symbols are misleading, therefore, they need not be *deliberately* deceptive. Indeed, the most powerful political symbols are disseminated by people who believe in them themselves.

Public officials can win mass support for actions that would elicit protest and resistance if undertaken by private groups. If private gas and electric companies could raise their rates whenever they pleased without any pretense of governmental supervision, any company that substantially raised its rates every year or two would certainly evoke massive protests and demands for public ownership or tight regulation.[1] But few people protest publicly when state public utilities commissions permit precisely the same rate rises. The blessing of a government agency reassures consumers and wins support for actions that would otherwise be resented.

If the wealthy, as private individuals, forced the poor or middle-class to give them a substantial part of their earnings, resistance would be massive and immediate. Yet governmental tax and subsidy policies that have exactly this effect are perceived as reasonable, even though particular taxes or subsidies are criticized by scattered interests. If private individuals forced millions of young men to leave home, submit to strict discipline, kill others, and be killed themselves, such "slavery" would be regarded as intolerable. But when legitimized by duly enacted draft laws, it is not only tolerated by most, but regarded as highly desirable and even necessary.

The point is that official governmental acts and statements are rarely *simple* in their impacts or their meanings. Almost never are

---

[1]This is precisely what happened in the late nineteenth century, giving rise to the existing state and federal regulatory laws.

their consequences clear and certain. Economists conclude that public utility laws typically do little to keep gas or electricity rates low. But it still seems likely to most people that the rates would be even higher without governmental regulation. Low tax rates for oil producers force other taxpayers to subsidize an affluent group, but the subsidy is justified on the grounds that it enlarges a vital national resource—and it probably does. In such cases the financial costs to large numbers of people are high (though they are largely or completely hidden), the method of calculating them is complex, and their fairness is hard for most people to judge. By contrast, the symbolic benefits—protection of the consumer, promotion of national security—are *easy* to see and to understand even though they often turn out to be trivial, misleading, or nonexistent when carefully studied.

The legitimacy of government—the belief that public officials represent the will of the people—therefore confers a mystique that can reassure people even when they have reason to be wary or alarmed. And it can arouse people to endure severe sacrifices, due to wars or regressive taxes, even if they have little to gain. In such cases the facts are hard to recognize or analyze, and anxious people want very much to believe that the government knows how to handle the economic, military, and other threats they fear but cannot cope with as individuals.

Not all public policy is symbolic or based upon deliberate or unintended mystification, of course. The impacts of many governmental acts upon people's everyday lives are so clear that there is little question whether they help or hurt. People in a slum neighborhood who want a playground or a traffic light know when they are getting what they need. The farm corporation that gets several hundred thousand dollars in "price support" subsidies knows precisely how public policy boosts its profits. To the taxpayer, of course, this same public policy may be invisible or perceived as an aid to the small family farmer or a desirable way of enhancing the nation's food production.

The key question, then, is under what conditions the acts of government become symbolic and help *create* beliefs, wants, and demands in mass publics. The question is both a highly practical one for the citizen or lobbyist and an intriguing one for the student of government; public policies have symbolic effects under conditions that we can identify, at least within rough limits. Because political symbolism is a *systematic* phenomenon, we can learn to understand and perhaps control it.

Symbol Analysis

Analysis of political symbolism allows us to see some things that are not otherwise obvious and to evaluate or judge them in a new way. How satisfied or dissatisfied people are with government does not depend only on how much they get. It depends even more on what society, and especially the government itself, cues them to expect, want, and believe they deserve. Corporate farm interests made rich by a price support program are often dissatisfied if they do not also get tax breaks, such as rapid depreciation allowances. Most of the poor, taught by schools, welfare workers, and governmental policies to feel inadequate for not having made money in a "land of equal opportunity," docilely accept meager welfare benefits and sometimes degrading "counseling" on how to live their lives. They may feel lucky if their benefits are raised ten dollars a month. In both these cases it is people's *expectations,* rather than how much they get, that chiefly influences how satisfied and how demanding they are. In both examples, and in thousands of others, government helps shape expectations rather than simply responding to them. Indeed, government acknowledges "the voice of the people" largely by influencing what that voice says.

The study of political symbolism necessarily focuses on *change* and the attitudinal and behavioral conditions of change. Symbols evoke either *change* or *reinforcement* of what people already believe and perceive. It becomes essential to know, for example, how a governmental action or statement may change beliefs or perceptions. A poll may show that virtually all Americans are convinced that the Chinese People's Republic is their eternal enemy and its people enslaved and hostile. But these poll results reflect a response to particular stimuli, and not necessarily to a stable state of affairs. More important than such a snapshot poll is the way such results change after the President of the United States visits China and the television networks broadcast pictures of beautiful Chinese cities and friendly-looking people. Statistics on support or opposition to the President are less important than what kinds of *change* in support will take place if unemployment rises or prices decline. Statistics on attitudes, in short, are not "hard data"—important in themselves. They are, rather, a way of learning something about how governments and other social groups evoke changes in the direction, intensity, or stability of attitudes. The symbolic perspective is a dynamic one.

Every mode of observing and interpreting the political scene has normative implications. It crudely or subtly suggests that the system, and particular aspects of it, are good or bad, right or wrong. Here, too, the symbolic perspective makes a difference. The conventional view of the political process sees public policy as reflecting what the people want—as expressed in their votes and responded to by legislatures and by the administrators and judges who carry out legislative policy. Systems theory, the most fashionable metaphor for explaining government, portrays public demands and support as the "inputs" of the system and legislative, executive, and judicial policy as the "out-puts." Both systems theory and the traditional outlook are highly re-assuring and justify the *status quo,* for they tell us that governmental action reflects what the people want.

The student of symbolism knows that this is often true, but does not avoid the less reassuring aspect of the political process: that gov-ernment can often shape people's wants before it reflects them. To the extent that governmental actions create popular beliefs and wants, the political process is not democratic, but potentially antidemocratic, for policies are not always based upon the people's will even when they seem to be. It is tempting to take the appearance for the reality. This is true whether the manipulation of public opinion by govern-mental officials is deliberate or unintentional. For this reason the symbolic perspective often raises questions about the legitimacy of political regimes, the obligation to support them, and the desirability of their policies.

Symbols and Their Creation

Some Characteristics of Symbols

How is it that on controversial public issues people come to hold conflicting views of the facts, the nature of the problem, and the proper course of action to solve it? Consider some recent public is-sues. Will antiballistic missile installations increase national security or actually decrease it by intensifying the international arms race? Will busing to desegregate public schools improve the quality of edu-cation or ruin the schools? Does a wage-price freeze help stop infla-tion or simply allow employers to keep the money they would otherwise pay their employees?

All of these issues have been hotly fought in recent years, and it is obvious that both sides cannot be right on the facts and impacts of proposed policies. The first step in understanding this kind of con-flict is to notice that the facts about such questions cannot be fully known and understood. Thus there is a large element of uncertainty, or ambiguity. Whenever ambiguity exists about matters that concern or threaten large numbers of people, public policies become "sym-bolic" in the sense that they evoke intense feelings and beliefs about a range of issues that may be quite different from the one that is pub-licly debated. Support for the ABM (antiballistic missile) may be based, perhaps subconsciously, upon deepseated inclinations to be tough with enemies or strong fears of unemployment in the aerospace industry. But both fears are expressed as concern for protection against foreign enemies. To its opponents, on the other hand, the ABM may arouse strong emotion not only because they think it unnecessary and economically wasteful but because it "symbolizes" a violent or aggressive posture they find repulsive. Such symbols are sometimes called "condensation symbols" because they condense into one event or act a whole range of anxieties, attitudes, remembrances of past victories or defeats, and expectations of future glories or catastrophes. To the extent that anything serves as a condensation symbol, reactions to it are not based upon observable facts that can be verified or falsified. Responses are based, rather, upon social suggestion—that is, upon what other people cue us to believe. They may turn out to be perfectly reasonable and appropriate responses, but often they are not.

Not all political acts, terms, or events are condensation symbols, of course. They may be only partly symbolic. We react to many political events as observable reality, as a part of our everyday lives with which we realistically cope. Such phenomena serve as "referential symbols." Often a political event is dealt with both as part of the factual world and as an expressive symbol. It may serve both functions for the same person or it may be chiefly referential for some people and chiefly expressive for others. And it may express quite different things to different groups of people.

When social workers refuse to give destitute people their welfare checks unless they agree to "counseling" on how to spend their money, raise their children, and run their homes, the social workers see counseling as help for the unfortunate. They refer to themselves as members of a "helping profession." Many of their clients see "counseling" as demeaning and repressive interference in their private lives and as coercion to make them live by middle-class standards and values. The same phenomenon symbolizes very different things to the two groups most directly involved with it.

What counseling symbolizes for the general public determines which group has power, status, and public support. Because social workers have been able to get their perspective on this issue widely accepted by the general public, they wield the greater power. Their clients are generally perceived as people who have much more wrong with them than lack of money. The notion that they need counseling evokes a view of the poor as personally inadequate and incompetent, unable to cope with life in the way other people do, requiring guidance and even coercion to behave well. Most people do not even perceive counseling as a political issue, so completely are they "socialized" to see social work as a helping profession. Indeed, convincing the public to perceive the exercise of authority and the allocation of values as a "professional" rather than a political issue is one of the most common and effective political techniques in contemporary society.

It is therefore the meanings of governmental actions and rhetoric to specific groups of people that are important to the analysis of political symbolism. The key issues are (1) how actions and words come to mean different things to different people and in different situations, and (2) the impact of such meanings upon the distribution of power and upon the inclination of people to be either militant, aroused, and violent, or willing to accept governmental action with satisfaction, apathy, or quiescence.

The Creation of Political Symbols: Language and "Information"

People underestimate the pervasiveness of political symbols partly because they are largely shaped and maintained unconsciously—through the language used to describe events and through unconscious emphasis of some kinds of information and disregard of other kinds. The nonobvious meanings of everyday activities are nowhere more striking than in analysis of the subtle meanings of the language we speak, hear, and read every day. What messages, for example, are conveyed by the appeals of politicians to vote for a particular candidate or to support policy A rather than policy B? There is, of course, an obvious level of meaning: a plea for support for the political cause or candidate.

It is equally clear, however, that this kind of political exhortation also tells the masses that what they support matters, that they do have an influence on how government works. People easily grow skeptical about the obvious message. They often question or resist specific appeals for support. But the subtle, nonobvious message is far harder to question or resist. To be asked for support is to be told that your support counts. In this way the *form* of political rhetoric shapes thought and belief more powerfully than can its content. Hortatory political language is only one example of the symbolic level at which language influences us. The legal language and administrative jargon to which we are constantly exposed also convey latent messages that reassure us that the political system functions so as to realize the will of the people.[2]

The metaphors we use, usually unconsciously, to describe political events and issues also subtly shape our political thought. A metaphor describes the unknown by comparing it to something that is well-known, and in doing so it highlights some features and conceals others. "A crusade for freedom" and "legalized murder" are two metaphoric descriptions of war that place it in quite different perspectives. A wage control program can be viewed either as "a battle

[2]For a discussion of their symbolic meanings, see Murray Edelman, *The Symbolic Uses of Politics* (Champaign: University of Illinois Press, 1964), Ch. 7.

against inflation" or as "a subsidy to employers." Every controversial political development is described and perceived by the use of conflicting metaphors, not necessarily because of a deliberate effort to influence or to mislead (though that, of course, happens too), but because we cannot speak or think about any complex matter without resorting to metaphor. It permeates our language whether or not we are aware of it.

The particular metaphor that describes a political issue for a person reinforces the other symbolic processes. A person who works in a defense industry and fears Russian aggression, is likely to adopt the political role of defender against a foreign enemy and to see the cold war as a crusade for freedom. Those who call it "legalized murder" will look to him like dupes or traitors. His beliefs, his self-concept, and his language reinforce each other and are, in fact, part of a single pattern of thought and behavior. They can be fully understood only as aspects of each other, and this is the important function of political language. It is always a vital part of a larger pattern of thought and action.

Political metaphors help shape both what we see as fact and how we *evaluate* political developments. Some think of abortion as a form of murder and some think of it as a form of freedom. Whichever metaphor is in a person's mind influences what he imagines when he reads a news story about an abortion clinic or about legalization of abortion. And, obviously, it influences whether he favors or opposes legal abortion.

The metaphoric mode in which people perceive complex political issues and events is an obstacle to complete understanding and to changes in perception and belief as new information becomes available. New information is ordinarily screened to conform to the metaphor rather than allowed to change it. Two people with opposing views can read the same news about abortion clinics and each find that it confirms their earlier opinions. In this way metaphors become self-perpetuating. They are the patterns into which we fit our observations of the world. If army communiqués describe the bombing of "structures" in Southeast Asian villages, people feel better than they would if they were told that our bombs were destroying people's houses or huts. For those who want to believe it, the word "structures" evokes an image of military installations rather than homes.

Statistics about governmental activities can readily create misleading beliefs and are an especially common form of impression management. In this case there is often a deliberate attempt to mislead, which is not typically true of other symbolic processes. But misleading statistics also depend for their effectiveness largely on the willingness, or eagerness, of the public to be convinced. In a society that puts a high premium on science and precision, and in which we are socialized to believe that "figures don't lie," statistics are usually highly persuasive. They are a form of information we are strongly tempted to accept and believe.

Nonetheless, figures often do lie, and it sometimes requires considerable sophistication to recognize their falsity. Unemployment is invariably understated in the statistics when it is high. This may occur, for example, because people who would like to have jobs but are convinced (often accurately) that there are none to be had are not counted as unemployed unless they actively seek work. A decline in the unemployment statistics often means, therefore, that a lot of people have become discouraged about the economy. But it is accepted as evidence of an upturn in the economy. "Body counts" showing far more enemy than American soldiers killed can easily create an impression of movement toward "victory" in a population eager for hard evidence. The impression is dubious. The figures are supplied by field commanders who can seldom actually count enemy bodies but know their promotions depend upon supplying statistics pleasing to their superiors; even if the statistics were accurate they would not, of course, have much to do with which side is winning. Even accurate figures can create quite misleading impressions. If the number of crimes increases by exactly the same number each year, a government can claim, quite accurately, that there has been a drastic decline in the rate of increase and so win credit for an effective fight against crime.

There is, then, a very strong temptation to accept or invent information that confirms what we already believe, gives events the meanings we want them to have, and serves our interests. The tendency to accept myth is sometimes virtually unrestrained. Where the temptation to accept it is less strong, empirical observation and reality-testing can offset or overcome it. Political belief and behavior cannot be understood without recognizing that there are severe limits on how well the human mind accepts and takes account of pertinent information.

Symbols and Reality

Fortunately, beliefs and perceptions about the world and about ourselves are also often realistic and based upon accurate observation. When a person is directly and critically affected by readily observable political events, he is likely to base his beliefs upon what he sees rather than upon symbolic cues. The poor in eighteenth- and nineteenth-century Europe rioted when food shortages occurred.[3] Peasants in Southeast Asia today riot or rebel when their patrons

---

[3] George F. Rude, *The Crowd in History* (New York: John Wiley, 1954).

stop providing them with at least a subsistence level of food, clothing, and shelter.[4] Blacks in American urban ghettos typically base their beliefs about progress toward racial equality upon what happens to them in their daily lives, not upon the enactment of civil rights laws.[5] In none of these cases is there much doubt or uncertainty about what is happening, and those most affected are realistic, though other groups may not be.

It is in ambiguous situations that evoke strong fears or hopes that symbolism becomes a powerful influence upon what people believe and what they think is happening. To upper middle-class whites, the enactment of civil rights laws is an encouraging signal that the lot of the ghetto black is improving, especially if there was a bitter struggle in Congress over passage of the law. Their evidence is news stories about the legislative outcome, not experience of life in the ghetto. In some lower middle-class whites, the same news stories create a belief that blacks are progressing too fast and threatening their jobs. When hopes or fears are strong and political events cannot be observed directly, governmental acts become especially powerful symbols. But every political belief involves some mix of direct observation and symbolic cuing, though in greatly varying proportions. The hungry food rioter is close to the realistic end of the realism-symbolism scale. Close to the other end of the scale is the German in the 1930s who followed and obeyed Hitler because he believed Hitler's claim that the Nazis would create a glorious thousand-year empire.

Even this understates the marvelous complexity of the human mind. The same person rarely retains exactly the same beliefs about a political issue over time; he or she responds to new events and new cues. In the wake of news of a particularly brutal crime, a person may take the position that fewer civil rights and longer prison terms for criminal offenders are necessary to reduce the crime rate. Shortly afterward, the same person may read a study of the effects of imprisonment that persuasively argues that prisons rarely "rehabilitate," often force the person who has violated the law once to adopt crime as a way of life, and therefore create more criminals than they cure. On controversial political issues, many people's beliefs and perceptions are likely to be consciously or unconsciously ambivalent and often quite unstable. Realistic observation keeps us from straying too far into fantasy most of the time. But given sufficient uncertainty about the facts and sufficiently strong fears or hopes, large groups of people indulge in mythical thinking about political issues. Let us now examine some of the effects and implications of such thinking.

---

[4]James Scott, "The Erosion of Patron-Client Bonds and Social Change in Rural Southeast Asia." Mimeographed.

[5]For a discussion and documentation of this point see Murray Edelman, *Politics as Symbolic Action* (Chicago: Markham, 1971), pp. 19–20.

Symbolic Politics and Political Quiescence

Legitimacy and Support

Why is there so little resistance to, and such overwhelming support from all strata of the population for a political system that yields the substantial inequalities in wealth, power, status, and sacrifice examined in the earlier chapters of this book? Support for the system and belief in its legitimacy is all the more striking in view of the fact that Americans are taught early that all men are created equal, and that they live in a land of equal opportunity.

Many governmental processes inculcate both generalized support for the political system and acquiescence in particular policies. Such processes are symbolic in character, for they create meanings and influence states of mind. If they also allocate values, they are both symbolic and instrumental.

The symbols that most powerfully inculcate support for the political system are those institutions we are taught to think of as the core of the democratic state—those that give the people control over the government. Probably the most reassuring are elections. Americans learn early in life to doubt that any state can be democratic without free elections, and they are inclined to assume that a country that holds elections must be democratic. Whatever else they accomplish, elections help create a belief in the reality of popular participation in government and popular control over policy. For the individual voter, elections also create a sense of personal participation and influence in government.

The belief is crucial whether or not it is accurate. Research discussed in Chapter 15 raises doubts that belief in popular control through elections is fully warranted. There is evidence that much of the electorate is neither especially interested in issues nor well-informed about them, and that votes are often cast on the basis of other considerations.[6] On the other hand, issues apparently do sometimes make a difference.[7] But if elections powerfully legitimate the political system and the regime, whether or not they are responsive to people's wants and demands, the realistic political analyst must recog-

---

[6]See especially Angus Campbell, Philip Converse, Warren Miller, and Donald Stokes, "*The American Voter* (New York: Wiley, 1960); Philip Converse, "The Nature of Belief Systems in Mass Publics," in *Ideology and Discontent*, ed. David Apter (New York: Free Press, 1964); Angus Campbell et al., *Elections and the Political Order* (New York: Wiley, 1966).

[7]For a study that tries to specify the conditions under which issues matter, and a review of the previous literature, see Gerald M. Pomper, "From Confusion to Clarity: Issues and American Voters, 1956–1968," *American Political Science Review* 66 (June 1972), pp. 415–428.

nize legitimation as one of their functions, and sometimes the major one.

Similarly, other institutions we are socialized to consider fundamental to democracy help inculcate broad support for the system and acquiescence in policies, even from those who do not like them. The publicized functioning of legislatures and courts promotes widespread confidence that majority will is reflected in the law, which is applied expertly and impartially to people who may have violated it. Here again, there is evidence that such belief is often not warranted. Legislative bodies chiefly reflect the needs of organized interests and strong pressure groups, and courts are more sensitive to the interests of some groups than others—regardless of the "mandate" of the voters in the last election.[8]

Besides legitimizing the political system, governmental actions also create support for, or acquiescence in, particular policies. A wide range of devices are used to evoke such acceptable responses to controversial governmental acts. It is a challenging exercise to identify them and learn to recognize new ones, for the analyst usually has to overcome his own identification with their popular or conventional meanings in order to recognize their symbolic functions.

Reassurance: Protection Against Threats

Some types of governmental action create the belief that government is providing effective protection against widely feared threats or undesirable developments. One policy area in which this effect is especially dramatic is government regulation of business to protect the consumer against high prices. We have antitrust laws to insure that businesses compete, rather than conspiring to concentrate economic power and charge what the traffic will bear. We have many laws to prevent corporations that enjoy a monopoly or special license in such fields as telephone, gas, and electric service, or radio broadcasting, from using their economic power to gouge the consumer with high prices or shoddy service. Antitrust actions are frequently in the news, as are the actions of public utility commissions, and politicians often declare their zeal to increase the effectiveness of protective legislation of this sort. Yet for many decades studies by economists and political scientists have shown that these laws and the agencies that administer them typically offer very little protection. They are usually highly sensitive to the economic interests of the businesses they "regulate," and far less so to the interests of consumers. The studies conclude that they become captives of these businesses,

[8]For an exposition of the pertinent evidence and theory, see David B. Truman, *The Governmental Process* New York: Knopf, 1951), Chs. 11–15.

rationalizing rate increases while ostensibly protecting the consumer.[9]

If the regulatory laws and commissions come close to reversing the economic function they are established to perform, why are they not abolished? They clearly serve political and psychological functions, both for politicians and for the mass public; politicians find that support for them or for strengthening them still brings in votes. Those who fear the concentration of economic power are reassured when the government responds to their anxiety by setting up an agency to keep prices fair or regulate product quality. It is rarely clear to consumers just which price ceilings and product standards protect them and which exploit them. In short, the issues are ambiguous and complex. This combination of ambiguity and widespread public anxiety is precisely the climate in which people are eager for reassurance that they are being protected, and therefore eager to believe that publicized governmental actions have the effects they are supposed to have.

In many other fields of governmental action the same conditions prevail; public policies are partly, perhaps often chiefly, symbolic in character. New civil rights laws reassure liberals that progress is being made. But policemen and courts can still ignore the laws or interpret them to permit the very denials of civil liberties they were intended to prevent. And many among the poor and minorities lack the knowledge and legal counsel to assert their rights. The civil rights laws serve as reassuring symbols for affluent liberals, whose own civil rights are fairly well protected. But for the black or radical who is beaten up after he is arrested on false charges, there is no ambiguity and no symbolic reassurance. For those who are worried about ecological catastrophe, the passage of laws against water and air pollution brings reassurance and a sense of victory. But again, it is usually far from clear that such laws provide the money or the capacity to act against influential industrial and governmental polluters. Nonetheless, such statutes and clean-up, paint-up, and anti-litter campaigns reassure many who would otherwise be aroused. Tokenism is a classic device for taking advantage of ambiguity and conveying a false sense of reassurance.

Reassurance: The Deprived Deserve It

Governmental or elitist actions also reassure people about worrisome conditions by instilling a conviction that the deprived deserve their fate and are personally benefitting from it. It is comforting to believe that those who are denied the good things of life suffer from personal pathology, deviance, or delinquency, and that they must be

[9]See Chapter 11 for references to these studies and an analysis of the impact of regulatory agencies on power centers.

controlled, guided, or incarcerated as a form of "correction" or "rehabilitation." Such a rehabilitative and psychiatric ideology has increasingly dominated the laws, rhetoric, and bureaucracies of all the public institutions that have the power to impose severe penalties upon the wayward and the dependent: prisons, mental hospitals, schools, and welfare departments. This is a "liberal" view, but its effects have been severely repressive, especially for the poor.[10] In this view, the person who steals is reacting not to poverty or alienating institutions but to psychopathic tendencies. The child who resists the school bureaucracy and its rules is "hostile" and must acquire "insight" by learning how inadequate he or she is. The person who is depressed or will not play conventional roles in life is a psychopath or schizophrenic who must be controlled, and possibly locked up, until he or she learns to behave in conventional ways. The welfare recipient is suffering less from lack of money than from personal inadequacies, for which he or she needs counseling and control. Because the staffs of these institutions enjoy wide latitude in defining deviance, the tendency is strong to perceive any behavior they dislike or that is uncommon in their own social circles as pathological and calling for "correction." Many people are unhappy or maladjusted; the problem lies in assuming that they themselves, rather than social institutions, are at fault.

For elites this way of defining the behavior of the poor and the unconventional has many advantages. It diverts attention from social and economic problems. It justifies repression of those who deviate from middle-class standards of behavior. It defines such repression as "rehabilitation," thereby enhancing the self-concepts of conservatives, liberals, professionals, and the administrative staff, who see themselves as altruistic. Finally, this ideology is accepted by many of the deprived themselves, making them docile and submissive. Docility and submission to authority are generously rewarded in schools, prisons, mental hospitals, and welfare agencies, while independence, insistence on personal dignity, and imagination are usually penalized, often severely.

The dissemination of the belief that the deprived are less deserving than others and must be controlled for their own good is a common and potent form of symbolic political action. Such labeling becomes a self-fulfilling prophecy, subtly or coercively requiring people to act

---

[10]Cf. *Struggle for Justice: A Report on Crime and Punishment in America,* prepared for the American Friends Service Committee (New York: Hill and Wang, 1971); August Hollingshead and Frederick C. Redlich, *Social Class and Mental Illness* (New York: Wiley, 1958); Gideon Sjoberg, Richard A. Brymer, and Buford Farris, "Bureaucracy and the Lower Class," in *The National Administrative System,* ed. Dean A. Yarwood (New York: Wiley, 1971), pp. 369–377; Aaron Cicourel and John I. Kitsuse, *The Educational Decision-Makers* (Indianapolis: Bobbs-Merrill, 1963).

as they are defined[11] and making it more likely that they will become recidivists—that they will revert to the behavior that got them into trouble in the first place. In a society in which economic and social rewards are very unevenly distributed, such social-psychological control supplements the use of coercive police powers and is more effective than naked coercion in maintaining quiescence. It minimizes resistance, maximizes support from the general public, and allays people's consciences.

The confusion between psychological help and political repression that is characteristic of the definition and treatment of "deviance" takes still another form, with even more far-reaching political consequences. The sociologists who study deviance have come to recognize that the person who is labeled an offender against morality or normality is sometimes more useful to society as a deviant (sick, delinquent, psychopathic) than as a nondeviant. This is because he serves as a reference point defining what behavior is acceptable and what is unacceptable and also making it clear that the deviant are segregated and penalized. Consequently, institutions that keep people deviant by labeling them and then forcing them to maintain a pathological role are doing what many demand that they do to preserve the common conventions.[12] Repression of a conspicuous group of people in the name of "help," "rehabilitation," or "correction" powerfully shapes the beliefs and behavior of mass publics. Here we have one of the most striking, significant, least obvious uses of political symbolism.

The Dynamics of Political Arousal

The Interpretation of Deprivation, Sacrifices, or Threats

For the student of mass political behavior, public quiescence and arousal are matters of central interest. We have just examined some of the ways large numbers of people are induced through governmental activity to remain quiescent, even though they may be deprived of much of the freedom, wealth, status, and dignity that others enjoy. Beliefs that arouse large numbers of people to militant action are also instilled by the use of symbols in ambiguous situations. We shall next examine the dynamics of the *escalation* of political conflict.

The symbols that promote quiescence create the widespread con-

[11]In addition to the studies cited in footnote 7, see Erving Goffman, *Asylums* (Garden City, N.Y.: Anchor, 1961).

[12]Lewis A. Coser, "Some Functions of Deviant Behavior and Normative Flexibility," *American Journal of Sociology*, Vol. 68 (September 1962), pp. 172–174; Robert A. Dentler and Kai T. Erikson, "The Functions of Deviance in Groups," *Social Problems*, Vol. 7 (1959), pp. 98–107.

viction that people are being protected from the threats they fear, or that those who behave unconventionally need to be restrained or punished for their own good and that of society. Protection of the public is the key symbolic theme in either case. The symbols that arouse mass publics to protest or violence evoke the opposite expectation— that a widely feared threat to their interests is growing more ominous, that those who behave unconventionally need to be restrained or punmust be resisted or, sometimes, exterminated. In the face of such a threat, people are led to set aside the lesser conflicts that ordinarily divide them and fight together against what they perceive as a more serious hazard to their common interests.

There might seem an easier explanation for political protest or militance—that those who are poor, oppressed, or trapped are driven to violence to try to better their condition. There is certainly a large element of truth in this view. It is often the poor and the manifestly oppressed who protest and engage in violence. But this is far from a complete explanation.

First, those who are most deprived are often quiescent. The occasional slave rebellions in the pre-Civil War South were atypical; the great majority of slaves lived out their lives without participating in any such movement. Only a small fraction of the poor ever engages in mass riots or join revolutionary movements. The "untouchables," the lowest Hindu caste in India, long accepted their miserable condition as a manifestation of the divine order. Clearly, deprivation alone does not produce or escalate political conflict.

Second, people who are relatively well off sometimes engage in a politics of protest and violence. Some affluent middle-class college students did so in massive numbers in the late 1960s. Revolutions typically occur after there has been substantial improvement in the condition of the deprived classes, not when they are most destitute.

Denial of the things people value is beyond question a major reason for political conflict; but the *meaning* of such deprivation is also critical. Is it seen as natural or divinely ordained or as unnecessary and unfairly imposed by the privileged? Is it seen as temporary, stable, or increasing? These *interpretations* of deprivation are influenced by symbols, and they are critical in influencing behavior.

How do people come to believe it necessary to resort to protest or violence outside the channels of conventional politics? How do large groups come to believe that those they fear are unrestrained by established governmental routines and represent an escalating threat that must be met by escalating counteraction?

The key condition is evidence that a group believed to be hostile is winning wider public support and preparing to attack, or to intensify attacks already in progress. Nothing helps American "hawks" win support for larger military budgets and incursions into foreign countries as much as allegations that hawkish sentiment and action is growing in foreign countries we believe are hostile. It is therefore hardly surprising that hawks in rival countries are careful to observe, publicize, and exaggerate the militaristic actions and rhetoric of their adversaries. As they observe and exaggerate their enemies' alleged escalations, rival hawks serve each others' interests; they win added public support for their opponents as well as for themselves. Nothing so powerfully contributes to antipolice sentiment and behavior in American cities or on college campuses as allegations or evidence that police are arbitrarily harassing, beating, or arresting the poor, black, or ideologically unconventional. Political conflicts of these kinds engage more people and greater passions on both sides as each adversary group comes to see the other as its enemy, bent upon its repression or extermination. A new and sudden step-up in harassment typically sets off widespread fear and support for escalation on the other side. This is the general pattern of escalating political conflict on any issue.

The Role of Myths in Escalating Conflicts

Another way to see this process is to recognize that people caught up in an escalating political conflict are likely to fit what they hear and see about it into a mythic form. A myth is a widely held belief based upon social cues rather than upon observation of the world. Myth subtly but powerfully shapes the meaning of events. Myths about political conflict fall into a small number of archetypical patterns. One is the myth of an enemy plotting against one's own group or nation and who therefore must be suppressed or exterminated. Another is the myth of a leader-hero-savior who represents a social order ordained by God or sanctioned by the people; he must be followed and obeyed, and sacrifice or suffering on his behalf are seen as ennobling.

In the modern world, people hardly need to be reminded that political conflicts often escalate to the point that the costs and suffering are extremely high. Political history is largely a chronicle of mass violence in the form of wars, massacres, revolutions, and genocides. To understand how men and women become willing, even anxious, to kill and die for political causes, we must examine some perceptions of the enemy and the self that recur whenever political conflict is escalating.

A central feature of this process is the personification of adversaries. Hostile or potentially hostile groups or nations are not seen as internally divided, though this is bound to be true of every formal organization or nation. Instead, the enemy is seen as monolithic and resolute: the loyal followers of the alien leader or oligarchy, who symbolize evil. This view simplifies the situation, substituting a vision of malevolence for the more realistic recognition that there is a large measure of drift in policymaking, that people change their positions from time to time, and that political leaders must respond to contending groups within their own countries in order to retain their positions. Simplification promotes solidarity against the enemy and eagerness to escalate attacks upon him.

Those who participate in an escalating political conflict develop a characteristic view both of themselves and of their adversaries. Believing that they must defend their lives, their honor, their most vital interests, or their country against hostile outsiders, they take on a well-defined political role: fighter in a noble cause. Such a role gives their lives meaning; it is cherished and not easily abandoned, even in the face of evidence casting doubt upon its validity. The cause, and the belief in its righteousness or necessity, come to be part of the person's self-concept, reinforcing his or her zeal and willingness to sacrifice, hurt, or kill. Political beliefs, social movements, and self-concepts are not as distinct in real life as they are in textbooks. When a person becomes emotionally involved in a political cause, he takes on a particular all-encompassing view of his own identity and political role.

In several important ways, then, people involved in escalating political conflict develop particular beliefs and perceptions of the world and of themselves that may distort reality; they hold such beliefs tenaciously and emotionally, and interpret new developments so as to be consistent with and reinforce them.

Symbols, Organization, and Ritualization

The Meaning of Events

The central theme of symbolic analysis of politics is the gap between perceptions or beliefs on the one hand and actual gains or losses in money, power, status, or tangible goods on the other. As political conflict escalates, this gap becomes wider.

The winner of symbolic victories may not be the winner of tangible victories. As an international war or "police action" escalates, the low- and middle-income citizens of the country that is victorious on the battlefield may find their taxes far more burdensome, their lives more regimented, their sons and relatives killed or wounded. But they are "the winners." Defenders of civil rights who win a court decision guaranteeing that accused persons be provided with lawyers and information about their procedural rights may later learn that actual practices in the stationhouse have changed little or not at all. Citizens whose outcries against arbitrary rate increases and poor service by a public utility bring about legislation to protect consumer interests have won a symbolic victory. But this form of political triumph rarely brings lower rates or better service for long. The regulatory agency often makes it easier to raise rates.

Other disparities between perceived and real changes in policy consequences become evident as political conflict widens and intensifies. Benefits often come to be perceived as deprivations and vice versa. As international conflict grows hotter, the armed forces gain larger appropriations for weapons, new powers to draft soldiers, higher status, and more influence in governmental decisions. It is the poor and the lower middle class whose sons are chiefly drafted to fight, whose incomes are disproportionately taxed, and whose influence in governmental decisions is least. Rather than appearing as real benefits and losses for a specific group of people, however, these changes are perceived and publicized as "costs" of defense, sacrifices the nation as a whole must valiantly assume to combat its enemies.

Even the identification of enemies and allies becomes confused and uncertain and may fail to correspond with observable reality as conflict escalates. Such confusion is not accidental, but a consistent and systematic aspect of political conflict. It is important to create perceptions that induce people to fight, and to sacrifice if necessary, to serve a noble cause and defeat an evil one. In international conflict, the belief is fostered that the country is uniting to defeat a common enemy. In fact, there are always internal divisions about whether and how seriously the fight should be waged and whether the enemy is really harmful or malevolent. These internal divisions partly reflect the differences in interest noted above. Escalation means that the more hawkish or militant groups are winning more support than their dovish rivals. As already noted, hawkish groups win support for their foreign counterparts as they win it for themselves, though this tacit cooperation is systematically masked by belief in the implacable hostility of the countries.

As civil rights conflict escalates, the same ambiguities appear. Here the symbolic conflict is between believers in "the rights of minorities" and believers in "law and order." These symbols unite people on both sides and bolster political support. At the same time, there are tangible gains and losses for both supporters and opponents of civil rights that do not correspond to the symbolic definition of the situation. As civil rights conflict grows more intense, the more militant groups on both sides win tangible benefits and the less militant ones lose. White supremacists and civil libertarians win followings and money as public opinion is polarized. The police get larger appropriations for men and weapons, higher status and more influence for top police officials, and greater authority over others. The more militant black groups, like the Black Panthers, gain moral and financial support at the expense of the Urban League and white liberals. To make this point is to recognize both that there is competition for tangible benefits within groups of symbolic allies and that escalation benefits militants and détente benefits moderates and compromisers. There is, then, a systematic link between symbol and fact, but it is a link that conceals or distorts the facts and thus can evoke political support for self-defeating policies.

The Role of Organizations in Ritualization

There are other ways in which the formation of organizations sometimes creates beliefs that do not conform to fact. When the discontented or the relatively powerless organize, it is commonly believed that they have become more powerful and can wrest new benefits from the establishment. To the extent that organization (of a labor union, for example) allows new sanctions to be imposed—as in strikes, boycotts, or threats to property—this belief is justified. Concessions are made in order to keep the peace and protect privileges from more serious encroachment. But once a routine procedure for new concessions is established, ongoing organizations typically take on quite a different function—one that is largely symbolic. They continue to make demands on behalf of their rank-and-file members, and sometimes strike or engage in other kinds of conflict. However, such conflict is largely ritualistic, in the sense that it serves primarily to justify the outcomes ultimately agreed upon by the leaders rather than to force major concessions or threaten the existence of adversaries. Ritualized political conflict convinces followers that their leaders are working zealously on their behalf and that the obstacles are formidable. Such conflict both legitimizes the leaders and justifies acceptance of minor gains, and sometimes even of losses.

Most political conflict is ritualistic. It is held within narrow limits, carried on through mutually accepted routines, and serves more to justify outcomes than to determine them, for they are largely predetermined by long-standing differences in bargaining resources. Election campaigns (especially in a two-party system), the procedures of regulatory administrative agencies, and most international arms and trade negotiations are examples of such ritualized conflict. To the minor degree that they make policy changes, their functions are generally recognized and reported in the news. Insofar as they serve to win wide public acceptance of leaders and of policy outcomes (i.e., serve symbolic functions), news reports typically miss their significance.

Political leaders retain followings (which is, of course, what makes them leaders) through a number of devices that are basically symbolic in character. We ordinarily think of a leader as a person who points the way for others through unusual abilities, wisdom, courage, or force of personality. But leaders can often retain their positions, whether or not they have these qualities, by creating in their followers a belief in their ability to cope. We have just seen that ritualized conflict creates such a belief. Other common political actions do so as well. The leader who is resolute and forceful, and seems confident in a situation that makes most people anxious and uncertain, reassures the public and creates a following, whether his actions succeed or fail. Those who are bewildered want very much to believe that their political leaders can cope. President Kennedy's seemingly resolute action in the disastrous Bay of Pigs invasion of Cuba in 1961 and President Nixon's dramatic though inconclusive visits to China and Russia in 1971 and 1972 illustrate the point. Survey data show that presidential popularity consistently rises after such dramatic actions, whether they succeed, fail, or are ambiguous in their consequences. Clearly, it is less the leader's skills, courage, and effectiveness that bring political success in such cases than his or her dramaturgy and the anxieties of mass publics.

Sometimes "leaders" are created chiefly by enemies of the groups they are ostensibly leading. This has been quite consistently true of crowds of discontented people who riot. The incident that sets off a riot is often a police action that is regarded as brutal, unfair, or racist. Or it may be some other event symbolizing oppression of a disadvantaged group. In any case, students of riots agree that they are typically unplanned reactions to an incident of this sort, not the result of plotting or agitation. Only people who are already discontented will riot; rebel leaders cannot create a following among a satisfied population.

Law enforcement officials and the privileged who feel threatened tend to look for riot leaders to blame for these situations. The myth of the outside agitator creating disorder among an otherwise happy or passive population is reassuring to those who oppose change; such a myth crops up regularly, regardless of the facts. Police therefore perceive as "ringleaders" rioters who are especially lively or visible, even if they have not "led" anybody. Even more commonly, the police pick out well-known people who have been active in earlier protest movements. In a very realistic sense, then, it is the opponents of the rioters who create their leaders; but the rioters themselves are also likely to feel reassured if they believe they have some leadership. In spontaneous protest and riot situations, therefore, leaders serve a political function for police and elites, evoking public support for punishing "ringleaders" or "agitators." They also serve a symbolic or expressive function for the protesters. This, again, is a rather common political situation in which appearances and beliefs diverge from reality. Symbolic functions become the important ones.

The Uses of Enemies

The choice or creation of political enemies is often a symbolic way of widening political support. Some political enemies are real enough. The migrant fruitpicker whose employer houses him and his family in a shanty without sanitary facilities, underpays him, and over-charges him for necessities has a real adversary. So does the prisoner arbitrarily thrown into solitary confinement because he displeases a guard. Jews in Nazi Germany had little doubt about who their enemies were. Those who have real enemies benefit from their elimination or loss of power.

There is another kind of political enemy, however, who *helps* his adversary politically by giving him a purpose, a cherished self-concept, and political support. For the Nazis, the Jews served as a politically useful enemy. Hitler portrayed the Jews to the German people as the satanic force he had to fight to preserve the country. Without this enemy to arouse their passions, minimize their internal differences, and unite them behind him, Hitler could hardly have achieved power or maintained it as long as he did. The Americans, the Russians, and the Chinese served similar functions for each other during the Cold War years. Without native radical movements, the FBI would win far less public support and far lower budgetary appropriations. In cases like these, the enemy is partly or entirely symbolic. He looks the same to his adversaries as real enemies do; but he helps them as much or more than he hurts them. It is in the interest of such enemies not to eliminate each other, but to perpetuate each other—and to create a popular belief in the enemy's strength and aggressive plans rather than his vulnerability.

Belief in real enemies is based upon empirical evidence and is rela-tively noncontroversial. Belief in symbolic enemies is based upon rumor and social suggestion and is often highly controversial. Such beliefs tell us more about the believers than about the ostensible enemies, for they bring political and social benefits for those who hold them. For this reason, they are not easily challenged by facts incompatible with them. A group that is eager to marshall political support for its cause is likely to define as the enemy whatever adver-sary that will most potently create and mobilize allies. A foreign coun-try long regarded as hostile, heretics among true believers, anarchists in the early decades of the twentieth century, Communists after the Russian Revolution, capitalists in the Soviet Union, the yellow peril, blacks—all have served such a political purpose.

Groups perceived as the enemy are consistently defined in ways that dehumanize them. They are seen as alien, strange, or subhuman, or a single feature or alleged mode of behavior is emphasized: their

color, alleged lack of intelligence (or uncanny shrewdness), clannish-
ness, and so on. This is politically effective because people can deliberately hurt or kill only those they do not acknowledge as sharing
their own human qualities.

Summary: The Significance of Symbolism

Politics consists only in part of giving and denying people the
things they want. Equally important is the generation of beliefs and
perceptions through political language and actions. Because this phenomenon shapes support and opposition to political causes, policies,
and candidates, it is basic to all governmental value allocations. And
because it depends upon social psychological processes, it is doubtless
more systematic and consistent in its functioning than is the allocation of tangible values through policymaking.

The publicized actions and rhetoric of governmental officials not
only reflect what people want but also influence how people think
and what they believe. The symbolic function of politics is particularly
important in ambiguous situations—when the facts are uncertain. Its
result is that most dramatic and controversial acts of government
are often perceived as more, less, or very different from their
actual nature. A tax program that enables many of the affluent to
escape taxes is perceived as taxation according to ability to pay. An
administrative program that enables businessmen to raise prices is
perceived as protection for the consumer. A foreign civil war is perceived as the spearhead of worldwide communist encroachment. A
welfare program that keeps families at the subsistence level, humili-
ates them, and requires them to live according to the middle-class
norms of their caseworker is perceived as overly generous, compassionate, or as coddling the lazy. Such perverse distortions are not
inevitable, and many govermental programs avoid them. The important thing is that they can and do occur frequently and for
systematic reasons.

They occur because people look to politics not only for realistic
understanding and control over their lives but also for reassurance
that their fears are unfounded and their own political roles are justified and noble. They also occur because the language we speak and the
process by which our minds accept or screen out information lend
themselves both to remarkable creative accomplishments and to
illusion and misperception. To recognize these dangers is not to grow
cynical or to despair. It is a necessary step toward the realistic assessment of politics and an attempt to avoid its pitfalls and realize its
promise. No analysis of the prospects for political change can fail
to take these processes into account.

Chapter 19

This chapter addresses the crucial questions about the future of the American political system. Some are merely analytical-descriptive: Will there be change? What kind? Others are evaluative-prescriptive: What kind of change *should* there be? How may such change come about? These questions force us to develop a very crude theory of how political change does and can occur, given the current political power structure and associated social and economic order of the

Political Change

United States. Applying this general framework to circumstances as they develop, we can generate some sense of the types of change that are most likely and ways to bring about changes we may consider desirable.

We shall first construct a crude theory describing when and how change occurs, and what determines the form such change will take. In practical terms, our theory will be little more than a set of analytical categories that facilitate thinking about change. In some respects, however, we shall be specifying factors and relationships among factors that make change of various kinds *more*, or *less* likely. Then we shall apply this framework to contemporary events in the United States, in an effort to assess the probable outcome of the forces now operating in this country. Finally, we shall suggest what seem to us to be some imperatives for the process of change in the United States. Once again, readers are reminded that our analyses are necessarily permeated with our value perspective, and that they should evaluate our work in the light of their own critical judgment.

Analysis of Political Change: A Framework

When is change likely to occur in the structure or policies of the American political system? What circumstances determine the form

it will take? Our approach is based on the premise that certain preconditions cause pressure to be exerted on the fundamental aspects
of the political system. If they are strong enough, modifications of
both mass and elite behavior follow, and—depending on the particular configuration of factors, forces, behavior, and events—political
change of various kinds and directions then occurs. We shall take
up three areas in which the preconditions of change are likely to be
generated and then identify some of the major factors that determine
the degree and kind of effect such conditions will have on the political
system. We shall then consider four alternative types of political
change possible in the United States, and the prerequisites and processes associated with each of them.

The Preconditions of Change

In one sense, political change is continuous. Governing elites regularly make adjustments in established policies, or undertake major
policy initiatives, in response to changing conditions. Such changes
may and often do result in alterations in domestic economic or social
relationships or in international affairs. One example is the emergence
of Cold War foreign policy and the related evolution of massive
defense and space programs. Another is the decision to institute a
"war on poverty." But these changes we term *marginal* because their
essential effect is to defend and promote the established economic
and political structures and the existing patterns of distribution of
wealth and status within the society. We shall reserve the term *fundamental* for those instances of substantial alteration in the economic
or political power structures or in key governmental policies bearing
upon distribution of wealth and status. Fundamental change is drastic
in character; it may come about, however, through either violent or
relatively peaceful means.

Our approach to the analysis of political change should permit us
to distinguish between these two types of change, and acknowledge
the relative improbability of the more fundamental type. *Marginal*
change is frequent, requiring few preconditions. But *fundamental*
change is infrequent and unlikely to occur without severe pressures
on the central concerns of politics that are widely perceived and
acted upon by masses and elites alike. We would expect fundamental
change only when the preconditions begin to disrupt or seriously
threaten the basic organization and operation of the economy, the
class structure, existing control over the uses of government's coercive powers, or the established patterns of distribution of wealth and
status. The more preconditions generate such effects, the more probable are changes in the structure and uses of political power, the
character of political institutions, and the key policies of government.
In short, the severity of dislocations in closely related policy areas

determines the probability of fundamental *political* change; we shall consider three such areas in the order of their importance for political change.

1. *Changes in the level and distribution of economic prosperity.* The most powerful source of pressure on the political system is the state of the economic system, for the obvious reason that it affects first the very survival, and then other avidly sought goals, of people in social settings. Despite its image of stability, American politics has always been highly sensitive to fluctuations and dislocations in the economy. Integration between the two systems is so intimate that political causes are alleged, and political remedies sought, for most perceived deprivations. When the economy is stable and unemployment limited, the political system is normally free of strain even though distribution of economic rewards is very unequal. But if either inflation or recession occurs, pressures begin to build up and distribution differences become salient and provocative. If a depression develops, pressures may become truly explosive.

Two possibilities deserve mention as sources of pressures that would promote fundamental political change. One, suggested by the "technological unfreedom" analysis, is that the economy can produce a vast oversupply of consumer goods and technological comfort, but that this will, nevertheless, generate a substantial level of discontent. This discontent will flow from the failure to produce the public goods —hospitals, recreation facilities, environmental amenities—necessary to human health, safety, and welfare. Consumer goods, material comfort, and leisure time signify little if the air and water are too polluted, the roads and cities too crowded, and the conditions of life generally too unsatisfying for human enjoyment. Or people may assume that with long-sought material goods finally within reach they should feel satisfaction, but instead experience frustration and unfulfillment. In either case, a severe reaction might set in. It could take the form of dissatisfaction with the standards and priorities of an economic order that can produce vast quantities of soon-obsolete consumer goods but not the public goods and human amenities that people increasingly seek. Or it could take the less rational form of a prolonged and system-changing assault upon those people generally perceived as presenting obstacles to the "good life"—under present circumstances, probably students, minorities, and the militant poor.

The other possible source of economic dislocation is serious depression. The economic system appears much more mechanistic in the interpretations and theories of economists than is actually the case. Neither the proverbial unseen hand of Adam Smith, nor even the manageable equilibriums of John Maynard Keynes, but the human judgments of many more or less "rational" men and women, shape the workings of the economic system. Their wants and desires and expectations, and particularly their judgments about the shape of the future, animate this system. If their sense of unfulfillment, or their perception of external events, or their pessimistic image of the future, should draw them away from profit-maximizing behavior, or from confidence in future profit-making opportunities, or from a high level of buying, the whole elaborate but fragile and interdependent structure of the economic system could come crashing down.

This is why boosterism is such a vital element of American business ideology, and the gambling, risk-taking entrepreneur such a heroic figure in our folk myths, in spite of the fact that real entrepreneurs take great care to act only when their risks are minimal. The great danger is that savings will exceed investments, and large money surpluses find no job-creating outlets. Stagnation and joblessness, and then depression, might well follow. Thus, continued prosperity and growth rest heavily on human factors, and more specifically, on optimistic assumptions about the future. In the absence of such faith (or the presence of pessimistic judgments), the result could still be a depression—despite all governmental efforts. And a depression creates an entirely new and highly unstable political situation.

It does so by seriously depriving very large numbers of people of things they want and need. At the same time, a social scientist must be wary of assuming that severe deprivation *inevitably* produces serious social instability, protest, or rebellion. As we have repeatedly noted, government not only influences what people get, but also what they expect to receive. It is one of the most awesome powers of modern governments that they have often been able to keep severely deprived people quiescent by creating in them a belief that their sufferings are in a noble cause or only temporary; that even during a major depression, prosperity is "just around the corner."

2. *Social tensions and underlying value changes.* A second— and potentially quite independent—major source of pressure on the political system is the rise of tensions and open conflict between major segments of the society. Such conflict is often associated with, and normally exacerbated by, rapid changes in the level and distribution of economic prosperity or other major technological changes. But it can also be generated by noneconomic factors and culminate in deep and widely felt animosities even during periods of economic affluence.

The tensions most likely to cause the heaviest pressure on the political system link current perceptions of deprivation to long-standing differences between segments of the population. If several such grievances overlap, so that the same people view themselves as constant losers despite their right to (and capacity to achieve) their goals, the potential for serious conflict is high. For such people, the legitimacy of the established economic and political order may be called into question. They may feel released from normal obligations to obey, and justified in the use of violence to gain their ends. Such action, of course, often promotes increased resistance on the part of their natural antagonists within the society. As polarization progresses, both sides become more prone to employ the most basic forms of power against the other.

Deep social divisions exist within the United States, rhetorical calls for solidarity and assertions of consensus notwithstanding. The most visible, long-standing and deeply-rooted of these is race. The extent to which racism is entrenched in the psychological makeup, political values, and institutional practices of white America may never be fully understood. But white-black/brown/red tensions escalate with every new assertion of the right to equal status. Should black militancy continue to rise, supported by similar claims by brown and red minorities, and white intransigence assume ever more peremptory forms, widespread open conflict seems inevitable. The urban ghetto riots of 1965-1968 may be only the beginning. Nor could the political system long endure such outbreaks without moving either to erase the causes or thoroughly suppress the symptoms. In either case, a substantially different political system would emerge.

More likely to produce fundamental change than the tensions created by the demands of relatively small and containable racial minorities are those grounded in class consciousness. Suppose most blue-collar workers and other wage-earners—black and white, men and women—should come to perceive themselves as jointly exploited for the benefit of a small group of owners and managers who already hold the vast majority of the nation's wealth. Justice, in their eyes, entitles them to a much larger share of the economic product. Their numbers alone would assure great impact, if their power could be organized and applied—though that is difficult. The idea of such a movement will seem undesirable or un-American to people who have been socialized into the dominant American political ideology. In the past, such class consciousness and assertiveness have also been discouraged by legal impediments, economic sanctions, and physical intimidation or coercion. Though forced to extreme measures, labor unions finally won the right to organize and bargain collectively during the Great Depression of the 1930s. Since then, class consciousness appears to have receded or been diverted by images of affluence, war, or racial tensions. If consciousness and militancy were revived, however, the potential pressure on the political system would be severe.

Other sources of tensions exist, though none compare with race and class as long-established antagonisms with continuing raw edges. Religious, regional, and rural-urban conflicts remain real, and could exert pressure on the political system if particular issues again raise perceptions of deprivation or create frustrations. But new forms of tension unrooted in old divisions also exist. One is the general lack of a sense of personal satisfaction that seems to pervade the United States in the 1970s. Despite such achievements as moon landings and the highest standard of living in the world, many observers see Americans as lacking contentment, self-confidence, and a sense of purpose. Work seems to be providing a less meaningful rationale for life, and to be less a source of pride, than in previous decades. Individuals seem to be aware of their apparent powerlessness to affect the course of events, or even matters that touch their own lives. Their alienation takes many forms, from compulsive TV-watching in the isolation of their own homes to apathy and cynicism. The hopes of millions were attached emotionally to charismatic political figures, only to be crushed in a staggering series of assassinations. A steadily rising crime rate, vast urban problems, and environmental decay have combined with these developments to create near-hysteria in many who look seriously at the problems of the society.

Perhaps the most striking new tension-producing feature of American social life, however, is the new set of values developed by young people. Contrasting sharply with the materialism, nationalism, conformity, and support for the economic and political *status quo* of their elders, the new value system has been termed a "counterculture." Its priorities are egalitarianism, humanism, participation, and self-fulfillment through a wide variety of individual activities. These priorities are acted out in various ways: many college students became heavily involved first in civil rights and then in anti-Vietnam War activities, some in highly militant forms; others simply dropped out of what they saw as a competitive, materialistic society and adopted communal or hippie life styles. A growing women's liberation movement is pressing for substantial change, reaching deep into the personal relationships and public roles of men and women, and potentially into basic societal values and assumptions.

3. *International tensions and events.*   The obvious interdependence of international and domestic affairs means that events overseas often spark economic and social tensions at home. Such developments may combine with ongoing economic and social trends or may generate wholly new types of tensions. They may serve either to generate massive new pressure on the political system or to deflect already powerful pressures away from it.

The most obvious source of restructured domestic relationships is war, or the immediately perceived threat of war. A relatively small, festering war in a distant place, such as Korea or Vietnam, is likely to create new social divisions or exacerbate tension between left and right; at the same time it promotes economic well-being and then inflation. A full-scale war, or even a small war close to home, tends to draw wider support and to eclipse all other issues that might otherwise divide people. More complex effects derive from the threat of armed conflict and from a posture and ideology that supports constant readiness for nuclear war, such as the Cold War, anticommunism, and defense expenditures of the 1950s and 1960s. This creates underlying tensions while it legitimates many actions, and diverts attention from others, in the name of patriotism and national security.

But war and the threat of war are only the most obvious sources of disruptive tensions and the prospect of political change. Of more basic causal significance are the economic circumstances of both the developed and undeveloped nations of the world. Depression or severe inflation in industrialized nations have important consequences for the American economy. Further, the availability of investment opportunities, raw materials, and markets in the Third World are of considerable importance to the stability and growth of the American economy. Sharp changes overseas—such as nationalization or severance of trade relations—may reverberate throughout segments of the U.S. economy and induce diplomatic pressure or military intervention to restore American advantage. International developments of a noneconomic nature may also have an impact on American life. The increasing militancy among American blacks during the 1950s and 1960s was due in part to the example of newly independent African and Asian nations, whose nonwhite leaders acquired power and led their countries effectively and with great pride.

This brief analysis of some sources of intrasocietal tensions and conflicts sufficient to raise the possibility of fundamental political change is merely illustrative, and not comprehensive. No doubt there are many other causes of pressure on the political system. But our point is that substantial pressures must be generated from some source before established econopolitical relationships are likely to undergo change of a fundamental kind. If there are several such pressures, and if they converge or overlap in such a way as to be mutually reinforcing (rather than pitting different groups against each other in a self-canceling and immobilizing fashion), the prospect of such change is greater. Any of the pressures we have touched upon may be merely temporary, or one may cancel out another, or all of them may be perceived as politically irrelevant, and thus not eventuate in change. But without them, or their equivalent, we see little prospect of any fundamental change.

The Political Impact of the Preconditions of Change

Preconditions are thus necessary, but not sufficient, causes of fundamental change. What is crucial for our purposes is the manner in which such preconditions become translated into effects on the political system. Multiple sources of tension clearly exist, some of them deep and others worsening. But there have always been some such tensions, and fundamental political change has not occurred in more than a century. Depressions and severe social tensions have given rise to militant parties and movements seeking fundamental change, but they have failed to achieve their goals. Social tensions must not only produce converging and mutually reinforcing percep- tions of deprivation, but must be translated into politics in particular ways before they are likely to generate fundamental change. We may identify several prerequisites that, if fulfilled, will make fundamental change more likely. Again, we do not see it as necessary or inevitable that all of these political effects be present in order for change to take place, but the prospect of change will increase as each is fulfilled. We shall frame the conditions as three basic questions.

(a) How fully do existing dislocations, tensions, and underlying value changes disrupt established patterns of distribution and detach masses of people from their previous commitments to the dominant political values, ideology, and behavior? *For fundamental change to occur, there must be a decrease in the supportive attitudes of people toward their government; its legitimacy must be eroded, and a vacuum of authority develop.* This is a long-term process, of course, and must be deep-seated enough to counteract the best efforts of the major socializing and interpreting agents (schools, mass media) of the exist- ing system. It also requires visible, legitimate leadership; but leaders are not likely to arise until the trend of popular change is already under way. Thus, the impetus toward change in values must be self- generated. Social and economic conditions, international events, or personal experience must create perceptions of serious personal deprivation that call into question the legitimacy or propriety of estab- lished political values and practices. Such perceptions of contradic- tion or unworkability in the present system must be strong enough to survive such explanations and diversions as the alleged failure of in- dividuals, racial antagonisms, symbolic appeals, anticommunism, and so forth. Not just one or two such perceptions, but an extended and cumulating series of them, are probably necessary to drive people to develop new priorities for political action and seriously consider al- ternatives to the present system. Without deep doubts about estab- lished values, at the very least, proposals or movements for change will be ignored, dismissed, or resisted by the very people who con- stitute an almost irreplaceable component in the process.

(b) How much (and what kind of) power can be mobilized by change-oriented elements within the society, and how does such power relate to elites' power resources? Almost by definition, those who feel personal deprivation in such a way as to commit themselves to fundamental change do not possess large or immediately effective power resources. A few wealthy, well-connected, or strategically-located persons may identify with the causes of the deprived, and serve as leaders or key supporters. But most persons with access to major power resources are probably either already members of the establishment or at least persuaded that the basic structures and values are acceptable and that only marginal change is required. *Fundamental change thus normally requires the mobilization of the latent power resources of the currently powerless.* Numbers become crucial. Regardless of how slight their individual power, if a substantial segment of the population becomes committed to unified action in support of fundamental change, their joint power is immense. Strategic location within the economy or society is also important. Effective strikes in vital service-providing fields (governmental functions, transportation, etc.) greatly multiply the power of relatively small numbers of people.

But the most crucial factors for mobilizing the powerless into a potentially successful force for fundamental change are *organization* and *communication.* Organization means the emergence of groups of people whose commitment is so complete that they subordinate all economic and other personal goals, and all factional interests of their particular group, single-minded efforts to awaken numbers of other people to the need for (and prepare them for the action necessary to) achieving fundamental change. Organization-building requires a supportive environment for group members, so that their commitments are regularly reinforced and new members are recruited. And it requires substantial agreement on (or at least only limited conflict over) the basic strategy by which change is to be accomplished.

The need for communication has both internal and external dimensions. There must be regular exchanges of information and effective coordination between the geographically (and perhaps in some ways ideologically) separated units of the growing organization. And there must be communication between the organizers and the people whom they seek to mobilize. Unless numbers of people can be brought to the support of the organized movement, or at least detached from their support for established ways and thus neutralized, the movement has little real prospect of success. It will either gradually become aware of its failure and dissipate, or be forced into isolation and resort to indiscriminate terrorism or other desperate and self-destructive measures.

The task of mobilizing numbers of people into a unified, change-seeking force is very difficult. Previously inert individuals must acquire a sense of political efficacy and hope strong enough to impel them to action. Various means of attracting attention and reaching people in terms they can readily identify with and understand are necessary: action, deliberate self-sacrifice, rational persuasion, and blatant propaganda all play parts at various stages. As organization progresses, a series of minor skirmishes in which victories over established institutions or procedures are scored probably contributes to awakening self-confidence and determination. The bases of solidarity among people must be developed over time and against a background of deep-seated suspicions, divisions, prejudices and misunderstandings. Without the development of such organization and its promotion of broad support, fundamental change seems unlikely.

(c) How do established elites react to forces seeking fundamental change? Because they hold the initiative and have a responsibility to act in response to events, existing elites' behavior plays a vital role in the evolving process of change. They may act to promote divisions and hostility within the population, and/or to isolate and discredit groups seeking change, thereby making mobilization difficult or impossible. They may appear to institute, or actually make, marginal changes in policies in order to reduce popular perceptions of deprivation, thereby undercutting (or, in some circumstances, promoting) the thrust toward fundamental change. They may introduce wholly new issues or appeals, such as space exploration, war, or the threat of war which redirect attention or mobilize support for the existing order. They may also engage in active repression of change-seeking groups. If done with sophistication and restraint, this may help to solve their problem. But if crudely handled, it can provide the movement with substantial new constituencies.

In each case, it is clear that elite response shapes the opportunities and problems of change-seekers. What determines how elites act? In part it depends on which segment of the establishment is currently dominant within the executive branch. The Eastern upper class, the managers of the great corporations, and welfare-state liberals tend to react with modest policy changes, deflection, and sophisticated repression. Those newer to real power and more steeped in the ideology than the practice of American government, such as the Southern and Southwestern individualist-conservatives, are more likely to react by exaggerating the threat, appealing to popular fears and prejudices, and escalating open repression.

Neither set of behaviors by itself determines whether the movement for change will *gain* or *lose* momentum as a result. What it does, essentially, is to shape the degree of polarization in the society. When accompanied by the disaffection, tensions, and loss of legitimacy described earlier, and when there is a cohesive organization ready to act with substantial popular support, a highly polarized situation ripe for fundamental change may be created. What is then required is a spark —the fortuitous event that creates the opportunity for the movement to cross the threshold to real and sweeping impact of some kind. Then, if the existing organization has the skill (or the sheer determination, which may often overcome lack of skill or the absence of some important conditions) to apply its power decisively, the whole structure of power may be sharply altered. Again, this need not be through violent revolution, although violence undoubtedly plays a major role in promoting change of a fundamental nature. Established elites are quite unlikely to release their grip on governmental power unless convinced that it is necessary or inevitable that they do so. Often the escalation of the stakes that results from serious and repeated mutual violence has created such conviction. A relatively low level of violence, if sustained amid credible threats of more to follow, has sometimes induced elites to acquiesce in, or even to institute, major changes sought in a relatively peaceful manner. Once the process of change has reached this point, developments are no longer even crudely predictable. The outcome depends on such factors as key individuals' personalities and chance.

We can summarize these general observations about the politics of change in terms consistent with our earlier speculations about the difference between top-down and bottom-up processes of change. Thus far, we have been speaking chiefly of fundamental change and its prerequisites. This is because marginal change is almost always possible, at the almost exclusive option of establishment elites. To be sure, there are limits within which such elites must select their policy options, but these are chiefly of their own making and only partially subject to popular preferences. In a fundamental change situation, however, elites have lost their predominance. They are either fragmented and beginning to contend with each other, or struggling to maintain themselves against the demands of a newly powerful antagonist arising from outside their ambit. Clearly, we are dealing with two contrasting levels and processes of change. Change initiated from the top down by established elites occurs because of their perceptions and needs, or perhaps through gradual changes in their membership. Such changes are likely to affect only minor policies, well within the established power systems—or, in short, to be *incremental* changes. Only when a thrust from outside the establishment (i.e., from below) begins to have an impact on elites' power and status does fundamental change become a possibility. The agency of change must be created by the previously powerless, and must build upon deep social tensions and/or value changes to force its way into the political arena. The more such thrust is generated from below, the more the system itself is the target, and the more likely is fundamental change.

Levels and Directions of Change: Four Scenarios

We have said nothing about the *direction* that either marginal or fundamental change may take. Clearly, either may go to the *left*, in the direction of wider distribution of power, wealth, and status within the society, or to the *right,* toward rigid insistence upon the *status quo* or even narrower and more restrictive distribution. A nearly infinite number of combinations of possible factors in the total political context could give rise to either marginal or fundamental changes in either direction. We shall reduce this wide range of possibilities to four, briefly describe the features of each, and try to specify what determines the direction they may take. In what seems to us their order of probability in the United States today, we shall discuss (1) erratic marginal change—perpetuation of the *status quo* with slight changes vacillating left and right but tending ultimately to an integrated and corporate-dominated econopolitical system; (2) reactionary marginal change culminating relatively promptly (in, say, 10 to 15 years) in near-fundamental change to a system best termed totalitarian electoral fascism; (3) sustained marginal change with a reformist emphasis, resulting after a longer time span in something like welfare-state capitalism; (4) revolution, generated by a left-oriented movement, which would result in a more rapid arrival of *either* fascism *or* socialism, depending upon unforeseeable circumstances developing as the revolution took place. In each case, we shall highlight those conditions and processes that our previous analysis suggests are of key importance.

1. *Erratic marginal change, culminating in a corporate-dominated system.* This scenario assumes that no major depression develops. Race conflict remains salient but more or less effectively suppressed through the isolation and containment of black/brown/red peoples. Class consciousness remains low and radicalism-populism proves to be a minor and transitory phenomenon, genuinely rejected by workers and middle class alike and ultimately dissipated or suppressed. Threats of nuclear war continue but no major land war is fought outside the western hemisphere. In short, basic conditions create no major new dislocations and leave established elites entrenched and with full capacity to orchestrate popular support for their decisions.

Under these conditions, the level of perceived deprivation remains not much higher than it is at present, the government retains its legitimacy and authority, and established values are not seriously challenged. Racial tensions continue to be the chief source of social conflict, and the mass of relatively powerless people is thus divided and distracted. Established elites are relatively unthreatened, and thus able to respond to what seem to them the most important needs of the nation. Their concerns center upon the continued stability and growth of the economy. More and more, the continued success of the dominant large corporations (and thus full employment and continued prosperity for most) depends upon the use of government power. Hence, government undertakes management of the basic conditions of social life, financing of research and development, underwriting of major risks through subsidies and guarantees, and military protection of overseas activities. And it repels all efforts to change such priorities.

Thus, elites perceive no acceptable alternatives to the growing (and, in the eyes of most, welcome) domination of both the society and the polity by the major corporations. Greater and greater integration between business and government occurs, until the two are nearly indistinguishable. Because established values remain unchanged, economic attainments are the principal measure of progress, and in any event a steadily rising standard of living remains an unchallenged necessity. Existing social problems will also be dealt with, but only when serious incidents occur; even then, they will be second priority and remedies will be applied to their symptoms rather than their causes. Occasionally, special efforts will be made to elicit popular support for space exploits, threats of nuclear war, or domestic "crusades" against the surface manifestations of problems that annoy many people. But the basic line of development will be an extension of the *status quo*, to the point that a corporate-managed society evolves. Conditions of life will not appear unfree or distasteful to most people, though to a small and permanent minority life will appear intolerably structured by the technological monsters of their own creation.

2. *Marginal reactionary change, culminating in fascism.* In this scenario, a stagnating economy causes unemployment to remain high and forces governments to cut back on services. The lowest levels of the white working class and all minorities feel the pinch quite seriously, though most of the middle class remains relatively affluent. Racial conflict is exacerbated by such conditions, and class consciousness is commensurately retarded. Social tensions multiply, there appear to be many severe problems but no solutions, and no clear moral or spiritual principles seem applicable. Amidst this general social fragmentation and purposelessness, various militant populist-type protest movements gain adherents. Some call for a general redistribution of wealth, others for a "return to fundamentals"; all are impatient with the continuing claims of minorities for equal status and opportunity. Governing elites, particularly those with roots in the corporate and financial world, grow alarmed at the obviously decaying social situations and worsening condition of the economy. They make a private alliance, tentative at first, either with incumbent politicians or with major populist leaders, enabling them to remain in or rise to power on this combination of elite and mass support.

A disorganized left offers little serious resistance, manifesting itself chiefly in isolated strikes and occasional terrorism. The new government uses the latter to justify exaggerated public attacks upon minorities, the left, and all forms of unorthodoxy and un-Americanism. Infiltration and surveillance are used in a broad campaign of intimidation. The general public, genuinely alarmed by the apparent reality of the alleged threat to national security, supports vigorous repression as necessary and justifiable.

Swept along by the hysteria, courts and juries find the means to jail people suspected of unorthodox actions or intentions. The Supreme Court, staffed by the nominees of the same elites, approves (and thereby legitimates) such uses of the police and judicial systems. The acknowledged vulnerability of the society appears to justify far-reaching supervision and control over behavior to prevent outbreaks.

At the same time, established elites recognize the necessity of promoting economic well-being, by which they mean serving the needs and preferences of various segments of the economy as fully as possible. Accordingly, they proceed much further than in the preceding scenario, regimenting the domestic working population, actively insisting upon opportunities for American investment and trade in various parts of the world, and employing American military power freely in behalf of both ends.

Political opposition begins to fade at the same time. Because of their similar perception of social conditions, and trends among those in authority and among voters, few recognized political leaders seriously dispute the propriety of existing public policy. Elections thus become contests between candidates who share a commitment to repression of dissent and promotion of the needs of the economy at practically any cost. Regardless of the winning political party, and because of the inability to perceive any alternative to surveillance and repression, such policies once undertaken become fixed, and can only intensify. In this manner—by the steady erosion of fixed standards of due process and fair procedures, coupled with rigid insistence upon the *status quo*—a police state evolves. The American version of fascism, well grounded in popular support, is complete.

3. *Marginal reformist change, culminating in welfare capitalism.* This scenario posits visible and continuing economic dislocation sufficient to convince a sizeable segment of the population—not just intellectuals and leftist organizers—that something is wrong with the economic order. It could be a mild depression or a continued recession that affects more than the lowest levels of workers. What is crucial is that it provide a basis for some degree of class consciousness or other shared consciousness of joint deprivation sufficient to overcome the divisiveness of group or racial conflicts. The latter, though unlikely to mellow substantially, could become somewhat less divisive if black/brown/red leaders began to interpret their plight in

class-based or economic, rather than exclusively racial terms. Young people would continue to be a source of new, more egalitarian, and humanistic values. For ever-increasing numbers of them, the older priorities would simply lack validity. Vitally important to the convergence of these conditions is the absence of war, for war would inject new obstacles into the path of a growing but fragile coalition seeking to span class, age, racial, and sexual divisions.

Considerable value change, gaining momentum continually as new waves of young people enter the society's mainstream, would make for a temporarily severe "generation gap." Before very long, however, elites themselves would be penetrated by the new standards, and key personnel at middle-management levels would begin to see likeminded persons permeating their areas of activity—including politics. Organizations of change-seeking persons would proliferate, venting their impatience with the recalcitrance of the established procedures in repeated outbreaks of violence. Unions in particular would regain their old militancy, as younger workers reinvigorated them, and waves of strikes demanding greater control over the conditions of work (not just higher wages and benefits) would take place.

Widening agreement among both elites and the general public on the justice of such causes would inhibit, but not entirely preclude, elite repression. Elites, perceiving themselves as severely threatened, would seek to undercut the new thrust by making marginal concessions to the demands. In time, as each adjustment granted new legitimacy to the rationale underlying the demands, and more and more elites became committed to the new values, a major turning-point would occur. The most likely would seem to be a sweeping victory for the more progressive political party in an election posing clear-cut alternatives between the new and the old values. After that, major institutional changes (such as the elimination of conservative rules in the Congress) would be possible, and fundamental change could then ensue.

The change would involve implementation of new value priorities: community, human rights, and esthetic concerns would replace competition, property rights, and materialism. Structural manifestations would include effective political control and direction of the corporate economy, decentralized management of most governmental and productive functions, and widespread participation by ordinary citizens in various stages of policymaking and its implementation. Technological developments would be subordinated to questions about the desirability of their impact. Economic "progress" would be viewed in terms of worldwide, rather than domestic, circumstances. Redistribution of wealth within the United States would be steadily extended, until resources and productivity were shared with other nations generally.

4. *Immediate fundamental change by revolution leading to fascism or socialism.* Revolution, though hard to contemplate in a heretofore highly stable, advanced industrial nation where the means of large-scale violence are thoroughly monopolized by government, is nevertheless a possibility that must be considered. Revolution requires substantial economic crisis, such as a severe depression, which would create wide unrest. Change in consciousness is thus not limited to the young. But there must be a united cadre group to serve as the principal moving force. Social tensions that place militant youth, black and white, in a position to join together, accompanied by at least some organized workers, are essential. The crucial factor is a continuing source of provocation that overrides racial suspicions and class differences and brings youth and workers together to serve as the nucleus of the instrument of change.

For such young people, and for those similarly affected by economic, social, or world conditions, value shifts are drastic. The government soon loses all legitimacy, and with it the power to restrain behavior. In response to the militant behavior of the young, polarization becomes sharp. Conditions nevertheless make a substantial segment of the population responsive to well-framed appeals by organizations of young militants. Major strikes in key industries and occasional victories in local conflicts mark their growing power and capability. Elite repression adds to the organizations' constituencies. At this point the situation is ripe for the final spark that can—if the organizations' leaders are perceptive and determined enough—eventuate in revolution. The spark would have to be so dramatic, and the response of major leaders and groups so indecisive or mutually conflicting, that an impasse would be apparent and police and military forces divided or immobilized. A hopelessly deadlocked presidential election, or savage repression of a major strike, or the imminent prospect of nuclear war, might be capable of providing such a spark.

If a total effort to seize power in the national government is made, with no reservations on the means or sacrifice involved, it might succeed. Actions limited to what is perceived as possible rarely exceed such bounds; those based on "impractical" aspirations sometimes achieve most of them, much to everyone's surprise. Once the attempt at revolution begins, of course, uncontrollable forces are set in motion. An effort undertaken in the absence of the conditions necessary to success can be totally self-destructive. Whoever mobilizes the means of violence most effectively emerges the winner. Their goals could be the faintly concealed fascism that appeals to many of the powers on the American right, or the democratic socialism that motivates the left. But revolutionary processes assure only that the old order will not survive, and there is no guarantee that what results will be an improvement on it. The result *might* be either fascism or democratic socialism. But there is no way to foresee the outcome until after the revolution has run its course.

These four scenarios are, of course, very gross characterizations, even caricatures. Many more (and more highly varied) factors would be involved in each process, leading to a great variety of results that would fall between the ends described here. We have presented only a few examples of the range of possibilities. But these four illustrations show how some major combinations of conditions and processes might interact to produce particular forms and directions of change. Without some such image of the process of change, and of the conditions requisite for particular types of change, we cannot assess the implications of contemporary events in the United States.

Prospects for Change in the American Political System

Analyzing processes of change from a position squarely in their midst requires us to press our sketchy framework very hard and risk the most embarrassing errors. But this is precisely what people must do if they are to act in ways that will be timely and effective in shaping their world. We must therefore try to show how the constructs we have developed contribute to individuals' understanding and potential impact on politics. As in the preceding scenarios, we shall do so in terms of preconditions, processes, key contingencies, and probable end results. The question before us is, quite simply, Where is the American political system heading in the 1970s? The answer requires not just prescient interpretation of weekly opinion polls and accurate forecasting of world events, but a combination of theory, widely divergent bodies of data, an intuitional sense of the core motivations and rhythms of American life—and remarkable good luck.

Preconditions

The early 1970s appear to be characterized by greater economic difficulties than were experienced at any time during the 1960s. Inflation and unemployment have led to unprecedented efforts at governmental control, with no assurance of success. Some branches of the growing ecology-environment movements appear to reject the classic standards of productivity and progress, substituting for them new limits on corporate freedom and demands for public goods and other amenities of life. The Third World is increasingly resistant to high yields on American investments and special trade advantages for American companies. Declining confidence in the future profitability of the economy is evidenced by conservative policies on the part of business and investors.

Social tensions in the United States are high. Racial conflict is deepening, as white resistance gains the tacit (and sometimes explicit) support of the national government, and blacks become more isolated, frustrated, and volatile. Class consciousness is still slight, and frequently undermined by racial divisions and other distractions. But it nevertheless seems to be reviving, and could spread if economic conditions worsen sharply. Young people as yet show no signs of reverting to the traditional values nor to the privatized, materialist quiescence of the 1950s. The level of tension is manifest in a variety of incidents too bizarre to be dismissed. It does not seem unduly alarmist to say that this might be the first stage of societal disintegration.

Political Impact

These already serious, and perhaps potentially explosive, conditions are still working their way into the political life of the nation. A substantial segment of young people, still clearly a minority, appears to have developed distinctive new values and priorities. But they remain essentially surrounded by continuing commitments to established values, practices, and systems of power—or perhaps by total inattention. Though the "silent majority" is in most respects either a meaningless term or a figment of powerholders' imaginations, there is no clear manifestation of widespread withdrawal of legitimacy from existing institutions. Malaise, uncertainty, and uneasiness surely exist, but they are not yet strong enough to pull large numbers of people away from habitual patterns.

Nor do there yet exist organizations that appear capable of effectively building a unified change-seeking movement. The peace movement was basically a single-issue, middle-class phenomenon. Many of its adherents remained committed to the familiar economic and political systems and saw only a single unwise policy requiring correction. The ecology-environment movement is (at the moment, at least) similar; it aims at correcting specific abuses, often without questioning the values or priorities that created them. Both serve to engage people, and perhaps to heighten their political awareness for a time, but only a relatively few become committed to fundamental change in the economic and social order as a result.

In summary, it seems clear that the left is weak, neither well nor cohesively organized, and subject to constant repression. The right is no better organized; but with substantial influence in government, it has no need to be. The prospects for left-oriented change may be expressed in terms of three contingencies: Will the American economy resume its stable growth and continue to satisfy the needs of most, given the world, domestic, and internal circumstances with which it is now faced? Assuming some degree of economic dislocation, can elites direct the discontent of the lower classes at the militant young and minorities in such a way as to contain them? Assuming that neither the money nor the will to solve the racial crisis can be found under the present (or perhaps any) system, can the resentments of minorities be contained or suppressed without creating system-altering consequences of some kind?

Prospects

As may be apparent, we are pessimistic about the future of the American republic. Tensions are high and climbing, but the signs point to change in directions that we deplore. No amount of unity-seeking rhetoric or patriotic ceremony surrounding the two-hundredth anniversary of the Declaration of Independence can undo deprivation and repression people can see and feel. If inequality persists (as we expect) and change is sought but prevented (as we also expect), only force can—*and will*—maintain the treasured "law and order." We see the United States in the 1970s as poised somewhere between (a) erratic marginal change eventually culminating in corporate-dominated society, and (b) reactionary marginal change moving steadily toward electoral fascism. The welfare-state scenario of change is a fading possibility, with revolution rising in its stead—but it is hardly threatening.

What can alter this set of probabilities? Only drastic changes in conditions, we would say: sustained recession or depression, another small war in a Third World location, mounting social disintegration, or other dramatic events. Not even crude elite repression can unify and render potent a movement that has no deep public discontent except racial hatreds on which to build. Americans, gripped by racial fixations and with one-tenth of the population semi-legitimately and forcibly relegated to subservient status, may simply be unable to cope with any other major problem. Racial conflict, escalating from time to time and likely to continue to do so, both inhibits political coalitions across racial boundaries and periodically supplants all other political concerns. The odds are that this factor will prevent all fundamental change except toward greater and greater suppression of minorities and their isolated white supporters. With this dynamic as the central motivator of political change, only one or another form of police state seems likely to evolve.

As analysts, we estimate probabilities. As citizens, we deplore our own estimates. As actors in politics, therefore, we must seek to maximize the chances for some more desirable result. That is why we do what we can to build an independent, active citizenry.

APPENDICES

The Declaration of Independence

**The Unanimous Declaration
of the Thirteen United States of America**

When in the Course of human events, it becomes necessary for one people to dissolve the political bands, which have connected them with another, and to assume among the powers of the earth, the separate and equal station to which the Laws of Nature and of Nature's God entitle them, a decent respect to the opinions of mankind requires that they should declare the causes which impel them to the separation.—We hold these truths to be self-evident, that all men are created equal, that they are endowed by their Creator with certain unalienable Rights, that among these are Life, Liberty and the pursuit of Happiness.—That to secure these rights, Governments are instituted among Men, deriving their just powers from the consent of the governed,—That whenever any Form of Government becomes destructive of these ends, it is the Right of the People to alter or to abolish it, and to institute new Government, laying its foundation on such principles and organizing its powers in such form, as to them shall seem most likely to effect their Safety and Happiness. Prudence, indeed, will dictate that Governments long established should not be changed for light and transient causes; and accordingly all experience hath shewn, that mankind are more disposed to suffer, while evils are sufferable, than to right themselves by abolishing the forms to which they are accustomed. But when a long train of abuses and usurpations, pursuing invariably the same Object evinces a design to reduce them under absolute Despotism, it is their right, it is their duty, to throw off such Government, and to provide new Guards for their future security.—Such has been the patient sufferance of these Colonies; and such now the necessity which constrains them to alter their former Systems of Government.

The history of the present King of Great Britain is a history of repeated injuries and usurpations, all having in direct object the establishment of an absolute Tyranny over these States. To prove this, let Facts be submitted to a candid world.— He has refused his Assent to Laws, the most wholesome and necessary for the public good.—He has forbidden his Governors to pass Laws of immediate and pressing importance, unless suspended in their operation till his Assent should be obtained, and when so suspended, he has utterly neglected to attend to them.—He has refused to pass other Laws for the accommodation of large districts of people, unless those people would relinquish the right of Representation in the Legislature, a right inestimable to them and formidable to tyrants only.—He has called together legislative bodies at places unusual, uncomfortable, and distant from the depository of their public Records, for the sole purpose of fatiguing them into compliance with his measures.—He has dissolved Representative Houses repeatedly for opposing with manly firmness his invasions on the rights of the people.—He has refused for a long time, after such dissolution, to cause others to be elected whereby the Legislative powers, incapable of Annihilation, have returned to the People at large for their exercise; the States remaining in the meantime exposed to all the dangers of invasion from without, and convulsions within.—He has endeavoured to prevent the population of these States; for that purpose obstructing the Laws for Naturalization of Foreigners; refusing to pass others to encourage their migrations hither, and raising the conditions of new Appropriations of Lands.—He has obstructed the Administration of Justice, by refusing his Assent to Laws for establishing Judiciary powers.—He has made Judges dependent on his Will alone, for the tenure of their offices, and the amount and payment of their salaries.—He has erected a multitude of New Offices, and sent hither swarms of Officers to harrass our people, and eat out their substance.—He has kept among us, in times of peace, Standing Armies without the Consent of our legislatures.—He has affected to render the Military independent of and superior to the Civil power.—He has combined with others to subject us to a jurisdiction foreign to our constitution, and unacknowledged by our laws; giving his Assent to their Acts of pretended Legislation. —For quartering large bodies of armed troops among us:— For protecting them, by a mock Trial, from punishment for any Murders which they should commit on the Inhabitants of these States:—For cutting off our Trade with all parts of the world:—For imposing Taxes on us without our Consent:—For depriving us in many cases, of the benefits of Trial by Jury:—For transporting us beyond Seas to be tried for pretended offenses:— For abolishing the free System of English Laws in a neighboring Province, establishing therein an Arbitrary

THE DECLARATION OF INDEPENDENCE

government, and enlarging its Boundaries so as to render it at once an example and fit instrument for introducing the same absolute rule into these Colonies:—For taking away our Charters, abolishing our most valuable Laws, and altering fundamentally the Forms of our Governments:—For suspending our own Legislatures, and declaring themselves invested with power to legislate for us in all cases whatsoever.—He has abdicated Government here, by declaring us out of his Protection and waging War against us.—He has plundered our seas, ravaged our Coasts, burnt our towns, and destroyed the lives of our people.— He is at this time transporting large Armies of Foreign Mercenaries to compleat the works of death, desolation and tyranny, already begun with circumstances of Cruelty & perfidy, scarcely paralleled in the most barbarous ages, and totally unworthy the Head of a civilized nation.—He has constrained our fellow Citizens taken Captive on the high Seas to bear Arms against their Country, to become the executioners of their friends and Brethren, or to fall themselves by their hands.—He has excited domestic insurrections amongst us, and has endeavoured to bring on the inhabitants of our frontiers, the Merciless Indian Savages, whose known rule of warfare, is an undistinguished destruction of all ages, sexes and conditions. In every stage of these Oppressions We have Petitioned for Redress in the most humble terms: Our repeated Petitions have been answered only by repeated injury. A Prince whose character is thus marked by every act which may define a Tyrant, is unfit to be the ruler of a free people. Nor have We been wanting in attentions to our British brethren. We have warned them from time to time of attempts by their legislature to extend an unwarrantable jurisdiction over us. We have reminded them of the circumstances of our emigration and settlement here. We have appealed to their native justice and magnanimity, and we have conjured them by the ties of our common kindred to disavow these usurpations, which would inevitably interrupt our connections and correspondence. They too have been deaf to the voice of justice and of consanguinity. We must, therefore, acquiesce in the necessity, which denounces our Separation, and hold them, as we hold the rest of mankind, Enemies in War, in Peace Friends.—

We, therefore, the Representatives of the United States of America, in General Congress, Assembled, appealing to the Supreme Judge of the world for the rectitude of our intentions do, in the Name, and by the Authority of the good People of these Colonies, solemnly publish and declare, That these United Colonies, are, and of Right ought to be Free and Independent States; that they are Absolved from all Allegiance to the British Crown, and that all political connection between them and the State of Great Britain, is and ought to be totally dissolved; and that as Free and Independent States, they have full Power to levy War, conclude Peace, contract Alliances, establish Commerce, and to do all other Acts and Things which Independent States may of right do.—And for the support of this Declaration, with a firm reliance on the protection of divine Providence, we mutually pledge to each other our Lives, our Fortunes and our sacred Honor.

The Constitution
of the United States of America

We the People of the United States, in Order to form a more perfect Union, establish Justice, insure domestic Tranquility, provide for the common defence, promote the general Welfare, and secure the Blessings of Liberty to ourselves and our Posterity, do ordain and establish this Constitution for the United States of America.

Article I

Section. 1. All legislative Powers herein granted shall be vested in a Congress of the United States, which shall consist of a Senate and House of Representatives.

Section. 2. The House of Representatives shall be composed of Members chosen every second Year by the People of the several States, and the Electors in each State shall have the Qualifications requisite for Electors of the most numerous Branch of the State Legislature.

No Person shall be a Representative who shall not have attained to the age of twenty five Years, and been seven Years a Citizen of the United States, and who shall not, when elected, be an Inhabitant of that State in which he shall be chosen.

Representatives and direct Taxes shall be apportioned among the several States which may be included within this Union, according to their respective Numbers, *which shall be determined by adding to the whole Number of free Persons, including those bound to Service for a Term of Years, and excluding Indians not taxed, three fifths of all other persons.*[1] The actual Enumeration shall be made within three Years after the first Meeting of the Congress of the United States, and within every subsequent Term of ten Years, in such Manner as they shall by Law direct. The Number of Representatives shall not exceed

[1] Italics are used throughout to indicate passages that have been altered by subsequent amendments. In this case see Amendment XIV.

one for every thirty Thousand, but each State shall have at Least one Representative; and until such enumeration shall be made, the State of New Hampshire shall be entitled to chuse three, Massachusetts eight, Rhode-Island and Providence Plantations one, Connecticut five, New-York six, New Jersey four, Pennsylvania eight, Delaware one, Maryland six, Virginia ten, North Carolina five, South Carolina five, and Georgia three.

When vacancies happen in the Representation from any State, the Executive Authority thereof shall issue Writs of Election to fill such Vacancies.

The House of Representatives shall chuse their Speaker and other Officers; and shall have the sole Power of Impeachment.

Section. 3. The Senate of the United States shall be composed of two Senators from each State, *chosen by the Legislature thereof,*[2] for six Years; and each Senator shall have one Vote.

Immediately after they shall be assembled in Consequence of the first Election, they shall be divided as equally as may be into three Classes. The Seats of the Senators of the first Class shall be vacated at the Expiration of the second Year, of the second Class at the Expiration of the fourth Year, and of the third Class at the Expiration of the sixth Year, so that one third may be chosen every second Year; *and if Vacancies happen by Resignation, or otherwise, during the Recess of the Legislature of any State, the Executive thereof may make temporary Appointments until the next Meeting of the Legislature, which shall then fill such Vacancies.*[3]

No Person shall be a Senator who shall not have attained to the Age of thirty Years, and been nine Years a Citizen of the United States, and who shall not, when elected, be an Inhabitant of that State for which he shall be chosen.

The Vice President of the United States shall be President of the Senate, but shall have no Vote, unless they be equally divided.

The Senate shall chuse their other Officers, and also a President pro tempore, in the Absence of the Vice President, or when he shall exercise the Office of President of the United States.

The Senate shall have the sole Power to try all Impeachments. When sitting for that Purpose, they shall be on Oath or Affirmation. When the President of the United States is tried, the Chief Justice shall preside: And no Person shall be convicted without the Concurrence of two thirds of the Members present.

Judgment in Cases of Impeachment shall not extend further than to removal from Office, and disqualification to hold and enjoy any Office of honor, Trust or Profit under the United States: but the Party

[2]See Amendment XVII.
[3]*Ibid.*

convicted shall nevertheless be liable and subject to Indictment, Trial, Judgment and Punishment, according to Law.

Section. 4. The Times, Places and Manner of holding Elections for Senators and Representatives, shall be prescribed in each State by the Legislature thereof; but the Congress may at any time by Law make or alter such Regulations, except as to the Places of chusing Senators.

The Congress shall assemble at least once in every Year, and such Meeting shall be on the first Monday in December, unless they shall by Law appoint a different Day.[4]

Section. 5. Each House shall be the Judge of the Elections, Returns and Qualifications of its own Members, and a Majority of each shall constitute a Quorum to do Business; but a smaller Number may adjourn from day to day, and may be authorized to compel the Attendance of absent Members, in such Manner, and under such Penalties as each House may provide.

Each House may determine the Rules of its Proceedings, punish its Members for disorderly Behavior, and, with the Concurrence of two thirds, expel a Member.

Each House shall keep a Journal of its Proceedings, and from time to time publish the same, excepting such Parts as may in their Judgment require Secrecy; and the Yeas and Nays of the Members of either House on any qeustion shall, at the Desire of one fifth of those Present, be entered on the Journal.

Neither House, during the Session of Congress, shall, without the Consent of the other, adjourn for more than three days, nor to any other Place than that in which the two Houses shall be sitting.

Section. 6. The Senators and Representatives shall receive a Compensation for their Services, to be ascertained by Law, and paid out of the Treasury of the United States. They shall in all Cases, except Treason, Felony and Breach of the Peace, be privileged from Arrest during their Attendance at the Session of their respective Houses, and in going to and returning from the same; and for any Speech or Debate in either House, they shall not be questioned in any other Place.

No Senator or Representative shall, during the Time for which he was elected, be appointed to any civil Office under the Authority of the United States, which shall have been created, or the Emoluments whereof shall have been encreased during such time; and no Person holding any Office under the United States, shall be a Member of either House during his Continuance in Office.

Section. 7. All Bills for raising Revenue shall originate in the House of Representatives; but the Senate may propose or concur with Amendments as on other Bills.

[4]See Amendment XX.

Every Bill which shall have passed the House of Representatives and the Senate, shall, before it become a Law, be presented to the President of the United States; if he approve he shall sign it, but if not he shall return it, with his Objections to that House in which it shall have originated, who shall enter the Objections at large on their Journal, and proceed to reconsider it. If after such Reconsideration two thirds of that House shall agree to pass the Bill, it shall be sent, together with the Objections, to the other House, by which it shall likewise be reconsidered, and if approved by two thirds of that House, it shall become a Law. But in all such Cases the Votes of both Houses shall be determined by Yeas and Nays, and the Names of the Persons voting for and against the Bill shall be entered on the Journal of each House respectively. If any Bill shall not be returned by the President within ten Days (Sundays excepted) after it shall have been presented to him, the Same shall be a Law, in like Manner as if he had signed it, unless Congress by their Adjournment prevent its Return, in which Case it shall not be a Law.

Every Order, Resolution, or Vote to which the Concurrence of the Senate and House of Representatives may be necessary (except on a question of Adjournment) shall be presented to the President of the United States; and before the Same shall take Effect, shall be approved by him, or being disapproved by him, shall be repassed by two thirds of the Senate and House of Representatives, according to the Rules and Limitations prescribed in the Case of a Bill.

Section. 8. The Congress shall have Power To lay and collect Taxes, Duties, Imposts and Excises, to pay the Debts and provide for the common Defence and general Welfare of the United States; but all Duties, Imposts and Excises shall be uniform throughout the United States;

To borrow Money on the credit of the United States;

To regulate Commerce with foreign Nations, and among the several States, and with the Indian Tribes;

To establish an uniform Rule of Naturalization, and uniform Laws on the subject of Bankruptcies throughout the United States;

To coin Money, regulate the Value thereof, and of foreign Coin, and fix the Standard of Weights and Measures;

To provide for the Punishment of counterfeiting the Securities and Current Coin of the United States;

To establish Post Offices and post Roads;

To promote the Progress of Science and useful Arts, by securing for limited Times to Authors and Inventors the exclusive Right to their respective Writings and Discoveries;

To constitute Tribunals inferior to the Supreme Court;

To define and punish Piracies and Felonies committed on the high Seas, and Offences against the Law of Nations;

To declare War, grant Letters of Marque and Reprisal, and make Rules concerning Captures on Land and Water;

To raise and support Armies, but no Appropriation of Money to that Use shall be for a longer Term than two Years;

To provide and maintain a Navy;

To make Rules for the Government and Regulation of the land and naval Forces;

To provide for calling forth the Militia to execute the Laws of the Union, suppress Insurrections and repel Invasions;

To provide for organizing, arming, and disciplining, the Militia, and for governing such Part of them as may be employed in the Service of the United States, reserving to the States respectively, the Appointment of the Officers, and the Authority of training the Militia according to the discipline prescribed by Congress;

To exercise exclusive Legislation in all Cases whatsoever, over such District (not exceeding ten Miles square) as may, by Cession of particular States, and the Acceptance of Congress, become the Seat of the Government of the United States, and to exercise like Authority over all Places purchased by the Consent of the Legislature of the State in which the Same shall be, for the Erection of Forts, Magazines, Arsenals, dock-Yards, and other needful Buildings;—And

To make all Laws which shall be necessary and proper for carrying into Execution the foregoing Powers, and all other Powers vested by this Constitution in the Government of the United States, or in any Department or Officer thereof.

Section. 9. The Migration or Importation of such Persons as any of the States now existing shall think proper to admit, shall not be prohibited by the Congress prior to the Year one thousand eight hundred and eight, but a Tax or duty may be imposed on such Importation, not exceeding ten dollars for each Person.

The Privilege of the Writ of Habeas Corpus shall not be suspended, unless when in Cases of Rebellion or Invasion the public Safety may require it.

No Bill of Attainder or ex post facto Law shall be passed.

No Capitation, or other direct, Tax shall be laid, unless in Proportion to the Census or Enumeration herein before directed to be taken.

No Tax or Duty shall be laid on Articles exported from any State.

No Preference shall be given by any Regulation of Commerce or Revenue to the Ports of one State over those of another: nor shall Vessels bound to, or from, one State, be obliged to enter, clear, or pay Duties in another.

No Money shall be drawn from the Treasury, but in Consequence of Appropriations made by Law; and a regular Statement and Account of the Receipts and Expenditures of all public Money shall be published from time to time.

No title of Nobility shall be granted by the United States: And no Person holding any Office of Profit or Trust under them, shall, without the Consent of the Congress, accept of any present, Emolument, Office, or Title, of any kind whatever, from any King, Prince, or foreign State.

Section. 10. No State shall enter into any Treaty, Alliance, or Confederation; grant Letters of Marque and Reprisal; coin Money; emit Bills of Credit; make any Thing but gold and silver Coin a Tender in Payment of Debts; pass any Bill of Attainder, ex post facto Law, or Law impairing the Obligation of Contracts, or Grant any Title of Nobility.

No State shall, without the Consent of the Congress, lay any Imposts or Duties on Imports or Exports, except what may be absolutely necessary for executing its inspection Laws: and the net Produce of all Duties and Imposts, laid by any State on Imports or Exports, shall be for the Use of the Treasury of the United States; and all such Laws be subject to the Revision and Control of the Congress.

No State shall, without the Consent of Congress, lay any Duty of Tonnage, keep Troops, or Ships of War in time of Peace, enter into any Agreement or Compact with another State, or with a foreign Power, or engage in War, unless actually invaded, or in such imminent Danger as will not admit of delay.

Article II

Section. 1. The executive Power shall be vested in a President of the United States of America. He shall hold his Office during the Term of four Years, and, together with the Vice President, chosen for the same Term be elected as follows:

Each State shall appoint, in such Manner as the Legislature thereof may direct, a Number of Electors, equal to the whole Number of Senators and Representatives to which the State may be entitled in the Congress: but no Senator or Representative, or Person holding an Office of Trust or Profit under the United States, shall be appointed an Elector.

The Electors shall meet in their respective States, and vote by Ballot for two Persons, of whom one at least shall not be an Inhabitant of the same State with themselves. And they shall make a List of all the Persons voted for, and of the Number of Votes for each; which List they shall sign and certify, and transmit sealed to the Seat of the Government of the United States, directed to the President of the Senate. The President of the Senate shall, in the Presence of the Senate and House of Representatives, open all the Certificates, and the Votes shall then be counted. The Person having the greatest Number of Votes shall be the President, if such Number be a Majority of the whole Number of Electors appointed; and if there be more than one who have such Majority, and have an equal Number of Votes, then the House of Representatives shall immediately chuse by Ballot one of them for President; and if no Person have a Majority, then from the five highest on the List the said House shall in like Manner chuse the President. But in chusing the President, the votes shall be taken by States, the Representation from each State having one Vote; A quorum for this purpose shall consist of a Member or Members from two thirds of the States, and a Majority of all the States shall be necessary to a Choice. In every Case, after the Choice of the President, the Person having the Greatest Number of Votes of the Electors shall be the Vice President. But if there should remain two or more who have equal Votes, the Senate shall chuse from them by Ballot the Vice President.[5]

The Congress may determine the Time of chusing the Electors, and the Day on which they shall give their Votes; which Day shall be the same throughout the United States.

No Person except a natural born Citizen, or a Citizen of the United States, at the time of the Adoption of this Constitution, shall be eligible to the Office of President; neither shall any Person be eligible to that Office who shall not have attained to the Age of thirty five Years, and been fourteen Years a Resident within the United States.

The Case of the Removal of the President from Office, or of his Death, Resignation, or Inability to discharge the Powers and Duties of the said Office, the Same shall devolve on the Vice President, and the Congress may by Law provide for the Case of Removal, Death, Resignation or Inability, both of the President and Vice President, declaring what Officer shall then act as President, and such Officer shall act accordingly, until the Disability be removed, or a President shall be elected.

The President shall, at stated Times, receive for his Services, a Compensation which shall neither be encreased nor diminished during the Period for which he shall have been elected, and he shall not receive within that Period any other Emolument from the United States, or any of them.

Before he enter on the Execution of his Office, he shall take the following Oath or Affirmation:—"I do solemnly swear (or affirm) that I will faithfully execute the Office of President of the United States, and will to the best of my Ability, preserve, protect, and defend the Constitution of the United States."

Section. 2. The President shall be Commander in Chief of the Army and Navy of the United States, and of the Militia of the several States, when called into the actual service of the United States; he

[5]See Amendment XII.

may require the Opinion, in writing, of the principal Officer in each of the executive Departments, upon any Subject relating to the Duties of their respective Offices, and he shall have Power to grant Reprieves and Pardons for Offences against the United States, except in Case of Impeachment.

He shall have Power, by and with the Advice and Consent of the Senate, to make Treaties, provided two thirds of the Senators present concur; and he shall nominate, and by and with the Advice and Consent of the Senate, shall appoint Ambassadors, and other public Ministers and Consuls, Judges of the supreme Court, and all other Officers of the United States, whose Appointments are not herein otherwise provided for, and which shall be established by Law; but the Congress may by Law vest the Appointment of such inferior Officers, as they think proper, in the President alone, in the Courts of Law, or in the Heads of Departments.

The President shall have Power to fill up all Vacancies that may happen during the Recess of the Senate, by granting Commissions which shall expire at the End of their next Session.

Section. 3. He shall from time to time give to the Congress Information of the State of the Union, and recommend to their Consideration such Measures as he shall judge necessary and expedient; he may, on extraordinary Occasions, convene both Houses, or either of them, and in Case of Disagreement between them, with Respect to the Time of Adjournment, he may adjourn them to such Time as he shall think proper; he shall receive Ambassadors and other public Ministers, he shall take Care that the Laws be faithfully executed, and shall Commission all the Officers of the United States.

Section. 4. The President, Vice President, and all civil Officers of the United States, shall be removed from Office on Impeachment for, and Conviction of, Treason, Bribery, or other Crimes and Misdemeanors.

Article III

Section. 1. The judicial Power of the United States, shall be vested in one supreme Court and in such inferior Courts as the Congress may from time to time ordain and establish. The Judges, both of the supreme and inferior Courts, shall hold their Offices during good Behavior, and shall, at stated Times, receive for their Services, a Compensation, which shall not be diminished during their Continuance in Office.

Section. 2. The Judicial Power shall extend to all Cases, in Law and Equity, arising under this Constitution, the Laws of the United States, and Treaties made, or which shall be made, under their Authority;—to all Cases affecting Ambassadors, other public Ministers and Consuls;—to all Cases of admiralty and maritime Jurisdiction;—to Controversies to which the United States shall be a Party;—to Controversies between two or more States;—*between a State and Citizens of another State;*[6]—between Citizens of different States;—between Citizens of the same State claiming Lands under Grants of different states, *and between a State, or the Citizens thereof, and foreign States, Citizens, or Subjects.*[7]

In all cases affecting Ambassadors, other public Ministers and Consuls, and those in which a State shall be Party, the supreme Court shall have original Jurisdiction. In all the other Cases before mentioned, the supreme Court shall have appellate Jurisdiction, both as to Law and Fact, with such Exceptions, and under such Regulations as the Congress shall make.

The Trial of all Crimes, except in Cases of Impeachment, shall be by Jury; and such Trial shall be held in the State where the said Crimes shall have been committed; but when not committed within any State, the Trial shall be at such Place or Places as the Congress may by Law have directed.

Section. 3. Treason against the United States, shall consist only in levying War against them, or in adhering to their Enemies, giving them Aid and Comfort. No person shall be convicted of Treason unless on the Testimony of two Witnesses to the same overt Act, or on Confession in open Court.

The Congress shall have Power to declare the Punishment of Treason, but no Attainder of Treason shall work Corruption of Blood, or Forfeiture except during the Life of the Person attainted.

Article IV

Section. 1. Full Faith and Credit shall be given in each State to the public Acts, Records, and judicial Proceedings of every other State. And the Congress may by general Laws prescribe the Manner in which such Acts, Records, and Proceedings shall be proved, and the Effect thereof.

Section. 2. The Citizens of each State shall be entitled to all Privileges and Immunities of Citizens in the several States.

A Person charged in any State with Treason, Felony, or other Crime, who shall flee from Justice, and be found in another State, shall on Demand of the executive Authority of the State from which he fled, be delivered up, to be removed to the State having Jurisdiction of the Crime.

No Person held to Service or Labour in one State, under the Laws thereof, escaping into another, shall, in Consequence of any Law or

[6]See Amendment XI.
[7]*Ibid.*

Regulation therein, be discharged from such Service or Labour, but shall be delivered up on Claim of the Party to whom such Service or Labour may be due.[8]

Section. 3. New States may be admitted by the Congress into this Union; but no new State shall be formed or erected within the Jurisdiction of any other State; nor any State be formed by the Junction of two or more States, or Parts of States, without the Consent of the Legislatures of the States concerned as well as of the Congress.

The Congress shall have Power to dispose of and make all needful Rules and Regulations respecting the Territory or other Property belonging to the United States; and nothing in this Constitution shall be so construed as to Prejudice any claims of the United States, or of any particular State.

Section. 4. The United States shall guarantee to every State in this Union a Republican Form of Government, and shall protect each of them against Invasion; and on Application of the Legislature, or of the Executive (when the Legislature cannot be convened) against domestic Violence.

Article V

The Congress, whenever two thirds of both Houses shall deem it necessary, shall propose Amendments to this Constitution, or, on the Application of the Legislatures of two thirds of the several States, shall call a Convention for proposing Amendments, which, in either Case, shall be valid to all Intents and Purposes, as Part of this Constitution, when ratified by the Legislatures of three fourths of the several States, or by Conventions in three fourths thereof, as the one or the other Mode of Ratification may be proposed by the Congress; Provided that no Amendment which may be made prior to the Year One thousand eight hundred and eight shall in any Manner affect the first and fourth Clauses in the Ninth Section of the first Article; and that no State, without its Consent, shall be deprived of its equal Suffrage in the Senate.

Article VI

All Debts contracted and Engagements entered into, before the Adoption of this Constitution shall be as valid against the United States under this Constitution, as under the Confederation.

This Constitution, and the Laws of the United States which shall be made in Pursuance thereof; and all Treaties made, or which shall be made, under the Authority of the United States, shall be the supreme Law of the Land; and the Judges in every State shall be

[8]See Amendment XIII.

bound thereby, any Thing in the Constitution or Laws of any State to the Contrary notwithstanding.

The Senators and Representatives before mentioned, and the Members of the several State Legislatures, and all executive and judicial Officers, both of the United States and of the several States, shall be bound by Oath or Affirmation, to support this Constitution; but no religious Test shall ever be required as a Qualification to any Office or public Trust under the United States.

Article VII

The Ratification of the Conventions of nine States, shall be sufficient for the Establishment of this Constitution between the States so ratifying the Same.

Done in Convention by the Unanimous Consent of the States present the Seventeenth Day of September in the Year of our Lord one thousand seven hundred and eighty seven and of the Independence of the United States of America the twelfth. In witness whereof We have hereunto subscribed our Names.

* * *

Articles in addition to, and amendment of, the Constitution of the United States of America, proposed by Congress, and ratified by the several States, pursuant to the Fifth Article of the original Constitution.

Amendment I

[Ratification of the first ten amendments was completed December 15, 1791]

Congress shall make no law respecting an establishment of religion, or prohibiting the free exercise thereof; or abridging the freedom of speech, or of the press; or the right of the people peaceably to assemble, and to petition the Government for a redress of grievances.

Amendment II

A well regulated Militia, being necessary to the security of a free State, the right of the people to keep and bear Arms, shall not be infringed.

Amendment III

No Soldier shall, in time of peace be quartered in any house, without the consent of the Owner, nor in time of war, but in a manner to be prescribed by law.

Amendment IV

The right of the people to be secure in their persons, houses, papers, and effects, against unreasonable searches and seizures, shall not be violated, and no Warrants shall issue, but upon probable cause, supported by Oath or affirmation, and particularly describing the place to be searched, and the persons or things to be seized.

Amendment V

No person shall be held to answer for a capital, or otherwise infamous crime, unless on a presentment or indictment of a Grand Jury, except in cases arising in the land or naval forces, or in the Militia, when an actual service in time of War or public danger; nor shall any person be subject for the same offence to be twice put in jeopardy of life or limb; nor shall be compelled in any criminal case to be a witness against himself, nor be deprived of life, liberty, or property, without due process of law; nor shall private property be taken for public use, without just compensation.

Amendment VI

In all criminal prosecutions, the accused shall enjoy the right to a speedy and public trial, by an impartial jury of the State and district wherein the crime shall have been committed, which district shall have been previously ascertained by law, and to be informed of the nature and cause of the accusation; to be confronted with the witness against him; to have compulsory process for obtaining witness in his favor, and to have the Assistance of Counsel for his defence.

Amendment VII

In Suits at common law, where the value in controversy shall exceed twenty dollars, the right of trial by jury shall be preserved, and no fact tried by a jury, shall be otherwise re-examined in any Court of the United States, than according to the rules of the common law.

Amendment VIII

Excessive bail shall not be required, nor excessive fines imposed, nor cruel and unusual punishments inflicted.

Amendment IX

The enumeration in the Constitution, of certain rights, shall not be construed to deny or disparage others retained by the people.

The powers not delegated to the United States by the Constitution, nor prohibited by it to the States, are reserved to the States respectively, or to the people.

Amendment XI

[January 8, 1798]

The Judicial power of the United States shall not be construed to extend to any suit in law or equity, commenced or prosecuted against one of the United States by Citizens of another State, or by Citizens or Subjects of any Foreign State.

Amendment XII

[September 25, 1804]

The Electors shall meet in their respective states and vote by ballot for President and Vice President, one of whom, at least, shall not be an inhabitant of the same state with themselves; they shall name in their ballots the person voted for as President, and in distinct ballots the person voted for as Vice President, and they shall make distinct lists of all persons voted for as President, and of all persons voted for as Vice President, and of the number of votes for each, which lists they shall sign and certify, and transmit sealed to the seat of the government of the United States, directed to the President of the Senate; —The President of the Senate shall, in the presence of the Senate and House of Representatives, open all the certificates and the votes shall then be counted;—The person having the greatest number of votes for President, shall be the President, if such number be a majority of the whole number of Electors appointed; and if no person have such majority, then from the persons having the highest numbers not exceeding three on the list of those voted for as President, the House of Representatives shall choose immediately, by ballot, the President. But in choosing the President, the votes shall be taken by states, the representation from each state having one vote; a quorum for this purpose shall consist of a member or members from two thirds of the states, and a majority of all the states shall be necessary to a choice. And if the House of Representatives shall not choose a President whenever the right of choice shall devolve upon them, *before the fourth day of March next following,*[9] then the Vice President shall act as President as in the case of the death or other constitutional disability

[9]See Amendment XX.

of the President.—The person having the greatest number of votes as Vice President, shall be the Vice President, if such number be a majority of the whole number of Electors appointed, and if no person have a majority, then from the two highest numbers on the list, the Senate shall choose the Vice President; a quorum for the purpose shall consist of two-thirds of the whole number of Senators, and a majority of the whole number shall be necessary to a choice. But no person constitutionally ineligible to the office of President shall be eligible to that of Vice President of the United States.

Amendment XIII

[December 18, 1865]

Section 1. Neither slavery nor involuntary servitude, except as a punishment for crime whereof the party shall have been duly convicted, shall exist within the United States, or any place subject to their jurisdiction.

Section 2.   Congress shall have power to enforce this article by appropriate legislation.

Amendment XIV

[July 28, 1868]

Section 1. All persons born or naturalized in the United States, and subject to the jurisdiction thereof, are citizens of the United States and of the State wherein they reside. No State shall make or enforce any law which shall abridge the privileges or immunities of citizens of the United States; nor shall any state deprive any person of life, liberty, or property, without due process of law; nor deny to any person within its jurisdiction the equal protection of the laws.

Section 2. Representatives shall be apportioned among the several States according to their respective numbers, counting the whole number of persons in each State, excluding Indians not taxed. But when the right to vote at any election for the choice of electors for President and Vice President of the United States, Representatives in Congress, the Executive and Judicial officers of a State, or the members of the Legislature thereof, is denied to any of the male inhabitants of such State, being twenty one years of age, and citizens of the United States, or in any way abridged, except for participation in rebellion, or other crime, the basis of representation therein shall be reduced in the proportion which the number of such male citizens shall bear to the whole number of male citizens twenty one years of age in such State.

Section 3. No person shall be a Senator or Representative in Congress, or elector of President and Vice President, or hold any office, civil or military, under the United States, or under any State, who, having previously taken an oath, as a member of Congress, or as an officer of the United States, or as a member of any State legislature, or as an executive or judicial officer of any State, to support the Constitution of the United States, shall have engaged in insurrection or rebellion against the same, or given aid or comfort to the enemies thereof. But Congress may by a vote of two thirds of each House, remove such disability.

Section 4. The validity of the public debt of the United States, authorized by law, including debts incurred for payment of pensions and bounties for services in suppressing insurrection or rebellion, shall not be questioned. But neither the United States nor any State shall assume or pay any debt or obligation incurred in aid of insurrection or rebellion against the United States, or any claim for the loss or emancipation of any slave; but all such debts, obligations, and claims shall be held illegal and void.

Section 5. The Congress shall have power to enforce, by appropriate legislation, the provisions of this article.

Amendment XV

[March 30, 1870]

Section 1. The right of citizens of the United States to vote shall not be denied or abridged by the United States or by any State on account of race, color, or previous condition of servitude.

Section 2. The Congress shall have power to enforce this article by appropriate legislation.

Amendment XVI

[February 25, 1913]

The Congress shall have power to lay and collect taxes on incomes, from whatever source derived, without apportionment among the several States, and without regard to any census or enumeration.

Amendment XVII

[May 31, 1913]

The Senate of the United States shall be composed of two Senators from each State, elected by the people thereof, for six years; and each Senator shall have one vote. The electors in each State shall have the qualifications requisite for electors of the most numerous branch of the State legislatures.

When vacancies happen in the representation of any State in the Senate, the executive authority of such State shall issue writs of election to fill such vacancies: *Provided,* That the legislature of any State may empower the executive thereof to make temporary appointments until the people fill the vacancies by election as the legislature may direct.

This amendment shall not be so construed as to affect the election or term of any Senator chosen before it becomes valid as part of the Constitution.

Amendment XVIII

[January 29, 1919]

Section 1. *After one year from the ratification of this article the manufacture, sale, or transportation of intoxicating liquors within, the importation thereof into, or the exportation thereof from the United States and all territory subject to the jurisdiction thereof for beverage purposes is hereby prohibited.*

Section 2. *The Congress and the several States shall have concurrent power to enforce this article by appropriate legislation.*

Section 3. *This article shall be inoperative unless it shall have been ratified as an amendment to the Constitution by the legislatures of the several States, as provided in the Constitution, within seven years from the date of submission hereof to the States by the Congress.*[10]

Amendment XIX

[August 26, 1920]

The right of citizens of the United States to vote shall not be denied or abridged by the United States or by any State on account of sex.

Congress shall have power to enforce this article by appropriate legislation.

Amendment XX

[February 6, 1933]

Section 1. The terms of the President and Vice President shall end at noon on the 20th day of January, and the terms of Senators and

---

[10]Repealed by Amendment XXI.

Representatives at noon on the 3rd day of January, of the years in which such terms would have ended if this article had not been ratified; and the terms of their successors shall then begin.

Section 2. The Congress shall assemble at least once in every year, and such meeting shall begin at noon on the 3rd day of January, unless they shall by law appoint a different day.

Section 3. If, at the time fixed for the beginning of the term of the President, the President elect shall have died, the Vice President elect shall become President. If a President shall not have been chosen before the time fixed for the beginning of his term, or if the President elect shall have failed to qualify, then the Vice President elect shall act as President until a President shall have qualified; and the Congress may by law provide for the case wherein neither a President elect nor a Vice President elect shall have qualified, declaring who shall then act as President, or the manner in which one who is to act shall be selected, and such person shall act accordingly until a President or Vice President shall have qualified.

Section 4. The Congress may by law provide for the case of the death of any of the persons from whom the House of Representatives may choose a President whenever the right of choice shall have devolved upon them, and for the case of the death of any of the persons from whom the Senate may choose a Vice President whenever the right of choice shall have devolved upon them.

Section 5. Sections 1 and 2 shall take effect on the 15th day of October following the ratification of this article.

Section 6. This article shall be inoperative unless it shall have been ratified as an amendment to the Constitution by the legislatures of three fourths of the several States within seven years from the date of its submission.

Amendment XXI

[December 5, 1933]

Section 1. The eighteenth article of amendment to the Constitution of the United States is hereby repealed.

Section 2.   The transportation or importation into any State, Territory, or possession of the United States for delivery or use therein of intoxicating liquors, in violation of the laws thereof, is hereby prohibited.

Section 3. This article shall be inoperative unless it shall have been ratified as an amendment to the Constitution by conventions in the several States, as provided in the Constitution, within seven years from the date of the submission hereof to the States by the Congress.

Amendment XXII

[February 26, 1951]

Section 1. No person shall be elected to the office of the President more than twice, and no person who has held the office of President, or acted as President, for more than two years of a term to which some other person was elected President shall be elected to the office of President more than once. But this Article shall not apply to any person holding the office of President when this Article was proposed by the Congress, and shall not prevent any person who may be holding the office of President, or acting as President, during the term within which this Article becomes operative from holding the office of President or acting as President during the remainder of such term.

Section 2. This article shall be inoperative unless it shall have been ratified as an amendment to the Constitution by the legislatures of three fourths of the several States within seven years from the date of its submission to the States by the Congress.

Amendment XXIII

[March 29, 1961]

Section 1. The District constituting the seat of Government of the United States shall appoint in such manner as the Congress may direct:

A number of electors of President and Vice President equal to the whole number of Senators and Representatives in Congress to which the District would be entitled if it were a State, but in no event more than the least populous State; they shall be in addition to those appointed by the States, but they shall be considered, for the purposes of the election of President and Vice President, to be electors appointed by a State; and they shall meet in the District and perform such duties as provided by the twelfth article of amendment.

Section 2. The Congress shall have power to enforce this article by appropriate legislation.

Amendment XXIV

[January 23, 1964]

Section 1. The right of citizens of the United States to vote in any primary or other election for President or Vice President, for electors for President or Vice President, or for Senator or Representative in Congress, shall not be denied or abridged by the United States or any state by reason of failure to pay any poll tax or other tax.

Section 2. The Congress shall have power to enforce this article by article by appropriate legislation.

Amendment XXV

[February 10, 1967]

Section 1. In case of the removal of the President from office or of his death or resignation, the Vice President shall become President.

Section 2. Whenever there is a vacancy in the office of the Vice President, the President shall nominate a Vice President who shall take office upon confirmation by a majority vote of both Houses of Congress.

Section 3. Whenever the President transmits to the President pro tempore of the Senate and the Speaker of the House of Representatives his written declaration that he is unable to discharge the powers and duties of his office, and until he transmits to them a written declaration to the contrary, such powers and duties shall be discharged by the Vice President as Acting President.

Section 4. Whenever the Vice President and a majority of either the principal officers of the executive departments or of such other body as Congress may by law provide, transmit to the President pro tempore of the Senate and the Speaker of the House of Representatives their written declaration that the President is unable to discharge the powers and duties of his office, the Vice President shall immediately assume the powers and duties of the office as Acting President.

Thereafter, when the President transmits to the President pro tempore of the Senate and the Speaker of the House of Representatives his written declaration that no inability exists, he shall resume the powers and duties of his office unless the Vice President and a majority of either the principal officers of the executive department[s] or of such other body as Congress may by law provide, transmit within four days to the President pro tempore of the Senate and the Speaker of the House of Representatives their written declaration that the President is unable to discharge the powers and duties of his office. Thereupon Congress shall decide the issue, assembling within forty-eight hours for that purpose if not in session. If the Congress, within twenty-one days after receipt of the latter written declaration, or, if Congress is not in session, within twenty-one days after Congress is required to assemble, determines by two-thirds vote of both Houses that the President is unable to discharge the powers and duties of his office, the Vice President shall continue to discharge the same as Acting President; otherwise, the President shall resume the powers and duties of his office.

Amendment XXVI

[June 30, 1971]

Section 1. The right of citizens of the United States, who are 18 years of age or older, to vote shall not be denied or abridged by the United States or by any state on account of age.

Section 2. The Congress shall have power to enforce this article by appropriate legislation.

Amendment XXVII

Which prohibits discrimination based on sex by any law or action of any government—federal, state, or local—went to the states for ratification in March 1972.

BIBLIOGRAPHY

The selections that follow have been drawn from the vast and rapidly growing literature on American politics. We have sought to identify additional reading, usually available in paperback, that will fill out each chapter in some important way. Sometimes these selections contrast sharply with our interpretation; at other times they extend it beyond the point that we consider supported by available evidence; or they represent reflections on approaches or methods worth examining. In no case, of course, can our selections be taken as a comprehensive bibliography. They are a beginning, and a highly diversified one.

Chapter 1

Politics as an attempt to describe and explain:

Dahl, Robert A. *Modern Political Analysis.* Englewood Cliffs, N.J.: Prentice-Hall, 1963.

Eulau, Heinz. *The Behavioral Persuasion in Politics.* New York: Random House, 1963.

Sorauf, Frank J. *Political Science: An Informal Overview.* Columbus, Ohio: Charles E. Merrill, 1963.

Politics as an extension of ethical concerns:

Kaplan, Abraham. *American Ethics and Public Policy.* New York: Oxford University Press, 1963.

Kariel, Henry S. *The Promise of Politics.* Englewood Cliffs, N.J.: Prentice-Hall, 1966.

Pranger, Robert J. *The Eclipse of Citizenship.* New York: Holt, Rinehart, Winston, 1968.

Approaches that mix the two in varying proportions:

Alinsky, Saul. *Reveille for Radicals.* New York: Vintage Books, 1969 (originally published in 1946).

Barber, James David. *Citizen Politics: An Introduction to Political Behavior.* Chicago: Markham, 1968.

Dalfiume, Richard M., ed. *American Politics Since 1945: A New York Times Book.* Chicago: Quadrangle Books, 1969.

Freedman, Leonard, ed. *Issues of the Seventies.* Belmont, Cal.: Wadsworth, 1970.

Gordon, Kermit, ed. *Agenda for the Nation.* Garden City, N.Y.: Doubleday, 1968.

Laing, R. D. *The Politics of Experience.* New York: Ballantine, 1967.

Lipset, Seymour Martin, ed. *Politics and the Social Sciences.* New York: Oxford University Press, 1969.

Myrdal, Gunnar. *Objectivity in the Social Sciences.* New York: Random House, 1969.

Schuman, David. *Preface to Politics.* Lexington, Mass.: D. C. Heath, 1973.

Chapter 2

Baran, Paul A., and Sweezey, Paul M. *Monopoly Capital*. New York: Monthly Review Press, 1966.

Edelman, Murray, and Fleming, R. W. *The Politics of Wage-Price Decisions*. Champaign-Urbana: University of Illinois Press, 1968.

Friedman, Milton. *Capitalism and Freedom*. Chicago: University of Chicago Press, 1962.

Galbraith, John K. *American Capitalism—The Concept of Countervailing Power*. Boston: Houghton Mifflin, 1952.

Galbraith, John K. *The Affluent Society*. New York: New American Library, 1958.

Galbraith, John K. *The New Industrial State*. New York: New American Library, 1968.

Hamilton, Walton. *The Politics of Industry*. Ann Arbor: University of Michigan Press, 1957.

Heller, Walter H., ed. *Perspectives on Economic Growth*. New York: John Wiley, 1968.

Mitchell, William C. "The American Polity and the Redistribution of Income," *American Behavioral Scientist* 13 (November/December 1969): 201–214.

Mustolf, Lloyd D. *Government and Economy*. Chicago: Scott, Foresman, 1965.

Potter, David M. *People of Plenty*. Chicago: Phoenix Books, 1954.

Reagan, Michael. *The Managed Economy*. New York: Oxford University Press, 1963.

Rostow, Walter W. *The Stages of Economic Growth*. Cambridge: Cambridge University Press, 1960.

Samuelson, Paul A. *Economics,* 9th ed. New York: McGraw-Hill, 1973.

Tanzer, Michael. *The Sick Society: An Economic Examination*. New York: Holt, Rinehart, & Winston, 1971.

Watson, Donald, ed. *Price Theory in Action*. Boston: Houghton Mifflin, 1965.

Wildavshy, Aaron. *The Politics of the Budgetary Process*. Boston: Little, Brown, 1964.

Zeitlin, Maurice. ed. *American Society, Inc.* Chicago: Markham, 1970.

Chapter 3

Barnet, Richard J. *The Economy of Death*. New York: Atheneum, 1969.

Bloomfield, Lincoln P., *et al. Khrushchev and the Arms Race*. Cambridge, Mass.: M.I.T. Press, 1966.

Boulding, Kenneth. *Conflict and Defense: A General Theory*. New York: Harper & Row, 1963.

Clayton, James L. *The Economic Impact of the Cold War*. New York: Harcourt Brace Jovanovich, 1970.

Hammond, Paul. *Organizing for Defense*. Princeton, N.J.: Princeton University Press, 1961.

Huntington, Samuel. *The Common Defense.* New York: Columbia University Press, 1961.

Kaufmann, William E. *The McNamara Strategy.* New York: Harper & Row, 1964.

Lapp, Ralph E. *The Weapons Culture.* New York: W. W. Norton, 1968.

Melman, Seymour. *Pentagon Capitalism.* New York: McGraw-Hill, 1970.

Melman, Seymour, ed. *The War Economy of the United States.* New York: St. Martin's Press, 1971.

Neiburg, H. L. *In the Name of Science.* Chicago: Quadrangle Books, 1966.

Peck, Merton J., and Scherer, Frederic H. *The Weapons Acquistion Process.* Cambridge, Mass.: Harvard Business School, 1962.

Thayer, George. *The War Business.* New York: Simon & Schuster, 1969.

Chapter 4

Bachrach, Peter, and Baratz, Morton. *Power and Poverty.* New York: Oxford University Press, 1970.

Baltzell, E. Digby. *Philadelphia Gentlemen: The Making of a National Upper Class.* Glencoe, Ill.: The Free Press, 1958.

Bottomore, T. B. *Classes in Modern Society.* New York: Vintage Books, 1966.

Clark, Kenneth, and Hopkins, Jeanette. *A Relevant War on Poverty.* New York: Harper & Row, 1969.

Dahrendorf, Ralf. *Class and Class Conflict in Industrial Societies.* Stanford, Cal.: Stanford University Press, 1959.

Donovan, John. *The Politics of Poverty.* New York: Pegasus, 1967.

DeGrazia, Sebastian. *The Political Community.* Chicago: University of Chicago Press, 1948.

Free, Lloyd A., and Cantril, Hadley. *The Political Beliefs of Americans.* New York: Simon & Schuster, 1968.

Ferman, Louis *et al. Poverty in America.* Ann Arbor: University of Michigan Press, 1965.

Harrington, Michael. *The Other America.* Baltimore: Penguin, 1967.

Kolko, Gabriel. *Wealth and Power in America.* New York: Praeger, 1962.

Kornhauser, William. *The Politics of Mass Society.* Glencoe, Ill: Free Press, 1959.

Lampman, Robert J. *The Share of Top Wealth-Holders in National Wealth.* Princeton: Princeton University Press, 1962.

Lenski, Gerhard. *Power and Privilege.* New York: McGraw-Hill, 1966.

Lunberg, Ferdinand. *The Rich and the Super-Rich.* New York: Bantam Books, 1968.

Matthews, Donald. *The Social Background of Political Decision-Makers.* New York: Random House, 1955.

Miller, S. M., and Roby, Pamela. *The Future of Inequality.* New York: Basic Books, 1970.

Mills, C. Wright. *The Power Elite.* New York: Oxford University Press, 1956.

Valentine, Charles. *Culture and Poverty.* Chicago: University of Chicago Press, 1961.

Chapter 5

Allen, Robert. *Black Awakening in Capitalist America*. New York: Doubleday, 1969.

Brown, Dee. *Bury My Heart at Wounded Knee*. New York: Holt, Rinehart, & Winston, 1970.

Carmichael, Stokely, and Hamilton, Charles V. *Black Power: The Politics of Liberation in America*. New York: Vintage Books, 1967.

Clark, Kenneth B. *Dark Ghetto: Dilemmas of Social Power:* New York: Harper & Row, 1965.

Cleaver, Eldridge. *Soul on Ice*. New York: McGraw-Hill, 1968.

Coleman, James S., *et al. Equality of Educational Opportunity*. Washington: Government Printing Office, 1966.

Coles, Robert. *Children of Crisis*. New York: Dell, 1964.

Deutsch, Martin, *et al. The Disadvantaged Child*. New York: Basic Books, 1967.

Elkins, Stanley. *Slavery*, 2nd ed. Chicago: University of Chicago Press, 1968.

Friedman, Lawrence M. *Government and Slum Housing*. Chicago: Rand McNally, 1968.

Knowles, Louis L., and Prewitt, Kenneth, eds. *Institutional Racism in America*. Englewood Cliffs, N.J.: Prentice-Hall, 1969.

Lewis, Oscar. *La Vida*. New York: Random House, 1966.

Lewis, Oscar. *The Children of Sanchez*. New York: Random House, 1961.

Liebow, Elliot. *Talley's Corner*. Boston: Little, Brown, 1967.

Malcolm X. *Autobiography*. New York: Grove Press, 1964.

Matthews, Donald R., and Prothro, James W. *Negroes and the New Southern Politics*. New York: Harcourt Brace Jovanovich, 1966.

Moynihan, Daniel. *Maximum Feasible Misunderstandings*. New York: The Free Press, 1969.

Parsons, Talcott, and Clark, Kenneth B., eds. *The Negro American*. Boston: Houghton Mifflin, 1966.

Prewitt, Kenneth, and Knowles, Louis. *Institutional Racism in America*. Englewood Cliffs, N.J.: Prentice-Hall, 1970.

Rendon, Armando. *Chicano Manifesto*. New York: Macmillan, 1971.

Report of the Advisory Commission on Civil Disorders. New York: Bantam Books, 1968.

Sexton, Patricia C. *Education and Income*. New York: Viking, 1961.

Van den Bergh, Pierre L. *Race and Racism*. New York: John Wiley, 1967.

Walker, Jack L., and Aberbach, Joel D. "The Meanings of Black Power: A Comparison of White and Black Interpretations of a Political Slogan," *American Political Science* Review 64 (June 1970): 367–388.

Zinn, Howard. *SNCC: The New Abolitionists*. Boston: Beacon Press, 1964.

Chapter 6

Becker, Carl. *Freedom and Responsibility in the American Way of Life*. New York: Vintage Books, 1960.

Boorstin, Daniel. *The Genuis of American Politics*. Chicago: University of Chicago Press, 1960.

Cantril, Albert, and Roll, Charles. *The Hopes and Fears of the American*

People. New York: Universe Books, 1971.

Cohane, John P. *White Papers of an Outraged Conservative.* Indianapolis: Bobbs-Merrill, 1972.

Devine, Donald. *The Political Culture of the United States.* Boston: Little, Brown, 1972.

Girvetz, Harry. *The Evolution of Liberalism.* New York: Collier Books, 1963.

Grimes, Alan P. *American Political Thought.* New York: Holt, Rinehart, & Winston, 1966.

Hartz, Louis M. *The Liberal Tradition in America.* New York: Harcourt Brace Jovanovich, 1955.

Lane, Robert. *Political Ideology: Why the American Common Man Believes What He Does.* New York: Free Press, 1962.

Lerner, Max. *America as a Civilization.* New York: Simon & Schuster, 1957.

McGiffert, Michael, ed. *The Character of Americans.* Homewood, Ill.: Dorsey Press, 1964.

Rossiter, Clinton. *Conservatism in America: The Thankless Persuasion.* New York: Vintage Books, 1955.

Chapter 7

Bond, Julian. *A Time to Speak, A Time to Act.* New York: Simon & Schuster, 1972.

Carmichael, Stokely, and Hamilton, Charles V. *Black Power: The Politics of Liberation in America.* New York: Vintage Books, 1967.

Cowan, Paul. *The Making of an Unamerican.* New York: Viking, 1969.

Dolbeare, Kenneth M., and Dolbeare, Patricia. *American Ideologies: The Competing Political Beliefs of the 1970's.* Chicago: Markham, 1971.

Harris, Fred. *Now Is the Time: A Populist Call to Action.* New York: Praeger, 1970.

Jacobs, Paul, and Landau, Saul, eds. *The New Radicals.* New York: Vintage Books, 1966.

Lowi, Theodore. *The End of Liberalism: Ideology, Policy and the Crisis of Authority.* New York: W. W. Norton, 1969.

Moore, Barrington. "Revolution in America," *The New York Review of Books,* 12 (30 January 1969): 6–12.

Newfield, Jack. *A Prophetic Minority.* New York: Signet Books, 1966.

Newfield, Jack, and Greenfield, Jeff. *A Populist Manifesto: The Making of a New Majority.* New York: Warner, 1972.

Seale, Bobby G. *Seize the Time: The Story of the Black Panther Party and Huey P. Newton.* New York: Random House, 1970.

Sherman, Howard. *Radical Political Economy.* New York: Basic Books, 1972.

Theodori, Massimo, ed. *The New Left: A Documentary History.* Indianapolis: Bobbs-Merrill, 1969.

Chapter 8

Banfield, Edward C., and Wilson, James Q. *City Politics.* New York: Vintage Books, 1963.

Bauer, Raymond; de Sola Pool, Ithiel; and Dexter, Louis Anthony. *American Business and Public Policy.* New York: Atherton Press, 1963.

Bell, Daniel, and Kristol, Irving, eds. *Capitalism Today.* New York: Mentor Books, 1971.

Cook, Fred J. *The Warfare State.* New York: Collier Books, 1962.

Elazar, Daniel. *American Federalism: A View From the States.* New York: Crowell, 1966.

Engler, Robert. *The Politics of Oil: A Study of Private Power and Political Directions.* Chicago: University of Chicago Press, 1967.

Galbraith, John K. *How to Control the Military.* Garden City, N.J.: Doubleday, 1969.

Harris, Richard. *A Sacred Trust.* New York: New American Library, 1966.

Kariel, Henry S. *The Decline of American Pluralism.* Stanford, Cal.: Stanford University Press, 1961.

Key, V. O. *Southern Politics.* New York: Vintage Books, 1949.

Lens, Sidney. *The Military-Industrial Complex.* Philadelphia: Pilgrim Press, 1970.

McConnell, Grant. *Private Power and American Democracy.* New York: Knopf, 1966.

Milbrath, Lester W. *The Washington Lobbyists.* Chicago: Rand McNally, 1963.

Miliband, Ralph. *The State in Capitalist Society.* New York: Basic Books, 1969.

Mintz, Morton, and Cohen, Jerry. *America Inc.: Who Owns and Operates the United States?* New York: Dell, 1971.

Neiburg, H. L. *In the Name of Science.* Chicago: Quadrangle Books, 1966.

Riker, William H. *Federalism: Origin, Operation, Significance.* Boston: Little, Brown, 1964.

Schattschneider, E. E. *The Semi-Sovereign People.* New York: Holt, Rinehart & Winston, 1960.

Silver, James W. *Mississippi—The Closed Society,* rev. ed. New York: Harcourt Jovanovich, 1966.

Sundquist, James. *Politics and Policy.* Washington: The Brookings Institution, 1968.

Sundquist, James. *Politics and Policy.* Washington: The Brookings Institution, 1969.

Truman, David. *The Governmental Process.* New York: Knopf, 1951.

Zeigler, Harmon. *Interest Groups in American Society.* Englewood Cliffs, N.J.: Prentice-Hall, 1964.

Chapter 9

Dahl, Robert A. *Who Governs?* New Haven, Conn.: Yale University Press, 1961.

David, Paul et al. *The Politics of National Party Conventions.* Washington: The Brookings Institution, 1957.

Domhoff, G. William. *Who Rules America?* Englewood Cliffs, N.J.; Prentice-Hall, 1967.

Duverger, Maurice. *Political Parties.* New York: John Wiley, 1963.

Edelman, Murray. *The Symbolic Uses of Politics.* Champaign-Urbana: University of Illinois Press, 1964.

Epstein, Leon. *Political Parties in Western Democracies.* New York: Praeger, 1967.

Hansen, Lee W., and Weisbrod, Burton A. *Benefits, Costs and Finance of Public Higher Education.* Chicago: Markham, 1969.

Hartnett, Rodney T. *College and University Trustees: Their Backgrounds, Roles, and Educational Attitudes.* Princeton, N.J.: Educational Testing Service, 1969.

Katz, Elihu, and Lazarsfeld, Paul F. *Personal Influence.* Glencoe, Ill.: Free Press, 1955.

Kelley, Stanley. *Professional Public Relations and Political Power.* Baltimore: Johns Hopkins, 1956.

Key, V.O. *Public Opinion and American Democracy.* New York: Knopf, 1961.

Klapp, Orrin. *Symbolic Leaders.* New York: Minerva Press, 1968.

Kolko, Gabriel. *Wealth and Power in the United States.* New York: Praeger, 1962.

Lang, Kurt, and Lang, Gladys. *Politics and Television.* Chicago: Quadrangle Books, 1968.

Lasswell, Harold. *Politics: Who Gets What, When, How.* Cleveland: Meridian Books, 1958.

Lowi, Theodore. "American Business, Public Policy, Case-Studies, and Political Theory," *World Politics,* 16 (July, 1954): 677–715.

Lundberg, Ferdinand. *The Rich and the Super-Rich.* New York: Bantam Books, 1968.

Matthews, Donald R. *Social Background of Political Decision Makers.* New York: Random House, 1954.

Michels, Robert. *Political Parties: A Sociological Study of the Oligarchical Tendencies of Modern Democracy.* Translated by Eden and Cedar Paul. New York: The Free Press, 1962.

Mills, C. Wright. *The Power Elite.* New York: Oxford University Press, 1959.

Polsby, Nelson W. *Community Power and Political Theory.* New Haven, Conn.: Yale University Press, 1963.

Prewitt, Kenneth. *The Recruitment of Political Leaders.* Indianapolis: Bobbs-Merrill, 1970.

Rose, Arnold. *The Power Structure.* New York: Oxford University Press, 1967.

Schattschneider, E. E. *The Semi-Sovereign People.* New York: Holt, Rinehart & Winston, 1960.

Ten Broek, Jacobus, ed. *The Law of the Poor.* San Francisco: Chandler, 1966.

Chapter 10

Andrews, William G. *Coordinate Magistrates: Constitutional Law by Congress and President.* New York: Van Nostrand, Reinhold, 1969.

Beard, Charles A. *An Economic Interpretation of the Constitution of the United States with New Introduction.* New York: Macmillan, 1954 (originally published in 1913).

Bickel, Alexander M. *The Least Dangerous Branch.* Indianapolis: Bobbs-Merrill, 1962.

Danelski, David J. *A Supreme Court Justice Is Appointed.* New York: Random House, 1964.

Krislov, Samuel. *The Supreme Court in the Political Process.* New York: Macmillan, 1965.

McCloskey, Robert G. *The American Supreme Court.* Chicago: University of Chicago Press, 1960.

Miller, Arthur S. *The Supreme Court and American Capitalism.* New York: The Free Press, 1968.

Mitau, G. Theodore. *Decade of Decision: The Supreme Court and the Constitutional Revolution, 1954–1964.* New York: Scribner's, 1967.

Pritchett, C. Herman. *The American Constitutional System,* 2nd ed. New York: McGraw-Hill, 1967.

Shapiro, Martin. *The Supreme Court and the Administrative Agencies.* New York: The Free Press, 1968.

Sutherland, Arthur E. *Constitution in America.* New York: Blaisdell, 1965

Chapter 11

Abraham, Henry J. *The Judicial Process,* 2nd ed. New York: Oxford University Press, 1968.

Becker, Theodore L., ed. *The Impact of Supreme Court Decisions.* New York: Oxford University Press, 1969.

Cardozo, Benjamin. *The Nature of the Judicial Process.* New Haven, Conn.: Yale University Press, 1921.

Casper, Jonathan D. *American Criminal Justice: The Defendant's Perspective.* Englewood Cliffs, N.J.: Prentice-Hall, 1972.

Cole, George F., ed. *Criminal Justice: Law and Politics.* Belmont, Cal.: Wadsworth, 1972.

Frank, Jerome. *Law and the Modern Mind.* New York: Doubleday, 1930.

Goldman, Sheldon, and Jahnige, Thomas P. *The Federal Courts as a Political System.* New York: Harper & Row, 1971.

Jacob, Herbert. *Justice in America,* 2nd ed. Boston: Little, Brown, 1972.

Klonoski, James R., and Mendelsohn, Robert I., eds. *The Politics of Local Justice.* Boston: Little, Brown, 1970.

Lewis, Anthony. *Gideon's Trumpet.* New York: Vintage, 1964.

Murphy, Walter F., and Tanenhaus, Joseph. *The Study of Public Law.* New York: Random House, 1972.

Rodgers, Harrell R., and Bullock, Charles S., III. *Law and Social Change: Civil Rights Laws and Their Consequences.* New York: McGraw-Hill, 1972.

Schmidhauser, John R. *The Supreme Court: Its Politics, Personalities, and Procedures.* New York: Holt, Rinehart & Winston, 1960.

Chapter 12

Bailey, Stephen K. *The New Congress.* New York: St. Martin's Press, 1966.

Berman, Daniel M. *A Bill Becomes a Law: Congress Enacts Civil Rights Legislation,* 2nd ed. New York: Macmillan, 1966.

Bibby, John, and Davidson, Roger. *On Capitol Hill: Studies in the Legislative Process.* New York: Holt, Rinehart, & Winston, 1967.

Burns, James MacGregor. *The Deadlock of Democracy.* Englewood Cliffs, N.J.: Prentice-Hall, 1963.

Fenno, Richard F., Jr. *The Power of the Purse: Appropriations Politics in Congress.* Boston: Little, Brown, 1966.

Froman, Lewis A., Jr. *Congressmen and the Constituencies.* Chicago: Rand McNally, 1963.

Green, Mark, *et al.* (Ralph Nader Congress Project). *Who Runs Congress?* New York: Grossman, 1972.

Herring, Pendleton. *Presidential Leadership.* New York: W. W. Norton, 1965.

Koenig, Louis W. *Congress and the President.* Chicago: Scott, Foresman, 1965.

March, James G., and Simon, Herbert A. *Organizations.* New York: John Wiley, 1958.

Mason, Alpheus T. *Harlan Fiske Stone: Pillar of the Law.* New York: Viking Press, 1956.

Matthews, Donald R. *U.S. Senators and Their World.* Chapel Hill, N.C.: University of North Carolina Press, 1960.

Murphy, Walter F. *Elements of Judicial Strategy.* Chicago: University of Chicago Press, 1964.

Polsby, Nelson W. *Congress and the Presidency.* Englewood Cliffs, N.J.: Prentice-Hall, 1964.

Chapter 13

Barnet, Richard J. *Roots of War.* New York: Antheneum, 1972.

Burns, James. *Presidential Government.* Boston: Houghton Mifflin, 1966.

Cornwell, Elmer. *Presidential Leadership of Public Opinion.* Bloomington: Indiana University Press, 1965.

Corwin, Edward. *The President: Office and Powers,* 4th ed. New York: New York University Press, 1957.

Dunn, Delmer. *Financing Presidential Campaigns.* Washington: The Brookings Institution, 1972.

Fenno, Richard F. *The President's Cabinet.* Cambridge, Mass: Harvard University Press, 1959.

Fisher, Louis. *President and Congress: Power and Policy.* New York: Free Press, 1972.

Herring, Pendleton. *Presidential Leadership.* New York: W. W. Norton, 1965.

Koenig, Louis, *The Chief Executive.* New York: Harcourt, Brace, & World, 1964.

McConnell, Grant. *The Modern Presidency.* New York: St. Martin's Press 1967.

Neustadt, Richard. *Presidential Power.* New York: Wiley, 1960.

Osbourne, John. *The Third Year of The Nixon Watch.* New York: Liveright, 1972.

Polsby, Nelson, and Wildavsky, Aaron. *Presidential Elections,* 2nd ed. New York: Scribner's, 1968.

Rossiter, Clinton. *The American Presidency.* New York: Harcourt, Brace & World, 1956.

Rostow, W. W. *The Diffusion of Power, 1957–1972.* New York: MacMillan, 1973.

Simon, Herbert A. *Administrative Behavior.* New York: Macmillan, 1957.

Sorensen, Theodore C. *Decision-Making in the White House.* New York: Columbia University Press, 1963.

White, Theodore H. *The Making of the President—1960.* New York: Atheneum, 1961.

Wildavsky, Aaron, ed. *The Presidency.* Boston: Little, Brown, 1969.

Chapter 14

Berelson, Bernard; Lazarsfeld, Paul F.; and McPhee, William N. *Voting.* Chicago: University of Chicago Press, 1954.

Campbell, Angus, *Elections and the Political Order.* New York: John Wiley, Donald E. *The American Voter.* New York: John Wiley, 1960.

Campbell, Angus, et. al. *Elections and the Political Order.* New York: John Wiley, 1966.

Converse, Philip. "The Nature of Belief Systems in Mass Publics." In *Ideology and Discontent,* ed. David Apter. London: Free Press of Glencoe, 1964.

Converse, Philip, and Dupeux, Georges. "The Politicization of the Electorate in France and the United States," *Public Opinion Quarterly* 26 (Spring 1962): 1–24.

Converse, Philip, *et al.* "Continuity and Change in American Politics: Parties and Issues in the 1968 Election," *American Political Science Review* 63 (December 1969): 1083–1105.

Downs, Anthony. *An Economic Theory of Democracy.* New York: Harper & Row, 1957.

Easton, David, and Dennis, Jack. *Children in the Political System.* New York: McGraw-Hill, 1969.

Easton, David, and Hess, Robert D. "Youth and the Political System." In *Culture and Social Character,* eds. S. M. Lipset and Leo Lowenthal. London: Free Press of Glencoe, 1962.

Flanigan, William H. *Political Behavior of the American Electorate.* Boston: Allyn & Bacon, 1968.

Greenstein, Fred I. *Children and Politics,* rev. ed. New Haven, Conn.: Yale University Press, 1968.

Hartz, Louis. *The Liberal Tradition in America.* New York: Harcourt Brace Jovanovich, 1955.

Hess, Robert D., and Torney, Judith V. *The Development of Political Attitudes in Children.* Chicago: Aldine, 1967.

Keech, William. *The Impact of Negro Voting.* Chicago: Rand-McNally, 1968.

Key, V. O. *The Responsible Electorate.* Cambridge, Mass.: Harvard University Press, 1966.

Langton, Kenneth. *Political Socialization.* New York: Oxford University Press, 1969.

Marvick, Dwayne. "The Political Socialization of American Negroes," *Annals* 361 (September 1965): 112–127.

Skolnick, Jerome H. *The Politics of Protest.* New York: Ballantine Books, 1969.

Stokes, Donald S., and Miller, Warren M. "Constituency Influence in Congress," *American Political Science Review* 57 (March 1963): 45–55.

U.S. Department of Health, Education, and Welfare. *Toward a Social Report.* Washington: Government Printing Office, 1969.

Wolfenstein, Martha, and Kliman, eds. *Children and the Death of the President.* Garden City, N.Y.: Doubleday, 1965.

Chapter 15

Cantril, Albert, and Roll, Charles. *The Hopes and Fears of the American People.* New York: Universe Books, 1972.

Clausen, John A., ed. *Socialization and Society.* Boston: Little, Brown, 1968.

Dawson, Richard, and Prewitt, Kenneth. *Political Socialization.* Boston: Little, Brown, 1969.

Devine, Donald. *The Political Culture of the United States.* Boston: Little, Brown, 1972.

Hamilton, Richard F. *Class and Politics in the United States.* New York: John Wiley, 1972.

Lane, Robert E. *Political Ideology: Why the American Common Man Believes What He Does.* New York: Free Press, 1962.

Lane, Robert E. *Political Thinking and Consciousness.* Chicago: Markham, 1962.

Lane, Robert E., and Sears, David O. *Public Opinion.* Englewood Cliffs, N.J.: Prentice-Hall, 1964.

Larson, Calvin, and Wasburn, Philo. *Power, Participation, and Ideology.* New York: David McKay, 1969.

Marcuse, Herbert. *One-Dimensional Man.* Boston: Beacon Press, 1964.

Schoenberger, Robert A. *The American Right Wing: Readings in Political Behavior.* New York: Holt, Rinehart & Winston, 1969.

Stouffer, Samuel. *Communism, Conformity and Civil Liberties.* New York: John Wiley, 1966 (originally published in 1956).

Chapter 16

Almond, Gabriel, and Verba, Sidney. *The Civic Culture.* Princeton, N.J.: Princeton University Press, 1963.

Altshuler, Alan A. *Community Control: The Black Demand for Participation in Large American Cities.* New York: Pegasus, 1970.

Campbell, Angus, et al. *The American Voter.* New York: John Wiley, 1960.

Campbell, Angus, et al. *Elections and the Political Order.* New York: John Wiley, 1966.

Clark, Kenneth, and Hopkins, Jeanette. *A Relevant War Against Poverty.* New York: Harper & Row, 1970.

Cummings, Milton C., Jr. *Congressmen and the Electorate.* New York: The Free Press, 1966.

Flanigan, William H. *Political Behavior of the American Electorate.* Boston: Allyn & Bacon, 1968.

Graham, Hugh Davis, and Gurr, Ted Robert (Task Force to the President's

Commission on Violence). *Violence in America.* New York: Signet Books, 1969.

Greenstein, Fred I. *The American Party System and The American People.* Englewood Cliffs, N.J.: Prentice-Hall, 1963.

Gurr, Ted Robert. *Why Men Rebel.* Princeton, N.J.: Princeton University Press, 1970.

Jennings, M. Kent, and Zeigler, Harmon, eds. *The Electoral Process.* Englewood Cliffs, N.J.: Prentice-Hall, 1966.

Key, V. O., Jr. *The Responsible Electorate.* Cambridge, Mass.: Harvard University Press, 1966.

Kramer, Ralph M. *Participation of the Poor: Comparative Case Studies in the War on Poverty.* Englewood Cliffs, N.J.: Prentice-Hall, 1969.

Mahood, H. R. *Pressure Groups in American Politics.* New York: Scribner's, 1967.

Moynihan, Daniel P. *Maximum Feasible Misunderstanding.* New York: The Free Press, 1969.

National Advisory Commission on Civil Disorders. *Report.* New York: Bantam Books, 1968.

Roszak, Theodore. *The Making of a Counter Culture.* Garden City, N.Y.: Doubleday, 1969.

Rubinstein, Richard E. *Rebels in Eden: Mass Political Violence in the United States.* Boston: Little, Brown, 1970.

Sorauf, Frank J. *Political Parties in the American System.* Boston: Little, Brown, 1964.

Sorauf, Frank J. *Party Politics in America.* Boston: Little, Brown, 1968.

Spiegel, Hans B. C., ed. *Citizen Participation in Urban Development.* Washington: NTL Institute for Applied Behavioral Science, 1968.

Sundquist, James L. *Politics and Policy: The Eisenhower, Kennedy, and Johnson Years.* Washington: The Brookings Institution, 1968.

Chapter 17

Barber, Richard J. *The American Corporation:* Its Power, Money, Its Politics. New York: E. P. Dutton, 1970.

Dahl, Robert A. *A Preface to Democratic Theory.* Chicago: University of Chicago Press, 1956.

Dahl, Robert A. *Who Governs? Democracy and Power in an American City.* New Haven, Conn.: Yale University Press, 1961.

Domhoff, G. William. *Who Rules America?* Englewood Cliffs, N.J.: Prentice-Hall, 1967.

Domhoff, G. William, and Ballard, Hoyt B. C. *Wright Mills and the Power Elite.* Boston: Beacon Press, 1968.

Kariel, Henry S. *The Decline of American Pluralism.* Stanford, Cal: Stanford University Press, 1961.

Kaufman, Arnold S. *The Radical Liberal: New Man in American Politics.* New York: Atherton Press, 1968.

Polsby, Nelson W. *Community Power and Political Theory.* New Haven, Conn.: Yale University Press, 1963.

Rose, Arnold M. *The Power Structure: Political Process in American Society.* New York: Oxford University Press, 1967.

Rowen, Hobart. *The Free Enterprisers: Kennedy, Johnson and The Business Establishment.* New York: G. P. Putnam, 1964.

Weinstein, James. *The Corporate Ideal in the Liberal State.* Boston: Beacon Press, 1968.

Zeitlin, Maurice, ed. *American Society, Inc.* Chicago: Markham, 1970.

Chapter 18

Dahl, Robert, *After the Revolution: Authority in the Good Society.* New Haven: Yale University Press, 1970.

Edleman, Murray. *The Symbolic Uses of Politics.* Champaign-Urbana: University of Illinois Press, 1964.

Edleman, Murray. *Politics as Symbolic Action: Mass Arousal and Quiescence.* Chicago: Markham, 1971.

Gravel, Mike. *Citizen Power: A People's Platform.* New York: Holt, Rinehart & Winston, 1972.

Kariel, Henry S. "Creating Political Reality," *The American Political Science Review* 64 (December 1970): 1088–1098.

Moore, Barrington. *Reflections on the Causes of Human Misery and Upon Certain Proposals to Eliminate Them.* Boston: Beacon Press, 1972.

Chapter 19

Berger, Peter, and Neuhaus, Richard J. *Movement and Revolution.* New York: Doubleday, 1970.

Cleaver, Eldridge. *On the Ideology of the Black Panther Party.* Mimeographed, circa 1969.

Cruse, Harold. *Rebellion or Revolution?* New York: William Morrow, 1968.

Harrington, Michael. *Toward A Democratic Left.* New York: Macmillan, 1968.

Hayden, Tom. *The Trial.* New York: Holt, Rinehart & Winston, 1970.

Hoffman, Abbie. *Revolution for the Hell of It.* New York: Dial Press, 1968.

Lasch, Christopher. *The Agony of the American Left.* New York: Vintage Books, 1969.

Lockwood, Lee. *Conversation with Eldridge Cleaver, Algiers.* New York: Delta Books, 1970.

Marcuse, Herbert. *Essay On Liberation.* Boston: Beacon Press, 1969.

Oppenheimer, Martin. *The Urban Guerrilla.* Chicago: Quadrangle Books, 1969.

Rubin, Jerry. *Do It! Scenarios of the Revolution.* New York: Simon & Schuster, 1970.

Scheer, Robert, ed. *Eldridge Cleaver: Post-Prison Writings.* New York: Random House, 1967.

Teodori, Massimo, ed. *The New Left: A Documentary History.* Indianapolis: Bobbs-Merrill, 1969.

Index

Interim Offensive Agreement, 65
International Monetary Confer-
    ence, 45
International monetary system,
    instability in, 28, 41

Jay, John, 262
Jefferson, Thomas, 159, 160, 262–
    66
Johnson, Lyndon, 402, 429, 431
Johnston, Laurie, 101–103
Jury and civic duty, 446–47

Kennedy, Edward M., 122
Kennedy, John F., 318, 320
Kennedy, Robert, 402
Keynes, John Maynard, 33–34, 503
King, Martin Luther, 167
Kolko, Gabriel, 210
Korean War, and U.S. foreign
    policy, 329

Labor-management conflicts, 237
Labor unions
    membership of, 439–40
    and political change, 515
Laird, Melvin, 64
Laissez faire, principle of, 150, 159
Law
    and Bill of Rights, 277–79
    and the courts, 261–88
    and criminal sanctions, 279–80
    and the elites, 282–88
    federal and state systems of,
        274–76
    international, 286–87
    and legal aid for poor, 284–86
    social control function of, 280–
        82
Lebanon, and U.S. foreign policy,
    330–31
Lipsitz, Lewis, 380, 392

McCarthy, Eugene, 402

McGovern, George, 433–36
Madison, James, 251, 256–57, 262
Magdoff, Harry, 341–44
Majority rule, 144
Males, occupational patterns of,
    353–56
Mao Tse Tung, 234
Marbury versus Madison, 266
Marshall, John, 262, 266, 270
Marxism, and class analysis, 381
Mass media
    and election of 1972, 435
    and elite influence, 397–99
    ideology of, 394
    influence of, 398–400
    and non-elites, 398–99
    and political power, 464
Mass publics: see Non-elites
Materialism
    and business ethic, 144–45
    and political value, 463
    and radicalism, 160, 162
Matthews, Donald, 208
Meany, George, 440–41
Medicaid program, 106
Medicare program, 106
Midwest, Chicanos in, 119
Military expenditures, 54, 194
    and domestic needs, 66, 74
    and domestic work force, 69–72
    effect of, on economy, 71–75
    and inflation, 58, 59, 62
    and military-industrial complex,
        54, 62, 66–75, 76–78, 194,
        204, 314
    public challenge to, 60–63
    for research and development,
        62
    space expenditures, 58
    taxation for, 93
    and unemployment, 63, 67, 71
    for Vietnam War, 58
Military-industrial complex, 54, 62,
    66–75, 76–78, 194, 204, 314
Military priorities
    decisional process, 76–78
    and domestic needs, 66, 74
    strategic explanation of, 75–76

Military priorities (*Cont.*)
  systemic explanation of, 78–81
Military superiority, 54–81, 137
  assumptions of, 54–62
  and domestic work force, 69–72
  and political analysis, 75–81
  strategic problem of, 56–58
Minimum wage law, 452
Minorities
  contemporary circumstances of, 114–24
  and criminal sanctions, 280
  goals of, 129–30
  income of, 137
  policies of 1960's toward, 110–14, 130–34
  and racism, 110–11, 114–24, 132, 137
  and radicalism, 65
  status of, 132
  and unemployment, 100, 120, 133, 137
  and War on Poverty, 130, 132, 134
  world-views, values, and goals of, 124–30

National Association for the Advancement of Colored People (NAACP), 166
Nationalism, cultural, among Blacks, 168–69
National security, through military superiority, 54–81
National Security Council, 327
Natural rights, 160, 162, 252–53, 462, 463
New Deal, social legislation, 103
Newsweek, 390
Nixon, Richard
  on conservative judges, 147
  on domestic scene, 146–48
  economic problems and policies of, 35–52
  election of, in 1968, 319
  election of, in 1972, 433–34, 436
  popularity of, 498
  on welfare, 147–48

Non-elites
  characteristics of, 188, 384
  class image and conditions of, 350–52, 378–83, 518
  and communism, 409, 410
  economic status of, 353–56, 380
  and education, 378
  and elites, 187–88, 216–19, 349–50, 442–45, 451–54
  and the establishment, 233–34
  health conditions of, 356–57
  ideology of, 385, 392–97, 407–16
  impact of, on policy, 451–54
  income of, 353–55, 380
  legal aid for, 284–86
  levels of job satisfaction of, 376–77, 383
  living conditions of, 357
  and mass media, 398–99
  and national breakdown, 417–19
  and national unity, 388–92
  occupational patterns of, 353–56
  political attitudes of, 385–97
  and political change, 515, 518
  and political participation, 421–22, 445–51
  and political parties, 426–28
  political power of, 189
  political values of, 187, 188, 395–97, 407–16, 518
  and priority of domestic problems, 390–92
  and racism, 413–15
  social mobility of, 357–60
  and social security protections, 452
  social setting of, 356–57
  and social welfare, 386–88
  subjective side of, life, 360–78
  and Supreme Court, 267–68
  and symbolism, 479, 483, 491–92
  trade union membership of, 439–40
  and unemployment, 33, 355–56
  and Vietnam War, 400, 405–406
North Central states, Black migration to, 115
Northeast
  Black migration to, 115

Puerto Ricans in, 119
Paine, Tom, 156
Parable of Pigs (Stutsman), 36–37
Pilisuk, Marc, 79
Pluralism
  and the Constitution, 256–57
  and political power, 465
Police
  nonwhite, 280
  and political conflicts, 494, 498
Point Four program, 332–33
Polk, James, 318
Political analysis
  and class analysis, 214–15, 350–52
  and ideology, 139–41, 148–53
  and military superiority, 75–81
  of minority-related policies, 132–34
  of poverty policy, 108
  problems in, and evaluation, 9–10, 16–20
  of symbolism, 480–82
Political Beliefs of Americans, The (Free and Cantril), 407
Political change
  and class consciousness, 505
  and dynamics of political arousal, 492–95
  and economic growth and stability, 503
  fundamental, 502, 511–12, 516–17, 519
  and international tensions, 506–507
  levels and directions of, 511–17
  marginal, 502, 511–17, 519
  and political power, 508–509
  and political values, 508, 515
  preconditions of, 502–507
  prospects for, 517–19
  and racism, 512, 514, 517–18, 519
  and social tensions, 504–506, 508
  and symbolism, 478–500
  and Vietnam War, 400–406
Political enemies, creation of, 499–500
Political equality, concept of, 14–15
Political legitimacy, and the Constitution, 240–41, 258–59
Political participation
  alternative forms of, 421, 445–51
  and voting, 421–45
Political parties, 464
  affiliation, 221, 395
  and the Constitution, 245–46
  and the electoral college, 246–47, 269
  and elites, 221, 227, 444–45
  and issues, 427, 428, 430–31
  minority, 152
  non-elites and, 426–28
  organization of, 421
  and political values, 515
  and third parties, 426–27, 428, 451
  and the two-party system, 426–27
  and voting behavior, 424–26
Political power
  of civil servants, 327–28
  concept of, 457
  consequences of, 461–65
  of corporations, 190–91, 193–95, 197, 200
  definition of, 458
  distribution of, 457, 465–74
  and economic power centers, 465, 473–77
  and elites, 185, 189, 224–31, 324, 344, 460–61, 465, 471–73
  forms of, 458–60
  and government, 464
  holders of, 460–61
  and mass media, 464
  and non-elites, 189
  of special-interest groups, 443–44
  and U.S. foreign policy, 317–20, 345–46
  and value priorities, 462–63, 508, 515
Political priorities, and decision-making process, 464
Political process, characteristics of, 151–53
Political socialization
  definition of, 393